# A.D.

## THE YEAR OF OUR LORD

NEW TESTAMENT

TYNDALE HOUSE PUBLISHERS, INC. • WHEATON, ILLINOIS
DISTRIBUTED BY BIBLES AT COST
1 (800) 778-8865

CONTRIBUTORS

Greg Laurie, General Editor
Karen Dagher, Harvest Ministries Editor
Danny Bond, Harvest Ministries Assistant Editor
Steve Benson, Tyndale House Editor
Timothy R. Botts and David Riley Associates, Graphic Designers

Greg Laurie is not only an evangelist and pastor, but he is the president of Harvest Ministries as well. Harvest Ministries sponsors Harvest Crusades. These crusades are public evangelistic events intended to present the message of Jesus Christ to people in a nonreligious environment. Begun in 1990, Harvest Crusades are known for their informal atmosphere, contemporary music, and simple, straightforward messages by Greg Laurie. To date, some 1.5 million people have attended the nondenominational Harvest Crusades. If you would like more information on Harvest Ministries and/or their crusades, write to Harvest Ministries, P.O. Box 4000, Riverside, CA 92514-4000. Or call (909) 687-6595. On the internet, type http://www.harvest.org.

# A.D.
## The Year of Our Lord

### Live the Difference

We all want to make a difference. We long for a walk with Jesus that is constantly growing, constantly getting deeper. A walk that leads to real change, not only in ourselves, but in the lives of those we touch.

The problem is: That walk is not as easy as it seems. The world is filled with people crazy about God but feeling overwhelmed by the day-to-day challenges of life. Don't let circumstances hold you back from your destiny. Live the difference that only a personal, exciting relationship with God can deliver.

2 Peter 1:5 says:

> *"Make every effort to apply the benefits of these promises to your life. Then your faith will produce a life of moral excellence. A life of moral excellence leads to knowing God better."*

Notice that it doesn't say *"perfect every benefit."* Instead, it says *"make every effort to apply."* It's like a math problem:

$$\begin{array}{r} \text{a life that wants God} \\ \underline{+\ \text{effort towards His plan}} \\ =\ \text{stronger every single day} \end{array}$$

This tells us that it is the *pursuit* of God (not the perfection of our attempts) that leads to moral excellence. You can do this! Step back for a minute from the intimidation of the big picture and, instead, take a look at a daily plan that gives us an "effort" for each new day to get closer to God for one year. If you have a bad day, pick right up again and take the reins with a new effort!

### What does a year of your life devoted to Jesus look like?

Imagine small *daily* steps leading to a walk with Jesus that looks like this:

- A passionate, intimate relationship with Jesus through a daily prayer time.
- A daily habit of reading, studying, and memorizing the Word of God.
- An active sharing of your faith as a daily, normal part of your life.
- Being active in your local church youth ministry each and every week.
- A heart for the people of the world developed through prayer, giving, and short- and long-term missions.
- Personal strong, Godly convictions.
- Get involved with your church and youth group and establish friendships with people that will know you, love you, and hold you to higher standards.
- A pursuit of the perfect will and plan of God for your life!

Why these descriptions? Because these are the message Jesus sent to us through His life. These are the parts of a walk with God that help you hear His voice and reach others with His great love.

## How do I start?

If you want your life to change, you have to do some things differently. But, where do you start? One of the most exciting aspects to a relationship with Jesus Christ is that it has the potential to always be growing and strengthening. God wants your friendship. God desires your friendship. Like any other friendship, it is based on real time and real communication. That's easy to say, but how does it fit into a busy life? Here are some practical suggestions to add to your day, week, or month that should kick start a deeper walk. Some work well alone while some can be done effectively in a group setting.

- Find a park or path and take a walk just spending time with God.
- Go to your campus after hours or on the weekend and pray for your school (students, teacher, administration).
- Buy a new Worship CD and have Personal Worship Time with just you and Jesus.
- As a gift to God, go perform an act of service or kindness for someone whom you don't even know.
- Dedicate an evening to Jesus, praying, worshiping, and studying.
- Write a letter to God telling how you really feel about Him. Place it inside your Bible at Psalm 139 and read how God really feels about you.
- Write your dreams on a piece of paper, then find a token to represent your biggest dream, Place both of these into a container or box and bury it as a time capsule. Set a time to open the time capsule at least six months later.
- Write down on a piece of paper all of the things in your life that are causing anxiety and then throw the paper into a fireplace or bonfire, symbolic of you giving them to Jesus and asking for His guidance.
- Write a word down on your hand everyday that summarizes what you were learning in your quiet time.
- Find as many adjectives in your daily Bible reading that describe God and keep a list as you go along.

## Making every "effort"

This sort of effort requires a daily commitment. For one year, take the opportunity each morning to give the day to God, and then commit to an item on the checklist. If you miss a day, don't freak out. Jump back on the bandwagon. God's mercies are new every morning. Remember: *"Sin is no longer your master, for you are no longer subject to the law, which enslaves you to sin. Instead you are free by God's grace. So since God's grace has set us free from the law, does that mean we can go on sinning? Of course not!" Romans 6:14-15.* Every day you build on a good day is a day you grow even stronger!

For your first month, try the list of "first steps." As you grow stronger with more and more successful days, you will get hungrier for more of God. At that point, try the "second steps," and after another month try the "third steps."

**FIRST STEPS:**
- Pray first thing in your day for strength to live the difference for Jesus (try to pray for at least 10 minutes). Also, pray for family, friends, and your country.
- Read one chapter in the Word of God. Begin in Matthew and work your way through the life of Jesus.
- Journal at least one paragraph of your thoughts, feelings, and prayers for the day.
- When your thoughts go away from God, take them captive. Stop and pray for God's strength. Speak positively and you will begin to think positively.
- Practice obeying God in the areas you read about in your daily Bible chapter.
- Tell at least five people about your decision to live the difference.
- Attend Youth Service, and develop friendships with other Christians. This is called fellowship. It is very important, because talking about your faith will cause it to grow.
- Attend Worship Service on Sunday and actively participate in Worship.
- End your day spending at least five minutes thanking God for giving you strength, provision, and protection, and then make a commitment to live for Him tomorrow.

**SECOND STEPS:**
- Begin praying for "Jesus Opportunities" to share your faith.
- Increase your time in prayer (at least fifteen minutes).
- Read at least one chapter in the Word of God.
- Write out the one verse or passage that most stood out to you as you studied.
- Journal at least one page of your thoughts, feelings and prayers. All you need is a note-book and something to write with. Write down the feelings you are experiencing as you walk with God. You will discover more clarity in your walk, because writing these things down pushes you to really think through what you are experiencing. Keep this journal close to your Bible, because it is a great reference on hard days. Many times, the answer to a daily struggle is in words God gave you on a different day.
- End your day with a re-commitment to live "all-out" the next day.
- Find an accountability partner and establish the guidelines for your relationship.
- Find a special place where you can sit, watch a sunset, walk in the woods, and tell God what is going on in your life.
- Establish Relationship Standards. Based on what you are learning in God's Word, pray that God will give you wisdom as to what kind of friends you should spend time with. Write these standards down and live by them.
- Prayerfully consider what television shows and movies you should watch before viewing them. Guard your heart by praying through your choice of magazines and Internet sites before checking them out. Find some Christian music that fits your tastes, and replace your secular music for two full weeks.

**THIRD STEPS:**
- Practice hearing and obeying God's voice during your day.
- Get involved with Youth Service. Ask your Youth Pastor how you can best help and serve.
- Look for and utilize "Jesus Opportunities" to share your faith.
- Increase your time in prayer (at least twenty minutes).
- Read at least two chapters in the Word of God.
- Journal at least two pages of your thoughts, feelings, and prayers.

- Ask God how He wants you to be involved with missions.
- Establish your "Top Ten Target List"* for sharing your faith.
- Invite at least one person to your Youth Service.
- Look for opportunities to show God you love him by obeying his word in your daily life.

**\*HOW TO MAKE A TOP TEN TARGET LIST:**
- Step 1: Form your List
    Pray about who would be the top ten people you would like to see come to Jesus.
- Step 2: Commit to pray
    Begin praying specifically and consistently for these ten people on your list.
- Step 3: Make a Plan
    Look at each name and pray for wisdom and help to determine what the most effective way to reach them would be—actually write these action steps down under each person's name.
- Step 4: Build the Bridge
    Begin to implement these action steps on a regular basis.
- Step 5: Make the Move
    Look for "Jesus Opportunities" to make a move on your bridge building actions—i.e. invite them to youth service, pray with them, etc.
- Step 6: Be a True Friend
    Continue to be a true friend in prayer and discipleship after they commit their life to Christ—be a true accountability partner to them.

## Now you have a plan.

Make each day a new day. If you fall down, get back up. God is so proud of you for doing this! His heart is to have a friendship with you, to communicate with you, and to help you love others and reach them for Him. The Bible tells us that our steps are ordered of the Lord. Give each effort to Him, and He will completely direct your path. A solid Christian walk is not easy and you will need to persevere, but God isn't asking you to be God. He is asking that you daily come to Him and give it your best shot.

> *"For God is working in you, giving you the desire to obey him and the power to do what pleases him"* Philippians 2:13.

Imagine a lifetime of having a great relationship with God and **having the power to do what pleases Him**. It all begins with what you do today. It all begins with a single effort.

> *"Make every effort to apply the benefits of these promises to your life. Then your faith will produce a life of moral excellence. A life of moral excellence leads to knowing God better"* 2 Peter 1:5.

# Welcome!

Congratulations! You are holding in your hands the best-selling book in the history of humanity—the Bible. It was given to us by God thousands of years ago. Although the Bible has been around for some time, the wisdom and knowledge contained within is still relevant today. In fact, everything you need to know about God and life is found in the pages of this book. It is the "user's manual of life" that we all have been searching for.

The Bible does not just teach us about life, though. It also shows us how to come into a *personal* relationship with the very God who inspired this book. This particular Bible contains features that have been specially designed to help you understand, discover, and deepen the personal relationship that God wants to have with you.

Perhaps you are not yet a believer in Jesus Christ, but you want to know more about Christianity. You may even want to be a believer, but you just don't know how to become one. In the How to Find God New Testament you will find a section entitled "How You Can Know God" (p. A1). Here, you will learn how to establish a life-changing relationship with Jesus.

Maybe you have just started in the Christian faith. You are a new believer. Here you will find out how to lay a good foundation for your faith and walk with God in the years ahead.

You may even be a believer who is mature in the faith. Here you will be refreshed and reminded of the essentials of the Christian faith and life.

## THE MAIN FEATURES

How to Find God contains four reading tracks: "Cornerstones," "First Steps," "Off and Running," and "Big Questions." Each reading track (except "Big Questions") is composed of two kinds of notes: up-front and *in-text*. The up-front notes appear before the Bible text and are made up of one to two paragraphs and two to eight numbered points that refer you to Scripture passages and their accompanying in-text notes.

## READING TRACK ONE: **CORNERSTONES**

Cornerstones—blocks of stone—were traditionally used to start a building's foundation. Likewise, the "Cornerstones" reading track helps you to begin to lay a solid foundation for your faith. Here you will learn about God's character, Jesus' life, and the Holy Spirit's role in the lives of believers. "Cornerstones" also contains notes on the essential Christian character traits that are developed and nurtured by a personal relationship with Jesus Christ. Some of those traits are love, forgiveness, purity, honesty, wisdom, peace, and joy.

### READING TRACK TWO: **FIRST STEPS**

The phrase *first steps* brings to mind the image of a young child taking his or her first unassisted steps. Like this young child, new believers in Christ need to learn how to walk all over again, so to speak. That is because the Christian life for most people is a completely new way of living. To help you learn to live this new life, the "First Steps" reading track gives you valuable building blocks for growing in your faith. Here you will discover the importance of and the "how to" of studying the Bible, praying, finding the right church, resisting temptation, and seeking God's will for your life.

### READING TRACK THREE: **OFF AND RUNNING**

"How does God's Word apply to my everyday life?" This is one of the most widely asked questions about the Bible today. The "Off and Running" reading track answers this question. Here you will discover how to put your faith into action. You will see what the Bible has to say about important topics like marriage, parenting, priorities, conversation, and job performance. By helping you apply biblical principles to these aspects of your life, "Off and Running" takes you to the next level of the Christian life—living it day to day.

### READING TRACK FOUR: **BIG QUESTIONS**

Life often presents us with difficult situations that cause us to ask hard questions. For instance, you may wonder how a good God could let something bad—like cancer—happen to you. Or you may wonder why Jesus Christ is the only way to God. Aren't other religions just as good? In the "Big Questions" reading track, you will find out what the Bible has to say about tough issues. Everything from alternative lifestyles to the second coming of Christ is covered here.

## ADDITIONAL FEATURES

Also included in this *New Believer's New Testament* are two features that will help you better understand the Bible and live out your faith. These features are:

- *How to Study the Bible*—a practical way for you to read through the Bible and a list of questions to ask yourself as you read.
- *Topical Index*—a list of various topics that are of special interest to believers, along with a list of verses that address each topic.

## HOW TO USE THE READING TRACKS

The *New Believer's New Testament* is easy to use. Simply turn to page A11 and begin reading the "Who Is God?" up-front note in the "Cornerstones" reading track. Look up the Scripture passages and in-text notes referred to at the end of this note. After you have read all the Scripture passages and in-text notes for "Who Is God?" move on to the next up-front note ("Who Is Jesus?") and begin the process over again.

You can read one up-front note and its Scripture passages and in-text notes a day. Or, if you prefer, browse through the table of contents and choose the topic(s) that interests you the most for your daily reading.

Colossians 3:16 says, "Let the words of Christ, in all their richness, live in your hearts and make you wise." God wants his Word to permeate every area of your life—your home, your business, your play time as well as your prayer time. So open your Bible and your heart, and God will speak to you from these pages. Don't let anything keep you from spending time each day in God's Word.

Greg Laurie

# H O W   Y O U   C A N   K N O W   GOD

## What Is Missing in Our Lives?

Purpose, meaning, a reason for living—these are all things we desire and search for in life. Despite steps each one of us takes to find purpose and meaning in life, we still feel empty, unfulfilled. That is because there is a spiritual emptiness in each of our lives. We each have a hole in our heart, a spiritual vacuum deep within our soul—a "God-shaped blank." Possessions won't fill this hole, nor will success. Relationships alone cannot satisfy this emptiness, and morality, in and of itself, falls miserably short of occupying this space. In fact, even religion cannot fill the void in our heart.

There is only one way to effectively fill that void. This way will not only help us to have a life that is full and rich on this earth, but—more important—will give us the absolute hope of spending eternity in the presence of God. Before we can truly appreciate this good news though, we need to understand the bad news, which is a serious problem we all have.

## THE PROBLEM: SIN

The Bible clearly identifies our serious problem as sin. Sin is not just an act but the actual nature of our being. In other words, we are not sinners because we sin. Rather, we sin because we are sinners! We are born with a nature to do wrong. King David, the Old Testament Israelite ruler, wrote, "For I was born a sinner—yes, from the moment my mother conceived me" (Psalm 51:5). Because we are born sinners, sinning comes to all of us naturally. That is why it is futile to think that the answer to all of life's problems comes from "within." According to the Bible, the *problem* is within! Scripture tells us, "The human heart is most deceitful and desperately wicked. Who really knows how bad it is?" (Jeremiah 17:9).

We are not basically good—we are basically sinful. This sinfulness spills out into every-thing we do. Every problem we experience in our society today can be traced back to our refusal to live God's way. Clear back to the Garden of Eden, Adam made his choice, and he suffered the consequences of it, setting the pattern that all humanity would follow. The Bible explains, "When Adam sinned, sin entered the entire human race. Adam's sin brought death, so death spread to everyone, for everyone sinned. . . . Yes, Adam's one sin brought condem-nation upon everyone" (Romans 5:12, 18).

"That's not fair!" you may protest. Why should we suffer because of what someone else has done? Yet, given the opportunity, each one of us would have done the same thing as Adam. In fact, not a single day passes that we do not face the same test that was set before Adam. God has given us the freedom to choose between two separate paths: the path that leads to life and the path that leads to death. The Bible says, "Today, I have given you the choice between life and death, between blessings and curses. I call on heaven and earth to witness the choice you make, Oh, that you would choose life, that you and your descendants might live!" (Deuteronomy 30:19).

## WITHOUT A LEG TO STAND ON

Someone may say, "But I live a good life. I try to be kind and considerate to others. I live by the Ten Commandments." But the truth of the matter is that the Ten Commandments, or the law, as they are called in the Bible, were not given to make us good but to show us how bad we are. The Bible tells us, "No one can ever be made right in God's sight by doing what his law commands. For the more we know God's law, the clearer it becomes that we aren't obeying it" (Romans 3:20). The purpose of the law is to make us realize how sinful we are. You might say that God's law was given to "shut our mouths" and show us that we desperately need his help and forgiveness for our terminal condition as sinners.

Look at the passages below to get a better understanding of the nature and seriousness of sin.

1. **We Have All Missed the Mark** (see Romans 3:23, p. 178). Romans 3:23 says, we have *all* sinned. For those that would claim to be the sole exception to this eternal truth, verse ten of this chapter plainly says, "No one is good—not even one (Romans 3:10). Another word for *good* is *righteous.* The word *righteous* means, "One who is as he or she ought to be." When the Bible says that no one is righteous, or good, it is not so much referring to behavior but to inner character.

   What exactly is "God's glorious standard" that Romans 3:23 says we have failed to meet? God's "glorious standard" is absolute perfection. Jesus said, "But you are to be per-fect, even as your Father in heaven is perfect" (Matthew 5:48). In other words, anyone who is not as good as God is not acceptable to him.

   One definition of *sin,* derived from the Greek word *hamartia,* is to "miss the mark." As far as the mark of perfection goes, we miss it by a mile. Although our sinful nature makes it impossible for us to live up to God's standard, we cannot blame sin on our nature alone. Sin is also a deliberate act.

2. **Sin Is a Deliberate Act** (see Ephesians 2:1-3, p. 238). Another word for *sins* in Ephe-sians 2:1 is *transgressions* or *trespasses.* This word speaks of a lapse or deviation from truth. In contrast to simply "missing the mark," this is a deliberate action. Because sin is a deliberate action, we cannot blame our sin on our society or our environment or our men-tal or physical state. Everyone has chosen to do what was wrong. If we protest this point, "we are only fooling ourselves and refusing to accept the truth" (1 John 1:8).

**3. The Ultimate Penalty for Sin Is Death** (see Romans 6:23, p. 182). According to the Bible, we have offended a Holy God. We have not done this once or twice, but so many times that we are unable to keep count. Romans 6:23 says, "The *wages* of sin is death. . . ." Wages are something that you are paid for work rendered. In other words, you earn your wages. Because we have all repeatedly sinned, we have earned the penalty of death, which is eternal torment and punishment in a place called hell.

Amid all this talk about sin and death, there is some good news. God has given us a way to escape the penalty of our sin. He has made it possible for us to have a relationship with him and enjoy the hope of eternal life without punishment.

# The Solution: Jesus Christ

God understood our problem and knew that we could do nothing about it. Because God loves us, he sent his own Son, Jesus Christ, to earth to bridge the chasm of sin that separates us from him.

## WHY JESUS CAN BRIDGE THE GAP

There has never been anyone like Jesus. For starters, Jesus was not conceived in the womb of his mother through natural means. Rather, he was supernaturally conceived in the womb of a young virgin named Mary. Because of his supernatural conception, Jesus, who is wholly God, also became wholly human.

Though Jesus is God, he chose to lay aside the privileges of his deity to live on earth as a man. The Bible, describing the sacrifice Christ made in becoming a man, says that Jesus "made himself nothing; he took the humble position of a slave and appeared in human form. And in human form he obediently humbled himself even further by dying a criminal's death on a cross" (Philippians 2:7-8). It is extremely important to note that Jesus did not cease to be God when he came to earth. He simply laid aside his divine privileges and walked the earth as a man. In doing so, he was personally able to experience the gamut of human emotions, ranging from happiness to deep sorrow. He felt what it was like to be tired, cold, and hungry.

Moreover, he came to this earth with a clear objective in mind: to bridge that gap between us and God.

When the Israelites of the Old Testament sinned, they would have the high priest go into the Temple and offer an animal sacrifice to God to atone for their sins. In a symbolic sense, this was a way of putting one's sins on the animal, which stood in the place of the guilty person. The Bible teaches, "Without the shedding of blood, there is no forgiveness of sins" (Hebrews 9:22).

The sacrificial rituals carried out by the Israelites in the Old Testament foreshadowed what Jesus would do when he came to this earth. He took the sin of the world upon himself when he hung on the cross so many years ago.

Numerous Old Testament prophecies pointed not only to his birth and life but also to his death, including the way in which he would die.

Jesus knew from the beginning that he had come expressly to die for the sins of humanity. He also knew that this sacrifice would be made on a Roman cross. He began his final journey to the cross of Calvary at a place called Caesarea Philippi, and he often spoke of his impending death with his disciples. Scripture records, "From then on Jesus began to tell his disciples plainly that he had to go to Jerusalem, and he told them what would happen to him there. He would suffer at the hands of the leaders and the leading priests and the teachers of religious law. He would be killed, and he would be raised on the third day" (Matthew 16:21).

He was eventually arrested on false charges after Judas Iscariot, one of his own disciples, betrayed him. But it was no accident. If humanity was going to be put in touch with God and have the barrier that separated them removed, something drastic had to be done. In essence, with one hand Jesus took hold of a Holy God, and with the other hand he took hold of the sinful human race. As crude nails were pounded into his hands, he bridged the gap for us!

We must not forget, however, that three days after his crucifixion, Jesus rose from the dead! If it is true that "you can't keep a good man down," then it is even truer that you can't keep the "God-man" down.

## WE PUT JESUS ON THE CROSS

The necessity of the death of Jesus Christ on the cross shows just how radical our situation was as fallen people. It's been said that you can tell the depth of a well by how much rope is lowered. When we look at "how much rope was lowered" from heaven, we realize how grave our situation really was.

For that reason, don't blame the people of that day for putting Jesus on the cross. We are just as guilty as they. In reality, it was not the Roman soldiers who put him on the cross, nor was it the Jewish leaders: it was our sins that made it necessary for Jesus to volunteer for this torturous and humiliating death.

Read the verses and notes below to see exactly what Jesus did for us.

**1. The Greatest Demonstration of Love** (see Romans 5:6-8, p. 180). Jesus did not die for us while we were his friends, but while we were his enemies, opposing him by our sinfulness. Yet, in spite of all of this, God demonstrated his love for us by dying on the cross. In this verse, the Apostle Paul explains that Jesus did not simply die for humanity as a whole, but that he died for us as individuals. Elsewhere, Paul writes, "[Christ] loved me and gave himself for me" (Galatians 2:20).

Whenever you are tempted to doubt God's love for you, take a long look at the cross on which Jesus died. Then realize that, for all practical purposes, it was not nails that held him to the cross, but love.

**2. Forsaken That We Might Be Forgiven** (see Luke 23:32-49, p. 104). Many of us have heard this story at some point in our lives. Yet the significance behind this heart-wrenching scene is often missed or misunderstood. This was not simply some "good teacher" being crucified for his beliefs. It was God in human form who hung on that cross, bridging the gap between sinful people and a holy God.

Matthew's Gospel tells us that when Jesus hung on that cross, he cried out, "My God, my God, why have you forsaken me?" (Matthew 27:46). Many Bible scholars believe that those words marked the precise moment at which God placed the sins of the world upon his Son. The Bible, speaking of God, says, "You are of purer eyes than to behold evil, and cannot look on wickedness" (Habakkuk 1:13, NKJV). For that reason, the holy Father had to "turn his face" and pour out his wrath upon his own Son. On the cross, Jesus received the wages that were due us. He was not heard that we might be heard. The ear of God was closed to Jesus for a time that it might never be closed to us.

**3. Christ, the Sole Mediator** (see 1 Timothy 2:5-6, p. 270). Why is there only one mediator who is qualified to bridge the gap between God and people? Haven't there been other religious leaders who have claimed to have *the* way to God? Haven't some of them also died as a result of their message?

While the answers to these questions may be yes, the truth is that not one of these other leaders was fully God and fully human. That is why Jesus is uniquely qualified to deal with sin. Jesus said, "I am the way, the truth, and the life. No one can come to the Father except through me" (John 14:6). Acts 4:12 tells us, "There is salvation in no one else! There is no other name in all of heaven for people to call on to save them." And, most important, Jesus Christ rose from the dead!

Though it is true that you must believe Jesus died on the cross for your sins in order to receive eternal life and be a true Christian, there is still something else you must do.

**The Response: Accept God's Offer**

To know Jesus Christ personally and have your sins forgiven, you must believe that you are a sinner separated from God and that your only hope is Jesus Christ, the Son of God, who came and died for your sins. To stop here, however, would be to stop short of salvation.

There are two things you must now do to enter into a relationship with the God from whom you have been separated.

## 1. TURN FROM YOUR SINS

As Jesus began his public ministry, his first message was "Turn from your sins" (Mark 1:15). In essence, Jesus was tellling the people to repent—to acknowledge their sinning, change their minds, and change the direction of their lives.

Look at it this way. In the past, we have been blinded by our sins, causing us to run from God. As we repent, we do a "U-turn" and start running toward him. It is not enough just to be sorry for our sins. We must also change our lifestyle, for the Bible teaches that "God can use sorrow in our lives to help us turn away from sin" (2 Corinthians 7:10). In other words, if you are really sorry for something, it will result in a change in your actions.

The apostle Paul summed up this change succinctly when he quoted Jesus, who had said that people must "turn from darkness to light, and from the power of Satan to God. Then they will receive forgiveness for their sins and be given a place among God's people, who are set apart by faith in me (Acts 26:18).

You see, there are some things only God can do and some things only you can do. Only God can remove your sins and give you the gift of eternal life, but only you can turn from your sins and receive Jesus as your Savior. That brings up the second thing you must do to respond to God's offer.

## 2. BELIEVE IN JESUS CHRIST AND RECEIVE HIM INTO YOUR LIFE

Having seen the enormity of your sin and having decided to turn from it, you then must believe in and receive Jesus Christ as your Lord and Savior. Becoming a Christian, however, is far more than following a creed or trying to live by certain standards. Jesus said that you must be "born again," or more literally, "born from above" (John 3:3). This spiritual rebirth happens when we personally believe in Jesus Christ, receive him by inviting him into our lives, and turn from our sins. In other words, we ask Jesus to come and take residence in our lives, making the changes he deems necessary. A person must take this all-important step in order to become a child of God.

Notice that this offer is yours for the asking, and it is free. You don't have to work for it, trying to clean up your life before you make this life-changing decision. The Bible says, "The free gift of God is eternal life through Christ Jesus our Lord" (Romans 6:23).

Being a Christian also means having a relationship with the living God. In Revelation 3:20, Jesus said, "Look! Here I stand at the door and knock. If you hear me calling and open the door, I will come in, and we will share a meal as friends." To better understand the meaning of this verse, it is important to understand the culture at the time it was written. Eating together in Bible times was a long, drawn-out affair. People would not sit on chairs behind tables in a formal setting as we do, but they would sit on the floor, reclining on pillows around a low table. The relaxed atmosphere made meals a time when you would not only satisfy your appetite but also receive a gratifying serving of enjoyable table conversation. You would share your heart and life with those who sat beside you.

Consequently, when Jesus says that he will "share a meal" with us, it implies intimacy, closeness, and friendship. He offers this to us, but we must first "hear him calling" us.

To hear God calling us, we must know how he speaks. One way in which God speaks to us is described in the Bible as a "still, small voice." This could be described in another way as that tug you may have felt on your heart from the Holy Spirit showing you your need for Jesus. He may even be speaking to you right now! It is at that point that you must "open the door." Only you can do that. Jesus will not force his way in.

## RECEIVING JESUS CHRIST INTO YOUR HEART

If you are ready to turn from your sins and believe in Jesus Christ so that you can receive the forgiveness of sin and the hope of eternal life, then take a moment to bow your head and pray a prayer like this one right now:

> God, I'm sorry for my sin. I turn from it right now. I thank you for sending Jesus Christ to die on the cross for my sin.
>
> Jesus, I ask you to come into my heart and life right now. Be my Lord, Savior, and friend. Help me to follow you all the days of my life as your disciple.
>
> Thank you for forgiving and receiving me right now. Thank

you that my sin is forgiven and that I am going to heaven. In Jesus' name I pray, amen.

## REDEDICATING YOUR LIFE TO JESUS CHRIST

Perhaps you are already a Christian but you have strayed from Jesus Christ. You have been a prodigal son or daughter. God will forgive you right now if you will return to him. He tells us in Scripture, "My wayward children, come back to me and I will heal your wayward hearts" (Jeremiah 3:22). If you would like to return to God and rededicate your life to him right now, you may want to pray something like this:

God, I am sorry for my sin. I am sorry that I have strayed from you. I ask you to forgive me now as I repent of my sin. I don't want to live like a prodigal any longer.
Renew and revive me as I once again follow you as my God. Thank you for your forgiveness. In Jesus' name I pray, amen.

Whether you prayed to make a first time commitment or a recommitment, you have made the right decision. God has forgiven and received you if you really meant it. Know that your relationship with Jesus Christ will bring radical and dramatic changes in your life. Describing this, the Bible says, "Those who become Christians become new persons. They are not the same anymore, for the old life is gone. A new life has begun!" (2 Corinthians 5:17). Now that is good news! But more importantly, God has changed your eternal destiny. Instead of fearing a eternal punishment in a place called hell, you will spend peaceful eternity in his presence in heaven.

Read the next section to see what else God has done for you now that you have taken this step.

## What God Has Done for You

What actually happens when Jesus Christ comes into your life? First, he saves you from your sins and the punishment you deserve as a result of them—eternity in hell. This is called salvation, or regeneration, and has to do with what takes place in your heart: God gives you new life.

Second, he justifies you. Justification has to do with your standing before God and includes the complete removal and forgiveness of your sins. Think about it! When you receive Jesus Christ into your life, you are completely forgiven. God's Word tells us, "Brothers, listen! In this man Jesus there is forgiveness for your sins! Everyone who believes in him is freed from all guilt and declared right with God [justified]— something the Jewish law could never do" (Acts 13:38-39). Speaking of our sins, God says, "I will never again remember [your] sins and lawless deeds" (Hebrews 10:17). What a wonderful promise!

Justification, however, is more than just the forgiveness and removal of the guilt and condemnation that accompany sin. While God has removed your sins and forgiven you of them, he has also placed the perfect righteousness of Jesus Christ "into your account," so to speak. You don't have to earn it or try to achieve it. It is yours as a gracious gift from the God who loves you. To understand justification more fully, read the following Scripture passages and notes below.

1. **God Promises Us His Gracious Forgiveness** (see 1 John 1:9, p. 317). The word *confess* means "to say the same thing as another" or "to agree with." To confess means that we are agreeing with God about our sin. We are seeing it as he does. We know that God hates sin. Therefore, to truly confess our sin means that we essentially feel the same way God feels about what we have done. After committing that sin, we will be determined to put it out of our lives and never do it again. That is true confession in the biblical sense. The reason many believers are not experiencing the forgiveness and joy they desire is because they have not yet truly confessed! Once we have met God's conditions, however, we will know his gracious forgiveness. We may not "feel" forgiven, but we are. We have his word on it.

2. **God Has Balanced Our Moral and Spiritual Budget** (see Romans 5:1-2, p. 180). When God makes us right in his sight, he does so by placing all of the righteousness of Christ to our credit. This balances the moral and spiritual budget for us. We now have sufficient "capital of character" to get on with the business of living.

   Up to this point, salvation has been God's responsibility. From this point on, it continues to be his responsibility except that we are responsible for the wise investment of our "capital of character"—that is, we are responsible for living as God desires us to. It is as if your checking account were empty, but then someone made a $100,000 deposit. What you do with that money is up to you.

3. **God Calls Us His Children** (see Luke 15:11-32, p. 91). This incredible story illustrates what happens when a person turns from sin and returns to God. First, notice that the father in the story did not give this prodigal son what he deserved— banishment. In the same way, we do not receive from God what we deserve—punishment for sin. Second, the young man was given what he did not deserve—the rights and privileges of full sonship. Likewise, although we are not worthy to be called children of God, he calls us sons and daughters. In summary, he doesn't give us what we deserve (judgment). He gives us what we don't deserve (forgiveness and justification).

Speaking of sons and daughters, read on to see how God has adopted you into his family.

## Adopted and Assured

We have looked at what happens when we are regenerated (when Christ comes into our lives) and when we are justified (when God forgives our sin and puts his righteousness in its place). Now let us look at another incredible thing God has done for us. He has adopted us into his family as his children!

*Adoption* means "to be given the rights of a son." In essence, you have been given the full rights of sonship in the family of God as though you were born that way. The story of the Prodigal Son illustrates this (Luke 15:11-32). The wayward son thought that after leaving home, he would no longer be considered a son but would instead be treated as a hired servant. Much to his surprise, when he made the long journey home, his father welcomed him and smothered him with kisses. He then gave orders to bring out the best robe and to put a ring on his finger, signifying full rights as a son. That is exactly what God has done for you! Take some time now to examine three Scripture passages that assure you of your adoption into God's family.

1. **God Disciplines His Children** (see Hebrews 12:5-9, p. 297). Recognizing you are now a child of God is not some distant hope but a present reality. One of the ways God will remind you of this is by correcting you and bringing you back into line like a loving father when you stray away from him.

   Before we were believers, we may have felt no sense of guilt for certain things we did or did not do. But now that we are Christians, God's Holy Spirit shows us the way to live, which includes correcting us. He does this not because he hates us, but because he loves us as his own dear children. Understanding this truth should help us in the way we behave.

2. **You Have an Approachable Father** (see Galatians 4:6, p. 232). The Aramaic word translated "dear Father" is *abba,* which is a word of affection that a young child would use endearingly toward his or her father. A western equivalent of that phrase would be "papa" or "daddy." God does not want to be viewed as some distant, disinterested father, but as a loving, approachable father to whom you can turn at any time because you are his child.

3. **His Promises Are Not Based upon Your Feelings** (see 1 John 5:11-13, p. 323). There will be times as a Christian when you may not "feel" God's presence. You may even be tempted to doubt that he has come into your life. But 1 John 5:13 does not say, "I write this to you who believe in the Son of God so that you may *feel* you have eternal life." This is because feelings come and go. They fluctuate. Nor does the Bible say, "I write this so that you may *hope*—if God is in a really good mood—that you have eternal life." It says, "so that you may *know*. . . ." Eternal life is yours! Stand on God's promise to you. You are forgiven, justified, adopted into his family, and assured of salvation. Now that is reason to rejoice!

To find out more about God, turn to "Who Is God?" p. A11, in the Cornerstones section.

FOUNDATIONAL TRUTHS OF THE FAITH

## Who Is God?

Thousands of years ago, Pharaoh, the Egyptian ruler, posed a question people are still asking today: "Who is the LORD that I should listen to him?" That's a good question, but it is not an easy subject to tackle. It is difficult for our limited minds to grasp the limitless, eternal God. It has been said, "If God were small enough for your minds, he wouldn't be big enough for your needs." For that reason, don't be exasperated if you can't fully understand who God is or why he does certain things. One day, Scripture promises, everything about God and his character will be made perfectly clear to us (1 Corinthians 13:12). But until then, we will find everything we need to know about him in his Word. Look up the following notes and passages to find out who God is.

1. **God Is All-Knowing, Ever Present, and All-Powerful.** The Creator of the Universe knows every intimate detail of his creation (see Matthew 10:29-31, p.15).
2. **God Is Holy.** God's incomparable holiness merits our worship (see Revelation 15:2-4, p. 343).
3. **God Is Loving and Just.** God's justice is tempered by his love (see 2 Peter 3:3-9, p. 314).
4. **God Is Personal.** This characteristic of God sets him apart from the so-called "gods" of other religions (see Acts 17:22-31, p. 162).
5. **God Is in Control.** It is important to remember that God is still in control, even if things around us seem to be in chaos (see Romans 11:33-36, p. 191).
6. **The God of the Bible Is the One True God.** While some insist on the existence of many gods, only the God of the Bible is the true, living God, worthy of our devotion (see 1 Corinthians 8:4-6, p. 206).

# Who Is Jesus?

Throughout history many people have attempted to answer this question. Some have done so accurately, but many have not. Our best source for answering this question is—once again—God's own Word. The Bible presents us with some inescapable truths about Jesus that demand a response. Anyone who seriously studies Scripture to learn more about Jesus must answer two probing questions: (1) What do you think of Jesus Christ? and (2) Who is he? The writer C. S. Lewis made this observation: "You must make your choice. Either this man was, and is, the Son of God: or else a madman or something worse. You can shut Him up for a fool, you can spit at Him and kill Him as a demon; or you can fall at His feet and call Him Lord and God. But let us not come with any patronising nonsense about His being a great human teacher. He has not left that open to us. He did not intend to" (*Mere Christianity,* rev. ed. [New York: Macmillan, 1952], 41).

Jesus was not just a good man. He was—and is—the God-man. Let's examine what the Bible has to say about Jesus.

1. **Jesus Is Human.** Jesus became our supreme example as God in human form (see Philippians 2:5-11, p. 248).
2. **Jesus Is Divine.** Even though Jesus became human, he still remained God (see Colossians 1:15-20, p. 254).
3. **Jesus Had a Specific Mission to Accomplish.** Jesus came to save humankind from sin (see Luke 4:16-21, p. 70).
4. **Jesus Made the Ultimate Sacrifice.** Jesus endured tremendous pain so that we could enjoy eternity with him (see 1 Peter 2:24, p. 307).
5. **Jesus Has Great Power to Transform People.** Jesus can change the most unlikely person into one of the most powerful witnesses on his behalf (see Acts 4:13, p. 140).
6. **Jesus Has an Eternal Dominion.** Jesus' Kingdom extends beyond the boundaries of space and time (see Revelation 1:4-8, p. 332).

# Who Is the Holy Spirit?

The Holy Spirit is the most mysterious member of the Trinity, which includes God the Father, God the Son (Jesus Christ), and God the Spirit (or the Holy Spirit). Many struggle with the idea of God being three persons, yet one. Quite honestly, we will never fully grasp the concept this side of heaven.

Some, however, have wrongly thought of the Holy Spirit as more of an "it" than a "him." That is probably due in part to biblical descriptions of him as being like the wind or coming upon Jesus in the form of a dove, among other comparisons.

Yet these descriptions must be balanced with the descriptions of the other members of the Trinity. For instance, Jesus referred to himself as "the bread of life" and "the good shepherd." In the same way, God the Father is referred to as "a refuge" and "a consuming fire." Does this mean that Jesus is a loaf of bread or a sheep farmer, or that the Father is a pile of rocks or a blast furnace? Of course not! These are simply metaphors used in Scripture to help communicate God's character. Likewise, the unique descriptions attributed to the Holy Spirit do not imply that the Holy Spirit is merely some "force" or "power." Jesus said this about the Holy Spirit: "When the Spirit of truth comes, he will guide you into all truth. . . . He will tell you about the future" (John 16:13). Note the use of the pronoun *he*. The Holy Spirit has a distinct personality, and he also has specific work that he wants to do in our lives as followers of Jesus Christ. Explore what the Bible says about him.

1. **Who the Holy Spirit Helps.** The Holy Spirit strengthens and empowers followers of Christ (see Acts 2:1-40, p. 136).
2. **How the Holy Spirit Works with the Father and the Son.** The Holy Spirit works alongside God the Father and Jesus, God's Son, to make our lives pleasing to God (see 1 Peter 1:2, p. 306).
3. **Why God Gives Us the Holy Spirit.** The Holy Spirit's presence in our lives is God's mark of ownership (see Ephesians 1:13-14, p. 238).
4. **How the Holy Spirit Works in Our Lives.** The Holy Spirit draws us to Christ, enters our life at conversion, and empowers us as we allow him to work in our life (see John 14:15-17, p. 126).
5. **When the Holy Spirit Can Be Sinned Against.** There are six specific ways we can sin against the Holy Spirit (see Acts 5:1-10, p. 142).
6. **Why Christians Need the Holy Spirit.** Living the Christian life is impossible without the Holy Spirit's help (see Galatians 5:16-26, p. 230).

## Who Is the Devil?

What is the Devil like? Does he really look like the red-suited, pitchfork-holding cartoon caricature seated on a throne in hell? Or does he roam through the earth disguised as an angel of light?

Unfortunately, far too many people do not have an accurate view of who the Devil is. Many underestimate him and his prowess, even going as far as to doubt his very existence. Someone once asked the great evangelist Charles Finney, "Mr. Finney, do you believe in a literal Devil?" Finney replied, "You try opposing him for a while, and you see if he's literal or not." You will find out how literal the Devil is the moment you make a commitment to Jesus Christ.

The Bible clearly shows us just how active and conniving the Devil really is. At the same time, Scripture also lets us know about the Devil's limitations and ultimate demise. The more we understand the tactics of this intelligent spirit being, the better equipped we will be to ward off his attacks. Below are some key passages of Scripture that answer some of the most commonly asked questions about the Devil—who is also referred to as Satan.

1. **Where Did Satan Come From?** Satan's pride led to his fall from heaven (see Revelation 12:7-9, p. 340).
2. **What Are Satan's Abilities?** Satan does have the power and access to do certain things in this world (see 2 Corinthians 4:3-4, p. 220).
3. **What Are Satan's Limitations?** While we should not underestimate Satan's power, we should realize that it is limited (see 2 Timothy 4:18, p. 278).
4. **How Does Satan Attack People?** Satan masterfully uses manipulation and distortion to deceive people (see 2 Corinthians 11:13-15, p. 226).
5. **Who Can Thwart Satan's Agenda?** Those who lay down their lives for Christ will defeat this evil foe (see Revelation 12:10-12, p. 340).

# What Are Angels?

According to recent surveys, most people believe in the existence of angels. A glut of books on the subject fill bookstore shelves. Still, our only reliable source on angels and their activity is the Bible. Just who are these mysterious creatures? What do they look like? Do they wear long, flowing robes and have large birdlike wings? And what is their purpose?

You might call angels "God's secret agents." They basically work undercover. Most of the time these secret agents remain invisible—except on those special occasions when God allows people to see them. No doubt God realized that if we were allowed to see them all of the time, they would become an object of our worship, which is to be reserved for God alone. Let's take some time to see what the Bible has to say about angels and their role in this world.

1. **Why Did God Create Angels?** God created angels as unique spiritual beings who worship Christ and care for his followers (see Hebrews 1:4-14, p. 286).
2. **What Do Angels Do in the Life of a Christian?** God has ordered the angels to protect his followers and keep them from harm (see Acts 27:23-24, p. 171).
3. **How Are Angels Involved in Our Prayers?** Our prayers can trigger spiritual warfare (see Colossians 2:18-19, p. 255).
4. **What Role Will Angels Play in the End Times?** Angels will play a strategic role in spreading the everlasting gospel (see Revelation 14:6-7, p. 342).

# What Are Demons?

Just as there are angels who look out for your welfare, there are angels who are bent upon your destruction. The Bible teaches that when Satan fell from heaven, he took one-third of the angels with him (Revelation 12:4). Although we do not know their exact number, Scripture tells us there are multitudes (Luke 2:13) and legions (Matthew 26:53) of angels. So Satan has a sizable, highly organized force under his control. These fallen angels, also known as demons, help Satan accomplish his purpose, which, in the words of Christ, is to steal, kill, and destroy. While the Bible does not give us specific details as to how demons work, we can be confident that everything we need to know about them is found in Scripture. We do not need to look elsewhere for insights into the spiritual world. See what God's Word has to say about these evil agents.

1. **What Do Demons Believe?** Strange as it may seem, demons acknowledge that there is only one God (see James 2:19, p. 304).
2. **Can Demons Personally Harm You?** Those people who have a true relationship with Christ cannot be overcome by demons; those who do not are "fair game" for these servants of Satan (see Acts 19:13-20, p. 164).
3. **What Makes Demons Powerless?** The name of Jesus used by the followers of Jesus makes the demons tremble (see Luke 10:1-20, p. 82).

# What Is Heaven?

The Bible gives us wonderful, vivid descriptions of heaven. From Scripture we know that heaven's streets are made of gold, and that pain, fear, and sorrow are not present there. But even with all of this detail, we still fall short of understanding "the big picture." That is because it is difficult for us to grasp the absolute perfection and glory of heaven.

All splendor aside, though, what truly makes heaven spectacular is that we will be forever in God's presence. As the psalmist so poignantly expressed, "You will show me the way of life, granting me the joy of your presence and the pleasures of living with you forever" (Psalm 16:11).

While we may not be able to have all of our questions about heaven answered here on earth, the Bible does answer some of our most probing questions.

1. **Who Will Enter Heaven?** Heaven is a place for those who have received Jesus Christ as Lord (see John 14:1-6, p. 124).
2. **When Does a Christian Enter Heaven?** When we take our last breath on earth, we will take our first breath in heaven (see 2 Corinthians 5:6-9, p. 222).
3. **Will We Recognize People in Heaven?** While our heavenly bodies may resemble our earthly bodies, we will in some ways be like the angels (see Matthew 22:23-33, p. 30).
4. **What Will Life in Heaven Be Like?** Our lives in heaven will no longer be consumed by the cares of this life, but we will be filled with joy being in the presence of our heavenly Father (see Revelation 7:13-17, p. 336).

# What Is Hell?

According to the Bible, you have two options to choose from when it comes to deciding where you will spend your life after death. One option is heaven. The other is hell. Interestingly enough, while there seems to be an increased belief in a place called hell, most people don't believe that they are headed there. Instead, they believe that hell is reserved for only the most hardened of criminals and other "evil" elements of our society. But God's Word judges people by a different set of criteria. You are not sent to hell for being a bad person any more than you are sent to heaven for being a good person. We all deserve to spend eternity in hell (Romans 3:22-23).

While God clearly says that those who reject the salvation offered through his Son, Jesus Christ, will spend eternity in this place of torment, he repeatedly gives each person ample opportunity to choose life—abundant life on earth and eternal life in heaven (2 Peter 3:9). If you haven't made that choice yet, or if you have decided and want a better understanding of what your nonbelieving friends will have to face, consider these facts about hell from the pages of Scripture.

1. **What Is Hell Like?** Hell is a place of unending, isolated torment (see Luke 16:19-31, p. 92).
2. **Who Will Go to Hell?** Those whose names do not appear in the Book of Life are destined to everlasting punishment (see Revelation 20:11-15, p. 346).
3. **What Is the Worst Punishment of Hell?** Hell's worst punishment is everlasting separation from God's presence (see 2 Thessalonians 1:7-10, p. 266).

**Love**

On one occasion Jesus was asked what command-ment was the most important. He replied, "The most important commandment is this: 'Hear, O Israel! The Lord our God is the one and only Lord. And you must love the Lord your God with all your heart, all your soul, all your mind, and all your strength.' The second is equally important: 'Love your neighbor as yourself'" (Mark 12:29-31).

These are the two most important commandments because if you truly love God with all your heart, soul, mind, and strength, you will want to do what pleases him. In the same way, if you really love others as much as you love yourself, you will be concerned for their welfare and will treat them accordingly. Before you can effec-tively love God, however, you must first realize how much he loves you.

Scripture explains that God showed his great love for us by sending Christ to die for us while we were still sinners who had no relationship with him (Romans 5:8). The more we realize this wonderful truth, the more our love for God will grow. The Bible correctly recognizes that our love for God comes as a result of his loving us first (1 John 4:19). These Scripture passages explore some different facets of the love we should have for God and for others.

1. **God Should Be the Greatest Love of Our Life.** Before we can fully love one another, however, we must fully love God and understand his love for us (see Matthew 22:37-38, p. 32).
2. **Christ's Love Sets the Standard.** Our love for others should model Christ's love for us (see Ephesians 5:1-2, p. 244).
3. **Love Surpasses All Spiritual Gifts.** A Christian who understands what love truly means and shows love in his or her life is the greatest testimony to others (see 1 Corin-thians 13:1-13, p. 214).
4. **Our Love for God Prepares Us for Service.** The depth of our love for God directly af-fects our ability to minister to others (see John 21:15-17, p. 132).
5. **Our Love for Others Mirrors the Condition of Our Heart.** The love we have for those around us is an indication of the strength of our Christian walk (see 1 John 2:9-11, p. 318).
6. **Our Love Should Grow.** The closer we grow to God, the more our love for others should increase (see 1 Thessalonians 3:12-13, p. 260).

**Forgiveness**

One of the great principles of the Christian life is forgive-ness. Jesus modeled this principle for us when he hung on the cross and prayed for the very people who had put him there (see Luke 23:34, p. 104). His words were so powerful and unexpected that they brought about the conversion of one of the thieves hanging on a cross next to him.

Because Jesus completely forgave us, he wants us to follow his example by forgiving others. As Scripture says: "Be kind to each other, tenderhearted, forgiving one another, just as God through Christ has forgiven you. Follow God's example in everything you do, because you are his dear children" (Ephesians 4:32–5:1). The Bible gives us several important characteristics of the forgiveness we should have for others.

1. **Forgiveness First Comes from God.** Our forgiveness of others should flow from God's forgiveness of us (see Mark 11:25, p. 56).
2. **Forgiveness Knows No Limits.** For a Christian, no wrong is too great or too small to forgive (see Matthew 18:21-35, p. 26).
3. **Forgiveness Is Not Selective.** You can't choose to forgive some people and not forgive others (see Matthew 5:43-48, p. 10).
4. **Forgiveness Breaks Down Walls.** When you choose to forgive, you experience true freedom (see Colossians 3:12-15, p. 257).

**Purity**

Purity is a quality we hear too little about today. Usually when we do hear something about purity, it is in reference to sexual purity. But purity goes beyond this to include wholesome thoughts, a sincere desire to do what is right, and a commitment to obey God's Word. Jesus alluded to the importance of purity by promising that those whose hearts were pure would see God (Matthew 5:8). In using the word heart, Jesus was saying that the center of our being—our will, our emotions, and our thought processes—needs to be cleansed of sin. The Bible texts below examine the idea of purity and how it affects us as followers of Jesus Christ.

1. **Don't Place Yourself in the Way of Unnecessary Temptation.** Know your moral weaknesses and avoid situations where the temptation to sin would be irresistible (see James 1:14-15, p. 299).
2. **Guard the Content of Your Thoughts.** Don't fill your mind with the world's moral filth (see 2 Timothy 2:22, p. 276).
3. **Beware of the Sins of the Heart.** The person who commits adultery in his heart is just as guilty as the person who actually carries it out (see Matthew 5:27-30, p. 8).
4. **Avoid Adulterous Relationships.** God specifically warns us against living in immoral relationships (see 1 Thessalonians 4:1-8, p. 262).
5. **If You Fall, Ask God to Forgive You and Purify Your Heart and Desires.** Only God can forgive you, restore your joy, and fill you with the right desires (see 1 John 1:9, p. 317).
6. **Keep an Eternal Perspective.** Don't waste your time chasing after earthly pleasures (see 2 Peter 3:10-11, p. 316).

**7. Live to Please God.** Surrendering your life to the leading of the Holy Spirit is the only way to live a life that is pleasing to God (see Romans 8:5-8, p. 184).

## Perseverance

There will be times in your Christian walk when you will feel emotionally "down." You may think that God has forgotten about you. Or you might become discouraged as you see others who have professed faith in Jesus Christ lose interest in spiritual things and fall away. You may begin to wonder whether you are next on the Devil's "hit list." But God will not allow you to be hit with more than you can handle spiritually. In fact, it is during times of trouble that you will actually be strengthened, not weakened.

As you read your Bible, you will come across words like *endurance* and *perseverance.* These words are often used when the Bible compares the Christian life to a race. The race referred to is a marathon, not a fifty-yard dash. Because the Christian life is a long-distance run, you need to pace yourself, to persevere, and most of all, to *finish* the race. Look up the following passages that describe how and why you need to persevere through the inevitable struggles of life.

**1. Perseverance Produces Results.** As you steadily grow in your understanding of God's Word and apply it to your life, you will win others to the Lord (see Luke 8:15, p. 78).
**2. Life's Trials Will Make You Stronger.** You shouldn't view difficulties as obstacles to your faith, but as opportunities for spiritual growth (see James 1:2-4, p. 300).
**3. Christ Endured Great Pain for Us.** Jesus modeled the ultimate in endurance so that we would be encouraged to keep our faith strong in the race of life (see Hebrews 12:1-3, p. 294).
**4. God Honors Those Who Persevere.** A wholehearted commitment to God will enable you to "finish well" with your faith intact (see 2 Timothy 4:7-8, p. 278).

## Honesty and Integrity

Honesty and integrity seem to be in short supply these days. Yet the Bible tells us that they are a part of the godly man's or woman's life. Unfortunately, the world tends to gloss over that aspect of the Christian life. It wants to characterize Christians as people who are out of touch with reality. But the Christian is simply someone who allows God to influence every aspect of his or her life—down to the practical, everyday dealings of business, finances, and relationships. The following passages examine how honesty and integrity should characterize our lives.

1. **We Should Be above Criticism.** Daniel's faithful and honest lifestyle made him "stand apart" from everyone else (see 2 Corinthians 7:2, p. 222).
2. **Our Conduct Should Cause Others to Glorify Christ.** Living a good, honest life around our unbelieving neighbors will ultimately bring glory to God (see 1 Peter 2:9-12, p. 310).
3. **We Need to Set an Example for Others.** We must seriously pursue a life of integrity in order to be a solid example for our fellow Christians (see Titus 2:6-8, p. 280).

## Faith and Works

When a person truly comes to Jesus Christ, this relationship will dramatically transform his or her life. We may see this transformation more immediately in the lives of some than others. For those whose lives are characterized by pronounced bad habits and blatant immoral living, the change in lifestyle will show others that something profound has indeed happened within that person's life. For others who may not be known for blatantly sinful living, the change may not be as outwardly pronounced, but it is just as significant. Remember, all of us were separated from God by sin, which was dealt with and atoned for at the cross of Jesus.

Our conversion will show itself in both fruit and works. This concept of "bearing fruit" is used often in Scripture to describe the results of someone's commitment to Jesus Christ. If we do not bear fruit, then it is apparent we have not really come to know Jesus Christ as Lord and Savior. Bearing fruit is not an option. It is the natural result of a person coming into union with God. Sometimes there is confusion in this area of fruit bearing, or works. See what the Bible has to say about the issue.

1. **Our Lives Should Show That God Is at Work in Our Hearts.** God desires that we demonstrate our spiritual growth through our outward actions (see Romans 7:4, p. 182).
2. **We Must Live Out Our Faith.** Faith without deeds is incomplete (see James 2:14-18, p. 302).
3. **God Saved Us for a Purpose.** While God himself gave us salvation, he planned that our salvation would lead to good works (see Ephesians 2:10, p. 240).
4. **Our Walk Should Match Our Talk.** God isn't as concerned with what we *say* we believe as with how we *live* what we believe (see Matthew 7:21-23, p. 12).

**Discernment**

An inspector who worked for Scotland Yard in the counterfeit department was once asked if he spent a lot of time handling counterfeit money. He said, "No." He then explained that he spent so much time handling the "real thing" that he could immediately detect the counterfeit. In the same way, as we become knowledgeable about God's Word, we, too, will be able to detect teachings and concepts that are contrary to Scripture. Make no mistake—counterfeit "truth" is out there in force. Look at the following Scripture passages to find out how you can keep from falling prey to false teachings.

1. **Beware of Satan's Clever Imitations.** Satan's work and agents may appear godly, but in the end they will be exposed for what they really are (see Matthew 13:24-30, p. 20).
2. **Recognize Satan's Strategies.** Lies and deceit are Satan's two main strategies to lead people away from the truth (see 1 Timothy 4:1-2, p. 270).
3. **Understand the Difference between the True Gospel and a False Gospel.** Scripture provides us with a "litmus test" to distinguish between truth and error (see 1 John 4:1-3, p. 320).
4. **Use God's Word to Evaluate Someone's Teachings.** The best way to detect a counterfeit is to become more familiar with the "real thing" (see Acts 17:11, p. 160).

**Peace**

Peace of mind—it seems almost elusive in a day when murders are commonplace, job security is nonexistent, and the moral fabric of society is tearing apart at the seams. Yet Jesus has promised that each one of us can experience true peace: "I am leaving you with a gift—peace of mind and heart. And the peace I give isn't like the peace the world gives. So don't be troubled or afraid" (John 14:27).

Unfortunately, some people are so caught up in the "pursuit of peace," that they have forgotten that Jesus has already given it to them. They have simply left that gift "unopened." And we cannot find peace outside of the parameters God has given us. As Augustine said many years ago, "Our souls are restless until they find their rest in God." Begin to "unwrap" this precious gift by examining what God's Word has to say about it.

1. **Peace Begins When We Relinquish Control of Our Lives to God.** When we give Jesus our burdens and allow him to guide us, we find rest (see Matthew 11:28-30, p. 16).

2. **Perfect Peace Builds upon Total Trust.** As God becomes a regular part of our daily lives, our worries begin to disappear (see John 16:33, p. 128).

3. **Our Peace Continues As We Follow the Holy Spirit.** We must stop allowing our old, sinful nature to control us before we can really experience peace (see Romans 8:5-8, p. 188).

4. **God's Peace Needs to Rule in Our Hearts.** We must constantly keep other things from crowding out God's peace in our lives (see Colossians 3:15, p. 256).

## Joy

One noticeable change that takes place in a new believer's life is the inner joy he or she receives. In fact, joy is listed as part of the "fruit of the Spirit" that should be evident in a believer's life (see Galatians 5:22). But this joy is different from the fleeting and temporary "happiness" that is usually dependent upon "good things" happening in someone's life. While sorrows will come a believer's way, the Holy Spirit gives him or her an inner joy and peace that cannot be taken away. Below are some of the ways in which you can experience God's joy in your life.

1. **Studying God's Word Helps Us to Experience His Joy.** As we study God's Word and honor God with our lives, we experience his joy in our lives (see 1 Thessalonians 1:6, p. 259).

2. **Knowing and Trusting God Is the Source of Inexpressible Joy.** The greatest joy we can experience comes only from a personal relationship with Jesus Christ (see 1 Peter 1:8, p. 308).

3. **Sharing Your Faith Results in Joy.** While laboring to introduce people to Jesus is difficult work, the end result will give you much to celebrate (see John 4:36, p. 111).

4. **Overlooking Petty Issues Frees Us to Experience Joy.** God wants us to experience his joy in our lives and to avoid those things that could hamper that joy (see 1 Corinthians 1:10-17, p. 198).

5. **Knowing Whom You Belong to and What the Future Holds Brings True Joy.** Realizing that you are a child of God and that you will spend eternity in heaven with him will bring you joy (see Romans 15:13, p. 196).

## Accountability

Once you receive Jesus Christ into your life as your personal Lord and Savior, not only do you obtain the privileged gift of eternal life, but you immediately acquire a great responsibility. You have been entrusted with the message of the gospel and are responsible for what you do with it in your life. In the end, we know that what we have done on this earth for Christ will be examined before almighty God and displayed before the rest of the world. The question we must all ask is this: Will what I am doing for Christ and his Kingdom stand the test of time? Those who have done much with what God has given them will be greatly rewarded. Take some time to see what God's Word has to say on this subject.

1. **The More We Know, the Greater Our Responsibility Will Be.** The Lord holds those who have been given positions of spiritual leadership to a higher accountability for what they do (see Luke 12:48, p. 88).
2. **We Are Responsible for Our Own Sins and Mistakes.** We cannot pass blame onto others for our own failings (see Romans 3:23, p. 178).
3. **We Need to Invest Our Abilities and Resources in God's Kingdom.** God has graciously given us abilities and resources to invest in the expansion of his Kingdom (see Luke 19:11-26, p. 96).
4. **The Value of Our Work on Earth Will Be Tested.** On Judgment Day, the quality of our faith and the work we have done for Jesus Christ will be revealed and rewarded accordingly (see 1 Corinthians 3:10-15, p. 200).

*What to do after you have accepted Christ . . .*

## Study the Bible

You might say that the Bible is the "user's manual of life" we have all been searching for. Everything we need to know about God and living a life that pleases him is found in its pages.

Tragically, some of us go through life without so much as picking up this amazing book, whose words were inspired by God. Yet, success or failure in the Christian life is determined by how much of the Bible we get into our hearts and minds and how obedient we are to the principles and teachings found within it. Just as we need to continually breathe oxygen to survive, we need to regularly study the Bible to grow and flourish spiritually. Here are some important reasons why we need to spend time in this life-changing book.

1. **Studying the Bible Is Necessary for Our Spiritual Growth.** The Bible performs three functions to help us mature spiritually (see 2 Timothy 3:16-17, p. 277).
2. **Studying the Bible Keeps Us Spiritually Strong.** The more we get into this book and apply its teachings, the more we will be able to stand our ground in the storms and trials of life (see Matthew 7:24-27, p. 12).
3. **Studying the Bible Makes Scripture a Central Part of Our Lives.** God desires that we make the Bible an integral part of our lives (see Colossians 3:16, p. 257).
4. **Studying the Bible Helps Us Apply Its Truth to Our Lives.** We will notice positive changes in our lives as we apply what we read in Scripture (see 2 Timothy 3:16-17, p. 277).

## Pray

The idea of talking to God can be intimidating. But it doesn't have to be. In fact, prayer can be a wonderful experience if we know how to do it God's way. Fortunately, we have God's Word to teach us how to pray. The Bible instructs us to pray at all times, in any posture, in any place, for any reason. In addition, it does not matter whether you pray in King James English or the most contemporary jargon. God only desires that you pray from a pure and sincere heart.

The disciples observed the profound effect prayer had in Jesus' life and ministry. They witnessed how Jesus would often go off by himself to spend time in prayer with his heavenly Father. They saw the power, peace, and tranquillity that emanated from his life, giving him the ability to stay calm in troubled circumstances. Jesus' prayer life so impressed these men that they asked him to teach them to pray (Luke 11:1-13). Certainly if the perfect Son of God often took time to pray during his life here on earth, how much more do we, mere men and women, need to pray?

Because prayer is an essential ingredient to walking with Jesus Christ, we need to examine its elements found in God's Word.

1. **Prayer Was Modeled for Us by Christ.** Jesus took the time to show his followers how to pray (see Matthew 6:5-15, p. 9).
2. **Prayer Is Not a Solitary Experience.** God has given us his Holy Spirit to aid us in prayer, even when we do not know what to pray (see Romans 8:26-27, p. 183).
3. **Prayer Allows Us to Voice Our Requests to God.** Prayer is God's appointed way for us to relate our concerns and present our needs to him (see James 4:2-3, p. 301).
4. **Prayer Enables Us to Seek Forgiveness.** When we pray sincerely for forgiveness, God will hear our prayers and restore us (see James 5:15-16, p. 304).
5. **Prayer Helps Us Overcome Worry.** In the midst of troubles, we can receive God's peace through prayer (see Philippians 4:6-7, p. 251).
6. **Prayer Increases Our Spiritual Knowledge and Maturity.** God will give us greater spiritual understanding through prayer (see Colossians 1:9, p. 253).

## Look for and Attend the Right Church

One of the essential building blocks of spiritual growth is fellowship with other believers by becoming part of a local church. The church (meaning the entire body of Christians) is not really an organization so much as an organism. It thrives by keeping its members spiritually active and well fed. The church provides you with spiritual instruction from God's Word, allows you to worship God with other believers, enables you to use your God-given gifts and abilities as God intended, and makes you accountable to spiritual leadership. Some people think they can get enough spiritual input from Christian television, radio programs, and books. While those things do have value, nothing can replace the need to become an active member of a church. Think about it—if joining in fellowship with other believers was not important, why did Jesus establish the church? (see Matthew 16:18). The Bible has plenty to say about the characteristics of a healthy, vibrant church and the necessity of Christian fellowship. Here are four helpful insights from God's Word on looking for and attending the right church.

1. **What to Look for in a Church.** You should look for a church that has the qualities and characteristics of the first century church (see Acts 2:42, 44-47, p. 139).
2. **Why We Need Fellowship with Other Believers.** Fellowship with other Christians sharpens your spiritual discernment and prepares you for Christ's return (see Hebrews 10:25, p. 293).
3. **Why the Church Needs You.** Not only will you benefit from the church, but the church will benefit from you and your God-given abilities (see Ephesians 4:11-16, p. 239).
4. **You Have a Place in the Church.** God has given each one of us a unique role to play in our place of fellowship (see 1 Corinthians 12:12-31, p. 213).

The real evidence of a true Christian is a changed life. The great British preacher Charles Haddon Spurgeon once said, "Of what value is the grace I profess to receive if it does not dramatically change the way that I live? If it doesn't change the way that I live, it will never change my eternal destiny."

## Obey God

A changed life begins with obedience to God. This means that you will have to stop doing certain things and start doing others. While God begins to change your heart and desires once you have surrendered your life to him, he still gives you the freedom to decide just how much of your life you will let him control. But know this: Whatever you give up to follow Jesus Christ will pale in comparison to what he will give you in return. For example, when you give up sinful behaviors for God, he will replace your sin with forgiveness and a clear conscience. With this incentive for obedience, look at six specific ways the Bible instructs us to obey God.

1. **Recognize That You Are a New Creation.** When you understand what God has done in your life, obedience becomes more of a desire than a mere duty (see 2 Corinthians 5:14-17, p. 223).
2. **Follow God Wholeheartedly.** When you follow God completely, you will finish the race of life well (see Hebrews 12:1-3, p. 296).

3. **Offer God More than Lip Service.** God looks at your heart more than your religious actions (see Matthew 23:25-28, p. 33).
4. **Live in God's Love.** Discover the secret of true and lasting joy (see John 15:9-11, p. 127).
5. **Put on God's Armor.** Obedience prepares you for the battles of life (see Romans 13:11-14, p. 191).
6. **Let God Occupy Your Thoughts.** Your thoughts will affect your actions (see Colossians 3:1-4, p. 255).

# Resist Temptation

Now that you are a follower of Jesus Christ, Satan is going to try to draw you away by tempting you to disobey God's Word. It is not a sin to be tempted—even Jesus was tempted (see Luke 4:1-13). We sin when we give in to that temptation. The good news is that God will never let a temptation become so strong that we can't handle it. In addition, he has given us specific ways to handle temptation. Here are three things to remember when dealing with temptation.

1. **Realize Who Is Tempting You.** Satan is the mastermind behind all of your temptations (see Ephesians 6:10-12, p. 243).
2. **Resist the Devil.** The Bible says that if you resist Satan's enticements, he will flee from you (see James 4:7-8, p. 303).
3. **Rejoice Because Victory Is Yours in Christ Jesus.** God promises that he will always provide a way of escape (see 1 Corinthians 10:13, p. 209).

# Live in God's Power

Some people look at the Christian life and say, "I couldn't begin to live that way and hold to those standards. It is too hard!" This is true. It is not hard to be a Christian—it is impossible (that is without the help of the Holy Spirit). You see, God has given you power to live the Christian life. The moment you asked Jesus Christ into your heart, he gave you the gift of his Holy Spirit (see "Who Is the Holy Spirit?" p. A12).

The Holy Spirit not only takes up residence in your heart, but he empowers you to live a holy life and to be an effective witness for Jesus Christ. The Holy Spirit's power is much like an investment. You need to draw upon his power daily to live out your faith. To find out more about how the Holy Spirit can empower and strengthen your Christian walk, look up the following passages of Scripture.

1. **God's Spirit Will Guide You.** The Holy Spirit will help you understand the truths of Scripture and the character of God (see John 16:13-15, p. 129).
2. **God's Spirit Will Empower Your Witness.** The Holy Spirit will give you greater courage and an increased ability to share your faith (see Acts 1:8, p. 137).
3. **God's Spirit Will Encourage You to Be Obedient.** You will have a Holy Spirit-inspired desire to obey God's commands (see Romans 8:13-14, p. 184).
4. **God's Spirit Will Help You Overcome Sin.** Sin will no longer have the power over you it had before you accepted Christ into your life (see Romans 8:9-14, p. 181).

# Share Your Faith

Next to personally knowing Jesus and walking with him, one of the greatest blessings of the Christian life is to actually lead someone to Jesus Christ. The good news is that God wants to use you—not just pastors, missionaries, and evangelists—as his instrument to speak to others.

Jesus gave us this very commission in Mark 16:15, where he says, "Go into all the world and preach the Good News to everyone, everywhere." This wonderful charge is known as the "great commission." But the way some Christians follow it, you would think it was the "great suggestion." Sharing our faith, however, is something that Jesus wants—and commands—us to do! How do we do this? First Peter 3:15-16 tells us to be ready to give an answer to anyone who asks us about the hope we have in Jesus. Here are five passages from God's Word that will help you to share your faith.

1. **You Don't Need Any Training to Share.** A changed heart is all you need to begin sharing your faith with others (see John 9:1-41, p. 117).
2. **Be Open to God's Leading.** Effectively sharing your faith begins with a willing heart (see Acts 8:4-8, 26-38, p. 147).
3. **Understand the Simplicity of the Gospel.** The message of the gospel is simple yet powerful (see 1 Corinthians 2:1-5, p. 199).
4. **Share Your Own Story.** Never underestimate the strength of your personal testimony (see Acts 26:1-23, p. 171).

## Seek God's Will

Have you ever wondered about the future? Have you pondered the answers to such important, life-changing decisions as whom you should marry or what career path you should pursue? More than likely, most of us have asked these questions and wondered if God has a definite plan or opinion in the matter. With that in mind, here is some good news: God is vitally interested in your life, and he does want to lead you in your decisions.

Jesus called his followers friends (see John 15:15). As God's friend you already have an "inside track" in discovering God's will for your life. It is called the Bible. There you will find God's general will for your life (such as putting God first in all you do and following God's guidelines for marriage), as well as some principles to follow when seeking his specific direction for your life. In the end, finding God's will comes down to living out what you read in the Bible and then living by faith. Here are six steps you can take as you seek God's will.

1. **Unconditionally Surrender Your Life.** Certain conditions must be met if you want to know God's will for your life (see Romans 12:1-2, p. 185).
2. **Realize That God Has a Plan for Your Life.** Your life has purpose and meaning, and God wants to reveal it to you (see Ephesians 1:7-9, p. 237).
3. **Act upon What God Has Already Revealed in Scripture.** God has already given us some specific guidelines to follow in his Word (see 1 Thessalonians 4:1-8, p. 261).
4. **Trust God Completely.** There is nothing more reassuring than entrusting an unknown future to a known God (see Philippians 4:6-7, p. 250).
5. **Listen for God's Voice.** Sometimes God speaks to us in a quiet voice (see John 10:27, p. 119).

## Live as a Disciple

When you hear the word *disciple,* do you immediately think of the Twelve who followed Jesus during his ministry on earth? Many people do not realize that Jesus still has disciples in this day and age. While every disciple is a believer, not every believer is necessarily a disciple. A disciple is someone who has made a wholehearted commitment to follow Jesus Christ as Savior and Lord. In one sense, you might call discipleship "radical Christian living." When you truly make a commitment to be Christ's disciple, you will be living the Christian life as it was meant to be lived. Anything short of discipleship is settling for less than what God desires. Here are four passages from the Bible that explain what it means to truly be a disciple of Jesus.

1. **A Disciple Takes Up His or Her Cross and Follows Christ.** Being a disciple takes work and commitment (see Luke 9:23-25, p. 81).
2. **A Disciple Counts the Cost.** Jesus' disciples are willing to give up everything to follow him (see Luke 14:25-33, p. 91).
3. **A Disciple Abides in Christ.** The source of a disciple's strength comes from his or her closeness to Christ (see John 15:1-17, p. 125).
4. **A Disciple Walks as Jesus Walked.** Disciples pattern their lives after Jesus, the ultimate example of how to live (see 1 John 2:3-6, p. 319).

**Give to God**

Money is such an important topic in the Bible that it is the main subject of nearly *half* the parables Jesus told. In addition, one out of every seven verses in the New Testament deals with the topic. To give you an idea of how this compares with other topics, Scripture offers about five hundred verses on prayer and fewer than five hundred on faith, while there are more than *two thousand* verses on money!

You may be wondering what money has to do with your faith. Now that Jesus Christ has come into your life, he wants to be Lord (to be in command) of every aspect of it. That includes your finances. Martin Luther astutely observed, "There are three conversions necessary: the conversion of the heart, the mind, and the purse [or wallet]." When we experience this "conversion of the purse" and give freely of our finances to the Lord's work (to our church, a missionary, or a ministry), we will make the best investment possible—an investment with eternal dividends. With that in mind, here are five questions to consider about wealth and giving.

1. **Why Should You Give a Portion of Your Financial Resources to God?** God wants to prove his faithfulness through your regular giving, or tithes (see 2 Corinthians 9:6-11, p. 225).
2. **How Much Should You Give?** God encourages us to give sacrificially (see Mark 12:41-44, p. 59).
3. **What Happens When You Give?** When you give with the right motives, you will experience joy and God's generous blessings (see 2 Corinthians 9:6-14, p. 227).
4. **How Should You View Material Wealth?** Accumulating wealth should never be a high priority because it is eternally worthless (see Matthew 6:19-34, p. 11).
5. **Can You Enjoy Wealth?** God may bless you materially, but you are responsible for using your material blessings wisely (see 1 Timothy 6:17-19, p. 271).

## Have Courage in Trials

Many Christians have the mistaken idea that once they make a commitment to Jesus Christ, life will be smooth sailing from that day forward. This is certainly not the case. While it is true that walking with Christ will help us avoid many of the problems we used to face, we are still going to experience what the Bible calls "trials."

Trials may come in the form of a crisis, a sudden illness, the loss of a loved one, or some drastic change in your life. You may go through a difficult time when you don't feel God's presence, when church may not be as exciting as it once was for you, or your prayers seem to go no higher than the ceiling. This may cause you to wonder if you have angered God or if he has left you. But God does not allow us to experience trials because he wants to see us suffer. Rather, he allows these difficulties into our lives to help us grow spiritually—to learn to live by faith, not by feelings. Look up the following passages to see the role trials play in our lives. Notice also God's promise to be with us during these times of trouble.

1. **Trials Sharpen Our Faith.** Hardships develop our character and purify our faith (see 1 Peter 1:3-7, p. 307).
2. **Trials Help Us Comfort Others.** Experiencing suffering deepens our compassion for others who suffer (see 2 Corinthians 1:3-7, p. 219).
3. **Trials Are Survivable.** We must keep our eternal perspective through the tough times (see 2 Corinthians 4:7-18, p. 221).
4. **Trials Test Our Foundation.** When we ground our lives in Christ, we can weather any storm (see Luke 6:47-49, p. 75).
5. **Jesus Is with Us in Life's Storms.** We are never outside of God's watchful eye and his abiding presence (see Mark 4:35-41, p. 47).
6. **God Gives Hope to Our Troubled Hearts.** We can have peace of mind in the middle of our greatest trials (see John 14:1-7, p. 123).

# OFF AND RUNNING

*How your faith affects the daily aspects of your life*

**Marriage**

How many times have you heard the cliché "They have a marriage made in heaven"? This statement implies that some marriages are destined to be good, while others are destined to be bad. Such thinking assumes that marriage has a life of its own, and the only way to find out if you are to have a "good" one or a "bad" one is to "give it a shot." What most people don't seem to understand, though, is that marriage is like a mirror. It reflects what it sees. If a marriage is strong, it is because the husband and wife have put a lot of hard work into it. If a marriage is weak, it is because the husband or wife or both have neglected it.

God never intended for anyone to have a weak marriage. His design for marriage is lifelong, fulfilling companionship. For a couple's marriage to thrive within his design, the couple must obey God and his Word and lay aside this world's distorted and perverse concept of marriage. The Bible contains truths that will not only help keep a couple together but will also keep their marriage strong. In fact, the lessons this book gives on marriage should serve as the foundation of every Christian couple's relationship. Whether you are married or single, the following verses will give you a godly perspective on marriage relationships.

1. **God Created Marriage.** We can learn more about God's marriage ideal from the world's first husband and wife (see Matthew 19:4-6, p. 27).
2. **Husbands and Wives Have Distinct Roles in Marriage.** A marriage works when a couple follows God's specific design for the husband and the wife (see Ephesians 5:21-33, p. 242).
3. **The Boundaries of Marriage Are to Be Honored and Enjoyed.** Sexual intimacy is meant to be enjoyed only within the bounds of the marriage relationship (see Hebrews 13:4, p. 297).

4. **Keeping Your Marriage Strong.** God promises punishment to those who commit adultery or lead immoral lives (see Hebrews 13:4, p. 296).

5. **Divorce Is Not Part of God's Plan.** Jesus teaches that marriage is meant to be a life-long commitment (see Mark 10:2-12, p. 54).

6. **A Christian Should Not Leave a Non-Christian Spouse.** An unbelieving husband or wife should not be abandoned, but loved (see 1 Corinthians 7:12-16, p. 206).

7. **Marriage Is Not for Everyone.** Although God blesses many with marriage, some are given a calling or ability to remain single (see 1 Corinthians 7:1-40, p. 204).

8. **There Is an Intimacy in Marriage That Can Be Found Nowhere Else.** God wants you to have a fulfilling, enjoyable sex life within the parameters of marriage (see 1 Corinthians 7:3-5, p. 204).

## Children

God's plan is to build, strengthen, and protect the family. Satan's plan is to undermine, weaken, and destroy it. Make no mistake: Satan has declared war on the family. Tragically, many of us have been willing accomplices. Why? Because the bulk of the problems in our culture today can be directly traced to the breakdown of the family or to homes in which biblical principles are ignored or disobeyed. This not only includes husbands and wives splitting apart, but also "alternative families," such as homosexual marriages and "live-in" lovers. Such relationships will never be blessed or honored by God, for they are clearly outside the parameters of his will. It has been said, "A family can survive without a country, but a country cannot survive without the family."

Fortunately, there is hope. The Bible gives us specific guidelines to follow when it comes to parenting. If they are put into practice, we will see amazing results. See what the Bible has to say about raising children who love and revere the Lord in a world that is often hostile to God and his values.

1. **Children Are Never Too Young to Learn about God.** Teaching your children to love the Lord in their early years will help them stay true to the Lord later in life (see Galatians 6:7-9, p. 234).

2. **Make Sure Your Children Hear the Gospel Message.** The gospel must first be preached in the home (see Acts 16:29-34, p. 158).

3. **Encourage Your Children's Spiritual Growth.** As the apostle Paul suggests, a loving father encourages his children to live a life pleasing to God (see 1 Thessalonians 2:11-12, p. 260).

4. **Watch the Legacy You Leave.** Your devotion to God—or lack of it—will make a resounding impression on the next generation (see Acts 21:5, p. 165).

**5. Discipline Your Children.** Parents who love their children and want them to grow up into young men and women of character will discipline them (see Hebrews 12:5-11, p. 297).

**6. Avoid Aggravating Your Children.** Your discipline must be tempered with love so that your children do not become resentful (see Colossians 3:20-21, p. 256).

## Priorities

As a Christian, one of the most dramatic changes in your life will be the way you spend your time. Your pursuits and ambitions in life will be different. After all, you are no longer living for yourself but for God. It may be a difficult transition at first, but here are a few pointers we can glean from God's Word.

**1. Place Christ before All Else.** To be a true follower of Jesus Christ, you need to be wholly devoted to him and let nothing else get in the way of your devotion (see Philippians 3:4-11, p. 250).

**2. Balance Christian Service with Worship.** Don't get so caught up in "serving" the Lord that you forget to worship him and get to know him better (see Luke 10:38-42, p. 84).

**3. Don't Waste Time Pursuing Things That Won't Last.** Your time on earth is short. Ask God to help you spend it on things that count (see 2 Timothy 4:5-8, p. 278).

**4. Spend Time Feeding Your Soul.** God offers blessings to you if you choose to spend time with him rather than devote your life to the pursuit of temporary satisfaction (see 1 Peter 2:1-3, p. 306).

**5. Keep Your Spiritual Zeal Alive.** Work hard to keep that "fire" in your heart burning brightly as you serve the Lord (see Romans 12:11, p. 186).

## Prayer Time

Before you became a Christian, you may have prayed before meals, on holidays, or perhaps during times of crisis. As a believer, however, prayer should become second nature. Prayer is no longer an option but should become part of all you do.

As you integrate prayer into every aspect of your life, you will not always see your prayers answered the way you would like them to be. When this happens, it is easy to grow discouraged and give up praying. But Jesus implored us to pray and never give up (Luke 18:1). Paul also instructed believers to "keep on praying" (1 Thessalonians 5:17). When we fail to pray, we miss out on one of the greatest blessings of the Christian life—fellowship with God himself, our power source for living. In addition, we are going against what God has instructed us to do.

The Bible gives us some perspective on how to experience the power of prayer in our lives. The following is a partial list of what should characterize your prayers as a believer.

1. **Pray Regularly.** God wants to hear our prayers throughout the day—not just in times of crisis or before meals (see Acts 10:2, p. 150).
2. **Pray without Hinderance.** Sins and other distractions can negatively affect your prayer life (see Luke 22:39-46, p. 101).
3. **Pray Expecting to Get Answers.** The Bible gives us guidelines to follow so that our prayers will be answered (see 1 John 5:14-15, p. 322).
4. **Pray Effectively.** Prayer can work powerfully in the face of a crisis when God's people come together and call out to him (see Acts 12:1-17, p. 152).
5. **Pray Persistently.** God honors persistent prayer (see Luke 18:1-8, p. 94).

## Conversation

As a Christian, it is extremely important to remember that you are a representative of Jesus Christ. One of the more visible ways you represent him is through your speech or conversations. It has been said that every person speaks about thirty thousand words in an average day. That is a considerable amount of "representation time"—especially when you consider the power of the spoken word. With our mouths we have the power to build up or destroy. This should give you even greater motivation to weigh your words before you speak them.

The Bible shares some practical advice when it comes to controlling the tongue. Below are a few passages of Scripture to guide you in this area.

1. **Think Before You Speak.** You demonstrate great wisdom and care when you weigh your words (see 1 Timothy 4:12, p. 272).
2. **Control Your Tongue.** As you learn to control your tongue, you will be able to control other aspects of your life (see James 3:1-12, p. 302).
3. **Refrain from Idle Talk.** We will be held accountable for every idle word we speak (see Matthew 12:35-37, p. 18).
4. **Make a Habit of Talking about the Lord.** When we talk about the Lord and his blessings with one another, God is pleased (see Acts 11:20, p. 151).
5. **Keep Your Conversation Gracious.** We should speak gently and sensibly as we share our faith with others (see Colossians 4:6, p. 258).
6. **Never Use Vulgar Speech.** Our conversations need to reflect God's goodness, not the world's coarseness (see 1 Peter 3:10, p. 308).
7. **Think of Ways to Encourage, Praise, and Build Up Others.** As a Christian, you should use your speech constructively (see 1 Thessalonians 5:11, p. 264).

**Relationships**

The people we associate with on a regular basis can either help or hinder our spiritual growth. For that reason God has given us some invaluable advice and strong warnings when it comes to choosing our friends. Look at the following Scripture passages to see what to pursue and what to avoid in your relationships with others.

1. **Find a Close Christian Friend.** A true Christian friend will help you get through times of trouble and temptation (see Galatians 6:1-3, p. 232).
2. **Don't Associate with Those Who Mock God.** God and his Word should be the focus of praise—not mockery—in your friendships (see 2 Timothy 3:1-5, p. 277).
3. **Avoid Relationships That Could Cause You to Sin.** Bad company corrupts good character (see 2 Corinthians 6:14–7:1, p. 224).
4. **Make Sure Your Friendships Honor God.** Seek the friendship of those who live as Christ intended (see 1 John 1:7, p. 318).

**Responsibility**

A common question that many new Christians have is, "Can I be a Christian and still do . . . ?" Some questions of "Christian liberty" can be answered easily, because the Bible directly addresses these questions. For instance, if someone asks, "Is it OK, as a Christian, to get drunk?" The answer is clearly no. The Bible says, "Don't be drunk with wine, because that will ruin your life. Instead, let the Holy Spirit fill and control you" (Ephesians 5:18). However, questions like, "Can I be a Christian and still drink alcoholic beverages?" or "Can I listen to any kind of music?" or "Can I go to any movie?" are not answered so easily. They are among the many "gray" areas of the Christian life that do not necessarily have a "chapter and verse" answer.

When you face a situation that the Bible does not directly address, you must consider whether or not your actions will please God. Here is a "litmus test" you can apply to those uncertain areas of life.

1. **Does This Activity Build Me Up Spiritually?** You need to avoid anything that has the potential to dull your spiritual senses and take away your hunger for God and his Word (see 1 Corinthians 10:23, p. 210).
2. **Does This Activity Bring Me under Its Power?** As a Christian, you only want to be controlled by the power of Jesus Christ (see 1 Corinthians 6:12, p. 202).

**3. Do I Have an Uneasy Conscience about This Activity?** You must be obedient to what God has told you to do, not swayed by what others are doing (see Romans 14:23, p. 194).

**4. Could This Activity Cause Other Christians to Stumble in Their Faith?** Stay away from things that could negatively influence other Christians around you (see Romans 14:3-21, p. 192).

## Job Performance

Some of the greatest challenges you may ever face as a Christian will come from the workplace. Perhaps you work in an unethical, morally questionable environment. Maybe you find it difficult to respect those who are over you. You might find your job tedious or meaningless. You may even wonder if you are making an impact on your co-workers for Christ. Whatever your vocation, your work can become more fulfilling and rewarding when you follow what the Bible has to say about your attitude toward your job or responsibilities. Take these biblical pointers to heart and see what a difference they will make!

**1. Work As If You Are Working for the Lord.** Keep in mind that you are ultimately serving the Lord, not just people (see Colossians 3:22-24, p. 258).

**2. Create a Spiritual Hunger in Those around You.** Your godly example can help increase your coworkers' desire to know more about Jesus (see Titus 2:9-10, p. 280).

**3. Strive to Be Responsible.** People will respect you and your message when you can prove that you are responsible (see 1 Thessalonians 4:11-12, p. 262).

**4. Honor Christ with Your Hard Work.** Don't allow nonbelievers to criticize the Lord because of your poor witness (see 1 Thessalonians 4:11-12, p. 263).

**5. Don't Neglect Your Spiritual Health.** Never place your desire for material wealth above your spiritual welfare (see Luke 12:15-21, p. 86).

## Attitude toward Self

Many are on a quest today to find personal happiness. They will do whatever is necessary to "find themselves." They are told that the answer is "within," so they search in all the wrong places trying to find meaning and purpose in life. The Bible, however, does not teach that the answer is within us. Rather, it teaches that the *problem* is within us. Jeremiah 17:9 tells us, "The heart is most deceitful and desperately wicked.

Who really knows how bad it is?" For that reason, all attempts to reform or improve ourselves will meet with failure. We do not need self-esteem as much as we need a realistic view of who we are and who God is. Once we honestly assess our own sinful condition and come to grips with our built-in weakness and vulnerability to sin, then we will be able to appreciate God's solution. In a nutshell, the way to true happiness comes not from seeking *it* but from seeking *God.* Here's what God's Word has to say about how we can be happy, fulfilled people.

1. **We Need to Recognize Our True Condition.** As we humble ourselves before a holy God, we will be blessed (see Matthew 5:3-5, p. 6).
2. **Our Needs Must Come Last.** Jesus gave us the ultimate example of what it means to be a servant (see Hebrews 13:11-13, p. 298).
3. **We Will Find Happiness in Loving God and Serving Others.** Loving God and others gives us real purpose and meaning in life (see Matthew 22:37-40, p. 32).
4. **We Must Surrender Our Dreams and Seek God's Will.** True followers of Christ entrust their future into God's hands, because he knows what is best for us (see Matthew 16:24-26, p. 24).

# How to Study the Bible

Now that you are a Christian, one thing you will want to do on a daily basis is study the Bible. You may, however, have some questions about this. For example, you may ask yourself, *How do I study the Bible?* Or, *Where do I begin reading?* This feature will answer those questions and give you the information you need to develop the basic techniques necessary for effective Bible study.

**Pray for Wisdom and Understanding.** The most often overlooked and under-valued aspect of Bible study is prayer. Yet prayer is essential to gaining wisdom and understanding when you read God's Word. Through prayer, you can approach God and acknowledge your incomplete knowledge of his Word, as well as your need for him to open your heart to his instruction. Therefore, determine to begin each study with prayer. Only God can give you the wisdom to understand his Word.

**Read in an Orderly Manner.** If you received a letter and read only a few sentences here and there, the letter would not make much sense to you. But if you read the letter in order, you would understand it. The same holds true when you read the Bible.

Sadly, many Christians do not realize the shallowness of this approach. They read a portion of Matthew, a verse or two from Ephesians, and then a chapter or so from Revelation and wonder why they do not have a good understanding of God's Word. Furthermore, they end up misinterpreting the meaning of these passages because they have failed to grasp the context from which they came.

To avoid developing this poor habit, you need to discipline yourself to read the Bible in an orderly manner. One way to do this is to use an established reading plan. A reading plan lists Scripture passages to be read in a certain order. Many of the existing plans were created with a goal in mind. Some plans break the whole Bible down into 365 daily readings. Others help you read through the Bible in the order that the events actually happened. For now, you may want to use the following plan as your reading guide. Start with the Gospel of John. This Gospel was written so that we might believe that Jesus is the Son of God. Then, after you have finished reading John, read the rest of the New Testament. Once you have finished the New Testament, you should read the books of the Old Testament. There you will see the coming of Jesus foreshadowed.

**Finish What You Start.** In life, the benefits of doing anything are often not realized until the task is completed. The same is true when reading a book from the Bible. Once you choose a book to read, read it from beginning to end. Although you may benefit spiritually by reading a verse from one book or a story from another, you will benefit more by reading the entire book from which the verse or story came. Reading the entire book puts each verse and story in its proper context. Thus, you will have a better understanding of what each verse and story means. In addition, by reading books from beginning to end you will become more familiar with the Bible as a whole. You may even discover passages that will one day become your favorites.

**Meditate on God's Word and Ask Questions.** Thinking about what you have read cannot be overemphasized. Meditating on what you have read helps you to discover the importance of the passage. It also helps you to examine your life in light of what God reveals in his Word.

One of the best ways to begin meditating on God's Word is to ask questions. Here are a few questions to help you get started:

■ What is the main subject of the passage?
■ To whom is this passage addressed?
■ Who is speaking?
■ About what or whom is the person speaking?
■ What is the key verse?
■ What does this passage teach me about God?

To see how the text might apply to you personally, ask yourself these questions:

■ Is there any sin mentioned in the passage that I need to confess or forsake?
■ Is there a command given that I should obey?
■ Is there a promise made that I can apply to my current circumstances?
■ Is there a prayer given that I could pray?

**Invest in a Few Good Resource Books.** The Bible alludes to many ancient customs that are completely unfamiliar to us today. Much of the subtle meaning behind these allusions that would give us greater insight into and appreciation for God's Word is therefore lost. To understand the culture in which the Bible was written, you may want to purchase a few good biblical resource books.

# The NEW Testament

# Matthew

## CHAPTER 1

### The Record of Jesus' Ancestors

This is a record of the ancestors of Jesus the Messiah, a descendant of King David and of Abraham:

2 Abraham was the father of Isaac.
Isaac was the father of Jacob.
Jacob was the father of Judah and his brothers.
3 Judah was the father of Perez and Zerah (their mother was Tamar).
Perez was the father of Hezron.
Hezron was the father of Ram.*
4 Ram was the father of Amminadab.
Amminadab was the father of Nahshon.
Nahshon was the father of Salmon.
5 Salmon was the father of Boaz (his mother was Rahab).
Boaz was the father of Obed (his mother was Ruth).
Obed was the father of Jesse.
6 Jesse was the father of King David.
David was the father of Solomon (his mother was Bathsheba, the widow of Uriah).
7 Solomon was the father of Rehoboam.
Rehoboam was the father of Abijah.
Abijah was the father of Asaph.*
8 Asaph was the father of Jehoshaphat.
Jehoshaphat was the father of Jehoram.*
Jehoram was the father* of Uzziah.
9 Uzziah was the father of Jotham.
Jotham was the father of Ahaz.
Ahaz was the father of Hezekiah.
10 Hezekiah was the father of Manasseh.
Manasseh was the father of Amos.*

Amos was the father of Josiah.
11 Josiah was the father of Jehoiachin* and his brothers (born at the time of the exile to Babylon).
12 After the Babylonian exile:
Jehoiachin was the father of Shealtiel.
Shealtiel was the father of Zerubbabel.
13 Zerubbabel was the father of Abiud.
Abiud was the father of Eliakim.
Eliakim was the father of Azor.
14 Azor was the father of Zadok.
Zadok was the father of Akim.
Akim was the father of Eliud.
15 Eliud was the father of Eleazar.
Eleazar was the father of Matthan.
Matthan was the father of Jacob.
16 Jacob was the father of Joseph, the husband of Mary.
Mary was the mother of Jesus, who is called the Messiah.

17All those listed above include fourteen generations from Abraham to King David, and fourteen from David's time to the Babylonian exile, and fourteen from the Babylonian exile to the Messiah.

### The Birth of Jesus the Messiah

18Now this is how Jesus the Messiah was born. His mother, Mary, was engaged to be married to Joseph. But while she was still a virgin, she became pregnant by the Holy Spirit. 19Joseph, her fiancé, being a just man, decided to break the engagement quietly, so as not to disgrace her publicly.

20As he considered this, he fell asleep, and an angel of the Lord appeared to him in a dream.

---

1:3 Greek Aram; also in 1:4. See 1 Chr 2:9-10.   1:7 Asaph is the same person as Asa; also in 1:8. See 1 Chr 3:10.   1:8a Greek Joram. See 1 Kgs 22:50 and note at 1 Chr 3:11.   1:8b Or ancestor; also in 1:11.   1:10 Amos is the same person as Amon. See 1 Chr 3:14.   1:11 Greek Jeconiah; also in 1:12. See 2 Kgs 24:6 and note at 1 Chr 3:16.

"Joseph, son of David," the angel said, "do not be afraid to go ahead with your marriage to Mary. For the child within her has been conceived by the Holy Spirit. 21And she will have a son, and you are to name him Jesus,* for he will save his people from their sins." 22All of this happened to fulfill the Lord's message through his prophet:

23 "Look! The virgin will conceive a child!
    She will give birth to a son,
    and he will be called Immanuel*
    (meaning, God is with us)."

24When Joseph woke up, he did what the angel of the Lord commanded. He brought Mary home to be his wife, 25but she remained a virgin until her son was born. And Joseph named him Jesus.

## CHAPTER 2
### The Visit of the Wise Men

Jesus was born in the town of Bethlehem in Judea, during the reign of King Herod. About that time some wise men* from eastern lands arrived in Jerusalem, asking, 2"Where is the newborn king of the Jews? We have seen his star as it arose,* and we have come to worship him."

3Herod was deeply disturbed by their question, as was all of Jerusalem. 4He called a meeting of the leading priests and teachers of religious law. "Where did the prophets say the Messiah would be born?" he asked them.

5"In Bethlehem," they said, "for this is what the prophet wrote:

6 'O Bethlehem of Judah,
    you are not just a lowly village in Judah,
    for a ruler will come from you
    who will be the shepherd for my people
      Israel.'* "

7Then Herod sent a private message to the wise men, asking them to come see him. At this meeting he learned the exact time when they first saw the star. 8Then he told them, "Go to Bethlehem and search carefully for the child. And when you find him, come back and tell me so that I can go and worship him, too!"

9After this interview the wise men went their way. Once again the star appeared to them, guiding them to Bethlehem. It went ahead of them and stopped over the place where the child was. 10When they saw the star, they were filled with joy! 11They entered the house where the child and his mother, Mary, were, and they fell down before him and worshiped him. Then they opened their treasure chests and gave him gifts of gold, frankincense, and myrrh. 12But when it was time to leave, they went home another way, because God had warned them in a dream not to return to Herod.

### The Escape to Egypt

13After the wise men were gone, an angel of the Lord appeared to Joseph in a dream. "Get up and flee to Egypt with the child and his mother," the angel said. "Stay there until I tell you to return, because Herod is going to try to kill the child." 14That night Joseph left for Egypt with the child and Mary, his mother, 15and they stayed there until Herod's death. This fulfilled what the Lord had spoken through the prophet: "I called my Son out of Egypt."*

16Herod was furious when he learned that the wise men had outwitted him. He sent soldiers to kill all the boys in and around Bethlehem who were two years old and under, because the wise men had told him the star first appeared to them about two years earlier.* 17Herod's brutal action fulfilled the prophecy of Jeremiah:

18 "A cry of anguish is heard in Ramah—
    weeping and mourning unrestrained.
    Rachel weeps for her children,
    refusing to be comforted—for they are
      dead."*

### The Return to Nazareth

19When Herod died, an angel of the Lord appeared in a dream to Joseph in Egypt and told him, 20"Get up and take the child and his mother back to the land of Israel, because those who were trying to kill the child are dead." 21So Joseph returned immediately to Israel with Jesus and his mother. 22But when he learned that the new ruler was Herod's son Archelaus, he was afraid. Then, in another dream, he was warned to go to Galilee. 23So they went and lived in a town called Nazareth. This fulfilled what was spoken by the prophets concerning the Messiah: "He will be called a Nazarene."

## CHAPTER 3
### John the Baptist Prepares the Way

In those days John the Baptist began preaching in the Judean wilderness. His message was,

1:21 *Jesus* means "The LORD saves." 1:23 Isa 7:14; 8:8, 10. 2:1 Or *royal astrologers*; Greek reads *Magi*; also in 2:7, 16. 2:2 Or *in the east.* 2:6 Mic 5:2; 2 Sam 5:2. 2:15 Hos 11:1. 2:16 Or *according to the time he calculated from the wise men.* 2:18 Jer 31:15.

2 "Turn from your sins and turn to God, because the Kingdom of Heaven is near.*" 3Isaiah had spoken of John when he said,

"He is a voice shouting in the wilderness:
'Prepare a pathway for the Lord's coming!
Make a straight road for him!'"*

4John's clothes were woven from camel hair, and he wore a leather belt; his food was locusts and wild honey. 5People from Jerusalem and from every section of Judea and from all over the Jordan Valley went out to the wilderness to hear him preach. 6And when they confessed their sins, he baptized them in the Jordan River.

7But when he saw many Pharisees and Sadducees coming to be baptized, he denounced them. "You brood of snakes!" he exclaimed. "Who warned you to flee God's coming judgment? 8Prove by the way you live that you have really turned from your sins and turned to God. 9Don't just say, 'We're safe—we're the descendants of Abraham.' That proves nothing. God can change these stones here into children of Abraham. 10Even now the ax of God's judgment is poised, ready to sever your roots. Yes, every tree that does not produce good fruit will be chopped down and thrown into the fire.

11 "I baptize with* water those who turn from their sins and turn to God. But someone is coming soon who is far greater than I am—so much greater that I am not even worthy to be his slave.* He will baptize you with the Holy Spirit and with fire.* 12He is ready to separate the chaff from the grain with his winnowing fork. Then he will clean up the threshing area, storing the grain in his barn but burning the chaff with never-ending fire."

## The Baptism of Jesus

13Then Jesus went from Galilee to the Jordan River to be baptized by John. 14But John didn't want to baptize him. "I am the one who needs to be baptized by you," he said, "so why are you coming to me?"

15But Jesus said, "It must be done, because we must do everything that is right.*" So then John baptized him.

16After his baptism, as Jesus came up out of the water, the heavens were opened and he saw the Spirit of God descending like a dove and settling on him. 17And a voice from heaven said, "This is my beloved Son, and I am fully pleased with him."

## CHAPTER 4
### The Temptation of Jesus

Then Jesus was led out into the wilderness by the Holy Spirit to be tempted there by the Devil. 2For forty days and forty nights he ate nothing and became very hungry. 3Then the Devil* came and said to him, "If you are the Son of God, change these stones into loaves of bread."

4But Jesus told him, "No! The Scriptures say,

'People need more than bread for their life;
they must feed on every word of God.'* "

5Then the Devil took him to Jerusalem, to the highest point of the Temple, 6and said, "If you are the Son of God, jump off! For the Scriptures say,

'He orders his angels to protect you.
And they will hold you with their hands
to keep you from striking your foot on a
stone.'* "

7Jesus responded, "The Scriptures also say, 'Do not test the Lord your God.'* "

8Next the Devil took him to the peak of a very high mountain and showed him the nations of the world and all their glory. 9"I will give it all to you," he said, "if you will only kneel down and worship me."

10"Get out of here, Satan," Jesus told him. "For the Scriptures say,

'You must worship the Lord your God;
serve only him.'* "

11Then the Devil went away, and angels came and cared for Jesus.

### The Ministry of Jesus Begins

12When Jesus heard that John had been arrested, he left Judea and returned to Galilee. 13But instead of going to Nazareth, he went to Capernaum, beside the Sea of Galilee, in the region of Zebulun and Naphtali. 14This fulfilled Isaiah's prophecy:

15 "In the land of Zebulun and of Naphtali,
beside the sea, beyond the Jordan River—
in Galilee where so many Gentiles live—
16 the people who sat in darkness
have seen a great light.
And for those who lived in the land where
death casts its shadow,
a light has shined."*

17From then on, Jesus began to preach, "Turn

3:2 Or has come or is coming soon.   3:3 Isa 40:3.   3:11a Or in.   3:11b Greek to carry his sandals.   3:11c Or in the Holy Spirit and in fire.   3:15 Or we must fulfill all righteousness.   4:3 Greek the tempter.   4:4 Deut 8:3.   4:6 Ps 91:11-12.   4:7 Deut 6:16.   4:10 Deut 6:13.   4:15-16 Isa 9:1-2.

from your sins and turn to God, because the Kingdom of Heaven is near.*"

### The First Disciples

18One day as Jesus was walking along the shore beside the Sea of Galilee, he saw two brothers—Simon, also called Peter, and Andrew—fishing with a net, for they were commercial fishermen. 19Jesus called out to them, "Come, be my disciples, and I will show you how to fish for people!" 20And they left their nets at once and went with him.

21A little farther up the shore he saw two other brothers, James and John, sitting in a boat with their father, Zebedee, mending their nets. And he called them to come, too. 22They immediately followed him, leaving the boat and their father behind.

### The Ministry of Jesus in Galilee

23Jesus traveled throughout Galilee teaching in the synagogues, preaching everywhere the Good News about the Kingdom. And he healed people who had every kind of sickness and disease. 24News about him spread far beyond the borders of Galilee so that the sick were soon coming to be healed from as far away as Syria. And whatever their illness and pain, or if they were possessed by demons, or were epileptics, or were paralyzed—he healed them all. 25Large crowds followed him wherever he went—people from Galilee, the Ten Towns,* Jerusalem, from all over Judea, and from east of the Jordan River.

CHAPTER **5**

### The Sermon on the Mount

One day as the crowds were gathering, Jesus went up the mountainside with his disciples and sat down to teach them.

### The Beatitudes

2This is what he taught them:

3 "God blesses those who realize their need
for him,*
for the Kingdom of Heaven is given to
them.
4 God blesses those who mourn,
for they will be comforted.
5 God blesses those who are gentle and lowly,
for the whole earth will belong to them.
6 God blesses those who are hungry and
thirsty for justice,
for they will receive it in full.
7 God blesses those who are merciful,
for they will be shown mercy.
8 God blesses those whose hearts are pure,
for they will see God.
9 God blesses those who work for peace,
for they will be called the children of
God.
10 God blesses those who are persecuted
because they live for God,
for the Kingdom of Heaven is theirs.

11 "God blesses you when you are mocked and persecuted and lied about because you are my followers. 12Be happy about it! Be very glad! For a great reward awaits you in heaven. And remember, the ancient prophets were persecuted, too.

### Teaching about Salt and Light

13"You are the salt of the earth. But what good is salt if it has lost its flavor? Can you make it useful again? It will be thrown out and trampled underfoot as worthless. 14You are the light of the world—like a city on a mountain, glowing in

4:17 Or *has come* or *is coming soon.*   4:25 Greek *Decapolis.*   5:3 Greek *the poor in spirit.*

# OFF AND RUNNING ◢◢◢◢

## We Need to Recognize Our True Condition
### Read MATTHEW 5:3-5

Jesus shows us the way to true happiness in this text. Interestingly, not a word is said about seeking "personal fulfillment." Here Jesus gives us a three-step prescription to spiritual health and happiness:

**1. See Yourself as You Really Are.** When you realize your need for God (verse 3), you see yourself as you really are: a sinner, in desperate need of God's forgiveness. This is the first "rung on the ladder." The phrase "need for God" in this verse comes from a verb meaning "to shrink, cower, or cringe," as beggars often did in that day. It speaks of someone who is destitute and completely dependent on others for help. Therefore, to "realize your need for God" is to admit that you are spiritually destitute apart from God.

**2. Take Action.** Another way to translate verse 4 is "happy are the unhappy." Because we see ourselves as we really are, we mourn over, or are sorry for, our condition. This leads us to begin making changes in our the night for all to see. 15Don't hide your light under a basket! Instead, put it on a stand and let it shine for all. 16In the same way, let your good deeds shine out for all to see, so that everyone will praise your heavenly Father.

## Teaching about the Law

17"Don't misunderstand why I have come. I did not come to abolish the law of Moses or the writings of the prophets. No, I came to fulfill them. 18I assure you, until heaven and earth disappear, even the smallest detail of God's law will remain until its purpose is achieved. 19So if you break the smallest commandment and teach others to do the same, you will be the least in the Kingdom of Heaven. But anyone who obeys God's laws and teaches them will be great in the Kingdom of Heaven.

20"But I warn you—unless you obey God better than the teachers of religious law and the Pharisees do, you can't enter the Kingdom of Heaven at all!

## Teaching about Anger

21"You have heard that the law of Moses says, 'Do not murder. If you commit murder, you are subject to judgment.'* 22But I say, if you are angry with someone,* you are subject to judgment! If you call someone an idiot,* you are in danger of being brought before the high council. And if you curse someone,* you are in danger of the fires of hell.

23"So if you are standing before the altar in the Temple, offering a sacrifice to God, and you suddenly remember that someone has some-thing against you, 24leave your sacrifice there beside the altar. Go and be reconciled to that person. Then come and offer your sacrifice to God. 25Come to terms quickly with your enemy before it is too late and you are dragged into court, handed over to an officer, and thrown in jail. 26I assure you that you won't be free again until you have paid the last penny.

## Teaching about Adultery

27"You have heard that the law of Moses says, 'Do not commit adultery.'* 28But I say, anyone who even looks at a woman with lust in his eye has already committed adultery with her in his heart. 29So if your eye—even if it is your good eye*—causes you to lust, gouge it out and throw it away. It is better for you to lose one part of your body than for your whole body to be thrown into hell. 30And if your hand—even if it is your stronger hand*—causes you to sin, cut it off and throw it away. It is better for you to lose one part of your body than for your whole body to be thrown into hell.

## Teaching about Divorce

31"You have heard that the law of Moses says, 'A man can divorce his wife by merely giving her a letter of divorce.'* 32But I say that a man who divorces his wife, unless she has been unfaithful, causes her to commit adultery. And anyone who marries a divorced woman commits adultery.

## Teaching about Vows

33"Again, you have heard that the law of Moses says, 'Do not break your vows; you must carry out the vows you have made to the Lord.'* 34But I say,

5:21 Exod 20:13; Deut 5:17.   5:22a Greek *your brother;* also in 5:23. Some manuscripts add *without cause.*   5:22b Greek uses an Aramaic term of contempt: *If you say to your brother, 'Raca.'*   5:22c Greek *if you say, 'You fool.'*   5:27 Exod 20:14; Deut 5:18.   5:29 Greek *your right eye.*   5:30 Greek *your right hand.*   5:31 Deut 24:1.   5:33 Num 30:2.

lives. Scripture tells us, "For God can use sorrow in our lives to help us turn away from sin and seek salvation. We will never regret that kind of sorrow. But sorrow without repentance is the kind that results in death" (2 Corinthians 7:10). Our true sorrow will lead to joy—salvation in Jesus Christ. But without that sorrow, there will be no joy.

**3. Pursue Meekness.** Seeing ourselves as we really are produces two vital spiritual qualities: gentleness and lowliness (verse 5). We are no longer inflated with pride. We have an accurate and honest assessment of ourselves that, in turn, affects how we approach others. This contradicts the world's way of thinking, which advocates standing up for your rights and asserting yourself in order to get "your piece of the pie." The meekness Jesus describes here is not some sort of weakness or cowardice, but rather "power under constraint," much like a powerful stallion submitting to the control of the bit.

The more we humble ourselves and admit our weaknesses, the more we will rely on God's grace—and the happier we will be with ourselves and others.

## Beware of the Sins of the Heart  Read MATTHEW 5:27-30

Some people have the mistaken notion that unless you commit the act of adultery, you have not really sinned. They think it is OK to fantasize about or look at someone, so long as you don't become involved in a sinful relationship with that person. But Jesus "cuts to the chase" in this passage. He lets us know that even a lustful glance is as sinful as committing the act of adultery.

In the original Greek, one of the meanings for the word Jesus uses for "look" is intentional and repeated gazing. Jesus' remedy for someone who has a problem in this area seems rather harsh, but you really have to look at the context and the culture of the day to understand this radical but important statement.

In the Jewish culture, the right eye and the right hand were thought of as the best one had. The right eye represented one's best vision and the right hand represented one's best skills. In essence, Jesus is saying that you should be willing to give up whatever is necessary to keep you from falling into this sin. That may mean terminating a relationship, canceling a cable channel or magazine subscription, or changing how or where you spend your spare time. In other words, remove yourself from those things that can have a spiritually destructive effect on your life. Then take practical steps to fill your mind with the things of God: "Fix your thoughts on what is true and honorable and right. Think about things that are pure and lovely and admirable. Think about things that are excellent and worthy of praise" (Philippians 4:8).

**CORNER STONES**

don't make any vows! If you say, 'By heaven!' it is a sacred vow because heaven is God's throne. ³⁵And if you say, 'By the earth!' it is a sacred vow because the earth is his footstool. And don't swear, 'By Jerusalem!' for Jerusalem is the city of the great King. ³⁶Don't even swear, 'By my head!' for you can't turn one hair white or black. ³⁷Just say a simple, 'Yes, I will,' or 'No, I won't.' Your word is enough. To strengthen your promise with a vow shows that something is wrong.*

### Teaching about Revenge

³⁸"You have heard that the law of Moses says, 'If an eye is injured, injure the eye of the person who did it. If a tooth gets knocked out, knock out the tooth of the person who did it.'* ³⁹But I say, don't resist an evil person! If you are slapped on the right cheek, turn the other, too. ⁴⁰If you are ordered to court and your shirt is taken from you, give your coat, too. ⁴¹If a soldier demands that you carry his gear for a mile,* carry it two miles. ⁴²Give to those who ask, and don't turn away from those who want to borrow.

### Teaching about Love for Enemies

⁴³"You have heard that the law of Moses says, 'Love your neighbor'* and hate your enemy.

⁴⁴But I say, love your enemies!* Pray for those who persecute you! ⁴⁵In that way, you will be acting as true children of your Father in heaven. For he gives his sunlight to both the evil and the good, and he sends rain on the just and on the unjust, too. ⁴⁶If you love only those who love you, what good is that? Even corrupt tax collectors do that much. ⁴⁷If you are kind only to your friends,* how are you different from anyone else? Even pagans do that. ⁴⁸But you are to be perfect, even as your Father in heaven is perfect.

## CHAPTER 6

### Teaching about Giving to the Needy

"Take care! Don't do your good deeds publicly, to be admired, because then you will lose the reward from your Father in heaven. ²When you give a gift to someone in need, don't shout about it as the hypocrites do—blowing trumpets in the synagogues and streets to call attention to their acts of charity! I assure you, they have received all the reward they will ever get. ³But when you give to someone, don't tell your left hand what your right hand is doing. ⁴Give

5:37 Or *Anything beyond this is from the evil one.*   5:38 Greek *'An eye for an eye and a tooth for a tooth.'* Exod 21:24; Lev 24:20; Deut 19:21.
5:41 Greek *milion* [4,854 feet or 1,478 meters].   5:43 Lev 19:18.   5:44 Some manuscripts add *Bless those who curse you, do good to those who hate you.*   5:47 Greek *your brothers.*

your gifts in secret, and your Father, who knows all secrets, will reward you.

*Teaching about Prayer and Fasting*

5 "And now about prayer. When you pray, don't be like the hypocrites who love to pray publicly on street corners and in the synagogues where everyone can see them. I assure you, that is all the reward they will ever get. 6 But when you pray, go away by yourself, shut the door behind you, and pray to your Father secretly. Then your Father, who knows all secrets, will reward you.

7 "When you pray, don't babble on and on as people of other religions do. They think their prayers are answered only by repeating their words again and again. 8 Don't be like them, because your Father knows exactly what you need even before you ask him! 9 Pray like this:

Our Father in heaven,
may your name be honored.
10 May your Kingdom come soon.
May your will be done here on earth,
just as it is in heaven.
11 Give us our food for today,*
12 and forgive us our sins,
just as we have forgiven those who have
sinned against us.
13 And don't let us yield to temptation,
but deliver us from the evil one.*

14 "If you forgive those who sin against you, your heavenly Father will forgive you. 15 But if you refuse to forgive others, your Father will not forgive your sins.

16 "And when you fast, don't make it obvious, as the hypocrites do, who try to look pale and disheveled so people will admire them for their fasting. I assure you, that is the only reward they will ever get. 17 But when you fast, comb your hair and wash your face. 18 Then no one will suspect you are fasting, except your Father, who knows what you do in secret. And your Father, who knows all secrets, will reward you.

*Teaching about Money and Possessions*

19 "Don't store up treasures here on earth, where they can be eaten by moths and get rusty, and where thieves break in and steal. 20 Store your treasures in heaven, where they will never become moth-eaten or rusty and where they will

6:11 Or *for tomorrow.* 6:13 Or *from evil.* Some manuscripts add *For yours is the kingdom and the power and the glory forever. Amen.*

## Prayer Was Modeled for Us by Christ Read MATTHEW 6:5-15

You have probably heard what has been called "the Lord's Prayer." Jesus gave us this particular prayer to show us *how* to pray. Incidentally, just because we call this prayer "the Lord's Prayer" does not mean that Jesus prayed it for himself. He had no reason to ask for forgiveness because he never sinned. Instead, it is more accurate to call this prayer "the Disciples' Prayer," for it was given by Jesus as a response to the disciples' request, "Lord, teach us how to pray."

To better understand this prayer, we can break it down into two sets of petitions:

The first three petitions focus on the glory of God.
- "Our Father in heaven": Recognize that you are addressing a holy God who sees you as his child.
- "May your name be honored": Begin your prayers with reverence and praise to God for who he is. This will enable you to put your needs or problems in their proper perspective.
- "May your Kingdom come soon. May your will be done here on earth, just as it is in heaven": Ask God for his will to reign supreme in your life. You cannot pray "your Kingdom come" until you pray "my kingdom go."

The second three petitions focus on our personal needs.
- "Give us our food for today": Make your physical and personal needs known to God. Remember, Scripture tells us that God will provide for all of our needs (see Philippians 4:19, p. 251).
- "And forgive us our sins, just as we have forgiven those who have sinned against us": Confess your sins to God. Psalm 66:18 says, "If I had not confessed the sin in my heart, my Lord would not have listened." If you are clinging to some sin, your prayer life will come to a screeching halt.
- "And don't let us yield to temptation, but deliver us from the evil one": Recognize your inclination to fall into sin, and pray that the opportunity to sin and the desire to do so will never coincide.

Make it a point to include these important aspects in your personal prayers. By doing so, you will begin to understand how immense your God is and how small your problems are in comparison to him.

FIRST STEPS

## Forgiveness Is Not Selective Read MATTHEW 5:43-48

As one Bible commentator has put it, "To return evil for good is devilish; to return good for good is human. To return good for evil is divine." Although we are not divine, we, as believers, do not have the liberty to choose whom we will forgive and not forgive. This means that we must do as Jesus has commanded and not only forgive our enemies, but love them as well.

Loving our enemies is certainly something that does not come easily—or naturally. In fact, if we wait for some feeling of love to suddenly overtake us, it simply won't happen. We must begin to pray for our enemies even before we are conscious of loving them. This is absolutely impossible to do apart from the help of the Holy Spirit. If you feel you fall short in the area of forgiveness, take heart. The Bible is full of examples of that "divine" ability to forgive, which can only come from the working of the Holy Spirit in our lives:

- God's Spirit enabled Abraham to give the best land to his traveling partner and nephew, Lot (Genesis 13:1-12).
- God's Spirit gave Joseph the ability to embrace and kiss the very brothers who had sold him into slavery (Genesis 45:1-15).
- God's Spirit kept David from taking advantage of an opportunity to kill King Saul, who was then seeking David's life (1 Samuel 24).
- God's Spirit caused Stephen (the first Christian martyr) to pray for those who were stoning him to death (see Acts 7:59-60, p. 147).

The ultimate example of forgiving one's enemies, however, comes from Jesus. He clearly modeled this principle for us when, while hanging on the cross, he prayed,

"Father, forgive these people, because they don't know what they are doing" (see Luke 23:34, p. 104). If the cruel torture of crucifixion would not silence Jesus' prayer for his enemies, what pain, prejudice, or unfair treatment could justify the silencing of our prayers for our enemies? Just as God's Spirit worked in the lives of the individuals above, he will enable you to love, pray, and do good to those who hate and hurt you.

**CORNER STONES**

---

be safe from thieves. 21Wherever your treasure is, there your heart and thoughts will also be.

22"Your eye is a lamp for your body. A pure eye lets sunshine into your soul. 23But an evil eye shuts out the light and plunges you into darkness. If the light you think you have is really darkness, how deep that darkness will be!

24"No one can serve two masters. For you will hate one and love the other, or be devoted to one and despise the other. You cannot serve both God and money.

25"So I tell you, don't worry about everyday life—whether you have enough food, drink, and clothes. Doesn't life consist of more than food and clothing? 26Look at the birds. They don't need to plant or harvest or put food in barns because your heavenly Father feeds them. And you are far more valuable to him than they are.

27Can all your worries add a single moment to your life? Of course not.

28"And why worry about your clothes? Look at the lilies and how they grow. They don't work or make their clothing, 29yet Solomon in all his glory was not dressed as beautifully as they are. 30And if God cares so wonderfully for flowers that are here today and gone tomorrow, won't he more surely care for you? You have so little faith!

31"So don't worry about having enough food or drink or clothing. 32Why be like the pagans who are so deeply concerned about these things? Your heavenly Father already knows all your needs, 33and he will give you all you need from day to day if you live for him and make the Kingdom of God your primary concern.

34"So don't worry about tomorrow, for tomorrow will bring its own worries. Today's trouble is enough for today.

CHAPTER **7**

## Don't Condemn Others

"Stop judging others, and you will not be judged. [2]For others will treat you as you treat them.* Whatever measure you use in judging others, it will be used to measure how you are judged. [3]And why worry about a speck in your friend's eye* when you have a log in your own? [4]How can you think of saying, 'Let me help you get rid of that speck in your eye,' when you can't see past the log in your own eye? [5]Hypocrite! First get rid of the log from your own eye; then perhaps you will see well enough to deal with the speck in your friend's eye.

[6]"Don't give what is holy to unholy people.* Don't give pearls to swine! They will trample the pearls, then turn and attack you.

## Effective Prayer

[7]"Keep on asking, and you will be given what you ask for. Keep on looking, and you will find. Keep on knocking, and the door will be opened. [8]For everyone who asks, receives. Everyone who seeks, finds. And the door is opened to everyone who knocks. [9]You parents—if your children ask for a loaf of bread, do you give them a stone instead? [10]Or if they ask for a fish, do you give them a snake? Of course not! [11]If you sinful people know how to give good gifts to your children, how much more will your heavenly Father give good gifts to those who ask him.

## The Golden Rule

[12]"Do for others what you would like them to do for you. This is a summary of all that is taught in the law and the prophets.

## The Narrow Gate

[13]"You can enter God's Kingdom only through the narrow gate. The highway to hell* is broad, and its gate is wide for the many who choose the easy way. [14]But the gateway to life is small, and the road is narrow, and only a few ever find it.

## The Tree and Its Fruit

[15]"Beware of false prophets who come disguised as harmless sheep, but are really wolves that will tear you apart. [16]You can detect them by the way they act, just as you can identify a tree by its fruit. You don't pick grapes from thornbushes, or figs from thistles. [17]A healthy tree produces good fruit, and an unhealthy tree produces bad fruit. [18]A good tree can't

7:2 Or For God will treat you as you treat others; Greek reads For with the judgment you judge you will be judged.   7:3 Greek your brother's eye; also in 7:5.   7:6 Greek Don't give the sacred to dogs.
7:13 Greek The way that leads to destruction.

## How Should You View Material Wealth? Read MATTHEW 6:19-34

This passage is part of Jesus' famous Sermon on the Mount. Here Jesus deals with possibly the greatest distraction to following him wholeheartedly: wealth. This series of verses gives us at least three warnings about wealth and one prescription to overcome its enslaving effects:

**1. We Must Watch How and What We Store.** Verse 19 says that we should not "store up treasures." The idea here is not simply saving, but stockpiling. Jesus is not condemning saving your resources or providing for your family (see 1 Timothy 5:8, p. 272). He is condemning the accumulation of possessions to flaunt or to impress others. We need to be able to enjoy what God has given us without making those possessions our primary ambition.

**2. We Must Keep Our Vision Clear.** While we can enjoy what God gives us, we need to understand that the material things of this world are only temporary. Our personal possessions and investments can be devalued by inflation or deflation, destroyed by natural disasters, or stolen by thieves. That is the problem with making the accumulation of "things" your life's passion. It is so fleeting, temporary, unfulfilling, and even enslaving. When we don't have this perspective, we can become easily enslaved to consumption and accumulation. Then we are no longer serving God but money, and our vision is dark, shutting out the light of God's Word (verses 22-24).

**3. We Should Not Worry about Material Things.** Worry is a powerful force that can divide or distract us. You can worry about your future, your job, your health, or even about what others think about you. But Jesus tells you to stop worrying, because God will *always* meet your needs (verses 25-30). Quite simply, worry is a waste of your valuable time as his servant on earth.

**4. We Must Put God First in Our Lives** Our main concern should not be the acquiring of material possessions or prestige. Our primary pursuit should be seeking the reign of Jesus Christ in our lives above all else (verses 31-34). It makes a lot of sense to place your temporary needs and worries in the hands of an eternal God.

FIRST STEPS

## Our Walk Should Match Our Talk Read MATTHEW 7:21

I n this verse, Jesus gets down to the heart of every person's belief. He states that calling him "Lord" is not enough to get into heaven. That is because anyone can say the word but not mean it. What counts is a person's changed life—a life of obedience to God's will.

Regarding the Christian life, it has been said, "It is not how high you can jump that matters, but how straight you can walk when you hit the ground again." You may be able to say all of the "right things," but if your faith does not impact the way you live, it is meaningless—even offensive. In truth, you do not have a real relationship with God.

An engraving on a cathedral wall in Germany bears these soul-searching words:

Thus speaketh Christ our Lord to us,
"You call me Master and obey me not;
You call me light and see me not;
You call me the Way and walk me not;
You call me life and live me not;
You call me wise and follow me not;
You call me fair and love me not;
You call me rich and ask me not;
You call me eternal and seek me not;
If I condemn you, blame me not."

The more we learn about what God has done for us, the more we will want to know what we can do for him. In addition, our motives will come from a pure heart, not from selfish ambition. God is looking for genuine believers whose walk matches their talk. Can you be counted as one?

CORNER STONES

produce bad fruit, and a bad tree can't produce good fruit. ¹⁹So every tree that does not produce good fruit is chopped down and thrown into the fire. ²⁰Yes, the way to identify a tree or a person is by the kind of fruit that is produced.

### True Disciples
²¹"Not all people who sound religious are really godly. They may refer to me as 'Lord,' but they still won't enter the Kingdom of Heaven. The decisive issue is whether they obey my Father in heaven. ²²On judgment day many will tell me, 'Lord, Lord, we prophesied in your name and cast out demons in your name and performed many miracles in your name.' ²³But I will reply, 'I never knew you. Go away; the things you did were unauthorized.*'

### Building on a Solid Foundation
²⁴"Anyone who listens to my teaching and obeys me is wise, like a person who builds a house on solid rock. ²⁵Though the rain comes in torrents

7:23 Or *unlawful.*

and the floodwaters rise and the winds beat against that house, it won't collapse, because it is built on rock. ²⁶But anyone who hears my teaching and ignores it is foolish, like a person who builds a house on sand. ²⁷When the rains and floods come and the winds beat against that house, it will fall with a mighty crash."

²⁸After Jesus finished speaking, the crowds were amazed at his teaching, ²⁹for he taught as one who had real authority—quite unlike the teachers of religious law.

CHAPTER **8**
### Jesus Heals a Man with Leprosy
Large crowds followed Jesus as he came down the mountainside. ²Suddenly, a man with leprosy approached Jesus. He knelt before him, worshiping. "Lord," the man said, "if you want to, you can make me well again."

³Jesus touched him. "I want to," he said. "Be

healed!" And instantly the leprosy disappeared. [4]Then Jesus said to him, "Go right over to the priest and let him examine you. Don't talk to anyone along the way. Take along the offering required in the law of Moses for those who have been healed of leprosy, so everyone will have proof of your healing."

### Faith of the Roman Officer

[5]When Jesus arrived in Capernaum, a Roman officer came and pleaded with him, [6]"Lord, my young servant lies in bed, paralyzed and racked with pain."

[7]Jesus said, "I will come and heal him."

[8]Then the officer said, "Lord, I am not worthy to have you come into my home. Just say the word from where you are, and my servant will be healed! [9]I know, because I am under the authority of my superior officers and I have authority over my soldiers. I only need to say, 'Go,' and they go, or 'Come,' and they come. And if I say to my slaves, 'Do this or that,' they do it."

[10]When Jesus heard this, he was amazed. Turning to the crowd, he said, "I tell you the truth, I haven't seen faith like this in all the land of Israel! [11]And I tell you this, that many Gentiles will come from all over the world and sit down with Abraham, Isaac, and Jacob at the feast in the Kingdom of Heaven. [12]But many Israelites—those for whom the Kingdom was prepared—will be cast into outer darkness, where there will be weeping and gnashing of teeth."

[13]Then Jesus said to the Roman officer, "Go on home. What you have believed has happened." And the young servant was healed that same hour.

### Jesus Heals Many People

[14]When Jesus arrived at Peter's house, Peter's mother-in-law was in bed with a high fever. [15]But when Jesus touched her hand, the fever left her. Then she got up and prepared a meal for him.

[16]That evening many demon-possessed people were brought to Jesus. All the spirits fled when he commanded them to leave; and he healed all the sick. [17]This fulfilled the word of the Lord through Isaiah, who said, "He took our sicknesses and removed our diseases."*

### The Cost of Following Jesus

[18]When Jesus noticed how large the crowd was growing, he instructed his disciples to cross to the other side of the lake.

[19]Then one of the teachers of religious law said to him, "Teacher, I will follow you no matter where you go!"

[20]But Jesus said, "Foxes have dens to live in, and birds have nests, but I, the Son of Man, have no home of my own, not even a place to lay my head."

[21]Another of his disciples said, "Lord, first let me return home and bury my father."

[22]But Jesus told him, "Follow me now! Let those who are spiritually dead care for their own dead."*

### Jesus Calms the Storm

[23]Then Jesus got into the boat and started across the lake with his disciples. [24]Suddenly, a terrible storm came up, with waves breaking into the boat. But Jesus was sleeping. [25]The disciples went to him and woke him up, shouting, "Lord, save us! We're going to drown!"

[26]And Jesus answered, "Why are you afraid? You have so little faith!" Then he stood up and rebuked the wind and waves, and suddenly all was calm. [27]The disciples just sat there in awe. "Who is this?" they asked themselves. "Even the wind and waves obey him!"

### Jesus Heals Two Demon-Possessed Men

[28]When Jesus arrived on the other side of the lake in the land of the Gadarenes,* two men who were possessed by demons met him. They lived in a cemetery and were so dangerous that no one could go through that area. [29]They began screaming at him, "Why are you bothering us, Son of God? You have no right to torture us before God's appointed time!" [30]A large herd of pigs was feeding in the distance, [31]so the demons begged, "If you cast us out, send us into that herd of pigs."

[32]"All right, go!" Jesus commanded them. So the demons came out of the men and entered the pigs, and the whole herd plunged down the steep hillside into the lake and drowned in the water. [33]The herdsmen fled to the nearby city, telling everyone what happened to the demon-possessed men. [34]The entire town came out to meet Jesus, but they begged him to go away and leave them alone.

## CHAPTER 9

### Jesus Heals a Paralyzed Man

Jesus climbed into a boat and went back across the lake to his own town. [2]Some people brought

8:17 Isa 53:4.   8:22 Greek *Let the dead bury their own dead.*   8:28 Some manuscripts read *Gerasenes;* other manuscripts read *Gergesenes.* See Mark 5:1; Luke 8:26.

to him a paralyzed man on a mat. Seeing their faith, Jesus said to the paralyzed man, "Take heart, son! Your sins are forgiven."

3"Blasphemy! This man talks like he is God!" some of the teachers of religious law said among themselves.

4Jesus knew what they were thinking, so he asked them, "Why are you thinking such evil thoughts? 5Is it easier to say, 'Your sins are forgiven' or 'Get up and walk'? 6I will prove that I, the Son of Man, have the authority on earth to forgive sins." Then Jesus turned to the paralyzed man and said, "Stand up, take your mat, and go on home, because you are healed!"

7And the man jumped up and went home! 8Fear swept through the crowd as they saw this happen right before their eyes. They praised God for sending a man with such great authority.

## Jesus Calls Matthew

9As Jesus was going down the road, he saw Matthew sitting at his tax-collection booth. "Come, be my disciple," Jesus said to him. So Matthew got up and followed him.

10That night Matthew invited Jesus and his disciples to be his dinner guests, along with his fellow tax collectors and many other notorious sinners. 11The Pharisees were indignant. "Why does your teacher eat with such scum*?" they asked his disciples.

12When he heard this, Jesus replied, "Healthy people don't need a doctor—sick people do." 13Then he added, "Now go and learn the meaning of this Scripture: 'I want you to be merciful; I don't want your sacrifices.'* For I have come to call sinners, not those who think they are already good enough."

## A Discussion about Fasting

14One day the disciples of John the Baptist came to Jesus and asked him, "Why do we and the Pharisees fast, but your disciples don't fast?"

15Jesus responded, "Should the wedding guests mourn while celebrating with the groom? Someday he will be taken from them, and then they will fast. 16And who would patch an old garment with unshrunk cloth? For the patch shrinks and pulls away from the old cloth, leaving an even bigger hole than before. 17And no one puts new wine into old wineskins. The old skins would burst from the pressure, spilling the wine and ruining the skins. New wine must be

stored in new wineskins. That way both the wine and the wineskins are preserved."

## Jesus Heals in Response to Faith

18As Jesus was saying this, the leader of a synagogue came and knelt down before him. "My daughter has just died," he said, "but you can bring her back to life again if you just come and lay your hand upon her."

19As Jesus and the disciples were going to the official's home, 20a woman who had had a hemorrhage for twelve years came up behind him. She touched the fringe of his robe, 21for she thought, "If I can just touch his robe, I will be healed."

22Jesus turned around and said to her, "Daughter, be encouraged! Your faith has made you well." And the woman was healed at that moment.

23When Jesus arrived at the official's home, he noticed the noisy crowds and heard the funeral music. 24He said, "Go away, for the girl isn't dead; she's only asleep." But the crowd laughed at him. 25When the crowd was finally outside, Jesus went in and took the girl by the hand, and she stood up! 26The report of this miracle swept through the entire countryside.

## Jesus Heals the Blind and Mute

27After Jesus left the girl's home, two blind men followed along behind him, shouting, "Son of David, have mercy on us!"

28They went right into the house where he was staying, and Jesus asked them, "Do you believe I can make you see?"

"Yes, Lord," they told him, "we do."

29Then he touched their eyes and said, "Because of your faith, it will happen." 30And suddenly they could see! Jesus sternly warned them, "Don't tell anyone about this." 31But instead, they spread his fame all over the region.

32When they left, some people brought to him a man who couldn't speak because he was possessed by a demon. 33So Jesus cast out the demon, and instantly the man could talk. The crowds marveled. "Nothing like this has ever happened in Israel!" they exclaimed.

34But the Pharisees said, "He can cast out demons because he is empowered by the prince of demons."

## The Need for Workers

35Jesus traveled through all the cities and villages of that area, teaching in the synagogues and announcing the Good News about the Kingdom. And wherever he went, he healed people of every sort of disease and illness. 36He felt great pity for the crowds that came, because their problems were so great and they didn't know where to go for help. They were like sheep without a shepherd. 37He said to his disciples, "The harvest is so great, but the workers are so few. 38So pray to the Lord who is in charge of the harvest; ask him to send out more workers for his fields."

## CHAPTER 10
### Jesus Sends Out the Twelve Apostles

Jesus called his twelve disciples to him and gave them authority to cast out evil spirits and to heal every kind of disease and illness. 2Here are the names of the twelve apostles:

first Simon (also called Peter),
then Andrew (Peter's brother),
James (son of Zebedee),
John (James's brother),
3 Philip,
Bartholomew,
Thomas,
Matthew (the tax collector),
James (son of Alphaeus),
Thaddaeus,
4 Simon (the Zealot*),
Judas Iscariot (who later betrayed him).

5Jesus sent the twelve disciples out with these instructions: "Don't go to the Gentiles or the Samaritans, 6but only to the people of Israel—God's lost sheep. 7Go and announce to them that the Kingdom of Heaven is near.* 8Heal the sick, raise the dead, cure those with leprosy, and cast out demons. Give as freely as you have received!

9"Don't take any money with you. 10Don't carry a traveler's bag with an extra coat and sandals or even a walking stick. Don't hesitate to accept hospitality, because those who work deserve to be fed.* 11Whenever you enter a city or village, search for a worthy man and stay in his home until you leave for the next town. 12When you are invited into someone's home, give it your blessing. 13If it turns out to be a worthy home, let your blessing stand; if it is not, take back the blessing. 14If a village doesn't welcome you or listen to you, shake off the dust of that place from your feet as you leave. 15I assure you, the wicked cities of Sodom and Gomorrah will

be better off on the judgment day than that place will be.

16"Look, I am sending you out as sheep among wolves. Be as wary as snakes and harmless as doves. 17But beware! For you will be handed over to the courts and beaten in the synagogues. 18And you must stand trial before governors and kings because you are my followers. This will be your opportunity to tell them about me—yes, to witness to the world. 19When you are arrested, don't worry about what to say in your defense, because you will be given the right words at the right time. 20For it won't be you doing the talking—it will be the Spirit of your Father speaking through you.

21"Brother will betray brother to death, fathers will betray their own children, and children will rise against their parents and cause them to be killed. 22And everyone will hate you because of your allegiance to me. But those who endure to the end will be saved. 23When you are persecuted in one town, flee to the next. I assure you that I, the Son of Man, will return before you have reached all the towns of Israel.

24"A student is not greater than the teacher. A servant is not greater than the master. 25The student shares the teacher's fate. The servant shares the master's fate. And since I, the master of the household, have been called the prince of demons,* how much more will it happen to you, the members of the household! 26But don't be afraid of those who threaten you. For the time is coming when everything will be revealed; all that is secret will be made public. 27What I tell you now in the darkness, shout abroad when daybreak comes. What I whisper in your ears, shout from the housetops for all to hear!

28"Don't be afraid of those who want to kill you. They can only kill your body; they cannot touch your soul. Fear only God, who can destroy both soul and body in hell. 29Not even a sparrow, worth only half a penny, can fall to the ground without your Father knowing it. 30And the very hairs on your head are all numbered. 31So don't be afraid; you are more valuable to him than a whole flock of sparrows.

32"If anyone acknowledges me publicly here on earth, I will openly acknowledge that person before my Father in heaven. 33But if anyone denies me here on earth, I will deny that person before my Father in heaven.

34"Don't imagine that I came to bring peace to the earth! No, I came to bring a sword. 35I

MATTHEW 11 ▶▶▶ *page 16*

## Peace Begins When We Relinquish Control of Our Lives to God Read MATTHEW 11:28-30

In this passage, Jesus teaches us three things we must do in order to find true peace, or "rest." Yet, for some odd reason, we sometimes find these things difficult to do:

**1. Come to Christ.** If you have already accepted Jesus Christ as Lord and Savior in your life, you have already completed this step. If you are still searching, you might be right at the door. But know this: You will not find peace from anyone or anything else. Sure, you may have temporary peace of mind when you feel financially secure or if you think you have discovered that "perfect" relationship. But when the bottom falls out, what happens then? Only Christ can guarantee you unending peace.

**2. Exchange Your Yoke for His Yoke.** A yoke is a heavy wooden harness that is placed over the neck of one or more oxen in order to help pull a wagon or other piece of equipment. It enables a farmer to direct the oxen. Shifting the analogy to humans, our "heavy yoke" could be the weight of guilt, or the burden of keeping God's commands and trying to please him through our own good works. Jesus wants you to exchange that load for his lighter load—God's grace. You can rest in knowing that you do not have to work for God's favor; you need only to accept his Son.

**3. Let Jesus Lead.** This is undoubtedly one of the hardest parts of this promise. That is because we want to be in control. But God says that we need to give him the reins so that he can "teach" us. Are you ready and willing to leave your abilities, your future, and your problems in God's hands? Then—and only then—will you experience God's promised "rest" for your soul.

**CORNER STONES**

have come to set a man against his father, and a daughter against her mother, and a daughter-in-law against her mother-in-law. ³⁶Your enemies will be right in your own household! ³⁷If you love your father or mother more than you love me, you are not worthy of being mine; or if you love your son or daughter more than me, you are not worthy of being mine. ³⁸If you refuse to take up your cross and follow me, you are not worthy of being mine. ³⁹If you cling to your life, you will lose it; but if you give it up for me, you will find it.

⁴⁰"Anyone who welcomes you is welcoming me, and anyone who welcomes me is welcoming the Father who sent me. ⁴¹If you welcome a prophet as one who speaks for God,* you will receive the same reward a prophet gets. And if you welcome good and godly people because of their godliness, you will be given a reward like theirs. ⁴²And if you give even a cup of cold water to one of the least of my followers, you will surely be rewarded."

## CHAPTER 11
### Jesus and John the Baptist
When Jesus had finished giving these instructions to his twelve disciples, he went off teaching and preaching in towns throughout the country.

²John the Baptist, who was now in prison, heard about all the things the Messiah was doing. So he sent his disciples to ask Jesus, ³"Are you really the Messiah we've been waiting for, or should we keep looking for someone else?"

⁴Jesus told them, "Go back to John and tell him about what you have heard and seen—⁵the blind see, the lame walk, the lepers are cured, the deaf hear, the dead are raised to life, and the Good News is being preached to the poor. ⁶And tell him: 'God blesses those who are not offended by me.*'"

⁷When John's disciples had gone, Jesus began talking about him to the crowds. "Who is this man in the wilderness that you went out to see? Did you find him weak as a reed, moved by every breath of wind? ⁸Or were you expecting to see a

10:41 Greek *welcome a prophet in the name of a prophet.* 11:6 Or *who don't fall away because of me.*

man dressed in expensive clothes? Those who dress like that live in palaces, not out in the wilderness. 9Were you looking for a prophet? Yes, and he is more than a prophet. 10John is the man to whom the Scriptures refer when they say,

'Look, I am sending my messenger before you,
and he will prepare your way before you.'*

11 "I assure you, of all who have ever lived, none is greater than John the Baptist. Yet even the most insignificant person in the Kingdom of Heaven is greater than he is! 12And from the time John the Baptist began preaching and baptizing until now, the Kingdom of Heaven has been forcefully advancing, and violent people attack it.* 13For before John came, all the teachings of the Scriptures looked forward to this present time. 14And if you are willing to accept what I say, he is Elijah, the one the prophets said would come.* 15Anyone who is willing to hear should listen and understand!

16"How shall I describe this generation? These people are like a group of children playing a game in the public square. They complain to their friends, 17'We played wedding songs, and you weren't happy, so we played funeral songs, but you weren't sad.' 18For John the Baptist didn't drink wine and he often fasted, and you say, 'He's demon possessed.' 19And I, the Son of Man, feast and drink, and you say, 'He's a glutton and a drunkard, and a friend of the worst sort of sinners!' But wisdom is shown to be right by what results from it."

## Judgment for the Unbelievers

20Then Jesus began to denounce the cities where he had done most of his miracles, because they hadn't turned from their sins and turned to God. 21 "What horrors await you, Korazin and Bethsaida! For if the miracles I did in you had been done in wicked Tyre and Sidon, their people would have sat in deep repentance long ago, clothed in sackcloth and throwing ashes on their heads to show their remorse. 22I assure you, Tyre and Sidon will be better off on the judgment day than you! 23And you people of Capernaum, will you be exalted to heaven? No, you will be brought down to the place of the dead.* For if the miracles I did for you had been done in Sodom, it would still be here today. 24I assure you, Sodom will be better off on the judgment day than you."

## Jesus' Prayer of Thanksgiving

25Then Jesus prayed this prayer: "O Father, Lord of heaven and earth, thank you for hiding the truth from those who think themselves so wise and clever, and for revealing it to the childlike. 26Yes, Father, it pleased you to do it this way!

27"My Father has given me authority over everything. No one really knows the Son except the Father, and no one really knows the Father except the Son and those to whom the Son chooses to reveal him."

28Then Jesus said, "Come to me, all of you who are weary and carry heavy burdens, and I will give you rest. 29Take my yoke upon you. Let me teach you, because I am humble and gentle, and you will find rest for your souls. 30For my yoke fits perfectly, and the burden I give you is light."

CHAPTER **12**
## Controversy about the Sabbath

At about that time Jesus was walking through some grainfields on the Sabbath. His disciples were hungry, so they began breaking off heads of wheat and eating the grain. 2Some Pharisees saw them do it and protested, "Your disciples shouldn't be doing that! It's against the law to work by harvesting grain on the Sabbath."

3But Jesus said to them, "Haven't you ever read in the Scriptures what King David did when he and his companions were hungry? 4He went into the house of God, and they ate the special bread reserved for the priests alone. That was breaking the law, too. 5And haven't you ever read in the law of Moses that the priests on duty in the Temple may work on the Sabbath? 6I tell you, there is one here who is even greater than the Temple! 7But you would not have condemned those who aren't guilty if you knew the meaning of this Scripture: 'I want you to be merciful; I don't want your sacrifices.'* 8For I, the Son of Man, am master even of the Sabbath."

9Then he went over to the synagogue, 10where he noticed a man with a deformed hand. The Pharisees asked Jesus, "Is it legal to work by healing on the Sabbath day?" (They were, of course, hoping he would say yes, so they could bring charges against him.)

11And he answered, "If you had one sheep, and it fell into a well on the Sabbath, wouldn't you get to work and pull it out? Of course you

11:10 Mal 3:1.  11:12 Or *until now, eager multitudes have been pressing into the Kingdom of Heaven.*  11:14 See Mal 4:5.  11:23 Greek *to Hades.*  12:7 Hos 6:6.

would. 12And how much more valuable is a person than a sheep! Yes, it is right to do good on the Sabbath." 13Then he said to the man, "Reach out your hand." The man reached out his hand, and it became normal, just like the other one. 14Then the Pharisees called a meeting and discussed plans for killing Jesus.

## Jesus, God's Chosen Servant

15But Jesus knew what they were planning. He left that area, and many people followed him. He healed all the sick among them, 16but he warned them not to say who he was. 17This fulfilled the prophecy of Isaiah concerning him:

18 "Look at my Servant,
   whom I have chosen.
He is my Beloved,
   and I am very pleased with him.
I will put my Spirit upon him,
   and he will proclaim justice to the
      nations.
19 He will not fight or shout;
   he will not raise his voice in public.
20 He will not crush those who are weak,
   or quench the smallest hope,
   until he brings full justice with his final
      victory.
21 And his name will be the hope
   of all the world."*

## Jesus and the Prince of Demons

22Then a demon-possessed man, who was both blind and unable to talk, was brought to Jesus. He healed the man so that he could both speak and see. 23The crowd was amazed. "Could it be that Jesus is the Son of David, the Messiah?" they wondered out loud.

24But when the Pharisees heard about the miracle, they said, "No wonder he can cast out demons. He gets his power from Satan,* the prince of demons."

25Jesus knew their thoughts and replied, "Any kingdom at war with itself is doomed. A city or home divided against itself is doomed. 26And if Satan is casting out Satan, he is fighting against himself. His own kingdom will not survive. 27And if I am empowered by the prince of demons,* what about your own followers? They cast out demons, too, so they will judge you for what you have said. 28But if I am casting out demons by the Spirit of God, then the Kingdom of God has arrived among you. 29Let me illustrate this. You can't enter a strong man's house and rob him without first tying him up. Only then can his house be robbed!* 30Anyone who isn't helping me opposes me, and anyone who isn't working with me is actually working against me.

31 "Every sin or blasphemy can be forgiven—except blasphemy against the Holy Spirit, which can never be forgiven. 32Anyone who blasphemes against me, the Son of Man, can be forgiven, but blasphemy against the Holy Spirit will never be forgiven, either in this world or in the world to come.

33 "A tree is identified by its fruit. Make a tree good, and its fruit will be good. Make a tree bad, and its fruit will be bad. 34You brood of snakes! How could evil men like you speak what is good and right? For whatever is in your heart determines what you say. 35A good person produces good words from a good heart, and an evil person produces evil words from an evil heart. 36And I tell you this, that you must give an account on judgment day of every idle word you speak. 37The words you say now reflect your fate then; either you will be justified by them or you will be condemned."

12:18-21 Isa 42:1-4.  12:24 Greek *Beelzeboul.*  12:27 Greek *by Beelzeboul.*  12:29 Or *One cannot rob Satan's kingdom without first tying him up. Only then can his demons be cast out.*

# OFF AND RUNNING

## Refrain from Idle Talk Read MATTHEW 12:35-37

The verse preceding this text says, "For whatever is in your heart determines what you say." Your speech mirrors the condition of your heart. Your heart represents your innermost thoughts, desires, and emotions. If your heart is filled with bitterness, your speech will be tainted by it. If it is filled with the love of God, your words will also express that love.

If we take seriously Jesus' warning about being held accountable for our idle words, then we should not only weigh our words, but we should also examine our hearts—the source of our speech. Here is a good rule to apply before you speak: THINK.

## The Sign of Jonah

38One day some teachers of religious law and Pharisees came to Jesus and said, "Teacher, we want you to show us a miraculous sign to prove that you are from God."

39But Jesus replied, "Only an evil, faithless generation would ask for a miraculous sign; but the only sign I will give them is the sign of the prophet Jonah. 40For as Jonah was in the belly of the great fish for three days and three nights, so I, the Son of Man, will be in the heart of the earth for three days and three nights. 41The people of Nineveh will rise up against this generation on judgment day and condemn it, because they repented at the preaching of Jonah. And now someone greater than Jonah is here—and you refuse to repent. 42The queen of Sheba* will also rise up against this generation on judgment day and condemn it, because she came from a distant land to hear the wisdom of Solomon. And now someone greater than Solomon is here—and you refuse to listen to him.

43"When an evil spirit leaves a person, it goes into the desert, seeking rest but finding none. 44Then it says, 'I will return to the person I came from.' So it returns and finds its former home empty, swept, and clean. 45Then the spirit finds seven other spirits more evil than itself, and they all enter the person and live there. And so that person is worse off than before. That will be the experience of this evil generation."

## The True Family of Jesus

46As Jesus was speaking to the crowd, his mother and brothers were outside, wanting to talk with him. 47Someone told Jesus, "Your mother and your brothers are outside, and they want to speak to you."

48Jesus asked, "Who is my mother? Who are my brothers?" 49Then he pointed to his disciples

12:42 Greek *The queen of the south.*

and said, "These are my mother and brothers. 50Anyone who does the will of my Father in heaven is my brother and sister and mother!"

## CHAPTER 13

## Story of the Farmer Scattering Seed

Later that same day, Jesus left the house and went down to the shore, 2where an immense crowd soon gathered. He got into a boat, where he sat and taught as the people listened on the shore. 3He told many stories such as this one:

"A farmer went out to plant some seed. 4As he scattered it across his field, some seeds fell on a footpath, and the birds came and ate them. 5Other seeds fell on shallow soil with underlying rock. The plants sprang up quickly, 6but they soon wilted beneath the hot sun and died because the roots had no nourishment in the shallow soil. 7Other seeds fell among thorns that shot up and choked out the tender blades. 8But some seeds fell on fertile soil and produced a crop that was thirty, sixty, and even a hundred times as much as had been planted. 9Anyone who is willing to hear should listen and understand!"

10His disciples came and asked him, "Why do you always tell stories when you talk to the people?"

11Then he explained to them, "You have been permitted to understand the secrets of the Kingdom of Heaven, but others have not. 12To those who are open to my teaching, more understanding will be given, and they will have an abundance of knowledge. But to those who are not listening, even what they have will be taken away from them. 13That is why I tell these stories, because people see what I do, but they don't really see. They hear what I say, but they don't really hear, and they don't understand. 14This fulfills the prophecy of Isaiah, which says:

**T**— Is it true?
**H**—Is it helpful?
**I**— Is it inspiring?
**N**—Is it necessary?
**K**—Is it kind?

If the content of what you want to say doesn't pass this test, you really do not need to say it. Otherwise, you will have to give an explanation when you stand before the Lord.

## Beware of Satan's Clever Imitations Read MATTHEW 13:24-30

This is known as the parable of the wheat and the tares. Jesus gave this illustration to expose the Satanic tactic of imitation and infiltration.

The thistles, or tares, were actually a plant that came from the darnel seed. In the initial stages of growth, this plant looked exactly like wheat. But in time the wild weed would show itself for what it really was—a plant that actually uprooted the wheat.

In essence, Satan has followed the pattern of the darnel seed in his attacks against the church. He has "flooded the market" with his imitations of the real thing. There are numerous examples of this throughout the Bible. In Exodus (the second book of the Old Testament), the Egyptian magicians imitated some of the miracles performed by God through Moses—like turning a rod into a snake, turning the waters of the Nile into blood, and bringing forth a plague of frogs. In Acts (the fifth book of the New Testament), the sorcerer Simon imitated Philip (see Acts 8:9-24, pp. 147-148).

In fact, whenever the church has experienced a great revival, a false movement has grown up by its side proclaiming half-truths and deceptions.

Satan knows that half of a truth is more dangerous than a lie. For those who have modified the truth have always injured the truth more than those who have denied it openly. Therefore we must guard against falling for half-truths and gospel imitations at all costs.

CORNER STONES

---

'You will hear my words,
  but you will not understand;
you will see what I do,
  but you will not perceive its meaning.
15 For the hearts of these people are hardened,
  and their ears cannot hear,
  and they have closed their eyes—
so their eyes cannot see,
  and their ears cannot hear,
  and their hearts cannot understand,
and they cannot turn to me
  and let me heal them.'*

16 "But blessed are your eyes, because they see; and your ears, because they hear. 17 I assure you, many prophets and godly people have longed to see and hear what you have seen and heard, but they could not.

18 "Now here is the explanation of the story I told about the farmer sowing grain: 19 The seed that fell on the hard path represents those who hear the Good News about the Kingdom and don't understand it. Then the evil one comes and snatches the seed away from their hearts. 20 The rocky soil represents those who hear the message and receive it with joy. 21 But like young plants in such soil, their roots don't go very deep. At first they get along fine, but they wilt as soon as they have problems or are persecuted

13:14-15 Isa 6:9-10.

because they believe the word. 22 The thorny ground represents those who hear and accept the Good News, but all too quickly the message is crowded out by the cares of this life and the lure of wealth, so no crop is produced. 23 The good soil represents the hearts of those who truly accept God's message and produce a huge harvest—thirty, sixty, or even a hundred times as much as had been planted."

*Story of the Wheat and Weeds*
24 Here is another story Jesus told: "The Kingdom of Heaven is like a farmer who planted good seed in his field. 25 But that night as everyone slept, his enemy came and planted weeds among the wheat. 26 When the crop began to grow and produce grain, the weeds also grew. 27 The farmer's servants came and told him, 'Sir, the field where you planted that good seed is full of weeds!'

28 " 'An enemy has done it!' the farmer exclaimed.

" 'Shall we pull out the weeds?' they asked.

29 "He replied, 'No, you'll hurt the wheat if you do. 30 Let both grow together until the harvest. Then I will tell the harvesters to sort out the weeds and burn them and to put the wheat in the barn.'"

## Illustration of the Mustard Seed

31Here is another illustration Jesus used: "The Kingdom of Heaven is like a mustard seed planted in a field. 32It is the smallest of all seeds, but it becomes the largest of garden plants and grows into a tree where birds can come and find shelter in its branches."

## Illustration of the Yeast

33Jesus also used this illustration: "The Kingdom of Heaven is like yeast used by a woman making bread. Even though she used a large amount* of flour, the yeast permeated every part of the dough."

34Jesus always used stories and illustrations like these when speaking to the crowds. In fact, he never spoke to them without using such parables. 35This fulfilled the prophecy that said,

"I will speak to you in parables.
  I will explain mysteries hidden since the
    creation of the world."*

## The Wheat and Weeds Explained

36Then, leaving the crowds outside, Jesus went into the house. His disciples said, "Please explain the story of the weeds in the field."

37."All right," he said. "I, the Son of Man, am the farmer who plants the good seed. 38The field is the world, and the good seed represents the people of the Kingdom. The weeds are the people who belong to the evil one. 39The enemy who planted the weeds among the wheat is the Devil. The harvest is the end of the world, and the harvesters are the angels.

40"Just as the weeds are separated out and burned, so it will be at the end of the world. 41I, the Son of Man, will send my angels, and they will remove from my Kingdom everything that causes sin and all who do evil, 42and they will throw them into the furnace and burn them. There will be weeping and gnashing of teeth. 43Then the godly will shine like the sun in their Father's Kingdom. Anyone who is willing to hear should listen and understand!

## Illustration of the Hidden Treasure

44"The Kingdom of Heaven is like a treasure that a man discovered hidden in a field. In his excitement, he hid it again and sold everything he owned to get enough money to buy the field—and to get the treasure, too!

## Illustration of the Pearl Merchant

45"Again, the Kingdom of Heaven is like a pearl merchant on the lookout for choice pearls.

46When he discovered a pearl of great value, he sold everything he owned and bought it!

## Illustration of the Fishing Net

47"Again, the Kingdom of Heaven is like a fishing net that is thrown into the water and gathers fish of every kind. 48When the net is full, they drag it up onto the shore, sit down, sort the good fish into crates, and throw the bad ones away. 49That is the way it will be at the end of the world. The angels will come and separate the wicked people from the godly, 50throwing the wicked into the fire. There will be weeping and gnashing of teeth. 51Do you understand?"

"Yes," they said, "we do."

52Then he added, "Every teacher of religious law who has become a disciple in the Kingdom of Heaven is like a person who brings out of the storehouse the new teachings as well as the old."

## Jesus Rejected at Nazareth

53When Jesus had finished telling these stories, he left that part of the country. 54He returned to Nazareth, his hometown. When he taught there in the synagogue, everyone was astonished and said, "Where does he get his wisdom and his miracles? 55He's just a carpenter's son, and we know Mary, his mother, and his brothers—James, Joseph, Simon, and Judas. 56All his sisters live right here among us. What makes him so great?" 57And they were deeply offended and refused to believe in him.

Then Jesus told them, "A prophet is honored everywhere except in his own hometown and among his own family." 58And so he did only a few miracles there because of their unbelief.

## CHAPTER 14

### The Death of John the Baptist

When Herod Antipas* heard about Jesus, 2he said to his advisers, "This must be John the Baptist come back to life again! That is why he can do such miracles." 3For Herod had arrested and imprisoned John as a favor to his wife Herodias (the former wife of Herod's brother Philip). 4John kept telling Herod, "It is illegal for you to marry her." 5Herod would have executed John, but he was afraid of a riot, because all the people believed John was a prophet.

6But at a birthday party for Herod, Herodias's daughter performed a dance that greatly pleased him, 7so he promised with an oath to

13:33 Greek 3 measures.  13:35 Ps 78:2.  14:1 Greek Herod the tetrarch. He was a son of King Herod and was ruler over one of the four districts in Palestine.

give her anything she wanted. 8At her mother's urging, the girl asked, "I want the head of John the Baptist on a tray!" 9The king was sorry, but because of his oath and because he didn't want to back down in front of his guests, he issued the necessary orders. 10So John was beheaded in the prison, 11and his head was brought on a tray and given to the girl, who took it to her mother. 12John's disciples came for his body and buried it. Then they told Jesus what had happened.

## Jesus Feeds Five Thousand

13As soon as Jesus heard the news, he went off by himself in a boat to a remote area to be alone. But the crowds heard where he was headed and followed by land from many villages. 14A vast crowd was there as he stepped from the boat, and he had compassion on them and healed their sick.

15That evening the disciples came to him and said, "This is a desolate place, and it is getting late. Send the crowds away so they can go to the villages and buy food for themselves."

16But Jesus replied, "That isn't necessary— you feed them."

17"Impossible!" they exclaimed. "We have only five loaves of bread and two fish!"

18"Bring them here," he said. 19Then he told the people to sit down on the grass. And he took the five loaves and two fish, looked up toward heaven, and asked God's blessing on the food. Breaking the loaves into pieces, he gave some of the bread and fish to each disciple, and the disciples gave them to the people. 20They all ate as much as they wanted, and they picked up twelve baskets of leftovers. 21About five thousand men had eaten from those five loaves, in addition to all the women and children!

## Jesus Walks on Water

22Immediately after this, Jesus made his disciples get back into the boat and cross to the other side of the lake while he sent the people home. 23Afterward he went up into the hills by himself to pray. Night fell while he was there alone. 24Meanwhile, the disciples were in trouble far away from land, for a strong wind had risen, and they were fighting heavy waves.

25About three o'clock in the morning* Jesus came to them, walking on the water. 26When the disciples saw him, they screamed in terror, thinking he was a ghost. 27But Jesus spoke to them at once. "It's all right," he said. "I am here! Don't be afraid."

28Then Peter called to him, "Lord, if it's really you, tell me to come to you by walking on water."

29"All right, come," Jesus said.

So Peter went over the side of the boat and walked on the water toward Jesus. 30But when he looked around at the high waves, he was terrified and began to sink. "Save me, Lord!" he shouted.

31Instantly Jesus reached out his hand and grabbed him. "You don't have much faith," Jesus said. "Why did you doubt me?" 32And when they climbed back into the boat, the wind stopped.

33Then the disciples worshiped him. "You really are the Son of God!" they exclaimed.

34After they had crossed the lake, they landed at Gennesaret. 35The news of their arrival spread quickly throughout the whole surrounding area, and soon people were bringing all their sick to be healed. 36The sick begged him to let them touch even the fringe of his robe, and all who touched it were healed.

## CHAPTER 15

### Jesus Teaches about Inner Purity

Some Pharisees and teachers of religious law now arrived from Jerusalem to interview Jesus. 2"Why do your disciples disobey our age-old traditions?" they demanded. "They ignore our tradition of ceremonial hand washing before they eat."

3Jesus replied, "And why do you, by your traditions, violate the direct commandments of God? 4For instance, God says, 'Honor your father and mother,' and 'Anyone who speaks evil of father or mother must be put to death.'* 5But you say, 'You don't need to honor your parents by caring for their needs if you give the money to God instead.' 6And so, by your own tradition, you nullify the direct commandment of God. 7You hypocrites! Isaiah was prophesying about you when he said,

8  'These people honor me with their lips,
   but their hearts are far away.
9  Their worship is a farce,
   for they replace God's commands with
      their own man-made teachings.'* "

10Then Jesus called to the crowds and said, "Listen to what I say and try to understand.

14:25 Greek *In the fourth watch of the night.*   15:4 Exod 20:12; 21:17; Lev 20:9; Deut 5:16.   15:8-9 Isa 29:13.

11You are not defiled by what you eat; you are defiled by what you say and do.*"

12Then the disciples came to him and asked, "Do you realize you offended the Pharisees by what you just said?"

13Jesus replied, "Every plant not planted by my heavenly Father will be rooted up, 14so ignore them. They are blind guides leading the blind, and if one blind person guides another, they will both fall into a ditch."

15Then Peter asked Jesus, "Explain what you meant when you said people aren't defiled by what they eat."

16"Don't you understand?" Jesus asked him. 17"Anything you eat passes through the stomach and then goes out of the body. 18But evil words come from an evil heart and defile the person who says them. 19For from the heart come evil thoughts, murder, adultery, all other sexual immorality, theft, lying, and slander. 20These are what defile you. Eating with unwashed hands could never defile you and make you unacceptable to God!"

### The Faith of a Gentile Woman
21Jesus then left Galilee and went north to the region of Tyre and Sidon. 22A Gentile* woman who lived there came to him, pleading, "Have mercy on me, O Lord, Son of David! For my daughter has a demon in her, and it is severely tormenting her."

23But Jesus gave her no reply—not even a word. Then his disciples urged him to send her away. "Tell her to leave," they said. "She is bothering us with all her begging."

24Then he said to the woman, "I was sent only to help the people of Israel—God's lost sheep—not the Gentiles."

25But she came and worshiped him and pleaded again, "Lord, help me!"

26"It isn't right to take food from the children and throw it to the dogs," he said.

27"Yes, Lord," she replied, "but even dogs are permitted to eat crumbs that fall beneath their master's table."

28"Woman," Jesus said to her, "your faith is great. Your request is granted." And her daughter was instantly healed.

### Jesus Heals Many People
29Jesus returned to the Sea of Galilee and climbed a hill and sat down. 30A vast crowd brought him the lame, blind, crippled, mute,

and many others with physical difficulties, and they laid them before Jesus. And he healed them all. 31The crowd was amazed! Those who hadn't been able to speak were talking, the crippled were made well, the lame were walking around, and those who had been blind could see again! And they praised the God of Israel.

### Jesus Feeds Four Thousand
32Then Jesus called his disciples to him and said, "I feel sorry for these people. They have been here with me for three days, and they have nothing left to eat. I don't want to send them away hungry, or they will faint along the road."

33The disciples replied, "And where would we get enough food out here in the wilderness for all of them to eat?"

34Jesus asked, "How many loaves of bread do you have?"

They replied, "Seven, and a few small fish."
35So Jesus told all the people to sit down on the ground. 36Then he took the seven loaves and the fish, thanked God for them, broke them into pieces, and gave them to the disciples, who distributed the food to the crowd.

37They all ate until they were full, and when the scraps were picked up, there were seven large baskets of food left over! 38There were four thousand men who were fed that day, in addition to all the women and children. 39Then Jesus sent the people home, and he got into a boat and crossed over to the region of Magadan.

## CHAPTER 16
### Leaders Demand a Miraculous Sign
One day the Pharisees and Sadducees came to test Jesus' claims by asking him to show them a miraculous sign from heaven.

2He replied, "You know the saying, 'Red sky at night means fair weather tomorrow, 3red sky in the morning means foul weather all day.' You are good at reading the weather signs in the sky, but you can't read the obvious signs of the times!* 4Only an evil, faithless generation would ask for a miraculous sign, but the only sign I will give them is the sign of the prophet Jonah." Then Jesus left them and went away.

### Yeast of the Pharisees and Sadducees
5Later, after they crossed to the other side of the lake, the disciples discovered they had forgotten to bring any food. 6"Watch out!" Jesus warned

15:11 Or *what comes out of the mouth defiles a person.* 15:22 Greek *Canaanite.* 16:2-3 Several manuscripts do not include any of the words in 16:2-3 after *He replied.*

them. "Beware of the yeast of the Pharisees and Sadducees."

7They decided he was saying this because they hadn't brought any bread. 8Jesus knew what they were thinking, so he said, "You have so little faith! Why are you worried about having no food? 9Won't you ever understand? Don't you remember the five thousand I fed with five loaves, and the baskets of food that were left over? 10Don't you remember the four thousand I fed with seven loaves, with baskets of food left over? 11How could you even think I was talking about food? So again I say, 'Beware of the yeast of the Pharisees and Sadducees.'"

12Then at last they understood that he wasn't speaking about yeast or bread but about the false teaching of the Pharisees and Sadducees.

## Peter's Declaration about Jesus

13When Jesus came to the region of Caesarea Philippi, he asked his disciples, "Who do people say that the Son of Man is?"

14"Well," they replied, "some say John the Baptist, some say Elijah, and others say Jeremiah or one of the other prophets."

15Then he asked them, "Who do you say I am?"

16Simon Peter answered, "You are the Messiah, the Son of the living God."

17Jesus replied, "You are blessed, Simon son of John,* because my Father in heaven has revealed this to you. You did not learn this from any human being. 18Now I say to you that you are Peter,* and upon this rock I will build my church, and all the powers of hell* will not conquer it. 19And I will give you the keys of the

Kingdom of Heaven. Whatever you lock on earth will be locked in heaven, and whatever you open on earth will be opened in heaven."

20Then he sternly warned them not to tell anyone that he was the Messiah.

## Jesus Predicts His Death

21From then on Jesus began to tell his disciples plainly that he had to go to Jerusalem, and he told them what would happen to him there. He would suffer at the hands of the leaders and the leading priests and the teachers of religious law. He would be killed, and he would be raised on the third day.

22But Peter took him aside and corrected him. "Heaven forbid, Lord," he said. "This will never happen to you!"

23Jesus turned to Peter and said, "Get away from me, Satan! You are a dangerous trap to me. You are seeing things merely from a human point of view, and not from God's."

24Then Jesus said to the disciples, "If any of you wants to be my follower, you must put aside your selfish ambition, shoulder your cross, and follow me. 25If you try to keep your life for yourself, you will lose it. But if you give up your life for me, you will find true life. 26And how do you benefit if you gain the whole world but lose your own soul* in the process? Is anything worth more than your soul? 27For I, the Son of Man, will come in the glory of my Father with his angels and will judge all people according to their deeds. 28And I assure you that some of you standing here right now will not die before you see me, the Son of Man, coming in my Kingdom."

16:17 Greek *Simon son of Jonah;* see John 1:42; 21:15-17.   16:18a *Peter* means "stone" or "rock."   16:18b Greek *and the gates of Hades.*
16:26 Or *your life.*

# OFF AND RUNNING

## We Must Surrender Our Dreams and Seek God's Will Read MATTHEW 16:24-26

Jesus' words in this passage may seem extremely harsh. Yet in reality they are compassionate, because they point the way to real life. Anyone who wants this real life must become a disciple of Jesus. That means obeying Jesus' commands and adopting an attitude of self-denial. This text makes three points on what it means to adopt that attitude and follow Jesus:

1. We Must "Lose Our Life." We "find life" not in seeking it but in coming into a proper alignment with God and his plan for us. As you "lose your life," you find it again. This "life" Jesus speaks of not only includes life after death, but also "life during life." Jesus tells us that he came to "give life in all its fullness" (John 10:10). You should never be afraid to trust an unknown future to a known God. God's plan for you is good. In fact, it is better than any plan you may have for yourself.

# CHAPTER 17

## The Transfiguration

Six days later Jesus took Peter and the two brothers, James and John, and led them up a high mountain. ²As the men watched, Jesus' appearance changed so that his face shone like the sun, and his clothing became dazzling white. ³Suddenly, Moses and Elijah appeared and began talking with Jesus. ⁴Peter blurted out, "Lord, this is wonderful! If you want me to, I'll make three shrines,* one for you, one for Moses, and one for Elijah."

⁵But even as he said it, a bright cloud came over them, and a voice from the cloud said, "This is my beloved Son, and I am fully pleased with him. Listen to him." ⁶The disciples were terrified and fell face down on the ground.

⁷Jesus came over and touched them. "Get up," he said, "don't be afraid." ⁸And when they looked, they saw only Jesus with them. ⁹As they descended the mountain, Jesus commanded them, "Don't tell anyone what you have seen until I, the Son of Man, have been raised from the dead."

¹⁰His disciples asked, "Why do the teachers of religious law insist that Elijah must return before the Messiah comes*?"

¹¹Jesus replied, "Elijah is indeed coming first to set everything in order. ¹²But I tell you, he has already come, but he wasn't recognized, and he was badly mistreated. And soon the Son of Man will also suffer at their hands." ¹³Then the disciples realized he had been speaking of John the Baptist.

## Jesus Heals a Demon-Possessed Boy

¹⁴When they arrived at the foot of the mountain, a huge crowd was waiting for them. A man came and knelt before Jesus and said, ¹⁵"Lord, have mercy on my son, because he has seizures and suffers terribly. He often falls into the fire or into the water. ¹⁶So I brought him to your disciples, but they couldn't heal him."

¹⁷Jesus replied, "You stubborn, faithless people! How long must I be with you until you believe? How long must I put up with you? Bring the boy to me." ¹⁸Then Jesus rebuked the demon in the boy, and it left him. From that moment the boy was well.

¹⁹Afterward the disciples asked Jesus privately, "Why couldn't we cast out that demon?"

²⁰"You didn't have enough faith," Jesus told them. "I assure you, even if you had faith as small as a mustard seed you could say to this mountain, 'Move from here to there,' and it would move. Nothing would be impossible."*

## Jesus Again Predicts His Death

²²One day after they had returned to Galilee, Jesus told them, "The Son of Man is going to be betrayed. ²³He will be killed, but three days later he will be raised from the dead." And the disciples' hearts were filled with grief.

## Payment of the Temple Tax

²⁴On their arrival in Capernaum, the tax collectors for the Temple tax came to Peter and asked him, "Doesn't your teacher pay the Temple tax?"

²⁵"Of course he does," Peter replied. Then he went into the house to talk to Jesus about it.

But before he had a chance to speak, Jesus asked him, "What do you think, Peter*? Do kings tax their own people or the foreigners they have conquered?"

17:4 Or *shelters;* Greek reads *tabernacles.* 17:10 Greek *that Elijah must come first.* 17:20 Some manuscripts add verse 21, *But this kind of demon won't leave unless you have prayed and fasted.* 17:25 Greek *Simon.*

---

**2. We Must Deny Ourselves.** To "deny ourselves" means that we put the will and purposes of God above our own. We discover God's will for our lives as we search, study, and obey God's Word.

**3. We Must Take Up Our Cross.** This speaks of "dying" to our own will and selfish ambition. Don't let this passage frighten you. It is through this dying to ourselves that we find God's plan and purpose for our lives.

The Christian life is not one of morbid misery and hyper self-examination. It is a life of peace and joy as we walk in harmony with the God who made us. Paul sums it up perfectly when he writes, "I have been crucified with Christ. I myself no longer live, but Christ lives in me. So I live my life in this earthly body by trusting in the Son of God, who loved me and gave himself for me" (Galatians 2:19-20). It is only when the bulb of a tulip goes into the ground and dies that a beautiful flower can grow in its place. Be willing to entrust yourself to God's plan for your life. You won't regret it.

## Forgiveness Knows No Limits Read MATTHEW 18:21-35

The religious leaders of that day taught that one who had been wronged was to forgive the person who wronged him two to three times—at the most! In this text, Peter, mustering up as much forgiveness as he could, wondered if forgiving someone seven times would be enough in Jesus' eyes. Imagine Peter's shock when Jesus told him that he should forgive up to "seventy times seven," or *490* times.

Does this mean that if someone needed forgiveness after the four-hundred-ninety-first time that we should say no? Of course not. Rather, Jesus was teaching that we should extend unlimited forgiveness to others. He then went on to tell this dramatic story of a man who was forgiven for so much (possibly $10 million), yet was unwilling to even work out terms with a person who owed him far less (around two thousand dollars). The point of Jesus' message is that we, as sinners, have been forgiven much. Therefore, we ought to forgive those who have hurt us, no matter how badly. For they owe us little, compared to what we had owed to God.

### CORNER STONES

26"They tax the foreigners," Peter replied.

"Well, then," Jesus said, "the citizens are free! 27However, we don't want to offend them, so go down to the lake and throw in a line. Open the mouth of the first fish you catch, and you will find a coin. Take the coin and pay the tax for both of us."

## CHAPTER 18

### The Greatest in the Kingdom

About that time the disciples came to Jesus and asked, "Which of us is greatest in the Kingdom of Heaven?"

2Jesus called a small child over to him and put the child among them. 3Then he said, "I assure you, unless you turn from your sins and become as little children, you will never get into the Kingdom of Heaven. 4Therefore, anyone who becomes as humble as this little child is the greatest in the Kingdom of Heaven. 5And anyone who welcomes a little child like this on my behalf is welcoming me. 6But if anyone causes one of these little ones who trusts in me to lose faith, it would be better for that person to be thrown into the sea with a large millstone tied around the neck.

7"How terrible it will be for anyone who causes others to sin. Temptation to do wrong is inevitable, but how terrible it will be for the person who does the tempting. 8So if your hand or foot causes you to sin, cut it off and throw it away. It is better to enter heaven* crippled or lame than to be thrown into the unquenchable fire with both of your hands and feet. 9And if your eye causes you to sin, gouge it out and throw it away. It is better to enter heaven half blind than to have two eyes and be thrown into hell.

10"Beware that you don't despise a single one of these little ones. For I tell you that in heaven their angels are always in the presence of my heavenly Father.*

### Story of the Lost Sheep

12"If a shepherd has one hundred sheep, and one wanders away and is lost, what will he do? Won't he leave the ninety-nine others and go out into the hills to search for the lost one? 13And if he finds it, he will surely rejoice over it more than over the ninety-nine that didn't wander away! 14In the same way, it is not my heavenly Father's will that even one of these little ones should perish.

### Correcting a Fellow Believer

15"If another believer* sins against you, go privately and point out the fault. If the other person listens and confesses it, you have won that person back. 16But if you are unsuccessful, take one or two others with you and go back again, so that everything you say may be confirmed by two or three witnesses. 17If that person still refuses to listen, take your case to the church. If the church decides you are right, but the other person won't accept it, treat that person as a pagan or a corrupt tax collector. 18I tell you this: Whatever you prohibit on earth is prohibited in

18:8 Greek *enter life*; also in 18:9.   18:10 Some manuscripts add verse 11, *And I, the Son of Man, have come to save the lost.*   18:15 Greek *your brother* heaven, and whatever you allow on earth is allowed in heaven.

19 "I also tell you this: If two of you agree down here on earth concerning anything you ask, my Father in heaven will do it for you. 20For where two or three gather together because they are mine,* I am there among them."

### Story of the Unforgiving Debtor

21Then Peter came to him and asked, "Lord, how often should I forgive someone* who sins against me? Seven times?"

22 "No!" Jesus replied, "seventy times seven!*

23 "For this reason, the Kingdom of Heaven can be compared to a king who decided to bring his accounts up to date with servants who had borrowed money from him. 24In the process, one of his debtors was brought in who owed him millions of dollars.* 25He couldn't pay, so the king ordered that he, his wife, his children, and everything he had be sold to pay the debt. 26But the man fell down before the king and begged him, 'Oh, sir, be patient with me, and I will pay it all.' 27Then the king was filled with pity for him, and he released him and forgave his debt.

28 "But when the man left the king, he went to a fellow servant who owed him a few thousand dollars.* He grabbed him by the throat and demanded instant payment. 29His fellow servant fell down before him and begged for a little more time. 'Be patient and I will pay it,' he pleaded. 30But his creditor wouldn't wait. He had the man arrested and jailed until the debt could be paid in full.

31 "When some of the other servants saw this, they were very upset. They went to the king and told him what had happened. 32Then the king called in the man he had forgiven and said, 'You evil servant! I forgave you that tremendous debt because you pleaded with me. 33Shouldn't you have mercy on your fellow servant, just as I had mercy on you?' 34Then the angry king sent the man to prison until he had paid every penny.

35 "That's what my heavenly Father will do to you if you refuse to forgive your brothers and sisters* in your heart."

## CHAPTER 19
### Discussion about Divorce and Marriage
After Jesus had finished saying these things, he left Galilee and went southward to the region of Judea and into the area east of the Jordan River. 2Vast crowds followed him there, and he healed their sick.

3Some Pharisees came and tried to trap him with this question: "Should a man be allowed to divorce his wife for any reason?"

4 "Haven't you read the Scriptures?" Jesus replied. "They record that from the beginning 'God made them male and female.'* 5And he said, 'This explains why a man leaves his father and mother and is joined to his wife, and the two are united into one.'* 6Since they are no longer two but one, let no one separate them, for God has joined them together."

7 "Then why did Moses say a man could merely write an official letter of divorce and send her away?"* they asked.

8Jesus replied, "Moses permitted divorce as a concession to your hard-hearted wickedness, but it was not what God had originally intended. 9And I tell you this, a man who divorces his wife and marries another commits adultery—unless his wife has been unfaithful.*"

10Jesus' disciples then said to him, "Then it is better not to marry!"

11 "Not everyone can accept this statement," Jesus said. "Only those whom God helps. 12Some are born as eunuchs, some have been made that way by others, and some choose not to marry for the sake of the Kingdom of Heaven. Let anyone who can, accept this statement."

### Jesus Blesses the Children
13Some children were brought to Jesus so he could lay his hands on them and pray for them. The disciples told them not to bother him. 14But Jesus said, "Let the children come to me. Don't stop them! For the Kingdom of Heaven belongs to such as these." 15And he put his hands on their heads and blessed them before he left.

### The Rich Young Man
16Someone came to Jesus with this question: "Teacher,* what good things must I do to have eternal life?"

17 "Why ask me about what is good?" Jesus replied. "Only God is good. But to answer your question, you can receive eternal life if you keep the commandments."

18 "Which ones?" the man asked.

And Jesus replied: " 'Do not murder. Do not commit adultery. Do not steal. Do not testify

18:20 Greek gather together in my name. 18:21 Greek my brother. 18:22 Or 77 times. 18:24 Greek 10,000 talents. 18:28 Greek 100 denarii. A denarius was the equivalent of a full day's wage. 18:35 Greek your brother. 19:4 Gen 1:27; 5:2. 19:5 Gen 2:24. 19:7 Deut 24:1. 19:9 Some manuscripts add And the man who marries a divorced woman commits adultery. 19:16 Some manuscripts read Good Teacher.

falsely. [19]Honor your father and mother. Love your neighbor as yourself.'* "

[20]"I've obeyed all these commandments," the young man replied. "What else must I do?"

[21]Jesus told him, "If you want to be perfect, go and sell all you have and give the money to the poor, and you will have treasure in heaven. Then come, follow me." [22]But when the young man heard this, he went sadly away because he had many possessions.

[23]Then Jesus said to his disciples, "I tell you the truth, it is very hard for a rich person to get into the Kingdom of Heaven. [24]I say it again—it is easier for a camel to go through the eye of a needle than for a rich person to enter the Kingdom of God!"

[25]The disciples were astounded. "Then who in the world can be saved?" they asked.

[26]Jesus looked at them intently and said, "Humanly speaking, it is impossible. But with God everything is possible."

[27]Then Peter said to him, "We've given up everything to follow you. What will we get out of it?"

[28]And Jesus replied, "I assure you that when I, the Son of Man, sit upon my glorious throne in the Kingdom,* you who have been my followers will also sit on twelve thrones, judging the twelve tribes of Israel. [29]And everyone who has given up houses or brothers or sisters or father or mother or children or property, for my sake, will receive a hundred times as much in return and will have eternal life. [30]But many who seem to be important now will be the least important then, and those who are considered least here will be the greatest then.*

## CHAPTER 20
### Story of the Vineyard Workers

"For the Kingdom of Heaven is like the owner of an estate who went out early one morning to hire workers for his vineyard. [2]He agreed to pay the normal daily wage* and sent them out to work.

[3]"At nine o'clock in the morning he was passing through the marketplace and saw some people standing around doing nothing. [4]So he hired them, telling them he would pay them whatever was right at the end of the day. [5]At noon and again around three o'clock he did the same thing. [6]At five o'clock that evening he was in town again and saw some more people stand-

ing around. He asked them, 'Why haven't you been working today?'

[7]"They replied, 'Because no one hired us.'

"The owner of the estate told them, 'Then go on out and join the others in my vineyard.'

[8]"That evening he told the foreman to call the workers in and pay them, beginning with the last workers first. [9]When those hired at five o'clock were paid, each received a full day's wage. [10]When those hired earlier came to get their pay, they assumed they would receive more. But they, too, were paid a day's wage. [11]When they received their pay, they protested, [12]'Those people worked only one hour, and yet you've paid them just as much as you paid us who worked all day in the scorching heat.'

[13]"He answered one of them, 'Friend, I haven't been unfair! Didn't you agree to work all day for the usual wage? [14]Take it and go. I wanted to pay this last worker the same as you. [15]Is it against the law for me to do what I want with my money? Should you be angry because I am kind?'

[16]"And so it is, that many who are first now will be last then; and those who are last now will be first then."

### Jesus Again Predicts His Death

[17]As Jesus was on the way to Jerusalem, he took the twelve disciples aside privately and told them what was going to happen to him. [18]"When we get to Jerusalem," he said, "the Son of Man will be betrayed to the leading priests and the teachers of religious law. They will sentence him to die. [19]Then they will hand him over to the Romans to be mocked, whipped, and crucified. But on the third day he will be raised from the dead."

### Jesus Teaches about Serving Others

[20]Then the mother of James and John, the sons of Zebedee, came to Jesus with her sons. She knelt respectfully to ask a favor. [21]"What is your request?" he asked.

She replied, "In your Kingdom, will you let my two sons sit in places of honor next to you, one at your right and the other at your left?"

[22]But Jesus told them, "You don't know what you are asking! Are you able to drink from the bitter cup of sorrow I am about to drink?"

"Oh yes," they replied, "we are able!"

[23]"You will indeed drink from it," he told them. "But I have no right to say who will sit on

19:18-19 Exod 20:12-16; Lev 19:18; Deut 5:16-20. 19:28 Greek *in the regeneration.* 19:30 Greek *But many who are first will be last; and the last, first.* 20:2 Greek *a denarius,* the payment for a full day's labor; also in 20:9, 10, 13.

the thrones next to mine. My Father has prepared those places for the ones he has chosen."

24When the ten other disciples heard what James and John had asked, they were indignant. 25But Jesus called them together and said, "You know that in this world kings are tyrants, and officials lord it over the people beneath them. 26But among you it should be quite different. Whoever wants to be a leader among you must be your servant, 27and whoever wants to be first must become your slave. 28For even I, the Son of Man, came here not to be served but to serve others, and to give my life as a ransom for many."

### Jesus Heals Two Blind Men
29As Jesus and the disciples left the city of Jericho, a huge crowd followed behind. 30Two blind men were sitting beside the road. When they heard that Jesus was coming that way, they began shouting, "Lord, Son of David, have mercy on us!" 31The crowd told them to be quiet, but they only shouted louder, "Lord, Son of David, have mercy on us!"

32Jesus stopped in the road and called, "What do you want me to do for you?"

33"Lord," they said, "we want to see!" 34Jesus felt sorry for them and touched their eyes. Instantly they could see! Then they followed him.

CHAPTER **21**
### The Triumphal Entry
As Jesus and the disciples approached Jerusalem, they came to the town of Bethphage on the Mount of Olives. Jesus sent two of them on ahead. 2"Go into the village over there," he said, "and you will see a donkey tied there, with its colt beside it. Untie them and bring them here. 3If anyone asks what you are doing, just say, 'The Lord needs them,' and he will immediately send them." 4This was done to fulfill the prophecy,

5 "Tell the people of Israel,*

 'Look, your King is coming to you.
 He is humble, riding on a donkey—
 even on a donkey's colt.'"*

6The two disciples did as Jesus said. 7They brought the animals to him and threw their garments over the colt, and he sat on it.*

8Most of the crowd spread their coats on the road ahead of Jesus, and others cut branches from the trees and spread them on the road. 9He was in the center of the procession, and the crowds all around him were shouting,

 "Praise God* for the Son of David!
 Bless the one who comes in the name of the Lord!
 Praise God in highest heaven!"*

10The entire city of Jerusalem was stirred as he entered. "Who is this?" they asked.

11And the crowds replied, "It's Jesus, the prophet from Nazareth in Galilee."

### Jesus Clears the Temple
12Jesus entered the Temple and began to drive out the merchants and their customers. He knocked over the tables of the money changers and the stalls of those selling doves. 13He said, "The Scriptures declare, 'My Temple will be called a place of prayer,' but you have turned it into a den of thieves!"*

14The blind and the lame came to him, and he healed them there in the Temple. 15The leading priests and the teachers of religious law saw these wonderful miracles and heard even the little children in the Temple shouting, "Praise God for the Son of David." But they were indignant 16and asked Jesus, "Do you hear what these children are saying?"

"Yes," Jesus replied. "Haven't you ever read the Scriptures? For they say, 'You have taught children and infants to give you praise.'* " 17Then he returned to Bethany, where he stayed overnight.

### Jesus Curses the Fig Tree
18In the morning, as Jesus was returning to Jerusalem, he was hungry, 19and he noticed a fig tree beside the road. He went over to see if there were any figs on it, but there were only leaves. Then he said to it, "May you never bear fruit again!" And immediately the fig tree withered up.

20The disciples were amazed when they saw this and asked, "How did the fig tree wither so quickly?"

21Then Jesus told them, "I assure you, if you have faith and don't doubt, you can do things like this and much more. You can even say to this mountain, 'May God lift you up and throw you into the sea,' and it will happen. 22If you believe, you will receive whatever you ask for in prayer."

### The Authority of Jesus Challenged
23When Jesus returned to the Temple and began teaching, the leading priests and other leaders

21:5a Greek *Tell the daughter of Zion.* Isa 62:11.   21:5b Zech 9:9.   21:7 Greek *over them, and he sat on them.*   21:9a Greek *Hosanna,* an exclamation of praise that literally means "save now"; also in 21:9b, 15.   21:9b Pss 118:25-26; 148:1.   21:13 Isa 56:7; Jer 7:11.   21:16 Ps 8:2.

## Will We Recognize People in Heaven? Read MATTHEW 22:23-33

A number of the people in Jesus' day had some aberrant views of life after death. The particular group of religious leaders mentioned here, the Sadducees, did not believe in life beyond the grave. So when Jesus answered their question (which they had asked to test him), he immediately addressed the error of their teaching: "Your problem is that you don't know the Scriptures, and you don't know the power of God" (verse 29). In refuting the error and arrogance of the Sadducees, Jesus revealed these three insights about life in heaven:

**1. We Will Not Be Married.** We will not participate in the same activities we do now, such as marriage and family life. In fact, it would appear that the majority of our time will be spent worshiping God (see Revelation 19:5, p. 345).

**2. We Will Recognize One Another.** Jesus said that we will be as the angels. We won't become angels, but we will probably have some of the same capabilities or characteristics. We will not simply be a spirit, but we will actually have a resurrected body. While no specific passage of Scripture guarantees that we will recognize one another in heaven, many verses suggest that we will. Jesus' disciples were able to recognize his resurrected body, so he must have retained certain physical characteristics. In the parable of Lazarus and the rich man (see Luke 16:19-31, p. 93), both men retained their identity. The Bible also says that we will have increased knowledge in heaven: "Now we see things imperfectly as in a poor mirror, but then we will see everything with perfect clarity. All that I know now is partial and incomplete, but then I will know everything completely, just as God knows me now" (1 Corinthians 13:12). With that kind of knowledge, we will probably recognize more people in heaven than we do here on earth!

**3. We Will Have a Distinct Personality.** Notice that at the end of the text Jesus refers to the Old Testament passage that says, "I *am* the God of Abraham, the God of Isaac, and the God of Jacob." Not only does this verse give great proof for a bodily resurrection, but it also refers to these men by name. When we read that God writes our names in the Book of Life, it indicates that we are distinct personalities in heaven. God didn't write a number—he wrote your *name*.

CORNER STONES

Some day, "in the blinking of an eye," Christ will call us home to heaven, and our bodies will be transformed into "heavenly bodies that will never die" (see 1 Corinthians 15:50-53, p. 215).

To live forever in these present bodies of ours would be a curse. But to live forever in new bodies—free of sickness and pain—in the presence of God will be a blessing.

---

came up to him. They demanded, "By whose authority did you drive out the merchants from the Temple?* Who gave you such authority?"

²⁴"I'll tell you who gave me the authority to do these things if you answer one question," Jesus replied. ²⁵"Did John's baptism come from heaven or was it merely human?"

They talked it over among themselves. "If we say it was from heaven, he will ask why we didn't believe him. ²⁶But if we say it was merely human, we'll be mobbed, because the people think he was a prophet." ²⁷So they finally replied, "We don't know."

21:23 Or *By whose authority do you do these things?*

And Jesus responded, "Then I won't answer your question either.

*Story of the Two Sons*
²⁸"But what do you think about this? A man with two sons told the older boy, 'Son, go out and work in the vineyard today.' ²⁹The son answered, 'No, I won't go,' but later he changed his mind and went anyway. ³⁰Then the father told the other son, 'You go,' and he said, 'Yes, sir, I will.' But he didn't go. ³¹Which of the two was obeying his father?"

They replied, "The first, of course."

Then Jesus explained his meaning: "I assure you, corrupt tax collectors and prostitutes will get into the Kingdom of God before you do. 32For John the Baptist came and showed you the way to life, and you didn't believe him, while tax collectors and prostitutes did. And even when you saw this happening, you refused to turn from your sins and believe him.

### Story of the Evil Farmers

33"Now listen to this story. A certain landowner planted a vineyard, built a wall around it, dug a pit for pressing out the grape juice, and built a lookout tower. Then he leased the vineyard to tenant farmers and moved to another country. 34At the time of the grape harvest he sent his servants to collect his share of the crop. 35But the farmers grabbed his servants, beat one, killed one, and stoned another. 36So the landowner sent a larger group of his servants to collect for him, but the results were the same.

37"Finally, the owner sent his son, thinking, 'Surely they will respect my son.'

38"But when the farmers saw his son coming, they said to one another, 'Here comes the heir to this estate. Come on, let's kill him and get the estate for ourselves!' 39So they grabbed him, took him out of the vineyard, and murdered him.

40"When the owner of the vineyard returns," Jesus asked, "what do you think he will do to those farmers?"

41The religious leaders replied, "He will put the wicked men to a horrible death and lease the vineyard to others who will give him his share of the crop after each harvest."

42Then Jesus asked them, "Didn't you ever read this in the Scriptures?

'The stone rejected by the builders
   has now become the cornerstone.
This is the Lord's doing,
   and it is marvelous to see.'*

43What I mean is that the Kingdom of God will be taken away from you and given to a nation that will produce the proper fruit. 44Anyone who stumbles over that stone will be broken to pieces, and it will crush anyone on whom it falls.*"

45When the leading priests and Pharisees heard Jesus, they realized he was pointing at them—that they were the farmers in his story. 46They wanted to arrest him, but they were afraid to try because the crowds considered Jesus to be a prophet.

## CHAPTER 22
### Story of the Great Feast

Jesus told them several other stories to illustrate the Kingdom. He said, 2"The Kingdom of Heaven can be illustrated by the story of a king who prepared a great wedding feast for his son. 3Many guests were invited, and when the banquet was ready, he sent his servants to notify everyone that it was time to come. But they all refused! 4So he sent other servants to tell them, 'The feast has been prepared, and choice meats have been cooked. Everything is ready. Hurry!' 5But the guests he had invited ignored them and went about their business, one to his farm, another to his store. 6Others seized his messengers and treated them shamefully, even killing some of them.

7"Then the king became furious. He sent out his army to destroy the murderers and burn their city. 8And he said to his servants, 'The wedding feast is ready, and the guests I invited aren't worthy of the honor. 9Now go out to the street corners and invite everyone you see.'

10"So the servants brought in everyone they could find, good and bad alike, and the banquet hall was filled with guests. 11But when the king came in to meet the guests, he noticed a man who wasn't wearing the proper clothes for a wedding. 12'Friend,' he asked, 'how is it that you are here without wedding clothes?' And the man had no reply. 13Then the king said to his aides, 'Bind him hand and foot and throw him out into the outer darkness, where there is weeping and gnashing of teeth.' 14For many are called, but few are chosen."

### Taxes for Caesar

15Then the Pharisees met together to think of a way to trap Jesus into saying something for which they could accuse him. 16They decided to send some of their disciples, along with the supporters of Herod, to ask him this question: "Teacher, we know how honest you are. You teach about the way of God regardless of the consequences. You are impartial and don't play favorites. 17Now tell us what you think about this: Is it right to pay taxes to the Roman government or not?"

18But Jesus knew their evil motives. "You hypocrites!" he said. "Whom are you trying to fool with your trick questions? 19Here, show me the Roman coin used for the tax." When they handed him the coin,* 20he asked, "Whose picture and title are stamped on it?"

---

21:42 Ps 118:22-23.   21:44 This verse is omitted in some early manuscripts.   22:19 Greek *a denarius.*

21"Caesar's," they replied.

"Well, then," he said, "give to Caesar what belongs to him. But everything that belongs to God must be given to God." 22His reply amazed them, and they went away.

### Discussion about Resurrection

23That same day some Sadducees stepped forward—a group of Jews who say there is no resurrection after death. They posed this question: 24"Teacher, Moses said, 'If a man dies without children, his brother should marry the widow and have a child who will be the brother's heir.'* 25Well, there were seven brothers. The oldest married and then died without children, so the second brother married the widow. 26This brother also died without children, and the wife was married to the next brother, and so on until she had been the wife of each of them. 27And then she also died. 28So tell us, whose wife will she be in the resurrection? For she was the wife of all seven of them!"

29Jesus replied, "Your problem is that you don't know the Scriptures, and you don't know the power of God. 30For when the dead rise, they won't be married. They will be like the angels in heaven. 31But now, as to whether there will be a resurrection of the dead—haven't you ever read about this in the Scriptures? Long after Abraham, Isaac, and Jacob had died, God said,* 32'I am the God of Abraham, the God of Isaac, and the God of Jacob.'* So he is the God of the living, not the dead."

33When the crowds heard him, they were impressed with his teaching.

### The Most Important Commandment

34But when the Pharisees heard that he had silenced the Sadducees with his reply, they thought up a fresh question of their own to ask him. 35One of them, an expert in religious law,

tried to trap him with this question: 36"Teacher, which is the most important commandment in the law of Moses?"

37Jesus replied, " 'You must love the Lord your God with all your heart, all your soul, and all your mind.'* 38This is the first and greatest commandment. 39A second is equally important: 'Love your neighbor as yourself.'* 40All the other commandments and all the demands of the prophets are based on these two commandments."

### Whose Son Is the Messiah?

41Then, surrounded by the Pharisees, Jesus asked them a question: 42"What do you think about the Messiah? Whose son is he?"

They replied, "He is the son of David."

43Jesus responded, "Then why does David, speaking under the inspiration of the Holy Spirit, call him Lord? For David said,

44 'The LORD said to my Lord,
  Sit in honor at my right hand
    until I humble your enemies beneath
      your feet.'*

45Since David called him Lord, how can he be his son at the same time?"

46No one could answer him. And after that, no one dared to ask him any more questions.

CHAPTER **23**
### Jesus Warns the Religious Leaders

Then Jesus said to the crowds and to his disciples, 2"The teachers of religious law and the Pharisees are the official interpreters of the Scriptures. 3So practice and obey whatever they say to you, but don't follow their example. For they don't practice what they teach. 4They crush you with impossible religious demands and never lift a finger to help ease the burden.

22:24 Deut 25:5-6.  22:31 Greek *in the Scriptures? God said.*  22:32 Exod 3:6.  22:37 Deut 6:5.  22:39 Lev 19:18.  22:44 Ps 110:1.

## OFF AND RUNNING ///
## We Will Find Happiness in Loving God and Others
### Read MATTHEW 22:37-39

In two commands Jesus summarized the entire Old Testament law. His summarization shows us what is important for us as his followers to do: to love God wholeheartedly and to love our neighbors as ourselves. When we do these two things, we will not only please God by our obedience, but we will also experience real happiness.

Ironically, real happiness is not found in fulfilling our own appetites and desires. Rather, it is found in loving God and others. This is not by chance, either. God designed it that way. He knew the value of loving

5"Everything they do is for show. On their arms they wear extra wide prayer boxes with Scripture verses inside,* and they wear extra long tassels on their robes. 6And how they love to sit at the head table at banquets and in the most prominent seats in the synagogue! 7They enjoy the attention they get on the streets, and they enjoy being called 'Rabbi.'* 8Don't ever let anyone call you 'Rabbi,' for you have only one teacher, and all of you are on the same level as brothers and sisters.* 9And don't address anyone here on earth as 'Father,' for only God in heaven is your spiritual Father. 10And don't let anyone call you 'Master,' for there is only one master, the Messiah. 11The greatest among you must be a servant. 12But those who exalt themselves will be humbled, and those who humble themselves will be exalted.

13"How terrible it will be for you teachers of religious law and you Pharisees. Hypocrites! For you won't let others enter the Kingdom of Heaven, and you won't go in yourselves.* 15Yes, how terrible it will be for you teachers of religious law and you Pharisees. For you cross land and sea to make one convert, and then you turn him into twice the son of hell as you yourselves are.

16"Blind guides! How terrible it will be for you! For you say that it means nothing to swear 'by God's Temple'—you can break that oath. But then you say that it is binding to swear 'by the gold in the Temple.' 17Blind fools! Which is greater, the gold, or the Temple that makes the gold sacred? 18And you say that to take an oath 'by the altar' can be broken, but to swear 'by the gifts on the altar' is binding! 19How blind! For which is greater, the gift on the altar, or the altar that makes the gift sacred? 20When you swear 'by the altar,' you are swearing by it and by everything on it. 21And when you swear 'by the

Temple,' you are swearing by it and by God, who lives in it. 22And when you swear 'by heaven,' you are swearing by the throne of God and by God, who sits on the throne.

23"How terrible it will be for you teachers of religious law and you Pharisees. Hypocrites! For you are careful to tithe even the tiniest part of your income,* but you ignore the important things of the law—justice, mercy, and faith. You should tithe, yes, but you should not leave undone the more important things. 24Blind guides! You strain your water so you won't accidentally swallow a gnat; then you swallow a camel!

25"How terrible it will be for you teachers of religious law and you Pharisees. Hypocrites! You are so careful to clean the outside of the cup and the dish, but inside you are filthy—full of greed and self-indulgence! 26Blind Pharisees! First wash the inside of the cup, and then the outside will become clean, too.

27"How terrible it will be for you teachers of religious law and you Pharisees. Hypocrites! You are like whitewashed tombs—beautiful on the outside but filled on the inside with dead people's bones and all sorts of impurity. 28You try to look like upright people outwardly, but inside your hearts are filled with hypocrisy and lawlessness.

29"How terrible it will be for you teachers of religious law and you Pharisees. Hypocrites! For you build tombs for the prophets your ancestors killed and decorate the graves of the godly people your ancestors destroyed. 30Then you say, 'We never would have joined them in killing the prophets.'

31"In saying that, you are accusing yourselves of being the descendants of those who murdered the prophets. 32Go ahead. Finish what they

23:5 Greek *They enlarge their phylacteries.* 23:7 *Rabbi,* from Aramaic, means "master" or "teacher." 23:8 Greek *brothers.* 23:13 Some manuscripts add verse 14, *How terrible it will be for you teachers of religious law and you Pharisees. Hypocrites! You shamelessly cheat widows out of their property, and then, to cover up the kind of people you really are, you make long prayers in public. Because of this, your punishment will be the greater.* 23:23 Greek *to tithe the mint, the dill, and the cumin.*

others even before he proved his love for us on the cross. He also knew how self-absorbed we are as humans and that we would fill our lives with empty pursuits in search of happiness if he didn't command us to love him and to love others.

As Paul tells us, all of our works will be tested by fire on Judgment Day (see 1 Corinthians 3:13, p. 200). Those works that were done out of selfishness will not last. But those works done out of love for God and others will. Because this love—and the works motivated by it—are everlasting, we will find real meaning in doing them. In addition, we will experience real joy in giving of ourselves to God and others out of love. It is in giving that we find purpose in life. From purpose we gain true happiness.

started. 33Snakes! Sons of vipers! How will you escape the judgment of hell? 34I will send you prophets and wise men and teachers of religious law. You will kill some by crucifixion and whip others in your synagogues, chasing them from city to city. 35As a result, you will become guilty of murdering all the godly people from righteous Abel to Zechariah son of Barachiah, whom you murdered in the Temple between the altar and the sanctuary. 36I assure you, all the accumulated judgment of the centuries will break upon the heads of this very generation.

### Jesus Grieves over Jerusalem

37"O Jerusalem, Jerusalem, the city that kills the prophets and stones God's messengers! How often I have wanted to gather your children together as a hen protects her chicks beneath her wings, but you wouldn't let me. 38And now look, your house is left to you, empty and desolate. 39For I tell you this, you will never see me again until you say, 'Bless the one who comes in the name of the Lord!'* "

CHAPTER **24**
### Jesus Foretells the Future

As Jesus was leaving the Temple grounds, his disciples pointed out to him the various Temple buildings. 2But he told them, "Do you see all these buildings? I assure you, they will be so completely demolished that not one stone will be left on top of another!"

3Later, Jesus sat on the slopes of the Mount of Olives. His disciples came to him privately and asked, "When will all this take place? And will there be any sign ahead of time to signal your return and the end of the world*?"

4Jesus told them, "Don't let anyone mislead you. 5For many will come in my name, saying, 'I am the Messiah.' They will lead many astray. 6And wars will break out near and far, but don't panic. Yes, these things must come, but the end won't follow immediately. 7The nations and kingdoms will proclaim war against each other, and there will be famines and earthquakes in many parts of the world. 8But all this will be only the beginning of the horrors to come.

9"Then you will be arrested, persecuted, and killed. You will be hated all over the world because of your allegiance to me. 10And many will turn away from me and betray and hate each other. 11And many false prophets will appear

and will lead many people astray. 12Sin will be rampant everywhere, and the love of many will grow cold. 13But those who endure to the end will be saved. 14And the Good News about the Kingdom will be preached throughout the whole world, so that all nations will hear it; and then, finally, the end will come.

15"The time will come when you will see what Daniel the prophet spoke about: the sacrilegious object that causes desecration* standing in the Holy Place"—reader, pay attention! 16"Then those in Judea must flee to the hills. 17A person outside the house* must not go inside to pack. 18A person in the field must not return even to get a coat. 19How terrible it will be for pregnant women and for mothers nursing their babies in those days. 20And pray that your flight will not be in winter or on the Sabbath. 21For that will be a time of greater horror than anything the world has ever seen or will ever see again. 22In fact, unless that time of calamity is shortened, the entire human race will be destroyed. But it will be shortened for the sake of God's chosen ones.

23"Then if anyone tells you, 'Look, here is the Messiah,' or 'There he is,' don't pay any attention. 24For false messiahs and false prophets will rise up and perform great miraculous signs and wonders so as to deceive, if possible, even God's chosen ones. 25See, I have warned you.

26"So if someone tells you, 'Look, the Messiah is out in the desert,' don't bother to go and look. Or, 'Look, he is hiding here,' don't believe it! 27For as the lightning lights up the entire sky, so it will be when the Son of Man comes. 28Just as the gathering of vultures shows there is a carcass nearby, so these signs indicate that the end is near.*

29"Immediately after those horrible days end,

the sun will be darkened,
    the moon will not give light,
the stars will fall from the sky,
    and the powers of heaven will be shaken.*

30And then at last, the sign of the coming of the Son of Man will appear in the heavens, and there will be deep mourning among all the nations of the earth. And they will see the Son of Man arrive on the clouds of heaven with power and great glory.* 31And he will send forth his angels with the sound of a mighty trumpet blast, and they will gather together his chosen ones from the farthest ends of the earth and heaven.

23:39 Ps 118:26. 24:3 Or *the age.* 24:15 Greek *the abomination of desolation.* See Dan 9:27; 11:31; 12:11. 24:17 Greek *on the roof.*
24:28 Greek *Wherever the carcass is, the vultures gather.* 24:29 See Isa 13:10; 34:4; Joel 2:10. 24:30 See Dan 7:13.

32"Now learn a lesson from the fig tree. When its buds become tender and its leaves begin to sprout, you know without being told that summer is near. 33Just so, when you see the events I've described beginning to happen, you can know his return is very near, right at the door. 34I assure you, this generation* will not pass from the scene before all these things take place. 35Heaven and earth will disappear, but my words will remain forever.

36"However, no one knows the day or the hour when these things will happen, not even the angels in heaven or the Son himself.* Only the Father knows.

37"When the Son of Man returns, it will be like it was in Noah's day. 38In those days before the Flood, the people were enjoying banquets and parties and weddings right up to the time Noah entered his boat. 39People didn't realize what was going to happen until the Flood came and swept them all away. That is the way it will be when the Son of Man comes.

40"Two men will be working together in the field; one will be taken, the other left. 41Two women will be grinding flour at the mill; one will be taken, the other left. 42So be prepared, because you don't know what day your Lord is coming.

43"Know this: A homeowner who knew exactly when a burglar was coming would stay alert and not permit the house to be broken into. 44You also must be ready all the time. For the Son of Man will come when least expected.

45"Who is a faithful, sensible servant, to whom the master can give the responsibility of managing his household and feeding his family? 46If the master returns and finds that the servant has done a good job, there will be a reward. 47I assure you, the master will put that servant in charge of all he owns. 48But if the servant is evil and thinks, 'My master won't be back for a while,' 49and begins oppressing the other servants, partying, and getting drunk— 50well, the master will return unannounced and unexpected. 51He will tear the servant apart and banish him with the hypocrites. In that place there will be weeping and gnashing of teeth.

CHAPTER **25**

## Story of the Ten Bridesmaids

"The Kingdom of Heaven can be illustrated by the story of ten bridesmaids* who took their lamps and went to meet the bridegroom. 2Five of them were foolish, and five were wise. 3The five who were foolish took no oil for their lamps, 4but the other five were wise enough to take along extra oil. 5When the bridegroom was delayed, they all lay down and slept. 6At midnight they were roused by the shout, 'Look, the bridegroom is coming! Come out and welcome him!'

7"All the bridesmaids got up and prepared their lamps. 8Then the five foolish ones asked the others, 'Please give us some of your oil because our lamps are going out.' 9But the others replied, 'We don't have enough for all of us. Go to a shop and buy some for yourselves.'

10"But while they were gone to buy oil, the bridegroom came, and those who were ready went in with him to the marriage feast, and the door was locked. 11Later, when the other five bridesmaids returned, they stood outside, calling, 'Sir, open the door for us!' 12But he called back, 'I don't know you!'

13"So stay awake and be prepared, because you do not know the day or hour of my return.

## Story of the Three Servants

14"Again, the Kingdom of Heaven can be illustrated by the story of a man going on a trip. He called together his servants and gave them money to invest for him while he was gone. 15He gave five bags of gold* to one, two bags of gold to another, and one bag of gold to the last—dividing it in proportion to their abilities—and then left on his trip. 16The servant who received the five bags of gold began immediately to invest the money and soon doubled it. 17The servant with two bags of gold also went right to work and doubled the money. 18But the servant who received the one bag of gold dug a hole in the ground and hid the master's money for safekeeping.

19"After a long time their master returned from his trip and called them to give an account of how they had used his money. 20The servant to whom he had entrusted the five bags of gold said, 'Sir, you gave me five bags of gold to invest, and I have doubled the amount.' 21The master was full of praise. 'Well done, my good and faithful servant. You have been faithful in handling this small amount, so now I will give you many more responsibilities. Let's celebrate together!'

22"Next came the servant who had received the two bags of gold, with the report, 'Sir, you

24:34 Or *this age*, or *this nation*.   24:36 Some manuscripts omit the phrase *or the Son himself*.   25:1 Or *virgins*; also in 25:7, 11.
25:15 Greek *talents*; also throughout the story. A talent is equal to 75 pounds or 34 kilograms.

gave me two bags of gold to invest, and I have doubled the amount.' 23The master said, 'Well done, my good and faithful servant. You have been faithful in handling this small amount, so now I will give you many more responsibilities. Let's celebrate together!'

24"Then the servant with the one bag of gold came and said, 'Sir, I know you are a hard man, harvesting crops you didn't plant and gathering crops you didn't cultivate. 25I was afraid I would lose your money, so I hid it in the earth and here it is.'

26"But the master replied, 'You wicked and lazy servant! You think I'm a hard man, do you, harvesting crops I didn't plant and gathering crops I didn't cultivate? 27Well, you should at least have put my money into the bank so I could have some interest. 28Take the money from this servant and give it to the one with the ten bags of gold. 29To those who use well what they are given, even more will be given, and they will have an abundance. But from those who are unfaithful,* even what little they have will be taken away. 30Now throw this useless servant into outer darkness, where there will be weeping and gnashing of teeth.'

### The Final Judgment

31"But when the Son of Man comes in his glory, and all the angels with him, then he will sit upon his glorious throne. 32All the nations will be gathered in his presence, and he will separate them as a shepherd separates the sheep from the goats. 33He will place the sheep at his right hand and the goats at his left. 34Then the King will say to those on the right, 'Come, you who are blessed by my Father, inherit the Kingdom prepared for you from the foundation of the world. 35For I was hungry, and you fed me. I was thirsty, and you gave me a drink. I was a stranger, and you invited me into your home. 36I was naked, and you gave me clothing. I was sick, and you cared for me. I was in prison, and you visited me.'

37"Then these righteous ones will reply, 'Lord, when did we ever see you hungry and feed you? Or thirsty and give you something to drink? 38Or a stranger and show you hospitality? Or naked and give you clothing? 39When did we ever see you sick or in prison, and visit you?' 40And the King will tell them, 'I assure you, when you did it to one of the least of these my brothers and sisters,* you were doing it to me!'

41"Then the King will turn to those on the left

and say, 'Away with you, you cursed ones, into the eternal fire prepared for the Devil and his demons! 42For I was hungry, and you didn't feed me. I was thirsty, and you didn't give me anything to drink. 43I was a stranger, and you didn't invite me into your home. I was naked, and you gave me no clothing. I was sick and in prison, and you didn't visit me.'

44"Then they will reply, 'Lord, when did we ever see you hungry or thirsty or a stranger or naked or sick or in prison, and not help you?' 45And he will answer, 'I assure you, when you refused to help the least of these my brothers and sisters, you were refusing to help me.' 46And they will go away into eternal punishment, but the righteous will go into eternal life."

## CHAPTER 26
### The Plot to Kill Jesus

When Jesus had finished saying these things, he said to his disciples, 2"As you know, the Passover celebration begins in two days, and I, the Son of Man, will be betrayed and crucified."

3At that same time the leading priests and other leaders were meeting at the residence of Caiaphas, the high priest, 4to discuss how to capture Jesus secretly and put him to death. 5"But not during the Passover," they agreed, "or there will be a riot."

### Jesus Anointed at Bethany

6Meanwhile, Jesus was in Bethany at the home of Simon, a man who had leprosy. 7During supper, a woman came in with a beautiful jar* of expensive perfume and poured it over his head. 8The disciples were indignant when they saw this. "What a waste of money," they said. 9"She could have sold it for a fortune and given the money to the poor."

10But Jesus replied, "Why berate her for doing such a good thing to me? 11You will always have the poor among you, but I will not be here with you much longer. 12She has poured this perfume on me to prepare my body for burial. 13I assure you, wherever the Good News is preached throughout the world, this woman's deed will be talked about in her memory."

### Judas Agrees to Betray Jesus

14Then Judas Iscariot, one of the twelve disciples, went to the leading priests 15and asked, "How much will you pay me to betray Jesus to you?" And they gave him thirty pieces of silver.

25:29 Or *who have nothing.*   25:40 Greek *my brothers.*   26:7 Greek *an alabaster jar.*

16From that time on, Judas began looking for the right time and place to betray Jesus.

## The Last Supper

17On the first day of the Festival of Unleavened Bread, the disciples came to Jesus and asked, "Where do you want us to prepare the Passover supper?"

18"As you go into the city," he told them, "you will see a certain man. Tell him, 'The Teacher says, My time has come, and I will eat the Passover meal with my disciples at your house.'" 19So the disciples did as Jesus told them and prepared the Passover supper there.

20When it was evening, Jesus sat down at the table with the twelve disciples. 21While they were eating, he said, "The truth is, one of you will betray me."

22Greatly distressed, one by one they began to ask him, "I'm not the one, am I, Lord?"

23He replied, "One of you who is eating with me now* will betray me. 24For I, the Son of Man, must die, as the Scriptures declared long ago. But how terrible it will be for my betrayer. Far better for him if he had never been born!"

25Judas, the one who would betray him, also asked, "Teacher, I'm not the one, am I?"

And Jesus told him, "You have said it yourself."

26As they were eating, Jesus took a loaf of bread and asked God's blessing on it. Then he broke it in pieces and gave it to the disciples, saying, "Take it and eat it, for this is my body." 27And he took a cup of wine and gave thanks to God for it. He gave it to them and said, "Each of you drink from it, 28for this is my blood, which seals the covenant* between God and his people. It is poured out to forgive the sins of many. 29Mark my words—I will not drink wine again until the day I drink it new with you in my Father's Kingdom." 30Then they sang a hymn and went out to the Mount of Olives.

## Jesus Predicts Peter's Denial

31"Tonight all of you will desert me," Jesus told them. "For the Scriptures say,

'God* will strike the Shepherd,
    and the sheep of the flock will be
        scattered.'*

32But after I have been raised from the dead, I will go ahead of you to Galilee and meet you there."

33Peter declared, "Even if everyone else deserts you, I never will."

34"Peter," Jesus replied, "the truth is, this very night, before the rooster crows, you will deny me three times."

35"No!" Peter insisted. "Not even if I have to die with you! I will never deny you!" And all the other disciples vowed the same.

## Jesus Prays in Gethsemane

36Then Jesus brought them to an olive grove called Gethsemane, and he said, "Sit here while I go on ahead to pray." 37He took Peter and Zebedee's two sons, James and John, and he began to be filled with anguish and deep distress. 38He told them, "My soul is crushed with grief to the point of death. Stay here and watch with me."

39He went on a little farther and fell face down on the ground, praying, "My Father! If it is possible, let this cup of suffering be taken away from me. Yet I want your will, not mine." 40Then he returned to the disciples and found them asleep. He said to Peter, "Couldn't you stay awake and watch with me even one hour? 41Keep alert and pray. Otherwise temptation will overpower you. For though the spirit is willing enough, the body is weak!"

42Again he left them and prayed, "My Father! If this cup cannot be taken away until I drink it, your will be done." 43He returned to them again and found them sleeping, for they just couldn't keep their eyes open.

44So he went back to pray a third time, saying the same things again. 45Then he came to the disciples and said, "Still sleeping? Still resting?* Look, the time has come. I, the Son of Man, am betrayed into the hands of sinners. 46Up, let's be going. See, my betrayer is here!"

## Jesus Is Arrested

47And even as he said this, Judas, one of the twelve disciples, arrived with a mob that was armed with swords and clubs. They had been sent out by the leading priests and other leaders of the people. 48Judas had given them a prearranged signal: "You will know which one to arrest when I go over and give him the kiss of greeting." 49So Judas came straight to Jesus. "Greetings, Teacher!" he exclaimed and gave him the kiss.

50Jesus said, "My friend, go ahead and do what you have come for." Then the others

26:23 Or *The one who has dipped his hand in the bowl with me.*  26:28 Some manuscripts read *the new covenant.*  26:31a Greek *I.*
26:31b Zech 13:7.  26:45 Or *Sleep on, take your rest.*

grabbed Jesus and arrested him. ⁵¹One of the men with Jesus pulled out a sword and slashed off an ear of the high priest's servant.

⁵²"Put away your sword," Jesus told him. "Those who use the sword will be killed by the sword. ⁵³Don't you realize that I could ask my Father for thousands* of angels to protect us, and he would send them instantly? ⁵⁴But if I did, how would the Scriptures be fulfilled that describe what must happen now?"

⁵⁵Then Jesus said to the crowd, "Am I some dangerous criminal, that you have come armed with swords and clubs to arrest me? Why didn't you arrest me in the Temple? I was there teaching every day. ⁵⁶But this is all happening to fulfill the words of the prophets as recorded in the Scriptures." At that point, all the disciples deserted him and fled.

## Jesus before the Council

⁵⁷Then the people who had arrested Jesus led him to the home of Caiaphas, the high priest, where the teachers of religious law and other leaders had gathered. ⁵⁸Meanwhile, Peter was following far behind and eventually came to the courtyard of the high priest's house. He went in, sat with the guards, and waited to see what was going to happen to Jesus.

⁵⁹Inside, the leading priests and the entire high council* were trying to find witnesses who would lie about Jesus, so they could put him to death. ⁶⁰But even though they found many who agreed to give false witness, there was no testimony they could use. Finally, two men were found ⁶¹who declared, "This man said, 'I am able to destroy the Temple of God and rebuild it in three days.'"

⁶²Then the high priest stood up and said to Jesus, "Well, aren't you going to answer these charges? What do you have to say for yourself?" ⁶³But Jesus remained silent. Then the high priest said to him, "I demand in the name of the living God that you tell us whether you are the Messiah, the Son of God."

⁶⁴Jesus replied, "Yes, it is as you say. And in the future you will see me, the Son of Man, sitting at God's right hand in the place of power and coming back on the clouds of heaven."*

⁶⁵Then the high priest tore his clothing to show his horror, shouting, "Blasphemy! Why do we need other witnesses? You have all heard his blasphemy. ⁶⁶What is your verdict?"

"Guilty!" they shouted. "He must die!"

⁶⁷Then they spit in Jesus' face and hit him with their fists. And some slapped him, ⁶⁸saying, "Prophesy to us, you Messiah! Who hit you that time?"

## Peter Denies Jesus

⁶⁹Meanwhile, as Peter was sitting outside in the courtyard, a servant girl came over and said to him, "You were one of those with Jesus the Galilean."

⁷⁰But Peter denied it in front of everyone. "I don't know what you are talking about," he said.

⁷¹Later, out by the gate, another servant girl noticed him and said to those standing around, "This man was with Jesus of Nazareth."

⁷²Again Peter denied it, this time with an oath. "I don't even know the man," he said.

⁷³A little later some other bystanders came over to him and said, "You must be one of them; we can tell by your Galilean accent."

⁷⁴Peter said, "I swear by God, I don't know the man." And immediately the rooster crowed. ⁷⁵Suddenly, Jesus' words flashed through Peter's mind: "Before the rooster crows, you will deny me three times." And he went away, crying bitterly.

CHAPTER **27**

## Judas Hangs Himself

Very early in the morning, the leading priests and other leaders met again to discuss how to persuade the Roman government to sentence Jesus to death. ²Then they bound him and took him to Pilate, the Roman governor.

³When Judas, who had betrayed him, realized that Jesus had been condemned to die, he was filled with remorse. So he took the thirty pieces of silver back to the leading priests and other leaders. ⁴"I have sinned," he declared, "for I have betrayed an innocent man."

"What do we care?" they retorted. "That's your problem." ⁵Then Judas threw the money onto the floor of the Temple and went out and hanged himself. ⁶The leading priests picked up the money. "We can't put it in the Temple treasury," they said, "since it's against the law to accept money paid for murder." ⁷After some discussion they finally decided to buy the potter's field, and they made it into a cemetery for foreigners. ⁸That is why the field is still called the Field of Blood. ⁹This fulfilled the prophecy of Jeremiah that says,

26:53 Greek *12 legions.* 26:59 Greek *the Sanhedrin.* 26:64 See Ps 110:1; Dan 7:13.

"They took* the thirty pieces of silver—
the price at which he was valued by the
people of Israel—
¹⁰ and purchased the potter's field,
as the Lord directed.*"

## Jesus' Trial before Pilate

¹¹Now Jesus was standing before Pilate, the Roman governor. "Are you the King of the Jews?" the governor asked him.

Jesus replied, "Yes, it is as you say."

¹²But when the leading priests and other leaders made their accusations against him, Jesus remained silent. ¹³"Don't you hear their many charges against you?" Pilate demanded. ¹⁴But Jesus said nothing, much to the governor's great surprise.

¹⁵Now it was the governor's custom to release one prisoner to the crowd each year during the Passover celebration—anyone they wanted. ¹⁶This year there was a notorious criminal in prison, a man named Barabbas.* ¹⁷As the crowds gathered before Pilate's house that morning, he asked them, "Which one do you want me to release to you—Barabbas, or Jesus who is called the Messiah?" ¹⁸(He knew very well that the Jewish leaders had arrested Jesus out of envy.)

¹⁹Just then, as Pilate was sitting on the judgment seat, his wife sent him this message: "Leave that innocent man alone, because I had a terrible nightmare about him last night."

²⁰Meanwhile, the leading priests and other leaders persuaded the crowds to ask for Barabbas to be released and for Jesus to be put to death. ²¹So when the governor asked again, "Which of these two do you want me to release to you?" the crowd shouted back their reply: "Barabbas!"

²²"But if I release Barabbas," Pilate asked them, "what should I do with Jesus who is called the Messiah?"

And they all shouted, "Crucify him!"

²³"Why?" Pilate demanded. "What crime has he committed?"

But the crowd only roared the louder, "Crucify him!"

²⁴Pilate saw that he wasn't getting anywhere and that a riot was developing. So he sent for a bowl of water and washed his hands before the crowd, saying, "I am innocent of the blood of this man. The responsibility is yours!"

²⁵And all the people yelled back, "We will take responsibility for his death—we and our children!"*

²⁶So Pilate released Barabbas to them. He ordered Jesus flogged with a lead-tipped whip, then turned him over to the Roman soldiers to crucify him.

## The Soldiers Mock Jesus

²⁷Some of the governor's soldiers took Jesus into their headquarters and called out the entire battalion. ²⁸They stripped him and put a scarlet robe on him. ²⁹They made a crown of long, sharp thorns and put it on his head, and they placed a stick in his right hand as a scepter. Then they knelt before him in mockery, yelling, "Hail! King of the Jews!" ³⁰And they spit on him and grabbed the stick and beat him on the head with it. ³¹When they were finally tired of mocking him, they took off the robe and put his own clothes on him again. Then they led him away to be crucified.

## The Crucifixion

³²As they were on the way, they came across a man named Simon, who was from Cyrene,* and they forced him to carry Jesus' cross. ³³Then they went out to a place called Golgotha (which means Skull Hill). ³⁴The soldiers gave him wine mixed with bitter gall, but when he had tasted it, he refused to drink it.

³⁵After they had nailed him to the cross, the soldiers gambled for his clothes by throwing dice.* ³⁶Then they sat around and kept guard as he hung there. ³⁷A signboard was fastened to the cross above Jesus' head, announcing the charge against him. It read: "This is Jesus, the King of the Jews."

³⁸Two criminals were crucified with him, their crosses on either side of his. ³⁹And the people passing by shouted abuse, shaking their heads in mockery. ⁴⁰"So! You can destroy the Temple and build it again in three days, can you? Well then, if you are the Son of God, save yourself and come down from the cross!"

⁴¹The leading priests, the teachers of religious law, and the other leaders also mocked Jesus. ⁴²"He saved others," they scoffed, "but he can't save himself! So he is the king of Israel, is he? Let him come down from the cross, and we will believe in him! ⁴³He trusted God—let God show his approval by delivering him! For he

27:9 Or *I took.* 27:9-10 Greek *as the Lord directed me.* Zech 11:12-13; Jer 32:6-9. 27:16 Some manuscripts read *Jesus Barabbas;* also in 27:17. 27:25 Greek *"His blood be on us and on our children."* 27:32 *Cyrene* was a city in northern Africa. 27:35 Greek *by casting lots.* A few late manuscripts add *This fulfilled the word of the prophet: "They divided my clothes among themselves and cast lots for my robe."* See Ps 22:18.

said, 'I am the Son of God.' " 44And the criminals who were crucified with him also shouted the same insults at him.

### The Death of Jesus

45At noon, darkness fell across the whole land until three o'clock. 46At about three o'clock, Jesus called out with a loud voice, "*Eli, Eli, lema sabachthani?*" which means, "My God, my God, why have you forsaken me?"*

47Some of the bystanders misunderstood and thought he was calling for the prophet Elijah. 48One of them ran and filled a sponge with sour wine, holding it up to him on a stick so he could drink. 49But the rest said, "Leave him alone. Let's see whether Elijah will come and save him."*

50Then Jesus shouted out again, and he gave up his spirit. 51At that moment the curtain in the Temple was torn in two, from top to bottom. The earth shook, rocks split apart, 52and tombs opened. The bodies of many godly men and women who had died were raised from the dead 53after Jesus' resurrection. They left the cemetery, went into the holy city of Jerusalem, and appeared to many people.*

54The Roman officer and the other soldiers at the crucifixion were terrified by the earthquake and all that had happened. They said, "Truly, this was the Son of God!"

55And many women who had come from Galilee with Jesus to care for him were watching from a distance. 56Among them were Mary Magdalene, Mary (the mother of James and Joseph), and Zebedee's wife, the mother of James and John.

### The Burial of Jesus

57As evening approached, Joseph, a rich man from Arimathea who was one of Jesus' followers, 58went to Pilate and asked for Jesus' body. And Pilate issued an order to release it to him. 59Joseph took the body and wrapped it in a long linen cloth. 60He placed it in his own new tomb, which had been carved out of the rock. Then he rolled a great stone across the entrance as he left. 61Both Mary Magdalene and the other Mary were sitting nearby watching.

### The Guard at the Tomb

62The next day—on the first day of the Passover ceremonies*—the leading priests and Pharisees

went to see Pilate. 63They told him, "Sir, we remember what that deceiver once said while he was still alive: 'After three days I will be raised from the dead.' 64So we request that you seal the tomb until the third day. This will prevent his disciples from coming and stealing his body and then telling everyone he came back to life! If that happens, we'll be worse off than we were at first."

65Pilate replied, "Take guards and secure it the best you can." 66So they sealed the tomb and posted guards to protect it.

## CHAPTER 28

### The Resurrection

Early on Sunday morning,* as the new day was dawning, Mary Magdalene and the other Mary went out to see the tomb. 2Suddenly there was a great earthquake, because an angel of the Lord came down from heaven and rolled aside the stone and sat on it. 3His face shone like lightning, and his clothing was as white as snow. 4The guards shook with fear when they saw him, and they fell into a dead faint.

5Then the angel spoke to the women. "Don't be afraid!" he said. "I know you are looking for Jesus, who was crucified. 6He isn't here! He has been raised from the dead, just as he said would happen. Come, see where his body was lying. 7And now, go quickly and tell his disciples he has been raised from the dead, and he is going ahead of you to Galilee. You will see him there. Remember, I have told you."

8The women ran quickly from the tomb. They were very frightened but also filled with great joy, and they rushed to find the disciples to give them the angel's message. 9And as they went, Jesus met them. "Greetings!" he said. And they ran to him, held his feet, and worshiped him. 10Then Jesus said to them, "Don't be afraid! Go tell my brothers to leave for Galilee, and they will see me there."

### The Report of the Guard

11As the women were on their way into the city, some of the men who had been guarding the tomb went to the leading priests and told them what had happened. 12A meeting of all the religious leaders was called, and they decided to bribe the soldiers. 13They told the soldiers, "You must say, 'Jesus' disciples came during the night

27:46 Ps 22:1.   27:49 Some manuscripts add *And another took a spear and pierced his side, and out came water and blood.*   27:51-53 Or *The earth shook, rocks split apart, tombs opened, and the bodies of many godly men and women who had died were raised from the dead. After Jesus' resurrection, they left the cemetery, went into the holy city of Jerusalem, and appeared to many people.*   27:62 Or *On the next day, which is after the Preparation.*   28:1 Greek *After the Sabbath, on the first day of the week.*

while we were sleeping, and they stole his body.' [14]If the governor hears about it, we'll stand up for you and everything will be all right." [15]So the guards accepted the bribe and said what they were told to say. Their story spread widely among the Jews, and they still tell it today.

### The Great Commission

[16]Then the eleven disciples left for Galilee, going to the mountain where Jesus had told them to go. [17]When they saw him, they worshiped him—but some of them still doubted!

[18]Jesus came and told his disciples, "I have been given complete authority in heaven and on earth. [19]Therefore, go and make disciples of all the nations, baptizing them in the name of the Father and the Son and the Holy Spirit. [20]Teach these new disciples to obey all the commands I have given you. And be sure of this: I am with you always, even to the end of the age."

# Mark

## John the Baptist Prepares the Way

Here begins the Good News about Jesus the Messiah, the Son of God.*

²In the book of the prophet Isaiah, God said,

"Look, I am sending my messenger before you,
  and he will prepare your way.*
³  He is a voice shouting in the wilderness:
  'Prepare a pathway for the Lord's coming!
  Make a straight road for him!'* "

⁴This messenger was John the Baptist. He lived in the wilderness and was preaching that people should be baptized to show that they had turned from their sins and turned to God to be forgiven.* ⁵People from Jerusalem and from all over Judea traveled out into the wilderness to see and hear John. And when they confessed their sins, he baptized them in the Jordan River. ⁶His clothes were woven from camel hair, and he wore a leather belt; his food was locusts and wild honey. ⁷He announced: "Someone is coming soon who is far greater than I am—so much greater that I am not even worthy to be his slave.* ⁸I baptize you with* water, but he will baptize you with the Holy Spirit!"

## The Baptism of Jesus

⁹One day Jesus came from Nazareth in Galilee, and he was baptized by John in the Jordan River. ¹⁰And when Jesus came up out of the water, he saw the heavens split open and the Holy Spirit descending like a dove on him. ¹¹And a voice came from heaven saying, "You are my beloved Son, and I am fully pleased with you."

## The Temptation of Jesus

¹²Immediately the Holy Spirit compelled Jesus to go into the wilderness. ¹³He was there for forty days, being tempted by Satan. He was out among the wild animals, and angels took care of him.

## The First Disciples

¹⁴Later on, after John was arrested by Herod Antipas, Jesus went to Galilee to preach God's Good News. ¹⁵"At last the time has come!" he announced. "The Kingdom of God is near! Turn from your sins and believe this Good News!"

¹⁶One day as Jesus was walking along the shores of the Sea of Galilee, he saw Simon* and his brother, Andrew, fishing with a net, for they were commercial fishermen. ¹⁷Jesus called out to them, "Come, be my disciples, and I will show you how to fish for people!" ¹⁸And they left their nets at once and went with him.

¹⁹A little farther up the shore Jesus saw Zebedee's sons, James and John, in a boat mending their nets. ²⁰He called them, too, and immediately they left their father, Zebedee, in the boat with the hired men and went with him.

## Jesus Casts Out an Evil Spirit

²¹Jesus and his companions went to the town of Capernaum, and every Sabbath day he went into the synagogue and taught the people. ²²They were amazed at his teaching, for he taught as one who had real authority—quite unlike the teachers of religious law.

²³A man possessed by an evil spirit was in the synagogue, ²⁴and he began shouting, "Why are you bothering us, Jesus of Nazareth? Have you come to destroy us? I know who you are—the Holy One sent from God!"

²⁵Jesus cut him short. "Be silent! Come out of the man." ²⁶At that, the evil spirit screamed

1:1 Some manuscripts do not include *the Son of God.*  1:2 Mal 3:1.  1:3 Isa 40:3.  1:4 Greek *preaching a baptism of repentance for the forgiveness of sins.*  1:7 Greek *to stoop down and untie his sandals.*  1:8 Or *in.*  1:16 *Simon* is called *Peter* in 3:16 and thereafter.

and threw the man into a convulsion, but then he left him.

²⁷Amazement gripped the audience, and they began to discuss what had happened. "What sort of new teaching is this?" they asked excitedly. "It has such authority! Even evil spirits obey his orders!" ²⁸The news of what he had done spread quickly through that entire area of Galilee.

## Jesus Heals Many People

²⁹After Jesus and his disciples left the synagogue, they went over to Simon and Andrew's home, and James and John were with them. ³⁰Simon's mother-in-law was sick in bed with a high fever. They told Jesus about her right away. ³¹He went to her bedside, and as he took her by the hand and helped her to sit up, the fever suddenly left, and she got up and prepared a meal for them.

³²That evening at sunset, many sick and demon-possessed people were brought to Jesus. ³³And a huge crowd of people from all over Capernaum gathered outside the door to watch. ³⁴So Jesus healed great numbers of sick people who had many different kinds of diseases, and he ordered many demons to come out of their victims. But because they knew who he was, he refused to allow the demons to speak.

## Jesus Preaches in Galilee

³⁵The next morning Jesus awoke long before daybreak and went out alone into the wilderness to pray. ³⁶Later Simon and the others went out to find him. ³⁷They said, "Everyone is asking for you."

³⁸But he replied, "We must go on to other towns as well, and I will preach to them, too, because that is why I came." ³⁹So he traveled throughout the region of Galilee, preaching in the synagogues and expelling demons from many people.

## Jesus Heals a Man with Leprosy

⁴⁰A man with leprosy came and knelt in front of Jesus, begging to be healed. "If you want to, you can make me well again," he said.

⁴¹Moved with pity,* Jesus touched him. "I want to," he said. "Be healed!" ⁴²Instantly the leprosy disappeared—the man was healed. ⁴³Then Jesus sent him on his way and told him sternly, ⁴⁴"Go right over to the priest and let him examine you. Don't talk to anyone along the way. Take along the offering required in the law of Moses for those who have been healed of

1:41 Some manuscripts read *Moved with anger.*

leprosy, so everyone will have proof of your healing."

⁴⁵But as the man went on his way, he spread the news, telling everyone what had happened to him. As a result, such crowds soon surrounded Jesus that he couldn't enter a town anywhere publicly. He had to stay out in the secluded places, and people from everywhere came to him there.

## CHAPTER 2

## Jesus Heals a Paralyzed Man

Several days later Jesus returned to Capernaum, and the news of his arrival spread quickly through the town. ²Soon the house where he was staying was so packed with visitors that there wasn't room for one more person, not even outside the door. And he preached the word to them. ³Four men arrived carrying a paralyzed man on a mat. ⁴They couldn't get to Jesus through the crowd, so they dug through the clay roof above his head. Then they lowered the sick man on his mat, right down in front of Jesus. ⁵Seeing their faith, Jesus said to the paralyzed man, "My son, your sins are forgiven."

⁶But some of the teachers of religious law who were sitting there said to themselves, ⁷"What? This is blasphemy! Who but God can forgive sins!"

⁸Jesus knew what they were discussing among themselves, so he said to them, "Why do you think this is blasphemy? ⁹Is it easier to say to the paralyzed man, 'Your sins are forgiven' or 'Get up, pick up your mat, and walk'? ¹⁰I will prove that I, the Son of Man, have the authority on earth to forgive sins." Then Jesus turned to the paralyzed man and said, ¹¹"Stand up, take your mat, and go on home, because you are healed!"

¹²The man jumped up, took the mat, and pushed his way through the stunned onlookers. Then they all praised God. "We've never seen anything like this before!" they exclaimed.

## Jesus Calls Levi (Matthew)

¹³Then Jesus went out to the lakeshore again and taught the crowds that gathered around him. ¹⁴As he walked along, he saw Levi son of Alphaeus sitting at his tax-collection booth. "Come, be my disciple," Jesus said to him. So Levi got up and followed him.

¹⁵That night Levi invited Jesus and his disciples to be his dinner guests, along with his fel-

low tax collectors and many other notorious sinners. (There were many people of this kind among the crowds that followed Jesus.) 16But when some of the teachers of religious law who were Pharisees* saw him eating with people like that, they said to his disciples, "Why does he eat with such scum*?"

17When Jesus heard this, he told them, "Healthy people don't need a doctor—sick people do. I have come to call sinners, not those who think they are already good enough."

### A Discussion about Fasting
18John's disciples and the Pharisees sometimes fasted. One day some people came to Jesus and asked, "Why do John's disciples and the Pharisees fast, but your disciples don't fast?"

19Jesus replied, "Do wedding guests fast while celebrating with the groom? Of course not. They can't fast while they are with the groom. 20But someday he will be taken away from them, and then they will fast. 21And who would patch an old garment with unshrunk cloth? For the new patch shrinks and pulls away from the old cloth, leaving an even bigger hole than before. 22And no one puts new wine into old wineskins. The wine would burst the wineskins, spilling the wine and ruining the skins. New wine needs new wineskins."

### A Discussion about the Sabbath
23One Sabbath day as Jesus was walking through some grainfields, his disciples began breaking off heads of wheat. 24But the Pharisees said to Jesus, "They shouldn't be doing that! It's against the law to work by harvesting grain on the Sabbath."

25But Jesus replied, "Haven't you ever read in the Scriptures what King David did when he and his companions were hungry? 26He went into the house of God (during the days when Abiathar was high priest), ate the special bread reserved for the priests alone, and then gave some to his companions. That was breaking the law, too." 27Then he said to them, "The Sabbath was made to benefit people, and not people to benefit the Sabbath. 28And I, the Son of Man, am master even of the Sabbath!"

## CHAPTER 3
### Jesus Heals on the Sabbath
Jesus went into the synagogue again and noticed a man with a deformed hand. 2Since it was the Sabbath, Jesus' enemies watched him closely. Would he heal the man's hand on the Sabbath? If he did, they planned to condemn him. 3Jesus said to the man, "Come and stand in front of everyone." 4Then he turned to his critics and asked, "Is it legal to do good deeds on the Sabbath, or is it a day for doing harm? Is this a day to save life or to destroy it?" But they wouldn't answer him. 5He looked around at them angrily, because he was deeply disturbed by their hard hearts. Then he said to the man, "Reach out your hand." The man reached out his hand, and it became normal again! 6At once the Pharisees went away and met with the supporters of Herod to discuss plans for killing Jesus.

### Crowds Follow Jesus
7Jesus and his disciples went out to the lake, followed by a huge crowd from all over Galilee, Judea, 8Jerusalem, Idumea, from east of the Jordan River, and even from as far away as Tyre and Sidon. The news about his miracles had spread far and wide, and vast numbers of people came to see him for themselves.

9Jesus instructed his disciples to bring around a boat and to have it ready in case he was crowded off the beach. 10There had been many healings that day. As a result, many sick people were crowding around him, trying to touch him. 11And whenever those possessed by evil spirits caught sight of him, they would fall down in front of him shrieking, "You are the Son of God!" 12But Jesus strictly warned them not to say who he was.

### Jesus Chooses the Twelve Apostles
13Afterward Jesus went up on a mountain and called the ones he wanted to go with him. And they came to him. 14Then he selected twelve of them to be his regular companions, calling them apostles.* He sent them out to preach, 15and he gave them authority to cast out demons. 16These are the names of the twelve he chose:

Simon (he renamed him Peter),
17 James and John (the sons of Zebedee, but Jesus nicknamed them "Sons of Thunder"*),
18 Andrew,
Philip,
Bartholomew,
Matthew,

2:16a Greek *the scribes of the Pharisees.*  2:16b Greek *with tax collectors and sinners.*  3:14 Some manuscripts do not include *calling them apostles.*  3:17 Greek *whom he named Boanerges, which means Sons of Thunder.*

Thomas,
James (son of Alphaeus),
Thaddaeus,
Simon (the Zealot*),
19 Judas Iscariot (who later betrayed him).

## Jesus and the Prince of Demons

20When Jesus returned to the house where he was staying, the crowds began to gather again, and soon he and his disciples couldn't even find time to eat. 21When his family heard what was happening, they tried to take him home with them. "He's out of his mind," they said.

22But the teachers of religious law who had arrived from Jerusalem said, "He's possessed by Satan,* the prince of demons. That's where he gets the power to cast out demons."

23Jesus called them over and said to them by way of illustration, "How can Satan cast out Satan? 24A kingdom at war with itself will collapse. 25A home divided against itself is doomed. 26And if Satan is fighting against himself, how can he stand? He would never survive. 27Let me illustrate this. You can't enter a strong man's house and rob him without first tying him up. Only then can his house be robbed!*

28"I assure you that any sin can be forgiven, including blasphemy; 29but anyone who blasphemes against the Holy Spirit will never be forgiven. It is an eternal sin." 30He told them this because they were saying he had an evil spirit.

## The True Family of Jesus

31Jesus' mother and brothers arrived at the house where he was teaching. They stood outside and sent word for him to come out and talk with them. 32There was a crowd around Jesus, and someone said, "Your mother and your brothers and sisters* are outside, asking for you."

33Jesus replied, "Who is my mother? Who are my brothers?" 34Then he looked at those around him and said, "These are my mother and brothers. 35Anyone who does God's will is my brother and sister and mother."

## CHAPTER 4
### Story of the Farmer Scattering Seed

Once again Jesus began teaching by the lakeshore. There was such a large crowd along the shore that he got into a boat and sat down and spoke from there. 2He began to teach the people by telling many stories such as this one:

3"Listen! A farmer went out to plant some seed. 4As he scattered it across his field, some seed fell on a footpath, and the birds came and ate it. 5Other seed fell on shallow soil with underlying rock. The plant sprang up quickly, 6but it soon wilted beneath the hot sun and died because the roots had no nourishment in the shallow soil. 7Other seed fell among thorns that shot up and choked out the tender blades so that it produced no grain. 8Still other seed fell on fertile soil and produced a crop that was thirty, sixty, and even a hundred times as much as had been planted." Then he said, 9"Anyone who is willing to hear should listen and understand!"

10Later, when Jesus was alone with the twelve disciples and with the others who were gathered around, they asked him, "What do your stories mean?"

11He replied, "You are permitted to understand the secret about the Kingdom of God. But I am using these stories to conceal everything about it from outsiders, 12so that the Scriptures might be fulfilled:

'They see what I do,
but they don't perceive its meaning.
They hear my words,
but they don't understand.
So they will not turn from their sins
and be forgiven.'*

13"But if you can't understand this story, how will you understand all the others I am going to tell? 14The farmer I talked about is the one who brings God's message to others. 15The seed that fell on the hard path represents those who hear the message, but then Satan comes at once and takes it away from them. 16The rocky soil represents those who hear the message and receive it with joy. 17But like young plants in such soil, their roots don't go very deep. At first they get along fine, but they wilt as soon as they have problems or are persecuted because they believe the word. 18The thorny ground represents those who hear and accept the Good News, 19but all too quickly the message is crowded out by the cares of this life, the lure of wealth, and the desire for nice things, so no crop is produced. 20But the good soil represents those who hear and accept God's message and produce a huge harvest—thirty, sixty, or even a hundred times as much as had been planted."

## Illustration of the Lamp

21Then Jesus asked them, "Would anyone light a lamp and then put it under a basket or under a bed to shut out the light? Of course not! A lamp is placed on a stand, where its light will shine.

22"Everything that is now hidden or secret will eventually be brought to light. 23Anyone who is willing to hear should listen and understand! 24And be sure to pay attention to what you hear. The more you do this, the more you will understand—and even more, besides. 25To those who are open to my teaching, more understanding will be given. But to those who are not listening, even what they have will be taken away from them."

## Illustration of the Growing Seed

26Jesus also said, "Here is another illustration of what the Kingdom of God is like: A farmer planted seeds in a field, 27and then he went on with his other activities. As the days went by, the seeds sprouted and grew without the farmer's help, 28because the earth produces crops on its own. First a leaf blade pushes through, then the heads of wheat are formed, and finally the grain ripens. 29And as soon as the grain is ready, the farmer comes and harvests it with a sickle."

## Illustration of the Mustard Seed

30Jesus asked, "How can I describe the Kingdom of God? What story should I use to illustrate it? 31It is like a tiny mustard seed. Though this is one of the smallest of seeds, 32it grows to become one of the largest of plants, with long branches where birds can come and find shelter."

33He used many such stories and illustrations to teach the people as much as they were able to understand. 34In fact, in his public teaching he taught only with parables, but afterward when he was alone with his disciples, he explained the meaning to them.

## Jesus Calms the Storm

35As evening came, Jesus said to his disciples, "Let's cross to the other side of the lake." 36He was already in the boat, so they started out, leaving the crowds behind (although other boats followed). 37But soon a fierce storm arose. High waves began to break into the boat until it was nearly full of water.

38Jesus was sleeping at the back of the boat with his head on a cushion. Frantically they woke him up, shouting, "Teacher, don't you even care that we are going to drown?"

39When he woke up, he rebuked the wind and said to the water, "Quiet down!" Suddenly the wind stopped, and there was a great calm. 40And he asked them, "Why are you so afraid? Do you still not have faith in me?"

---

# Jesus Is with Us in Life's Storms Read MARK 4:35-41

This story illustrates how God is with us and in control of even the most desperate of circumstances. Here we find the disciples, several of whom were seasoned fishermen and sailors, frantically worried that they would perish in this storm. Although Jesus was with them in the middle of it, they thought he was oblivious to the severity of their situation. Yet Jesus wanted them to discover three important lessons.

**1. Jesus Is Aware of Your Situation.**
Although Jesus, being human, needed physical sleep for his weary body, he was still fully aware of the disciples' predicament. The moment one of them cried to him, he responded immediately and powerfully. Though the shrieking of the storm did not wake him, the cry of one of his disciples did. Matthew 10:29 says, "Not even a sparrow . . . can fall to the ground without your Father knowing it."

**2. Jesus Will Answer Your Call for Help.**
The Lord will do the same for you in the midst of your trials. Sometimes he just lets us reach the point of desperation so we will recognize that he is our only hope. He wants us to remember that he is "on board" with us, so to speak.

**3. You Can Make It Through.** Every one of us is going to face hardship. But only the child of God has the promise that God's presence is with him or her in the midst of the storm. As surely as Jesus said to the disciples, "Let's cross to the other side of the lake" (verse 35), God has promised to finish the work he has begun in your life. He will not leave you stranded in the middle of your problem. Although he didn't promise smooth sailing, he did promise safe passage. Paul reminds us that "I am sure that God, who began the good work within you, will continue his work until it is finally finished on that day when Christ Jesus comes back again" (Philippians 1:6).

41And they were filled with awe and said among themselves, "Who is this man, that even the wind and waves obey him?"

## CHAPTER 5

### Jesus Heals a Demon-Possessed Man

So they arrived at the other side of the lake, in the land of the Gerasenes.* 2Just as Jesus was climbing from the boat, a man possessed by an evil spirit ran out from a cemetery to meet him. 3This man lived among the tombs and could not be restrained, even with a chain. 4Whenever he was put into chains and shackles—as he often was—he snapped the chains from his wrists and smashed the shackles. No one was strong enough to control him. 5All day long and throughout the night, he would wander among the tombs and in the hills, screaming and hitting himself with stones.

6When Jesus was still some distance away, the man saw him. He ran to meet Jesus and fell down before him. 7He gave a terrible scream, shrieking, "Why are you bothering me, Jesus, Son of the Most High God? For God's sake, don't torture me!" 8For Jesus had already said to the spirit, "Come out of the man, you evil spirit."

9Then Jesus asked, "What is your name?"

And the spirit replied, "Legion, because there are many of us here inside this man." 10Then the spirits begged him again and again not to send them to some distant place. 11There happened to be a large herd of pigs feeding on the hillside nearby. 12"Send us into those pigs," the evil spirits begged. 13Jesus gave them permission. So the evil spirits came out of the man and entered the pigs, and the entire herd of two thousand pigs plunged down the steep hillside into the lake, where they drowned.

14The herdsmen fled to the nearby city and the surrounding countryside, spreading the news as they ran. Everyone rushed out to see for themselves. 15A crowd soon gathered around Jesus, but they were frightened when they saw the man who had been demon possessed, for he was sitting there fully clothed and perfectly sane. 16Those who had seen what happened to the man and to the pigs told everyone about it, 17and the crowd began pleading with Jesus to go away and leave them alone.

18When Jesus got back into the boat, the man who had been demon possessed begged to go, too. 19But Jesus said, "No, go home to your friends, and tell them what wonderful things the Lord has done for you and how merciful he has been." 20So the man started off to visit the Ten Towns* of that region and began to tell everyone about the great things Jesus had done for him; and everyone was amazed at what he told them.

### Jesus Heals in Response to Faith

21When Jesus went back across to the other side of the lake, a large crowd gathered around him on the shore. 22A leader of the local synagogue, whose name was Jairus, came and fell down before him, 23pleading with him to heal his little daughter. "She is about to die," he said in desperation. "Please come and place your hands on her; heal her so she can live."

24Jesus went with him, and the crowd thronged behind. 25And there was a woman in the crowd who had had a hemorrhage for twelve years. 26She had suffered a great deal from many doctors through the years and had spent everything she had to pay them, but she had gotten no better. In fact, she was worse. 27She had heard about Jesus, so she came up behind him through the crowd and touched the fringe of his robe. 28For she thought to herself, "If I can just touch his clothing, I will be healed." 29Immediately the bleeding stopped, and she could feel that she had been healed!

30Jesus realized at once that healing power had gone out from him, so he turned around in the crowd and asked, "Who touched my clothes?"

31His disciples said to him, "All this crowd is pressing around you. How can you ask, 'Who touched me?' "

32But he kept on looking around to see who had done it. 33Then the frightened woman, trembling at the realization of what had happened to her, came and fell at his feet and told him what she had done. 34And he said to her, "Daughter, your faith has made you well. Go in peace. You have been healed."

35While he was still speaking to her, messengers arrived from Jairus's home with the message, "Your daughter is dead. There's no use troubling the Teacher now."

36But Jesus ignored their comments and said to Jairus, "Don't be afraid. Just trust me." 37Then Jesus stopped the crowd and wouldn't let anyone go with him except Peter and James and John. 38When they came to the home of the synagogue leader, Jesus saw the commotion and the weeping and wailing. 39He went inside and spoke to the people. "Why all this weeping and commotion?" he asked. "The child isn't dead; she is only asleep."

40The crowd laughed at him, but he told them all to go outside. Then he took the girl's father and mother and his three disciples into the room where the girl was lying. 41Holding her hand, he said to her, "Get up, little girl!"* 42And the girl, who was twelve years old, immediately stood up and walked around! Her parents were absolutely overwhelmed. 43Jesus commanded them not to tell anyone what had happened, and he told them to give her something to eat.

## CHAPTER 6

### Jesus Rejected at Nazareth

Jesus left that part of the country and returned with his disciples to Nazareth, his hometown. 2The next Sabbath he began teaching in the synagogue, and many who heard him were astonished. They asked, "Where did he get all his wisdom and the power to perform such miracles? 3He's just the carpenter, the son of Mary and brother of James, Joseph,* Judas, and Simon. And his sisters live right here among us." They were deeply offended and refused to believe in him.

4Then Jesus told them, "A prophet is honored everywhere except in his own hometown and among his relatives and his own family." 5And because of their unbelief, he couldn't do any mighty miracles among them except to place his hands on a few sick people and heal them. 6And he was amazed at their unbelief.

### Jesus Sends Out the Twelve Apostles

Then Jesus went out from village to village, teaching. 7And he called his twelve disciples together and sent them out two by two, with authority to cast out evil spirits. 8He told them to take nothing with them except a walking stick—no food, no traveler's bag, no money. 9He told them to wear sandals but not to take even an extra coat. 10"When you enter each village, be a guest in only one home," he said. 11"And if a village won't welcome you or listen to you, shake off its dust from your feet as you leave. It is a sign that you have abandoned that village to its fate."

12So the disciples went out, telling all they met to turn from their sins. 13And they cast out many demons and healed many sick people, anointing them with olive oil.

### The Death of John the Baptist

14Herod Antipas, the king, soon heard about Jesus, because people everywhere were talking about him. Some were saying,* "This must be John the Baptist come back to life again. That is why he can do such miracles." 15Others thought Jesus was the ancient prophet Elijah. Still others thought he was a prophet like the other great prophets of the past. 16When Herod heard about Jesus, he said, "John, the man I beheaded, has come back from the dead." 17For Herod had sent soldiers to arrest and imprison John as a favor to Herodias. She had been his brother Philip's wife, but Herod had married her. 18John kept telling Herod, "It is illegal for you to marry your brother's wife." 19Herodias was enraged and wanted John killed in revenge, but without Herod's approval she was powerless. 20And Herod respected John, knowing that he was a good and holy man, so he kept him under his protection. Herod was disturbed whenever he talked with John, but even so, he liked to listen to him.

21Herodias's chance finally came. It was Herod's birthday, and he gave a party for his palace aides, army officers, and the leading citizens of Galilee. 22Then his daughter, also named Herodias,* came in and performed a dance that greatly pleased them all. "Ask me for anything you like," the king said to the girl, "and I will give it to you." 23Then he promised, "I will give you whatever you ask, up to half of my kingdom!"

24She went out and asked her mother, "What should I ask for?"

Her mother told her, "Ask for John the Baptist's head!"

25So the girl hurried back to the king and told him, "I want the head of John the Baptist, right now, on a tray!"

26Then the king was very sorry, but he was embarrassed to break his oath in front of his guests. 27So he sent an executioner to the prison to cut off John's head and bring it to him. The soldier beheaded John in the prison, 28brought his head on a tray, and gave it to the girl, who took it to her mother. 29When John's disciples heard what had happened, they came for his body and buried it in a tomb.

5:41 Greek text uses Aramaic "Talitha cumi" and then translates it as "Get up, little girl."   6:3 Greek Joses; see Matt 13:55.   6:14 Some manuscripts read He was saying.   6:22 Some manuscripts read the daughter of Herodias herself.

## Jesus Feeds Five Thousand

30The apostles returned to Jesus from their ministry tour and told him all they had done and what they had taught. 31Then Jesus said, "Let's get away from the crowds for a while and rest." There were so many people coming and going that Jesus and his apostles didn't even have time to eat. 32They left by boat for a quieter spot. 33But many people saw them leaving, and people from many towns ran ahead along the shore and met them as they landed. 34A vast crowd was there as he stepped from the boat, and he had compassion on them because they were like sheep without a shepherd. So he taught them many things.

35Late in the afternoon his disciples came to him and said, "This is a desolate place, and it is getting late. 36Send the crowds away so they can go to the nearby farms and villages and buy themselves some food."

37But Jesus said, "You feed them."

"With what?" they asked. "It would take a small fortune* to buy food for all this crowd!"

38"How much food do you have?" he asked. "Go and find out."

They came back and reported, "We have five loaves of bread and two fish." 39Then Jesus told the crowd to sit down in groups on the green grass. 40So they sat in groups of fifty or a hundred.

41Jesus took the five loaves and two fish, looked up toward heaven, and asked God's blessing on the food. Breaking the loaves into pieces, he kept giving the bread and fish to the disciples to give to the people. 42They all ate as much as they wanted, 43and they picked up twelve baskets of leftover bread and fish. 44Five thousand men had eaten from those five loaves!

## Jesus Walks on Water

45Immediately after this, Jesus made his disciples get back into the boat and head out across the lake to Bethsaida, while he sent the people home. 46Afterward he went up into the hills by himself to pray.

47During the night, the disciples were in their boat out in the middle of the lake, and Jesus was alone on land. 48He saw that they were in serious trouble, rowing hard and struggling against the wind and waves. About three o'clock in the morning* he came to them, walking on the water. He started to go past them, 49but when they saw him walking on the water, they screamed in terror, thinking he was a ghost. 50They were all terrified when they saw him. But Jesus spoke to them at once. "It's all right," he said. "I am here! Don't be afraid." 51Then he climbed into the boat, and the wind stopped. They were astonished at what they saw. 52They still didn't understand the significance of the miracle of the multiplied loaves, for their hearts were hard and they did not believe.

53When they arrived at Gennesaret on the other side of the lake, they anchored the boat 54and climbed out. The people standing there recognized him at once, 55and they ran throughout the whole area and began carrying sick people to him on mats. 56Wherever he went—in villages and cities and out on the farms—they laid the sick in the market plazas and streets. The sick begged him to let them at least touch the fringe of his robe, and all who touched it were healed.

## CHAPTER 7

### Jesus Teaches about Inner Purity

One day some Pharisees and teachers of religious law arrived from Jerusalem to confront Jesus. 2They noticed that some of Jesus' disciples failed to follow the usual Jewish ritual of hand washing before eating. 3(The Jews, especially the Pharisees, do not eat until they have poured water over their cupped hands,* as required by their ancient traditions. 4Similarly, they eat nothing bought from the market unless they have immersed their hands in water. This is but one of many traditions they have clung to— such as their ceremony of washing cups, pitchers, and kettles.*) 5So the Pharisees and teachers of religious law asked him, "Why don't your disciples follow our age-old customs? For they eat without first performing the hand-washing ceremony."

6Jesus replied, "You hypocrites! Isaiah was prophesying about you when he said,

7 'These people honor me with their lips,
    but their hearts are far away.
  Their worship is a farce,
    for they replace God's commands with
      their own man-made teachings.'*

8For you ignore God's specific laws and substitute your own traditions."

9Then he said, "You reject God's laws in order

6:37 Greek *200 denarii.* A denarius was the equivalent of a full day's wage.   6:48 Greek *About the fourth watch of the night.*   7:3 Greek *washed with the fist.*   7:4 Some Greek manuscripts add *and dining couches.*   7:7 Isa 29:13.

to hold on to your own traditions. 10For instance, Moses gave you this law from God: 'Honor your father and mother,' and 'Anyone who speaks evil of father or mother must be put to death.'* 11But you say it is all right for people to say to their parents, 'Sorry, I can't help you. For I have vowed to give to God what I could have given to you.'* 12You let them disregard their needy parents. 13As such, you break the law of God in order to protect your own tradition. And this is only one example. There are many, many others."

14Then Jesus called to the crowd to come and hear. "All of you listen," he said, "and try to understand. 15You are not defiled by what you eat; you are defiled by what you say and do!*"

17Then Jesus went into a house to get away from the crowds, and his disciples asked him what he meant by the statement he had made. 18"Don't you understand either?" he asked. "Can't you see that what you eat won't defile you? 19Food doesn't come in contact with your heart, but only passes through the stomach and then comes out again." (By saying this, he showed that every kind of food is acceptable.)

20And then he added, "It is the thought-life that defiles you. 21For from within, out of a person's heart, come evil thoughts, sexual immorality, theft, murder, 22adultery, greed, wickedness, deceit, eagerness for lustful pleasure, envy, slander, pride, and foolishness. 23All these vile things come from within; they are what defile you and make you unacceptable to God."

### The Faith of a Gentile Woman

24Then Jesus left Galilee and went north to the region of Tyre.* He tried to keep it secret that he was there, but he couldn't. As usual, the news of his arrival spread fast. 25Right away a woman came to him whose little girl was possessed by an evil spirit. She had heard about Jesus, and now she came and fell at his feet. 26She begged him to release her child from the demon's control.

Since she was a Gentile, born in Syrian Phoenicia, 27Jesus told her, "First I should help my own family, the Jews.* It isn't right to take food from the children and throw it to the dogs."

28She replied, "That's true, Lord, but even the dogs under the table are given some crumbs from the children's plates."

29"Good answer!" he said. "And because you have answered so well, I have healed your daughter." 30And when she arrived home, her little girl was lying quietly in bed, and the demon was gone.

### Jesus Heals a Deaf and Mute Man

31Jesus left Tyre and went to Sidon, then back to the Sea of Galilee and the region of the Ten Towns.* 32A deaf man with a speech impediment was brought to him, and the people begged Jesus to lay his hands on the man to heal him. 33Jesus led him to a private place away from the crowd. He put his fingers into the man's ears. Then, spitting onto his own fingers, he touched the man's tongue with the spittle. 34And looking up to heaven, he sighed and commanded, "Be opened!"* 35Instantly the man could hear perfectly and speak plainly!

36Jesus told the crowd not to tell anyone, but the more he told them not to, the more they spread the news, 37for they were completely amazed. Again and again they said, "Everything he does is wonderful. He even heals those who are deaf and mute."

## CHAPTER **8**
### Jesus Feeds Four Thousand

About this time another great crowd had gathered, and the people ran out of food again. Jesus called his disciples and told them, 2"I feel sorry for these people. They have been here with me for three days, and they have nothing left to eat. 3And if I send them home without feeding them, they will faint along the road. For some of them have come a long distance."

4"How are we supposed to find enough food for them here in the wilderness?" his disciples asked.

5"How many loaves of bread do you have?" he asked.

"Seven," they replied. 6So Jesus told all the people to sit down on the ground. Then he took the seven loaves, thanked God for them, broke them into pieces, and gave them to his disciples, who distributed the bread to the crowd. 7A few small fish were found, too, so Jesus also blessed these and told the disciples to pass them out.

8They ate until they were full, and when the scraps were picked up, there were seven large baskets of food left over! 9There were about four thousand people in the crowd that day, and he

---

7:10 Exod 20:12; 21:17; Lev 20:9; Deut 5:16.   7:11 Greek *'What I could have given to you is Corban' (that is, a gift).*   7:15 Some manuscripts add verse 16, *Anyone who is willing to hear should listen and understand.*   7:24 Some Greek manuscripts add *and Sidon.*   7:27 Greek *Let the children eat first.*   7:31 Greek *Decapolis.*   7:34 Greek text uses Aramaic *"Ephphatha"* and then translates it as *"Be opened."*

sent them home after they had eaten. [10]Immediately after this, he got into a boat with his disciples and crossed over to the region of Dalmanutha.

### Pharisees Demand a Miraculous Sign

[11]When the Pharisees heard that Jesus had arrived, they came to argue with him. Testing him to see if he was from God, they demanded, "Give us a miraculous sign from heaven to prove yourself."

[12]When he heard this, he sighed deeply and said, "Why do you people keep demanding a miraculous sign? I assure you, I will not give this generation any such sign." [13]So he got back into the boat and left them, and he crossed to the other side of the lake.

### Yeast of the Pharisees and Herod

[14]But the disciples discovered they had forgotten to bring any food, so there was only one loaf of bread with them in the boat. [15]As they were crossing the lake, Jesus warned them, "Beware of the yeast of the Pharisees and of Herod."

[16]They decided he was saying this because they hadn't brought any bread. [17]Jesus knew what they were thinking, so he said, "Why are you so worried about having no food? Won't you ever learn or understand? Are your hearts too hard to take it in? [18]'You have eyes—can't you see? You have ears—can't you hear?'* Don't you remember anything at all? [19]What about the five thousand men I fed with five loaves of bread? How many baskets of leftovers did you pick up afterward?"

"Twelve," they said.

[20]"And when I fed the four thousand with seven loaves, how many large baskets of leftovers did you pick up?"

"Seven," they said.

[21]"Don't you understand even yet?" he asked them.

### Jesus Heals a Blind Man

[22]When they arrived at Bethsaida, some people brought a blind man to Jesus, and they begged him to touch and heal the man. [23]Jesus took the blind man by the hand and led him out of the village. Then, spitting on the man's eyes, he laid his hands on him and asked, "Can you see anything now?"

[24]The man looked around. "Yes," he said, "I see people, but I can't see them very clearly. They look like trees walking around."

[25]Then Jesus placed his hands over the man's eyes again. As the man stared intently, his sight was completely restored, and he could see everything clearly. [26]Jesus sent him home, saying, "Don't go back into the village on your way home."

### Peter's Declaration about Jesus

[27]Jesus and his disciples left Galilee and went up to the villages of Caesarea Philippi. As they were walking along, he asked them, "Who do people say I am?"

[28]"Well," they replied, "some say John the Baptist, some say Elijah, and others say you are one of the other prophets."

[29]Then Jesus asked, "Who do you say I am?"

Peter replied, "You are the Messiah." [30]But Jesus warned them not to tell anyone about him.

### Jesus Predicts His Death

[31]Then Jesus began to tell them that he, the Son of Man, would suffer many terrible things and be rejected by the leaders, the leading priests, and the teachers of religious law. He would be killed, and three days later he would rise again. [32]As he talked about this openly with his disciples, Peter took him aside and told him he shouldn't say things like that.*

[33]Jesus turned and looked at his disciples and then said to Peter very sternly, "Get away from me, Satan! You are seeing things merely from a human point of view, not from God's."

[34]Then he called his disciples and the crowds to come over and listen. "If any of you wants to be my follower," he told them, "you must put aside your selfish ambition, shoulder your cross, and follow me. [35]If you try to keep your life for yourself, you will lose it. But if you give up your life for my sake and for the sake of the Good News, you will find true life. [36]And how do you benefit if you gain the whole world but lose your own soul* in the process? [37]Is anything worth more than your soul? [38]If a person is ashamed of me and my message in these adulterous and sinful days, I, the Son of Man, will be ashamed of that person when I return in the glory of my Father with the holy angels."

## CHAPTER 9

Jesus went on to say, "I assure you that some of you standing here right now will not die before you see the Kingdom of God arrive in great power!"

8:18 Jer 5:21.  8:32 Or *and began to correct him.*  8:36 Or *your life;* also in 8:37.

## The Transfiguration

2Six days later Jesus took Peter, James, and John to the top of a mountain. No one else was there. As the men watched, Jesus' appearance changed, 3and his clothing became dazzling white, far whiter than any earthly process could ever make it. 4Then Elijah and Moses appeared and began talking with Jesus.

5"Teacher, this is wonderful!" Peter exclaimed. "We will make three shrines*—one for you, one for Moses, and one for Elijah." 6He didn't really know what to say, for they were all terribly afraid.

7Then a cloud came over them, and a voice from the cloud said, "This is my beloved Son. Listen to him." 8Suddenly they looked around, and Moses and Elijah were gone, and only Jesus was with them. 9As they descended the mountainside, he told them not to tell anyone what they had seen until he, the Son of Man, had risen from the dead. 10So they kept it to themselves, but they often asked each other what he meant by "rising from the dead."

11Now they began asking him, "Why do the teachers of religious law insist that Elijah must return before the Messiah comes?"

12Jesus responded, "Elijah is indeed coming first to set everything in order. Why then is it written in the Scriptures that the Son of Man must suffer and be treated with utter contempt? 13But I tell you, Elijah has already come, and he was badly mistreated, just as the Scriptures predicted."

## Jesus Heals a Boy Possessed by an Evil Spirit

14At the foot of the mountain they found a great crowd surrounding the other disciples, as some teachers of religious law were arguing with them. 15The crowd watched Jesus in awe as he came toward them, and then they ran to greet him. 16"What is all this arguing about?" he asked.

17One of the men in the crowd spoke up and said, "Teacher, I brought my son for you to heal him. He can't speak because he is possessed by an evil spirit that won't let him talk. 18And whenever this evil spirit seizes him, it throws him violently to the ground and makes him foam at the mouth and grind his teeth and become rigid.* So I asked your disciples to cast out the evil spirit, but they couldn't do it."

19Jesus said to them, "You faithless people! How long must I be with you until you believe? How long must I put up with you? Bring the boy

to me." 20So they brought the boy. But when the evil spirit saw Jesus, it threw the child into a violent convulsion, and he fell to the ground, writhing and foaming at the mouth. 21"How long has this been happening?" Jesus asked the boy's father.

He replied, "Since he was very small. 22The evil spirit often makes him fall into the fire or into water, trying to kill him. Have mercy on us and help us. Do something if you can."

23"What do you mean, 'If I can'?" Jesus asked. "Anything is possible if a person believes."

24The father instantly replied, "I do believe, but help me not to doubt!"

25When Jesus saw that the crowd of onlookers was growing, he rebuked the evil spirit. "Spirit of deafness and muteness," he said, "I command you to come out of this child and never enter him again!" 26Then the spirit screamed and threw the boy into another violent convulsion and left him. The boy lay there motionless, and he appeared to be dead. A murmur ran through the crowd, "He's dead." 27But Jesus took him by the hand and helped him to his feet, and he stood up.

28Afterward, when Jesus was alone in the house with his disciples, they asked him, "Why couldn't we cast out that evil spirit?"

29Jesus replied, "This kind can be cast out only by prayer.*"

## Jesus Again Predicts His Death

30Leaving that region, they traveled through Galilee. Jesus tried to avoid all publicity 31in order to spend more time with his disciples and teach them. He said to them, "The Son of Man is going to be betrayed. He will be killed, but three days later he will rise from the dead." 32But they didn't understand what he was saying, and they were afraid to ask him what he meant.

## The Greatest in the Kingdom

33After they arrived at Capernaum, Jesus and his disciples settled in the house where they would be staying. Jesus asked them, "What were you discussing out on the road?" 34But they didn't answer, because they had been arguing about which of them was the greatest. 35He sat down and called the twelve disciples over to him. Then he said, "Anyone who wants to be the first must take last place and be the servant of everyone else."

36Then he put a little child among them. Taking the child in his arms, he said to them,

9:5 Or shelters; Greek reads tabernacles. 9:18 Or become weak. 9:29 Some manuscripts add and fasting.

37"Anyone who welcomes a little child like this on my behalf welcomes me, and anyone who welcomes me welcomes my Father who sent me."

## Using the Name of Jesus

38John said to Jesus, "Teacher, we saw a man using your name to cast out demons, but we told him to stop because he isn't one of our group."

39"Don't stop him!" Jesus said. "No one who performs miracles in my name will soon be able to speak evil of me. 40Anyone who is not against us is for us. 41If anyone gives you even a cup of water because you belong to the Messiah, I assure you, that person will be rewarded.

42"But if anyone causes one of these little ones who trusts in me to lose faith, it would be better for that person to be thrown into the sea with a large millstone tied around the neck. 43If your hand causes you to sin, cut it off. It is better to enter heaven* with only one hand than to go into the unquenchable fires of hell with two hands.* 45If your foot causes you to sin, cut it off. It is better to enter heaven with only one foot than to be thrown into hell with two feet.* 47And if your eye causes you to sin, gouge it out. It is better to enter the Kingdom of God half blind than to have two eyes and be thrown into hell, 48'where the worm never dies and the fire never goes out.'*

49"For everyone will be purified with fire.* 50Salt is good for seasoning. But if it loses its flavor, how do you make it salty again? You must have the qualities of salt among yourselves and live in peace with each other."

## CHAPTER 10
### Discussion about Divorce and Marriage
Then Jesus left Capernaum and went southward to the region of Judea and into the area east of the Jordan River. As always there were the crowds, and as usual he taught them.

2Some Pharisees came and tried to trap him with this question: "Should a man be allowed to divorce his wife?"

3"What did Moses say about divorce?" Jesus asked them.

4"Well, he permitted it," they replied. "He said a man merely has to write his wife an official letter of divorce and send her away."*

5But Jesus responded, "He wrote those instructions only as a concession to your hardhearted wickedness. 6But God's plan was seen from the beginning of creation, for 'He made them male and female.'* 7This explains why a man leaves his father and mother and is joined to his wife,* 8and the two are united into one.'* Since they are no longer two but one, 9let no one separate them, for God has joined them together."

10Later, when he was alone with his disciples in the house, they brought up the subject again. 11He told them, "Whoever divorces his wife and marries someone else commits adultery against her. 12And if a woman divorces her husband and remarries, she commits adultery."

### Jesus Blesses the Children
13One day some parents brought their children to Jesus so he could touch them and bless them, but the disciples told them not to bother him.

9:43a Greek *enter life;* also in 9:45.   9:43b Some manuscripts add verse 44 (which is identical with 9:48).   9:45 Some manuscripts add verse 46 (which is identical with 9:48).   9:48 Isa 66:24.   9:49 Greek *salted with fire.* Some manuscripts add *and every sacrifice will be salted with salt.*   10:4 Deut 24:1.   10:6 Gen 1:27; 5:2.   10:7 Some manuscripts do not include *and is joined to his wife.*   10:7-8 Gen 2:24.

# OFF AND RUNNING
## Divorce Is Not Part of God's Plan Read MARK 10:2-12

At the time Jesus was asked this question about divorce, some people had a liberal attitude toward it. Much like today, one could dissolve a marriage for practically any reason. But Jesus reminded the people of God's original plan for marriage (verses 6-9). God desires that a man and woman make a lifelong commitment to each other. Divorce should not even be a consideration.

Perhaps one of the greatest deterrents for divorce is to see how much God really hates it:

"You cry out, 'Why has the LORD abandoned us?' I'll tell you why! Because the LORD witnessed the vows you and your wife made to each other on your wedding day when you were young. But you have been disloyal to her, though she remained your faithful companion, the wife of your marriage vows. Didn't the LORD make you one with your wife? In body and spirit you are his. And what does he want? Godly children from your union. So guard yourself; remain loyal to the wife of your youth. 'For I hate divorce!'" (Malachi 2:14-16).

14But when Jesus saw what was happening, he was very displeased with his disciples. He said to them, "Let the children come to me. Don't stop them! For the Kingdom of God belongs to such as these. 15I assure you, anyone who doesn't have their kind of faith will never get into the Kingdom of God." 16Then he took the children into his arms and placed his hands on their heads and blessed them.

## The Rich Man

17As he was starting out on a trip, a man came running up to Jesus, knelt down, and asked, "Good Teacher, what should I do to get eternal life?"

18"Why do you call me good?" Jesus asked. "Only God is truly good. 19But as for your question, you know the commandments: 'Do not murder. Do not commit adultery. Do not steal. Do not testify falsely. Do not cheat. Honor your father and mother.'* "

20"Teacher," the man replied, "I've obeyed all these commandments since I was a child."

21Jesus felt genuine love for this man as he looked at him. "You lack only one thing," he told him. "Go and sell all you have and give the money to the poor, and you will have treasure in heaven. Then come, follow me." 22At this, the man's face fell, and he went sadly away because he had many possessions.

23Jesus looked around and said to his disciples, "How hard it is for rich people to get into the Kingdom of God!" 24This amazed them. But Jesus said again, "Dear children, it is very hard* to get into the Kingdom of God. 25It is easier for a camel to go through the eye of a needle than for a rich person to enter the Kingdom of God!"

26The disciples were astounded. "Then who in the world can be saved?" they asked.

27Jesus looked at them intently and said, "Humanly speaking, it is impossible. But not with God. Everything is possible with God."

28Then Peter began to mention all that he and the other disciples had left behind. "We've given up everything to follow you," he said.

29And Jesus replied, "I assure you that everyone who has given up house or brothers or sisters or mother or father or children or property, for my sake and for the Good News, 30will receive now in return, a hundred times over, houses, brothers, sisters, mothers, children, and property—with persecutions. And in the world to come they will have eternal life. 31But many who seem to be important now will be the least important then, and those who are considered least here will be the greatest then.* "

## Jesus Again Predicts His Death

32They were now on the way to Jerusalem, and Jesus was walking ahead of them. The disciples were filled with dread and the people following behind were overwhelmed with fear. Taking the twelve disciples aside, Jesus once more began to describe everything that was about to happen to him in Jerusalem. 33"When we get to Jerusalem," he told them, "the Son of Man will be betrayed to the leading priests and the teachers of religious law. They will sentence him to die and hand him over to the Romans. 34They will mock him, spit on him, beat him with their

10:19 Exod 20:12-16; Deut 5:16-20. 10:24 Some manuscripts add *for those who trust in riches.* 10:31 Greek *But many who are first will be last; and the last, first.*

---

Just as one should count the cost of getting married, one should also count the cost of getting divorced. Not only does it devastate the "companionship" God desires between a husband and wife, but it will also greatly affect any children they may have. As God says here, he wants his people to bring up godly children from the union between husband and wife. When a home is broken by divorce, it can become more difficult to raise children in obedience to the Lord.

Does God ever permit divorce? While the Bible cites two instances (adultery, and if a nonbelieving spouse chooses to leave a believing spouse), God's will is that a married couple stay together. Any confusion about the subject arises when we try to accommodate the divine standard to the lack of standards in our contemporary morality.

Winston Churchill astutely observed, "Victory is not obtained through evacuation." If you are married, ask God to strengthen your marriage today. Remember that God has joined you and your spouse together. Stand by your commitment. Don't retreat from your problems, but ask God to help you face and overcome them. Cultivate "oneness" and friendship in your marriage, and get back to God's original design.

## Forgiveness First Comes from God Read MARK 11:25

As verse 25 of this passage implies, an attitude of unforgiveness can actually hinder our prayer life.

In verse 25, Jesus is not saying that God's forgiveness is dependent upon your forgiveness of others. God's acceptance and forgiveness is entirely dependent upon what he did for you at the cross. He is simply stressing that if you are truly a forgiven person, you—of all people—should be willing to forgive others. At the same time, if you are not willing to forgive others, one would wonder if you personally know anything of God's forgiveness.

Don't let unforgiveness rob you of your joy. Forgive as Christ forgave you.

CORNER STONES

whips, and kill him, but after three days he will rise again."

### Jesus Teaches about Serving Others

35Then James and John, the sons of Zebedee, came over and spoke to him. "Teacher," they said, "we want you to do us a favor."

36"What is it?" he asked.

37"In your glorious Kingdom, we want to sit in places of honor next to you," they said, "one at your right and the other at your left."

38But Jesus answered, "You don't know what you are asking! Are you able to drink from the bitter cup of sorrow I am about to drink? Are you able to be baptized with the baptism of suffering I must be baptized with?"

39"Oh yes," they said, "we are able!"

And Jesus said, "You will indeed drink from my cup and be baptized with my baptism, 40but I have no right to say who will sit on the thrones next to mine. God has prepared those places for the ones he has chosen."

41When the ten other disciples discovered what James and John had asked, they were indignant. 42So Jesus called them together and said, "You know that in this world kings are tyrants, and officials lord it over the people beneath them. 43But among you it should be quite different. Whoever wants to be a leader among you must be your servant, 44and whoever wants to be first must be the slave of all. 45For even I, the Son of Man, came here not to be served but to serve others, and to give my life as a ransom for many."

10:52 Or *on the way.*

### Jesus Heals Blind Bartimaeus

46And so they reached Jericho. Later, as Jesus and his disciples left town, a great crowd was following. A blind beggar named Bartimaeus (son of Timaeus) was sitting beside the road as Jesus was going by. 47When Bartimaeus heard that Jesus from Nazareth was nearby, he began to shout out, "Jesus, Son of David, have mercy on me!"

48"Be quiet!" some of the people yelled at him.

But he only shouted louder, "Son of David, have mercy on me!"

49When Jesus heard him, he stopped and said, "Tell him to come here."

So they called the blind man. "Cheer up," they said. "Come on, he's calling you!" 50Bartimaeus threw aside his coat, jumped up, and came to Jesus.

51"What do you want me to do for you?" Jesus asked.

"Teacher," the blind man said, "I want to see!"

52And Jesus said to him, "Go your way. Your faith has healed you." And instantly the blind man could see! Then he followed Jesus down the road.*

CHAPTER **11**
### The Triumphal Entry

As Jesus and his disciples approached Jerusalem, they came to the towns of Bethphage and Bethany, on the Mount of Olives. Jesus sent two of them on ahead. 2"Go into that village over there," he told them, "and as soon as you enter it, you will see a colt tied there that has never been ridden. Untie it and bring it here. 3If anyone asks what you are doing, just say, 'The Lord needs it and will return it soon.'"

4The two disciples left and found the colt standing in the street, tied outside a house. 5As they were untying it, some bystanders demanded, "What are you doing, untying that colt?" 6They said what Jesus had told them to say, and they were permitted to take it. 7Then they brought the colt to Jesus and threw their garments over it, and he sat on it.

8Many in the crowd spread their coats on the road ahead of Jesus, and others cut leafy branches in the fields and spread them along the way. 9He was in the center of the procession, and the crowds all around him were shouting,

"Praise God!*
   Bless the one who comes in the name of
      the Lord!
10 Bless the coming kingdom of our ancestor
      David!
   Praise God in highest heaven!"*

11So Jesus came to Jerusalem and went into the Temple. He looked around carefully at everything, and then he left because it was late in the afternoon. Then he went out to Bethany with the twelve disciples.

## Jesus Curses the Fig Tree

12The next morning as they were leaving Bethany, Jesus felt hungry. 13He noticed a fig tree a little way off that was in full leaf, so he went over to see if he could find any figs on it. But there were only leaves because it was too early in the season for fruit. 14Then Jesus said to the tree, "May no one ever eat your fruit again!" And the disciples heard him say it.

## Jesus Clears the Temple

15When they arrived back in Jerusalem, Jesus entered the Temple and began to drive out the merchants and their customers. He knocked over the tables of the money changers and the stalls of those selling doves, 16and he stopped everyone from bringing in merchandise. 17He taught them, "The Scriptures declare, 'My Temple will be called a place of prayer for all nations,' but you have turned it into a den of thieves."*

18When the leading priests and teachers of religious law heard what Jesus had done, they began planning how to kill him. But they were afraid of him because the people were so enthusiastic about Jesus' teaching. 19That evening Jesus and the disciples* left the city.

20The next morning as they passed by the fig tree he had cursed, the disciples noticed it was withered from the roots. 21Peter remembered what Jesus had said to the tree on the previous day and exclaimed, "Look, Teacher! The fig tree you cursed has withered!"

22Then Jesus said to the disciples, "Have faith in God. 23I assure you that you can say to this mountain, 'May God lift you up and throw you into the sea,' and your command will be obeyed. All that's required is that you really believe and do not doubt in your heart. 24Listen to me! You can pray for anything, and if you believe, you will have it. 25But when you are praying, first forgive anyone you are holding a grudge against, so that your Father in heaven will forgive your sins, too.*"

## The Authority of Jesus Challenged

27By this time they had arrived in Jerusalem again. As Jesus was walking through the Temple area, the leading priests, the teachers of religious law, and the other leaders came up to him. They demanded, 28"By whose authority did you drive out the merchants from the Temple?* Who gave you such authority?"

29"I'll tell who gave me authority to do these things if you answer one question," Jesus replied. 30"Did John's baptism come from heaven or was it merely human? Answer me!"

31They talked it over among themselves. "If we say it was from heaven, he will ask why we didn't believe him. 32But do we dare say it was merely human?" For they were afraid that the people would start a riot, since everyone thought that John was a prophet. 33So they finally replied, "We don't know."

And Jesus responded, "Then I won't answer your question either."

CHAPTER **12**
## Story of the Evil Farmers

Then Jesus began telling them stories: "A man planted a vineyard, built a wall around it, dug a pit for pressing out the grape juice, and built a lookout tower. Then he leased the vineyard to tenant farmers and moved to another country.

11:9 Greek *Hosanna,* an exclamation of praise that literally means "save now"; also in 11:10.   11:9-10 Pss 118:25-26; 148:1.   11:17 Isa 56:7; Jer 7:11.   11:19 Greek *they;* some manuscripts read *he.*   11:25 Some manuscripts add verse 26, *But if you do not forgive, neither will your Father who is in heaven forgive your sins.*   11:28 Or *By whose authority do you do these things?*

2At grape-picking time he sent one of his servants to collect his share of the crop. 3But the farmers grabbed the servant, beat him up, and sent him back empty-handed.

4"The owner then sent another servant, but they beat him over the head and treated him shamefully. 5The next servant he sent was killed. Others who were sent were either beaten or killed, 6until there was only one left—his son whom he loved dearly. The owner finally sent him, thinking, 'Surely they will respect my son.'

7"But the farmers said to one another, 'Here comes the heir to this estate. Let's kill him and get the estate for ourselves!' 8So they grabbed him and murdered him and threw his body out of the vineyard.

9"What do you suppose the owner of the vineyard will do?" Jesus asked. "I'll tell you—he will come and kill them all and lease the vineyard to others. 10Didn't you ever read this in the Scriptures?

'The stone rejected by the builders
    has now become the cornerstone.
11  This is the Lord's doing,
    and it is marvelous to see.'* "

12The Jewish leaders wanted to arrest him for using this illustration because they realized he was pointing at them—they were the wicked farmers in his story. But they were afraid to touch him because of the crowds. So they left him and went away.

## Taxes for Caesar

13The leaders sent some Pharisees and supporters of Herod to try to trap Jesus into saying something for which he could be arrested. 14"Teacher," these men said, "we know how honest you are. You are impartial and don't play favorites. You sincerely teach the ways of God. Now tell us—is it right to pay taxes to the Roman government or not? 15Should we pay them, or should we not?"

Jesus saw through their hypocrisy and said, "Whom are you trying to fool with your trick questions? Show me a Roman coin,* and I'll tell you." 16When they handed it to him, he asked, "Whose picture and title are stamped on it?"

"Caesar's," they replied.

17"Well, then," Jesus said, "give to Caesar what belongs to him. But everything that belongs to God must be given to God." This reply completely amazed them.

## Discussion about Resurrection

18Then the Sadducees stepped forward—a group of Jews who say there is no resurrection after death. They posed this question: 19"Teacher, Moses gave us a law that if a man dies, leaving a wife without children, his brother should marry the widow and have a child who will be the brother's heir.* 20Well, there were seven brothers. The oldest of them married and then died without children. 21So the second brother married the widow, but soon he too died and left no children. Then the next brother married her and died without children. 22This continued until all the brothers had married her and died, and still there were no children. Last of all, the woman died, too. 23So tell us, whose wife will she be in the resurrection? For all seven were married to her."

24Jesus replied, "Your problem is that you don't know the Scriptures, and you don't know the power of God. 25For when the dead rise, they won't be married. They will be like the angels in heaven. 26But now, as to whether the dead will be raised—haven't you ever read about this in the writings of Moses, in the story of the burning bush? Long after Abraham, Isaac, and Jacob had died, God said to Moses,* 'I am the God of Abraham, the God of Isaac, and the God of Jacob.'* 27So he is the God of the living, not the dead. You have made a serious error."

## The Most Important Commandment

28One of the teachers of religious law was standing there listening to the discussion. He realized that Jesus had answered well, so he asked, "Of all the commandments, which is the most important?"

29Jesus replied, "The most important commandment is this: 'Hear, O Israel! The Lord our God is the one and only Lord. 30And you must love the Lord your God with all your heart, all your soul, all your mind, and all your strength.'* 31The second is equally important: 'Love your neighbor as yourself.'* No other commandment is greater than these."

32The teacher of religious law replied, "Well said, Teacher. You have spoken the truth by saying that there is only one God and no other. 33And I know it is important to love him with all my heart and all my understanding and all my strength, and to love my neighbors as myself. This is more important than to offer all of

12:10-11 Ps 118:22-23.   12:15 Greek *a denarius.*   12:19 Deut 25:5-6.   12:26a Greek *in the story of the bush? God said to him.*
12:26b Exod 3:6.   12:29-30 Deut 6:4-5.   12:31 Lev 19:18.

the burnt offerings and sacrifices required in the law."

34Realizing this man's understanding, Jesus said to him, "You are not far from the Kingdom of God." And after that, no one dared to ask him any more questions.

### Whose Son Is the Messiah?

35Later, as Jesus was teaching the people in the Temple, he asked, "Why do the teachers of religious law claim that the Messiah will be the son of David? 36For David himself, speaking under the inspiration of the Holy Spirit, said,

'The LORD said to my Lord,
Sit in honor at my right hand
    until I humble your enemies beneath
        your feet.'*

37Since David himself called him Lord, how can he be his son at the same time?" And the crowd listened to him with great interest.

38Here are some of the other things he taught them at this time: "Beware of these teachers of religious law! For they love to parade in flowing robes and to have everyone bow to them as they walk in the marketplaces. 39And how they love the seats of honor in the synagogues and at banquets. 40But they shamelessly cheat widows out of their property, and then, to cover up the kind of people they really are, they make long prayers in public. Because of this, their punishment will be the greater."

### The Widow's Offering

41Jesus went over to the collection box in the Temple and sat and watched as the crowds dropped in their money. Many rich people put in large amounts. 42Then a poor widow came and dropped in two pennies.* 43He called his disciples to him and said, "I assure you, this poor widow has given more than all the others have given. 44For they gave a tiny part of their surplus, but she, poor as she is, has given everything she has."

## CHAPTER 13
### Jesus Foretells the Future

As Jesus was leaving the Temple that day, one of his disciples said, "Teacher, look at these tremendous buildings! Look at the massive stones in the walls!"

2Jesus replied, "These magnificent buildings

will be so completely demolished that not one stone will be left on top of another."

3Later, Jesus sat on the slopes of the Mount of Olives across the valley from the Temple. Peter, James, John, and Andrew came to him privately and asked him, 4"When will all this take place? And will there be any sign ahead of time to show us when all this will be fulfilled?"

5Jesus replied, "Don't let anyone mislead you, 6because many will come in my name, claiming to be the Messiah.* They will lead many astray. 7And wars will break out near and far, but don't panic. Yes, these things must come, but the end won't follow immediately. 8Nations and kingdoms will proclaim war against each other, and there will be earth-

13:6 Greek name, saying, 'I am.'

---

## How Much Should You Give?
### Read MARK 12:41-44

Generosity is not measured by the size of the gift itself, but by the motivation. In this story, we see how Jesus valued the small offering of this poor widow over the large sums of money from the wealthy people. Jesus knew that she had given all she had. He could see that her heart was in the right place.

The great psalmist, David, king of Israel, said he would not give to the Lord that which cost him nothing. In other words, we are not to give our "leftovers" to God, but our best. When you think about it, is that really too much to ask? After all, he gave his best to us when he sent us his own dear Son to die in our place.

Our attitude toward giving should be like that of the generous believers in Macedonia, who eagerly came to the aid of the church in Jerusalem during its time of need: "For I can testify that they gave not only what they could afford but far more. And they did it of their own free will. They begged us again and again for the gracious privilege of sharing in the gift for the Christians in Jerusalem" (2 Corinthians 8:3-4).

When you question how much of your income should be spent on God's work, remember this promise: "God loves the person who gives cheerfully. And God will generously provide all you need" (2 Corinthians 9:7-8).

FIRST STEPS

12:36 Ps 110:1.   12:42 Greek 2 lepta, which is a kodrantes.

quakes in many parts of the world, and famines. But all this will be only the beginning of the horrors to come. 9But when these things begin to happen, watch out! You will be handed over to the courts and beaten in the synagogues. You will be accused before governors and kings of being my followers. This will be your opportunity to tell them about me.* 10And the Good News must first be preached to every nation. 11But when you are arrested and stand trial, don't worry about what to say in your defense. Just say what God tells you to. Then it is not you who will be speaking, but the Holy Spirit.

12"Brother will betray brother to death, fathers will betray their own children, and children will rise against their parents and cause them to be killed. 13And everyone will hate you because of your allegiance to me. But those who endure to the end will be saved.

14"The time will come when you will see the sacrilegious object that causes desecration* standing where it should not be"—reader, pay attention! "Then those in Judea must flee to the hills. 15A person outside the house* must not go back into the house to pack. 16A person in the field must not return even to get a coat. 17How terrible it will be for pregnant women and for mothers nursing their babies in those days. 18And pray that your flight will not be in winter. 19For those will be days of greater horror than at any time since God created the world. And it will never happen again. 20In fact, unless the Lord shortens that time of calamity, the entire human race will be destroyed. But for the sake of his chosen ones he has shortened those days.

21"And then if anyone tells you, 'Look, here is the Messiah,' or, 'There he is,' don't pay any attention. 22For false messiahs and false prophets will rise up and perform miraculous signs and wonders so as to deceive, if possible, even God's chosen ones. 23Watch out! I have warned you!

24"At that time, after those horrible days end,

the sun will be darkened,
the moon will not give light,
25 the stars will fall from the sky,
and the powers of heaven will be shaken.*

26Then everyone will see the Son of Man arrive on the clouds with great power and glory.*

27And he will send forth his angels to gather together his chosen ones from all over the world—from the farthest ends of the earth and heaven.

28"Now, learn a lesson from the fig tree. When its buds become tender and its leaves begin to sprout, you know without being told that summer is near. 29Just so, when you see the events I've described beginning to happen, you can be sure that his return is very near, right at the door. 30I assure you, this generation* will not pass from the scene until all these events have taken place. 31Heaven and earth will disappear, but my words will remain forever.

32"However, no one knows the day or hour when these things will happen, not even the angels in heaven or the Son himself. Only the Father knows. 33And since you don't know when they will happen, stay alert and keep watch.*

34"The coming of the Son of Man can be compared with that of a man who left home to go on a trip. He gave each of his employees instructions about the work they were to do, and he told the gatekeeper to watch for his return. 35So keep a sharp lookout! For you do not know when the homeowner will return—at evening, midnight, early dawn, or late daybreak. 36Don't let him find you sleeping when he arrives without warning. 37What I say to you I say to everyone: Watch for his return!"

## CHAPTER 14
### Jesus Anointed at Bethany

It was now two days before the Passover celebration and the Festival of Unleavened Bread. The leading priests and the teachers of religious law were still looking for an opportunity to capture Jesus secretly and put him to death. 2"But not during the Passover," they agreed, "or there will be a riot."

3Meanwhile, Jesus was in Bethany at the home of Simon, a man who had leprosy. During supper, a woman came in with a beautiful jar of expensive perfume.* She broke the seal and poured the perfume over his head. 4Some of those at the table were indignant. "Why was this expensive perfume wasted?" they asked. 5"She could have sold it for a small fortune* and given the money to the poor!" And they scolded her harshly.

13:9 Or *This will be your testimony against them.* 13:14 Greek *the abomination of desolation.* See Dan 9:27; 11:31; 12:11. 13:15 Greek *on the roof.* 13:24-25 See Isa 13:10; 34:4; Joel 2:10. 13:26 See Dan 7:13. 13:30 Or *this age,* or *this nation.* 13:33 Some manuscripts add *and pray.* 14:3 Greek *an alabaster jar of expensive ointment, pure nard.* 14:5 Greek *300 denarii.* A denarius was the equivalent of a full day's wage.

⁶But Jesus replied, "Leave her alone. Why berate her for doing such a good thing to me? ⁷You will always have the poor among you, and you can help them whenever you want to. But I will not be here with you much longer. ⁸She has done what she could and has anointed my body for burial ahead of time. ⁹I assure you, wherever the Good News is preached throughout the world, this woman's deed will be talked about in her memory."

## Judas Agrees to Betray Jesus

¹⁰Then Judas Iscariot, one of the twelve disciples, went to the leading priests to arrange to betray Jesus to them. ¹¹The leading priests were delighted when they heard why he had come, and they promised him a reward. So he began looking for the right time and place to betray Jesus.

## The Last Supper

¹²On the first day of the Festival of Unleavened Bread (the day the Passover lambs were sacrificed), Jesus' disciples asked him, "Where do you want us to go to prepare the Passover supper?"

¹³So Jesus sent two of them into Jerusalem to make the arrangements. "As you go into the city," he told them, "a man carrying a pitcher of water will meet you. Follow him. ¹⁴At the house he enters, say to the owner, 'The Teacher asks, Where is the guest room where I can eat the Passover meal with my disciples?' ¹⁵He will take you upstairs to a large room that is already set up. That is the place; go ahead and prepare our supper there." ¹⁶So the two disciples went on ahead into the city and found everything just as Jesus had said, and they prepared the Passover supper there.

¹⁷In the evening Jesus arrived with the twelve disciples. ¹⁸As they were sitting around the table eating, Jesus said, "The truth is, one of you will betray me, one of you who is here eating with me."

¹⁹Greatly distressed, one by one they began to ask him, "I'm not the one, am I?"

²⁰He replied, "It is one of you twelve, one who is eating with me now.* ²¹For I, the Son of Man, must die, as the Scriptures declared long ago. But how terrible it will be for my betrayer. Far better for him if he had never been born!"

²²As they were eating, Jesus took a loaf of bread and asked God's blessing on it. Then he broke it in pieces and gave it to the disciples, saying, "Take it, for this is my body."

²³And he took a cup of wine and gave thanks to God for it. He gave it to them, and they all drank from it. ²⁴And he said to them, "This is my blood, poured out for many, sealing the covenant* between God and his people. ²⁵I solemnly declare that I will not drink wine again until that day when I drink it new in the Kingdom of God." ²⁶Then they sang a hymn and went out to the Mount of Olives.

## Jesus Predicts Peter's Denial

²⁷"All of you will desert me," Jesus told them. "For the Scriptures say,

'God* will strike the Shepherd,
    and the sheep will be scattered.'*

²⁸But after I am raised from the dead, I will go ahead of you to Galilee and meet you there."

²⁹Peter said to him, "Even if everyone else deserts you, I never will."

³⁰"Peter," Jesus replied, "the truth is, this very night, before the rooster crows twice, you will deny me three times."

³¹"No!" Peter insisted. "Not even if I have to die with you! I will never deny you!" And all the others vowed the same.

## Jesus Prays in Gethsemane

³²And they came to an olive grove called Gethsemane, and Jesus said, "Sit here while I go and pray." ³³He took Peter, James, and John with him, and he began to be filled with horror and deep distress. ³⁴He told them, "My soul is crushed with grief to the point of death. Stay here and watch with me."

³⁵He went on a little farther and fell face down on the ground. He prayed that, if it were possible, the awful hour awaiting him might pass him by. ³⁶"Abba,* Father," he said, "everything is possible for you. Please take this cup of suffering away from me. Yet I want your will, not mine."

³⁷Then he returned and found the disciples asleep. "Simon!" he said to Peter. "Are you asleep? Couldn't you stay awake and watch with me even one hour? ³⁸Keep alert and pray. Otherwise temptation will overpower you. For though the spirit is willing enough, the body is weak."

³⁹Then Jesus left them again and prayed, repeating his pleadings. ⁴⁰Again he returned to

14:20 Or *one who is dipping bread into the bowl with me.*   14:24 Some manuscripts read *the new covenant.*   14:27a Greek *I.*   14:27b Zech 13:7.   14:36 *Abba* is an Aramaic term for "father."

them and found them sleeping, for they just couldn't keep their eyes open. And they didn't know what to say.

41When he returned to them the third time, he said, "Still sleeping? Still resting?* Enough! The time has come. I, the Son of Man, am betrayed into the hands of sinners. 42Up, let's be going. See, my betrayer is here!"

## Jesus Is Betrayed and Arrested

43And immediately, as he said this, Judas, one of the twelve disciples, arrived with a mob that was armed with swords and clubs. They had been sent out by the leading priests, the teachers of religious law, and the other leaders. 44Judas had given them a prearranged signal: "You will know which one to arrest when I go over and give him the kiss of greeting. Then you can take him away under guard."

45As soon as they arrived, Judas walked up to Jesus. "Teacher!" he exclaimed, and gave him the kiss. 46Then the others grabbed Jesus and arrested him. 47But someone pulled out a sword and slashed off an ear of the high priest's servant.

48Jesus asked them, "Am I some dangerous criminal, that you come armed with swords and clubs to arrest me? 49Why didn't you arrest me in the Temple? I was there teaching every day. But these things are happening to fulfill what the Scriptures say about me."

50Meanwhile, all his disciples deserted him and ran away. 51There was a young man following along behind, clothed only in a linen nightshirt. When the mob tried to grab him, 52they tore off his clothes, but he escaped and ran away naked.

## Jesus before the Council

53Jesus was led to the high priest's home where the leading priests, other leaders, and teachers of religious law had gathered. 54Meanwhile, Peter followed far behind and then slipped inside the gates of the high priest's courtyard. For a while he sat with the guards, warming himself by the fire.

55Inside, the leading priests and the entire high council* were trying to find witnesses who would testify against Jesus, so they could put him to death. But their efforts were in vain. 56Many false witnesses spoke against him, but they contradicted each other. 57Finally, some men stood up to testify against him with this lie: 58"We heard him say, 'I will destroy this Temple made with human hands, and in three days I will build another, made without human

hands.'" 59But even then they didn't get their stories straight!

60Then the high priest stood up before the others and asked Jesus, "Well, aren't you going to answer these charges? What do you have to say for yourself?" 61Jesus made no reply. Then the high priest asked him, "Are you the Messiah, the Son of the blessed God?"

62Jesus said, "I am, and you will see me, the Son of Man, sitting at God's right hand in the place of power and coming back on the clouds of heaven."*

63Then the high priest tore his clothing to show his horror and said, "Why do we need other witnesses? 64You have all heard his blasphemy. What is your verdict?" And they all condemned him to death.

65Then some of them began to spit at him, and they blindfolded him and hit his face with their fists. "Who hit you that time, you prophet?" they jeered. And even the guards were hitting him as they led him away.

## Peter Denies Jesus

66Meanwhile, Peter was below in the courtyard. One of the servant girls who worked for the high priest 67noticed Peter warming himself at the fire. She looked at him closely and then said, "You were one of those with Jesus, the Nazarene."

68Peter denied it. "I don't know what you're talking about," he said, and he went out into the entryway. Just then, a rooster crowed.*

69The servant girl saw him standing there and began telling the others, "That man is definitely one of them!" 70Peter denied it again.

A little later some other bystanders began saying to Peter, "You must be one of them because you are from Galilee."

71Peter said, "I swear by God, I don't know this man you're talking about." 72And immediately the rooster crowed the second time. Suddenly, Jesus' words flashed through Peter's mind: "Before the rooster crows twice, you will deny me three times." And he broke down and cried.

## CHAPTER 15
### Jesus' Trial before Pilate
Very early in the morning the leading priests, other leaders, and teachers of religious law—the entire high council*—met to discuss their next step. They bound Jesus and took him to Pilate, the Roman governor.

14:41 Or *Sleep on, take your rest.*   14:55 Greek *the Sanhedrin.*   14:62 See Ps 110:1; Dan 7:13.   14:68 Some manuscripts do not include *Just then, a rooster crowed.*   15:1 Greek *the Sanhedrin;* also in 15:43.

2Pilate asked Jesus, "Are you the King of the Jews?"

Jesus replied, "Yes, it is as you say."

3Then the leading priests accused him of many crimes, 4and Pilate asked him, "Aren't you going to say something? What about all these charges against you?" 5But Jesus said nothing, much to Pilate's surprise.

6Now it was the governor's custom to release one prisoner each year at Passover time—anyone the people requested. 7One of the prisoners at that time was Barabbas, convicted along with others for murder during an insurrection. 8The mob began to crowd in toward Pilate, asking him to release a prisoner as usual. 9"Should I give you the King of the Jews?" Pilate asked. 10(For he realized by now that the leading priests had arrested Jesus out of envy.) 11But at this point the leading priests stirred up the mob to demand the release of Barabbas instead of Jesus. 12"But if I release Barabbas," Pilate asked them, "what should I do with this man you call the King of the Jews?"

13They shouted back, "Crucify him!"

14"Why?" Pilate demanded. "What crime has he committed?"

But the crowd only roared the louder, "Crucify him!"

15So Pilate, anxious to please the crowd, released Barabbas to them. He ordered Jesus flogged with a lead-tipped whip, then turned him over to the Roman soldiers to crucify him.

### The Soldiers Mock Jesus

16The soldiers took him into their headquarters* and called out the entire battalion. 17They dressed him in a purple robe and made a crown of long, sharp thorns and put it on his head. 18Then they saluted, yelling, "Hail! King of the Jews!" 19And they beat him on the head with a stick, spit on him, and dropped to their knees in mock worship. 20When they were finally tired of mocking him, they took off the purple robe and put his own clothes on him again. Then they led him away to be crucified.

### The Crucifixion

21A man named Simon, who was from Cyrene,* was coming in from the country just then, and they forced him to carry Jesus' cross. (Simon is the father of Alexander and Rufus.) 22And they brought Jesus to a place called Golgotha (which means Skull Hill).

23They offered him wine drugged with myrrh, but he refused it. 24Then they nailed him to the cross. They gambled for his clothes, throwing dice* to decide who would get them.

25It was nine o'clock in the morning when the crucifixion took place. 26A signboard was fastened to the cross above Jesus' head, announcing the charge against him. It read: "The King of the Jews." 27Two criminals were crucified with him, their crosses on either side of his.* 29And the people passing by shouted abuse, shaking their heads in mockery. "Ha! Look at you now!" they yelled at him. "You can destroy the Temple and rebuild it in three days, can you? 30Well then, save yourself and come down from the cross!"

31The leading priests and teachers of religious law also mocked Jesus. "He saved others," they scoffed, "but he can't save himself! 32Let this Messiah, this king of Israel, come down from the cross so we can see it and believe him!" Even the two criminals who were being crucified with Jesus ridiculed him.

### The Death of Jesus

33At noon, darkness fell across the whole land until three o'clock. 34Then, at that time Jesus called out with a loud voice, "Eloi, Eloi, lema sabachthani?" which means, "My God, my God, why have you forsaken me?"*

35Some of the bystanders misunderstood and thought he was calling for the prophet Elijah. 36One of them ran and filled a sponge with sour wine, holding it up to him on a stick so he could drink. "Leave him alone. Let's see whether Elijah will come and take him down!" he said.

37Then Jesus uttered another loud cry and breathed his last. 38And the curtain in the Temple was torn in two, from top to bottom. 39When the Roman officer who stood facing him saw how he had died, he exclaimed, "Truly, this was the Son of God!"

40Some women were there, watching from a distance, including Mary Magdalene, Mary (the mother of James the younger and of Joseph*), and Salome. 41They had been followers of Jesus and had cared for him while he was in Galilee. Then they and many other women had come with him to Jerusalem.

### The Burial of Jesus

42This all happened on Friday, the day of preparation,* the day before the Sabbath. As evening

---

15:16 Greek *the courtyard, which is the praetorium.*　　15:21 *Cyrene* was a city in northern Africa.　　15:24 Greek *casting lots.* See Ps 22:18.
15:27 Some manuscripts add verse 28, *And the Scripture was fulfilled that said, "He was counted among those who were rebels."* See Isa 53:12.
15:34 Ps 22:1.　　15:40 Greek *Joses;* also in 15:47. See Matt 27:56.　　15:42 Greek *on the day of preparation.*

approached, [43]an honored member of the high council, Joseph from Arimathea (who was waiting for the Kingdom of God to come), gathered his courage and went to Pilate to ask for Jesus' body. [44]Pilate couldn't believe that Jesus was already dead, so he called for the Roman military officer in charge and asked him. [45]The officer confirmed the fact, and Pilate told Joseph he could have the body. [46]Joseph bought a long sheet of linen cloth, and taking Jesus' body down from the cross, he wrapped it in the cloth and laid it in a tomb that had been carved out of the rock. Then he rolled a stone in front of the entrance. [47]Mary Magdalene and Mary the mother of Joseph saw where Jesus' body was laid.

CHAPTER **16**
*The Resurrection*
The next evening, when the Sabbath ended, Mary Magdalene and Salome and Mary the mother of James went out and purchased burial spices to put on Jesus' body. [2]Very early on Sunday morning,* just at sunrise, they came to the tomb. [3]On the way they were discussing who would roll the stone away from the entrance to the tomb. [4]But when they arrived, they looked up and saw that the stone—a very large one—had already been rolled aside. [5]So they entered the tomb, and there on the right sat a young man clothed in a white robe. The women were startled, [6]but the angel said, "Do not be so surprised. You are looking for Jesus, the Nazarene, who was crucified. He isn't here! He has been raised from the dead! Look, this is where they laid his body. [7]Now go and give this message to his disciples, including Peter: Jesus is going ahead of you to Galilee. You will see him there, just as he told you before he died!" [8]The women fled from the tomb, trembling and bewildered, saying nothing to anyone because they were too frightened to talk.*

*[Shorter Ending of Mark]*

Then they reported all these instructions briefly to Peter and his companions. Afterward Jesus himself sent them out from east to west with the sacred and unfailing message of salvation that gives eternal life. Amen.

*[Longer Ending of Mark]*

[9]It was early on Sunday morning when Jesus rose from the dead, and the first person who saw him was Mary Magdalene, the woman from whom he had cast out seven demons. [10]She went and found the disciples, who were grieving and weeping. [11]But when she told them that Jesus was alive and she had seen him, they didn't believe her.

[12]Afterward he appeared to two who were walking from Jerusalem into the country, but they didn't recognize him at first because he had changed his appearance. [13]When they realized who he was, they rushed back to tell the others, but no one believed them.

[14]Still later he appeared to the eleven disciples as they were eating together. He rebuked them for their unbelief—their stubborn refusal to believe those who had seen him after he had risen.

[15]And then he told them, "Go into all the world and preach the Good News to everyone, everywhere. [16]Anyone who believes and is baptized will be saved. But anyone who refuses to believe will be condemned. [17]These signs will accompany those who believe: They will cast out demons in my name, and they will speak new languages.* [18]They will be able to handle snakes with safety, and if they drink anything poisonous, it won't hurt them. They will be able to place their hands on the sick and heal them."

[19]When the Lord Jesus had finished talking with them, he was taken up into heaven and sat down in the place of honor at God's right hand. [20]And the disciples went everywhere and preached, and the Lord worked with them, confirming what they said by many miraculous signs.

**16:2** Greek *on the first day of the week;* also in 16:9.   **16:8** The most reliable early manuscripts conclude the Gospel of Mark at verse 8. Other manuscripts include various endings to the Gospel. Two of the more noteworthy endings are printed here.   **16:17** Or *new tongues.* Some manuscripts omit *new.*

# Luke

## CHAPTER 1

*Introduction*

Most honorable Theophilus:

Many people have written accounts about the events that took place* among us. 2They used as their source material the reports circulating among us from the early disciples and other eyewitnesses of what God has done in fulfillment of his promises. 3Having carefully investigated all of these accounts from the beginning, I have decided to write a careful summary for you, 4to reassure you of the truth of all you were taught.

### The Birth of John the Baptist Foretold

5It all begins with a Jewish priest, Zechariah, who lived when Herod was king of Judea. Zechariah was a member of the priestly order of Abijah. His wife, Elizabeth, was also from the priestly line of Aaron. 6Zechariah and Elizabeth were righteous in God's eyes, careful to obey all of the Lord's commandments and regulations. 7They had no children because Elizabeth was barren, and now they were both very old.

8One day Zechariah was serving God in the Temple, for his order was on duty that week. 9As was the custom of the priests, he was chosen by lot to enter the sanctuary and burn incense in the Lord's presence. 10While the incense was being burned, a great crowd stood outside, praying.

11Zechariah was in the sanctuary when an angel of the Lord appeared, standing to the right of the incense altar. 12Zechariah was overwhelmed with fear. 13But the angel said, "Don't be afraid, Zechariah! For God has heard your prayer, and your wife, Elizabeth, will bear you a son! And you are to name him John. 14You will have great joy and gladness, and many will rejoice with you at his birth, 15for he will be great

in the eyes of the Lord. He must never touch wine or hard liquor, and he will be filled with the Holy Spirit, even before his birth.* 16And he will persuade many Israelites to turn to the Lord their God. 17He will be a man with the spirit and power of Elijah, the prophet of old. He will precede the coming of the Lord, preparing the people for his arrival. He will turn the hearts of the fathers to their children, and he will change disobedient minds to accept godly wisdom."*

18Zechariah said to the angel, "How can I know this will happen? I'm an old man now, and my wife is also well along in years."

19Then the angel said, "I am Gabriel! I stand in the very presence of God. It was he who sent me to bring you this good news! 20And now, since you didn't believe what I said, you won't be able to speak until the child is born. For my words will certainly come true at the proper time."

21Meanwhile, the people were waiting for Zechariah to come out, wondering why he was taking so long. 22When he finally did come out, he couldn't speak to them. Then they realized from his gestures that he must have seen a vision in the Temple sanctuary.

23He stayed at the Temple until his term of service was over, and then he returned home. 24Soon afterward his wife, Elizabeth, became pregnant and went into seclusion for five months. 25"How kind the Lord is!" she exclaimed. "He has taken away my disgrace of having no children!"

### The Birth of Jesus Foretold

26In the sixth month of Elizabeth's pregnancy, God sent the angel Gabriel to Nazareth, a village in Galilee, 27to a virgin named Mary. She was engaged to be married to a man named Joseph,

1:1 Or *have been fulfilled.* 1:15 Or *even from birth.* 1:17 See Mal 4:5-6.

a descendant of King David. 28Gabriel appeared to her and said, "Greetings, favored woman! The Lord is with you!*"

29Confused and disturbed, Mary tried to think what the angel could mean. 30"Don't be frightened, Mary," the angel told her, "for God has decided to bless you! 31You will become pregnant and have a son, and you are to name him Jesus. 32He will be very great and will be called the Son of the Most High. And the Lord God will give him the throne of his ancestor David. 33And he will reign over Israel* forever; his Kingdom will never end!"

34Mary asked the angel, "But how can I have a baby? I am a virgin."

35The angel replied, "The Holy Spirit will come upon you, and the power of the Most High will overshadow you. So the baby born to you will be holy, and he will be called the Son of God. 36What's more, your relative Elizabeth has become pregnant in her old age! People used to say she was barren, but she's already in her sixth month. 37For nothing is impossible with God."

38Mary responded, "I am the Lord's servant, and I am willing to accept whatever he wants. May everything you have said come true." And then the angel left.

## Mary Visits Elizabeth

39A few days later Mary hurried to the hill country of Judea, to the town 40where Zechariah lived. She entered the house and greeted Elizabeth. 41At the sound of Mary's greeting, Elizabeth's child leaped within her, and Elizabeth was filled with the Holy Spirit.

42Elizabeth gave a glad cry and exclaimed to Mary, "You are blessed by God above all other women, and your child is blessed. 43What an honor this is, that the mother of my Lord should visit me! 44When you came in and greeted me, my baby jumped for joy the instant I heard your voice! 45You are blessed, because you believed that the Lord would do what he said."

## The Magnificat: Mary's Song of Praise

46Mary responded,

"Oh, how I praise the Lord.
47    How I rejoice in God my Savior!
48 For he took notice of his lowly servant girl,
       and now generation after generation
          will call me blessed.
49 For he, the Mighty One, is holy,

and he has done great things for me.
50 His mercy goes on from generation to
       generation,
    to all who fear him.
51 His mighty arm does tremendous things!
    How he scatters the proud and haughty
       ones!
52 He has taken princes from their thrones
    and exalted the lowly.
53 He has satisfied the hungry with good things
    and sent the rich away with empty hands.
54 And how he has helped his servant Israel!
    He has not forgotten his promise to be
       merciful.
55 For he promised our ancestors—Abraham
       and his children—
    to be merciful to them forever."

56Mary stayed with Elizabeth about three months and then went back to her own home.

## The Birth of John the Baptist

57Now it was time for Elizabeth's baby to be born, and it was a boy. 58The word spread quickly to her neighbors and relatives that the Lord had been very kind to her, and everyone rejoiced with her.

59When the baby was eight days old, all the relatives and friends came for the circumcision ceremony. They wanted to name him Zechariah, after his father. 60But Elizabeth said, "No! His name is John!"

61"What?" they exclaimed. "There is no one in all your family by that name." 62So they asked the baby's father, communicating to him by making gestures. 63He motioned for a writing tablet, and to everyone's surprise he wrote, "His name is John!" 64Instantly Zechariah could speak again, and he began praising God.

65Wonder fell upon the whole neighborhood, and the news of what had happened spread throughout the Judean hills. 66Everyone who heard about it reflected on these events and asked, "I wonder what this child will turn out to be? For the hand of the Lord is surely upon him in a special way."

## Zechariah's Prophecy

67Then his father, Zechariah, was filled with the Holy Spirit and gave this prophecy:

68 "Praise the Lord, the God of Israel,
       because he has visited his people and
          redeemed them.

1:28 Some manuscripts add *Blessed are you among women.*   1:33 Greek *over the house of Jacob.*

## Is the Bible Believable? Read LUKE 1:1-4

In writing this Gospel, Luke took painstaking efforts to confirm the accuracy of his work. He made it clear that he meticulously put this book together, going so far as to "recheck" the disciples' accounts "from the beginning."

Although Luke and other writers of the books of the Bible have taken great pains to accurately record the events within, some people have tried to point out alleged contradictions or inconsistencies in the Bible. These same people argue that the Bible is not credible based on what they believe to be contradictions. But here are three reasons why the Bible is believable:

**1. God Is the Author.** Despite the fact that the Bible was written by more than forty authors, we must recognize one important fact: The people who put the pen to the paper were but instruments in the hand of God. The real author of the Bible is God. As the apostle Paul wrote, "All Scripture is inspired by God" (2 Timothy 3:16). God chose to speak through these different people much like an artist uses different brushes to paint on a canvas. Each one had his own unique style, but the truth was the same.

**2. The Main Story of the Bible Is Too Complex to Be a Hoax.** The renowned historian Will Durant, who devoted his life to the study of records of antiquity, made this observation concerning the accounts of Jesus and the early church in Scripture: "That a few simple men should in one generation have invented so powerful and appealing a personality, so lofty an ethic, and so inspiring a vision of human brotherhood, would be a miracle far more incredible than any recorded in the Gospels. After two centuries of Higher Criticism the outlines of life, character, and teaching of Christ remain reasonably clear, and constitute the most fascinating feature in the history of Western man" [*Caesar and Christ,* in The Story of Civilization, vol. 3 (New York: Simon & Schuster, 1944), p. 557].

**3. Scientific Evidence Supports the Bible's Accuracy.** Archaeological findings have supported many of the complex historical passages found in the Bible. In addition, the Bible has greater documented accuracy than any other ancient literary work [see Norman L. Geisler & William E. Nix, *A General Introduction to the Bible* (Chicago: Moody Press, Moody Bible Institute, 1986)].

In spite of the evidence, God's Word must be accepted by faith. You, as an individual, must come to recognize that the words of the Lord are perfect, trustworthy, and right (see Hebrews 11:7-12). Your belief in and practice of the truths found in this book—God's message to us—will make the most profound impact on your life for time and eternity.

---

69 He has sent us a mighty Savior
from the royal line of his servant David,
70 just as he promised
through his holy prophets long ago.
71 Now we will be saved from our enemies
and from all who hate us.
72 He has been merciful to our ancestors
by remembering his sacred covenant
with them,
73 the covenant he gave to our ancestor
Abraham.
74 We have been rescued from our enemies,
so we can serve God without fear,
75 in holiness and righteousness forever.

76 "And you, my little son,
will be called the prophet of the Most
High,
because you will prepare the way for the
Lord.
77 You will tell his people how to find
salvation
through forgiveness of their sins.
78 Because of God's tender mercy,
the light from heaven is about to break
upon us,
79 to give light to those who sit in darkness
and in the shadow of death,
and to guide us to the path of peace."

80John grew up and became strong in spirit. Then he lived out in the wilderness until he began his public ministry to Israel.

## CHAPTER 2
### The Birth of Jesus

At that time the Roman emperor, Augustus, decreed that a census should be taken throughout the Roman Empire. 2(This was the first census taken when Quirinius was governor of Syria.) 3All returned to their own towns to register for this census. 4And because Joseph was a descendant of King David, he had to go to Bethlehem in Judea, David's ancient home. He traveled there from the village of Nazareth in Galilee. 5He took with him Mary, his fiancée, who was obviously pregnant by this time.

6And while they were there, the time came for her baby to be born. 7She gave birth to her first child, a son. She wrapped him snugly in strips of cloth and laid him in a manger, because there was no room for them in the village inn.

### The Shepherds and Angels

8That night some shepherds were in the fields outside the village, guarding their flocks of sheep. 9Suddenly, an angel of the Lord appeared among them, and the radiance of the Lord's glory surrounded them. They were terribly frightened, 10but the angel reassured them. "Don't be afraid!" he said. "I bring you good news of great joy for everyone! 11The Savior—yes, the Messiah, the Lord—has been born tonight in Bethlehem, the city of David! 12And this is how you will recognize him: You will find a baby lying in a manger, wrapped snugly in strips of cloth!"

13Suddenly, the angel was joined by a vast host of others—the armies of heaven—praising God:

14 "Glory to God in the highest heaven,
    and peace on earth to all whom God
       favors.*"

15When the angels had returned to heaven, the shepherds said to each other, " Come on, let's go to Bethlehem! Let's see this wonderful thing that has happened, which the Lord has told us about."

16They ran to the village and found Mary and Joseph. And there was the baby, lying in the manger. 17Then the shepherds told everyone what had happened and what the angel had said to them about this child. 18All who heard the shepherds'

story were astonished, 19but Mary quietly treasured these things in her heart and thought about them often. 20The shepherds went back to their fields and flocks, glorifying and praising God for what the angels had told them, and because they had seen the child, just as the angel had said.

### Jesus Is Presented in the Temple

21Eight days later, when the baby was circumcised, he was named Jesus, the name given him by the angel even before he was conceived.

22Then it was time for the purification offering, as required by the law of Moses after the birth of a child; so his parents took him to Jerusalem to present him to the Lord. 23The law of the Lord says, "If a woman's first child is a boy, he must be dedicated to the Lord."* 24So they offered a sacrifice according to what was required in the law of the Lord—"either a pair of turtledoves or two young pigeons."*

### The Prophecy of Simeon

25Now there was a man named Simeon who lived in Jerusalem. He was a righteous man and very devout. He was filled with the Holy Spirit, and he eagerly expected the Messiah to come and rescue Israel. 26The Holy Spirit had revealed to him that he would not die until he had seen the Lord's Messiah. 27That day the Spirit led him to the Temple. So when Mary and Joseph came to present the baby Jesus to the Lord as the law required, 28Simeon was there. He took the child in his arms and praised God, saying,

29 "Lord, now I can die in peace!
     As you promised me,
30 I have seen the Savior
31    you have given to all people.
32 He is a light to reveal God to the nations,
     and he is the glory of your people Israel!"

33Joseph and Mary were amazed at what was being said about Jesus. 34Then Simeon blessed them, and he said to Mary, "This child will be rejected by many in Israel, and it will be their undoing. But he will be the greatest joy to many others. 35Thus, the deepest thoughts of many hearts will be revealed. And a sword will pierce your very soul."

### The Prophecy of Anna

36Anna, a prophet, was also there in the Temple. She was the daughter of Phanuel, of the tribe of Asher, and was very old. She was a widow, for her husband had died when they had been married only seven years. 37She was now eighty-four years old. She never left the Temple but stayed there day and night, worshiping God with fasting and prayer. 38She came along just as Simeon was talking with Mary and Joseph, and she began praising God. She talked about Jesus to everyone who had been waiting for the promised King to come and deliver Jerusalem.

39When Jesus' parents had fulfilled all the requirements of the law of the Lord, they returned home to Nazareth in Galilee. 40There the child grew up healthy and strong. He was filled with wisdom beyond his years, and God placed his special favor upon him.

## Jesus Speaks with the Teachers

41Every year Jesus' parents went to Jerusalem for the Passover festival. 42When Jesus was twelve years old, they attended the festival as usual. 43After the celebration was over, they started home to Nazareth, but Jesus stayed behind in Jerusalem. His parents didn't miss him at first, 44because they assumed he was with friends among the other travelers. But when he didn't show up that evening, they started to look for him among their relatives and friends. 45When they couldn't find him, they went back to Jerusalem to search for him there. 46Three days later they finally discovered him. He was in the Temple, sitting among the religious teachers, discussing deep questions with them. 47And all who heard him were amazed at his understanding and his answers.

48His parents didn't know what to think. "Son!" his mother said to him. "Why have you done this to us? Your father and I have been frantic, searching for you everywhere."

49"But why did you need to search?" he asked. "You should have known that I would be in my Father's house."* 50But they didn't understand what he meant.

51Then he returned to Nazareth with them and was obedient to them; and his mother stored all these things in her heart. 52So Jesus grew both in height and in wisdom, and he was loved by God and by all who knew him.

CHAPTER **3**
## John the Baptist Prepares the Way

It was now the fifteenth year of the reign of Tiberius, the Roman emperor. Pilate was gover-

nor over Judea; Herod Antipas was ruler* over Galilee; his brother Philip was ruler* over Iturea and Traconitis; Lysanias was ruler over Abilene. 2Annas and Caiaphas were the high priests. At this time a message from God came to John son of Zechariah, who was living out in the wilderness. 3Then John went from place to place on both sides of the Jordan River, preaching that people should be baptized to show that they had turned from their sins and turned to God to be forgiven.* 4Isaiah had spoken of John when he said,

"He is a voice shouting in the wilderness:
'Prepare a pathway for the Lord's coming!
    Make a straight road for him!
5  Fill in the valleys,
    and level the mountains and hills!
Straighten the curves,
    and smooth out the rough places!
6  And then all people will see
    the salvation sent from God.'"*

7Here is a sample of John's preaching to the crowds that came for baptism: "You brood of snakes! Who warned you to flee God's coming judgment? 8Prove by the way you live that you have really turned from your sins and turned to God. Don't just say, 'We're safe—we're the descendants of Abraham.' That proves nothing. God can change these stones here into children of Abraham. 9Even now the ax of God's judgment is poised, ready to sever your roots. Yes, every tree that does not produce good fruit will be chopped down and thrown into the fire."

10The crowd asked, "What should we do?"

11John replied, "If you have two coats, give one to the poor. If you have food, share it with those who are hungry."

12Even corrupt tax collectors came to be baptized and asked, "Teacher, what should we do?"

13"Show your honesty," he replied. "Make sure you collect no more taxes than the Roman government requires you to."

14"What should we do?" asked some soldiers.

John replied, "Don't extort money, and don't accuse people of things you know they didn't do. And be content with your pay."

15Everyone was expecting the Messiah to come soon, and they were eager to know whether John might be the Messiah. 16John answered their questions by saying, "I baptize with* water; but someone is coming soon who is greater than I am—so much greater that I am

2:49 Or "Didn't you realize that I should be involved with my Father's affairs?"    3:1a Greek Herod was tetrarch. Herod Antipas was a son of King Herod.
3:1b Greek tetrarch; also in 3:19.    3:3 Greek preaching a baptism of repentance for the forgiveness of sins.    3:4-6 Isa 40:3-5.    3:16a Or in.

## Jesus Had a Specific Mission to Accomplish Read LUKE 4:16-21

Jesus quoted from Isaiah 61:1-2 to describe the purpose of his ministry. This portion of Scripture describes five goals of Jesus' personal ministry on earth:

**1. Preach the Good News to the Poor.** Jesus ministered to people from all walks of life—from the wealthy tax collectors, to the "blue collar" fishermen, to the beggars on the street. It was not people's financial status that he was concerned with. Rather, he looked beyond people's outward need to their inward need. He saw the poverty of their soul. And to those who will listen, Jesus offers the good news of the gospel.

**2. Heal the Brokenhearted.** When your heart is broken, you may feel as though no one understands or cares. Yet Jesus understands. He knows what it is like to be abandoned by friends. He has experienced what it is like to be let down. He understands the sting of death. For that reason, he wants to heal your broken heart.

**3. Bring Deliverance to the Captives.** The Bible teaches that before we give our lives to God, we are held captive by sin. If you find yourself a slave to some vice or sin that you just can't overcome, Jesus wants to release you from that spiritual bondage. Just admit your sinful condition and turn from it, and ask God to give you a new heart. Then begin to yield yourself to the help and power of the Holy Spirit, and you will know true freedom.

**4. Give Sight to the Blind.** The Bible also teaches that before we give our lives to Jesus Christ, we are spiritually blind: "Satan, the god of this evil world, has blinded the minds of those who don't believe, so they are unable to see the glorious light of the Good News that is shining upon them. They don't understand the message we preach about the glory of Christ, who is the exact likeness of God" (2 Corinthians 4:4). Jesus wants to open our eyes so that we can understand and respond to the gospel message.

**5. Bring Liberty to the Oppressed.** The word *downtrodden* can also be translated "those who are crushed with life." Jesus understands your worries and hurts, and he wants to lift those burdens from your shoulders.

CORNER STONES

---

not even worthy to be his slave.* He will baptize you with the Holy Spirit and with fire.* [17]He is ready to separate the chaff from the grain with his winnowing fork. Then he will clean up the threshing area, storing the grain in his barn but burning the chaff with never-ending fire." [18]John used many such warnings as he announced the Good News to the people.

[19]John also publicly criticized Herod Antipas, ruler of Galilee, for marrying Herodias, his brother's wife, and for many other wrongs he had done. [20]So Herod put John in prison, adding this sin to his many others.

### The Baptism of Jesus

[21]One day when the crowds were being baptized, Jesus himself was baptized. As he was praying, the heavens opened, [22]and the Holy Spirit descended on him in the form of a dove. And a voice from heaven said, "You are my beloved Son, and I am fully pleased with you.*"

### The Record of Jesus' Ancestors

[23]Jesus was about thirty years old when he began his public ministry.

Jesus was known as the son of Joseph.
Joseph was the son of Heli.
[24] Heli was the son of Matthat.
Matthat was the son of Levi.
Levi was the son of Melki.
Melki was the son of Jannai.
Jannai was the son of Joseph.
[25] Joseph was the son of Mattathias.

**3:16b** Greek *to untie his sandals.*   **3:16c** Or *in the Holy Spirit and in fire.*   **3:22** Some manuscripts read *and today I have become your Father.*

Mattathias was the son of Amos.
Amos was the son of Nahum.
Nahum was the son of Esli.
Esli was the son of Naggai.
26 Naggai was the son of Maath.
Maath was the son of Mattathias.
Mattathias was the son of Semein.
Semein was the son of Josech.
Josech was the son of Joda.
27 Joda was the son of Joanan.
Joanan was the son of Rhesa.
Rhesa was the son of Zerubbabel.
Zerubbabel was the son of Shealtiel.
Shealtiel was the son of Neri.
28 Neri was the son of Melki.
Melki was the son of Addi.
Addi was the son of Cosam.
Cosam was the son of Elmadam.
Elmadam was the son of Er.
29 Er was the son of Joshua.
Joshua was the son of Eliezer.
Eliezer was the son of Jorim.
Jorim was the son of Matthat.
Matthat was the son of Levi.
30 Levi was the son of Simeon.
Simeon was the son of Judah.
Judah was the son of Joseph.
Joseph was the son of Jonam.
Jonam was the son of Eliakim.
31 Eliakim was the son of Melea.
Melea was the son of Menna.
Menna was the son of Mattatha.
Mattatha was the son of Nathan.
Nathan was the son of David.
32 David was the son of Jesse.
Jesse was the son of Obed.
Obed was the son of Boaz.
Boaz was the son of Salmon.*
Salmon was the son of Nahshon.
33 Nahshon was the son of Amminadab.
Amminadab was the son of Admin.
Admin was the son of Arni.*
Arni was the son of Hezron.
Hezron was the son of Perez.
Perez was the son of Judah.
34 Judah was the son of Jacob.
Jacob was the son of Isaac.
Isaac was the son of Abraham.
Abraham was the son of Terah.
Terah was the son of Nahor.
35 Nahor was the son of Serug.
Serug was the son of Reu.
Reu was the son of Peleg.

Peleg was the son of Eber.
Eber was the son of Shelah.
36 Shelah was the son of Cainan.
Cainan was the son of Arphaxad.
Arphaxad was the son of Shem.
Shem was the son of Noah.
Noah was the son of Lamech.
37 Lamech was the son of Methuselah.
Methuselah was the son of Enoch.
Enoch was the son of Jared.
Jared was the son of Mahalalel.
Mahalalel was the son of Kenan.
38 Kenan was the son of Enosh.*
Enosh was the son of Seth.
Seth was the son of Adam.
Adam was the son of God.

CHAPTER **4**
*The Temptation of Jesus*
Then Jesus, full of the Holy Spirit, left the Jordan River. He was led by the Spirit to go out into the wilderness, 2where the Devil tempted him for forty days. He ate nothing all that time and was very hungry.

3Then the Devil said to him, "If you are the Son of God, change this stone into a loaf of bread."

4But Jesus told him, "No! The Scriptures say, 'People need more than bread for their life.'* "

5Then the Devil took him up and revealed to him all the kingdoms of the world in a moment of time. 6The Devil told him, "I will give you the glory of these kingdoms and authority over them—because they are mine to give to anyone I please. 7I will give it all to you if you will bow down and worship me."

8Jesus replied, "The Scriptures say,

'You must worship the Lord your God;
    serve only him.'* "

9Then the Devil took him to Jerusalem, to the highest point of the Temple, and said, "If you are the Son of God, jump off! 10For the Scriptures say,

'He orders his angels to protect and guard you.
11 And they will hold you with their hands
    to keep you from striking your foot on a
        stone.'* "

12Jesus responded, "The Scriptures also say, 'Do not test the Lord your God.'* "
13When the Devil had finished tempting Jesus, he left him until the next opportunity came.

3:32 Greek *Sala;* see Ruth 4:22.   3:33 *Arni* is the same person as Ram; see 1 Chr 2:9-10.   3:38 Greek *Enos;* see Gen 5:6.   4:4 Deut 8:3.
4:8 Deut 6:13.   4:10-11 Ps 91:11-12.   4:12 Deut 6:16.

## Jesus Rejected at Nazareth

14Then Jesus returned to Galilee, filled with the Holy Spirit's power. Soon he became well known throughout the surrounding country. 15He taught in their synagogues and was praised by everyone.

16When he came to the village of Nazareth, his boyhood home, he went as usual to the synagogue on the Sabbath and stood up to read the Scriptures. 17The scroll containing the messages of Isaiah the prophet was handed to him, and he unrolled the scroll to the place where it says:

18 "The Spirit of the Lord is upon me,
    for he has appointed me to preach Good
      News to the poor.
He has sent me to proclaim
    that captives will be released,
    that the blind will see,
    that the downtrodden will be freed from
      their oppressors,
19    and that the time of the Lord's favor has
      come.*"

20He rolled up the scroll, handed it back to the attendant, and sat down. Everyone in the synagogue stared at him intently. 21Then he said, "This Scripture has come true today before your very eyes!"

22All who were there spoke well of him and were amazed by the gracious words that fell from his lips. "How can this be?" they asked. "Isn't this Joseph's son?"

23Then he said, "Probably you will quote me that proverb, 'Physician, heal yourself'—meaning, 'Why don't you do miracles here in your hometown like those you did in Capernaum?' 24But the truth is, no prophet is accepted in his own hometown.

25"Certainly there were many widows in Israel who needed help in Elijah's time, when there was no rain for three and a half years and hunger stalked the land. 26Yet Elijah was not sent to any of them. He was sent instead to a widow of Zarephath—a foreigner in the land of Sidon. 27Or think of the prophet Elisha, who healed Naaman, a Syrian, rather than the many lepers in Israel who needed help."

28When they heard this, the people in the synagogue were furious. 29Jumping up, they mobbed him and took him to the edge of the hill on which the city was built. They intended to push him over the cliff, 30but he slipped away through the crowd and left them.

## Jesus Casts Out a Demon

31Then Jesus went to Capernaum, a town in Galilee, and taught there in the synagogue every Sabbath day. 32There, too, the people were amazed at the things he said, because he spoke with authority.

33Once when he was in the synagogue, a man possessed by a demon began shouting at Jesus, 34"Go away! Why are you bothering us, Jesus of Nazareth? Have you come to destroy us? I know who you are—the Holy One sent from God."

35Jesus cut him short. "Be silent!" he told the demon. "Come out of the man!" The demon threw the man to the floor as the crowd watched; then it left him without hurting him further.

36Amazed, the people exclaimed, "What authority and power this man's words possess! Even evil spirits obey him and flee at his command!" 37The story of what he had done spread like wildfire throughout the whole region.

## Jesus Heals Many People

38After leaving the synagogue that day, Jesus went to Simon's home, where he found Simon's mother-in-law very sick with a high fever. "Please heal her," everyone begged. 39Standing at her bedside, he spoke to the fever, rebuking it, and immediately her temperature returned to normal. She got up at once and prepared a meal for them.

40As the sun went down that evening, people throughout the village brought sick family members to Jesus. No matter what their diseases were, the touch of his hand healed every one. 41Some were possessed by demons; and the demons came out at his command, shouting, "You are the Son of God." But because they knew he was the Messiah, he stopped them and told them to be silent.

## Jesus Continues to Preach

42Early the next morning Jesus went out into the wilderness. The crowds searched everywhere for him, and when they finally found him, they begged him not to leave them. 43But he replied, "I must preach the Good News of the Kingdom of God in other places, too, because that is why I was sent." 44So he continued to travel around, preaching in synagogues throughout Judea.*

## CHAPTER 5
### The First Disciples

One day as Jesus was preaching on the shore of the Sea of Galilee,* great crowds pressed in on him to listen to the word of God. 2He noticed two empty

---

4:18-19 Or *and to proclaim the acceptable year of the Lord.* Isa 61:1-2.   4:44 Some manuscripts read *Galilee.*   5:1 Greek *Lake Gennesaret,* another name for the Sea of Galilee.

boats at the water's edge, for the fishermen had left them and were washing their nets. ³Stepping into one of the boats, Jesus asked Simon,* its owner, to push it out into the water. So he sat in the boat and taught the crowds from there.

⁴When he had finished speaking, he said to Simon, "Now go out where it is deeper and let down your nets, and you will catch many fish."

⁵"Master," Simon replied, "we worked hard all last night and didn't catch a thing. But if you say so, we'll try again." ⁶And this time their nets were so full they began to tear! ⁷A shout for help brought their partners in the other boat, and soon both boats were filled with fish and on the verge of sinking.

⁸When Simon Peter realized what had happened, he fell to his knees before Jesus and said, "Oh, Lord, please leave me—I'm too much of a sinner to be around you." ⁹For he was awestruck by the size of their catch, as were the others with him. ¹⁰His partners, James and John, the sons of Zebedee, were also amazed.

Jesus replied to Simon, "Don't be afraid! From now on you'll be fishing for people!" ¹¹And as soon as they landed, they left everything and followed Jesus.

## Jesus Heals a Man with Leprosy

¹²In one of the villages, Jesus met a man with an advanced case of leprosy. When the man saw Jesus, he fell to the ground, face down in the dust, begging to be healed. "Lord," he said, "if you want to, you can make me well again."

¹³Jesus reached out and touched the man. "I want to," he said. "Be healed!" And instantly the leprosy disappeared. ¹⁴Then Jesus instructed him not to tell anyone what had happened. He said, "Go right to the priest and let him examine you. Take along the offering required in the law of Moses for those who have been healed of leprosy, so everyone will have proof of your healing." ¹⁵Yet despite Jesus' instructions, the report of his power spread even faster, and vast crowds came to hear him preach and to be healed of their diseases. ¹⁶But Jesus often withdrew to the wilderness for prayer.

## Jesus Heals a Paralyzed Man

¹⁷One day while Jesus was teaching, some Pharisees and teachers of religious law were sitting nearby. (It seemed that these men showed up from every village in all Galilee and Judea, as well as from Jerusalem.) And the Lord's healing power

was strongly with Jesus. ¹⁸Some men came carrying a paralyzed man on a sleeping mat. They tried to push through the crowd to Jesus, ¹⁹but they couldn't reach him. So they went up to the roof, took off some tiles, and lowered the sick man down into the crowd, still on his mat, right in front of Jesus. ²⁰Seeing their faith, Jesus said to the man, "Son, your sins are forgiven."

²¹"Who does this man think he is?" the Pharisees and teachers of religious law said to each other. "This is blasphemy! Who but God can forgive sins?"

²²Jesus knew what they were thinking, so he asked them, "Why do you think this is blasphemy? ²³Is it easier to say, 'Your sins are forgiven' or 'Get up and walk'? ²⁴I will prove that I, the Son of Man, have the authority on earth to forgive sins." Then Jesus turned to the paralyzed man and said, "Stand up, take your mat, and go on home, because you are healed!"

²⁵And immediately, as everyone watched, the man jumped to his feet, picked up his mat, and went home praising God. ²⁶Everyone was gripped with great wonder and awe. And they praised God, saying over and over again, "We have seen amazing things today."

## Jesus Calls Levi (Matthew)

²⁷Later, as Jesus left the town, he saw a tax-collector named Levi sitting at his tax-collection booth. "Come, be my disciple!" Jesus said to him. ²⁸So Levi got up, left everything, and followed him.

²⁹Soon Levi held a banquet in his home with Jesus as the guest of honor. Many of Levi's fellow tax collectors and other guests were there. ³⁰But the Pharisees and their teachers of religious law complained bitterly to Jesus' disciples, "Why do you eat and drink with such scum*?"

³¹Jesus answered them, "Healthy people don't need a doctor—sick people do. ³²I have come to call sinners to turn from their sins, not to spend my time with those who think they are already good enough."

## A Discussion about Fasting

³³The religious leaders complained that Jesus' disciples were feasting instead of fasting. "John the Baptist's disciples always fast and pray," they declared, "and so do the disciples of the Pharisees. Why are yours always feasting?"

³⁴Jesus asked, "Do wedding guests fast while celebrating with the groom? ³⁵Someday he will be taken away from them, and then they will fast."

5:3 *Simon* is called *Peter* in 6:14 and thereafter.　5:30 Greek *with tax collectors and sinners.*

36Then Jesus gave them this illustration: "No one tears a piece of cloth from a new garment and uses it to patch an old garment. For then the new garment would be torn, and the patch wouldn't even match the old garment. 37And no one puts new wine into old wineskins. The new wine would burst the old skins, spilling the wine and ruining the skins. 38New wine must be put into new wineskins. 39But no one who drinks the old wine seems to want the fresh and the new. 'The old is better,' they say."

## CHAPTER 6
### A Discussion about the Sabbath

One Sabbath day as Jesus was walking through some grainfields, his disciples broke off heads of wheat, rubbed off the husks in their hands, and ate the grains. 2But some Pharisees said, "You shouldn't be doing that! It's against the law to work by harvesting grain on the Sabbath."

3Jesus replied, "Haven't you ever read in the Scriptures what King David did when he and his companions were hungry? 4He went into the house of God, ate the special bread reserved for the priests alone, and then gave some to his friends. That was breaking the law, too." 5And Jesus added, "I, the Son of Man, am master even of the Sabbath."

### Jesus Heals on the Sabbath

6On another Sabbath day, a man with a deformed right hand was in the synagogue while Jesus was teaching. 7The teachers of religious law and the Pharisees watched closely to see whether Jesus would heal the man on the Sabbath, because they were eager to find some legal charge to bring against him. 8But Jesus knew their thoughts. He said to the man with the deformed hand, "Come and stand here where everyone can see." So the man came forward. 9Then Jesus said to his critics, "I have a question for you. Is it legal to do good deeds on the Sabbath, or is it a day for doing harm? Is this a day to save life or to destroy it?" 10He looked around at them one by one and then said to the man, "Reach out your hand." The man reached out his hand, and it became normal again! 11At this, the enemies of Jesus were wild with rage and began to discuss what to do with him.

### Jesus Chooses the Twelve Apostles

12One day soon afterward Jesus went to a mountain to pray, and he prayed to God all night. 13At daybreak he called together all of his disciples and chose twelve of them to be apostles. Here are their names:

14 Simon (he also called him Peter),
    Andrew (Peter's brother),
    James,
    John,
    Philip,
    Bartholomew,
15 Matthew,
    Thomas,
    James (son of Alphaeus),
    Simon (the Zealot),
16 Judas (son of James),
    Judas Iscariot (who later betrayed him).

### Crowds Follow Jesus

17When they came down the slopes of the mountain, the disciples stood with Jesus on a large, level area, surrounded by many of his followers and by the crowds. There were people from all over Judea and from Jerusalem and from as far north as the seacoasts of Tyre and Sidon. 18They had come to hear him and to be healed, and Jesus cast out many evil spirits. 19Everyone was trying to touch him, because healing power went out from him, and they were all cured.

### The Beatitudes

20Then Jesus turned to his disciples and said,

"God blesses you who are poor,
    for the Kingdom of God is given to you.
21 God blesses you who are hungry now,
    for you will be satisfied.
God blesses you who weep now,
    for the time will come when you will
        laugh with joy.
22 God blesses you who are hated and
        excluded and mocked and cursed
    because you are identified with me, the
        Son of Man.

23"When that happens, rejoice! Yes, leap for joy! For a great reward awaits you in heaven. And remember, the ancient prophets were also treated that way by your ancestors.

### Sorrows Foretold

24 "What sorrows await you who are rich,
    for you have your only happiness now.
25 What sorrows await you who are satisfied
        and prosperous now,
    for a time of awful hunger is before you.

What sorrows await you who laugh
carelessly,
for your laughing will turn to mourning
and sorrow.
26 What sorrows await you who are praised by
the crowds,
for their ancestors also praised false
prophets.

## Love for Enemies

27 "But if you are willing to listen, I say, love your enemies. Do good to those who hate you. 28 Pray for the happiness of those who curse you. Pray for those who hurt you. 29 If someone slaps you on one cheek, turn the other cheek. If someone demands your coat, offer your shirt also. 30 Give what you have to anyone who asks you for it; and when things are taken away from you, don't try to get them back. 31 Do for others as you would like them to do for you.

32 "Do you think you deserve credit merely for loving those who love you? Even the sinners do that! 33 And if you do good only to those who do good to you, is that so wonderful? Even sinners do that much! 34 And if you lend money only to those who can repay you, what good is that? Even sinners will lend to their own kind for a full return.

35 "Love your enemies! Do good to them! Lend to them! And don't be concerned that they might not repay. Then your reward from heaven will be very great, and you will truly be acting as children of the Most High, for he is kind to the unthankful and to those who are wicked. 36 You must be compassionate, just as your Father is compassionate.

## Don't Condemn Others

37 "Stop judging others, and you will not be judged. Stop criticizing others, or it will all come back on you. If you forgive others, you will be forgiven. 38 If you give, you will receive. Your gift will return to you in full measure, pressed down, shaken together to make room for more, and running over. Whatever measure you use in giving—large or small—it will be used to measure what is given back to you."

39 Then Jesus gave the following illustration: "What good is it for one blind person to lead another? The first one will fall into a ditch and pull the other down also. 40 A student is not greater than the teacher. But the student who works hard will become like the teacher.

41 "And why worry about a speck in your friend's eye* when you have a log in your own?

42 How can you think of saying, 'Friend,* let me help you get rid of that speck in your eye,' when you can't see past the log in your own eye? Hypocrite! First get rid of the log from your own eye; then perhaps you will see well enough to deal with the speck in your friend's eye.

## The Tree and Its Fruit

43 "A good tree can't produce bad fruit, and a bad tree can't produce good fruit. 44 A tree is identified by the kind of fruit it produces. Figs never grow on thornbushes or grapes on bramble

**6:41** Greek *your brother's eye;* also in 6:42. **6:42** Greek *Brother.*

---

## Trials Test Our Foundation
Read LUKE 6:48-49

From all outward appearances, these homes probably looked alike. They may have even had similar floor plans. The only thing that set them apart was their foundation. This became apparent when the storm hit. In the same way, when the storms of life hit us, the true foundation of our lives will be revealed. Upon which foundation have you built your life?

**The Faulty (or Nonexistent) Foundation.** The person who builds upon this foundation is known as a "hearer." This individual may be quick to read, listen, or talk about what Jesus has to say in his Word but will fail to apply those teachings to his or her own life. When the storms of life come—and they will—this person will be spiritually weakened and will likely "throw in the towel" on his or her faith because he or she does not have a good foothold.

**The Rock Solid Foundation.** The person who builds upon this foundation is known as a "doer." This individual not only listens to Jesus' teachings, but follows them in his or her day-to-day life. Such a person will be able to withstand even the most devastating tempest, because he or she is grounded in the teachings of the Lord.

If you find yourself on the faulty foundation, you still have time to remodel. But you are the only architect who can make that change.

bushes. 45A good person produces good deeds from a good heart, and an evil person produces evil deeds from an evil heart. Whatever is in your heart determines what you say.

### Building on a Solid Foundation

46"So why do you call me 'Lord,' when you won't obey me? 47I will show you what it's like when someone comes to me, listens to my teaching, and then obeys me. 48It is like a person who builds a house on a strong foundation laid upon the underlying rock. When the floodwaters rise and break against the house, it stands firm because it is well built. 49But anyone who listens and doesn't obey is like a person who builds a house without a foundation. When the floods sweep down against that house, it will crumble into a heap of ruins."

CHAPTER **7**

### Faith of the Roman Officer

When Jesus had finished saying all this, he went back to Capernaum. 2Now the highly valued slave of a Roman officer was sick and near death. 3When the officer heard about Jesus, he sent some respected Jewish leaders to ask him to come and heal his slave. 4So they earnestly begged Jesus to come with them and help the man. "If anyone deserves your help, it is he," they said, 5"for he loves the Jews and even built a synagogue for us."

6So Jesus went with them. But just before they arrived at the house, the officer sent some friends to say, "Lord, don't trouble yourself by coming to my home, for I am not worthy of such an honor. 7I am not even worthy to come and meet you. Just say the word from where you are, and my servant will be healed. 8I know because I am under the authority of my superior officers, and I have authority over my soldiers. I only need to say, 'Go,' and they go, or 'Come,' and they come. And if I say to my slaves, 'Do this or that,' they do it."

9When Jesus heard this, he was amazed. Turning to the crowd, he said, "I tell you, I haven't seen faith like this in all the land of Israel!" 10And when the officer's friends returned to his house, they found the slave completely healed.

### Jesus Raises a Widow's Son

11Soon afterward Jesus went with his disciples to the village of Nain, with a great crowd following

him. 12A funeral procession was coming out as he approached the village gate. The boy who had died was the only son of a widow, and many mourners from the village were with her. 13When the Lord saw her, his heart overflowed with compassion. "Don't cry!" he said. 14Then he walked over to the coffin and touched it, and the bearers stopped. "Young man," he said, "get up." 15Then the dead boy sat up and began to talk to those around him! And Jesus gave him back to his mother.

16Great fear swept the crowd, and they praised God, saying, "A mighty prophet has risen among us," and "We have seen the hand of God at work today." 17The report of what Jesus had done that day spread all over Judea and even out across its borders.

### Jesus and John the Baptist

18The disciples of John the Baptist told John about everything Jesus was doing. So John called for two of his disciples, 19and he sent them to the Lord to ask him, "Are you the Messiah we've been expecting, or should we keep looking for someone else?"

20John's two disciples found Jesus and said to him, "John the Baptist sent us to ask, 'Are you the Messiah we've been expecting, or should we keep looking for someone else?'"

21At that very time, he cured many people of their various diseases, and he cast out evil spirits and restored sight to the blind. 22Then he told John's disciples, "Go back to John and tell him what you have seen and heard—the blind see, the lame walk, the lepers are cured, the deaf hear, the dead are raised to life, and the Good News is being preached to the poor. 23And tell him, 'God blesses those who are not offended by me.*'"

24After they left, Jesus talked to the crowd about John. "Who is this man in the wilderness that you went out to see? Did you find him weak as a reed, moved by every breath of wind? 25Or were you expecting to see a man dressed in expensive clothes? No, people who wear beautiful clothes and live in luxury are found in palaces, not in the wilderness. 26Were you looking for a prophet? Yes, and he is more than a prophet. 27John is the man to whom the Scriptures refer when they say,

'Look, I am sending my messenger before
    you,
    and he will prepare your way before
        you.'*

7:23 Or *who don't fall away because of me.*    7:27 Mal 3:1.

page 77 ▶ ▶ ▶ LUKE 8

28I tell you, of all who have ever lived, none is greater than John. Yet even the most insignificant person in the Kingdom of God is greater than he is!"

29When they heard this, all the people, including the unjust tax collectors, agreed that God's plan was right,* for they had been baptized by John. 30But the Pharisees and experts in religious law had rejected God's plan for them, for they had refused John's baptism.

31"How shall I describe this generation?" Jesus asked. "With what will I compare them? 32They are like a group of children playing a game in the public square. They complain to their friends, 'We played wedding songs, and you weren't happy, so we played funeral songs, but you weren't sad.' 33For John the Baptist didn't drink wine and he often fasted, and you say, 'He's demon possessed.' 34And I, the Son of Man, feast and drink, and you say, 'He's a glutton and a drunkard, and a friend of the worst sort of sinners!' 35But wisdom is shown to be right by the lives of those who follow it.*"

## Jesus Anointed by a Sinful Woman

36One of the Pharisees asked Jesus to come to his home for a meal, so Jesus accepted the invitation and sat down to eat. 37A certain immoral woman heard he was there and brought a beautiful jar* filled with expensive perfume. 38Then she knelt behind him at his feet, weeping. Her tears fell on his feet, and she wiped them off with her hair. Then she kept kissing his feet and putting perfume on them.

39When the Pharisee who was the host saw what was happening and who the woman was, he said to himself, "This proves that Jesus is no prophet. If God had really sent him, he would know what kind of woman is touching him. She's a sinner!"

40Then Jesus spoke up and answered his thoughts. "Simon," he said to the Pharisee, "I have something to say to you."

"All right, Teacher," Simon replied, "go ahead."

41Then Jesus told him this story: "A man loaned money to two people—five hundred pieces of silver* to one and fifty pieces to the other. 42But neither of them could repay him, so he kindly forgave them both, canceling their debts. Who do you suppose loved him more after that?"

43Simon answered, "I suppose the one for whom he canceled the larger debt."

"That's right," Jesus said. 44Then he turned to the woman and said to Simon, "Look at this woman kneeling here. When I entered your home, you didn't offer me water to wash the dust from my feet, but she has washed them with her tears and wiped them with her hair. 45You didn't give me a kiss of greeting, but she has kissed my feet again and again from the time I first came in. 46You neglected the courtesy of olive oil to anoint my head, but she has anointed my feet with rare perfume. 47I tell you, her sins—and they are many—have been forgiven, so she has shown me much love. But a person who is forgiven little shows only little love." 48Then Jesus said to the woman, "Your sins are forgiven."

49The men at the table said among themselves, "Who does this man think he is, going around forgiving sins?"

50And Jesus said to the woman, "Your faith has saved you; go in peace."

CHAPTER **8**

## Women Who Followed Jesus

Not long afterward Jesus began a tour of the nearby cities and villages to announce the Good News concerning the Kingdom of God. He took his twelve disciples with him, 2along with some women he had healed and from whom he had cast out evil spirits. Among them were Mary Magdalene, from whom he had cast out seven demons; 3Joanna, the wife of Chuza, Herod's business manager; Susanna; and many others who were contributing from their own resources to support Jesus and his disciples.

## Story of the Farmer Scattering Seed

4One day Jesus told this story to a large crowd that had gathered from many towns to hear him: 5"A farmer went out to plant some seed. As he scattered it across his field, some seed fell on a footpath, where it was stepped on, and the birds came and ate it. 6Other seed fell on shallow soil with underlying rock. This seed began to grow, but soon it withered and died for lack of moisture. 7Other seed fell among thorns that shot up and choked out the tender blades. 8Still other seed fell on fertile soil. This seed grew and produced a crop one hundred times as much as had been planted." When he had said this, he called out, "Anyone who is willing to hear should listen and understand!"

9His disciples asked him what the story

7:29 Or praised God.   7:35 Or But wisdom is justified by all her children.   7:37 Greek an alabaster jar.   7:41 Greek 500 denarii. A denarius was the equivalent of a full day's wage.

## Perseverance Produces Results Read LUKE 8:15

In verses 4 through 8 of this chapter, Jesus tells the well-known parable of the sower to illustrate four different reactions to his message. The verses following that parable explain what those responses are.

The seed that falls on the roadside represents those who hear the gospel, but who do not allow it to penetrate their hearts and minds (verse 12). The seed that lands on the rocky soil depicts those who hear God's Word and initially receive it with joy, but their "commitment" is shown to be shallow and superficial through time (verse 13). The seed that lands among the thorns portrays those who appear to believe, but who let the cares of this life slowly choke out any growth (verse 14). The seed that falls on the fertile soil is the seed that actually takes root to produce spiritual fruit.

What is the difference between this group of individuals and the rest? The key to their success can be broken down into three steps: (1) They *listen* to God's Word; (2) they *obey* God's Word; and (3) they *persevere* to "produce a huge harvest."

Describing their perseverance in the faith, Jesus uses the Greek word *hupomone*, which speaks of "a patient enduring." It is this type of perseverance that produces spiritual fruit in the form of new believers.

By letting God's Word take root in your heart and life, you will not only grow stronger and be able to withstand the storms of life, but your life will help to draw many others to the Lord Jesus Christ.

CORNER STONES

---

meant. [10]He replied, "You have been permitted to understand the secrets of the Kingdom of God. But I am using these stories to conceal everything about it from outsiders, so that the Scriptures might be fulfilled:

'They see what I do,
    but they don't really see;
they hear what I say,
    but they don't understand.'*

[11]"This is the meaning of the story: The seed is God's message. [12]The seed that fell on the hard path represents those who hear the message, but then the Devil comes and steals it away and prevents them from believing and being saved. [13]The rocky soil represents those who hear the message with joy. But like young plants in such soil, their roots don't go very deep. They believe for a while, but they wilt when the hot winds of testing blow. [14]The thorny ground represents those who hear and accept the message, but all too quickly the message is crowded out by the cares and riches and pleasures of this life. And so they never grow into maturity. [15]But the good soil represents honest, good-hearted people who hear God's message, cling to it, and steadily produce a huge harvest.

8:10 Isa 6:9.

### Illustration of the Lamp

[16]"No one would light a lamp and then cover it up or put it under a bed. No, lamps are mounted in the open, where they can be seen by those entering the house. [17]For everything that is hidden or secret will eventually be brought to light and made plain to all. [18]So be sure to pay attention to what you hear. To those who are open to my teaching, more understanding will be given. But to those who are not listening, even what they think they have will be taken away from them."

### The True Family of Jesus

[19]Once when Jesus' mother and brothers came to see him, they couldn't get to him because of the crowds. [20]Someone told Jesus, "Your mother and your brothers are outside, and they want to see you."

[21]Jesus replied, "My mother and my brothers are all those who hear the message of God and obey it."

### Jesus Calms the Storm

[22]One day Jesus said to his disciples, "Let's cross over to the other side of the lake." So they got into a boat and started out. [23]On the way across, Jesus lay down for a nap, and while he was

sleeping the wind began to rise. A fierce storm developed that threatened to swamp them, and they were in real danger.

24The disciples woke him up, shouting, "Master, Master, we're going to drown!"

So Jesus rebuked the wind and the raging waves. The storm stopped and all was calm! 25Then he asked them, "Where is your faith?"

And they were filled with awe and amazement. They said to one another, "Who is this man, that even the winds and waves obey him?"

## Jesus Heals a Demon-Possessed Man

26So they arrived in the land of the Gerasenes,* across the lake from Galilee. 27As Jesus was climbing out of the boat, a man who was possessed by demons came out to meet him. Homeless and naked, he had lived in a cemetery for a long time. 28As soon as he saw Jesus, he shrieked and fell to the ground before him, screaming, "Why are you bothering me, Jesus, Son of the Most High God? Please, I beg you, don't torture me!" 29For Jesus had already commanded the evil spirit to come out of him. This spirit had often taken control of the man. Even when he was shackled with chains, he simply broke them and rushed out into the wilderness, completely under the demon's power.

30"What is your name?" Jesus asked.

"Legion," he replied—for the man was filled with many demons. 31The demons kept begging Jesus not to send them into the Bottomless Pit. 32A large herd of pigs was feeding on the hillside nearby, and the demons pleaded with him to let them enter into the pigs. Jesus gave them permission. 33So the demons came out of the man and entered the pigs, and the whole herd plunged down the steep hillside into the lake, where they drowned.

34When the herdsmen saw it, they fled to the nearby city and the surrounding countryside, spreading the news as they ran. 35A crowd soon gathered around Jesus, for they wanted to see for themselves what had happened. And they saw the man who had been possessed by demons sitting quietly at Jesus' feet, clothed and sane. And the whole crowd was afraid. 36Then those who had seen what happened told the others how the demon-possessed man had been healed. 37And all the people in that region begged Jesus to go away and leave them alone, for a great wave of fear swept over them.

So Jesus returned to the boat and left, crossing back to the other side of the lake. 38The man who had been demon possessed begged to go, too, but Jesus said, 39"No, go back to your family and tell them all the wonderful things God has done for you." So he went all through the city telling about the great thing Jesus had done for him.

## Jesus Heals in Response to Faith

40On the other side of the lake the crowds received Jesus with open arms because they had been waiting for him. 41And now a man named Jairus, a leader of the local synagogue, came and fell down at Jesus' feet, begging him to come home with him. 42His only child was dying, a little girl twelve years old.

As Jesus went with him, he was surrounded by the crowds. 43And there was a woman in the crowd who had had a hemorrhage for twelve years. She had spent everything she had on doctors* and still could find no cure. 44She came up behind Jesus and touched the fringe of his robe. Immediately, the bleeding stopped.

45"Who touched me?" Jesus asked.

Everyone denied it, and Peter said, "Master, this whole crowd is pressing up against you."

46But Jesus told him, "No, someone deliberately touched me, for I felt healing power go out from me." 47When the woman realized that Jesus knew, she began to tremble and fell to her knees before him. The whole crowd heard her explain why she had touched him and that she had been immediately healed. 48"Daughter," he said to her, "your faith has made you well. Go in peace."

49While he was still speaking to her, a messenger arrived from Jairus's home with the message, "Your little girl is dead. There's no use troubling the Teacher now."

50But when Jesus heard what had happened, he said to Jairus, "Don't be afraid. Just trust me, and she will be all right."

51When they arrived at the house, Jesus wouldn't let anyone go in with him except Peter, James, John, and the little girl's father and mother. 52The house was filled with people weeping and wailing, but he said, "Stop the weeping! She isn't dead; she is only asleep."

53But the crowd laughed at him because they all knew she had died. 54Then Jesus took her by the hand and said in a loud voice, "Get up, my child!" 55And at that moment her life returned, and she immediately stood up! Then Jesus told

---

8:26 Some manuscripts read *Gadarenes;* other manuscripts read *Gergesenes.* See Matt 8:28; Mark 5:1.  8:43 Some manuscripts omit *She had spent everything she had on doctors.*

them to give her something to eat. 56Her parents were overwhelmed, but Jesus insisted that they not tell anyone what had happened.

## CHAPTER 9
### Jesus Sends Out the Twelve Apostles

One day Jesus called together his twelve apostles and gave them power and authority to cast out demons and to heal all diseases. 2Then he sent them out to tell everyone about the coming of the Kingdom of God and to heal the sick. 3"Don't even take along a walking stick," he instructed them, "nor a traveler's bag, nor food, nor money. Not even an extra coat. 4When you enter each village, be a guest in only one home. 5If the people of the village won't receive your message when you enter it, shake off its dust from your feet as you leave. It is a sign that you have abandoned that village to its fate."

6So they began their circuit of the villages, preaching the Good News and healing the sick.

### Herod's Confusion

7When reports of Jesus' miracles reached Herod Antipas,* he was worried and puzzled because some were saying, "This is John the Baptist come back to life again." 8Others were saying, "It is Elijah or some other ancient prophet risen from the dead."

9"I beheaded John," Herod said, "so who is this man about whom I hear such strange stories?" And he tried to see him.

### Jesus Feeds Five Thousand

10When the apostles returned, they told Jesus everything they had done. Then he slipped quietly away with them toward the town of Bethsaida. 11But the crowds found out where he was going, and they followed him. And he welcomed them, teaching them about the Kingdom of God and curing those who were ill. 12Late in the afternoon the twelve disciples came to him and said, "Send the crowds away to the nearby villages and farms, so they can find food and lodging for the night. There is nothing to eat here in this deserted place."

13But Jesus said, "You feed them."

"Impossible!" they protested. "We have only five loaves of bread and two fish. Or are you expecting us to go and buy enough food for this whole crowd?" 14For there were about five thousand men there.

"Just tell them to sit down on the ground in groups of about fifty each," Jesus replied. 15So the people all sat down. 16Jesus took the five loaves and two fish, looked up toward heaven, and asked God's blessing on the food. Breaking the loaves into pieces, he kept giving the bread and fish to the disciples to give to the people. 17They all ate as much as they wanted, and they picked up twelve baskets of leftovers!

### Peter's Declaration about Jesus

18One day as Jesus was alone, praying, he came over to his disciples and asked them, "Who do people say I am?"

19"Well," they replied, "some say John the Baptist, some say Elijah, and others say you are one of the other ancient prophets risen from the dead."

20Then he asked them, "Who do you say I am?"

Peter replied, "You are the Messiah sent from God!"

### Jesus Predicts His Death

21Jesus warned them not to tell anyone about this. 22"For I, the Son of Man, must suffer many terrible things," he said. "I will be rejected by the leaders, the leading priests, and the teachers of religious law. I will be killed, but three days later I will be raised from the dead."

23Then he said to the crowd, "If any of you wants to be my follower, you must put aside your selfish ambition, shoulder your cross daily, and follow me. 24If you try to keep your life for yourself, you will lose it. But if you give up your life for me, you will find true life. 25And how do you benefit if you gain the whole world but lose or forfeit your own soul in the process? 26If a person is ashamed of me and my message, I, the Son of Man, will be ashamed of that person when I return in my glory and in the glory of the Father and the holy angels. 27And I assure you that some of you standing here right now will not die before you see the Kingdom of God."

### The Transfiguration

28About eight days later Jesus took Peter, James, and John to a mountain to pray. 29And as he was praying, the appearance of his face changed, and his clothing became dazzling white. 30Then two men, Moses and Elijah, appeared and began talking with Jesus. 31They were glorious to see. And they were speaking of how he was about to fulfill God's plan by dying in Jerusalem. 32Peter and the others were very drowsy and

9:7 Greek *Herod the tetrarch.* He was a son of King Herod and was ruler over one of the four districts in Palestine.

had fallen asleep. Now they woke up and saw Jesus' glory and the two men standing with him. 33As Moses and Elijah were starting to leave, Peter, not even knowing what he was saying, blurted out, "Master, this is wonderful! We will make three shrines*—one for you, one for Moses, and one for Elijah." 34But even as he was saying this, a cloud came over them; and terror gripped them as it covered them.

35Then a voice from the cloud said, "This is my Son, my Chosen One.* Listen to him." 36When the voice died away, Jesus was there alone. They didn't tell anyone what they had seen until long after this happened.

### Jesus Heals a Demon-Possessed Boy

37The next day, after they had come down the mountain, a huge crowd met Jesus. 38A man in the crowd called out to him, "Teacher, look at my boy, who is my only son. 39An evil spirit keeps seizing him, making him scream. It throws him into convulsions so that he foams at the mouth. It is always hitting and injuring him. It hardly ever leaves him alone. 40I begged your disciples to cast the spirit out, but they couldn't do it."

41"You stubborn, faithless people," Jesus said, "how long must I be with you and put up with you? Bring him here." 42As the boy came forward, the demon knocked him to the ground and threw him into a violent convulsion. But Jesus rebuked the evil spirit and healed the boy. Then he gave him back to his father. 43Awe gripped the people as they saw this display of God's power.

### Jesus Again Predicts His Death

While everyone was marveling over all the wonderful things he was doing, Jesus said to his disciples, 44"Listen to me and remember what I say. The Son of Man is going to be betrayed." 45But they didn't know what he meant. Its significance was hidden from them, so they could not understand it, and they were afraid to ask him about it.

### The Greatest in the Kingdom

46Then there was an argument among them as to which of them would be the greatest. 47But Jesus knew their thoughts, so he brought a little child to his side. 48Then he said to them, "Anyone who welcomes a little child like this on my behalf welcomes me, and anyone who

9:33 Or *shelters*; Greek reads *tabernacles*. 9:35 Some manuscripts read *This is my beloved Son.*

## A Disciple Takes Up His or Her Cross and Follows Christ
Read LUKE 9:23-25

Choosing to be a disciple of Jesus Christ takes more than just some verbal affirmation. It takes daily sacrifice and commitment. But when you follow Christ's guidelines for discipleship, you will find that the end result is far better than you could ever have imagined. Here are three things a true disciple of Christ should do:

**1. Your Desires Must Take a Backseat to His Desires for Your Life.** Being a disciple means recognizing that God's plans for your life are ultimately better than your own. That may mean making some sacrifices in your life, such as spending more of your time in God's Word than in the newspaper, volunteering your services for teaching children's Sunday school, or putting off that vacation to work on a ministry project. Yet, in relinquishing your own plans, you will find yourself drawn closer to the Lord.

**2. You Must Take Up Your Cross Daily.** Jesus is not simply referring to a religious symbol. At this time in history, a cross symbolized the cruelest of deaths. Anyone seen carrying a cross was headed for a horrible death. Some have misunderstood this statement by Jesus to mean that your cross is your personal inconvenience or problem. In this passage, however, Jesus is talking about the act of dying to yourself. In essence, he wants you to lay yourself at his feet and say, "I want your will more than my own." Once you have taken up that cross, you will experience the abundant life that Jesus promises to those who follow him.

**3. You Must Lose Yourself to Save Yourself.** Verse 24 may sound like a contradiction when you first read it. Yet, if you truly want to find happiness and fulfillment, you must relinquish full control of your life to Jesus Christ. Paul wrote, "I myself no longer live, but Christ lives in me" (Galatians 2:20). Taking up the cross is no more a burden to the disciple than wings are to a bird, or sails are to a ship. A surrendered life holds the key to a fulfilling walk.

Though it is true that it costs to be a disciple, it is also true that it costs a lot more not to be!

## What Makes Demons Powerless? Read LUKE 10:1-20

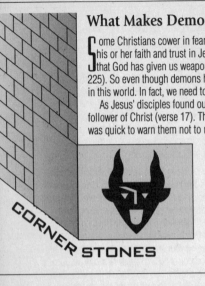

**CORNER STONES**

Some Christians cower in fear of Satan and his army of demons. Yet every person who has put his or her faith and trust in Jesus Christ comes under God's protection. In fact, Scripture says that God has given us weapons to break down Satan's strongholds (2 Corinthians 10:4-5, p. 225). So even though demons have real powers, we do not have to be paralyzed at their presence in this world. In fact, we need to recognize the power Christ has given us in the face of our enemy.

As Jesus' disciples found out, demons are drastically limited in their power before the true follower of Christ (verse 17). The power they had was not of themselves but from God. And Jesus was quick to warn them not to rejoice in the power they had been given over demons. Rather, Jesus told them to rejoice that their names were "registered as citizens of heaven" (verse 20).

Today you may find people who allege to have "conversations" with demons and reminding them how powerless they are. Yet even Michael the archangel, when arguing with Satan about Moses' body, did not taunt the devil, but simply said, "The Lord rebuke you" (see Jude 1:9, p. 329). Our focus should not be upon the power we have been given but on the Giver of that power.

---

welcomes me welcomes my Father who sent me. Whoever is the least among you is the greatest."

### Using the Name of Jesus

49John said to Jesus, "Master, we saw someone using your name to cast out demons. We tried to stop him because he isn't in our group."

50But Jesus said, "Don't stop him! Anyone who is not against you is for you."

### Opposition from Samaritans

51As the time drew near for his return to heaven, Jesus resolutely set out for Jerusalem. 52He sent messengers ahead to a Samaritan village to prepare for his arrival. 53But they were turned away. The people of the village refused to have anything to do with Jesus because he had resolved to go to Jerusalem. 54When James and John heard about it, they said to Jesus, "Lord, should we order down fire from heaven to burn them up*?" 55But Jesus turned and rebuked them.* 56So they went on to another village.

### The Cost of Following Jesus

57As they were walking along someone said to Jesus, "I will follow you no matter where you go."

58But Jesus replied, "Foxes have dens to live in, and birds have nests, but I, the Son of Man, have no home of my own, not even a place to lay my head."

59He said to another person, "Come, be my disciple."

The man agreed, but he said, "Lord, first let me return home and bury my father."

60Jesus replied, "Let those who are spiritually dead care for their own dead.* Your duty is to go and preach the coming of the Kingdom of God."

61Another said, "Yes, Lord, I will follow you, but first let me say good-bye to my family."

62But Jesus told him, "Anyone who puts a hand to the plow and then looks back is not fit for the Kingdom of God."

## CHAPTER 10
### Jesus Sends Out His Disciples

The Lord now chose seventy-two* other disciples and sent them on ahead in pairs to all the towns and villages he planned to visit. 2These were his instructions to them: "The harvest is so great, but the workers are so few. Pray to the Lord who is in charge of the harvest, and ask him to send out more workers for his fields. 3Go now, and remember that I am sending you out as lambs among wolves. 4Don't take along any money, or a traveler's bag, or even an extra pair of sandals. And don't stop to greet anyone on the road.

5"Whenever you enter a home, give it your blessing. 6If those who live there are worthy, the blessing will stand; if they are not, the blessing

9:54 Some manuscripts add *as Elijah did.*  9:55 Some manuscripts add *And he said, "You don't realize what your hearts are like. 56For the Son of Man has not come to destroy men's lives, but to save them."*  9:60 Greek *Let the dead bury their own dead.*  10:1 Some manuscripts read *70;* also in 10:17.

will return to you. 7When you enter a town, don't move around from home to home. Stay in one place, eating and drinking what they provide you. Don't hesitate to accept hospitality, because those who work deserve their pay.

8 "If a town welcomes you, eat whatever is set before you 9and heal the sick. As you heal them, say, 'The Kingdom of God is near you now.' 10But if a town refuses to welcome you, go out into its streets and say, 11 'We wipe the dust of your town from our feet as a public announcement of your doom. And don't forget the Kingdom of God is near!' 12The truth is, even wicked Sodom will be better off than such a town on the judgment day.

13 "What horrors await you, Korazin and Bethsaida! For if the miracles I did in you had been done in wicked Tyre and Sidon, their people would have sat in deep repentance long ago, clothed in sackcloth and throwing ashes on their heads to show their remorse. 14Yes, Tyre and Sidon will be better off on the judgment day than you. 15And you people of Capernaum, will you be exalted to heaven? No, you will be brought down to the place of the dead.*"

16Then he said to the disciples, "Anyone who accepts your message is also accepting me. And anyone who rejects you is rejecting me. And anyone who rejects me is rejecting God who sent me."

17When the seventy-two disciples returned, they joyfully reported to him, "Lord, even the demons obey us when we use your name!"

18 "Yes," he told them, "I saw Satan falling from heaven as a flash of lightning! 19And I have given you authority over all the power of the enemy, and you can walk among snakes and scorpions and crush them. Nothing will injure you. 20But don't rejoice just because evil spirits obey you; rejoice because your names are registered as citizens of heaven."

### Jesus' Prayer of Thanksgiving

21Then Jesus was filled with the joy of the Holy Spirit and said, "O Father, Lord of heaven and earth, thank you for hiding the truth from those who think themselves so wise and clever, and for revealing it to the childlike. Yes, Father, it pleased you to do it this way.

22 "My Father has given me authority over everything. No one really knows the Son except the Father, and no one really knows the Father except the Son and those to whom the Son chooses to reveal him."

23Then when they were alone, he turned to the disciples and said, "How privileged you are to see what you have seen. 24I tell you, many prophets and kings have longed to see and hear what you have seen and heard, but they could not."

### The Most Important Commandment

25One day an expert in religious law stood up to test Jesus by asking him this question: "Teacher, what must I do to receive eternal life?"

26Jesus replied, "What does the law of Moses say? How do you read it?"

27The man answered, " 'You must love the Lord your God with all your heart, all your soul, all your strength, and all your mind.' And, 'Love your neighbor as yourself.' " *

28 "Right!" Jesus told him. "Do this and you will live!"

29The man wanted to justify his actions, so he asked Jesus, "And who is my neighbor?"

### Story of the Good Samaritan

30Jesus replied with an illustration: "A Jewish man was traveling on a trip from Jerusalem to Jericho, and he was attacked by bandits. They stripped him of his clothes and money, beat him up, and left him half dead beside the road.

31 "By chance a Jewish priest came along; but when he saw the man lying there, he crossed to the other side of the road and passed him by. 32A Temple assistant* walked over and looked at him lying there, but he also passed by on the other side.

33 "Then a despised Samaritan came along, and when he saw the man, he felt deep pity. 34Kneeling beside him, the Samaritan soothed his wounds with medicine and bandaged them. Then he put the man on his own donkey and took him to an inn, where he took care of him. 35The next day he handed the innkeeper two pieces of silver* and told him to take care of the man. 'If his bill runs higher than that,' he said, 'I'll pay the difference the next time I am here.'

36 "Now which of these three would you say was a neighbor to the man who was attacked by bandits?" Jesus asked.

37The man replied, "The one who showed him mercy."

Then Jesus said, "Yes, now go and do the same."

10:15 Greek *to Hades.*   10:27 Deut 6:5; Lev 19:18.   10:32 Greek *A Levite.*   10:35 Greek *2 denarii.* A denarius was the equivalent of a full day's wage.

## Jesus Visits Martha and Mary

38As Jesus and the disciples continued on their way to Jerusalem, they came to a village where a woman named Martha welcomed them into her home. 39Her sister, Mary, sat at the Lord's feet, listening to what he taught. 40But Martha was worrying over the big dinner she was preparing. She came to Jesus and said, "Lord, doesn't it seem unfair to you that my sister just sits here while I do all the work? Tell her to come and help me."

41But the Lord said to her, "My dear Martha, you are so upset over all these details! 42There is really only one thing worth being concerned about. Mary has discovered it—and I won't take it away from her."

## CHAPTER 11

### Teaching about Prayer

Once when Jesus had been out praying, one of his disciples came to him as he finished and said, "Lord, teach us to pray, just as John taught his disciples."

2He said, "This is how you should pray:

"Father, may your name be honored.
May your Kingdom come soon.
3 Give us our food day by day.
4 And forgive us our sins—
just as we forgive those who have sinned
against us.
And don't let us yield to temptation.*"

5Then, teaching them more about prayer, he used this illustration: "Suppose you went to a friend's house at midnight, wanting to borrow three loaves of bread. You would say to him, 6'A friend of mine has just arrived for a visit, and I have nothing for him to eat.' 7He would call out from his bedroom, 'Don't bother me. The door is locked for the night, and we are all in bed. I can't help you this time.' 8But I tell you this—though he won't do it as a friend, if you keep knocking long enough, he will get up and give you what you want so his reputation won't be damaged.*

9"And so I tell you, keep on asking, and you will be given what you ask for. Keep on looking, and you will find. Keep on knocking, and the door will be opened. 10For everyone who asks, receives. Everyone who seeks, finds. And the door is opened to everyone who knocks.

11"You fathers—if your children ask* for a fish, do you give them a snake instead? 12Or if they ask for an egg, do you give them a scorpion? Of course not! 13If you sinful people know how to give good gifts to your children, how much more will your heavenly Father give the Holy Spirit to those who ask him."

### Jesus and the Prince of Demons

14One day Jesus cast a demon out of a man who couldn't speak, and the man's voice returned to him. The crowd was amazed, 15but some said, "No wonder he can cast out demons. He gets his power from Satan,* the prince of demons!" 16Trying to test Jesus, others asked for a miraculous sign from heaven to see if he was from God.

17He knew their thoughts, so he said, "Any kingdom at war with itself is doomed. A divided home is also doomed. 18You say I am empowered by the prince of demons.* But if Satan is fighting against himself by empowering me to cast out his demons, how can his kingdom survive? 19And if I am empowered by

11:2-4 Some manuscripts add additional portions of the Lord's Prayer as it reads in Matt 6:9-13.    11:8 Greek *in order to avoid shame,* or *because of [your] persistence.*    11:11 Some manuscripts add *for bread, do you give them a stone? Or if they ask.*    11:15 Greek *Beelzeboul.*    11:18 Greek *by Beelzeboul;* also in 11:19.

# OFF AND RUNNING

## Balance Christian Service with Worship Read LUKE 10:38-42

It is easy to lose sight of Jesus in the midst of all our activity for him. This story shows the necessity of balancing our work with our worship. Here we see two personalities, represented by Martha and Mary.

**Martha: the Doer.** Martha was a practical type of person who wanted to get things done. Deep down, she probably wanted to please the Lord, but she made the common mistake of offering work for worship. She received Jesus into her house, then neglected Jesus in the process. Jesus wanted her attention, and she offered him a flurry of activity. As a result, she felt tired and overworked. Like Martha, we can become weary in our work for the Lord when we fail to take time to sit at his feet and draw from the spiritual resources available to us.

**Mary: the Worshiper.** Mary had a balanced life. She recognized that there was a time to work and a time to the prince of demons, what about your own followers? They cast out demons, too, so they will judge you for what you have said. 20But if I am casting out demons by the power of God, then the Kingdom of God has arrived among you. 21For when Satan,* who is completely armed, guards his palace, it is safe—22until someone who is stronger attacks and overpowers him, strips him of his weapons, and carries off his belongings.

23"Anyone who isn't helping me opposes me, and anyone who isn't working with me is actually working against me.

24"When an evil spirit leaves a person, it goes into the desert, searching for rest. But when it finds none, it says, 'I will return to the person I came from.' 25So it returns and finds that its former home is all swept and clean. 26Then the spirit finds seven other spirits more evil than itself, and they all enter the person and live there. And so that person is worse off than before."

27As he was speaking, a woman in the crowd called out, "God bless your mother—the womb from which you came, and the breasts that nursed you!"

28He replied, "But even more blessed are all who hear the word of God and put it into practice."

## The Sign of Jonah

29As the crowd pressed in on Jesus, he said, "These are evil times, and this evil generation keeps asking me to show them a miraculous sign. But the only sign I will give them is the sign of the prophet Jonah. 30What happened to him was a sign to the people of Nineveh that God had sent him. What happens to me will be a sign

that God has sent me, the Son of Man, to these people.

31"The queen of Sheba* will rise up against this generation on judgment day and condemn it, because she came from a distant land to hear the wisdom of Solomon. And now someone greater than Solomon is here—and you refuse to listen to him. 32The people of Nineveh, too, will rise up against this generation on judgment day and condemn it, because they repented at the preaching of Jonah. And now someone greater than Jonah is here—and you refuse to repent.

## Receiving the Light

33"No one lights a lamp and then hides it or puts it under a basket. Instead, it is put on a lampstand to give light to all who enter the room. 34Your eye is a lamp for your body. A pure eye lets sunshine into your soul. But an evil eye shuts out the light and plunges you into darkness. 35Make sure that the light you think you have is not really darkness. 36If you are filled with light, with no dark corners, then your whole life will be radiant, as though a floodlight is shining on you."

## Jesus Criticizes the Religious Leaders

37As Jesus was speaking, one of the Pharisees invited him home for a meal. So he went in and took his place at the table. 38His host was amazed to see that he sat down to eat without first performing the ceremonial washing required by Jewish custom. 39Then the Lord said to him, "You Pharisees are so careful to clean the outside of the cup and the dish, but inside you are still filthy—full of greed and wickedness! 40Fools! Didn't God make the inside as well as the outside? 41So give to the needy

11:21 Greek the strong one.    11:31 Greek the queen of the south.

worship, a time to do and a time to pray. She knew when it was time to take off the apron and converse with this most honored guest. While Martha essentially wanted to "get the dishes done," Mary wanted to seize this wonderful moment to sit at the feet of the Creator of the universe.

Few things are as damaging to the Christian life as trying to work for Christ without taking time to commune with him. In his letter to young Timothy, the apostle Paul writes, "Hardworking farmers are the first to enjoy the fruit of their labor" (2 Timothy 2:6). In other words, you can't effectively feed others until you yourself have been fed.

What we do *with* Christ is far more important than what we do *for* Christ. Those who strike a balance between work and worship will keep themselves from spiritual burnout and will become more effective in their service to the Lord.

what you greedily possess, and you will be clean all over.

42 "But how terrible it will be for you Pharisees! For you are careful to tithe even the tiniest part of your income,* but you completely forget about justice and the love of God. You should tithe, yes, but you should not leave undone the more important things.

43 "How terrible it will be for you Pharisees! For how you love the seats of honor in the synagogues and the respectful greetings from everyone as you walk through the markets! 44Yes, how terrible it will be for you. For you are like hidden graves in a field. People walk over them without knowing the corruption they are stepping on."

45 "Teacher," said an expert in religious law, "you have insulted us, too, in what you just said."

46 "Yes," said Jesus, "how terrible it will be for you experts in religious law! For you crush people beneath impossible religious demands, and you never lift a finger to help ease the burden. 47How terrible it will be for you! For you build tombs for the very prophets your ancestors killed long ago. 48Murderers! You agree with your ancestors that what they did was right. You would have done the same yourselves. 49This is what God in his wisdom said about you:* 'I will send prophets and apostles to them, and they will kill some and persecute the others.'

50 "And you of this generation will be held responsible for the murder of all God's prophets from the creation of the world—51from the murder of Abel to the murder of Zechariah, who was killed between the altar and the sanctuary. Yes, it will surely be charged against you.

52 "How terrible it will be for you experts in religious law! For you hide the key to knowledge from the people. You don't enter the Kingdom yourselves, and you prevent others from entering."

53As Jesus finished speaking, the Pharisees

and teachers of religious law were furious. From that time on they grilled him with many hostile questions, 54trying to trap him into saying something they could use against him.

CHAPTER **12**

*A Warning against Hypocrisy*

Meanwhile, the crowds grew until thousands were milling about and crushing each other. Jesus turned first to his disciples and warned them, "Beware of the yeast of the Pharisees—beware of their hypocrisy. 2The time is coming when everything will be revealed; all that is secret will be made public. 3Whatever you have said in the dark will be heard in the light, and what you have whispered behind closed doors will be shouted from the housetops for all to hear!

4 "Dear friends, don't be afraid of those who want to kill you. They can only kill the body; they cannot do any more to you. 5But I'll tell you whom to fear. Fear God, who has the power to kill people and then throw them into hell.

6 "What is the price of five sparrows? A couple of pennies? Yet God does not forget a single one of them. 7And the very hairs on your head are all numbered. So don't be afraid; you are more valuable to him than a whole flock of sparrows.

8 "And I assure you of this: If anyone acknowledges me publicly here on earth, I, the Son of Man, will openly acknowledge that person in the presence of God's angels. 9But if anyone denies me here on earth, I will deny that person before God's angels. 10Yet those who speak against the Son of Man may be forgiven, but anyone who speaks blasphemies against the Holy Spirit will never be forgiven.

11 "And when you are brought to trial in the synagogues and before rulers and authorities, don't worry about what to say in your defense, 12for the Holy Spirit will teach you what needs to be said even as you are standing there."

11:42 Greek *to tithe the mint and the rue and every herb.*   11:49 Greek *Therefore, the wisdom of God said.*

# OFF AND RUNNING

## Don't Neglect Your Spiritual Health Read LUKE 12:16-21

As this parable illustrates, it is easy to allow other pursuits to cloud our spiritual vision. We have to make enough money to get that new car, buy that house, or take that dream vacation. Sometimes we can get so caught up in chasing after money and success that we leave God out of the equation altogether.

## Story of the Rich Fool

¹³Then someone called from the crowd, "Teacher, please tell my brother to divide our father's estate with me."

¹⁴Jesus replied, "Friend, who made me a judge over you to decide such things as that?" ¹⁵Then he said, "Beware! Don't be greedy for what you don't have. Real life is not measured by how much we own."

¹⁶And he gave an illustration: "A rich man had a fertile farm that produced fine crops. ¹⁷In fact, his barns were full to overflowing. ¹⁸So he said, 'I know! I'll tear down my barns and build bigger ones. Then I'll have room enough to store everything. ¹⁹And I'll sit back and say to myself, My friend, you have enough stored away for years to come. Now take it easy! Eat, drink, and be merry!'

²⁰"But God said to him, 'You fool! You will die this very night. Then who will get it all?'

²¹"Yes, a person is a fool to store up earthly wealth but not have a rich relationship with God."

## Teaching about Money and Possessions

²²Then turning to his disciples, Jesus said, "So I tell you, don't worry about everyday life—whether you have enough food to eat or clothes to wear. ²³For life consists of far more than food and clothing. ²⁴Look at the ravens. They don't need to plant or harvest or put food in barns because God feeds them. And you are far more valuable to him than any birds! ²⁵Can all your worries add a single moment to your life? Of course not! ²⁶And if worry can't do little things like that, what's the use of worrying over bigger things?

²⁷"Look at the lilies and how they grow. They don't work or make their clothing, yet Solomon in all his glory was not dressed as beautifully as they are. ²⁸And if God cares so wonderfully for flowers that are here today and gone tomorrow, won't he more surely care for you? You have so little faith! ²⁹And don't worry about food—

12:38 Greek *in the second or third watch.*

what to eat and drink. Don't worry whether God will provide it for you. ³⁰These things dominate the thoughts of most people, but your Father already knows your needs. ³¹He will give you all you need from day to day if you make the Kingdom of God your primary concern.

³²"So don't be afraid, little flock. For it gives your Father great happiness to give you the Kingdom.

³³"Sell what you have and give to those in need. This will store up treasure for you in heaven! And the purses of heaven have no holes in them. Your treasure will be safe—no thief can steal it and no moth can destroy it. ³⁴Wherever your treasure is, there your heart and thoughts will also be.

## Be Ready for the Lord's Coming

³⁵"Be dressed for service and well prepared, ³⁶as though you were waiting for your master to return from the wedding feast. Then you will be ready to open the door and let him in the moment he arrives and knocks. ³⁷There will be special favor for those who are ready and waiting for his return. I tell you, he himself will seat them, put on an apron, and serve them as they sit and eat! ³⁸He may come in the middle of the night or just before dawn.* But whenever he comes, there will be special favor for his servants who are ready!

³⁹"Know this: A homeowner who knew exactly when a burglar was coming would not permit the house to be broken into. ⁴⁰You must be ready all the time, for the Son of Man will come when least expected."

⁴¹Peter asked, "Lord, is this illustration just for us or for everyone?"

⁴²And the Lord replied, "I'm talking to any faithful, sensible servant to whom the master gives the responsibility of managing his household and feeding his family. ⁴³If the master returns and finds that the servant has done a good job, there will be a reward. ⁴⁴I assure you, the master will put that servant in charge of all he

God's answer to this dilemma is for us to seek first his reign and will in our lives. Then everything else will come into balance. It is simple. The more you channel your energy, your ambition, and your life into this one, holy pursuit, the less obsessed you will be with the cares and concerns of this world. For the sake of your spiritual health, seek God's kingdom in all that you do. Failure to do so will only guarantee confusion, failure, emptiness, and dissatisfaction.

## The More We Know, the Greater Our Responsibility Will Be
Read LUKE 12:48

According to this verse, you will be held accountable for what you know. This can refer to your personal behavior, as well as the work you do for God's Kingdom. For instance, you now know that you should not lie, cheat, steal, or live an immoral lifestyle. If you disregard God's commands, you know that you will reap the consequences. On the other hand, you must also share your spiritual knowledge with others—especially those who are on their way to spending eternity in hell. Our attitude should be as Paul's, who wrote, "For we speak as messengers who have been approved by God to be entrusted with the Good News. Our purpose is to please God, not people. He is the one who examines the motives of our hearts" (1 Thessalonians 2:4).

What are you doing with the spiritual knowledge and insight God has given you? Are you using it to his glory?

CORNER STONES

---

owns. ⁴⁵But if the servant thinks, 'My master won't be back for a while,' and begins oppressing the other servants, partying, and getting drunk—⁴⁶well, the master will return unannounced and unexpected. He will tear the servant apart and banish him with the unfaithful. ⁴⁷The servant will be severely punished, for though he knew his duty, he refused to do it.

⁴⁸"But people who are not aware that they are doing wrong will be punished only lightly. Much is required from those to whom much is given, and much more is required from those to whom much more is given.

### Jesus Causes Division
⁴⁹"I have come to bring fire to the earth, and I wish that my task were already completed! ⁵⁰There is a terrible baptism ahead of me, and I am under a heavy burden until it is accomplished. ⁵¹Do you think I have come to bring peace to the earth? No, I have come to bring strife and division! ⁵²From now on families will be split apart, three in favor of me, and two against—or the other way around. ⁵³There will be a division between father and son, mother and daughter, mother-in-law and daughter-in-law."

⁵⁴Then Jesus turned to the crowd and said, "When you see clouds beginning to form in the west, you say, 'Here comes a shower.' And you are right. ⁵⁵When the south wind blows, you say, 'Today will be a scorcher.' And it is. ⁵⁶You hypocrites! You know how to interpret the appear-

ance of the earth and the sky, but you can't interpret these present times.

⁵⁷"Why can't you decide for yourselves what is right? ⁵⁸If you are on the way to court and you meet your accuser, try to settle the matter before it reaches the judge, or you may be sentenced and handed over to an officer and thrown in jail. ⁵⁹And if that happens, you won't be free again until you have paid the last penny."

## CHAPTER 13
### A Call to Repentance
About this time Jesus was informed that Pilate had murdered some people from Galilee as they were sacrificing at the Temple in Jerusalem. ²"Do you think those Galileans were worse sinners than other people from Galilee?" he asked. "Is that why they suffered? ³Not at all! And you will also perish unless you turn from your evil ways and turn to God. ⁴And what about the eighteen men who died when the Tower of Siloam fell on them? Were they the worst sinners in Jerusalem? ⁵No, and I tell you again that unless you repent, you will also perish."

### Illustration of the Barren Fig Tree
⁶Then Jesus used this illustration: "A man planted a fig tree in his garden and came again and again to see if there was any fruit on it, but he was always disappointed. ⁷Finally, he said to his gardener, 'I've waited three years, and there hasn't been a single fig! Cut it down. It's taking up space we can use for something else.'

⁸"The gardener answered, 'Give it one more

chance. Leave it another year, and I'll give it special attention and plenty of fertilizer. 9If we get figs next year, fine. If not, you can cut it down.'"

### Jesus Heals on the Sabbath
10One Sabbath day as Jesus was teaching in a synagogue, 11he saw a woman who had been crippled by an evil spirit. She had been bent double for eighteen years and was unable to stand up straight. 12When Jesus saw her, he called her over and said, "Woman, you are healed of your sickness!" 13Then he touched her, and instantly she could stand straight. How she praised and thanked God!

14But the leader in charge of the synagogue was indignant that Jesus had healed her on the Sabbath day. "There are six days of the week for working," he said to the crowd. "Come on those days to be healed, not on the Sabbath."

15But the Lord replied, "You hypocrite! You work on the Sabbath day! Don't you untie your ox or your donkey from their stalls on the Sabbath and lead them out for water? 16Wasn't it necessary for me, even on the Sabbath day, to free this dear woman* from the bondage in which Satan has held her for eighteen years?" 17This shamed his enemies. And all the people rejoiced at the wonderful things he did.

### Illustration of the Mustard Seed
18Then Jesus said, "What is the Kingdom of God like? How can I illustrate it? 19It is like a tiny mustard seed planted in a garden; it grows and becomes a tree, and the birds come and find shelter among its branches."

### Illustration of the Yeast
20He also asked, "What else is the Kingdom of God like? 21It is like yeast used by a woman making bread. Even though she used a large amount* of flour, the yeast permeated every part of the dough."

### The Narrow Door
22Jesus went through the towns and villages, teaching as he went, always pressing on toward Jerusalem. 23Someone asked him, "Lord, will only a few be saved?"

He replied, 24"The door to heaven is narrow. Work hard to get in, because many will try to enter, 25but when the head of the house has locked the door, it will be too late. Then you will

stand outside knocking and pleading, 'Lord, open the door for us!' But he will reply, 'I do not know you.' 26You will say, 'But we ate and drank with you, and you taught in our streets.' 27And he will reply, 'I tell you, I don't know you. Go away, all you who do evil.'

28"And there will be great weeping and gnashing of teeth, for you will see Abraham, Isaac, Jacob, and all the prophets within the Kingdom of God, but you will be thrown out. 29Then people will come from all over the world to take their places in the Kingdom of God. 30And note this: Some who are despised now will be greatly honored then; and some who are greatly honored now will be despised then.*"

### Jesus Grieves over Jerusalem
31A few minutes later some Pharisees said to him, "Get out of here if you want to live, because Herod Antipas wants to kill you!"

32Jesus replied, "Go tell that fox that I will keep on casting out demons and doing miracles of healing today and tomorrow; and the third day I will accomplish my purpose. 33Yes, today, tomorrow, and the next day I must proceed on my way. For it wouldn't do for a prophet of God to be killed except in Jerusalem!

34"O Jerusalem, Jerusalem, the city that kills the prophets and stones God's messengers! How often I have wanted to gather your children together as a hen protects her chicks beneath her wings, but you wouldn't let me. 35And now look, your house is left to you empty. And you will never see me again until you say, 'Bless the one who comes in the name of the Lord!'* "

## CHAPTER 14
### Jesus Heals on the Sabbath
One Sabbath day Jesus was in the home of a leader of the Pharisees. The people were watching him closely, 2because there was a man there whose arms and legs were swollen.* 3Jesus asked the Pharisees and experts in religious law, "Well, is it permitted in the law to heal people on the Sabbath day, or not?" 4When they refused to answer, Jesus touched the sick man and healed him and sent him away. 5Then he turned to them and asked, "Which of you doesn't work on the Sabbath? If your son* or your cow falls into a pit, don't you proceed at once to get him out?" 6Again they had no answer.

13:16 Greek this woman, a daughter of Abraham. 13:21 Greek 3 measures. 13:30 Greek Some are last who will be first, and some are first who will be last. 13:35 Ps 118:26. 14:2 Traditionally translated who had dropsy. 14:5 Some manuscripts read donkey.

## Jesus Teaches about Humility

7When Jesus noticed that all who had come to the dinner were trying to sit near the head of the table, he gave them this advice: 8"If you are invited to a wedding feast, don't always head for the best seat. What if someone more respected than you has also been invited? 9The host will say, 'Let this person sit here instead.' Then you will be embarrassed and will have to take whatever seat is left at the foot of the table!

10"Do this instead—sit at the foot of the table. Then when your host sees you, he will come and say, 'Friend, we have a better place than this for you!' Then you will be honored in front of all the other guests. 11For the proud will be humbled, but the humble will be honored."

12Then he turned to his host. "When you put on a luncheon or a dinner," he said, "don't invite your friends, brothers, relatives, and rich neighbors. For they will repay you by inviting you back. 13Instead, invite the poor, the crippled, the lame, and the blind. 14Then at the resurrection of the godly, God will reward you for inviting those who could not repay you."

## Story of the Great Feast

15Hearing this, a man sitting at the table with Jesus exclaimed, "What a privilege it would be to have a share in the Kingdom of God!"

16Jesus replied with this illustration: "A man prepared a great feast and sent out many invitations. 17When all was ready, he sent his servant around to notify the guests that it was time for them to come. 18But they all began making excuses. One said he had just bought a field and wanted to inspect it, so he asked to be excused. 19Another said he had just bought five pair of oxen and wanted to try them out. 20Another had just been married, so he said he couldn't come.

21"The servant returned and told his master what they had said. His master was angry and said, 'Go quickly into the streets and alleys of the city and invite the poor, the crippled, the lame, and the blind.' 22After the servant had done this, he reported, 'There is still room for more.' 23So his master said, 'Go out into the country lanes and behind the hedges and urge anyone you find to come, so that the house will be full. 24For none of those I invited first will get even the smallest taste of what I had prepared for them.'"

## The Cost of Being a Disciple

25Great crowds were following Jesus. He turned around and said to them, 26"If you want to be

14:26 Greek *you must hate.*

my follower you must love me more than* your own father and mother, wife and children, brothers and sisters—yes, more than your own life. Otherwise, you cannot be my disciple. 27And you cannot be my disciple if you do not carry your own cross and follow me.

28"But don't begin until you count the cost. For who would begin construction of a building without first getting estimates and then checking to see if there is enough money to pay the bills? 29Otherwise, you might complete only the foundation before running out of funds. And then how everyone would laugh at you! 30They would say, 'There's the person who started that building and ran out of money before it was finished!'

31"Or what king would ever dream of going to war without first sitting down with his counselors and discussing whether his army of ten thousand is strong enough to defeat the twenty thousand soldiers who are marching against him? 32If he is not able, then while the enemy is still far away, he will send a delegation to discuss terms of peace. 33So no one can become my disciple without giving up everything for me.

34"Salt is good for seasoning. But if it loses its flavor, how do you make it salty again? 35Flavorless salt is good neither for the soil nor for fertilizer. It is thrown away. Anyone who is willing to hear should listen and understand!"

CHAPTER **15**
## Story of the Lost Sheep

Tax collectors and other notorious sinners often came to listen to Jesus teach. 2This made the Pharisees and teachers of religious law complain that he was associating with such despicable people—even eating with them!

3So Jesus used this illustration: 4"If you had one hundred sheep, and one of them strayed away and was lost in the wilderness, wouldn't you leave the ninety-nine others to go and search for the lost one until you found it? 5And then you would joyfully carry it home on your shoulders. 6When you arrived, you would call together your friends and neighbors to rejoice with you because your lost sheep was found. 7In the same way, heaven will be happier over one lost sinner who returns to God than over ninety-nine others who are righteous and haven't strayed away!

### Story of the Lost Coin

8 "Or suppose a woman has ten valuable silver coins* and loses one. Won't she light a lamp and look in every corner of the house and sweep every nook and cranny until she finds it? 9And when she finds it, she will call in her friends and neighbors to rejoice with her because she has found her lost coin. 10In the same way, there is joy in the presence of God's angels when even one sinner repents."

### Story of the Lost Son

11To illustrate the point further, Jesus told them this story: "A man had two sons. 12The younger son told his father, 'I want my share of your estate now, instead of waiting until you die.' So his father agreed to divide his wealth between his sons.

13 "A few days later this younger son packed all his belongings and took a trip to a distant land, and there he wasted all his money on wild living. 14About the time his money ran out, a great famine swept over the land, and he began to starve. 15He persuaded a local farmer to hire him to feed his pigs. 16The boy became so hungry that even the pods he was feeding the pigs looked good to him. But no one gave him anything.

17 "When he finally came to his senses, he said to himself, 'At home even the hired men have food enough to spare, and here I am, dying of hunger! 18I will go home to my father and say, "Father, I have sinned against both heaven and you, 19and I am no longer worthy of being called your son. Please take me on as a hired man." '

20 "So he returned home to his father. And while he was still a long distance away, his father saw him coming. Filled with love and compassion, he ran to his son, embraced him, and kissed him. 21His son said to him, 'Father, I have sinned against both heaven and you, and I am no longer worthy of being called your son.*'

22 "But his father said to the servants, 'Quick! Bring the finest robe in the house and put it on him. Get a ring for his finger, and sandals for his feet. 23And kill the calf we have been fattening in the pen. We must celebrate with a feast, 24for this son of mine was dead and has now returned to life. He was lost, but now he is found.' So the party began.

25 "Meanwhile, the older son was in the fields working. When he returned home, he heard

music and dancing in the house, 26and he asked one of the servants what was going on. 27'Your brother is back,' he was told, 'and your father has killed the calf we were fattening and has prepared a great feast. We are celebrating because of his safe return.'

28 "The older brother was angry and wouldn't go in. His father came out and begged him, 29but he replied, 'All these years I've worked hard for you and never once refused to do a single thing you told me to. And in all that time you never gave me even one young goat for a feast with my friends. 30Yet when this son of yours comes back

---

## A Disciple Counts the Cost
### Read LUKE 14:25-33

At the time Jesus said these words, he had become quite a popular figure. Crowds flocked around him wherever he went. But they did not always do so for the right reasons. Consequently, Jesus directed his solemn and searching words to those people who followed him for selfish purposes or because it was the thing to do.

Likewise, Jesus doesn't want you to follow him only when it is convenient or socially acceptable. He wants you to be his disciple for the long haul—regardless of how easy or difficult it might be. That is why you must count the cost of being a true disciple of Jesus Christ. What does it mean to count the cost? The following four questions will give you a concrete idea:

- Do you love Jesus more than anyone or anything else in your life?
- Do you love Jesus and desire his will for your life over your own?
- Are you willing to accept ridicule and sacrifice for the cause of Christ?
- Will you commit to following Jesus, whether or not it is popular or expedient?

If you have carefully examined your heart, counted the cost, and can truthfully answer yes to these questions, then you are on the road to discipleship and are now ready to spend the rest of your life as his disciple and friend.

Jesus is not looking for halfhearted followers. He wants wholehearted commitment.

15:8 Greek 10 drachmas. A drachma was the equivalent of a full day's wage. 15:21 Some manuscripts add Please take me on as a hired man.

## What Is Hell Like? Read LUKE 16:19-31

Jesus gave us a rare glimpse of life in hell in this parable. Here is what he revealed about this dark place of punishment.

**People's Lifestyles on Earth Will Not Be the Same in Eternity.** Things dramatically changed for the rich man when he passed into eternity. Because he did not have a personal relationship with God, he immediately entered into the dark torment of hell, penniless and in agony. Those whose hearts are not right with God face the same future as the rich man in this story. After death they will be held in hell until they are brought before God at what is called the Great White Throne Judgment (see "Why Would a Good God Send Anyone to Hell?" p. 287).

**Hell Is a Place of Flames and Torment.** The rich man in this parable experienced unrelenting heat and an unquenchable thirst. He was in so much agony that he called out to Abraham to have Lazarus come and dip his finger in water to cool his (the rich man's) tongue. If you have ever been badly burned, then you have an idea of the torment that awaits those who will spend eternity in hell. Add to that darkness and isolation, and you have an incredibly bleak scenario.

**People Do Not "Have a Good Time" in Hell.** Some people say, "I want to go to hell. All of my friends will be there." That may be true. But hell holds no parties. As this parable states, the rich man is so alarmed by his situation that he wants Lazarus to go and warn his brothers, so that they will not join him in torment.

If you want to know about the reality of hell, you don't need some tabloid account of someone who has supposedly had an out-of-body experience. You can study the words of the living God, who died and rose again, and who can tell you exactly what to expect in eternity. Our acceptance or rejection of his words determines on which side of the divide we will spend the rest of our lives.

CORNER STONES

---

after squandering your money on prostitutes, you celebrate by killing the finest calf we have.'

31 "His father said to him, 'Look, dear son, you and I are very close, and everything I have is yours. 32 We had to celebrate this happy day. For your brother was dead and has come back to life! He was lost, but now he is found!'"

## CHAPTER 16
*Story of the Shrewd Manager*

Jesus told this story to his disciples: "A rich man hired a manager to handle his affairs, but soon a rumor went around that the manager was thoroughly dishonest. 2 So his employer called him in and said, 'What's this I hear about your stealing from me? Get your report in order, because you are going to be dismissed.'

3 "The manager thought to himself, 'Now what? I'm through here, and I don't have the strength to go out and dig ditches, and I'm too proud to beg. 4 I know just the thing! And then I'll have plenty of friends to take care of me when I leave!'

5 "So he invited each person who owed money to his employer to come and discuss the situation. He asked the first one, 'How much do you owe him?' 6 The man replied, 'I owe him eight hundred gallons of olive oil.' So the manager told him, 'Tear up that bill and write another one for four hundred gallons.*'

7 " 'And how much do you owe my employer?' he asked the next man. 'A thousand bushels of wheat,' was the reply. 'Here,' the manager said, 'take your bill and replace it with one for only eight hundred bushels.*'

8 "The rich man had to admire the dishonest rascal for being so shrewd. And it is true that the citizens of this world are more shrewd than the godly are. 9 I tell you, use your worldly resources to

16:6 Greek *100 baths . . . 50 [baths]*.   16:7 Greek *100 korous . . . 80 [korous]*.

benefit others and make friends. In this way, your generosity stores up a reward for you in heaven.*

10"Unless you are faithful in small matters, you won't be faithful in large ones. If you cheat even a little, you won't be honest with greater responsibilities. 11And if you are untrustworthy about worldly wealth, who will trust you with the true riches of heaven? 12And if you are not faithful with other people's money, why should you be trusted with money of your own?

13"No one can serve two masters. For you will hate one and love the other, or be devoted to one and despise the other. You cannot serve both God and money."

14The Pharisees, who dearly loved their money, naturally scoffed at all this. 15Then he said to them, "You like to look good in public, but God knows your evil hearts. What this world honors is an abomination in the sight of God.

16"Until John the Baptist began to preach, the laws of Moses and the messages of the prophets were your guides. But now the Good News of the Kingdom of God is preached, and eager multitudes are forcing their way in. 17But that doesn't mean that the law has lost its force in even the smallest point. It is stronger and more permanent than heaven and earth.

18"Anyone who divorces his wife and marries someone else commits adultery, and anyone who marries a divorced woman commits adultery."

### The Rich Man and Lazarus

19Jesus said, "There was a certain rich man who was splendidly clothed and who lived each day in luxury. 20At his door lay a diseased beggar named Lazarus. 21As Lazarus lay there longing for scraps from the rich man's table, the dogs would come and lick his open sores. 22Finally, the beggar died and was carried by the angels to be with Abraham.* The rich man also died and was buried, 23and his soul went to the place of the dead.* There, in torment, he saw Lazarus in the far distance with Abraham.

24"The rich man shouted, 'Father Abraham, have some pity! Send Lazarus over here to dip the tip of his finger in water and cool my tongue, because I am in anguish in these flames.'

25"But Abraham said to him, 'Son, remember that during your lifetime you had everything you wanted, and Lazarus had nothing. So now he is here being comforted, and you are in anguish. 26And besides, there is a great chasm separating us. Anyone who wanted to cross over to you

from here is stopped at its edge, and no one there can cross over to us.'

27"Then the rich man said, 'Please, Father Abraham, send him to my father's home. 28For I have five brothers, and I want him to warn them about this place of torment so they won't have to come here when they die.'

29"But Abraham said, 'Moses and the prophets have warned them. Your brothers can read their writings anytime they want to.'

30"The rich man replied, 'No, Father Abraham! But if someone is sent to them from the dead, then they will turn from their sins.'

31"But Abraham said, 'If they won't listen to Moses and the prophets, they won't listen even if someone rises from the dead.'"

## CHAPTER 17

### Teachings about Forgiveness and Faith

One day Jesus said to his disciples, "There will always be temptations to sin, but how terrible it will be for the person who does the tempting. 2It would be better to be thrown into the sea with a large millstone tied around the neck than to face the punishment in store for harming one of these little ones. 3I am warning you! If another believer* sins, rebuke him; then if he repents, forgive him. 4Even if he wrongs you seven times a day and each time turns again and asks forgiveness, forgive him."

5One day the apostles said to the Lord, "We need more faith; tell us how to get it."

6"Even if you had faith as small as a mustard seed," the Lord answered, "you could say to this mulberry tree, 'May God uproot you and throw you into the sea,' and it would obey you!

7"When a servant comes in from plowing or taking care of sheep, he doesn't just sit down and eat. 8He must first prepare his master's meal and serve him his supper before eating his own. 9And the servant is not even thanked, because he is merely doing what he is supposed to do. 10In the same way, when you obey me you should say, 'We are not worthy of praise. We are servants who have simply done our duty.'"

### Ten Healed of Leprosy

11As Jesus continued on toward Jerusalem, he reached the border between Galilee and Samaria. 12As he entered a village there, ten lepers stood at a distance, 13crying out, "Jesus, Master, have mercy on us!"

14He looked at them and said, "Go show yourselves to the priests." And as they went, their leprosy disappeared.

15One of them, when he saw that he was healed, came back to Jesus, shouting, "Praise God, I'm healed!" 16He fell face down on the ground at Jesus' feet, thanking him for what he had done. This man was a Samaritan.

17Jesus asked, "Didn't I heal ten men? Where are the other nine? 18Does only this foreigner return to give glory to God?" 19And Jesus said to the man, "Stand up and go. Your faith has made you well."

### The Coming of the Kingdom

20One day the Pharisees asked Jesus, "When will the Kingdom of God come?"

Jesus replied, "The Kingdom of God isn't ushered in with visible signs.* 21You won't be able to say, 'Here it is!' or 'It's over there!' For the Kingdom of God is among you.*"

22Later he talked again about this with his disciples. "The time is coming when you will long to share in the days of the Son of Man, but you won't be able to," he said. 23"Reports will reach you that the Son of Man has returned and that he is in this place or that. Don't believe such reports or go out to look for him. 24For when the Son of Man returns, you will know it beyond all doubt. It will be as evident as the lightning that flashes across the sky. 25But first the Son of Man must suffer terribly* and be rejected by this generation.

26"When the Son of Man returns, the world will be like the people were in Noah's day. 27In those days before the flood, the people enjoyed banquets and parties and weddings right up to the time Noah entered his boat and the flood came to destroy them all.

28"And the world will be as it was in the days of Lot. People went about their daily business—eating and drinking, buying and selling, farming and building—29until the morning Lot left Sodom. Then fire and burning sulfur rained down from heaven and destroyed them all. 30Yes, it will be 'business as usual' right up to the hour when the Son of Man returns.* 31On that day a person outside the house* must not go into the house to pack. A person in the field must not return to town. 32Remember what happened to Lot's wife! 33Whoever clings to this life will lose it, and whoever loses this life will save it. 34That night two people will be asleep in one bed; one will be taken away, and the other will be left. 35Two women will be grinding flour together at the mill; one will be taken, the other left.*"

37"Lord, where will this happen?" the disciples asked.

Jesus replied, "Just as the gathering of vultures shows there is a carcass nearby, so these signs indicate that the end is near."*

## CHAPTER 18

### Story of the Persistent Widow

One day Jesus told his disciples a story to illustrate their need for constant prayer and to show them that they must never give up. 2"There was a judge in a certain city," he said, "who was a godless man with great contempt for everyone. 3A widow of that city came to him repeatedly, appealing for justice against someone who had harmed her. 4The judge ignored her for a while, but eventually she wore him out. 'I fear neither God nor man,' he said to himself, 5'but this woman is driving me crazy. I'm going to see that she gets justice, because she is wearing me out with her constant requests!'"

6Then the Lord said, "Learn a lesson from this evil judge. 7Even he rendered a just decision

17:20 Or *by your speculations.* 17:21 Or *within you.* 17:25 Or *suffer many things.* 17:30 Or *on the day the Son of Man is revealed.* 17:31 Greek *on the roof.* 17:35 Some manuscripts add verse 36, *Two men will be working in the field; one will be taken, the other left.* 17:37 Greek *Wherever the carcass is, the vultures gather.*

# OFF AND RUNNING

## Pray Persistently  Read LUKE 18:1-8

This parable illustrates the need for persistence in prayer. Interestingly enough, Jesus chose two unlikely characters for this parable: a poor, widowed woman, and a corrupt judge. These characters hardly seem like the proper comparison for describing our relationship with God, but Jesus wants us to focus upon several important contrasts in this story:

- The widow had to go to a corrupt judge. . . . We can go to our heavenly Father (see Ephesians 3:14, p. 239).
- The widow was a stranger. . . . We are God's children (see John 1:12, p. 107).

in the end, so don't you think God will surely give justice to his chosen people who plead with him day and night? Will he keep putting them off? [8]I tell you, he will grant justice to them quickly! But when I, the Son of Man, return, how many will I find who have faith?"

### Story of the Pharisee and Tax Collector
[9]Then Jesus told this story to some who had great self-confidence and scorned everyone else: [10]"Two men went to the Temple to pray. One was a Pharisee, and the other was a dishonest tax collector. [11]The proud Pharisee stood by himself and prayed this prayer: 'I thank you, God, that I am not a sinner like everyone else, especially like that tax collector over there! For I never cheat, I don't sin, I don't commit adultery, [12]I fast twice a week, and I give you a tenth of my income.'

[13]"But the tax collector stood at a distance and dared not even lift his eyes to heaven as he prayed. Instead, he beat his chest in sorrow, saying, 'O God, be merciful to me, for I am a sinner.' [14]I tell you, this sinner, not the Pharisee, returned home justified before God. For the proud will be humbled, but the humble will be honored."

### Jesus Blesses the Children
[15]One day some parents brought their little children to Jesus so he could touch them and bless them, but the disciples told them not to bother him. [16]Then Jesus called for the children and said to the disciples, "Let the children come to me. Don't stop them! For the Kingdom of God belongs to such as these. [17]I assure you, anyone who doesn't have their kind of faith will never get into the Kingdom of God."

### The Rich Man
[18]Once a religious leader asked Jesus this question: "Good teacher, what should I do to get eternal life?"

18:20 Exod 20:12-16; Deut 5:16-20.

[19]"Why do you call me good?" Jesus asked him. "Only God is truly good. [20]But as for your question, you know the commandments: 'Do not commit adultery. Do not murder. Do not steal. Do not testify falsely. Honor your father and mother.'* "

[21]The man replied, "I've obeyed all these commandments since I was a child."

[22]"There is still one thing you lack," Jesus said. "Sell all you have and give the money to the poor, and you will have treasure in heaven. Then come, follow me." [23]But when the man heard this, he became sad because he was very rich.

[24]Jesus watched him go and then said to his disciples, "How hard it is for rich people to get into the Kingdom of God! [25]It is easier for a camel to go through the eye of a needle than for a rich person to enter the Kingdom of God!"

[26]Those who heard this said, "Then who in the world can be saved?"

[27]He replied, "What is impossible from a human perspective is possible with God."

[28]Peter said, "We have left our homes and followed you."

[29]"Yes," Jesus replied, "and I assure you, everyone who has given up house or wife or brothers or parents or children, for the sake of the Kingdom of God, [30]will be repaid many times over in this life, as well as receiving eternal life in the world to come."

### Jesus Again Predicts His Death
[31]Gathering the twelve disciples around him, Jesus told them, "As you know, we are going to Jerusalem. And when we get there, all the predictions of the ancient prophets concerning the Son of Man will come true. [32]He will be handed over to the Romans to be mocked, treated shamefully, and spit upon. [33]They will whip him and kill him, but on the third day he will rise again."

[34]But they didn't understand a thing he said.

---

- The widow had no access to the judge. . . . We have constant access to God (see Hebrews 10:19, p. 293).
- The widow came to the court of law. . . . We come to the throne of grace (see Hebrews 4:16, p. 288).
- The widow had no lawyer. . . . We have Jesus as our advocate (see 1 John 2:1, p. 317).
- The widow had to wear down the judge before he really listened. . . . We already know that God hears our requests (see Matthew 7:7-11, p. 11).

If this poor woman received what she deserved from a corrupt judge, how much more will we receive from our loving heavenly Father. As Jesus illustrated, persistence pays off. Keep on praying!

## We Need to Invest Our Abilities and Resources in God's Kingdom Read LUKE 19:11-26

This parable explains what Jesus expects of us as we await his return to earth. The nobleman in this story represents Christ. The servants refer to us, his followers. In essence, the crux of the parable is that we are to work diligently on his behalf until he returns.

In this parable, each man was given ten pounds of silver. Likewise, every believer has been given equal opportunity to invest his or her life in God's Kingdom, a common responsibility. It is the simple commission to proclaim the gospel to the world and make disciples. We then see three levels of investment.

**1. The Servant with Tremendous Gain.** This ambitious servant gave the king back ten times the amount he originally had been given. This type of person is truly a disciple. He or she actively shares his or her faith with one person after another, then takes these individuals under his or her wing to help them mature in their faith.

**2. The Servant with Splendid Gain.** The second servant was a little less ambitious than the first, but he did make some gain. This type of person seems somewhat satisfied with the status quo. He or she gets the gospel out slowly but surely, but he or she doesn't see the same results as the first type of person. This person fails to use all of the resources God has given him or her, so he or she always falls a little short of his or her full potential.

**3. The Servant with No Gain.** The third servant wanted to "play it safe," so he buried his money. He did so because he had a false perception of his master. He claimed that his master was hard and unfair. In the same way, this person is often motivated out of fear of God rather than a love for God. He or she sees witnessing as a duty rather than a privilege. That is why Paul tells us that Christ's love needs to be the motivating force in all that we do (see 2 Corinthians 5:14, pp. 220-221). We can only give out what we ourselves have taken in. And this person knows little of the Savior he or she serves.

In the Kingdom of God, God expects investment as well as results. Don't take this sacred trust he has given to you and bury it in the ground. Use it. Multiply it. Remember, God isn't asking you to work *for* him. He is asking to work *through* you. Yield to the power of the Holy Spirit and ask God for directions as to how you can be used by him. Then you will see results.

**CORNER STONES**

Its significance was hidden from them, and they failed to grasp what he was talking about.

### Jesus Heals a Blind Beggar
35As they approached Jericho, a blind beggar was sitting beside the road. 36When he heard the noise of a crowd going past, he asked what was happening. 37They told him that Jesus of Nazareth was going by. 38So he began shouting, "Jesus, Son of David, have mercy on me!" 39The crowds ahead of Jesus tried to hush the man, but he only shouted louder, "Son of David, have mercy on me!"

40When Jesus heard him, he stopped and ordered that the man be brought to him. 41Then Jesus asked the man, "What do you want me to do for you?"

"Lord," he pleaded, "I want to see!"

42And Jesus said, "All right, you can see! Your faith has healed you." 43Instantly the man could see, and he followed Jesus, praising God. And all who saw it praised God, too.

## CHAPTER 19
### Jesus and Zacchaeus
Jesus entered Jericho and made his way through the town. 2There was a man there named Zacchaeus. He was one of the most influential Jews in the Roman tax-collecting business, and he had become very rich. 3He tried to get a look at Jesus, but he was too short to see over the crowds. 4So he ran ahead and climbed a syca-

more tree beside the road, so he could watch from there.

⁵When Jesus came by, he looked up at Zacchaeus and called him by name. "Zacchaeus!" he said. "Quick, come down! For I must be a guest in your home today."

⁶Zacchaeus quickly climbed down and took Jesus to his house in great excitement and joy. ⁷But the crowds were displeased. "He has gone to be the guest of a notorious sinner," they grumbled.

⁸Meanwhile, Zacchaeus stood there and said to the Lord, "I will give half my wealth to the poor, Lord, and if I have overcharged people on their taxes, I will give them back four times as much!"

⁹Jesus responded, "Salvation has come to this home today, for this man has shown himself to be a son of Abraham. ¹⁰And I, the Son of Man, have come to seek and save those like him who are lost."

## Story of the Ten Servants

¹¹The crowd was listening to everything Jesus said. And because he was nearing Jerusalem, he told a story to correct the impression that the Kingdom of God would begin right away. ¹²He said, "A nobleman was called away to a distant empire to be crowned king and then return. ¹³Before he left, he called together ten servants and gave them ten pounds of silver* to invest for him while he was gone. ¹⁴But his people hated him and sent a delegation after him to say they did not want him to be their king.

¹⁵"When he returned, the king called in the servants to whom he had given the money. He wanted to find out what they had done with the money and what their profits were. ¹⁶The first servant reported a tremendous gain—ten times as much as the original amount! ¹⁷'Well done!' the king exclaimed. 'You are a trustworthy servant. You have been faithful with the little I entrusted to you, so you will be governor of ten cities as your reward.'

¹⁸"The next servant also reported a good gain—five times the original amount. ¹⁹'Well done!' the king said. 'You can be governor over five cities.'

²⁰"But the third servant brought back only the original amount of money and said, 'I hid it and kept it safe. ²¹I was afraid because you are a

hard man to deal with, taking what isn't yours and harvesting crops you didn't plant.'

²²" 'You wicked servant!' the king roared. 'Hard, am I? If you knew so much about me and how tough I am, ²³why didn't you deposit the money in the bank so I could at least get some interest on it?' ²⁴Then turning to the others standing nearby, the king ordered, 'Take the money from this servant, and give it to the one who earned the most.'

²⁵" 'But, master,' they said, 'that servant has enough already!'

²⁶" 'Yes,' the king replied, 'but to those who use well what they are given, even more will be given. But from those who are unfaithful,* even what little they have will be taken away. ²⁷And now about these enemies of mine who didn't want me to be their king—bring them in and execute them right here in my presence.' "

## The Triumphal Entry

²⁸After telling this story, Jesus went on toward Jerusalem, walking ahead of his disciples. ²⁹As they came to the towns of Bethphage and Bethany, on the Mount of Olives, he sent two disciples ahead. ³⁰"Go into that village over there," he told them, "and as you enter it, you will see a colt tied there that has never been ridden. Untie it and bring it here. ³¹If anyone asks what you are doing, just say, 'The Lord needs it.' "

³²So they went and found the colt, just as Jesus had said. ³³And sure enough, as they were untying it, the owners asked them, "Why are you untying our colt?"

³⁴And the disciples simply replied, "The Lord needs it." ³⁵So they brought the colt to Jesus and threw their garments over it for him to ride on.

³⁶Then the crowds spread out their coats on the road ahead of Jesus. ³⁷As they reached the place where the road started down from the Mount of Olives, all of his followers began to shout and sing as they walked along, praising God for all the wonderful miracles they had seen.

³⁸ "Bless the King who comes in the name of
the Lord!
Peace in heaven
and glory in highest heaven!"*

³⁹But some of the Pharisees among the crowd said, "Teacher, rebuke your followers for saying things like that!"

⁴⁰He replied, "If they kept quiet, the stones along the road would burst into cheers!"

19:13 Greek *10 minas;* 1 mina was worth about 3 months' wages.   19:26 Or *who have nothing.*   19:38 Pss 118:26; 148:1.

## Jesus Weeps over Jerusalem

41But as they came closer to Jerusalem and Jesus saw the city ahead, he began to cry. 42"I wish that even today you would find the way of peace. But now it is too late, and peace is hidden from you. 43Before long your enemies will build ramparts against your walls and encircle you and close in on you. 44They will crush you to the ground, and your children with you. Your enemies will not leave a single stone in place, because you have rejected the opportunity God offered you."

## Jesus Clears the Temple

45Then Jesus entered the Temple and began to drive out the merchants from their stalls. 46He told them, "The Scriptures declare, 'My Temple will be a place of prayer,' but you have turned it into a den of thieves."*

47After that, he taught daily in the Temple, but the leading priests, the teachers of religious law, and the other leaders of the people began planning how to kill him. 48But they could think of nothing, because all the people hung on every word he said.

## CHAPTER 20
### The Authority of Jesus Challenged

One day as Jesus was teaching and preaching the Good News in the Temple, the leading priests and teachers of religious law and other leaders came up to him. 2They demanded, "By whose authority did you drive out the merchants from the Temple?* Who gave you such authority?"

3"Let me ask you a question first," he replied. 4"Did John's baptism come from heaven, or was it merely human?"

5They talked it over among themselves. "If we say it was from heaven, he will ask why we didn't believe him. 6But if we say it was merely human, the people will stone us, because they are convinced he was a prophet." 7Finally they replied, "We don't know."

8And Jesus responded, "Then I won't answer your question either."

## Story of the Evil Farmers

9Now Jesus turned to the people again and told them this story: "A man planted a vineyard, leased it out to tenant farmers, and moved to another country to live for several years. 10At grape-picking time, he sent one of his servants to collect his share of the crop. But the farmers attacked the servant, beat him up, and sent him back empty-handed. 11So the owner sent another servant, but the same thing happened; he was beaten up and treated shamefully, and he went away empty-handed. 12A third man was sent and the same thing happened. He, too, was wounded and chased away.

13" 'What will I do?' the owner asked himself. 'I know! I'll send my cherished son. Surely they will respect him.'

14"But when the farmers saw his son, they said to each other, 'Here comes the heir to this estate. Let's kill him and get the estate for ourselves!' 15So they dragged him out of the vineyard and murdered him.

"What do you suppose the owner of the vineyard will do to those farmers?" Jesus asked. 16"I'll tell you—he will come and kill them all and lease the vineyard to others."

"But God forbid that such a thing should ever happen," his listeners protested.

17Jesus looked at them and said, "Then what do the Scriptures mean?

'The stone rejected by the builders
has now become the cornerstone.'*

18All who stumble over that stone will be broken to pieces, and it will crush anyone on whom it falls."

19When the teachers of religious law and the leading priests heard this story, they wanted to arrest Jesus immediately because they realized he was pointing at them—that they were the farmers in the story. But they were afraid there would be a riot if they arrested him.

## Taxes for Caesar

20Watching for their opportunity, the leaders sent secret agents pretending to be honest men. They tried to get Jesus to say something that could be reported to the Roman governor so he would arrest Jesus. 21They said, "Teacher, we know that you speak and teach what is right and are not influenced by what others think. You sincerely teach the ways of God. 22Now tell us— is it right to pay taxes to the Roman government or not?"

23He saw through their trickery and said, 24"Show me a Roman coin.* Whose picture and title are stamped on it?"

"Caesar's," they replied.

25"Well then," he said, "give to Caesar what belongs to him. But everything that belongs to

19:46 Isa 56:7; Jer 7:11.  20:2 Or *By whose authority do you do these things?*  20:17 Ps 118:22.  20:24 Greek *a denarius.*

God must be given to God." ²⁶So they failed to trap him in the presence of the people. Instead, they were amazed by his answer, and they were silenced.

### Discussion about Resurrection

²⁷Then some Sadducees stepped forward—a group of Jews who say there is no resurrection after death. ²⁸They posed this question: "Teacher, Moses gave us a law that if a man dies, leaving a wife but no children, his brother should marry the widow and have a child who will be the brother's heir.* ²⁹Well, there were seven brothers. The oldest married and then died without children. ³⁰His brother married the widow, but he also died. Still no children. ³¹And so it went, one after the other, until each of the seven had married her and died, leaving no children. ³²Finally, the woman died, too. ³³So tell us, whose wife will she be in the resurrection? For all seven were married to her!"

³⁴Jesus replied, "Marriage is for people here on earth. ³⁵But that is not the way it will be in the age to come. For those worthy of being raised from the dead won't be married then. ³⁶And they will never die again. In these respects they are like angels. They are children of God raised up to new life. ³⁷But now, as to whether the dead will be raised—even Moses proved this when he wrote about the burning bush. Long after Abraham, Isaac, and Jacob had died, he referred to the Lord* as 'the God of Abraham, the God of Isaac, and the God of Jacob.'* ³⁸So he is the God of the living, not the dead. They are all alive to him."

³⁹"Well said, Teacher!" remarked some of the teachers of religious law who were standing there. ⁴⁰And that ended their questions; no one dared to ask any more.

### Whose Son Is the Messiah?

⁴¹Then Jesus presented them with a question. "Why is it," he asked, "that the Messiah is said to be the son of David? ⁴²For David himself wrote in the book of Psalms:

'The LORD said to my Lord,
  Sit in honor at my right hand
⁴³  until I humble your enemies,
    making them a footstool under your feet.'*

⁴⁴Since David called him Lord, how can he be his son at the same time?"

⁴⁵Then, with the crowds listening, he turned to his disciples and said, ⁴⁶"Beware of these teachers of religious law! For they love to parade in flowing robes and to have everyone bow to them as they walk in the marketplaces. And how they love the seats of honor in the synagogues and at banquets. ⁴⁷But they shamelessly cheat widows out of their property, and then, to cover up the kind of people they really are, they make long prayers in public. Because of this, their punishment will be the greater."

## CHAPTER 21
### The Widow's Offering

While Jesus was in the Temple, he watched the rich people putting their gifts into the collection box. ²Then a poor widow came by and dropped in two pennies.* ³"I assure you," he said, "this poor widow has given more than all the rest of them. ⁴For they have given a tiny part of their surplus, but she, poor as she is, has given everything she has."

### Jesus Foretells the Future

⁵Some of his disciples began talking about the beautiful stonework of the Temple and the memorial decorations on the walls. But Jesus said, ⁶"The time is coming when all these things will be so completely demolished that not one stone will be left on top of another."

⁷"Teacher," they asked, "when will all this take place? And will there be any sign ahead of time?"

⁸He replied, "Don't let anyone mislead you. For many will come in my name, claiming to be the Messiah* and saying, 'The time has come!' But don't believe them. ⁹And when you hear of wars and insurrections, don't panic. Yes, these things must come, but the end won't follow immediately." ¹⁰Then he added, "Nations and kingdoms will proclaim war against each other. ¹¹There will be great earthquakes, and there will be famines and epidemics in many lands, and there will be terrifying things and great miraculous signs in the heavens.

¹²"But before all this occurs, there will be a time of great persecution. You will be dragged into synagogues and prisons, and you will be accused before kings and governors of being my followers. ¹³This will be your opportunity to tell them about me. ¹⁴So don't worry about how to answer the charges against you, ¹⁵for I will give you the right words and such wisdom that none

of your opponents will be able to reply! 16Even those closest to you—your parents, brothers, relatives, and friends—will betray you. And some of you will be killed. 17And everyone will hate you because of your allegiance to me. 18But not a hair of your head will perish! 19By standing firm, you will win your souls.

20"And when you see Jerusalem surrounded by armies, then you will know that the time of its destruction has arrived. 21Then those in Judea must flee to the hills. Let those in Jerusalem escape, and those outside the city should not enter it for shelter. 22For those will be days of God's vengeance, and the prophetic words of the Scriptures will be fulfilled. 23How terrible it will be for pregnant women and for mothers nursing their babies. For there will be great distress in the land and wrath upon this people. 24They will be brutally killed by the sword or sent away as captives to all the nations of the world. And Jerusalem will be conquered and trampled down by the Gentiles until the age of the Gentiles comes to an end.

25"And there will be strange events in the skies—signs in the sun, moon, and stars. And down here on earth the nations will be in turmoil, perplexed by the roaring seas and strange tides. 26The courage of many people will falter because of the fearful fate they see coming upon the earth, because the stability of the very heavens will be broken up. 27Then everyone will see the Son of Man arrive on the clouds with power and great glory.* 28So when all these things begin to happen, stand straight and look up, for your salvation is near!"

29Then he gave them this illustration: "Notice the fig tree, or any other tree. 30When the leaves come out, you know without being told that summer is near. 31Just so, when you see the events I've described taking place, you can be sure that the Kingdom of God is near. 32I assure you, this generation* will not pass from the scene until all these events have taken place. 33Heaven and earth will disappear, but my words will remain forever.

34"Watch out! Don't let me find you living in careless ease and drunkenness, and filled with the worries of this life. Don't let that day catch you unaware, 35as in a trap. For that day will come upon everyone living on the earth. 36Keep a constant watch. And pray that, if possible, you may escape these horrors and stand before the Son of Man."

37Every day Jesus went to the Temple to teach, and each evening he returned to spend the night on the Mount of Olives. 38The crowds gathered early each morning to hear him.

CHAPTER **22**

## Judas Agrees to Betray Jesus

The Festival of Unleavened Bread, which begins with the Passover celebration, was drawing near. 2The leading priests and teachers of religious law were actively plotting Jesus' murder. But they wanted to kill him without starting a riot, a possibility they greatly feared.

3Then Satan entered into Judas Iscariot, who was one of the twelve disciples, 4and he went over to the leading priests and captains of the Temple guard to discuss the best way to betray Jesus to them. 5They were delighted that he was ready to help them, and they promised him a reward. 6So he began looking for an opportunity to betray Jesus so they could arrest him quietly when the crowds weren't around.

## The Last Supper

7Now the Festival of Unleavened Bread arrived, when the Passover lambs were sacrificed. 8Jesus sent Peter and John ahead and said, "Go and prepare the Passover meal, so we can eat it together."

9"Where do you want us to go?" they asked him.

10He replied, "As soon as you enter Jerusalem, a man carrying a pitcher of water will meet you. Follow him. At the house he enters, 11say to the owner, 'The Teacher asks, Where is the guest room where I can eat the Passover meal with my disciples?' 12He will take you upstairs to a large room that is already set up. That is the place. Go ahead and prepare our supper there." 13They went off to the city and found everything just as Jesus had said, and they prepared the Passover supper there.

14Then at the proper time Jesus and the twelve apostles sat down together at the table. 15Jesus said, "I have looked forward to this hour with deep longing, anxious to eat this Passover meal with you before my suffering begins. 16For I tell you now that I won't eat it again until it comes to fulfillment in the Kingdom of God."

17Then he took a cup of wine, and when he had given thanks for it, he said, "Take this and share it among yourselves. 18For I will not drink wine again until the Kingdom of God has come."

21:27 See Dan 7:13.   21:32 Or *this age,* or *this nation.*

19Then he took a loaf of bread; and when he had thanked God for it, he broke it in pieces and gave it to the disciples, saying, "This is my body, given for you. Do this in remembrance of me." 20After supper he took another cup of wine and said, "This wine is the token of God's new covenant to save you—an agreement sealed with the blood I will pour out for you.*

21"But here at this table, sitting among us as a friend, is the man who will betray me. 22For I, the Son of Man, must die since it is part of God's plan. But how terrible it will be for my betrayer!" 23Then the disciples began to ask each other which of them would ever do such a thing.

24And they began to argue among themselves as to who would be the greatest in the coming Kingdom. 25Jesus told them, "In this world the kings and great men order their people around, and yet they are called 'friends of the people.' 26But among you, those who are the greatest should take the lowest rank, and the leader should be like a servant. 27Normally the master sits at the table and is served by his servants. But not here! For I am your servant. 28You have remained true to me in my time of trial. 29And just as my Father has granted me a Kingdom, I now grant you the right 30to eat and drink at my table in that Kingdom. And you will sit on thrones, judging the twelve tribes of Israel.

## Jesus Predicts Peter's Denial

31"Simon, Simon, Satan has asked to have all of you, to sift you like wheat. 32But I have pleaded in prayer for you, Simon, that your faith should not fail. So when you have repented and turned to me again, strengthen and build up your brothers."

33Peter said, "Lord, I am ready to go to prison with you, and even to die with you."

34But Jesus said, "Peter, let me tell you something. The rooster will not crow tomorrow morning until you have denied three times that you even know me."

35Then Jesus asked them, "When I sent you out to preach the Good News and you did not have money, a traveler's bag, or extra clothing, did you lack anything?"

"No," they replied.

36"But now," he said, "take your money and a traveler's bag. And if you don't have a sword, sell your clothes and buy one! 37For the time has come for this prophecy about me to be fulfilled: 'He was counted among those who were reb-

els.'* Yes, everything written about me by the prophets will come true."

38"Lord," they replied, "we have two swords among us."

"That's enough," he said.

## Jesus Prays on the Mount of Olives

39Then, accompanied by the disciples, Jesus left the upstairs room and went as usual to the Mount of Olives. 40There he told them, "Pray that you will not be overcome by temptation."

41He walked away, about a stone's throw, and knelt down and prayed, 42"Father, if you are willing, please take this cup of suffering away from me. Yet I want your will, not mine." 43Then an angel from heaven appeared and strengthened him. 44He prayed more fervently, and he was in such agony of spirit that his sweat fell to the ground like great drops of blood.* 45At last he stood up again and returned to the disciples, only to find them asleep, exhausted from grief. 46"Why are you sleeping?" he asked. "Get up and pray. Otherwise temptation will overpower you."

## Jesus Is Betrayed and Arrested

47But even as he said this, a mob approached, led by Judas, one of his twelve disciples. Judas walked over to Jesus and greeted him with a kiss. 48But Jesus said, "Judas, how can you betray me, the Son of Man, with a kiss?"

49When the other disciples saw what was about to happen, they exclaimed, "Lord, should we fight? We brought the swords!" 50And one of them slashed at the high priest's servant and cut off his right ear.

51But Jesus said, "Don't resist anymore." And he touched the place where the man's ear had been and healed him. 52Then Jesus spoke to the leading priests and captains of the Temple guard and the other leaders who headed the mob. "Am I some dangerous criminal," he asked, "that you have come armed with swords and clubs to arrest me? 53Why didn't you arrest me in the Temple? I was there every day. But this is your moment, the time when the power of darkness reigns."

## Peter Denies Jesus

54So they arrested him and led him to the high priest's residence, and Peter was following far behind. 55The guards lit a fire in the courtyard and sat around it, and Peter joined them there.

22:19-20 Some manuscripts omit 22:19b-20, given for you . . . I will pour out for you. 22:37 Isa 53:12. 22:43-44 These verses are not included in many ancient manuscripts.

56A servant girl noticed him in the firelight and began staring at him. Finally she said, "This man was one of Jesus' followers!"

57Peter denied it. "Woman," he said, "I don't even know the man!"

58After a while someone else looked at him and said, "You must be one of them!"

"No, man, I'm not!" Peter replied.

59About an hour later someone else insisted, "This must be one of Jesus' disciples because he is a Galilean, too."

60But Peter said, "Man, I don't know what you are talking about." And as soon as he said these words, the rooster crowed. 61At that moment the Lord turned and looked at Peter. Then Peter remembered that the Lord had said, "Before the rooster crows tomorrow morning, you will deny me three times." 62And Peter left the courtyard, crying bitterly.

63Now the guards in charge of Jesus began mocking and beating him. 64They blindfolded him; then they hit him and asked, "Who hit you that time, you prophet?" 65And they threw all sorts of terrible insults at him.

### Jesus before the Council

66At daybreak all the leaders of the people assembled, including the leading priests and the teachers of religious law. Jesus was led before this high council,* 67and they said, "Tell us if you are the Messiah."

But he replied, "If I tell you, you won't believe me. 68And if I ask you a question, you won't answer. 69But the time is soon coming when I, the Son of Man, will be sitting at God's right hand in the place of power."*

70They all shouted, "Then you claim you are the Son of God?"

And he replied, "You are right in saying that I am."

71"What need do we have for other witnesses?" they shouted. "We ourselves heard him say it."

## CHAPTER 23

### Jesus' Trial before Pilate

Then the entire council took Jesus over to Pilate, the Roman governor. 2They began at once to state their case: "This man has been leading our people to ruin by telling them not to pay their taxes to the Roman government and by claiming he is the Messiah, a king."

3So Pilate asked him, "Are you the King of the Jews?"

Jesus replied, "Yes, it is as you say."

4Pilate turned to the leading priests and to the crowd and said, "I find nothing wrong with this man!"

5Then they became desperate. "But he is causing riots everywhere he goes, all over Judea, from Galilee to Jerusalem!"

6"Oh, is he a Galilean?" Pilate asked. 7When they answered that he was, Pilate sent him to Herod Antipas, because Galilee was under Herod's jurisdiction, and Herod happened to be in Jerusalem at the time.

8Herod was delighted at the opportunity to see Jesus, because he had heard about him and had been hoping for a long time to see him perform a miracle. 9He asked Jesus question after question, but Jesus refused to answer. 10Meanwhile, the leading priests and the teachers of religious law stood there shouting their accusations. 11Now Herod and his soldiers began mocking and ridiculing Jesus. Then they put a royal robe on him and sent him back to Pilate. 12Herod and Pilate, who had been enemies before, became friends that day.

13Then Pilate called together the leading priests and other religious leaders, along with the people, 14and he announced his verdict. "You brought this man to me, accusing him of leading a revolt. I have examined him thoroughly on this point in your presence and find him innocent. 15Herod came to the same conclusion and sent him back to us. Nothing this man has done calls for the death penalty. 16So I will have him flogged, but then I will release him."*

18Then a mighty roar rose from the crowd, and with one voice they shouted, "Kill him, and release Barabbas to us!" 19(Barabbas was in prison for murder and for taking part in an insurrection in Jerusalem against the government.) 20Pilate argued with them, because he wanted to release Jesus. 21But they shouted, "Crucify him! Crucify him!"

22For the third time he demanded, "Why? What crime has he committed? I have found no reason to sentence him to death. I will therefore flog him and let him go."

23But the crowd shouted louder and louder for Jesus' death, and their voices prevailed. 24So Pilate sentenced Jesus to die as they demanded. 25As they had requested, he released Barabbas,

22:66 Greek *before their Sanhedrin.*   22:69 See Ps 110:1.   23:16 Some manuscripts add verse 17, *For it was necessary for him to release one [prisoner] for them during the feast.*

# What Is Backsliding? Read LUKE 22:31-62

As believers we have been given a "new nature"—a part of us that spiritually hungers after God, a supernatural inclination to do what is right. Unfortunately, being human, we also have an "old nature"—a natural inclination to do wrong. Sometimes Christians begin to fall back spiritually or "backslide."

Perhaps the best way to understand the dangers of backsliding is to examine the biblical account of how one believer fell into this trap. He was none other than Simon Peter, one of Jesus' closest disciples. In Luke 22 we are given the account of his spiritual regression. His story serves as a warning that even the most mature believers have the potential to fall if they let their guard down.

**Self-Confidence and False Security.** Not only did Peter reveal his unfounded confidence in himself (his claim that he would "die" with Jesus), but he also directly contradicted the Lord's prediction that he would fall (verse 34). He denied his own weakness to sin. The Bible warns, "If you think you are standing strong, be careful, for you, too, may fall into the same sin" (1 Corinthians 10:12).

**Prayerlessness.** Even after Jesus specifically instructed Peter to pray, he decided to sleep instead. In Matthew's account of this incident, Jesus had even warned them, "For though the spirit is willing enough, the body is weak!" (Matthew 26:41). Yet he felt no weakness and saw no need to be prayerful and watchful. Prayerlessness is as much a sin as directly breaking a commandment, for throughout Scripture God has specifically instructed us to pray.

**Following God at a Distance.** A lack of closeness and fellowship with the Lord will always be at the foundation of all spiritual regression. Although Peter was still following Jesus, he wasn't following as closely as he could have been. There are some Christians who want to try to live in both worlds. They want to be believers, but they don't want to be too committed. You endanger yourself when you live this way.

**Warming Up at the Enemies' Fire.** Following in the distance, Peter became cold and was attracted to the fire. Peter hoped to go unnoticed in the larger crowd, so he settled in with the very people who were responsible for arresting his Lord. The Bible tells us, "Oh, the joys of those who do not follow the advice of the wicked, or stand around with sinners, or join in with scoffers" (Psalm 1:1). Tragically, Peter was doing exactly the opposite. When that spiritual passion in our heart begins to die, that fire for Jesus Christ will grow cold, and we will look elsewhere for warmth.

**Denial and Disassociations.** Peter reached this final step of spiritual regression when he denied knowing or ever being with Jesus. Matthew's Gospel tells us that he began to curse and swear, which means that he took an oath, saying, "May God kill and damn me if I am not speaking the truth (26:74)." Peter had lost all sense of reality and seemingly all awareness of God.

Despite Peter's fall, he was restored. In verse 61, his eyes met those of Jesus, and Peter cried bitterly. As he grieved over his sin, Jesus saw his heart. The Bible says, "God can use sorrow in our lives to help us turn away from sin and seek salvation" (2 Corinthians 7:10). Interestingly enough, three days later, after Jesus' resurrection, the angel at the tomb specifically told Mary, "Now go and give this message to his disciples, *including Peter:* 'Jesus is going ahead of you to Galilee. You will see him there" (Mark 16:7, emphasis added). Jesus wanted Peter to know that he still loved him.

As Christians we will sin. Scripture says, "If we say that we have no sin, we are only fooling ourselves and refusing to accept the truth" (1 John 1:8). But the Holy Spirit will lovingly convict us of that sin and lead us back to the cross, where we can confess it and turn from it. Remember, when we sin we should run to—not away from—the Lord.

BIG QUESTIONS

the man in prison for insurrection and murder. But he delivered Jesus over to them to do as they wished.

## The Crucifixion

26As they led Jesus away, Simon of Cyrene,* who was coming in from the country just then, was forced to follow Jesus and carry his cross. 27Great crowds trailed along behind, including many grief-stricken women. 28But Jesus turned and said to them, "Daughters of Jerusalem, don't weep for me, but weep for yourselves and for your children. 29For the days are coming when they will say, 'Fortunate indeed are the women who are childless, the wombs that have not borne a child and the breasts that have never nursed.' 30People will beg the mountains to fall on them and the hills to bury them. 31For if these things are done when the tree is green, what will happen when it is dry?*"

32Two others, both criminals, were led out to be executed with him. 33Finally, they came to a place called The Skull.* All three were crucified there—Jesus on the center cross, and the two criminals on either side.

34Jesus said, "Father, forgive these people, because they don't know what they are doing."* And the soldiers gambled for his clothes by throwing dice.*

35The crowd watched, and the leaders laughed and scoffed. "He saved others," they said, "let him save himself if he is really God's Chosen One, the Messiah." 36The soldiers mocked him, too, by offering him a drink of sour wine. 37They called out to him, "If you are the King of the Jews, save yourself!" 38A signboard was nailed to the cross above him with these words: "This is the King of the Jews."

39One of the criminals hanging beside him scoffed, "So you're the Messiah, are you? Prove it by saving yourself—and us, too, while you're at it!"

40But the other criminal protested, "Don't you fear God even when you are dying? 41We deserve to die for our evil deeds, but this man hasn't done anything wrong." 42Then he said, "Jesus, remember me when you come into your Kingdom."

43And Jesus replied, "I assure you, today you will be with me in paradise."

## The Death of Jesus

44By this time it was noon, and darkness fell across the whole land until three o'clock. 45The light from the sun was gone. And suddenly, the thick veil hanging in the Temple was torn apart. 46Then Jesus shouted, "Father, I entrust my spirit into your hands!"* And with those words he breathed his last.

47When the captain of the Roman soldiers handling the executions saw what had happened, he praised God and said, "Surely this man was innocent.*" 48And when the crowd that came to see the crucifixion saw all that had happened, they went home in deep sorrow.* 49But Jesus' friends, including the women who had followed him from Galilee, stood at a distance watching.

## The Burial of Jesus

50Now there was a good and righteous man named Joseph. He was a member of the Jewish high council, 51but he had not agreed with the decision and actions of the other religious leaders. He was from the town of Arimathea in Judea, and he had been waiting for the Kingdom of God to come. 52He went to Pilate and asked for Jesus' body. 53Then he took the body down from the cross and wrapped it in a long linen cloth and laid it in a new tomb that had been carved out of rock. 54This was done late on Friday afternoon, the day of preparation* for the Sabbath.

55As his body was taken away, the women from Galilee followed and saw the tomb where they placed his body. 56Then they went home and prepared spices and ointments to embalm him. But by the time they were finished it was the Sabbath, so they rested all that day as required by the law.

## CHAPTER 24
### The Resurrection

But very early on Sunday morning* the women came to the tomb, taking the spices they had prepared. 2They found that the stone covering the entrance had been rolled aside. 3So they went in, but they couldn't find the body of the Lord Jesus. 4They were puzzled, trying to think what could have happened to it. Suddenly, two men appeared to them, clothed in dazzling robes. 5The women were terrified and bowed

23:26 Cyrene was a city in northern Africa. 23:31 Or If these things are done to me, the living tree, what will happen to you, the dry tree? 23:33 Sometimes rendered Calvary, which comes from the Latin word for "skull." 23:34a This sentence is not included in many ancient manuscripts. 23:34b Greek by casting lots. See Ps 22:18. 23:46 Ps 31:5. 23:47 Or righteous. 23:48 Greek beating their breasts. 23:54 Greek on the day of preparation. 24:1 Greek But on the first day of the week, very early in the morning.

low before them. Then the men asked, "Why are you looking in a tomb for someone who is alive? 6He isn't here! He has risen from the dead! Don't you remember what he told you back in Galilee, 7that the Son of Man must be betrayed into the hands of sinful men and be crucified, and that he would rise again the third day?"

8Then they remembered that he had said this. 9So they rushed back to tell his eleven disciples—and everyone else—what had happened. 10The women who went to the tomb were Mary Magdalene, Joanna, Mary the mother of James, and several others. They told the apostles what had happened, 11but the story sounded like nonsense, so they didn't believe it. 12However, Peter ran to the tomb to look. Stooping, he peered in and saw the empty linen wrappings; then he went home again, wondering what had happened.*

### The Walk to Emmaus

13That same day two of Jesus' followers were walking to the village of Emmaus, seven miles* out of Jerusalem. 14As they walked along they were talking about everything that had happened. 15Suddenly, Jesus himself came along and joined them and began walking beside them. 16But they didn't know who he was, because God kept them from recognizing him.

17"You seem to be in a deep discussion about something," he said. "What are you so concerned about?"

They stopped short, sadness written across their faces. 18Then one of them, Cleopas, replied, "You must be the only person in Jerusalem who hasn't heard about all the things that have happened there the last few days."

19"What things?" Jesus asked.

"The things that happened to Jesus, the man from Nazareth," they said. "He was a prophet who did wonderful miracles. He was a mighty teacher, highly regarded by both God and all the people. 20But our leading priests and other religious leaders arrested him and handed him over to be condemned to death, and they crucified him. 21We had thought he was the Messiah who had come to rescue Israel. That all happened three days ago. 22Then some women from our group of his followers were at his tomb early this morning, and they came back with an amazing report. 23They said his body was missing, and they had seen angels who told them Jesus is alive! 24Some of our men ran out to see, and

sure enough, Jesus' body was gone, just as the women had said."

25Then Jesus said to them, "You are such foolish people! You find it so hard to believe all that the prophets wrote in the Scriptures. 26Wasn't it clearly predicted by the prophets that the Messiah would have to suffer all these things before entering his time of glory?" 27Then Jesus quoted passages from the writings of Moses and all the prophets, explaining what all the Scriptures said about himself.

28By this time they were nearing Emmaus and the end of their journey. Jesus would have gone on, 29but they begged him to stay the night with them, since it was getting late. So he went home with them. 30As they sat down to eat, he took a small loaf of bread, asked God's blessing on it, broke it, then gave it to them. 31Suddenly, their eyes were opened, and they recognized him. And at that moment he disappeared!

32They said to each other, "Didn't our hearts feel strangely warm as he talked with us on the road and explained the Scriptures to us?" 33And within the hour they were on their way back to Jerusalem, where the eleven disciples and the other followers of Jesus were gathered. When they arrived, they were greeted with the report, 34"The Lord has really risen! He appeared to Peter*!"

### Jesus Appears to the Disciples

35Then the two from Emmaus told their story of how Jesus had appeared to them as they were walking along the road and how they had recognized him as he was breaking the bread. 36And just as they were telling about it, Jesus himself was suddenly standing there among them. He said, "Peace be with you."* 37But the whole group was terribly frightened, thinking they were seeing a ghost! 38"Why are you frightened?" he asked. "Why do you doubt who I am? 39Look at my hands. Look at my feet. You can see that it's really me. Touch me and make sure that I am not a ghost, because ghosts don't have bodies, as you see that I do!" 40As he spoke, he held out his hands for them to see, and he showed them his feet.*

41Still they stood there doubting, filled with joy and wonder. Then he asked them, "Do you have anything here to eat?" 42They gave him a piece of broiled fish, 43and he ate it as they watched.

44Then he said, "When I was with you before,

I told you that everything written about me by Moses and the prophets and in the Psalms must all come true." [45]Then he opened their minds to understand these many Scriptures. [46]And he said, "Yes, it was written long ago that the Messiah must suffer and die and rise again from the dead on the third day. [47]With my authority, take this message of repentance to all the nations, beginning in Jerusalem: 'There is forgiveness of sins for all who turn to me.' [48]You are witnesses of all these things.

[49]"And now I will send the Holy Spirit, just as my Father promised. But stay here in the city until the Holy Spirit comes and fills you with power from heaven."

## The Ascension

[50]Then Jesus led them to Bethany, and lifting his hands to heaven, he blessed them. [51]While he was blessing them, he left them and was taken up to heaven.* [52]They worshiped him and* then returned to Jerusalem filled with great joy. [53]And they spent all of their time in the Temple, praising God.

24:51 Some manuscripts do not include *and was taken up to heaven.*  24:52 Some manuscripts do not include *worshiped him and.*

# John

## CHAPTER 1

### Christ, the Eternal Word

In the beginning the Word already existed. He was with God, and he was God. ²He was in the beginning with God. ³He created everything there is. Nothing exists that he didn't make. ⁴Life itself was in him, and this life gives light to everyone. ⁵The light shines through the darkness, and the darkness can never extinguish it.

⁶God sent John the Baptist ⁷to tell everyone about the light so that everyone might believe because of his testimony. ⁸John himself was not the light; he was only a witness to the light. ⁹The one who is the true light, who gives light to everyone, was going to come into the world.

¹⁰But although the world was made through him, the world didn't recognize him when he came. ¹¹Even in his own land and among his own people, he was not accepted. ¹²But to all who believed him and accepted him, he gave the right to become children of God. ¹³They are reborn! This is not a physical birth resulting from human passion or plan—this rebirth comes from God.

¹⁴So the Word became human and lived here on earth among us. He was full of unfailing love and faithfulness.* And we have seen his glory, the glory of the only Son of the Father.

¹⁵John pointed him out to the people. He shouted to the crowds, "This is the one I was talking about when I said, 'Someone is coming who is far greater than I am, for he existed long before I did.'"

¹⁶We have all benefited from the rich blessings he brought to us—one gracious blessing after another.* ¹⁷For the law was given through Moses; God's unfailing love and faithfulness came through Jesus Christ. ¹⁸No one has ever seen God. But his only Son, who is himself God,* is near to the Father's heart; he has told us about him.

### The Testimony of John the Baptist

¹⁹This was the testimony of John when the Jewish leaders sent priests and Temple assistants* from Jerusalem to ask John whether he claimed to be the Messiah. ²⁰He flatly denied it. "I am not the Messiah," he said.

²¹"Well then, who are you?" they asked. "Are you Elijah?"

"No," he replied.

"Are you the Prophet?"*

"No."

²²"Then who are you? Tell us, so we can give an answer to those who sent us. What do you have to say about yourself?"

²³John replied in the words of Isaiah:

"I am a voice shouting in the wilderness,
  'Prepare a straight pathway for the Lord's
     coming!'"*

²⁴Then those who were sent by the Pharisees ²⁵asked him, "If you aren't the Messiah or Elijah or the Prophet, what right do you have to baptize?"

²⁶John told them, "I baptize with* water, but right here in the crowd is someone you do not know, ²⁷who will soon begin his ministry. I am not even worthy to be his slave.*" ²⁸This incident took place at Bethany, a village east of the Jordan River, where John was baptizing.

### Jesus, the Lamb of God

²⁹The next day John saw Jesus coming toward him and said, "Look! There is the Lamb of God who takes away the sin of the world! ³⁰He is the one I was talking about when I said, 'Soon a

1:14 Greek *grace and truth*; also in 1:17.   1:16 Greek *grace upon grace*.   1:18 Some manuscripts read *his one and only Son*.   1:19 Greek *and Levites*.   1:21 See Deut 18:15, 18; Mal 4:5-6.   1:23 Isa 40:3.   1:26 Or *in*; also in 1:31, 33.   1:27 Greek *to untie his sandals*.

man is coming who is far greater than I am, for he existed long before I did.' 31I didn't know he was the one, but I have been baptizing with water in order to point him out to Israel."

32Then John said, "I saw the Holy Spirit descending like a dove from heaven and resting upon him. 33I didn't know he was the one, but when God sent me to baptize with water, he told me, 'When you see the Holy Spirit descending and resting upon someone, he is the one you are looking for. He is the one who baptizes with the Holy Spirit.' 34I saw this happen to Jesus, so I testify that he is the Son of God.*"

### The First Disciples

35The following day, John was again standing with two of his disciples. 36As Jesus walked by, John looked at him and then declared, "Look! There is the Lamb of God!" 37Then John's two disciples turned and followed Jesus.

38Jesus looked around and saw them following. "What do you want?" he asked them.

They replied, "Rabbi" (which means Teacher), "where are you staying?"

39"Come and see," he said. It was about four o'clock in the afternoon when they went with him to the place, and they stayed there the rest of the day.

40Andrew, Simon Peter's brother, was one of these men who had heard what John said and then followed Jesus. 41The first thing Andrew did was to find his brother, Simon, and tell him, "We have found the Messiah" (which means the Christ).

42Then Andrew brought Simon to meet Jesus. Looking intently at Simon, Jesus said, "You are Simon, the son of John—but you will be called Cephas" (which means Peter*).

43The next day Jesus decided to go to Galilee. He found Philip and said to him, "Come, be my disciple." 44Philip was from Bethsaida, Andrew and Peter's hometown.

45Philip went off to look for Nathanael and told him, "We have found the very person Moses and the prophets wrote about! His name is Jesus, the son of Joseph from Nazareth."

46"Nazareth!" exclaimed Nathanael. "Can anything good come from there?"

"Just come and see for yourself," Philip said.

47As they approached, Jesus said, "Here comes an honest man—a true son of Israel."

48"How do you know about me?" Nathanael asked.

And Jesus replied, "I could see you under the fig tree before Philip found you."

49Nathanael replied, "Teacher, you are the Son of God—the King of Israel!"

50Jesus asked him, "Do you believe all this just because I told you I had seen you under the fig tree? You will see greater things than this." 51Then he said, "The truth is, you will all see heaven open and the angels of God going up and down upon the Son of Man."*

## CHAPTER 2
### The Wedding at Cana

The next day* Jesus' mother was a guest at a wedding celebration in the village of Cana in Galilee. 2Jesus and his disciples were also invited to the celebration. 3The wine supply ran out during the festivities, so Jesus' mother spoke to him about the problem. "They have no more wine," she told him.

4"How does that concern you and me?" Jesus asked. "My time has not yet come."

5But his mother told the servants, "Do whatever he tells you."

6Six stone waterpots were standing there; they were used for Jewish ceremonial purposes and held twenty to thirty gallons* each. 7Jesus told the servants, "Fill the jars with water." When the jars had been filled to the brim, 8he said, "Dip some out and take it to the master of ceremonies." So they followed his instructions.

9When the master of ceremonies tasted the water that was now wine, not knowing where it had come from (though, of course, the servants knew), he called the bridegroom over. 10"Usually a host serves the best wine first," he said. "Then, when everyone is full and doesn't care, he brings out the less expensive wines. But you have kept the best until now!"

11This miraculous sign at Cana in Galilee was Jesus' first display of his glory. And his disciples believed in him.

12After the wedding he went to Capernaum for a few days with his mother, his brothers, and his disciples.

### Jesus Clears the Temple

13It was time for the annual Passover celebration, and Jesus went to Jerusalem. 14In the Temple area he saw merchants selling cattle, sheep, and doves for sacrifices; and he saw money changers behind their counters. 15Jesus made a whip from some

---

1:34 Some manuscripts read *the chosen One of God.*   1:42 The names *Cephas* and *Peter* both mean "rock."   1:51 See Gen 28:10-17, the account of Jacob's ladder.   2:1 Greek *On the third day;* see 1:35, 43.   2:6 Greek *2 or 3 measures* [75 to 113 liters].

ropes and chased them all out of the Temple. He drove out the sheep and oxen, scattered the money changers' coins over the floor, and turned over their tables. 16Then, going over to the people who sold doves, he told them, "Get these things out of here. Don't turn my Father's house into a marketplace!"

17Then his disciples remembered this prophecy from the Scriptures: "Passion for God's house burns within me."*

18"What right do you have to do these things?" the Jewish leaders demanded. "If you have this authority from God, show us a miraculous sign to prove it."

19"All right," Jesus replied. "Destroy this temple, and in three days I will raise it up."

20"What!" they exclaimed. "It took forty-six years to build this Temple, and you can do it in three days?" 21But by "this temple," Jesus meant his body. 22After he was raised from the dead, the disciples remembered that he had said this. And they believed both Jesus and the Scriptures.

23Because of the miraculous signs he did in Jerusalem at the Passover celebration, many people were convinced that he was indeed the Messiah. 24But Jesus didn't trust them, because he knew what people were really like. 25No one needed to tell him about human nature.

## CHAPTER 3

### Jesus and Nicodemus

After dark one evening, a Jewish religious leader named Nicodemus, a Pharisee, 2came to speak with Jesus. "Teacher," he said, "we all know that God has sent you to teach us. Your miraculous signs are proof enough that God is with you."

3Jesus replied, "I assure you, unless you are born again,* you can never see the Kingdom of God."

4"What do you mean?" exclaimed Nicodemus. "How can an old man go back into his mother's womb and be born again?"

5Jesus replied, "The truth is, no one can enter the Kingdom of God without being born of water and the Spirit.* 6Humans can reproduce only human life, but the Holy Spirit gives new life from heaven. 7So don't be surprised at my statement that you* must be born again. 8Just as you can hear the wind but can't tell where it comes from or where it is going, so you can't explain how people are born of the Spirit."

9"What do you mean?" Nicodemus asked.

10Jesus replied, "You are a respected Jewish teacher, and yet you don't understand these things? 11I assure you, I am telling you what we know and have seen, and yet you won't believe us. 12But if you don't even believe me when I tell you about things that happen here on earth, how can you possibly believe if I tell you what is going on in heaven? 13For only I, the Son of Man,* have come to earth and will return to heaven again. 14And as Moses lifted up the bronze snake on a pole in the wilderness, so I, the Son of Man, must be lifted up on a pole,* 15so that everyone who believes in me will have eternal life.

16"For God so loved the world that he gave his only Son, so that everyone who believes in him will not perish but have eternal life. 17God did not send his Son into the world to condemn it, but to save it.

18"There is no judgment awaiting those who trust him. But those who do not trust him have already been judged for not believing in the only Son of God. 19Their judgment is based on this fact: The light from heaven came into the world, but they loved the darkness more than the light, for their actions were evil. 20They hate the light because they want to sin in the darkness. They stay away from the light for fear their sins will be exposed and they will be punished. 21But those who do what is right come to the light gladly, so everyone can see that they are doing what God wants."

### John the Baptist Exalts Jesus

22Afterward Jesus and his disciples left Jerusalem, but they stayed in Judea for a while and baptized there.

23At this time John the Baptist was baptizing at Aenon, near Salim, because there was plenty of water there and people kept coming to him for baptism. 24This was before John was put into prison. 25At that time a certain Jew began an argument with John's disciples over ceremonial cleansing. 26John's disciples came to him and said, "Teacher, the man you met on the other side of the Jordan River, the one you said was the Messiah, is also baptizing people. And everybody is going over there instead of coming here to us."

27John replied, "God in heaven appoints each person's work. 28You yourselves know how plainly I told you that I am not the Messiah. I am here to prepare the way for him—that is all. 29The bride will go where the bridegroom is. A

2:17 Or "Concern for God's house will be my undoing." Ps 69:9.   3:3 Or born from above; also in 3:7.   3:5 Or spirit. The Greek word for Spirit can also be translated wind; see 3:8.   3:7 The Greek word for you is plural; also in 3:12.   3:13 Some manuscripts add who lives in heaven. 3:14 Greek must be lifted up.

bridegroom's friend rejoices with him. I am the bridegroom's friend, and I am filled with joy at his success. 30He must become greater and greater, and I must become less and less.

31"He has come from above and is greater than anyone else. I am of the earth, and my understanding is limited to the things of earth, but he has come from heaven.* 32He tells what he has seen and heard, but how few believe what he tells them! 33Those who believe him discover that God is true. 34For he is sent by God. He speaks God's words, for God's Spirit is upon him without measure or limit. 35The Father loves his Son, and he has given him authority over everything. 36And all who believe in God's Son have eternal life. Those who don't obey the Son will never experience eternal life, but the wrath of God remains upon them."

## CHAPTER 4
### Jesus and the Samaritan Woman

Jesus* learned that the Pharisees had heard, "Jesus is baptizing and making more disciples than John" 2(though Jesus himself didn't baptize them—his disciples did). 3So he left Judea to return to Galilee.

4He had to go through Samaria on the way. 5Eventually he came to the Samaritan village of Sychar, near the parcel of ground that Jacob gave to his son Joseph. 6Jacob's well was there; and Jesus, tired from the long walk, sat wearily beside the well about noontime. 7Soon a Samaritan woman came to draw water, and Jesus said to her, "Please give me a drink." 8He was alone at the time because his disciples had gone into the village to buy some food.

9The woman was surprised, for Jews refuse to have anything to do with Samaritans. She said to Jesus, "You are a Jew, and I am a Samaritan woman. Why are you asking me for a drink?"

10Jesus replied, "If you only knew the gift God has for you and who I am, you would ask me, and I would give you living water."

11"But sir, you don't have a rope or a bucket," she said, "and this is a very deep well. Where would you get this living water? 12And besides, are you greater than our ancestor Jacob who gave us this well? How can you offer better water than he and his sons and his cattle enjoyed?"

13Jesus replied, "People soon become thirsty again after drinking this water. 14But the water I give them takes away thirst altogether. It be-

comes a perpetual spring within them, giving them eternal life."

15"Please, sir," the woman said, "give me some of that water! Then I'll never be thirsty again, and I won't have to come here to haul water."

16"Go and get your husband," Jesus told her.

17"I don't have a husband," the woman replied.

Jesus said, "You're right! You don't have a husband—18for you have had five husbands, and you aren't even married to the man you're living with now."

19"Sir," the woman said, "you must be a prophet. 20So tell me, why is it that you Jews insist that Jerusalem is the only place of worship, while we Samaritans claim it is here at Mount Gerizim,* where our ancestors worshiped?"

21Jesus replied, "Believe me, the time is coming when it will no longer matter whether you worship the Father here or in Jerusalem. 22You Samaritans know so little about the one you worship, while we Jews know all about him, for salvation comes through the Jews. 23But the time is coming and is already here when true worshipers will worship the Father in spirit and in truth. The Father is looking for anyone who will worship him that way. 24For God is Spirit, so those who worship him must worship in spirit and in truth."

25The woman said, "I know the Messiah will come—the one who is called Christ. When he comes, he will explain everything to us."

26Then Jesus told her, "I am the Messiah!"*

27Just then his disciples arrived. They were astonished to find him talking to a woman, but none of them asked him why he was doing it or what they had been discussing. 28The woman left her water jar beside the well and went back to the village and told everyone, 29"Come and meet a man who told me everything I ever did! Can this be the Messiah?" 30So the people came streaming from the village to see him.

31Meanwhile, the disciples were urging Jesus to eat. 32"No," he said, "I have food you don't know about."

33"Who brought it to him?" the disciples asked each other.

34Then Jesus explained: "My nourishment comes from doing the will of God, who sent me, and from finishing his work. 35Do you think the work of harvesting will not begin until the summer ends four months from now? Look around

3:31 Some manuscripts omit *but he has come from heaven.* 4:1 Some manuscripts read *The Lord.* 4:20 Greek *on this mountain.* 4:26 Greek *"I am, the one speaking to you."*

you! Vast fields are ripening all around us and are ready now for the harvest. 36The harvesters are paid good wages, and the fruit they harvest is people brought to eternal life. What joy awaits both the planter and the harvester alike! 37You know the saying, 'One person plants and someone else harvests.' And it's true. 38I sent you to harvest where you didn't plant; others had already done the work, and you will gather the harvest."

## Many Samaritans Believe

39Many Samaritans from the village believed in Jesus because the woman had said, "He told me everything I ever did!" 40When they came out to see him, they begged him to stay at their village. So he stayed for two days, 41long enough for many of them to hear his message and believe. 42Then they said to the woman, "Now we believe because we have heard him ourselves, not just because of what you told us. He is indeed the Savior of the world."

## Jesus Heals an Official's Son

43At the end of the two days' stay, Jesus went on into Galilee. 44He had previously said, "A prophet is honored everywhere except in his own country." 45The Galileans welcomed him, for they had been in Jerusalem at the Passover celebration and had seen all his miraculous signs.

46In the course of his journey through Galilee, he arrived at the town of Cana, where he had turned the water into wine. There was a government official in the city of Capernaum whose son was very sick. 47When he heard that Jesus had come from Judea and was traveling in Galilee, he went over to Cana. He found Jesus and begged him to come to Capernaum with him to heal his son, who was about to die.

48Jesus asked, "Must I do miraculous signs and wonders before you people will believe in me?"

49The official pleaded, "Lord, please come now before my little boy dies."

50Then Jesus told him, "Go back home. Your son will live!" And the man believed Jesus' word and started home.

51While he was on his way, some of his servants met him with the news that his son was alive and well. 52He asked them when the boy had begun to feel better, and they replied, "Yesterday afternoon at one o'clock his fever suddenly disappeared!" 53Then the father realized it was the same time that Jesus had told him,

"Your son will live." And the officer and his entire household believed in Jesus. 54This was Jesus' second miraculous sign in Galilee after coming from Judea.

## CHAPTER 5
### Jesus Heals a Lame Man

Afterward Jesus returned to Jerusalem for one of the Jewish holy days. 2Inside the city, near the Sheep Gate, was the pool of Bethesda,* with five covered porches. 3Crowds of sick people—blind, lame, or paralyzed—lay on the porches.* 5One of the men lying there had been sick for thirty-eight years. 6When Jesus saw him and knew how long he had been ill, he asked him, "Would you like to get well?"

7"I can't, sir," the sick man said, "for I have no one to help me into the pool when the water is stirred up. While I am trying to get there, someone else always gets in ahead of me."

8Jesus told him, "Stand up, pick up your sleeping mat, and walk!"

9Instantly, the man was healed! He rolled up the mat and began walking! But this miracle happened on the Sabbath day. 10So the Jewish leaders objected. They said to the man who was cured, "You can't work on the Sabbath! It's illegal to carry that sleeping mat!"

11He replied, "The man who healed me said to me, 'Pick up your sleeping mat and walk.'"

12"Who said such a thing as that?" they demanded.

13The man didn't know, for Jesus had disappeared into the crowd. 14But afterward Jesus found him in the Temple and told him, "Now you are well; so stop sinning, or something even worse may happen to you." 15Then the man went to find the Jewish leaders and told them it was Jesus who had healed him.

### Jesus Claims to Be the Son of God

16So the Jewish leaders began harassing Jesus for breaking the Sabbath rules. 17But Jesus replied, "My Father never stops working, so why should I?" 18So the Jewish leaders tried all the more to kill him. In addition to disobeying the Sabbath rules, he had spoken of God as his Father, thereby making himself equal with God.

19Jesus replied, "I assure you, the Son can do nothing by himself. He does only what he sees the Father doing. Whatever the Father does, the Son also does. 20For the Father loves the Son and

5:2 Some manuscripts read *Beth-zatha;* other manuscripts read *Bethsaida.* 5:3 Some manuscripts add *waiting for a certain movement of the water,* 4*for an angel of the Lord came from time to time and stirred up the water. And the first person to step down into it afterward was healed.*

tells him everything he is doing, and the Son will do far greater things than healing this man. You will be astonished at what he does. 21He will even raise from the dead anyone he wants to, just as the Father does. 22And the Father leaves all judgment to his Son, 23so that everyone will honor the Son, just as they honor the Father. But if you refuse to honor the Son, then you are certainly not honoring the Father who sent him.

24"I assure you, those who listen to my message and believe in God who sent me have eternal life. They will never be condemned for their sins, but they have already passed from death into life.

25"And I assure you that the time is coming, in fact it is here, when the dead will hear my voice—the voice of the Son of God. And those who listen will live. 26The Father has life in himself, and he has granted his Son to have life in himself. 27And he has given him authority to judge all mankind because he is the Son of Man. 28Don't be so surprised! Indeed, the time is coming when all the dead in their graves will hear the voice of God's Son, 29and they will rise again. Those who have done good will rise to eternal life, and those who have continued in evil will rise to judgment. 30But I do nothing without consulting the Father. I judge as I am told. And my judgment is absolutely just, because it is according to the will of God who sent me; it is not merely my own.

*Witnesses to Jesus*

31"If I were to testify on my own behalf, my testimony would not be valid. 32But someone else is also testifying about me, and I can assure you that everything he says about me is true. 33In fact, you sent messengers to listen to John the Baptist, and he preached the truth. 34But the best testimony about me is not from a man, though I have reminded you about John's testimony so you might be saved. 35John shone brightly for a while, and you benefited and rejoiced. 36But I have a greater witness than John—my teachings and my miracles. They have been assigned to me by the Father, and they testify that the Father has sent me. 37And the Father himself has also testified about me. You have never heard his voice or seen him face to face, 38and you do not have his message in your hearts, because you do not believe me—the one he sent to you.

39"You search the Scriptures because you believe they give you eternal life. But the Scriptures point to me! 40Yet you refuse to come to me so that I can give you this eternal life.

41"Your approval or disapproval means nothing to me, 42because I know you don't have God's love within you. 43For I have come to you representing my Father, and you refuse to welcome me, even though you readily accept others who represent only themselves. 44No wonder you can't believe! For you gladly honor each other, but you don't care about the honor that comes from God alone.

45"Yet it is not I who will accuse you of this before the Father. Moses will accuse you! Yes, Moses, on whom you set your hopes. 46But if you had believed Moses, you would have believed me because he wrote about me. 47And since you don't believe what he wrote, how will you believe what I say?"

## CHAPTER 6

*Jesus Feeds Five Thousand*

After this, Jesus crossed over the Sea of Galilee, also known as the Sea of Tiberias. 2And a huge crowd kept following him wherever he went, because they saw his miracles as he healed the sick. 3Then Jesus went up into the hills and sat down with his disciples around him. 4(It was nearly time for the annual Passover celebration.) 5Jesus soon saw a great crowd of people climbing the hill, looking for him. Turning to Philip, he asked, "Philip, where can we buy bread to feed all these people?" 6He was testing Philip, for he already knew what he was going to do.

7Philip replied, "It would take a small fortune* to feed them!"

8Then Andrew, Simon Peter's brother, spoke up. 9"There's a young boy here with five barley loaves and two fish. But what good is that with this huge crowd?"

10"Tell everyone to sit down," Jesus ordered. So all of them—the men alone numbered five thousand—sat down on the grassy slopes. 11Then Jesus took the loaves, gave thanks to God, and passed them out to the people. Afterward he did the same with the fish. And they all ate until they were full. 12"Now gather the leftovers," Jesus told his disciples, "so that nothing is wasted." 13There were only five barley loaves to start with, but twelve baskets were filled with the pieces of bread the people did not eat!

14When the people saw this miraculous sign, they exclaimed, "Surely, he is the Prophet* we have been expecting!" 15Jesus saw that they were ready to take him by force and make him king, so he went higher into the hills alone.

6:7 Greek *200 denarii*. A denarius was the equivalent of a full day's wage.  6:14 See Deut 18:15, 18.

## Jesus Walks on Water

16That evening his disciples went down to the shore to wait for him. 17But as darkness fell and Jesus still hadn't come back, they got into the boat and headed out across the lake toward Capernaum. 18Soon a gale swept down upon them as they rowed, and the sea grew very rough. 19They were three or four miles* out when suddenly they saw Jesus walking on the water toward the boat. They were terrified, 20but he called out to them, "I am here! Don't be afraid." 21Then they were eager to let him in, and immediately the boat arrived at their destination!

## Jesus, the Bread of Life

22The next morning, back across the lake, crowds began gathering on the shore, waiting to see Jesus. For they knew that he and his disciples had come over together and that the disciples had gone off in their boat, leaving him behind. 23Several boats from Tiberias landed near the place where the Lord had blessed the bread and the people had eaten. 24When the crowd saw that Jesus wasn't there, nor his disciples, they got into the boats and went across to Capernaum to look for him. 25When they arrived and found him, they asked, "Teacher, how did you get here?"

26Jesus replied, "The truth is, you want to be with me because I fed you, not because you saw the miraculous sign. 27But you shouldn't be so concerned about perishable things like food. Spend your energy seeking the eternal life that I, the Son of Man, can give you. For God the Father has sent me for that very purpose."

28They replied, "What does God want us to do?"

29Jesus told them, "This is what God wants you to do: Believe in the one he has sent."

30They replied, "You must show us a miraculous sign if you want us to believe in you. What will you do for us? 31After all, our ancestors ate manna while they journeyed through the wilderness! As the Scriptures say, 'Moses gave them bread from heaven to eat.'* "

32Jesus said, "I assure you, Moses didn't give them bread from heaven. My Father did. And now he offers you the true bread from heaven. 33The true bread of God is the one who comes down from heaven and gives life to the world."

34"Sir," they said, "give us that bread every day of our lives."

35Jesus replied, "I am the bread of life. No one who comes to me will ever be hungry again.

Those who believe in me will never thirst. 36But you haven't believed in me even though you have seen me. 37However, those the Father has given me will come to me, and I will never reject them. 38For I have come down from heaven to do the will of God who sent me, not to do what I want. 39And this is the will of God, that I should not lose even one of all those he has given me, but that I should raise them to eternal life at the last day. 40For it is my Father's will that all who see his Son and believe in him should have eternal life—that I should raise them at the last day."

41Then the people* began to murmur in disagreement because he had said, "I am the bread from heaven." 42They said, "This is Jesus, the son of Joseph. We know his father and mother. How can he say, 'I came down from heaven'?"

43But Jesus replied, "Don't complain about what I said. 44For people can't come to me unless the Father who sent me draws them to me, and at the last day I will raise them from the dead. 45As it is written in the Scriptures, 'They will all be taught by God.'* Everyone who hears and learns from the Father comes to me. 46(Not that anyone has ever seen the Father; only I, who was sent from God, have seen him.)

47"I assure you, anyone who believes in me already has eternal life. 48Yes, I am the bread of life! 49Your ancestors ate manna in the wilderness, but they all died. 50However, the bread from heaven gives eternal life to everyone who eats it. 51I am the living bread that came down out of heaven. Anyone who eats this bread will live forever; this bread is my flesh, offered so the world may live."

52Then the people began arguing with each other about what he meant. "How can this man give us his flesh to eat?" they asked.

53So Jesus said again, "I assure you, unless you eat the flesh of the Son of Man and drink his blood, you cannot have eternal life within you. 54But those who eat my flesh and drink my blood have eternal life, and I will raise them at the last day. 55For my flesh is the true food, and my blood is the true drink. 56All who eat my flesh and drink my blood remain in me, and I in them. 57I live by the power of the living Father who sent me; in the same way, those who partake of me will live because of me. 58I am the true bread from heaven. Anyone who eats this bread will live forever and not die as your ancestors did, even though they ate the manna."

6:19 Greek 25 or 30 stadia [4.6 or 5.5 kilometers]. 6:31 Exod 16:4; Ps 78:24. 6:41 Greek Jewish people; also in 6:52. 6:45 Isa 54:13.

59He said these things while he was teaching in the synagogue in Capernaum.

## Many Disciples Desert Jesus

60Even his disciples said, "This is very hard to understand. How can anyone accept it?"

61Jesus knew within himself that his disciples were complaining, so he said to them, "Does this offend you? 62Then what will you think if you see me, the Son of Man, return to heaven again? 63It is the Spirit who gives eternal life. Human effort accomplishes nothing. And the very words I have spoken to you are spirit and life. 64But some of you don't believe me." (For Jesus knew from the beginning who didn't believe, and he knew who would betray him.) 65Then he said, "That is what I meant when I said that people can't come to me unless the Father brings them to me."

66At this point many of his disciples turned away and deserted him. 67Then Jesus turned to the Twelve and asked, "Are you going to leave, too?"

68Simon Peter replied, "Lord, to whom would we go? You alone have the words that give eternal life. 69We believe them, and we know you are the Holy One of God."

70Then Jesus said, "I chose the twelve of you, but one is a devil." 71He was speaking of Judas, son of Simon Iscariot, one of the Twelve, who would betray him.

## CHAPTER 7

### Jesus and His Brothers

After this, Jesus stayed in Galilee, going from village to village. He wanted to stay out of Judea where the Jewish leaders were plotting his death. 2But soon it was time for the Festival of Shelters, 3and Jesus' brothers urged him to go to Judea for the celebration. "Go where your followers can see your miracles!" they scoffed. 4"You can't become a public figure if you hide like this! If you can do such wonderful things, prove it to the world!" 5For even his brothers didn't believe in him.

6Jesus replied, "Now is not the right time for me to go. But you can go anytime, and it will make no difference. 7The world can't hate you, but it does hate me because I accuse it of sin and evil. 8You go on. I am not yet* ready to go to this festival, because my time has not yet come." 9So Jesus remained in Galilee.

### Jesus Teaches Openly at the Temple

10But after his brothers had left for the festival, Jesus also went, though secretly, staying out of

7:8 Some manuscripts omit *yet.*

public view. 11The Jewish leaders tried to find him at the festival and kept asking if anyone had seen him. 12There was a lot of discussion about him among the crowds. Some said, "He's a wonderful man," while others said, "He's nothing but a fraud, deceiving the people." 13But no one had the courage to speak favorably about him in public, for they were afraid of getting in trouble with the Jewish leaders.

14Then, midway through the festival, Jesus went up to the Temple and began to teach. 15The Jewish leaders were surprised when they heard him. "How does he know so much when he hasn't studied everything we've studied?" they asked.

16So Jesus told them, "I'm not teaching my own ideas, but those of God who sent me. 17Anyone who wants to do the will of God will know whether my teaching is from God or is merely my own. 18Those who present their own ideas are looking for praise for themselves, but those who seek to honor the one who sent them are good and genuine. 19None of you obeys the law of Moses! In fact, you are trying to kill me."

20The crowd replied, "You're demon possessed! Who's trying to kill you?"

21Jesus replied, "I worked on the Sabbath by healing a man, and you were offended. 22But you work on the Sabbath, too, when you obey Moses' law of circumcision. (Actually, this tradition of circumcision is older than the law of Moses; it goes back to Abraham.) 23For if the correct time for circumcising your son falls on the Sabbath, you go ahead and do it, so as not to break the law of Moses. So why should I be condemned for making a man completely well on the Sabbath? 24Think this through and you will see that I am right."

### Is Jesus the Messiah?

25Some of the people who lived there in Jerusalem said among themselves, "Isn't this the man they are trying to kill? 26But here he is, speaking in public, and they say nothing to him. Can it be that our leaders know that he really is the Messiah? 27But how could he be? For we know where this man comes from. When the Messiah comes, he will simply appear; no one will know where he comes from."

28While Jesus was teaching in the Temple, he called out, "Yes, you know me, and you know where I come from. But I represent one you don't know, and he is true. 29I know him because I have come from him, and he sent me to you." 30Then the leaders tried to arrest him; but no one laid a hand on him, because his time had not yet come.

31Many among the crowds at the Temple believed in him. "After all," they said, "would you expect the Messiah to do more miraculous signs than this man has done?"

32When the Pharisees heard that the crowds were murmuring such things, they and the leading priests sent Temple guards to arrest Jesus. 33But Jesus told them, "I will be here a little longer. Then I will return to the one who sent me. 34You will search for me but not find me. And you won't be able to come where I am."

35The Jewish leaders were puzzled by this statement. "Where is he planning to go?" they asked. "Maybe he is thinking of leaving the country and going to the Jews in other lands, or maybe even to the Gentiles! 36What does he mean when he says, 'You will search for me but not find me,' and 'You won't be able to come where I am'?"

### Jesus Promises Living Water

37On the last day, the climax of the festival, Jesus stood and shouted to the crowds, "If you are thirsty, come to me! 38If you believe in me, come and drink! For the Scriptures declare that rivers of living water will flow out from within."* 39(When he said "living water," he was speaking of the Spirit, who would be given to everyone believing in him. But the Spirit had not yet been given, because Jesus had not yet entered into his glory.)

### Division and Unbelief

40When the crowds heard him say this, some of them declared, "This man surely is the Prophet."* 41Others said, "He is the Messiah." Still others said, "But he can't be! Will the Messiah come from Galilee? 42For the Scriptures clearly state that the Messiah will be born of the royal line of David, in Bethlehem, the village where King David was born."* 43So the crowd was divided in their opinion about him. 44And some wanted him arrested, but no one touched him.

45The Temple guards who had been sent to arrest him returned to the leading priests and Pharisees. "Why didn't you bring him in?" they demanded.

46"We have never heard anyone talk like this!" the guards responded.

47"Have you been led astray, too?" the Phari-

sees mocked. 48"Is there a single one of us rulers or Pharisees who believes in him? 49These ignorant crowds do, but what do they know about it? A curse on them anyway!"

50Nicodemus, the leader who had met with Jesus earlier, then spoke up. 51"Is it legal to convict a man before he is given a hearing?" he asked.

52They replied, "Are you from Galilee, too? Search the Scriptures and see for yourself—no prophet ever comes from Galilee!"

[*The most ancient Greek manuscripts do not include John 7:53–8:11.*]

53Then the meeting broke up and everybody went home.

## CHAPTER 8
### A Woman Caught in Adultery

Jesus returned to the Mount of Olives, 2but early the next morning he was back again at the Temple. A crowd soon gathered, and he sat down and taught them. 3As he was speaking, the teachers of religious law and Pharisees brought a woman they had caught in the act of adultery. They put her in front of the crowd.

4"Teacher," they said to Jesus, "this woman was caught in the very act of adultery. 5The law of Moses says to stone her. What do you say?"

6They were trying to trap him into saying something they could use against him, but Jesus stooped down and wrote in the dust with his finger. 7They kept demanding an answer, so he stood up again and said, "All right, stone her. But let those who have never sinned throw the first stones!" 8Then he stooped down again and wrote in the dust.

9When the accusers heard this, they slipped away one by one, beginning with the oldest, until only Jesus was left in the middle of the crowd with the woman. 10Then Jesus stood up again and said to her, "Where are your accusers? Didn't even one of them condemn you?"

11"No, Lord," she said.

And Jesus said, "Neither do I. Go and sin no more."

### Jesus, the Light of the World

12Jesus said to the people, "I am the light of the world. If you follow me, you won't be stumbling through the darkness, because you will have the light that leads to life."

7:37-38 Or *"Let anyone who is thirsty come to me and drink.* 38*For the Scriptures declare that rivers of living water will flow from the heart of those who believe in me."* 7:40 See Deut 18:15, 18. 7:42 See Mic 5:2.

13The Pharisees replied, "You are making false claims about yourself!"

14Jesus told them, "These claims are valid even though I make them about myself. For I know where I came from and where I am going, but you don't know this about me. 15You judge me with all your human limitations,* but I am not judging anyone. 16And if I did, my judgment would be correct in every respect because I am not alone—I have with me the Father who sent me. 17Your own law says that if two people agree about something, their witness is accepted as fact.* 18I am one witness, and my Father who sent me is the other."

19"Where is your father?" they asked.

Jesus answered, "Since you don't know who I am, you don't know who my Father is. If you knew me, then you would know my Father, too." 20Jesus made these statements while he was teaching in the section of the Temple known as the Treasury. But he was not arrested, because his time had not yet come.

## The Unbelieving People Warned

21Later Jesus said to them again, "I am going away. You will search for me and die in your sin. You cannot come where I am going."

22The Jewish leaders asked, "Is he planning to commit suicide? What does he mean, 'You cannot come where I am going'?"

23Then he said to them, "You are from below; I am from above. You are of this world; I am not. 24That is why I said that you will die in your sins; for unless you believe that I am who I say I am, you will die in your sins."

25"Tell us who you are," they demanded.

Jesus replied, "I am the one I have always claimed to be.* 26I have much to say about you and much to condemn, but I won't. For I say only what I have heard from the one who sent me, and he is true." 27But they still didn't understand that he was talking to them about his Father.

28So Jesus said, "When you have lifted up the Son of Man on the cross, then you will realize that I am he and that I do nothing on my own, but I speak what the Father taught me. 29And the one who sent me is with me—he has not deserted me. For I always do those things that are pleasing to him." 30Then many who heard him say these things believed in him.

## Jesus and Abraham

31Jesus said to the people* who believed in him, "You are truly my disciples if you keep obeying my teachings. 32And you will know the truth, and the truth will set you free."

33"But we are descendants of Abraham," they said. "We have never been slaves to anyone on earth. What do you mean, 'set free'?"

34Jesus replied, "I assure you that everyone who sins is a slave of sin. 35A slave is not a permanent member of the family, but a son is part of the family forever. 36So if the Son sets you free, you will indeed be free. 37Yes, I realize that you are descendants of Abraham. And yet some of you are trying to kill me because my message does not find a place in your hearts. 38I am telling you what I saw when I was with my Father. But you are following the advice of your father."

39"Our father is Abraham," they declared.

"No," Jesus replied, "for if you were children of Abraham, you would follow his good example.* 40I told you the truth I heard from God, but you are trying to kill me. Abraham wouldn't do a thing like that. 41No, you are obeying your real father when you act that way."

They replied, "We were not born out of wedlock! Our true Father is God himself."

42Jesus told them, "If God were your Father, you would love me, because I have come to you from God. I am not here on my own, but he sent me. 43Why can't you understand what I am saying? It is because you are unable to do so! 44For you are the children of your father the Devil, and you love to do the evil things he does. He was a murderer from the beginning and has always hated the truth. There is no truth in him. When he lies, it is consistent with his character; for he is a liar and the father of lies. 45So when I tell the truth, you just naturally don't believe me! 46Which of you can truthfully accuse me of sin? And since I am telling you the truth, why don't you believe me? 47Anyone whose Father is God listens gladly to the words of God. Since you don't, it proves you aren't God's children."

48The people retorted, "You Samaritan devil! Didn't we say all along that you were possessed by a demon?"

49"No," Jesus said, "I have no demon in me. For I honor my Father—and you dishonor me. 50And though I have no wish to glorify myself, God wants to glorify me. Let him be the judge. 51I assure you, anyone who obeys my teaching will never die!"

52The people said, "Now we know you are possessed by a demon. Even Abraham and the prophets died, but you say that those who obey

---

8:15 Or *judge me by human standards.*  8:17 See Deut 19:15.  8:25 Or *"Why do I speak to you at all?"*  8:31 Greek *Jewish people;* also in 8:48, 52, 57.  8:39 Some manuscripts read *if you are children of Abraham, follow his example.*

your teaching will never die! 53Are you greater than our father Abraham, who died? Are you greater than the prophets, who died? Who do you think you are?"

54Jesus answered, "If I am merely boasting about myself, it doesn't count. But it is my Father who says these glorious things about me. You say, 'He is our God,' 55but you do not even know him. I know him. If I said otherwise, I would be as great a liar as you! But it is true—I know him and obey him. 56Your ancestor Abraham rejoiced as he looked forward to my coming. He saw it and was glad."

57The people said, "You aren't even fifty years old. How can you say you have seen Abraham?*"

58Jesus answered, "The truth is, I existed before Abraham was even born!"* 59At that point they picked up stones to kill him. But Jesus hid himself from them and left the Temple.

CHAPTER **9**

*Jesus Heals a Man Born Blind*

As Jesus was walking along, he saw a man who had been blind from birth. 2"Teacher," his disciples asked him, "why was this man born blind? Was it a result of his own sins or those of his parents?"

3"It was not because of his sins or his parents' sins," Jesus answered. "He was born blind so the power of God could be seen in him. 4All of us must quickly carry out the tasks assigned us by the one who sent me, because there is little time left before the night falls and all work comes to an end. 5But while I am still here in the world, I am the light of the world."

6Then he spit on the ground, made mud with the saliva, and smoothed the mud over the blind man's eyes. 7He told him, "Go and wash in the pool of Siloam" (Siloam means Sent). So the man went and washed, and came back seeing!

8His neighbors and others who knew him as a blind beggar asked each other, "Is this the same man—that beggar?" 9Some said he was, and others said, "No, but he surely looks like him!" And the beggar kept saying, "I am the same man!"

10They asked, "Who healed you? What happened?"

11He told them, "The man they call Jesus made mud and smoothed it over my eyes and told me, 'Go to the pool of Siloam and wash off the mud.' I went and washed, and now I can see!"

12"Where is he now?" they asked.

"I don't know," he replied.

13Then they took the man to the Pharisees. 14Now as it happened, Jesus had healed the man on a Sabbath. 15The Pharisees asked the man all about it. So he told them, "He smoothed the mud over my eyes, and when it was washed away, I could see!"

16Some of the Pharisees said, "This man Jesus is not from God, for he is working on the Sabbath." Others said, "But how could an ordinary sinner do such miraculous signs?" So there was a deep division of opinion among them.

---

## You Don't Need Any Training to Share Read JOHN 9:1-41

Perhaps one of the biggest reasons many Christians haven't shared their faith is that they feel God could never use them to draw people to himself. You might say, "I am not qualified to speak for God!" In reality, once you invite Jesus Christ into your life as Savior and Lord, you can begin to tell others about your newfound faith.

This passage tells the story of a blind man whose sight was restored when Jesus touched his eyes. After Jesus healed this man, certain religious rulers known as Pharisees challenged him, asking him some rather complex questions about Jesus. The man's response was classic. He said, "I know this: I was blind, and now I can see!"

In many ways, we as believers are like this formerly blind man. We, too, were once blinded by the power and deception of sin. Scripture tells us that "Satan, the god of this evil world" made us "blind" and "unable to see the glorious light of the Good News" (2 Corinthians 4:4). But one day God lovingly "opened our eyes" to see our real spiritual need, and we responded to the message of the Gospel.

Although we may not yet be great scholars of Scripture, we still know more about the gospel than many, and we can start with that. Like that blind man, we can, in a spiritual sense, say to others, "Once I was blind, but now I can see. . . ." As we study the Bible on a regular basis, we will be able to answer many of the questions people have about our faith.

17Then the Pharisees once again questioned the man who had been blind and demanded, "This man who opened your eyes—who do you say he is?"

The man replied, "I think he must be a prophet."

18The Jewish leaders wouldn't believe he had been blind, so they called in his parents. 19They asked them, "Is this your son? Was he born blind? If so, how can he see?"

20His parents replied, "We know this is our son and that he was born blind, 21but we don't know how he can see or who healed him. He is old enough to speak for himself. Ask him." 22They said this because they were afraid of the Jewish leaders, who had announced that anyone saying Jesus was the Messiah would be expelled from the synagogue. 23That's why they said, "He is old enough to speak for himself. Ask him."

24So for the second time they called in the man who had been blind and told him, "Give glory to God by telling the truth,* because we know Jesus is a sinner."

25"I don't know whether he is a sinner," the man replied. "But I know this: I was blind, and now I can see!"

26"But what did he do?" they asked. "How did he heal you?"

27"Look!" the man exclaimed. "I told you once. Didn't you listen? Why do you want to hear it again? Do you want to become his disciples, too?"

28Then they cursed him and said, "You are his disciple, but we are disciples of Moses. 29We know God spoke to Moses, but as for this man, we don't know anything about him."

30"Why, that's very strange!" the man replied. "He healed my eyes, and yet you don't know anything about him! 31Well, God doesn't listen to sinners, but he is ready to hear those who worship him and do his will. 32Never since the world began has anyone been able to open the eyes of someone born blind. 33If this man were not from God, he couldn't do it."

34"You were born in sin!" they answered. "Are you trying to teach us?" And they threw him out of the synagogue.

## Spiritual Blindness

35When Jesus heard what had happened, he found the man and said, "Do you believe in the Son of Man*?"

36The man answered, "Who is he, sir, because I would like to."

37"You have seen him," Jesus said, "and he is speaking to you!"

38"Yes, Lord," the man said, "I believe!" And he worshiped Jesus.

39Then Jesus told him, "I have come to judge the world. I have come to give sight to the blind and to show those who think they see that they are blind."

40The Pharisees who were standing there heard him and asked, "Are you saying we are blind?"

41"If you were blind, you wouldn't be guilty," Jesus replied. "But you remain guilty because you claim you can see.

## CHAPTER 10
### The Good Shepherd and His Sheep

"I assure you, anyone who sneaks over the wall of a sheepfold, rather than going through the gate, must surely be a thief and a robber! 2For a shepherd enters through the gate. 3The gatekeeper opens the gate for him, and the sheep hear his voice and come to him. He calls his own sheep by name and leads them out. 4After he has gathered his own flock, he walks ahead of them, and they follow him because they recognize his voice. 5They won't follow a stranger; they will run from him because they don't recognize his voice."

6Those who heard Jesus use this illustration didn't understand what he meant, 7so he explained it to them. "I assure you, I am the gate for the sheep," he said. 8"All others who came before me were thieves and robbers. But the true sheep did not listen to them. 9Yes, I am the gate. Those who come in through me will be saved. Wherever they go, they will find green pastures. 10The thief's purpose is to steal and kill and destroy. My purpose is to give life in all its fullness.

11"I am the good shepherd. The good shepherd lays down his life for the sheep. 12A hired hand will run when he sees a wolf coming. He will leave the sheep because they aren't his and he isn't their shepherd. And so the wolf attacks them and scatters the flock. 13The hired hand runs away because he is merely hired and has no real concern for the sheep.

14"I am the good shepherd; I know my own sheep, and they know me, 15just as my Father knows me and I know the Father. And I lay down

9:24 Or *Give glory to God, not to Jesus*; Greek reads *Give glory to God.*   9:35 Some manuscripts read *the Son of God.*

my life for the sheep. 16I have other sheep, too, that are not in this sheepfold. I must bring them also, and they will listen to my voice; and there will be one flock with one shepherd.

17"The Father loves me because I lay down my life that I may have it back again. 18No one can take my life from me. I lay down my life voluntarily. For I have the right to lay it down when I want to and also the power to take it again. For my Father has given me this command."

19When he said these things, the people* were again divided in their opinions about him. 20Some of them said, "He has a demon, or he's crazy. Why listen to a man like that?" 21Others said, "This doesn't sound like a man possessed by a demon! Can a demon open the eyes of the blind?"

### Jesus Claims to Be the Son of God

22It was now winter, and Jesus was in Jerusalem at the time of Hanukkah.* 23He was at the Temple, walking through the section known as Solomon's Colonnade. 24The Jewish leaders surrounded him and asked, "How long are you going to keep us in suspense? If you are the Messiah, tell us plainly."

25Jesus replied, "I have already told you, and you don't believe me. The proof is what I do in the name of my Father. 26But you don't believe me because you are not part of my flock. 27My sheep recognize my voice; I know them, and they follow me. 28I give them eternal life, and they will never perish. No one will snatch them away from me, 29for my Father has given them to me, and he is more powerful than anyone else. So no one can take them from me. 30The Father and I are one."

31Once again the Jewish leaders picked up stones to kill him. 32Jesus said, "At my Father's direction I have done many things to help the people. For which one of these good deeds are you killing me?"

33They replied, "Not for any good work, but for blasphemy, because you, a mere man, have made yourself God."

34Jesus replied, "It is written in your own law that God said to certain leaders of the people, 'I say, you are gods!'* 35And you know that the Scriptures cannot be altered. So if those people, who received God's message, were called 'gods,' 36why do you call it blasphemy when the Holy One who was sent into the world by the Father says, 'I am the Son of God'? 37Don't believe me unless I carry out my Father's work. 38But if I do his work, believe in what I have done, even if you don't believe me. Then you will realize that the Father is in me, and I am in the Father."

39Once again they tried to arrest him, but he got away and left them. 40He went beyond the Jordan River to stay near the place where John was first baptizing. 41And many followed him. "John didn't do miracles," they remarked to one another, "but all his predictions about this man have come true." 42And many believed in him there.

## CHAPTER 11
### The Death of Lazarus

A man named Lazarus was sick. He lived in Bethany with his sisters, Mary and Martha. 2This is the Mary who poured the expensive perfume on the Lord's feet and wiped them with her hair.* Her brother, Lazarus, was sick. 3So the two sisters sent a message to Jesus telling him, "Lord, the one you love is very sick."

4But when Jesus heard about it he said, "Lazarus's sickness will not end in death. No, it is for the glory of God. I, the Son of God, will receive glory from this." 5Although Jesus loved Martha, Mary, and Lazarus, 6he stayed where he was for the next two days and did not go to them. 7Finally after two days, he said to his disciples, "Let's go to Judea again."

8But his disciples objected. "Teacher," they said, "only a few days ago the Jewish leaders in Judea were trying to kill you. Are you going there again?"

9Jesus replied, "There are twelve hours of daylight every day. As long as it is light, people can walk safely. They can see because they have the light of this world. 10Only at night is there danger of stumbling because there is no light." 11Then he said, "Our friend Lazarus has fallen asleep, but now I will go and wake him up."

12The disciples said, "Lord, if he is sleeping, that means he is getting better!" 13They thought Jesus meant Lazarus was having a good night's rest, but Jesus meant Lazarus had died.

14Then he told them plainly, "Lazarus is dead. 15And for your sake, I am glad I wasn't there, because this will give you another opportunity to believe in me. Come, let's go see him."

16Thomas, nicknamed the Twin,* said to his fellow disciples, "Let's go, too—and die with Jesus."

10:19 Greek *Jewish people*.   10:22 Or *the Festival of Dedication*.   10:34 Ps 82:6.   11:2 This incident is recorded in chapter 12.   11:16 Greek *the one who was called Didymus.*

17When Jesus arrived at Bethany, he was told that Lazarus had already been in his grave for four days. 18Bethany was only a few miles* down the road from Jerusalem, 19and many of the people* had come to pay their respects and console Martha and Mary on their loss. 20When Martha got word that Jesus was coming, she went to meet him. But Mary stayed at home. 21Martha said to Jesus, "Lord, if you had been here, my brother would not have died. 22But even now I know that God will give you whatever you ask."

23Jesus told her, "Your brother will rise again."

24"Yes," Martha said, "when everyone else rises, on resurrection day."

25Jesus told her, "I am the resurrection and the life.* Those who believe in me, even though they die like everyone else, will live again. 26They are given eternal life for believing in me and will never perish. Do you believe this, Martha?"

27"Yes, Lord," she told him. "I have always believed you are the Messiah, the Son of God, the one who has come into the world from God." 28Then she left him and returned to Mary. She called Mary aside from the mourners and told her, "The Teacher is here and wants to see you." 29So Mary immediately went to him.

30Now Jesus had stayed outside the village, at the place where Martha met him. 31When the people who were at the house trying to console Mary saw her leave so hastily, they assumed she was going to Lazarus's grave to weep. So they followed her there. 32When Mary arrived and saw Jesus, she fell down at his feet and said, "Lord, if you had been here, my brother would not have died."

33When Jesus saw her weeping and saw the other people wailing with her, he was moved with indignation and was deeply troubled. 34"Where have you put him?" he asked them.

They told him, "Lord, come and see." 35Then Jesus wept. 36The people who were standing nearby said, "See how much he loved him." 37But some said, "This man healed a blind man. Why couldn't he keep Lazarus from dying?"

## Jesus Raises Lazarus from the Dead

38And again Jesus was deeply troubled. Then they came to the grave. It was a cave with a stone rolled across its entrance. 39"Roll the stone aside," Jesus told them.

But Martha, the dead man's sister, said, "Lord, by now the smell will be terrible because he has been dead for four days."

40Jesus responded, "Didn't I tell you that you will see God's glory if you believe?" 41So they rolled the stone aside. Then Jesus looked up to heaven and said, "Father, thank you for hearing me. 42You always hear me, but I said it out loud for the sake of all these people standing here, so they will believe you sent me." 43Then Jesus shouted, "Lazarus, come out!" 44And Lazarus came out, bound in graveclothes, his face wrapped in a headcloth. Jesus told them, "Unwrap him and let him go!"

## The Plot to Kill Jesus

45Many of the people who were with Mary believed in Jesus when they saw this happen. 46But some went to the Pharisees and told them what Jesus had done. 47Then the leading priests and Pharisees called the high council* together to discuss the situation. "What are we going to do?" they asked each other. "This man certainly performs many miraculous signs. 48If we leave him alone, the whole nation will follow him, and then the Roman army will come and destroy both our Temple and our nation."

49And one of them, Caiaphas, who was high priest that year, said, "How can you be so stupid? 50Why should the whole nation be destroyed? Let this one man die for the people."

51This prophecy that Jesus should die for the entire nation came from Caiaphas in his position as high priest. He didn't think of it himself; he was inspired to say it. 52It was a prediction that Jesus' death would be not for Israel only, but for the gathering together of all the children of God scattered around the world.

53So from that time on the Jewish leaders began to plot Jesus' death. 54As a result, Jesus stopped his public ministry among the people and left Jerusalem. He went to a place near the wilderness, to the village of Ephraim, and stayed there with his disciples.

55It was now almost time for the celebration of Passover, and many people from the country arrived in Jerusalem several days early so they could go through the cleansing ceremony before the Passover began. 56They wanted to see Jesus, and as they talked in the Temple, they asked each other, "What do you think? Will he come for the Passover?" 57Meanwhile, the leading priests and Pharisees had publicly announced that anyone seeing Jesus must report him immediately so they could arrest him.

11:18 Greek *was about 15 stadia* [about 2.8 kilometers].   11:19 Greek *Jewish people;* also 11:31, 33, 36, 45, 54.   11:25 Some manuscripts do not include *and the life.*   11:47 Greek *the Sanhedrin.*

# CHAPTER 12

## Jesus Anointed at Bethany

Six days before the Passover ceremonies began, Jesus arrived in Bethany, the home of Lazarus— the man he had raised from the dead. 2A dinner was prepared in Jesus' honor. Martha served, and Lazarus sat at the table with him. 3Then Mary took a twelve-ounce jar* of expensive perfume made from essence of nard, and she anointed Jesus' feet with it and wiped his feet with her hair. And the house was filled with fragrance.

4But Judas Iscariot, one of his disciples—the one who would betray him—said, 5"That perfume was worth a small fortune.* It should have been sold and the money given to the poor." 6Not that he cared for the poor—he was a thief who was in charge of the disciples' funds, and he often took some for his own use.

7Jesus replied, "Leave her alone. She did it in preparation for my burial. 8You will always have the poor among you, but I will not be here with you much longer."

9When all the people* heard of Jesus' arrival, they flocked to see him and also to see Lazarus, the man Jesus had raised from the dead. 10Then the leading priests decided to kill Lazarus, too, 11for it was because of him that many of the people had deserted them and believed in Jesus.

## The Triumphal Entry

12The next day, the news that Jesus was on the way to Jerusalem swept through the city. A huge crowd of Passover visitors 13took palm branches and went down the road to meet him. They shouted,

"Praise God!*
Bless the one who comes in the name of the Lord!
Hail to the King of Israel!"*

14Jesus found a young donkey and sat on it, fulfilling the prophecy that said:

15 "Don't be afraid, people of Israel.*
Look, your King is coming,
    sitting on a donkey's colt."*

16His disciples didn't realize at the time that this was a fulfillment of prophecy. But after Jesus entered into his glory, they remembered that these Scriptures had come true before their eyes.

17Those in the crowd who had seen Jesus call Lazarus back to life were telling others all about it. 18That was the main reason so many went out to meet him—because they had heard about this mighty miracle. 19Then the Pharisees said to each other, "We've lost. Look, the whole world has gone after him!"

## Jesus Predicts His Death

20Some Greeks who had come to Jerusalem to attend the Passover 21paid a visit to Philip, who was from Bethsaida in Galilee. They said, "Sir, we want to meet Jesus." 22Philip told Andrew about it, and they went together to ask Jesus.

23Jesus replied, "The time has come for the Son of Man to enter into his glory. 24The truth is, a kernel of wheat must be planted in the soil. Unless it dies it will be alone—a single seed. But its death will produce many new kernels—a plentiful harvest of new lives. 25Those who love their life in this world will lose it. Those who despise their life in this world will keep it for eternal life. 26All those who want to be my disciples must come and follow me, because my servants must be where I am. And if they follow me, the Father will honor them. 27Now my soul is deeply troubled. Should I pray, 'Father, save me from what lies ahead'? But that is the very reason why I came! 28Father, bring glory to your name."

Then a voice spoke from heaven, saying, "I have already brought it glory, and I will do it again." 29When the crowd heard the voice, some thought it was thunder, while others declared an angel had spoken to him.

30Then Jesus told them, "The voice was for your benefit, not mine. 31The time of judgment for the world has come, when the prince of this world* will be cast out. 32And when I am lifted up on the cross,* I will draw everyone to myself." 33He said this to indicate how he was going to die.

34"Die?" asked the crowd. "We understood from Scripture that the Messiah would live forever. Why are you saying the Son of Man will die? Who is this Son of Man you are talking about?"

35Jesus replied, "My light will shine out for you just a little while longer. Walk in it while you can, so you will not stumble when the darkness falls. If you walk in the darkness, you cannot see where you are going. 36Believe in the light while there is still time; then you will become children of the light." After saying these things, Jesus went away and was hidden from them.

## The Unbelief of the People

37But despite all the miraculous signs he had done, most of the people did not believe in him.

12:3 Greek took 1 litra [327 grams].   12:5 Greek 300 denarii. A denarius was equivalent to a full day's wage.   12:9 Greek Jewish people; also in 12:11.   12:13a Greek Hosanna, an exclamation of praise that literally means "save now."   12:13b Ps 118:25-26; Zeph 3:15.   12:15a Greek daughter of Zion.   12:15b Zech 9:9.   12:31 The prince of this world is a name for Satan.   12:32 Greek lifted up from the earth.

38This is exactly what Isaiah the prophet had predicted:

"Lord, who has believed our message?
To whom will the Lord reveal his saving
power?"*

39But the people couldn't believe, for as Isaiah also said,

40 "The Lord has blinded their eyes
and hardened their hearts—
so their eyes cannot see,
and their hearts cannot understand,
and they cannot turn to me
and let me heal them."*

41Isaiah was referring to Jesus when he made this prediction, because he was given a vision of the Messiah's glory. 42Many people, including some of the Jewish leaders, believed in him. But they wouldn't admit it to anyone because of their fear that the Pharisees would expel them from the synagogue. 43For they loved human praise more than the praise of God.

44Jesus shouted to the crowds, "If you trust me, you are really trusting God who sent me. 45For when you see me, you are seeing the one who sent me. 46I have come as a light to shine in this dark world, so that all who put their trust in me will no longer remain in the darkness. 47If anyone hears me and doesn't obey me, I am not his judge—for I have come to save the world and not to judge it. 48But all who reject me and my message will be judged at the day of judgment by the truth I have spoken. 49I don't speak on my own authority. The Father who sent me gave me his own instructions as to what I should say. 50And I know his instructions lead to eternal life; so I say whatever the Father tells me to say!"

CHAPTER **13**

## Jesus Washes His Disciples' Feet

Before the Passover celebration, Jesus knew that his hour had come to leave this world and return to his Father. He now showed the disciples the full extent of his love.* 2It was time for supper, and the Devil had already enticed Judas, son of Simon Iscariot, to carry out his plan to betray Jesus. 3Jesus knew that the Father had given him authority over everything and that he had come from God and would return to God. 4So he got up from the table, took off his robe, wrapped a towel around his waist, 5and

poured water into a basin. Then he began to wash the disciples' feet and to wipe them with the towel he had around him.

6When he came to Simon Peter, Peter said to him, "Lord, why are you going to wash my feet?"

7Jesus replied, "You don't understand now why I am doing it; someday you will."

8"No," Peter protested, "you will never wash my feet!"

Jesus replied, "But if I don't wash you, you won't belong to me."

9Simon Peter exclaimed, "Then wash my hands and head as well, Lord, not just my feet!"

10Jesus replied, "A person who has bathed all over does not need to wash, except for the feet,* to be entirely clean. And you are clean, but that isn't true of everyone here." 11For Jesus knew who would betray him. That is what he meant when he said, "Not all of you are clean."

12After washing their feet, he put on his robe again and sat down and asked, "Do you understand what I was doing? 13You call me 'Teacher' and 'Lord,' and you are right, because it is true. 14And since I, the Lord and Teacher, have washed your feet, you ought to wash each other's feet. 15I have given you an example to follow. Do as I have done to you. 16How true it is that a servant is not greater than the master. Nor are messengers more important than the one who sends them. 17You know these things—now do them! That is the path of blessing.

## Jesus Predicts His Betrayal

18"I am not saying these things to all of you; I know so well each one of you I chose. The Scriptures declare, 'The one who shares my food has turned against me,'* and this will soon come true. 19I tell you this now, so that when it happens you will believe I am the Messiah. 20Truly, anyone who welcomes my messenger is welcoming me, and anyone who welcomes me is welcoming the Father who sent me."

21Now Jesus was in great anguish of spirit, and he exclaimed, "The truth is, one of you will betray me!"

22The disciples looked at each other, wondering whom he could mean. 23One of Jesus' disciples, the one Jesus loved, was sitting next to Jesus at the table.* 24Simon Peter motioned to him to ask who would do this terrible thing. 25Leaning toward Jesus, he asked, "Lord, who is it?"

26Jesus said, "It is the one to whom I give the bread dipped in the sauce." And when he had

12:38 Isa 53:1.   12:40 Isa 6:10.   13:1 Or *He loved his disciples to the very end.*   13:10 Some manuscripts do not include *except for the feet.*
13:18 Ps 41:9.   13:23 Greek *was reclining on Jesus' bosom.* The "disciple whom Jesus loved" was probably John.

dipped it, he gave it to Judas, son of Simon Iscariot. ²⁷As soon as Judas had eaten the bread, Satan entered into him. Then Jesus told him, "Hurry. Do it now." ²⁸None of the others at the table knew what Jesus meant. ²⁹Since Judas was their treasurer, some thought Jesus was telling him to go and pay for the food or to give some money to the poor. ³⁰So Judas left at once, going out into the night.

### Jesus Predicts Peter's Denial

³¹As soon as Judas left the room, Jesus said, "The time has come for me, the Son of Man, to enter into my glory, and God will receive glory because of all that happens to me. ³²And God will bring* me into my glory very soon. ³³Dear children, how brief are these moments before I must go away and leave you! Then, though you search for me, you cannot come to me—just as I told the Jewish leaders. ³⁴So now I am giving you a new commandment: Love each other. Just as I have loved you, you should love each other. ³⁵Your love for one another will prove to the world that you are my disciples."

³⁶Simon Peter said, "Lord, where are you going?"

And Jesus replied, "You can't go with me now, but you will follow me later."

³⁷"But why can't I come now, Lord?" he asked. "I am ready to die for you."

³⁸Jesus answered, "Die for me? No, before the rooster crows tomorrow morning, you will deny three times that you even know me.

CHAPTER **14**

### Jesus, the Way to the Father

"Don't be troubled. You trust God, now trust in me. ²There are many rooms in my Father's home, and I am going to prepare a place for you. If this were not so, I would tell you plainly. ³When everything is ready, I will come and get you, so that you will always be with me where I am. ⁴And you know where I am going and how to get there."

⁵"No, we don't know, Lord," Thomas said. "We haven't any idea where you are going, so how can we know the way?"

⁶Jesus told him, "I am the way, the truth, and the life. No one can come to the Father except through me. ⁷If you had known who I am, then you would have known who my Father is.* From now on you know him and have seen him!"

13:32 Some manuscripts read *And if God is glorified in him [the Son of Man], God will bring.* 14:7 Some manuscripts read *If you really have known me, you will know who my Father is.*

⁸Philip said, "Lord, show us the Father and we will be satisfied."

⁹Jesus replied, "Philip, don't you even yet know who I am, even after all the time I have

## God Gives Hope to Our Troubled Hearts Read JOHN 14:1-4

Have you ever felt troubled and uncertain about your future? Have you ever questioned whether God realizes that your world has turned upside down? The disciples may have been experiencing these feelings when Jesus gave them this message. He had just told them that he was going to leave them, and they were extremely concerned. Yet he tells them to not be troubled, then gives them three reasons why they should have peace in their hearts:

**1. We Can Take God at His Word.** When Jesus said, "You trust God, now trust in me," he was reminding his disciples to trust in God's Word (verse 1). Scripture had spoken not only of Jesus' impending crucifixion but also of his resurrection. Somehow they had missed that. Sometimes we forget to look at the whole picture when our circumstances seem overwhelming. But we must remember that the words found in these pages will "remain forever" (Matthew 24:35). We can always take God's promises at face value.

**2. We Are Going to Heaven.** The next time you face some kind of difficulty—be it an illness, a family problem, or an unexpected change in your life—remember that you are going to heaven (verse 2). That will help to keep everything in perspective. Your trials are only temporary. One day you will be in the presence of the Lord, and there will be no more fear, no more death, no more pain, and no more sorrow.

**3. Jesus Is Coming Back for Us.** Notice that Jesus says, "I will come and get you" (verse 3). The Lord is not merely going to send for us. He is going to personally escort us to the Father's house. The Bible tells us to *"comfort* and encourage each other with these words" (1 Thessalonians 4:18). In the midst of your trials, remember that God cares for you so much that he is coming back so that you can be with him forever.

FIRST STEPS

## Who Will Enter Heaven? Read JOHN 14:2-6

Hollywood has often depicted the gates of heaven as the place where you "plead your case" for the merits of your entrance. In this passage, Jesus clearly explains that the only ones who will enter heaven will be those who have accepted him as the way, the truth, and the life—not those who have the best "arguments" or who have performed the greatest number of good deeds.

Heaven is not a court but a prepared place for prepared people. If you are a Christian, you can rest assured that your reservation for heaven was made the moment you received Christ. And when it comes to accommodations, you don't need to worry, for Jesus himself has promised to prepare a place for you.

The Bible tells us to prepare to meet our God. Is your reservation in place?

**CORNER STONES**

been with you? Anyone who has seen me has seen the Father! So why are you asking to see him? 10Don't you believe that I am in the Father and the Father is in me? The words I say are not my own, but my Father who lives in me does his work through me. 11Just believe that I am in the Father and the Father is in me. Or at least believe because of what you have seen me do.

12"The truth is, anyone who believes in me will do the same works I have done, and even greater works, because I am going to be with the Father. 13You can ask for anything in my name, and I will do it, because the work of the Son brings glory to the Father. 14Yes, ask anything in my name, and I will do it!

*Jesus Promises the Holy Spirit*

15"If you love me, obey my commandments. 16And I will ask the Father, and he will give you another Counselor,* who will never leave you. 17He is the Holy Spirit, who leads into all truth. The world at large cannot receive him, because it isn't looking for him and doesn't recognize him. But you do, because he lives with you now and later will be in you. 18No, I will not abandon you as orphans—I will come to you. 19In just a little while the world will not see me again, but you will. For I will live again, and you will, too. 20When I am raised to life again, you will know that I am in my Father, and you are in me, and I am in you. 21Those who obey my commandments are the ones who love me. And because they love me, my Father will love them, and I will love them. And I will reveal myself to each one of them."

22Judas (not Judas Iscariot, but the other dis-

ciple with that name) said to him, "Lord, why are you going to reveal yourself only to us and not to the world at large?"

23Jesus replied, "All those who love me will do what I say. My Father will love them, and we will come to them and live with them. 24Anyone who doesn't love me will not do what I say. And remember, my words are not my own. This message is from the Father who sent me. 25I am telling you these things now while I am still with you. 26But when the Father sends the Counselor as my representative—and by the Counselor I mean the Holy Spirit—he will teach you everything and will remind you of everything I myself have told you.

27"I am leaving you with a gift—peace of mind and heart. And the peace I give isn't like the peace the world gives. So don't be troubled or afraid. 28Remember what I told you: I am going away, but I will come back to you again. If you really love me, you will be very happy for me, because now I can go to the Father, who is greater than I am. 29I have told you these things before they happen so that you will believe when they do happen.

30"I don't have much more time to talk to you, because the prince of this world approaches. He has no power over me, 31but I will do what the Father requires of me, so that the world will know that I love the Father. Come, let's be going.

## CHAPTER 15
*Jesus, the True Vine*

"I am the true vine, and my Father is the gardener. 2He cuts off every branch that doesn't

14:16 Or *Comforter,* or *Encourager,* or *Advocate.* Greek *Paraclete;* also in 14:26.

produce fruit, and he prunes the branches that do bear fruit so they will produce even more. ³You have already been pruned for greater fruitfulness by the message I have given you. ⁴Remain in me, and I will remain in you. For a branch cannot produce fruit if it is severed from the vine, and you cannot be fruitful apart from me.

⁵"Yes, I am the vine; you are the branches. Those who remain in me, and I in them, will produce much fruit. For apart from me you can do nothing. ⁶Anyone who parts from me is thrown away like a useless branch and withers. Such branches are gathered into a pile to be burned. ⁷But if you stay joined to me and my words remain in you, you may ask any request you like, and it will be granted! ⁸My true disciples produce much fruit. This brings great glory to my Father.

⁹"I have loved you even as the Father has loved me. Remain in my love. ¹⁰When you obey me, you remain in my love, just as I obey my Father and remain in his love. ¹¹I have told you this so that you will be filled with my joy. Yes, your joy will overflow! ¹²I command you to love each other in the same way that I love you. ¹³And here is how to measure it—the greatest love is shown when people lay down their lives for their friends. ¹⁴You are my friends if you obey me. ¹⁵I no longer call you servants, because a master doesn't confide in his servants. Now you are my friends, since I have told you everything the Father told me. ¹⁶You didn't choose me. I chose you. I appointed you to go and produce fruit that will last, so that the Father will give you whatever you ask for, using my name. ¹⁷I command you to love each other.

### The World's Hatred

¹⁸"When the world hates you, remember it hated me before it hated you. ¹⁹The world would love you if you belonged to it, but you don't. I chose you to come out of the world, and so it hates you. ²⁰Do you remember what I told you? 'A servant is not greater than the master.' Since they persecuted me, naturally they will persecute you. And if they had listened to me, they would listen to you! ²¹The people of the world will hate you because you belong to me, for they don't know God who sent me. ²²They would not be guilty if I had not come and spoken to them. But now they have no excuse for their sin. ²³Anyone who hates me hates my Father, too. ²⁴If I hadn't done such miraculous signs among them that no one else could do, they would not be counted guilty. But as it is, they saw all that I

## A Disciple Abides in Christ
Read JOHN 15:1-17

Jesus knows that his true followers desire to live productive, fulfilling, joy-filled lives. In this passage, he lays out four predominant characteristics of a growing disciple:

**1. A Disciple Stays Close to the Master.** Jesus encourages us to remain in him (verses 4-5). Another way to translate that is "to abide in him." The word *abide* signifies a permanence of position. It means that you sink your roots deep into your relationship with Jesus, allowing him to fill every part of your life and daily activities. If you maintain this unbroken fellowship with God, a changed lifestyle will result.

**2. A Disciple Is Fruitful.** Just as a branch can only be fruitful when attached to the vine, we can only be productive when we draw our strength from Jesus (verses 6, 16). The Bible describes the fruit Jesus is talking about as love, joy, peace, patience, kindness, goodness, faithfulness, gentleness, and self-control (see Galatians 5:22, p. 234).

**3. A Disciple Obeys the Master.** Another clear sign that you are Christ's disciple is your obedience to the principles and guidelines found in his Word, the Bible (verse 10). Then, and only then, will you discover what it means to live in God's love.

**4. A Disciple Loves Others.** Jesus gave us the ultimate example of love by laying down his life for us. He, in essence, is asking us to do nothing less. Although that may not mean actually dying for someone, it may mean placing someone else's needs before our own.

In verse 11 we find Jesus' reason for sharing these principles: He wants us to be filled with joy. If you try to find happiness by pursuing it in and of itself, it will elude you. The only way to find happiness is through the pursuit of God. If you prioritize your life as Jesus has laid out in these verses, then "your joy will overflow."

FIRST STEPS

## How the Holy Spirit Works in Our Lives Read JOHN 14:15-17

The Bible uses three different Greek prepositions in the New Testament to describe the different ways in which the Holy Spirit works in our lives. This verse shows two of these ways, and a third can be found elsewhere in Scripture:

**1. He Works *with* Us as Nonbelievers (*para*).** Prior to our conversion to faith in Jesus Christ, the Holy Spirit convicts us of our sin and reveals Christ as the answer (see John 16:8, p. 126). Some might dismiss his working as the prodding of one's personal conscience. Yet it is the Holy Spirit who opens our eyes to our terminally sinful condition, exposing our lack of righteousness so that we will see the need to turn our lives over to Jesus Christ.

**2. He Comes *into* Our Lives When We Turn to Christ (*en*).** Once we accept Jesus Christ as our Savior and invite him into our lives, the Holy Spirit moves into our lives and sets up residence, so to speak. First, he produces the process of salvation in our heart. As Jesus said, "No one can enter the Kingdom of God without being born of . . . the Spirit" (John 3:5). Second, he assures us that we have done the right thing. For Scripture tells us, "For his Holy Spirit speaks to us deep in our hearts and tells us that we are God's children" (Romans 8:16). He gives us the inner knowledge that Christ is living in us. Now he can begin changing us from the inside out and develop the new nature within us.

**3. He Will Come *upon* Us to Empower Us as Believers (*epi*).** This aspect of the Holy Spirit's work is described in Luke 24:49, where Jesus says, "And now I will send the Holy Spirit, just as my Father promised." Here Jesus describes the dynamic empowering of the Holy Spirit upon our lives. This is what the early Christians experienced in Acts chapter 2, and it dramatically emboldened their witness for Jesus Christ. This power is available to believers today, for Scripture says of the giving of his Spirit, "This promise is to you and your children, and even to the Gentiles—all who have been called by the Lord our God!" (Acts 2:39).

CORNER STONES

did and yet hated both of us—me and my Father. 25This has fulfilled what the Scriptures said: 'They hated me without cause.'*

26"But I will send you the Counselor*—the Spirit of truth. He will come to you from the Father and will tell you all about me. 27And you must also tell others about me because you have been with me from the beginning.

CHAPTER **16**
"I have told you these things so that you won't fall away. 2For you will be expelled from the synagogues, and the time is coming when those who kill you will think they are doing God a service. 3This is because they have never known the Father or me. 4Yes, I'm telling you these things now, so that when they happen, you will remember I warned you. I didn't tell you earlier because I was going to be with you for a while longer.

*The Work of the Holy Spirit*
5"But now I am going away to the one who sent me, and none of you has asked me where I am going. 6Instead, you are very sad. 7But it is actually best for you that I go away, because if I don't, the Counselor* won't come. If I do go away, he will come because I will send him to you. 8And when he comes, he will convince the world of its sin, and of God's righteousness, and of the coming judgment. 9The world's sin is unbelief in me. 10Righteousness is available because I go to the Father, and you will see me no more. 11Judgment will come because the prince of this world has already been judged.

12"Oh, there is so much more I want to tell you, but you can't bear it now. 13When the Spirit of truth comes, he will guide you into all truth. He will not be presenting his own ideas; he will be telling you what he has heard. He will tell you

15:25 Pss 35:19; 69:4.  15:26 Or *Comforter*, or *Encourager*, or *Advocate*. Greek *Paraclete*.  16:7 Or *Comforter*, or *Encourager*, or *Advocate*. Greek *Paraclete*.

about the future. ¹⁴He will bring me glory by revealing to you whatever he receives from me. ¹⁵All that the Father is mine; this is what I mean when I say that the Spirit will reveal to you whatever he receives from me.

### Sadness Will Be Turned to Joy

¹⁶"In just a little while I will be gone, and you won't see me anymore. Then, just a little while after that, you will see me again."

¹⁷The disciples asked each other, "What does he mean when he says, 'You won't see me, and then you will see me'? And what does he mean when he says, 'I am going to the Father'? ¹⁸And what does he mean by 'a little while'? We don't understand."

¹⁹Jesus realized they wanted to ask him, so he said, "Are you asking yourselves what I meant? I said in just a little while I will be gone, and you won't see me anymore. Then, just a little while after that, you will see me again. ²⁰Truly, you will weep and mourn over what is going to happen to me, but the world will rejoice. You will grieve, but your grief will suddenly turn to wonderful joy when you see me again. ²¹It will be like a woman experiencing the pains of labor. When her child is born, her anguish gives place to joy because she has brought a new person into the world. ²²You have sorrow now, but I will see you again; then you will rejoice, and no one can rob you of that joy. ²³At that time you won't need to ask me for anything. The truth is, you can go directly to the Father and ask him, and he will grant your request because you use my name. ²⁴You haven't done this before. Ask, using my name, and you will receive, and you will have abundant joy.

²⁵"I have spoken of these matters in parables, but the time will come when this will not be necessary, and I will tell you plainly all about the Father. ²⁶Then you will ask in my name. I'm not saying I will ask the Father on your behalf, ²⁷for the Father himself loves you dearly because you love me and believe that I came from God. ²⁸Yes, I came from the Father into the world, and I will leave the world and return to the Father."

²⁹Then his disciples said, "At last you are speaking plainly and not in parables. ³⁰Now we understand that you know everything and don't need anyone to tell you anything.* From this we believe that you came from God."

³¹Jesus asked, "Do you finally believe? ³²But the time is coming—in fact, it is already here— when you will be scattered, each one going his

16:30 Or don't need that anyone should ask you anything.

---

## Live in God's Love Read JOHN 15:9-11

This passage is a portion of Jesus' last message to his disciples before his death. In preparing them for his departure, he wanted to emphasize his love for them and how that love should affect their lives. He wanted them to realize that they could experience true and lasting joy in their walk with God—even if he could not personally be with them. For that reason this intimate message and command from Christ applies to us today as well. In this text Jesus gives four simple points that will enable us to live in his love:

**1. Realize That You Have the Love of Jesus and Your Heavenly Father.** Jesus is not simply some authoritative figure who demands our respect. He is a personal being who loved us so much that he died in our place. In return, he requires our obedience. Knowing that you are loved by Jesus frees you to love him in return. The best way to show your love for him is to obey his commands. Trying to obey his commands out of obligation rather than love can produce resentment toward him. That is because there is no joy in mere obligation. But obeying Jesus out of love produces joy.

**2. Live within God's Love by Obeying His Commands.** This is one of the earmarks of a true follower of Christ. It is easy to boast of our great love for God or the wonderful affection and devotion we feel toward him. But as the saying goes, The proof is in the pudding. If we really love God, we will obey him. If we do not obey him, it is questionable as to just how deep our love for him really is.

**3. Follow Jesus' Example.** Jesus is our perfect model of obedience. Pay careful attention to how Jesus obeyed his heavenly Father throughout the Gospels of Matthew, Mark, Luke, and John.

**4. Experience the Reward of Obedience: Overflowing Joy.** The obedient Christian is the happy Christian. If you want more joy in your life, make sure that you are following the guidelines God has given you in his Word.

Do you find it hard to obey God and his principles? If so, it is probably time to reexamine your priorities and make sure that getting to know your Creator is right at the top of the list. Then you will discover the joy that comes from living in God's love every day.

own way, leaving me alone. Yet I am not alone because the Father is with me. [33]I have told you all this so that you may have peace in me. Here on earth you will have many trials and sorrows. But take heart, because I have overcome the world."

## CHAPTER 17
### The Prayer of Jesus

When Jesus had finished saying all these things, he looked up to heaven and said, "Father, the time has come. Glorify your Son so he can give glory back to you. [2]For you have given him authority over everyone in all the earth. He gives eternal life to each one you have given him. [3]And this is the way to have eternal life—to know you, the only true God, and Jesus Christ, the one you sent to earth. [4]I brought glory to you here on earth by doing everything you told me to do. [5]And now, Father, bring me into the glory we shared before the world began.

[6]"I have told these men about you. They were in the world, but then you gave them to me. Actually, they were always yours, and you gave them to me; and they have kept your word. [7]Now they know that everything I have is a gift from you, [8]for I have passed on to them the words you gave me; and they accepted them and know that I came from you, and they believe you sent me.

[9]"My prayer is not for the world, but for those you have given me, because they belong to you. [10]And all of them, since they are mine, belong to you; and you have given them back to me, so they are my glory! [11]Now I am departing the world; I am leaving them behind and coming to you. Holy Father, keep them and care for them—all those you have given me—so that they will be united just as we are. [12]During my time here, I have kept them safe.* I guarded them so that not one was lost, except the one headed for destruction, as the Scriptures foretold.

[13]"And now I am coming to you. I have told them many things while I was with them so they would be filled with my joy. [14]I have given them your word. And the world hates them because they do not belong to the world, just as I do not. [15]I'm not asking you to take them out of the world, but to keep them safe from the evil one. [16]They are not part of this world any more than I am. [17]Make them pure and holy by teaching them your words of truth. [18]As you sent me into the world, I am sending them into the world. [19]And I give myself entirely to you so they also might be entirely yours.

[20]"I am praying not only for these disciples but also for all who will ever believe in me because of their testimony. [21]My prayer for all of them is that they will be one, just as you and I are one, Father—that just as you are in me and I am in you, so they will be in us, and the world will believe you sent me.

[22]"I have given them the glory you gave me, so that they may be one, as we are—[23]I in them and you in me, all being perfected into one. Then the world will know that you sent me and will understand that you love them as much as you love me. [24]Father, I want these whom you've given me to be with me, so they can see my glory. You gave me the glory because you loved me even before the world began!

[25]"O righteous Father, the world doesn't know you, but I do; and these disciples know you sent me. [26]And I have revealed you to them and will keep on revealing you. I will do this so that your love for me may be in them and I in them."

## CHAPTER 18
### Jesus Is Betrayed and Arrested

After saying these things, Jesus crossed the Kidron Valley with his disciples and entered a grove of olive trees. [2]Judas, the betrayer, knew this place, because Jesus had gone there many times with his disciples. [3]The leading priests and Pharisees had given Judas a battalion of Roman soldiers and Temple guards to accompany him. Now with blazing torches, lanterns, and weapons, they arrived at the olive grove.

[4]Jesus fully realized all that was going to happen to him. Stepping forward to meet them, he asked, "Whom are you looking for?"

[5]"Jesus of Nazareth," they replied.

"I am he,"* Jesus said. Judas was standing there with them when Jesus identified himself. [6]And as he said, "I am he," they all fell backward to the ground! [7]Once more he asked them, "Whom are you searching for?"

And again they replied, "Jesus of Nazareth."

[8]"I told you that I am he," Jesus said. "And since I am the one you want, let these others go." [9]He did this to fulfill his own statement: "I have not lost a single one of those you gave me."*

[10]Then Simon Peter drew a sword and slashed off the right ear of Malchus, the high

17:12 Greek *I have kept in your name those whom you have given me.*   18:5 Greek *I am;* also in 18:6, 8.   18:9 See John 6:39 and 17:12.

priest's servant. ¹¹But Jesus said to Peter, "Put your sword back into its sheath. Shall I not drink from the cup the Father has given me?"

### Annas Questions Jesus

¹²So the soldiers, their commanding officer, and the Temple guards arrested Jesus and tied him up. ¹³First they took him to Annas, the father-in-law of Caiaphas, the high priest that year. ¹⁴Caiaphas was the one who had told the other Jewish leaders, "Better that one should die for all."

### Peter's First Denial

¹⁵Simon Peter followed along behind, as did another of the disciples. That other disciple was acquainted with the high priest, so he was allowed to enter the courtyard with Jesus. ¹⁶Peter stood outside the gate. Then the other disciple spoke to the woman watching at the gate, and she let Peter in. ¹⁷The woman asked Peter, "Aren't you one of Jesus' disciples?"

"No," he said, "I am not."

¹⁸The guards and the household servants were standing around a charcoal fire they had made because it was cold. And Peter stood there with them, warming himself.

### The High Priest Questions Jesus

¹⁹Inside, the high priest began asking Jesus about his followers and what he had been teaching them. ²⁰Jesus replied, "What I teach is widely known, because I have preached regularly in the synagogues and the Temple. I have been heard by people* everywhere, and I teach nothing in private that I have not said in public. ²¹Why are you asking me this question? Ask those who heard me. They know what I said."

²²One of the Temple guards standing there struck Jesus on the face. "Is that the way to answer the high priest?" he demanded.

²³Jesus replied, "If I said anything wrong, you must give evidence for it. Should you hit a man for telling the truth?"

²⁴Then Annas bound Jesus and sent him to Caiaphas, the high priest.

### Peter's Second and Third Denials

²⁵Meanwhile, as Simon Peter was standing by the fire, they asked him again, "Aren't you one of his disciples?"

"I am not," he said.

²⁶But one of the household servants of the high priest, a relative of the man whose ear Peter had cut off, asked, "Didn't I see you out there in

18:20 Greek *Jewish people*; also in 18:38.

the olive grove with Jesus?" ²⁷Again Peter denied it. And immediately a rooster crowed.

### Jesus' Trial before Pilate

²⁸Jesus' trial before Caiaphas ended in the early hours of the morning. Then he was taken to the headquarters of the Roman governor. His accusers didn't go in themselves because it would

## God's Spirit Will Guide You
Read JOHN 16:13-15

The work of the Holy Spirit in the life of a Christian is multidimensional. We are told that, among other things, the Holy Spirit "speaks to us deep in our hearts and tells us that we are God's children" (Romans 8:16). In this passage, we see that the Holy Spirit serves as a teacher and a guide.

**The Holy Spirit Will Help Us Understand the Bible.** Before you became a Christian, understanding the Bible may have been like walking around with blinders on. But those "blinders" you once had were taken off, so to speak, when the Holy Spirit took up residence in your heart. The Holy Spirit teaches you the truth of the Scripture, helping you grasp hard-to-understand passages.

**The Holy Spirit Will Reveal More and More about God and Jesus.** The Bible makes it abundantly clear that one of the primary roles of the Holy Spirit is to glorify Christ. The moment you invited Jesus into your heart, God's Spirit began to help you grasp the awesome, praiseworthy attributes of Jesus. Those who do not have a personal relationship with Christ cannot see or understand the full glory of God, because they do not have the Holy Spirit's assistance.

The Holy Spirit wants to be actively involved in your life, helping you grow in the knowledge of God and his Word so that you can better understand God's will for your life. Every time you open the Bible, pray for the Holy Spirit to show you how the passages you read can apply to your life.

defile them, and they wouldn't be allowed to celebrate the Passover feast. 29So Pilate, the governor, went out to them and asked, "What is your charge against this man?"

30"We wouldn't have handed him over to you if he weren't a criminal!" they retorted.

31"Then take him away and judge him by your own laws," Pilate told them.

"Only the Romans are permitted to execute someone," the Jewish leaders replied. 32This fulfilled Jesus' prediction about the way he would die.*

33Then Pilate went back inside and called for Jesus to be brought to him. "Are you the King of the Jews?" he asked him.

34Jesus replied, "Is this your own question, or did others tell you about me?"

35"Am I a Jew?" Pilate asked. "Your own people and their leading priests brought you here. Why? What have you done?"

36Then Jesus answered, "I am not an earthly king. If I were, my followers would have fought when I was arrested by the Jewish leaders. But my Kingdom is not of this world."

37Pilate replied, "You are a king then?"

"You say that I am a king, and you are right," Jesus said. "I was born for that purpose. And I came to bring truth to the world. All who love the truth recognize that what I say is true."

38"What is truth?" Pilate asked. Then he went out again to the people and told them, "He is not guilty of any crime. 39But you have a custom of asking me to release someone from prison each year at Passover. So if you want me to, I'll release the King of the Jews."

40But they shouted back, "No! Not this man, but Barabbas!" (Barabbas was a criminal.)

## CHAPTER 19
### Jesus Sentenced to Death

Then Pilate had Jesus flogged with a lead-tipped whip. 2The soldiers made a crown of long, sharp thorns and put it on his head, and they put a royal purple robe on him. 3"Hail! King of the Jews!" they mocked, and they hit him with their fists.

4Pilate went outside again and said to the people, "I am going to bring him out to you now, but understand clearly that I find him not guilty." 5Then Jesus came out wearing the crown of thorns and the purple robe. And Pilate said, "Here is the man!"

6When they saw him, the leading priests

and Temple guards began shouting, "Crucify! Crucify!"

"You crucify him," Pilate said. "I find him not guilty."

7The Jewish leaders replied, "By our laws he ought to die because he called himself the Son of God."

8When Pilate heard this, he was more frightened than ever. 9He took Jesus back into the headquarters again and asked him, "Where are you from?" But Jesus gave no answer. 10"You won't talk to me?" Pilate demanded. "Don't you realize that I have the power to release you or to crucify you?"

11Then Jesus said, "You would have no power over me at all unless it were given to you from above. So the one who brought me to you has the greater sin."

12Then Pilate tried to release him, but the Jewish leaders told him, "If you release this man, you are not a friend of Caesar. Anyone who declares himself a king is a rebel against Caesar."

13When they said this, Pilate brought Jesus out to them again. Then Pilate sat down on the judgment seat on the platform that is called the Stone Pavement (in Hebrew, *Gabbatha*). 14It was now about noon of the day of preparation for the Passover. And Pilate said to the people,* "Here is your king!"

15"Away with him," they yelled. "Away with him—crucify him!"

"What? Crucify your king?" Pilate asked.

"We have no king but Caesar," the leading priests shouted back.

16Then Pilate gave Jesus to them to be crucified.

### The Crucifixion

So they took Jesus and led him away. 17Carrying the cross by himself, Jesus went to the place called Skull Hill (in Hebrew, *Golgotha*). 18There they crucified him. There were two others crucified with him, one on either side, with Jesus between them. 19And Pilate posted a sign over him that read, "Jesus of Nazareth, the King of the Jews." 20The place where Jesus was crucified was near the city; and the sign was written in Hebrew, Latin, and Greek, so that many people could read it.

21Then the leading priests said to Pilate, "Change it from 'The King of the Jews' to 'He said, I am King of the Jews.'"

22Pilate replied, "What I have written, I have written. It stays exactly as it is."

18:32 See John 12:32-33.  19:14 Greek *Jewish people*; also in 19:20.

23When the soldiers had crucified Jesus, they divided his clothes among the four of them. They also took his robe, but it was seamless, woven in one piece from the top. 24So they said, "Let's not tear it but throw dice* to see who gets it." This fulfilled the Scripture that says, "They divided my clothes among themselves and threw dice for my robe."* 25So that is what they did.

Standing near the cross were Jesus' mother, and his mother's sister, Mary (the wife of Clopas), and Mary Magdalene. 26When Jesus saw his mother standing there beside the disciple he loved, he said to her, "Woman, he is your son." 27And he said to this disciple, "She is your mother." And from then on this disciple took her into his home.

## The Death of Jesus
28Jesus knew that everything was now finished, and to fulfill the Scriptures he said, "I am thirsty."* 29A jar of sour wine was sitting there, so they soaked a sponge in it, put it on a hyssop branch, and held it up to his lips. 30When Jesus had tasted it, he said, "It is finished!" Then he bowed his head and gave up his spirit.

31The Jewish leaders didn't want the victims hanging there the next day, which was the Sabbath (and a very special Sabbath at that, because it was the Passover), so they asked Pilate to hasten their deaths by ordering that their legs be broken. Then their bodies could be taken down. 32So the soldiers came and broke the legs of the two men crucified with Jesus. 33But when they came to Jesus, they saw that he was dead already, so they didn't break his legs. 34One of the soldiers, however, pierced his side with a spear, and blood and water flowed out. 35This report is from an eyewitness giving an accurate account; it is presented so that you also can believe. 36These things happened in fulfillment of the Scriptures that say, "Not one of his bones will be broken,"* 37and "They will look on him whom they pierced."*

## The Burial of Jesus
38Afterward Joseph of Arimathea, who had been a secret disciple of Jesus (because he feared the Jewish leaders), asked Pilate for permission to take Jesus' body down. When Pilate gave him permission, he came and took the body away. 39Nicodemus, the man who had come to Jesus at night, also came, bringing about seventy-five pounds* of embalming ointment made from myrrh and aloes. 40Together they wrapped Jesus' body in a long

linen cloth with the spices, as is the Jewish custom of burial. 41The place of crucifixion was near a garden, where there was a new tomb, never used before. 42And so, because it was the day of preparation before the Passover and since the tomb was close at hand, they laid Jesus there.

CHAPTER 20
## The Resurrection
Early Sunday morning,* while it was still dark, Mary Magdalene came to the tomb and found that the stone had been rolled away from the entrance. 2She ran and found Simon Peter and the other disciple, the one whom Jesus loved. She said, "They have taken the Lord's body out of the tomb, and I don't know where they have put him!"

3Peter and the other disciple ran to the tomb to see. 4The other disciple outran Peter and got there first. 5He stooped and looked in and saw the linen cloth lying there, but he didn't go in. 6Then Simon Peter arrived and went inside. He also noticed the linen wrappings lying there, 7while the cloth that had covered Jesus' head was folded up and lying to the side. 8Then the other disciple also went in, and he saw and believed—9for until then they hadn't realized that the Scriptures said he would rise from the dead. 10Then they went home.

## Jesus Appears to Mary Magdalene
11Mary was standing outside the tomb crying, and as she wept, she stooped and looked in. 12She saw two white-robed angels sitting at the head and foot of the place where the body of Jesus had been lying. 13"Why are you crying?" the angels asked her.

"Because they have taken away my Lord," she replied, "and I don't know where they have put him."

14She glanced over her shoulder and saw someone standing behind her. It was Jesus, but she didn't recognize him. 15"Why are you crying?" Jesus asked her. "Who are you looking for?"

She thought he was the gardener. "Sir," she said, "if you have taken him away, tell me where you have put him, and I will go and get him."

16"Mary!" Jesus said.

She turned toward him and exclaimed, "Teacher!"*

17"Don't cling to me," Jesus said, "for I haven't

## Our Love for God Prepares Us for Service Read JOHN 21:15-17

Peter knew that he had let Jesus down by denying him three times prior to the Crucifixion. But Peter also knew that Jesus had forgiven him. So Jesus tested Peter by asking him the searching question, "Do you love me?" three times.

Peter's response to Jesus' questions has great significance in the original language of the text. When Jesus posed the questions, he had basically asked, "Peter, do you love me with a sacrificial, committed love?" Peter, however, responded with a different word for "love" than Jesus had suggested. Peter essentially said, "Lord, I like you. I love you as a friend."

At least Peter was being honest. He told Jesus the truth about his commitment. Interestingly enough, Jesus still enlisted Peter in his service, to feed and care for his sheep. Jesus just wanted Peter to affirm his devotion to the Lord before giving him his directions for ministry.

As this story implies, we must love God before we can serve him faithfully. Do you love God? Here are five ways to tell if you really love God and are growing in that love for him:

**1. If You Love the Lord, You Will Long for Personal Communion with Him.** Can you relate to the words of the psalmist, "As the deer pants for streams of water, so I long for you, O God" (Psalm 42:1)? When you really love God, you will delight in praising and worshiping him. That is because your praise and worship will overflow from a heart filled with love for God. And this love will cause you to look forward to spending time with him and his people.

**2. If You Love God, You Will Love the Things He Loves.** We know what God loves by what he has declared in his Word, the Bible. So if you love God, you will love his Word. Bible study will not be a drudgery, but a delight.

**3. If You Love the Lord, You Will Hate What He Hates.** As the Lord's nature becomes your nature, his likes and dislikes become your likes and dislikes. His outlook becomes your outlook. We know from his Word that he hates sin. If we love him, then we should also hate sin.

**4. If You Love the Lord, You Will Long for His Return.** Jesus described himself as a bridegroom (Mark 2:19). His bride is the church—the body of believers (Ephesians 5:23-29). When Jesus returns, he will be united with his bride. Therefore, if you love the Lord, you will long for his return as a bride and bridegroom long to be together.

**5. If You Love the Lord, You Will Keep His Commandments.** Jesus says, "If you love me, obey my commandments" (John 14:15). That does not mean that you will never sin. Though it is impossible for any of us who love God to go on an endless course of sin, it is quite possible to fall into individual sins. But if we love God, we will repent of those sins and seek his forgiveness, and our lifestyle will conform to the truths we find in his Word.

Do you love the Lord? Like Peter, you may be tempted to believe that you have no love for Jesus when you sin. Maybe you feel that God could never use you in his service again. Be honest with God; then start rebuilding that relationship by following the steps above. As you reaffirm your love for him, God will open up opportunities for you to serve him and share that love with others. A committed heart leads to committed service.

CORNER STONES

yet ascended to the Father. But go find my brothers and tell them that I am ascending to my Father and your Father, my God and your God."

18Mary Magdalene found the disciples and told them, "I have seen the Lord!" Then she gave them his message.

*Jesus Appears to His Disciples*

19That evening, on the first day of the week, the disciples were meeting behind locked doors because they were afraid of the Jewish leaders. Suddenly, Jesus was standing there among them! "Peace be with you," he said. 20As he spoke, he held out his hands for them to see, and he showed them his side. They were filled with joy when they saw their Lord! 21He spoke to them again and said, "Peace be with you. As the Father has sent me, so I send you." 22Then he breathed on them and said to them, "Receive the Holy Spirit. 23If you forgive anyone's sins, they are forgiven. If you refuse to forgive them, they are unforgiven."

### Jesus Appears to Thomas

24One of the disciples, Thomas (nicknamed the Twin*), was not with the others when Jesus came. 25They told him, "We have seen the Lord!" But he replied, "I won't believe it unless I see the nail wounds in his hands, put my fingers into them, and place my hand into the wound in his side."

26Eight days later the disciples were together again, and this time Thomas was with them. The doors were locked; but suddenly, as before, Jesus was standing among them. He said, "Peace be with you." 27Then he said to Thomas, "Put your finger here and see my hands. Put your hand into the wound in my side. Don't be faithless any longer. Believe!"

28"My Lord and my God!" Thomas exclaimed.

29Then Jesus told him, "You believe because you have seen me. Blessed are those who haven't seen me and believe anyway."

### Purpose of the Book

30Jesus' disciples saw him do many other miraculous signs besides the ones recorded in this book. 31But these are written so that you may believe* that Jesus is the Messiah, the Son of God, and that by believing in him you will have life.

## CHAPTER 21

### Jesus Appears to Seven Disciples

Later Jesus appeared again to the disciples beside the Sea of Galilee.* This is how it happened. 2Several of the disciples were there—Simon Peter, Thomas (nicknamed the Twin*), Nathanael from Cana in Galilee, the sons of Zebedee, and two other disciples.

3Simon Peter said, "I'm going fishing."

"We'll come, too," they all said. So they went out in the boat, but they caught nothing all night.

4At dawn the disciples saw Jesus standing on the beach, but they couldn't see who he was. 5He called out, "Friends, have you caught any fish?"

"No," they replied.

6Then he said, "Throw out your net on the right-hand side of the boat, and you'll get plenty of fish!" So they did, and they couldn't draw in the net because there were so many fish in it.

7Then the disciple whom Jesus loved said to Peter, "It is the Lord!" When Simon Peter heard that it was the Lord, he put on his tunic (for he had stripped for work), jumped into the water, and swam ashore. 8The others stayed with the boat and pulled the loaded net to the shore, for they were only out about three hundred feet.* 9When they got there, they saw that a charcoal fire was burning and fish were frying over it, and there was bread.

10"Bring some of the fish you've just caught," Jesus said. 11So Simon Peter went aboard and dragged the net to the shore. There were 153 large fish, and yet the net hadn't torn.

12"Now come and have some breakfast!" Jesus said. And no one dared ask him if he really was the Lord because they were sure of it. 13Then Jesus served them the bread and the fish. 14This was the third time Jesus had appeared to his disciples since he had been raised from the dead.

### Jesus Challenges Peter

15After breakfast Jesus said to Simon Peter, "Simon son of John, do you love me more than these?"

"Yes, Lord," Peter replied, "you know I love you."

"Then feed my lambs," Jesus told him.

16Jesus repeated the question: "Simon son of John, do you love me?"

"Yes, Lord," Peter said, "you know I love you."

"Then take care of my sheep," Jesus said.

17Once more he asked him, "Simon son of John, do you love me?"

Peter was grieved that Jesus asked the question a third time. He said, "Lord, you know everything. You know I love you."

Jesus said, "Then feed my sheep. 18The truth is, when you were young, you were able to do as you liked and go wherever you wanted to. But when you are old, you will stretch out your hands, and others will direct you and take you where you don't want to go." 19Jesus said this to let him know what kind of death he would die

---

20:24 Greek *the one who was called Didymus.*  20:31 Some manuscripts read *may continue to believe.*  21:1 Greek *Sea of Tiberias,* another name for the Sea of Galilee.  21:2 Greek *the one who was called Didymus.*  21:8 Greek *200 cubits* [90 meters].

to glorify God. Then Jesus told him, "Follow me."

20Peter turned around and saw the disciple Jesus loved following them—the one who had leaned over to Jesus during supper and asked, "Lord, who among us will betray you?" 21Peter asked Jesus, "What about him, Lord?"

22Jesus replied, "If I want him to remain alive until I return, what is that to you? You follow me." 23So the rumor spread among the community of believers* that that disciple wouldn't die.

21:23 Greek *the brothers.*

But that isn't what Jesus said at all. He only said, "If I want him to remain alive until I return, what is that to you?"

## Conclusion

24This is that disciple who saw these events and recorded them here. And we all know that his account of these things is accurate.

25And I suppose that if all the other things Jesus did were written down, the whole world could not contain the books.

# Acts

## CHAPTER 1

### The Promise of the Holy Spirit

Dear Theophilus:

In my first book* I told you about everything Jesus began to do and teach 2until the day he ascended to heaven after giving his chosen apostles further instructions from the Holy Spirit. 3During the forty days after his crucifixion, he appeared to the apostles from time to time and proved to them in many ways that he was actually alive. On these occasions he talked to them about the Kingdom of God.

4In one of these meetings as he was eating a meal with them, he told them, "Do not leave Jerusalem until the Father sends you what he promised. Remember, I have told you about this before. 5John baptized with* water, but in just a few days you will be baptized with the Holy Spirit."

### The Ascension of Jesus

6When the apostles were with Jesus, they kept asking him, "Lord, are you going to free Israel now and restore our kingdom?"

7"The Father sets those dates," he replied, "and they are not for you to know. 8But when the Holy Spirit has come upon you, you will receive power and will tell people about me everywhere—in Jerusalem, throughout Judea, in Samaria, and to the ends of the earth."

9It was not long after he said this that he was taken up into the sky while they were watching, and he disappeared into a cloud. 10As they were straining their eyes to see him, two white-robed men suddenly stood there among them. 11They said, "Men of Galilee, why are you standing here staring at the sky? Jesus has been taken away from you into heaven. And someday, just as you saw him go, he will return!"

### Matthias Replaces Judas

12The apostles were at the Mount of Olives when this happened, so they walked the half mile* back to Jerusalem. 13Then they went to the upstairs room of the house where they were staying. Here is the list of those who were present:

> Peter,
> John,
> James,
> Andrew,
> Philip,
> Thomas,
> Bartholomew,
> Matthew,
> James (son of Alphaeus),
> Simon (the Zealot),
> and Judas (son of James).

14They all met together continually for prayer, along with Mary the mother of Jesus, several other women, and the brothers of Jesus.

15During this time, on a day when about 120 believers* were present, Peter stood up and addressed them as follows:

16"Brothers, it was necessary for the Scriptures to be fulfilled concerning Judas, who guided the Temple police to arrest Jesus. This was predicted long ago by the Holy Spirit, speaking through King David. 17Judas was one of us, chosen to share in the ministry with us."

18(Judas bought a field with the money he received for his treachery, and falling there, he burst open, spilling out his intestines. 19The news of his death spread rapidly among all the people of Jerusalem, and they gave the place the Aramaic name Akeldama, which means "Field of Blood.")

1:1 The reference is to the book of Luke.　1:5 Or in; also in 1:5b.　1:12 Greek a Sabbath day's journey.　1:15 Greek brothers.

## Who the Holy Spirit Helps Read ACTS 2:1-41

Who is the Holy Spirit here to help? The Holy Spirit has been given to all believers to deepen their spiritual walk and to enable them to make an impact upon their world for Jesus Christ. This passage illustrates three aspects of the Holy Spirit's unique work in the lives of believers:

**1. The Holy Spirit Fills All Believers.** In the Old Testament, the Holy Spirit was given only to a select few to perform specific tasks. This chapter indicates a change in that pattern. The Holy Spirit was poured out on all the believers in the house that day (verse 4), and he continued to be present in each of their lives from that day forward. This outpouring of the Holy Spirit was used by God to establish the church—and to spread the message of the gospel around the world (see verse 39).

**2. The Holy Spirit Draws Attention to the Savior.** Notice that Peter did not focus on the unique happening that had just taken place but turned the crowd's attention to the message of Jesus Christ and their need for repentance. Likewise, the Holy Spirit does not draw attention to himself but to the Savior. And when he fills your life, he radically increases your ability to share the gospel with others.

**3. The Holy Spirit Inspired Peter's Message.** Peter's sermon, inspired by the Holy Spirit, led many in the crowd to a point of decision: "What should we do?"(verse 37). The people were not attracted to Peter but to his message. As stated in point 2 above, one of the primary roles of the Holy Spirit is to draw people to God. As stated above, the Holy Spirit worked powerfully this day, and three thousand people responded to the message.

The Holy Spirit is promised to all who repent and receive Jesus Christ into their lives. Many people fail to understand who the Holy Spirit is and what dimension of power is available to them through him. It may help to examine what took place after the disciples received the filling of the Holy Spirit that Jesus had promised (see Acts 1:8, p. 135).

**CORNER STONES**

20Peter continued, "This was predicted in the book of Psalms, where it says, 'Let his home become desolate, with no one living in it.' And again, 'Let his position be given to someone else.'*

21"So now we must choose another man to take Judas's place. It must be someone who has been with us all the time that we were with the Lord Jesus—22from the time he was baptized by John until the day he was taken from us into heaven. Whoever is chosen will join us as a witness of Jesus' resurrection."

23So they nominated two men: Joseph called Barsabbas (also known as Justus) and Matthias. 24Then they all prayed for the right man to be chosen. "O Lord," they said, "you know every heart. Show us which of these men you have chosen 25as an apostle to replace Judas the traitor in this ministry, for he has deserted us and gone where he belongs." 26Then they cast lots, and in this way Matthias was chosen and became an apostle with the other eleven.

CHAPTER **2**
*The Holy Spirit Comes*
On the day of Pentecost, seven weeks after Jesus' resurrection,* the believers were meeting together in one place. 2Suddenly, there was a sound from heaven like the roaring of a mighty windstorm in the skies above them, and it filled the house where they were meeting. 3Then, what looked like flames or tongues of fire appeared and settled on each of them. 4And everyone present was filled with the Holy Spirit and began speaking in other languages,* as the Holy Spirit gave them this ability.

5Godly Jews from many nations were living in Jerusalem at that time. 6When they heard this sound, they came running to see what it was all

1:20 Pss 69:25; 109:8.  2:1 Greek *When the day of Pentecost arrived.* This annual celebration came 50 days after the Passover ceremonies. See Lev 23:16.  2:4 Or *in other tongues.*

about, and they were bewildered to hear their own languages being spoken by the believers.

7They were beside themselves with wonder. "How can this be?" they exclaimed. "These people are all from Galilee, 8and yet we hear them speaking the languages of the lands where we were born! 9Here we are—Parthians, Medes, Elamites, people from Mesopotamia, Judea, Cappadocia, Pontus, the province of Asia, 10Phrygia, Pamphylia, Egypt, and the areas of Libya toward Cyrene, visitors from Rome (both Jews and converts to Judaism), 11Cretans, and Arabians. And we all hear these people speaking in our own languages about the wonderful things God has done!" 12They stood there amazed and perplexed. "What can this mean?" they asked each other. 13But others in the crowd were mocking. "They're drunk, that's all!" they said.

### Peter Preaches to a Crowd

14Then Peter stepped forward with the eleven other apostles and shouted to the crowd, "Listen carefully, all of you, fellow Jews and residents of Jerusalem! Make no mistake about this. 15Some of you are saying these people are drunk. It isn't true! It's much too early for that. People don't get drunk by nine o'clock in the morning. 16No, what you see this morning was predicted centuries ago by the prophet Joel:

17 'In the last days, God said,
   I will pour out my Spirit upon all people.
   Your sons and daughters will prophesy,
      your young men will see visions,
      and your old men will dream dreams.
18 In those days I will pour out my Spirit
      upon all my servants, men and women
      alike,
   and they will prophesy.
19 And I will cause wonders in the heavens
      above
   and signs on the earth below—
      blood and fire and clouds of smoke.
20 The sun will be turned into darkness,
      and the moon will turn bloodred,
   before that great and glorious day of the
      Lord arrives.
21 And anyone who calls on the name of the
      Lord
   will be saved.'*

22"People of Israel, listen! God publicly endorsed Jesus of Nazareth by doing wonderful miracles, wonders, and signs through him, as

2:17-21 Joel 2:28-32.

you well know. 23But you followed God's prearranged plan. With the help of lawless Gentiles, you nailed him to the cross and murdered him. 24However, God released him from the horrors of death and raised him back to life again, for death could not keep him in its grip. 25King David said this about him:

'I know the Lord is always with me.
   I will not be shaken, for he is right beside
      me.
26 No wonder my heart is filled with joy,
      and my mouth shouts his praises!
   My body rests in hope.
27 For you will not leave my soul among the
      dead*

2:27 Greek in Hades; also in 2:31.

## God's Spirit Will Empower Your Witness Read ACTS 1:8

One of the greatest things the Holy Spirit wants to do in the life of the believer is empower his or her witness. The word for *power* in this verse comes from the Greek word *dunamis*, from which we get the words *dynamite*, *dynamic*, and *dynamo*. God didn't give us the power of the Holy Spirit to *feel* something, but to *accomplish* something.

Sometimes the Holy Spirit's power acts like dynamite in our lives, blasting us with zeal, jolting us out of complacency, and motivating us to greater spiritual growth. At other times God's Spirit is like a dynamic, generating power that will help us live from day to day at a level we could not achieve on our own. We need to remember the encouraging words the apostle Paul gave to young Timothy: "For God has not given us a spirit of fear and timidity, but of power, love, and self-discipline" (2 Timothy 1:7).

Are you timid in your witness for Christ? Is it hard for you to speak up for what you believe? Then you need to tap in to that power he has made available to you through his Spirit. God's Holy Spirit will give you an added dimension of boldness, power, and persuasiveness in your witness that you have never experienced before.

or allow your Holy One to rot in the
grave.
28 You have shown me the way of life,
and you will give me wonderful joy in
your presence.'*

29"Dear brothers, think about this! David
wasn't referring to himself when he spoke these
words I have quoted, for he died and was buried,
and his tomb is still here among us. 30But he was
a prophet, and he knew God had promised with
an oath that one of David's own descendants
would sit on David's throne as the Messiah.
31David was looking into the future and predict-
ing the Messiah's resurrection. He was saying
that the Messiah would not be left among the
dead and that his body would not rot in the
grave.

32"This prophecy was speaking of Jesus,
whom God raised from the dead, and we all are
witnesses of this. 33Now he sits on the throne of
highest honor in heaven, at God's right hand.
And the Father, as he had promised, gave him
the Holy Spirit to pour out upon us, just as you
see and hear today. 34For David himself never
ascended into heaven, yet he said,

'The LORD said to my Lord,
Sit in honor at my right hand
35    until I humble your enemies,
making them a footstool under your
feet.'*

36So let it be clearly known by everyone in Israel
that God has made this Jesus whom you crucified to be both Lord and Messiah!"

37Peter's words convicted them deeply, and
they said to him and to the other apostles,
"Brothers, what should we do?"

38Peter replied, "Each of you must turn from
your sins and turn to God, and be baptized in
the name of Jesus Christ for the forgiveness of
your sins. Then you will receive the gift of the
Holy Spirit. 39This promise is to you and to your
children, and even to the Gentiles*—all who
have been called by the Lord our God." 40Then
Peter continued preaching for a long time,
strongly urging all his listeners, "Save yourselves
from this generation that has gone astray!"

41Those who believed what Peter said were
baptized and added to the church—about three
thousand in all. 42They joined with the other
believers and devoted themselves to the apostles' teaching and fellowship, sharing in the
Lord's Supper and in prayer.

### The Believers Meet Together

43A deep sense of awe came over them all, and
the apostles performed many miraculous signs
and wonders. 44And all the believers met together constantly and shared everything they
had. 45They sold their possessions and shared
the proceeds with those in need. 46They worshiped together at the Temple each day, met in
homes for the Lord's Supper, and shared their
meals with great joy and generosity—47all the
while praising God and enjoying the goodwill of
all the people. And each day the Lord added to
their group those who were being saved.

## CHAPTER 3
### Peter Heals a Crippled Beggar

Peter and John went to the Temple one afternoon to take part in the three o'clock prayer
service. 2As they approached the Temple, a man
lame from birth was being carried in. Each day
he was put beside the Temple gate, the one
called the Beautiful Gate, so he could beg from
the people going into the Temple. 3When he saw
Peter and John about to enter, he asked them for
some money.

4Peter and John looked at him intently, and
Peter said, "Look at us!" 5The lame man looked
at them eagerly, expecting a gift. 6But Peter said,
"I don't have any money for you. But I'll give
you what I have. In the name of Jesus Christ of
Nazareth, get up and walk!"

7Then Peter took the lame man by the right
hand and helped him up. And as he did, the
man's feet and anklebones were healed and
strengthened. 8He jumped up, stood on his feet,
and began to walk! Then, walking, leaping, and
praising God, he went into the Temple with
them.

9All the people saw him walking and heard
him praising God. 10When they realized he was
the lame beggar they had seen so often at the
Beautiful Gate, they were absolutely astounded!
11They all rushed out to Solomon's Colonnade,
where he was holding tightly to Peter and John.
Everyone stood there in awe of the wonderful
thing that had happened.

### Peter Preaches in the Temple

12Peter saw his opportunity and addressed the
crowd. "People of Israel," he said, "what is so
astounding about this? And why look at us as
though we had made this man walk by our own
power and godliness? 13For it is the God of

2:25-28 Ps 16:8-11.   2:34-35 Ps 110:1.   2:39 Greek *to those far away.*

Abraham, the God of Isaac, the God of Jacob, the God of all our ancestors who has brought glory to his servant Jesus by doing this. This is the same Jesus whom you handed over and rejected before Pilate, despite Pilate's decision to release him. 14You rejected this holy, righteous one and instead demanded the release of a murderer. 15You killed the author of life, but God raised him to life. And we are witnesses of this fact!

16"The name of Jesus has healed this man—and you know how lame he was before. Faith in Jesus' name has caused this healing before your very eyes.

17"Friends,* I realize that what you did to Jesus was done in ignorance; and the same can be said of your leaders. 18But God was fulfilling what all the prophets had declared about the Messiah beforehand—that he must suffer all these things. 19Now turn from your sins and turn to God, so you can be cleansed of your sins. 20Then wonderful times of refreshment will come from the presence of the Lord, and he will send Jesus your Messiah to you again. 21For he must remain in heaven until the time for the final restoration of all things, as God promised long ago through his prophets. 22Moses said, 'The Lord your God will raise up a Prophet like me from among your own people. Listen carefully to everything he tells you.'* 23Then Moses said, 'Anyone who will not listen to that Prophet will be cut off from God's people and utterly destroyed.'*

24"Starting with Samuel, every prophet spoke about what is happening today. 25You are the children of those prophets, and you are included in the covenant God promised to your ancestors. For God said to Abraham, 'Through your descendants all the families on earth will be blessed.'* 26When God raised up his servant, he sent him first to you people of Israel, to bless you by turning each of you back from your sinful ways."

CHAPTER **4**

*Peter and John before the Council*

While Peter and John were speaking to the people, the leading priests, the captain of the Temple guard, and some of the Sadducees came over to them. 2They were very disturbed that Peter and John were claiming, on the authority of Jesus, that there is a resurrection of the dead. 3They arrested them and, since it was already

3:17 Greek *Brothers.*   3:22 Deut 18:15.   3:23 Deut 18:19; Lev 23:29.   3:25 Gen 22:18.

## What to Look for in a Church
Read ACTS 2:42, 44-47

The first-century church turned the world upside down with its message (see Acts 17:6, p. 159). What made the early church so dynamic was the commitment of its members to follow Christ wholeheartedly. When you look for a church to attend, make sure it has these five characteristics of a healthy church:

**1. Look for a Church That Meets Together Regularly.** The early believers did not view church as a social club, but as a place for devoted fellowship and valuable instruction. We miss out on a tremendous blessing when we neglect meeting together with God's people. When we are spiritually weak, we should not run *from* church but *to* church!

**2. Look for a Church That Places a High Priority on Bible Study.** The first-century Christians "devoted themselves to the apostles' teaching." The apostles' teachings on the life and ministry of Jesus eventually became the Gospel portion of the New Testament. Studying the Bible is important to every Christian's spiritual growth. Without Bible study, Christians cannot know and understand God's commands and truth.

**3. Look for a Church That Is a Place of Corporate Worship and Prayer.** The early church recognized the importance of corporate worship and prayer. Corporate worship focused their attention on the praiseworthy character of God and gave them an opportunity to express their thanks to God. Corporate prayer allowed them to express their thanks to God as well, but it was also an opportunity to seek God together and present their requests before him as a body.

**4. Look for a Church That Looks after Its Members.** The early believers shared food, clothing, and housing with each other. The Bible reminds us to care for fellow believers who are in need (see 2 Corinthians 9:1-15).

**5. Look for a Church That Is Growing.** Church growth is not our responsibility but God's. If we do our part as a church, God will do his. We see proof of this in verse 47.

## Jesus Has Great Power to Transform People Read ACTS 4:1-13

The entire book of Acts is a testimony to the transformation that takes place in the life of a true follower of Jesus Christ. Consider the case of Peter and John. Immediately after Christ's crucifixion, Peter and John went into hiding. In fact, Peter denied knowing Jesus three times before Jesus even died! These men were far from bold. Yet when Jesus came back to life, met with them, and told them to wait for the promised Holy Spirit once he returned to heaven, everything changed.

Why were Peter and John so bold? What made their witness so effective, and how can our lives be so dramatically transformed?

**Peter and John Spent Time with Jesus.** For three years Peter and John followed Jesus throughout Israel. During this time they saw Jesus perform many miracles. They also listened to his teaching and observed his lifestyle. But they weren't just casual observers. They talked with Jesus and shared their lives with him. In doing so, they made Jesus a significant part of their lives. Even though we did not walk alongside Jesus during his time on earth, we can invite him into our hearts. In addition, we have his teachings to study and the ability to spend time with him in prayer. In other words, we don't have to live in Bible times to have a relationship with Jesus.

**Peter and John Modeled Their Lives after Jesus' Life and Teachings.** Christ's life and resurrection had such an impact on Peter and John that they began to imitate Jesus in their behavior. We can see the impact Jesus made on these two disciples in the first few chapters of Acts. Here Peter and John speak boldly for Jesus in public, heal a crippled beggar, and endure persecution for Jesus. Their actions prove an important point: We need to put into practice what we have learned from spending time with Jesus.

**Peter and John Put Their Confidence in Christ, Not in Their Own Abilities.** Remember, Peter and John were common fishermen. They had no impressive credentials to flash in front of these

people. They simply relied upon Jesus to guide them and help them through any obstacles, and that gave them all the confidence they needed. We should do no less.

If you want to see the power of Jesus Christ in action today, take a look at some of the lives he has turned around. Some of the greatest evidence for Jesus Christ today consists of the countless lives that have been dramatically changed by his touch.

CORNER STONES

---

evening, jailed them until morning. ⁴But many of the people who heard their message believed it, so that the number of believers totaled about five thousand men, not counting women and children.*

⁵The next day the council of all the rulers and elders and teachers of religious law met in Jerusalem. ⁶Annas the high priest was there, along with Caiaphas, John, Alexander, and other relatives of the high priest. ⁷They brought in the two disciples and demanded, "By what power, or in whose name, have you done this?"

⁸Then Peter, filled with the Holy Spirit, said to them, "Leaders and elders of our nation, ⁹are we being questioned because we've done a good

deed for a crippled man? Do you want to know how he was healed? ¹⁰Let me clearly state to you and to all the people of Israel that he was healed in the name and power of Jesus Christ from Nazareth, the man you crucified, but whom God raised from the dead. ¹¹For Jesus is the one referred to in the Scriptures, where it says,

'The stone that you builders rejected
has now become the cornerstone.'*

¹²There is salvation in no one else! There is no other name in all of heaven for people to call on to save them."

¹³The members of the council were amazed when they saw the boldness of Peter and John,

4:4 Greek 5,000 adult males.　4:11 Ps 118:22.

## Why Is Jesus Christ the Only Way to God? Read ACTS 4:12

One of the most common criticisms of Christianity is that it is too narrow. Many people just cannot believe that there is only one way to heaven.

Because Christians have championed this truth, they have been criticized for implying that they are better than those who do not believe in Jesus Christ. But it is important to note that the reason Christians believe Jesus Christ is the only way to heaven is because he himself said it. Jesus said, "I am the way, the truth, and the life. No one can come to the Father except through me" (John 14:6).

If humankind could have reached God any other way, Jesus would not have had to die. His voluntary death on the cross clearly illustrates the fact that there is no other way. Those who reject his loving offer of forgiveness—which is extended to all of humankind—do so at their own peril.

---

for they could see that they were ordinary men who had had no special training. They also recognized them as men who had been with Jesus. [14]But since the man who had been healed was standing right there among them, the council had nothing to say. [15]So they sent Peter and John out of the council chamber* and conferred among themselves.

[16]"What should we do with these men?" they asked each other. "We can't deny they have done a miraculous sign, and everybody in Jerusalem knows about it. [17]But perhaps we can stop them from spreading their propaganda. We'll warn them not to speak to anyone in Jesus' name again." [18]So they called the apostles back in and told them never again to speak or teach about Jesus.

[19]But Peter and John replied, "Do you think God wants us to obey you rather than him? [20]We cannot stop telling about the wonderful things we have seen and heard."

[21]The council then threatened them further, but they finally let them go because they didn't know how to punish them without starting a riot. For everyone was praising God [22]for this miraculous sign—the healing of a man who had been lame for more than forty years.

### The Believers Pray for Courage

[23]As soon as they were freed, Peter and John found the other believers and told them what

the leading priests and elders had said. [24]Then all the believers were united as they lifted their voices in prayer: "O Sovereign Lord, Creator of heaven and earth, the sea, and everything in them—[25]you spoke long ago by the Holy Spirit through our ancestor King David, your servant, saying,

'Why did the nations rage?
Why did the people waste their time with futile plans?
[26] The kings of the earth prepared for battle;
the rulers gathered together
against the Lord
and against his Messiah.'*

[27]"That is what has happened here in this city! For Herod Antipas, Pontius Pilate the governor, the Gentiles, and the people of Israel were all united against Jesus, your holy servant, whom you anointed. [28]In fact, everything they did occurred according to your eternal will and plan. [29]And now, O Lord, hear their threats, and give your servants great boldness in their preaching. [30]Send your healing power; may miraculous signs and wonders be done through the name of your holy servant Jesus."

[31]After this prayer, the building where they were meeting shook, and they were all filled with the Holy Spirit. And they preached God's message with boldness.

# When the Holy Spirit Can Be Sinned Against Read ACTS 5:1-10

One way Scripture supports the concept that the Holy Spirit is a person rather than a force is by showing how one can sin against him. It is important to understand that the Holy Spirit is indeed *God* at work and that to commit a sin against him is to commit a sin against God. In this passage we see one way in which we can sin against the Holy Spirit. But other passages inform us of at least five additional ways in which a person can sin against the Spirit.

**1. Lying to the Holy Spirit.** Ananias and Sapphira lied to the Holy Spirit by pretending to be thoroughly devoted to God when they really were not. One way people continue to do this today is by "going through the [spiritual] motions" without really meaning it in their hearts.

**2. Grieving the Holy Spirit.** Only believers can grieve the Holy Spirit (see Ephesians 4:30, p. 242). We grieve the Holy Spirit when we carry anger in our heart, slander others, or do things that we know go against the new nature that is inside of us.

**3. Quenching the Holy Spirit.** When the Holy Spirit convicts us of something we need to change in our life and we ignore his promptings, we are extinguishing his power in our life (1 Thessalonians 5:19). He is still in our life, but we are holding back from giving him complete control.

**4. Resisting the Holy Spirit.** When Stephen, the first recorded Christian martyr, spoke to his persecutors, he shared the message of Jesus Christ but closed with the words: "You stubborn people! . . . Must you forever resist the Holy Spirit?" (Acts 7:51). People who commit this sin may know that the Holy Spirit is trying to bring them to Jesus, but their pride keeps them from acknowledging Christ as Savior and Lord. The danger with this sin is that every time a person resists God's Spirit, he or she makes it more difficult for him or herself to come to Christ.

**5. Insulting the Holy Spirit.** To insult the Holy Spirit means to treat "the blood of the covenant as if it were common and unholy" (Hebrews 10:29). The person who commits this sin essentially dismisses the great price that Jesus paid for him or her at the cross of Calvary. This person has refused to accept the tremendous gift of salvation that God has offered to him or her.

**6. Blaspheming the Holy Spirit.** The two sins listed above, resisting and insulting the Holy Spirit, can lead to what is termed the "unforgivable sin": blasphemy against the Holy Spirit (see Matthew 12:31-32, p. 18). Since the Bible tells us that Christ is the only way of salvation, and the Holy Spirit's initial work in our life as a nonbeliever is to draw us to Christ, to blaspheme the Holy Spirit is to reject Jesus Christ as our Lord and Savior. That is the point of no return. Every time a person resists the Spirit and insults him, he or she gets a step closer to this ultimate sin.

CORNER STONES

*The Believers Share Their Possessions*
32All the believers were of one heart and mind, and they felt that what they owned was not their own; they shared everything they had. 33And the apostles gave powerful witness to the resurrection of the Lord Jesus, and God's great favor was upon them all. 34There was no poverty among them, because people who owned land or houses sold them 35and brought the money to the apostles to give to others in need.

36For instance, there was Joseph, the one the apostles nicknamed Barnabas (which means "Son of Encouragement"). He was from the tribe of Levi and came from the island of Cyprus. 37He sold a field he owned and brought the money to the apostles for those in need.

## CHAPTER 5
*Ananias and Sapphira*
There was also a man named Ananias who, with his wife, Sapphira, sold some property. 2He brought part of the money to the apostles, but he claimed it was the full amount. His wife had agreed to this deception.

3Then Peter said, "Ananias, why has Satan filled your heart? You lied to the Holy Spirit, and

## Aren't Other Religions Just As Good As Christianity? Read ACTS 4:12

Some people say that all religions basically say and teach the same thing, so they must all be "true." To quote another well-used phrase, "If a person is really sincere in what he or she believes, he or she will get to heaven."

In reality, all belief systems cannot be true, because they contradict one another. Many would like to think that all religions blend together beautifully, but they do not. Look at the differences between what the followers of three major world religions believe compared with what Christians believe.

### The Existence of a Personal God.
- Buddhists deny the existence of a personal God.
- Hindus believe in two major gods, Vishnu and Siva, as well as in millions of lesser gods.
- Muslims believe in one God named Allah.
- Christians believe that God is a being who created humans in his own image and who loves them and wants to have a personal relationship with them.

### The Subject of Salvation.
- Buddhists believe salvation is by self-effort only.
- Hindus believe you achieve salvation by devotion, works, and self-control.
- Muslims believe that people earn their own salvation and pay for their own sins.
- Christians believe that Jesus Christ died for their sins. If people turn from their sins and follow Jesus, they can be forgiven and have the hope of being with Jesus in heaven.

### The Person of Jesus Christ.
- Buddhists believe that Jesus Christ was a good teacher, though less important then Buddha.
- Hindus believe that Jesus was just one of many incarnations—or sons —of God. Yet they also assert that Christ was not the unique Son of God. He was no more divine then any other man, and he did not die for people's sins.
- Muslims believe that Jesus Christ was the greatest of the prophets below Muhammad. In addition, they do not believe that Christ died for people's sin.
- Christians believe that Jesus is God as well as man, that he was sinless, and that he died to redeem humankind.

As you can see, you cannot believe in all of the major religious beliefs. That is because each religion eventually contradicts the claims of Christianity [Fritz Ridenour, *So What's the Difference?* (Glendale: Gospel Light Publications, 1967)].

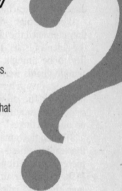

BIG QUESTIONS

you kept some of the money for yourself. ⁴The property was yours to sell or not sell, as you wished. And after selling it, the money was yours to give away. How could you do a thing like this? You weren't lying to us but to God."

⁵As soon as Ananias heard these words, he fell to the floor and died. Everyone who heard about it was terrified. ⁶Then some young men wrapped him in a sheet and took him out and buried him.

⁷About three hours later his wife came in, not knowing what had happened. ⁸Peter asked her, "Was this the price you and your husband received for your land?"

"Yes," she replied, "that was the price."

⁹And Peter said, "How could the two of you even think of doing a thing like this—conspiring together to test the Spirit of the Lord? Just outside that door are the young men who buried your husband, and they will carry you out, too."

¹⁰Instantly, she fell to the floor and died. When the young men came in and saw that she was dead, they carried her out and buried her beside her husband. ¹¹Great fear gripped the entire church and all others who heard what had happened.

### The Apostles Heal Many

¹²Meanwhile, the apostles were performing many miraculous signs and wonders among the

people. And the believers were meeting regularly at the Temple in the area known as Solomon's Colonnade. 13No one else dared to join them, though everyone had high regard for them. 14And more and more people believed and were brought to the Lord—crowds of both men and women. 15As a result of the apostles' work, sick people were brought out into the streets on beds and mats so that Peter's shadow might fall across some of them as he went by. 16Crowds came in from the villages around Jerusalem, bringing their sick and those possessed by evil spirits, and they were all healed.

## The Apostles Meet Opposition

17The high priest and his friends, who were Sadducees, reacted with violent jealousy. 18They arrested the apostles and put them in the jail. 19But an angel of the Lord came at night, opened the gates of the jail, and brought them out. Then he told them, 20"Go to the Temple and give the people this message of life!" 21So the apostles entered the Temple about daybreak and immediately began teaching.

When the high priest and his officials arrived, they convened the high council,* along with all the elders of Israel. Then they sent for the apostles to be brought for trial. 22But when the Temple guards went to the jail, the men were gone. So they returned to the council and reported, 23"The jail was locked, with the guards standing outside, but when we opened the gates, no one was there!"

24When the captain of the Temple guard and the leading priests heard this, they were perplexed, wondering where it would all end. 25Then someone arrived with the news that the men they had jailed were out in the Temple, teaching the people.

26The captain went with his Temple guards and arrested them, but without violence, for they were afraid the people would kill them if they treated the apostles roughly. 27Then they brought the apostles in before the council. 28"Didn't we tell you never again to teach in this man's name?" the high priest demanded. "Instead, you have filled all Jerusalem with your teaching about Jesus, and you intend to blame us for his death!"

29But Peter and the apostles replied, "We must obey God rather than human authority. 30The God of our ancestors raised Jesus from the dead after you killed him by crucifying him.

31Then God put him in the place of honor at his right hand as Prince and Savior. He did this to give the people of Israel an opportunity to turn from their sins and turn to God so their sins would be forgiven. 32We are witnesses of these things and so is the Holy Spirit, who is given by God to those who obey him."

33At this, the high council was furious and decided to kill them. 34But one member had a different perspective. He was a Pharisee named Gamaliel, who was an expert on religious law and was very popular with the people. He stood up and ordered that the apostles be sent outside the council chamber for a while. 35Then he addressed his colleagues as follows: "Men of Israel, take care what you are planning to do to these men! 36Some time ago there was that fellow Theudas, who pretended to be someone great. About four hundred others joined him, but he was killed, and his followers went their various ways. The whole movement came to nothing. 37After him, at the time of the census, there was Judas of Galilee. He got some people to follow him, but he was killed, too, and all his followers were scattered.

38"So my advice is, leave these men alone. If they are teaching and doing these things merely on their own, it will soon be overthrown. 39But if it is of God, you will not be able to stop them. You may even find yourselves fighting against God."

40The council accepted his advice. They called in the apostles and had them flogged. Then they ordered them never again to speak in the name of Jesus, and they let them go. 41The apostles left the high council rejoicing that God had counted them worthy to suffer dishonor for the name of Jesus. 42And every day, in the Temple and in their homes,* they continued to teach and preach this message: "The Messiah you are looking for is Jesus."

CHAPTER **6**
## Seven Men Chosen to Serve

But as the believers* rapidly multiplied, there were rumblings of discontent. Those who spoke Greek complained against those who spoke Hebrew, saying that their widows were being discriminated against in the daily distribution of food. 2So the Twelve called a meeting of all the believers.

"We apostles should spend our time preaching and teaching the word of God, not adminis-

5:21 Greek *Sanhedrin;* also in 5:27, 41.   5:42 Greek *from house to house.*   6:1 Greek *disciples;* also in 6:2, 7.

tering a food program," they said. ³"Now look around among yourselves, brothers, and select seven men who are well respected and are full of the Holy Spirit and wisdom. We will put them in charge of this business. ⁴Then we can spend our time in prayer and preaching and teaching the word."

⁵This idea pleased the whole group, and they chose the following: Stephen (a man full of faith and the Holy Spirit), Philip, Procorus, Nicanor, Timon, Parmenas, and Nicolas of Antioch (a Gentile convert to the Jewish faith, who had now become a Christian). ⁶These seven were presented to the apostles, who prayed for them as they laid their hands on them.

⁷God's message was preached in ever-widening circles. The number of believers greatly increased in Jerusalem, and many of the Jewish priests were converted, too.

### Stephen Is Arrested

⁸Stephen, a man full of God's grace and power, performed amazing miracles and signs among the people. ⁹But one day some men from the Synagogue of Freed Slaves, as it was called, started to debate with him. They were Jews from Cyrene, Alexandria, Cilicia, and the province of Asia. ¹⁰None of them was able to stand against the wisdom and Spirit by which Stephen spoke.

¹¹So they persuaded some men to lie about Stephen, saying, "We heard him blaspheme Moses, and even God." ¹²Naturally, this roused the crowds, the elders, and the teachers of religious law. So they arrested Stephen and brought him before the high council.* ¹³The lying witnesses said, "This man is always speaking against the Temple and against the law of Moses. ¹⁴We have heard him say that this Jesus of Nazareth will destroy the Temple and change the customs Moses handed down to us." ¹⁵At this point everyone in the council stared at Stephen because his face became as bright as an angel's.

## CHAPTER 7
### Stephen Addresses the Council

Then the high priest asked Stephen, "Are these accusations true?"

²This was Stephen's reply: "Brothers and honorable fathers, listen to me. Our glorious God appeared to our ancestor Abraham in Mesopotamia before he moved to Haran.* ³God told him, 'Leave your native land and your rela-

tives, and come to the land that I will show you.'* ⁴So Abraham left the land of the Chaldeans and lived in Haran until his father died. Then God brought him here to the land where you now live. ⁵But God gave him no inheritance here, not even one square foot of land. God did promise, however, that eventually the whole country would belong to Abraham and his descendants—though he had no children yet. ⁶But God also told him that his descendants would live in a foreign country where they would be mistreated as slaves for four hundred years. ⁷'But I will punish the nation that enslaves them,' God told him, 'and in the end they will come out and worship me in this place.'* ⁸God also gave Abraham the covenant of circumcision at that time. And so Isaac, Abraham's son, was circumcised when he was eight days old. Isaac became the father of Jacob, and Jacob was the father of the twelve patriarchs of the Jewish nation.

⁹"These sons of Jacob were very jealous of their brother Joseph, and they sold him to be a slave in Egypt. But God was with him ¹⁰and delivered him from his anguish. And God gave him favor before Pharaoh, king of Egypt. God also gave Joseph unusual wisdom, so that Pharaoh appointed him governor over all of Egypt and put him in charge of all the affairs of the palace.

¹¹"But a famine came upon Egypt and Canaan. There was great misery for our ancestors, as they ran out of food. ¹²Jacob heard that there was still grain in Egypt, so he sent his sons* to buy some. ¹³The second time they went, Joseph revealed his identity to his brothers, and they were introduced to Pharaoh. ¹⁴Then Joseph sent for his father, Jacob, and all his relatives to come to Egypt, seventy-five persons in all. ¹⁵So Jacob went to Egypt. He died there, as did all his sons. ¹⁶All of them were taken to Shechem and buried in the tomb Abraham had bought from the sons of Hamor in Shechem.

¹⁷"As the time drew near when God would fulfill his promise to Abraham, the number of our people in Egypt greatly increased. ¹⁸But then a new king came to the throne of Egypt who knew nothing about Joseph. ¹⁹This king plotted against our people and forced parents to abandon their newborn babies so they would die.

²⁰"At that time Moses was born—a beautiful child in God's eyes. His parents cared for him at home for three months. ²¹When at last they had to abandon him, Pharaoh's daughter found him

6:12 Greek *Sanhedrin;* also in 6:15.   7:2 *Mesopotamia* was the region now called Iraq. *Haran* was a city in what is now called Syria.   7:3 Gen 12:1.   7:5-7 Gen 12:7; 15:13-14; Exod 3:12.   7:12 Greek *our fathers;* also in 7:15.

and raised him as her own son. 22Moses was taught all the wisdom of the Egyptians, and he became mighty in both speech and action.

23"One day when he was forty years old, he decided to visit his relatives, the people of Israel. 24During this visit, he saw an Egyptian mistreating a man of Israel. So Moses came to his defense and avenged him, killing the Egyptian. 25Moses assumed his brothers would realize that God had sent him to rescue them, but they didn't.

26"The next day he visited them again and saw two men of Israel fighting. He tried to be a peacemaker. 'Men,' he said, 'you are brothers. Why are you hurting each other?'

27"But the man in the wrong pushed Moses aside and told him to mind his own business. 'Who made you a ruler and judge over us?' he asked. 28'Are you going to kill me as you killed that Egyptian yesterday?' 29When Moses heard that, he fled the country and lived as a foreigner in the land of Midian, where his two sons were born.

30"Forty years later, in the desert near Mount Sinai, an angel appeared to Moses in the flame of a burning bush. 31Moses saw it and wondered what it was. As he went to see, the voice of the Lord called out to him, 32'I am the God of your ancestors—the God of Abraham, Isaac, and Jacob.' Moses shook with terror and dared not look.

33"And the Lord said to him, 'Take off your sandals, for you are standing on holy ground. 34You can be sure that I have seen the misery of my people in Egypt. I have heard their cries. So I have come to rescue them. Now go, for I will send you to Egypt.'* 35And so God sent back the same man his people had previously rejected by demanding, 'Who made you a ruler and judge over us?' Through the angel who appeared to him in the burning bush, Moses was sent to be their ruler and savior. 36And by means of many miraculous signs and wonders, he led them out of Egypt, through the Red Sea, and back and forth through the wilderness for forty years.

37"Moses himself told the people of Israel, 'God will raise up a Prophet like me from among your own people.'* 38Moses was with the assembly of God's people in the wilderness. He was the mediator between the people of Israel and the angel who gave him life-giving words on Mount Sinai to pass on to us.

39"But our ancestors rejected Moses and

wanted to return to Egypt. 40They told Aaron, 'Make us some gods who can lead us, for we don't know what has become of this Moses, who brought us out of Egypt.' 41So they made an idol shaped like a calf, and they sacrificed to it and rejoiced in this thing they had made. 42Then God turned away from them and gave them up to serve the sun, moon, and stars as their gods! In the book of the prophets it is written,

'Was it to me you were bringing sacrifices
      during those forty years in the
           wilderness, Israel?
43 No, your real interest was in your pagan
           gods—
      the shrine of Molech,
      the star god Rephan,
      and the images you made to worship
           them.
So I will send you into captivity
      far away in Babylon.'*

44"Our ancestors carried the Tabernacle* with them through the wilderness. It was constructed in exact accordance with the plan shown to Moses by God. 45Years later, when Joshua led the battles against the Gentile nations that God drove out of this land, the Tabernacle was taken with them into their new territory. And it was used there until the time of King David.

46"David found favor with God and asked for the privilege of building a permanent Temple for the God of Jacob.* 47But it was Solomon who actually built it. 48However, the Most High doesn't live in temples made by human hands. As the prophet says,

49 'Heaven is my throne,
      and the earth is my footstool.
Could you ever build me a temple as good
      as that?'
      asks the Lord.
'Could you build a dwelling place for me?
50      Didn't I make everything in heaven and
           earth?'*

51"You stubborn people! You are heathen at heart and deaf to the truth. Must you forever resist the Holy Spirit? But your ancestors did, and so do you! 52Name one prophet your ancestors didn't persecute! They even killed the ones who predicted the coming of the Righteous One—the Messiah whom you betrayed and

7:31-34 Exod 3:5-10.   7:37 Deut 18:15.   7:42-43 Amos 5:25-27.   7:44 Greek *the tent of witness.*   7:46 Some manuscripts read *the house of Jacob.*   7:49-50 Isa 66:1-2.

murdered. 53You deliberately disobeyed God's law, though you received it from the hands of angels.*"

54The Jewish leaders were infuriated by Stephen's accusation, and they shook their fists in rage.* 55But Stephen, full of the Holy Spirit, gazed steadily upward into heaven and saw the glory of God, and he saw Jesus standing in the place of honor at God's right hand. 56And he told them, "Look, I see the heavens opened and the Son of Man standing in the place of honor at God's right hand!"

57Then they put their hands over their ears, and drowning out his voice with their shouts, they rushed at him. 58They dragged him out of the city and began to stone him. The official witnesses took off their coats and laid them at the feet of a young man named Saul.*

59And as they stoned him, Stephen prayed, "Lord Jesus, receive my spirit." 60And he fell to his knees, shouting, "Lord, don't charge them with this sin!" And with that, he died.

## CHAPTER 8

Saul was one of the official witnesses at the killing of Stephen.

### Persecution Scatters the Believers

A great wave of persecution began that day, sweeping over the church in Jerusalem, and all the believers except the apostles fled into Judea and Samaria. 2(Some godly men came and buried Stephen with loud weeping.) 3Saul was going everywhere to devastate the church. He went from house to house, dragging out both men and women to throw them into jail.

### Philip Preaches in Samaria

4But the believers who had fled Jerusalem went everywhere preaching the Good News about Jesus. 5Philip, for example, went to the city of Samaria and told the people there about the Messiah. 6Crowds listened intently to what he had to say because of the miracles he did. 7Many evil spirits were cast out, screaming as they left their victims. And many who had been paralyzed or lame were healed. 8So there was great joy in that city.

9A man named Simon had been a sorcerer there for many years, claiming to be someone great. 10The Samaritan people, from the least to

7:53 Greek *received the Law as it was ordained by angels.* 7:54 Greek *they were grinding their teeth against him.* 7:58 Saul *is later called Paul; see 13:9.*

## Be Open to God's Leading
Read ACTS 8:4-8, 26-38

This text shows two forms of evangelism. In the beginning of this passage, we see Philip engaged in "mass evangelism" (verses 4-8). Toward the end of the chapter, we see Philip taking part in personal, "one-on-one evangelism" with the Ethiopian (verses 26-38). The text also gives us three principles to follow for effective evangelism:

**1. Philip Was Led by God's Spirit.** This principle (verse 29) can make all the difference in sharing one's faith. This leading will often come in the form of an "impression" or a burden—such as a compelling desire to talk to someone about your faith (see Acts 17:16-31, pp. 159–160). Like Philip, we should simply be open and available to what God would have us to do.

**2. Philip Obeyed God's Leading.** Philip did exactly what the Lord told him to do without delay (verse 27). Jesus said, "My sheep recognize my voice; I know them, and they follow me" (John 10:27). So when God said, "Go," Philip went! Likewise, we need to be on duty at all times, ready to "preach the word of God" (2 Timothy 4:2).

**3. Philip Knew Scripture.** Philip used the Scripture this man was reading as a starting point. Then he used a number of other passages to tell the Ethiopian about Jesus (verse 35). Knowing God's Word is essential for any person who wants to lead others to Jesus Christ. Arguments will not have nearly the impact that God's Word will when we share our faith with others.

The same God who led Philip in his evangelistic work also wants to direct your steps. You might start each day with a prayer like the prophet Isaiah: "Lord, I'll go! Send me" (Isaiah 6:8). Remember, God is not looking so much for a person's ability as his or her availability. God is not looking for "strong" people to be his witnesses so much as he is looking for people through whom he can show his strength.

FIRST STEPS

the greatest, often spoke of him as "the Great One—the Power of God." [11]He was very influential because of the magic he performed. [12]But now the people believed Philip's message of Good News concerning the Kingdom of God and the name of Jesus Christ. As a result, many men and women were baptized. [13]Then Simon himself believed and was baptized. He began following Philip wherever he went, and he was amazed by the great miracles and signs Philip performed.

[14]When the apostles back in Jerusalem heard that the people of Samaria had accepted God's message, they sent Peter and John there. [15]As soon as they arrived, they prayed for these new Christians to receive the Holy Spirit. [16]The Holy Spirit had not yet come upon any of them, for they had only been baptized in the name of the Lord Jesus. [17]Then Peter and John laid their hands upon these believers, and they received the Holy Spirit.

[18]When Simon saw that the Holy Spirit was given when the apostles placed their hands upon people's heads, he offered money to buy this power. [19]"Let me have this power, too," he exclaimed, "so that when I lay my hands on people, they will receive the Holy Spirit!"

[20]But Peter replied, "May your money perish with you for thinking God's gift can be bought! [21]You can have no part in this, for your heart is not right before God. [22]Turn from your wickedness and pray to the Lord. Perhaps he will forgive your evil thoughts, [23]for I can see that you are full of bitterness and held captive by sin."

[24]"Pray to the Lord for me," Simon exclaimed, "that these terrible things won't happen to me!"

[25]After testifying and preaching the word of the Lord in Samaria, Peter and John returned to Jerusalem. And they stopped in many Samaritan villages along the way to preach the Good News to them, too.

### Philip and the Ethiopian Eunuch

[26]As for Philip, an angel of the Lord said to him, "Go south* down the desert road that runs from Jerusalem to Gaza." [27]So he did, and he met the treasurer of Ethiopia, a eunuch of great authority under the queen of Ethiopia.* The eunuch had gone to Jerusalem to worship, [28]and he was now returning. Seated in his carriage, he was reading aloud from the book of the prophet Isaiah.

[29]The Holy Spirit said to Philip, "Go over and walk along beside the carriage."

[30]Philip ran over and heard the man reading from the prophet Isaiah; so he asked, "Do you understand what you are reading?"

[31]The man replied, "How can I, when there is no one to instruct me?" And he begged Philip to come up into the carriage and sit with him. [32]The passage of Scripture he had been reading was this:

"He was led as a sheep to the slaughter.
And as a lamb is silent before the shearers,
    he did not open his mouth.
[33] He was humiliated and received no justice.
    Who can speak of his descendants?
    For his life was taken from the earth."*

[34]The eunuch asked Philip, "Was Isaiah talking about himself or someone else?" [35]So Philip began with this same Scripture and then used many others to tell him the Good News about Jesus.

[36]As they rode along, they came to some water, and the eunuch said, "Look! There's some water! Why can't I be baptized?"* [38]He ordered the carriage to stop, and they went down into the water, and Philip baptized him.

[39]When they came up out of the water, the Spirit of the Lord caught Philip away. The eunuch never saw him again but went on his way rejoicing. [40]Meanwhile, Philip found himself farther north at the city of Azotus! He preached the Good News there and in every city along the way until he came to Caesarea.

## CHAPTER 9
### Saul's Conversion

Meanwhile, Saul was uttering threats with every breath. He was eager to destroy the Lord's followers,* so he went to the high priest. [2]He requested letters addressed to the synagogues in Damascus, asking their cooperation in the arrest of any followers of the Way he found there. He wanted to bring them—both men and women—back to Jerusalem in chains.

[3]As he was nearing Damascus on this mission, a brilliant light from heaven suddenly beamed down upon him! [4]He fell to the ground and heard a voice saying to him, "Saul! Saul! Why are you persecuting me?"

8:26 Or *Go at noon.*   8:27 Greek *under the Candace, the queen of Ethiopia.*   8:32-33 Isa 53:7-8.   8:36 Some manuscripts add verse 37, *"You can," Philip answered, "if you believe with all your heart." And the eunuch replied, "I believe that Jesus Christ is the Son of God."*   9:1 Greek *disciples.*

5"Who are you, sir?" Saul asked.

And the voice replied, "I am Jesus, the one you are persecuting! 6Now get up and go into the city, and you will be told what you are to do."

7The men with Saul stood speechless with surprise, for they heard the sound of someone's voice, but they saw no one! 8As Saul picked himself up off the ground, he found that he was blind. 9So his companions led him by the hand to Damascus. He remained there blind for three days. And all that time he went without food and water.

10Now there was a believer* in Damascus named Ananias. The Lord spoke to him in a vision, calling, "Ananias!"

"Yes, Lord!" he replied.

11The Lord said, "Go over to Straight Street, to the house of Judas. When you arrive, ask for Saul of Tarsus. He is praying to me right now. 12I have shown him a vision of a man named Ananias coming in and laying his hands on him so that he can see again."

13"But Lord," exclaimed Ananias, "I've heard about the terrible things this man has done to the believers in Jerusalem! 14And we hear that he is authorized by the leading priests to arrest every believer in Damascus."

15But the Lord said, "Go and do what I say. For Saul is my chosen instrument to take my message to the Gentiles and to kings, as well as to the people of Israel. 16And I will show him how much he must suffer for me."

17So Ananias went and found Saul. He laid his hands on him and said, "Brother Saul, the Lord Jesus, who appeared to you on the road, has sent me so that you may get your sight back and be filled with the Holy Spirit." 18Instantly something like scales fell from Saul's eyes, and he regained his sight. Then he got up and was baptized. 19Afterward he ate some food and was strengthened.

## Saul in Damascus and Jerusalem

Saul stayed with the believers* in Damascus for a few days. 20And immediately he began preaching about Jesus in the synagogues, saying, "He is indeed the Son of God!"

21All who heard him were amazed. "Isn't this the same man who persecuted Jesus' followers with such devastation in Jerusalem?" they asked. "And we understand that he came here to arrest them and take them in chains to the leading priests."

22Saul's preaching became more and more powerful, and the Jews in Damascus couldn't refute his proofs that Jesus was indeed the Messiah. 23After a while the Jewish leaders decided to kill him. 24But Saul was told about their plot, and that they were watching for him day and night at the city gate so they could murder him. 25So during the night, some of the other believers* let him down in a large basket through an opening in the city wall.

26When Saul arrived in Jerusalem, he tried to meet with the believers, but they were all afraid of him. They thought he was only pretending to be a believer! 27Then Barnabas brought him to the apostles and told them how Saul had seen the Lord on the way to Damascus. Barnabas also told them what the Lord had said to Saul and how he boldly preached in the name of Jesus in Damascus. 28Then the apostles accepted Saul, and after that he was constantly with them in Jerusalem, preaching boldly in the name of the Lord. 29He debated with some Greek-speaking Jews, but they plotted to murder him. 30When the believers* heard about it, however, they took him to Caesarea and sent him on to his hometown of Tarsus.

31The church then had peace throughout Judea, Galilee, and Samaria, and it grew in strength and numbers. The believers were walking in the fear of the Lord and in the comfort of the Holy Spirit.

## Peter Heals Aeneas and Raises Dorcas

32Peter traveled from place to place to visit the believers, and in his travels he came to the Lord's people in the town of Lydda. 33There he met a man named Aeneas, who had been paralyzed and bedridden for eight years. 34Peter said to him, "Aeneas, Jesus Christ heals you! Get up and make your bed!" And he was healed instantly. 35Then the whole population of Lydda and Sharon turned to the Lord when they saw Aeneas walking around.

36There was a believer in Joppa named Tabitha (which in Greek is Dorcas*). She was always doing kind things for others and helping the poor. 37About this time she became ill and died. Her friends prepared her for burial and laid her in an upstairs room. 38But they had heard that Peter was nearby at Lydda, so they sent two men to beg him, "Please come as soon as possible!"

9:10 Greek disciple; also in 9:36.   9:19 Greek disciples; also in 9:26.   9:25 Greek his disciples.   9:30 Greek brothers.   9:36 The names Tabitha in Aramaic and Dorcas in Greek both mean "gazelle."

39So Peter returned with them; and as soon as he arrived, they took him to the upstairs room. The room was filled with widows who were weeping and showing him the coats and other garments Dorcas had made for them. 40But Peter asked them all to leave the room; then he knelt and prayed. Turning to the body he said, "Get up, Tabitha." And she opened her eyes! When she saw Peter, she sat up! 41He gave her his hand and helped her up. Then he called in the widows and all the believers, and he showed them that she was alive.

42The news raced through the whole town, and many believed in the Lord. 43And Peter stayed a long time in Joppa, living with Simon, a leatherworker.

## CHAPTER 10
### Cornelius Calls for Peter

In Caesarea there lived a Roman army officer named Cornelius, who was a captain of the Italian Regiment. 2He was a devout man who feared the God of Israel, as did his entire household. He gave generously to charity and was a man who regularly prayed to God. 3One afternoon about three o'clock, he had a vision in which he saw an angel of God coming toward him. "Cornelius!" the angel said.

4Cornelius stared at him in terror. "What is it, sir?" he asked the angel.

And the angel replied, "Your prayers and gifts to the poor have not gone unnoticed by God! 5Now send some men down to Joppa to find a man named Simon Peter. 6He is staying with Simon, a leatherworker who lives near the shore. Ask him to come and visit you."

7As soon as the angel was gone, Cornelius called two of his household servants and a devout soldier, one of his personal attendants. 8He told them what had happened and sent them off to Joppa.

### Peter Visits Cornelius

9The next day as Cornelius's messengers were nearing the city, Peter went up to the flat roof to pray. It was about noon, 10and he was hungry. But while lunch was being prepared, he fell into a trance. 11He saw the sky open, and something like a large sheet was let down by its four corners. 12In the sheet were all sorts of animals, reptiles, and birds. 13Then a voice said to him, "Get up, Peter; kill and eat them."

14"Never, Lord," Peter declared. "I have never in all my life eaten anything forbidden by our Jewish laws.*"

15The voice spoke again, "If God says something is acceptable, don't say it isn't."* 16The same vision was repeated three times. Then the sheet was pulled up again to heaven.

17Peter was very perplexed. What could the vision mean? Just then the men sent by Cornelius found the house and stood outside at the gate. 18They asked if this was the place where Simon Peter was staying. 19Meanwhile, as Peter was puzzling over the vision, the Holy Spirit said to him, "Three men have come looking for you. 20Go down and go with them without hesitation. All is well, for I have sent them."

21So Peter went down and said, "I'm the man you are looking for. Why have you come?"

22They said, "We were sent by Cornelius, a Roman officer. He is a devout man who fears the God of Israel and is well respected by all the Jews. A holy angel instructed him to send for you so you can go to his house and give him a message." 23So Peter invited the men to be his guests for the night. The next day he went with them, accompanied by some other believers* from Joppa.

24They arrived in Caesarea the following day. Cornelius was waiting for him and had called together his relatives and close friends to meet Peter. 25As Peter entered his home, Cornelius fell to the floor before him in worship. 26But Peter pulled him up and said, "Stand up! I'm a human being like you!" 27So Cornelius got up, and they talked together and went inside where the others were assembled.

28Peter told them, "You know it is against the Jewish laws for me to come into a Gentile home like this. But God has shown me that I should never think of anyone as impure. 29So I came as soon as I was sent for. Now tell me why you sent for me."

30Cornelius replied, "Four days ago I was praying in my house at three o'clock in the afternoon. Suddenly, a man in dazzling clothes was standing in front of me. 31He told me, 'Cornelius, your prayers have been heard, and your gifts to the poor have been noticed by God! 32Now send some men to Joppa and summon Simon Peter. He is staying in the home of Simon, a leatherworker who lives near the shore.' 33So I sent for you at once, and it was good of you to come. Now here we are, waiting before God to hear the message the Lord has given you."

10:14 Greek *anything common and unclean.*    10:15 Greek *"What God calls clean you must not call unclean."*    10:23 Greek *brothers.*

## The Gentiles Hear the Good News

34Then Peter replied, "I see very clearly that God doesn't show partiality. 35In every nation he accepts those who fear him and do what is right. 36I'm sure you have heard about the Good News for the people of Israel—that there is peace with God through Jesus Christ, who is Lord of all. 37You know what happened all through Judea, beginning in Galilee after John the Baptist began preaching. 38And no doubt you know that God anointed Jesus of Nazareth with the Holy Spirit and with power. Then Jesus went around doing good and healing all who were oppressed by the Devil, for God was with him.

39"And we apostles are witnesses of all he did throughout Israel and in Jerusalem. They put him to death by crucifying him, 40but God raised him to life three days later. Then God allowed him to appear, 41not to the general public,* but to us whom God had chosen beforehand to be his witnesses. We were those who ate and drank with him after he rose from the dead. 42And he ordered us to preach everywhere and to testify that Jesus is ordained of God to be the judge of all—the living and the dead. 43He is the one all the prophets testified about, saying that everyone who believes in him will have their sins forgiven through his name."

## The Gentiles Receive the Holy Spirit

44Even as Peter was saying these things, the Holy Spirit fell upon all who had heard the message. 45The Jewish believers who came with Peter were amazed that the gift of the Holy Spirit had been poured out upon the Gentiles, too. 46And there could be no doubt about it, for they heard them speaking in tongues and praising God.

Then Peter asked, 47"Can anyone object to their being baptized, now that they have received the Holy Spirit just as we did?" 48So he gave orders for them to be baptized in the name of Jesus Christ. Afterward Cornelius asked him to stay with them for several days.

## CHAPTER 11

### Peter Explains His Actions

Soon the news reached the apostles and other believers* in Judea that the Gentiles had received the word of God. 2But when Peter arrived back in Jerusalem, some of the Jewish believers*

criticized him. 3"You entered the home of Gentiles* and even ate with them!" they said.

4Then Peter told them exactly what had happened. 5"One day in Joppa," he said, "while I was praying, I went into a trance and saw a vision. Something like a large sheet was let down by its four corners from the sky. And it came right down to me. 6When I looked inside the sheet, I saw all sorts of small animals, wild animals, reptiles, and birds that we are not allowed to eat. 7And I heard a voice say, 'Get up, Peter; kill and eat them.'

8" 'Never, Lord,' I replied. 'I have never eaten anything forbidden by our Jewish laws.*'

9"But the voice from heaven came again, 'If God says something is acceptable, don't say it isn't.'*

10"This happened three times before the sheet and all it contained was pulled back up to heaven. 11Just then three men who had been sent from Caesarea arrived at the house where I was staying. 12The Holy Spirit told me to go with them and not to worry about their being Gentiles. These six brothers here accompanied me, and we soon arrived at the home of the man who had sent for us. 13He told us how an angel had appeared to him in his home and had told him, 'Send messengers to Joppa to find Simon Peter. 14He will tell you how you and all your household will be saved!'

15"Well, I began telling them the Good News, but just as I was getting started, the Holy Spirit fell on them, just as he fell on us at the beginning. 16Then I thought of the Lord's words when he said, 'John baptized with* water, but you will be baptized with the Holy Spirit.' 17And since God gave these Gentiles the same gift he gave us when we believed in the Lord Jesus Christ, who was I to argue?"

18When the others heard this, all their objections were answered and they began praising God. They said, "God has also given the Gentiles the privilege of turning from sin and receiving eternal life."

## The Church in Antioch of Syria

19Meanwhile, the believers who had fled from Jerusalem during the persecution after Stephen's death traveled as far as Phoenicia, Cyprus, and Antioch of Syria. They preached the Good News, but only to Jews. 20However, some of the believers who went to Antioch from Cyprus and Cyrene began preaching to Gentiles* about the

10:41 Greek *the people.*   11:1 Greek *brothers.*   11:2 Greek *those of the circumcision.*   11:3 Greek *of uncircumcised men.*   11:8 Greek *anything common or unclean.*   11:9 Greek *'What God calls clean you must not call unclean.'*   11:16 Or *in;* also in 11:16b.   11:20 Greek *the Greeks;* other manuscripts read *the Hellenists.*

Lord Jesus. 21The power of the Lord was upon them, and large numbers of these Gentiles believed and turned to the Lord.

22When the church at Jerusalem heard what had happened, they sent Barnabas to Antioch. 23When he arrived and saw this proof of God's favor, he was filled with joy, and he encouraged the believers to stay true to the Lord. 24Barnabas was a good man, full of the Holy Spirit and strong in faith. And large numbers of people were brought to the Lord.

25Then Barnabas went on to Tarsus to find Saul. 26When he found him, he brought him back to Antioch. Both of them stayed there with the church for a full year, teaching great numbers of people. (It was there at Antioch that the believers* were first called Christians.)

27During this time, some prophets traveled from Jerusalem to Antioch. 28One of them named Agabus stood up in one of the meetings to predict by the Spirit that a great famine was coming upon the entire Roman world. (This was fulfilled during the reign of Claudius.) 29So the believers in Antioch decided to send relief to the brothers and sisters* in Judea, everyone giving as much as they could. 30This they did, entrusting their gifts to Barnabas and Saul to take to the elders of the church in Jerusalem.

## CHAPTER 12
*James Is Killed and Peter Is Imprisoned*
About that time King Herod Agrippa* began to persecute some believers in the church. 2He had the apostle James (John's brother) killed with a sword. 3When Herod saw how much this pleased the Jewish leaders, he arrested Peter during the Passover celebration* 4and imprisoned him, placing him under the guard of four squads of four soldiers each. Herod's intention was to bring Peter out for public trial after the Passover. 5But while Peter was in prison, the church prayed very earnestly for him.

*Peter's Miraculous Escape from Prison*
6The night before Peter was to be placed on trial, he was asleep, chained between two soldiers, with others standing guard at the prison gate. 7Suddenly, there was a bright light in the cell, and an angel of the Lord stood before Peter. The angel tapped him on the side to awaken him and said, "Quick! Get up!" And the chains fell off his wrists. 8Then the angel told him, "Get dressed and put on your sandals." And he did. "Now put on your coat and follow me," the angel ordered.

9So Peter left the cell, following the angel. But all the time he thought it was a vision. He didn't realize it was really happening. 10They passed the first and second guard posts and came to the iron gate to the street, and this opened to them all by itself. So they passed through and started walking down the street, and then the angel suddenly left him.

11Peter finally realized what had happened. "It's really true!" he said to himself. "The Lord has sent his angel and saved me from Herod and from what the Jews were hoping to do to me!"

12After a little thought, he went to the home of Mary, the mother of John Mark, where many were gathered for prayer. 13He knocked at the door in the gate, and a servant girl named Rhoda

11:26 Greek *disciples;* also in 11:29.  11:29 Greek *the brothers.*  12:1 Greek *Herod the king.* He was the nephew of Herod Antipas and a grandson of Herod the Great.  12:3 Greek *the days of unleavened bread.*

# OFF AND RUNNING
## Pray Effectively Read ACTS 12:1-17

This Bible story vividly illustrates how God works in response to the prayers of his people. Though all appeared hopeless for Peter, the body of believers did all that they could for him—they called on God. What made the prayers of these believers so effective? Their secret is found in verse 5. There we see the three basic steps these Christians took in response to what appeared to be a hopeless situation:

**1. They Directed Their Prayer to God.** Ironically, many times our prayers often contain little thought of God himself. We fill our mind with thoughts about our own needs instead of our heavenly Father. But Jesus himself encouraged us to respectfully consider whom we are praying to when he gave us the Lord's Prayer (see Matthew 6:9-13, p. 9). This will allow you to take your eyes off of your dilemma and to place them on Jesus, and it will also help to align your will or desire with his.

**2. They Prayed Earnestly.** These believers offered constant, fervent prayer on Peter's behalf. Another way came to open it. 14When she recognized Peter's voice, she was so overjoyed that, instead of opening the door, she ran back inside and told everyone, "Peter is standing at the door!"

15"You're out of your mind," they said. When she insisted, they decided, "It must be his angel."

16Meanwhile, Peter continued knocking. When they finally went out and opened the door, they were amazed. 17He motioned for them to quiet down and told them what had happened and how the Lord had led him out of jail. "Tell James and the other brothers what happened," he said. And then he went to another place.

18At dawn, there was a great commotion among the soldiers about what had happened to Peter. 19Herod Agrippa ordered a thorough search for him. When he couldn't be found, Herod interrogated the guards and sentenced them to death. Afterward Herod left Judea to stay in Caesarea for a while.

### The Death of Herod Agrippa

20Now Herod was very angry with the people of Tyre and Sidon. So they sent a delegation to make peace with him because their cities were dependent upon Herod's country for their food. They made friends with Blastus, Herod's personal assistant, 21and an appointment with Herod was granted. When the day arrived, Herod put on his royal robes, sat on his throne, and made a speech to them. 22The people gave him a great ovation, shouting, "It is the voice of a god, not of a man!"

23Instantly, an angel of the Lord struck Herod with a sickness, because he accepted the people's

13:1a Greek who was called Niger.   13:1b Greek Herod the tetrarch.

worship instead of giving the glory to God. So he was consumed with worms and died.

24But God's Good News was spreading rapidly, and there were many new believers.

25When Barnabas and Saul had finished their mission in Jerusalem, they returned to Antioch, taking John Mark with them.

## CHAPTER 13
### Barnabas and Saul Are Sent Out

Among the prophets and teachers of the church at Antioch of Syria were Barnabas, Simeon (called "the black man"*), Lucius (from Cyrene), Manaen (the childhood companion of King Herod Antipas*), and Saul. 2One day as these men were worshiping the Lord and fasting, the Holy Spirit said, "Dedicate Barnabas and Saul for the special work I have for them." 3So after more fasting and prayer, the men laid their hands on them and sent them on their way.

### Paul's First Missionary Journey

4Sent out by the Holy Spirit, Saul and Barnabas went down to the seaport of Seleucia and then sailed for the island of Cyprus. 5There, in the town of Salamis, they went to the Jewish synagogues and preached the word of God. (John Mark went with them as their assistant.)

6Afterward they preached from town to town across the entire island until finally they reached Paphos, where they met a Jewish sorcerer, a false prophet named Bar-Jesus. 7He had attached himself to the governor, Sergius Paulus, a man of considerable insight and understanding. The governor invited Barnabas and Saul to visit him, for he wanted to hear the word of God. 8But

---

to translate this verse is, "They prayed with agony." It is the same phrase used to describe the way Jesus prayed in the garden of Gethsemane. Their prayers had intensity. Many of our prayers have no power because they have little or no heart in them. If we put so little heart into our prayers, we cannot expect God to put much heart into answering them.

**3. They Prayed as a Body.** There is power in united prayer. Jesus said in Matthew 18:19, "I also tell you this: If two of you agree down here on earth concerning anything you ask, my Father in heaven will do it for you." What Jesus meant is that if two or more people who share the same God-given burden are sure of God's will and are in agreement with the Spirit of God and one another as they pray—they will see dynamic results.

Someone once said, "Satan trembles when he sees the weakest saint upon his knees." If you are in a bleak situation today, consider how God worked through the prayers of these early Christians. Don't give up. If you follow these principles, you will see results done God's way and in God's timing.

Elymas, the sorcerer (as his name means in Greek), interfered and urged the governor to pay no attention to what Saul and Barnabas said. He was trying to turn the governor away from the Christian faith.

9Then Saul, also known as Paul, filled with the Holy Spirit, looked the sorcerer in the eye and said, 10"You son of the Devil, full of every sort of trickery and villainy, enemy of all that is good, will you never stop perverting the true ways of the Lord? 11And now the Lord has laid his hand of punishment upon you, and you will be stricken awhile with blindness." Instantly mist and darkness fell upon him, and he began wandering around begging for someone to take his hand and lead him. 12When the governor saw what had happened, he believed and was astonished at what he learned about the Lord.

*Paul Preaches in Antioch of Pisidia*
13Now Paul and those with him left Paphos by ship for Pamphylia,* landing at the port town of Perga. There John Mark left them and returned to Jerusalem. 14But Barnabas and Paul traveled inland to Antioch of Pisidia.*

On the Sabbath they went to the synagogue for the services. 15After the usual readings from the books of Moses and from the Prophets, those in charge of the service sent them this message: "Brothers, if you have any word of encouragement for us, come and give it!"

16So Paul stood, lifted his hand to quiet them, and started speaking. "People of Israel," he said, "and you devout Gentiles who fear the God of Israel, listen to me.

17"The God of this nation of Israel chose our ancestors and made them prosper in Egypt. Then he powerfully led them out of their slavery. 18He put up with them* through forty years of wandering around in the wilderness. 19Then he destroyed seven nations in Canaan and gave their land to Israel as an inheritance. 20All this took about 450 years. After that, judges ruled until the time of Samuel the prophet. 21Then the people begged for a king, and God gave them Saul son of Kish, a man of the tribe of Benjamin, who reigned for forty years. 22But God removed him from the kingship and replaced him with David, a man about whom God said, 'David son of Jesse is a man after my own heart, for he will do everything I want him to.'*

23"And it is one of King David's descendants,

Jesus, who is God's promised Savior of Israel! 24But before he came, John the Baptist preached the need for everyone in Israel to turn from sin and turn to God and be baptized. 25As John was finishing his ministry he asked, 'Do you think I am the Messiah? No! But he is coming soon— and I am not even worthy to be his slave.*'

26"Brothers—you sons of Abraham, and also all of you devout Gentiles who fear the God of Israel—this salvation is for us! 27The people in Jerusalem and their leaders fulfilled prophecy by condemning Jesus to death. They didn't recognize him or realize that he is the one the prophets had written about, though they hear the prophets' words read every Sabbath. 28They found no just cause to execute him, but they asked Pilate to have him killed anyway.

29"When they had fulfilled all the prophecies concerning his death, they took him down from the cross and placed him in a tomb. 30But God raised him from the dead! 31And he appeared over a period of many days to those who had gone with him from Galilee to Jerusalem— these are his witnesses to the people of Israel.

32"And now Barnabas and I are here to bring you this Good News. God's promise to our ancestors has come true in our own time, 33in that God raised Jesus. This is what the second psalm is talking about when it says concerning Jesus,

'You are my Son.
    Today I have become your Father.*'

34For God had promised to raise him from the dead, never again to die. This is stated in the Scripture that says, 'I will give you the sacred blessings I promised to David.'* 35Another psalm explains more fully, saying, 'You will not allow your Holy One to rot in the grave.'* 36Now this is not a reference to David, for after David had served his generation according to the will of God, he died and was buried, and his body decayed. 37No, it was a reference to someone else—someone whom God raised and whose body did not decay.

38"Brothers, listen! In this man Jesus there is forgiveness for your sins. 39Everyone who believes in him is freed from all guilt and declared right with God—something the Jewish law could never do. 40Be careful! Don't let the prophets' words apply to you. For they said,

41 'Look you mockers,

13:13-14 *Pamphylia* and *Pisidia* were districts in the land now called Turkey.   13:18 Other manuscripts read *He cared for them;* compare Deut 1:31.   13:22 1 Sam 13:14.   13:25 Greek *to untie his sandals.*   13:33 Or *Today I reveal you as my Son.* Ps 2:7.   13:34 Isa 55:3. 13:35 Ps 16:10.

be amazed and die!
For I am doing something in your own day,
   something you wouldn't believe
   even if someone told you about it.'* "

⁴²As Paul and Barnabas left the synagogue that day, the people asked them to return again and speak about these things the next week. ⁴³Many Jews and godly converts to Judaism who worshiped at the synagogue followed Paul and Barnabas, and the two men urged them, "By God's grace, remain faithful."

### Paul Turns to the Gentiles

⁴⁴The following week almost the entire city turned out to hear them preach the word of the Lord. ⁴⁵But when the Jewish leaders saw the crowds, they were jealous; so they slandered Paul and argued against whatever he said.

⁴⁶Then Paul and Barnabas spoke out boldly and declared, "It was necessary that this Good News from God be given first to you Jews. But since you have rejected it and judged yourselves unworthy of eternal life—well, we will offer it to Gentiles. ⁴⁷For this is as the Lord commanded us when he said,

'I have made you a light to the Gentiles,
   to bring salvation to the farthest corners
   of the earth.'* "

⁴⁸When the Gentiles heard this, they were very glad and thanked the Lord for his message; and all who were appointed to eternal life became believers. ⁴⁹So the Lord's message spread throughout that region.

⁵⁰Then the Jewish leaders stirred up both the influential religious women and the leaders of the city, and they incited a mob against Paul and Barnabas and ran them out of town. ⁵¹But they shook off the dust of their feet against them and went to the city of Iconium. ⁵²And the believers* were filled with joy and with the Holy Spirit.

## CHAPTER 14

### Paul and Barnabas in Iconium

In Iconium,* Paul and Barnabas went together to the synagogue and preached with such power that a great number of both Jews and Gentiles believed. ²But the Jews who spurned God's message stirred up distrust among the Gentiles against Paul and Barnabas, saying all sorts of evil things about them. ³The apostles stayed there a long time, preaching boldly

about the grace of the Lord. The Lord proved their message was true by giving them power to do miraculous signs and wonders. ⁴But the people of the city were divided in their opinion about them. Some sided with the Jews, and some with the apostles.

⁵A mob of Gentiles and Jews, along with their leaders, decided to attack and stone them. ⁶When the apostles learned of it, they fled for their lives. They went to the region of Lycaonia, to the cities of Lystra and Derbe and the surrounding area, ⁷and they preached the Good News there.

### Paul and Barnabas in Lystra and Derbe

⁸While they were at Lystra, Paul and Barnabas came upon a man with crippled feet. He had been that way from birth, so he had never walked. ⁹He was listening as Paul preached, and Paul noticed him and realized he had faith to be healed. ¹⁰So Paul called to him in a loud voice, "Stand up!" And the man jumped to his feet and started walking.

¹¹When the listening crowd saw what Paul had done, they shouted in their local dialect, "These men are gods in human bodies!" ¹²They decided that Barnabas was the Greek god Zeus and that Paul, because he was the chief speaker, was Hermes. ¹³The temple of Zeus was located on the outskirts of the city. The priest of the temple and the crowd brought oxen and wreaths of flowers, and they prepared to sacrifice to the apostles at the city gates.

¹⁴But when Barnabas and Paul heard what was happening, they tore their clothing in dismay and ran out among the people, shouting, ¹⁵"Friends,* why are you doing this? We are merely human beings like yourselves! We have come to bring you the Good News that you should turn from these worthless things to the living God, who made heaven and earth, the sea, and everything in them. ¹⁶In earlier days he permitted all the nations to go their own ways, ¹⁷but he never left himself without a witness. There were always his reminders, such as sending you rain and good crops and giving you food and joyful hearts." ¹⁸But even so, Paul and Barnabas could scarcely restrain the people from sacrificing to them.

¹⁹Now some Jews arrived from Antioch and Iconium and turned the crowds into a murderous mob. They stoned Paul and dragged him out of the city, apparently dead. ²⁰But as the believ-

13:41 Hab 1:5.   13:47 Isa 49:6.   13:52 Greek *the disciples.*   14:1 *Iconium,* as well as *Lystra* and *Derbe* (14:6), were cities in the land now called Turkey.   14:15 Greek *Men.*

ers* stood around him, he got up and went back into the city. The next day he left with Barnabas for Derbe.

## Paul and Barnabas Return to Antioch of Syria

21After preaching the Good News in Derbe and making many disciples, Paul and Barnabas returned again to Lystra, Iconium, and Antioch of Pisidia, 22where they strengthened the believers. They encouraged them to continue in the faith, reminding them that they must enter into the Kingdom of God through many tribulations. 23Paul and Barnabas also appointed elders in every church and prayed for them with fasting, turning them over to the care of the Lord, in whom they had come to trust. 24Then they traveled back through Pisidia to Pamphylia. 25They preached again in Perga, then went on to Attalia.

26Finally, they returned by ship to Antioch of Syria, where their journey had begun and where they had been committed to the grace of God for the work they had now completed. 27Upon arriving in Antioch, they called the church together and reported about their trip, telling all that God had done and how he had opened the door of faith to the Gentiles, too. 28And they stayed there with the believers in Antioch for a long time.

## CHAPTER 15
### The Council at Jerusalem

While Paul and Barnabas were at Antioch of Syria, some men from Judea arrived and began to teach the Christians*: "Unless you keep the ancient Jewish custom of circumcision taught by Moses, you cannot be saved." 2Paul and Barnabas, disagreeing with them, argued forcefully and at length. Finally, Paul and Barnabas were sent to Jerusalem, accompanied by some local believers, to talk to the apostles and elders about this question. 3The church sent the delegates to Jerusalem, and they stopped along the way in Phoenicia and Samaria to visit the believers.* They told them—much to everyone's joy—that the Gentiles, too, were being converted.

4When they arrived in Jerusalem, Paul and Barnabas were welcomed by the whole church, including the apostles and elders. They reported on what God had been doing through their ministry. 5But then some of the men who had been Pharisees before their conversion stood up and declared that all Gentile converts must be circumcised and be required to follow the law of Moses.

6So the apostles and church elders got together to decide this question. 7At the meeting, after a long discussion, Peter stood and addressed them as follows: "Brothers, you all know that God chose me from among you some time ago to preach to the Gentiles so that they could hear the Good News and believe. 8God, who knows people's hearts, confirmed that he accepts Gentiles by giving them the Holy Spirit, just as he gave him to us. 9He made no distinction between us and them, for he also cleansed their hearts through faith. 10Why are you now questioning God's way by burdening the Gentile believers* with a yoke that neither we nor our ancestors were able to bear? 11We believe that we are all saved the same way, by the special favor of the Lord Jesus."

12There was no further discussion, and everyone listened as Barnabas and Paul told about the miraculous signs and wonders God had done through them among the Gentiles.

13When they had finished, James stood and said, "Brothers, listen to me. 14Peter* has told you about the time God first visited the Gentiles to take from them a people for himself. 15And this conversion of Gentiles agrees with what the prophets predicted. For instance, it is written:

16 'Afterward I will return,
    and I will restore the fallen kingdom of
      David.
   From the ruins I will rebuild it,
    and I will restore it,
17 so that the rest of humanity might find the
      Lord,
    including the Gentiles—
    all those I have called to be mine.
   This is what the Lord says,
18      he who made these things known long
      ago.'*

19And so my judgment is that we should stop troubling the Gentiles who turn to God, 20except that we should write to them and tell them to abstain from eating meat sacrificed to idols, from sexual immorality, and from consuming blood or eating the meat of strangled animals. 21For these laws of Moses have been preached in Jewish synagogues in every city on every Sabbath for many generations."

## The Letter for Gentile Believers

22Then the apostles and elders and the whole church in Jerusalem chose delegates, and they sent them to Antioch of Syria with Paul and Barnabas to report on this decision. The men chosen were two of the church leaders*—Judas (also called Barsabbas) and Silas. 23This is the letter they took along with them:

"This letter is from the apostles and elders, your brothers in Jerusalem. It is written to the Gentile believers in Antioch, Syria, and Cilicia. Greetings!

24"We understand that some men from here have troubled you and upset you with their teaching, but they had no such instructions from us. 25So it seemed good to us, having unanimously agreed on our decision, to send you these official representatives, along with our beloved Barnabas and Paul, 26who have risked their lives for the sake of our Lord Jesus Christ. 27So we are sending Judas and Silas to tell you what we have decided concerning your question.

28"For it seemed good to the Holy Spirit and to us to lay no greater burden on you than these requirements: 29You must abstain from eating food offered to idols, from consuming blood or eating the meat of strangled animals, and from sexual immorality. If you do this, you will do well. Farewell."

30The four messengers went at once to Antioch, where they called a general meeting of the Christians and delivered the letter. 31And there was great joy throughout the church that day as they read this encouraging message.

32Then Judas and Silas, both being prophets, spoke extensively to the Christians, encouraging and strengthening their faith. 33They stayed for a while, and then Judas and Silas were sent back to Jerusalem, with the blessings of the Christians, to those who had sent them.* 35Paul and Barnabas stayed in Antioch to assist many others who were teaching and preaching the word of the Lord there.

## Paul and Barnabas Separate

36After some time Paul said to Barnabas, "Let's return to each city where we previously preached the word of the Lord, to see how the new believers are getting along." 37Barnabas agreed and wanted to take along John Mark. 38But Paul disagreed strongly, since John Mark had deserted

them in Pamphylia and had not shared in their work. 39Their disagreement over this was so sharp that they separated. Barnabas took John Mark with him and sailed for Cyprus. 40Paul chose Silas, and the believers sent them off, entrusting them to the Lord's grace. 41So they traveled throughout Syria and Cilicia to strengthen the churches there.

## CHAPTER 16
### Paul's Second Missionary Journey

Paul and Silas went first to Derbe and then on to Lystra. There they met Timothy, a young disciple whose mother was a Jewish believer, but whose father was a Greek. 2Timothy was well thought of by the believers* in Lystra and Iconium, 3so Paul wanted him to join them on their journey. In deference to the Jews of the area, he arranged for Timothy to be circumcised before they left, for everyone knew that his father was a Greek. 4Then they went from town to town, explaining the decision regarding the commandments that were to be obeyed, as decided by the apostles and elders in Jerusalem. 5So the churches were strengthened in their faith and grew daily in numbers.

### A Call from Macedonia

6Next Paul and Silas traveled through the area of Phrygia and Galatia, because the Holy Spirit had told them not to go into the province of Asia at that time. 7Then coming to the borders of Mysia, they headed for the province of Bithynia,* but again the Spirit of Jesus did not let them go. 8So instead, they went on through Mysia to the city of Troas.

9That night Paul had a vision. He saw a man from Macedonia in northern Greece, pleading with him, "Come over here and help us." 10So we* decided to leave for Macedonia at once, for we could only conclude that God was calling us to preach the Good News there.

### Lydia of Philippi Believes in Jesus

11We boarded a boat at Troas and sailed straight across to the island of Samothrace, and the next day we landed at Neapolis. 12From there we reached Philippi, a major city of the district of Macedonia and a Roman colony; we stayed there several days.

13On the Sabbath we went a little way outside the city to a riverbank, where we supposed that some people met for prayer, and we sat down to

---

15:22 Greek were leaders among the brothers. 15:33 Some manuscripts add verse 34, But Silas decided to stay there. 16:2 Greek brothers; also in 16:40. 16:6-7 Phrygia, Galatia, Asia, Mysia, and Bithynia were all districts in the land now called Turkey. 16:10 Luke, the writer of this book, here joined Paul and accompanied him on his journey.

speak with some women who had come together. [14]One of them was Lydia from Thyatira, a merchant of expensive purple cloth. She was a worshiper of God. As she listened to us, the Lord opened her heart, and she accepted what Paul was saying. [15]She was baptized along with other members of her household, and she asked us to be her guests. "If you agree that I am faithful to the Lord," she said, "come and stay at my home." And she urged us until we did.

## Paul and Silas in Prison

[16]One day as we were going down to the place of prayer, we met a demon-possessed slave girl. She was a fortune-teller who earned a lot of money for her masters. [17]She followed along behind us shouting, "These men are servants of the Most High God, and they have come to tell you how to be saved."

[18]This went on day after day until Paul got so exasperated that he turned and spoke to the demon within her. "I command you in the name of Jesus Christ to come out of her," he said. And instantly it left her.

[19]Her masters' hopes of wealth were now shattered, so they grabbed Paul and Silas and dragged them before the authorities at the marketplace. [20]"The whole city is in an uproar because of these Jews!" they shouted. [21]"They are teaching the people to do things that are against Roman customs."

[22]A mob quickly formed against Paul and Silas, and the city officials ordered them stripped and beaten with wooden rods. [23]They were severely beaten, and then they were thrown into prison. The jailer was ordered to make sure they didn't escape. [24]So he took no chances but put them into the inner dungeon and clamped their feet in the stocks.

[25]Around midnight, Paul and Silas were praying and singing hymns to God, and the other prisoners were listening. [26]Suddenly, there was a great earthquake, and the prison was shaken to its foundations. All the doors flew open, and the chains of every prisoner fell off! [27]The jailer woke up to see the prison doors wide open. He assumed the prisoners had escaped, so he drew his sword to kill himself. [28]But Paul shouted to him, "Don't do it! We are all here!"

[29]Trembling with fear, the jailer called for lights and ran to the dungeon and fell down before Paul and Silas. [30]He brought them out and asked, "Sirs, what must I do to be saved?"

[31]They replied, "Believe on the Lord Jesus and you will be saved, along with your entire household." [32]Then they shared the word of the Lord with him and all who lived in his household. [33]That same hour the jailer washed their wounds, and he and everyone in his household were immediately baptized. [34]Then he brought them into his house and set a meal before them. He and his entire household rejoiced because they all believed in God.

[35]The next morning the city officials sent the police to tell the jailer, "Let those men go!" [36]So the jailer told Paul, "You and Silas are free to leave. Go in peace."

[37]But Paul replied, "They have publicly beaten us without trial and jailed us—and we are Roman citizens. So now they want us to leave secretly? Certainly not! Let them come themselves to release us!"

[38]When the police made their report, the city officials were alarmed to learn that Paul and Silas were Roman citizens. [39]They came to the jail and apologized to them. Then they brought them out and begged them to leave the city. [40]Paul and Silas then returned to the home of Lydia, where they met with the believers and encouraged them once more before leaving town.

# OFF AND RUNNING

## Make Sure Your Children Hear the Gospel Message
Read ACTS 16:29-34

In this wonderful story, we see how one man looked out for the spiritual welfare of his family. He took the opportunity at hand to expose his family to the message of Christ through the testimony of Paul and Silas.

We, too, need to take advantage of every opportunity to share Christ with our family—and particularly our children. They are never too young (or too old) to be taught about the things of God. Here are four suggestions to help you share the gospel with your family:

**1. Set Aside Time for Family Devotions.** Study the Bible, pray together, and share how God has been working in your life.

CHAPTER **17**

*Paul Preaches in Thessalonica*

Now Paul and Silas traveled through the towns of Amphipolis and Apollonia and came to Thessalonica, where there was a Jewish synagogue. 2As was Paul's custom, he went to the synagogue service, and for three Sabbaths in a row he interpreted the Scriptures to the people. 3He was explaining and proving the prophecies about the sufferings of the Messiah and his rising from the dead. He said, "This Jesus I'm telling you about is the Messiah." 4Some who listened were persuaded and became converts, including a large number of godly Greek men and also many important women of the city.*

5But the Jewish leaders were jealous, so they gathered some worthless fellows from the streets to form a mob and start a riot. They attacked the home of Jason, searching for Paul and Silas so they could drag them out to the crowd.* 6Not finding them there, they dragged out Jason and some of the other believers* instead and took them before the city council. "Paul and Silas have turned the rest of the world upside down, and now they are here disturbing our city," they shouted. 7"And Jason has let them into his home. They are all guilty of treason against Caesar, for they profess allegiance to another king, Jesus."

8The people of the city, as well as the city officials, were thrown into turmoil by these reports. 9But the officials released Jason and the other believers after they had posted bail.

*Paul and Silas in Berea*

10That very night the believers sent Paul and Silas to Berea. When they arrived there, they went to the synagogue. 11And the people of Berea were more open-minded than those in Thessalonica, and they listened eagerly to Paul's message. They searched the Scriptures day after day to check up on Paul and Silas, to see if they were really teaching the truth. 12As a result, many Jews believed, as did some of the prominent Greek women and many men.

13But when some Jews in Thessalonica learned that Paul was preaching the word of God in Berea, they went there and stirred up trouble. 14The believers acted at once, sending Paul on to the coast, while Silas and Timothy remained behind. 15Those escorting Paul went with him to Athens; then they returned to Berea with a message for Silas and Timothy to hurry and join him.

*Paul Preaches in Athens*

16While Paul was waiting for them in Athens, he was deeply troubled by all the idols he saw everywhere in the city. 17He went to the synagogue to debate with the Jews and the God-fearing Gentiles, and he spoke daily in the public square to all who happened to be there.

18He also had a debate with some of the Epicurean and Stoic philosophers. When he told them about Jesus and his resurrection, they said, "This babbler has picked up some strange ideas." Others said, "He's pushing some foreign religion."

19Then they took him to the Council of Philosophers.* "Come and tell us more about this new religion," they said. 20"You are saying some rather startling things, and we want to know what it's all about." 21(It should be explained that all the Athenians as well as the foreigners in Athens seemed to spend all their time discussing the latest ideas.)

17:4 Some manuscripts read *many of the wives of the leading men.*   17:5 Or *the city council.*   17:6 Greek *brothers;* also in 17:10, 14.
17:19 Greek *the Areopagus.*

**2. Invite Other Believers to Your Home.** This jailer invited Paul and Silas over for dinner, and we read how the whole household rejoiced because all were now believers. This type of fellowship can be an enriching time for your family.

**3. Bring Your Children to Church with You.** Your children will probably learn lessons here that they will carry with them the rest of their lives. If they are young enough, bring them. If they are older, strongly encourage them to join you.

**4. Pray for Your Children Daily.** As a parent, you cannot "make" your children Christians, but you can pray that their hearts will be sensitive and open to the gospel message.

## Use God's Word to Evaluate Someone's Teachings
Read ACTS 17:11

The group of people in this passage—the Bereans—actually searched the written Word of God to see if Paul's words were true. In the original Greek, the word for "searched" could also be translated "scrutinized." They did this because they knew that they could trust God's Word and use it as the standard against which to evaluate others' teachings.

The same is true for us today. Everything we need to know about God is found in the pages of Scripture. Applying ourselves in the study of his Word helps us determine whether someone's teachings are true or false. If we fail to study the Bible, we may be lured into believing false teachings. But if we consistently study God's Word, it—along with the illumination of the Holy Spirit—will enable us to distinguish truth from error.

Here is a trustworthy saying to keep in mind: If someone says they "have a new 'word' or 'revelation' from the Lord," rest assured that it is not true. If it is true, it is not new. If it is new, it is not true! If it is not in the Word, it is not of the Lord.

**CORNER STONES**

---

22So Paul, standing before the Council,* addressed them as follows: "Men of Athens, I notice that you are very religious, 23for as I was walking along I saw your many altars. And one of them had this inscription on it—'To an Unknown God.' You have been worshiping him without knowing who he is, and now I wish to tell you about him.

24"He is the God who made the world and everything in it. Since he is Lord of heaven and earth, he doesn't live in man-made temples, 25and human hands can't serve his needs—for he has no needs. He himself gives life and breath to everything, and he satisfies every need there is. 26From one man he created all the nations throughout the whole earth. He decided beforehand which should rise and fall, and he determined their boundaries.

27"His purpose in all of this was that the nations should seek after God and perhaps feel their way toward him and find him—though he is not far from any one of us. 28For in him we live and move and exist. As one of your own poets says, 'We are his offspring.' 29And since this is true, we shouldn't think of God as an idol designed by craftsmen from gold or silver or stone. 30God overlooked people's former ignorance about these things, but now he commands everyone everywhere to turn away from idols and turn to him.* 31For he has set a day for

judging the world with justice by the man he has appointed, and he proved to everyone who this is by raising him from the dead."

32When they heard Paul speak of the resurrection of a person who had been dead, some laughed, but others said, "We want to hear more about this later." 33That ended Paul's discussion with them, 34but some joined him and became believers. Among them were Dionysius, a member of the Council,* a woman named Damaris, and others.

CHAPTER **18**

*Paul Meets Priscilla and Aquila in Corinth*
Then Paul left Athens and went to Corinth.* 2There he became acquainted with a Jew named Aquila, born in Pontus, who had recently arrived from Italy with his wife, Priscilla. They had been expelled from Italy as a result of Claudius Caesar's order to deport all Jews from Rome. 3Paul lived and worked with them, for they were tentmakers* just as he was.

4Each Sabbath found Paul at the synagogue, trying to convince the Jews and Greeks alike. 5And after Silas and Timothy came down from Macedonia, Paul spent his full time preaching and testifying to the Jews, telling them, "The Messiah you are looking for is Jesus." 6But when the Jews opposed him and insulted him, Paul

---

17:22 Or *in the middle of Mars Hill;* Greek reads *in the middle of the Areopagus.* 17:30 Greek *everywhere to repent.* 17:34 Greek *an Areopagite.* 18:1 *Athens* and *Corinth* were major cities in Achaia, the region on the southern end of the Greek peninsula. 18:3 Or *leatherworkers.*

shook the dust from his robe and said, "Your blood be upon your own heads—I am innocent. From now on I will go to the Gentiles."

7After that he stayed with Titius Justus, a Gentile who worshiped God and lived next door to the synagogue. 8Crispus, the leader of the synagogue, and all his household believed in the Lord. Many others in Corinth also became believers and were baptized.

9One night the Lord spoke to Paul in a vision and told him, "Don't be afraid! Speak out! Don't be silent! 10For I am with you, and no one will harm you because many people here in this city belong to me." 11So Paul stayed there for the next year and a half, teaching the word of God.

12But when Gallio became governor of Achaia, some Jews rose in concerted action against Paul and brought him before the governor for judgment. 13They accused Paul of "persuading people to worship God in ways that are contrary to the law." 14But just as Paul started to make his defense, Gallio turned to Paul's accusers and said, "Listen, you Jews, if this were a case involving some wrongdoing or a serious crime, I would be obliged to listen to you. 15But since it is merely a question of words and names and your Jewish laws, you take care of it. I refuse to judge such matters." 16And he drove them out of the courtroom. 17The mob had grabbed Sosthenes, the leader of the synagogue, and had beaten him right there in the courtroom. But Gallio paid no attention.

### Paul Returns to Antioch of Syria

18Paul stayed in Corinth for some time after that and then said good-bye to the brothers and sisters* and sailed for the coast of Syria, taking Priscilla and Aquila with him. (Earlier, at Cenchrea, Paul had shaved his head according to Jewish custom, for he had taken a vow.) 19When they arrived at the port of Ephesus, Paul left the others behind. But while he was there, he went to the synagogue to debate with the Jews. 20They asked him to stay longer, but he declined. 21So he left, saying, "I will come back later,* God willing." Then he set sail from Ephesus. 22The next stop was at the port of Caesarea. From there he went up and visited the church at Jerusalem* and then went back to Antioch.

23After spending some time in Antioch, Paul went back to Galatia and Phrygia, visiting all the believers,* encouraging them and helping them to grow in the Lord.

### Apollos Instructed at Ephesus

24Meanwhile, a Jew named Apollos, an eloquent speaker who knew the Scriptures well, had just arrived in Ephesus from Alexandria in Egypt. 25He had been taught the way of the Lord and talked to others with great enthusiasm and accuracy about Jesus. However, he knew only about John's baptism. 26When Priscilla and Aquila heard him preaching boldly in the synagogue, they took him aside and explained the way of God more accurately.

27Apollos had been thinking about going to Achaia, and the brothers and sisters in Ephesus encouraged him in this. They wrote to the believers in Achaia, asking them to welcome him. When he arrived there, he proved to be of great benefit to those who, by God's grace, had believed. 28He refuted all the Jews with powerful arguments in public debate. Using the Scriptures, he explained to them, "The Messiah you are looking for is Jesus."

## CHAPTER 19

### Paul's Third Missionary Journey

While Apollos was in Corinth, Paul traveled through the interior provinces. Finally, he came to Ephesus, where he found several believers.* 2"Did you receive the Holy Spirit when you believed?" he asked them.

"No," they replied, "we don't know what you mean. We haven't even heard that there is a Holy Spirit."

3"Then what baptism did you experience?" he asked.

And they replied, "The baptism of John."

4Paul said, "John's baptism was to demonstrate a desire to turn from sin and turn to God. John himself told the people to believe in Jesus, the one John said would come later."

5As soon as they heard this, they were baptized in the name of the Lord Jesus. 6Then when Paul laid his hands on them, the Holy Spirit came on them, and they spoke in other tongues and prophesied. 7There were about twelve men in all.

### Paul Ministers in Ephesus

8Then Paul went to the synagogue and preached boldly for the next three months, arguing persuasively about the Kingdom of God. 9But some rejected his message and publicly spoke against the Way, so Paul left the synagogue and took the believers with him. Then he began preaching

18:18 Greek brothers; also in 18:27.   18:21 Some manuscripts read "I must by all means be at Jerusalem for the upcoming festival, but I will come back later."   18:22 Greek the church.   18:23 Greek disciples; also in 18:27.   19:1 Greek disciples; also in 19:9, 30.

## God Is Personal  Read ACTS 17:22-33

Paul's audience in this passage included people of two different beliefs. There were those who did not believe in life after death and lived only for pleasure. They were known as the Epicureans. There were also those who believed that God existed in every material object and strived to be at peace with the world. These people were known as the Stoics. In speaking to these two groups, Paul showed them how their philosophies fell short of grasping the true nature of God. He did this by bringing out the following truths about who God is.

### God Is the All-Powerful Creator
- God made heaven and earth, and every living creature.
- God is too great to be housed in man-made temples or shrines.
- God created all the people of the world from one man.
- God is the architect behind the world stage.

### God Is the Personal Supreme Being
- His purpose behind creation was to draw people to himself.
- He is concerned about people's needs.
- He is not far from any of us.
- He makes it easy for us to know him personally (salvation through Jesus Christ).
- He can and will judge every thought and motive on Judgment Day.

The people who listened to Paul speak responded in one of three ways: (1) Some mocked him; (2) some procrastinated and said they would make a decision after listening to him again later; and (3) some believed him and accepted Jesus as their Savior. People today react to the gospel message in much the same way. However, if someone really wants to know the powerful God who created him or her and who is personally interested in his or her life, only the last response will do.

CORNERSTONES

---

daily at the lecture hall of Tyrannus. [10]This went on for the next two years, so that people throughout the province of Asia—both Jews and Greeks—heard the Lord's message.

[11]God gave Paul the power to do unusual miracles, [12]so that even when handkerchiefs or cloths that had touched his skin were placed on sick people, they were healed of their diseases, and any evil spirits within them came out.

[13]A team of Jews who were traveling from town to town casting out evil spirits tried to use the name of the Lord Jesus. The incantation they used was this: "I command you by Jesus, whom Paul preaches, to come out!" [14]Seven sons of Sceva, a leading priest, were doing this. [15]But when they tried it on a man possessed by an evil spirit, the spirit replied, "I know Jesus, and I know Paul. But who are you?" [16]And he leaped on them and attacked them with such violence that they fled from the house, naked and badly injured.

[17]The story of what happened spread quickly all through Ephesus, to Jews and Greeks alike. A solemn fear descended on the city, and the name of the Lord Jesus was greatly honored. [18]Many who became believers confessed their sinful practices. [19]A number of them who had been practicing magic brought their incantation books and burned them at a public bonfire. The value of the books was several million dollars.* [20]So the message about the Lord spread widely and had a powerful effect.

### The Riot in Ephesus
[21]Afterward Paul felt impelled by the Holy Spirit* to go over to Macedonia and Achaia before returning to Jerusalem. "And after that," he said, "I must go on to Rome!" [22]He sent his two assistants, Timothy and Erastus, on ahead to Macedonia while he stayed awhile longer in the province of Asia.

[23]But about that time, serious trouble developed in Ephesus concerning the Way. [24]It began

19:19 Greek *50,000 pieces of silver*, each of which was the equivalent of a day's wage.  19:21 Or *purposed in his spirit.*

with Demetrius, a silversmith who had a large business manufacturing silver shrines of the Greek goddess Artemis.* He kept many crafts-men busy. 25He called the craftsmen together, along with others employed in related trades, and addressed them as follows:

"Gentlemen, you know that our wealth comes from this business. 26As you have seen and heard, this man Paul has persuaded many people that handmade gods aren't gods at all. And this is happening not only here in Ephesus but throughout the entire province! 27Of course, I'm not just talking about the loss of public respect for our business. I'm also concerned that the temple of the great goddess Artemis will lose its influence and that Artemis—this magnificent goddess worshiped throughout the province of Asia and all around the world—will be robbed of her prestige!"

28At this their anger boiled, and they began shouting, "Great is Artemis of the Ephesians!" 29A crowd began to gather, and soon the city was filled with confusion. Everyone rushed to the amphitheater, dragging along Gaius and Aristar-chus, who were Paul's traveling companions from Macedonia. 30Paul wanted to go in, but the believers wouldn't let him. 31Some of the offi-cials of the province, friends of Paul, also sent a message to him, begging him not to risk his life by entering the amphitheater.

32Inside, the people were all shouting, some one thing and some another. Everything was in confusion. In fact, most of them didn't even know why they were there. 33Alexander was thrust forward by some of the Jews, who encour-aged him to explain the situation. He motioned for silence and tried to speak in defense. 34But when the crowd realized he was a Jew, they started shouting again and kept it up for two hours: "Great is Artemis of the Ephesians! Great is Artemis of the Ephesians!"

35At last the mayor was able to quiet them down enough to speak. "Citizens of Ephesus," he said. "Everyone knows that Ephesus is the official guardian of the temple of the great Artemis, whose image fell down to us from heaven. 36Since this is an indisputable fact, you shouldn't be disturbed, no matter what is said. Don't do anything rash. 37You have brought these men here, but they have stolen nothing from the temple and have not spoken against our goddess. 38If Demetrius and the craftsmen have a case against them, the courts are in ses-sion and the judges can take the case at once. Let them go through legal channels. 39And if there are complaints about other matters, they can be settled in a legal assembly. 40I am afraid we are in danger of being charged with rioting by the Roman government, since there is no cause for all this commotion. And if Rome demands an explanation, we won't know what to say." 41Then he dismissed them, and they dispersed.

CHAPTER 20

*Paul Goes to Macedonia and Greece*

When it was all over, Paul sent for the believers* and encouraged them. Then he said good-bye and left for Macedonia. 2Along the way, he en-couraged the believers in all the towns he passed through. Then he traveled down to Greece, 3where he stayed for three months. He was pre-paring to sail back to Syria when he discovered a plot by some Jews against his life, so he de-cided to return through Macedonia.

4Several men were traveling with him. They were Sopater of Berea, the son of Pyrrhus; Aris-tarchus and Secundus, from Thessalonica; Ga-ius, from Derbe; Timothy; and Tychicus and Trophimus, who were from the province of Asia. 5They went ahead and waited for us at Troas. 6As soon as the Passover season* ended, we boarded a ship at Philippi in Macedonia and five days later arrived in Troas, where we stayed a week.

*Paul's Final Visit to Troas*

7On the first day of the week, we gathered to observe the Lord's Supper.* Paul was preaching; and since he was leaving the next day, he talked until midnight. 8The upstairs room where we met was lighted with many flickering lamps. 9As Paul spoke on and on, a young man named Eutychus, sitting on the windowsill, became very drowsy. Finally, he sank into a deep sleep and fell three stories to his death below. 10Paul went down, bent over him, and took him into his arms. "Don't worry," he said, "he's alive!" 11Then they all went back upstairs and ate the Lord's Supper together.* And Paul continued talking to them until dawn; then he left. 12Meanwhile, the young man was taken home unhurt, and everyone was greatly relieved.

*Paul Meets the Ephesian Elders*

13Paul went by land to Assos, where he had arranged for us to join him, and we went on

19:24 Artemis is otherwise known as Diana.   20:1 Greek *disciples.*   20:6 Greek *the days of unleavened bread.*   20:7 Greek *to break bread.*
20:11 Greek *broke the bread.*

## Can Demons Personally Harm You? Read ACTS 19:13-20

While Christians have the promise of angelic protection over their lives, non-Christians are open targets for the Devil and his demon forces. As this passage relates, demons will only respond to or avoid the "genuine" believer. They will not answer to someone who simply uses the name of Jesus without really knowing who Jesus is. Religion will not keep them away, nor will symbols like a crucifix. Certainly the Devil hates what Jesus did on the literal cross, but wearing a cross will not drive these evil spirits away.

The only thing that will secure you from the Devil's domination—and even possession—of your soul is the presence of Jesus Christ in your life. Once you trust in him, you come under divine protection and become his property. He said that you are his sheep and that no one can take you out of his hand (see John 10:27-29, p. 119). But if you are not a Christian, you are open game that the Devil can take at his will.

CORNER STONES

---

ahead by ship. ¹⁴He joined us there and we sailed together to Mitylene. ¹⁵The next day we passed the island of Kios. The following day, we crossed to the island of Samos. And a day later we arrived at Miletus.

¹⁶Paul had decided against stopping at Ephesus this time because he didn't want to spend further time in the province of Asia. He was hurrying to get to Jerusalem, if possible, for the Festival of Pentecost. ¹⁷But when we landed at Miletus, he sent a message to the elders of the church at Ephesus, asking them to come down to meet him.

¹⁸When they arrived he declared, "You know that from the day I set foot in the province of Asia until now ¹⁹I have done the Lord's work humbly—yes, and with tears. I have endured the trials that came to me from the plots of the Jews. ²⁰Yet I never shrank from telling you the truth, either publicly or in your homes. ²¹I have had one message for Jews and Gentiles alike—the necessity of turning from sin and turning to God, and of faith in our Lord Jesus.

²²"And now I am going to Jerusalem, drawn there irresistibly by the Holy Spirit,* not knowing what awaits me, ²³except that the Holy Spirit has told me in city after city that jail and suffering lie ahead. ²⁴But my life is worth nothing unless I use it for doing the work assigned me by the Lord Jesus—the work of telling others the Good News about God's wonderful kindness and love.

²⁵"And now I know that none of you to whom I have preached the Kingdom will ever

see me again. ²⁶Let me say plainly that I have been faithful. No one's damnation can be blamed on me,* ²⁷for I didn't shrink from declaring all that God wants for you.

²⁸"And now beware! Be sure that you feed and shepherd God's flock—his church, purchased with his blood—over whom the Holy Spirit has appointed you as elders.* ²⁹I know full well that false teachers, like vicious wolves, will come in among you after I leave, not sparing the flock. ³⁰Even some of you will distort the truth in order to draw a following. ³¹Watch out! Remember the three years I was with you—my constant watch and care over you night and day, and my many tears for you.

³²"And now I entrust you to God and the word of his grace—his message that is able to build you up and give you an inheritance with all those he has set apart for himself.

³³"I have never coveted anyone's money or fine clothing. ³⁴You know that these hands of mine have worked to pay my own way, and I have even supplied the needs of those who were with me. ³⁵And I have been a constant example of how you can help the poor by working hard. You should remember the words of the Lord Jesus: 'It is more blessed to give than to receive.' "

³⁶When he had finished speaking, he knelt and prayed with them. ³⁷They wept aloud as they embraced him in farewell, ³⁸sad most of all because he had said that they would never see him again. Then they accompanied him down to the ship.

20:22 Or *by my spirit,* or *by an inner compulsion;* Greek reads *by the spirit.*   20:26 Greek *I am innocent of the blood of all.*   20:28 Greek *overseers.*

# CHAPTER 21

*Paul's Journey to Jerusalem*

After saying farewell to the Ephesian elders, we sailed straight to the island of Cos. The next day we reached Rhodes and then went to Patara. ²There we boarded a ship sailing for the Syrian province of Phoenicia. ³We sighted the island of Cyprus, passed it on our left, and landed at the harbor of Tyre, in Syria, where the ship was to unload. ⁴We went ashore, found the local believers,* and stayed with them a week. These disciples prophesied through the Holy Spirit that Paul should not go on to Jerusalem. ⁵When we returned to the ship at the end of the week, the entire congregation, including wives and children, came down to the shore with us. There we knelt, prayed, ⁶and said our farewells. Then we went aboard, and they returned home.

⁷The next stop after leaving Tyre was Ptolemais, where we greeted the brothers and sisters* but stayed only one day. ⁸Then we went on to Caesarea and stayed at the home of Philip the Evangelist, one of the seven men who had been chosen to distribute food. ⁹He had four unmarried daughters who had the gift of prophecy.

¹⁰During our stay of several days, a man named Agabus, who also had the gift of prophecy, arrived from Judea. ¹¹When he visited us, he took Paul's belt and bound his own feet and hands with it. Then he said, "The Holy Spirit declares, 'So shall the owner of this belt be bound by the Jewish leaders in Jerusalem and turned over to the Romans.'" ¹²When we heard this, we who were traveling with him, as well as the local believers, begged Paul not to go on to Jerusalem.

¹³But he said, "Why all this weeping? You are breaking my heart! For I am ready not only to be jailed at Jerusalem but also to die for the sake of the Lord Jesus." ¹⁴When it was clear that we couldn't persuade him, we gave up and said, "The will of the Lord be done."

*Paul Arrives at Jerusalem*

¹⁵Shortly afterward we packed our things and left for Jerusalem. ¹⁶Some believers from Caesarea accompanied us, and they took us to the home of Mnason, a man originally from Cyprus and one of the early disciples. ¹⁷All the brothers and sisters in Jerusalem welcomed us cordially.

¹⁸The next day Paul went in with us to meet with James, and all the elders of the Jerusalem church were present. ¹⁹After greetings were exchanged, Paul gave a detailed account of the things God had accomplished among the Gentiles through his ministry.

²⁰After hearing this, they praised God. But then they said, "You know, dear brother, how many thousands of Jews have also believed, and they all take the law of Moses very seriously. ²¹Our Jewish Christians here at Jerusalem have been told that you are teaching all the Jews living in the Gentile world to turn their backs on the laws of Moses. They say that you teach people not to circumcise their children or follow other Jewish customs. ²²Now what can be done? For they will certainly hear that you have come.

²³"Here's our suggestion. We have four men here who have taken a vow and are preparing to shave their heads. ²⁴Go with them to the Temple and join them in the purification ceremony, and pay for them to have their heads shaved. Then everyone will know that the rumors are all false and that you yourself observe the Jewish laws.

²⁵"As for the Gentile Christians, all we ask of them is what we already told them in a letter: They should not eat food offered to idols, nor consume blood, nor eat meat from strangled animals, and they should stay away from all sexual immorality."

*Paul Is Arrested*

²⁶So Paul agreed to their request, and the next day he went through the purification ritual with the men and went to the Temple. Then he publicly announced the date when their vows would end and sacrifices would be offered for each of them.

²⁷The seven days were almost ended when some Jews from the province of Asia saw Paul in the Temple and roused a mob against him. They grabbed him, ²⁸yelling, "Men of Israel! Help! This is the man who teaches against our people and tells everybody to disobey the Jewish laws. He speaks against the Temple—and he even defiles it by bringing Gentiles in!" ²⁹(For earlier that day they had seen him in the city with Trophimus, a Gentile from Ephesus,* and they assumed Paul had taken him into the Temple.) ³⁰The whole population of the city was rocked by these accusations, and a great riot followed. Paul was dragged out of the Temple, and immediately the gates were closed behind him. ³¹As they were trying to kill him, word reached the commander of the Roman regiment that all Jerusalem was in an uproar. ³²He

21:4 Greek *disciples;* also in 21:16.  21:7 Greek *brothers;* also in 21:17.  21:29 Greek *Trophimus, the Ephesian.*

immediately called out his soldiers and officers and ran down among the crowd. When the mob saw the commander and the troops coming, they stopped beating Paul. 33The commander arrested him and ordered him bound with two chains. Then he asked the crowd who he was and what he had done. 34Some shouted one thing and some another. He couldn't find out the truth in all the uproar and confusion, so he ordered Paul to be taken to the fortress. 35As they reached the stairs, the mob grew so violent the soldiers had to lift Paul to their shoulders to protect him. 36And the crowd followed behind shouting, "Kill him, kill him!"

### Paul Speaks to the Crowd

37As Paul was about to be taken inside, he said to the commander, "May I have a word with you?"

"Do you know Greek?" the commander asked, surprised. 38"Aren't you the Egyptian who led a rebellion some time ago and took four thousand members of the Assassins out into the desert?"

39"No," Paul replied, "I am a Jew from Tarsus in Cilicia, which is an important city. Please, let me talk to these people." 40The commander agreed, so Paul stood on the stairs and motioned to the people to be quiet. Soon a deep silence enveloped the crowd, and he addressed them in their own language, Aramaic.*

CHAPTER **22**

"Brothers and esteemed fathers," Paul said, "listen to me as I offer my defense." 2When they heard him speaking in their own language,* the silence was even greater. 3"I am a Jew, born in Tarsus, a city in Cilicia, and I was brought up and educated here in Jerusalem under Gamaliel. At his feet I learned to follow our Jewish laws and customs very carefully. I became very zealous to honor God in everything I did, just as all of you are today. 4And I persecuted the followers of the Way, hounding some to death, binding and delivering both men and women to prison. 5The high priest and the whole council of leaders can testify that this is so. For I received letters from them to our Jewish brothers in Damascus, authorizing me to bring the Christians from there to Jerusalem, in chains, to be punished.

6"As I was on the road, nearing Damascus, about noon a very bright light from heaven suddenly shone around me. 7I fell to the ground

and heard a voice saying to me, 'Saul, Saul, why are you persecuting me?'

8" 'Who are you, sir?' I asked. And he replied, 'I am Jesus of Nazareth, the one you are persecuting.' 9The people with me saw the light but didn't hear the voice.

10"I said, 'What shall I do, Lord?' And the Lord told me, 'Get up and go into Damascus, and there you will be told all that you are to do.'

11"I was blinded by the intense light and had to be led into Damascus by my companions. 12A man named Ananias lived there. He was a godly man in his devotion to the law, and he was well thought of by all the Jews of Damascus. 13He came to me and stood beside me and said, 'Brother Saul, receive your sight.' And that very hour I could see him!

14"Then he told me, 'The God of our ancestors has chosen you to know his will and to see the Righteous One and hear him speak. 15You are to take his message everywhere, telling the whole world what you have seen and heard. 16And now, why delay? Get up and be baptized, and have your sins washed away, calling on the name of the Lord.'

17"One day after I returned to Jerusalem, I was praying in the Temple, and I fell into a trance. 18I saw a vision of Jesus saying to me, 'Hurry! Leave Jerusalem, for the people here won't believe you when you give them your testimony about me.'

19" 'But Lord,' I argued, 'they certainly know that I imprisoned and beat those in every synagogue who believed on you. 20And when your witness Stephen was killed, I was standing there agreeing. I kept the coats they laid aside as they stoned him.'

21"But the Lord said to me, 'Leave Jerusalem, for I will send you far away to the Gentiles!' "

22The crowd listened until Paul came to that word; then with one voice they shouted, "Away with such a fellow! Kill him! He isn't fit to live!" 23They yelled, threw off their coats, and tossed handfuls of dust into the air.

### Paul Reveals His Roman Citizenship

24The commander brought Paul inside and ordered him lashed with whips to make him confess his crime. He wanted to find out why the crowd had become so furious. 25As they tied Paul down to lash him, Paul said to the officer standing there, "Is it legal for you to whip a Roman citizen who hasn't even been tried?"

21:40 Or *Hebrew.*  22:2 Greek *in Aramaic.*

26The officer went to the commander and asked, "What are you doing? This man is a Roman citizen!"

27So the commander went over and asked Paul, "Tell me, are you a Roman citizen?"

"Yes, I certainly am," Paul replied.

28"I am, too," the commander muttered, "and it cost me plenty!"

"But I am a citizen by birth!"

29The soldiers who were about to interrogate Paul quickly withdrew when they heard he was a Roman citizen, and the commander was frightened because he had ordered him bound and whipped.

### Paul before the High Council

30The next day the commander freed Paul from his chains and ordered the leading priests into session with the Jewish high council.* He had Paul brought in before them to try to find out what the trouble was all about.

## CHAPTER 23

Gazing intently at the high council,* Paul began: "Brothers, I have always lived before God in all good conscience!"

2Instantly Ananias the high priest commanded those close to Paul to slap him on the mouth. 3But Paul said to him, "God will slap you, you whitewashed wall! What kind of judge are you to break the law yourself by ordering me struck like that?"

4Those standing near Paul said to him, "Is that the way to talk to God's high priest?"

5"I'm sorry, brothers. I didn't realize he was the high priest," Paul replied, "for the Scriptures say, 'Do not speak evil of anyone who rules over you.'* "

6Paul realized that some members of the high council were Sadducees and some were Pharisees, so he shouted, "Brothers, I am a Pharisee, as were all my ancestors! And I am on trial because my hope is in the resurrection of the dead!"

7This divided the council—the Pharisees against the Sadducees—8for the Sadducees say there is no resurrection or angels or spirits, but the Pharisees believe in all of these. 9So a great clamor arose. Some of the teachers of religious law who were Pharisees jumped up to argue that Paul was all right. "We see nothing wrong with him," they shouted. "Perhaps a spirit or an angel spoke to him." 10The shouting grew louder and louder, and the men were tugging at Paul from both sides, pulling him this way and that. Finally, the commander, fearing they would tear him apart, ordered his soldiers to take him away from them and bring him back to the fortress.

11That night the Lord appeared to Paul and said, "Be encouraged, Paul. Just as you have told the people about me here in Jerusalem, you must preach the Good News in Rome."

### The Plan to Kill Paul

12The next morning a group of Jews got together and bound themselves with an oath to neither eat nor drink until they had killed Paul. 13There were more than forty of them. 14They went to the leading priests and other leaders and told them what they had done. "We have bound ourselves under oath to neither eat nor drink until we have killed Paul. 15You and the high council should tell the commander to bring Paul back to the council again," they requested. "Pretend you want to examine his case more fully. We will kill him on the way."

16But Paul's nephew heard of their plan and went to the fortress and told Paul. 17Paul called one of the officers and said, "Take this young man to the commander. He has something important to tell him."

18So the officer did, explaining, "Paul, the prisoner, called me over and asked me to bring this young man to you because he has something to tell you."

19The commander took him by the arm, led him aside, and asked, "What is it you want to tell me?"

20Paul's nephew told him, "Some Jews are going to ask you to bring Paul before the Jewish high council tomorrow, pretending they want to get some more information. 21But don't do it! There are more than forty men hiding along the way ready to jump him and kill him. They have vowed not to eat or drink until they kill him. They are ready, expecting you to agree to their request."

22"Don't let a soul know you told me this," the commander warned the young man as he sent him away.

### Paul Is Sent to Caesarea

23Then the commander called two of his officers and ordered, "Get two hundred soldiers ready to leave for Caesarea at nine o'clock tonight. Also take two hundred spearmen and

22:30 Greek Sanhedrin.   23:1 Greek Sanhedrin; also in 23:6, 15, 20, 28.   23:5 Exod 22:28.

seventy horsemen. 24Provide horses for Paul to ride, and get him safely to Governor Felix." 25Then he wrote this letter to the governor:

26"From Claudius Lysias, to his Excellency, Governor Felix. Greetings! 27This man was seized by some Jews, and they were about to kill him when I arrived with the troops. When I learned that he was a Roman citizen, I removed him to safety. 28Then I took him to their high council to try to find out what he had done. 29I soon discovered it was something regarding their religious law—certainly nothing worthy of imprisonment or death. 30But when I was informed of a plot to kill him, I immediately sent him on to you. I have told his accusers to bring their charges before you."

31So that night, as ordered, the soldiers took Paul as far as Antipatris. 32They returned to the fortress the next morning, while the horsemen took him on to Caesarea. 33When they arrived in Caesarea, they presented Paul and the letter to Governor Felix. 34He read it and then asked Paul what province he was from. "Cilicia," Paul answered.

35"I will hear your case myself when your accusers arrive," the governor told him. Then the governor ordered him kept in the prison at Herod's headquarters.

CHAPTER **24**
*Paul Appears before Felix*
Five days later Ananias, the high priest, arrived with some of the Jewish leaders and the lawyer* Tertullus, to press charges against Paul. 2When Paul was called in, Tertullus laid charges against Paul in the following address to the governor:

"Your Excellency, you have given peace to us Jews and have enacted reforms for us. 3And for all of this we are very grateful to you. 4But lest I bore you, kindly give me your attention for only a moment as I briefly outline our case against this man. 5For we have found him to be a troublemaker, a man who is constantly inciting the Jews throughout the world to riots and rebellions against the Roman government. He is a ringleader of the sect known as the Nazarenes. 6Moreover he was trying to defile the Temple when we arrested him.* 8You can find out the truth of our accusations by examining him your-

self." 9Then the other Jews chimed in, declaring that everything Tertullus said was true.

10Now it was Paul's turn. The governor motioned for him to rise and speak. Paul said, "I know, sir, that you have been a judge of Jewish affairs for many years, and this gives me confidence as I make my defense. 11You can quickly discover that it was no more than twelve days ago that I arrived in Jerusalem to worship at the Temple. 12I didn't argue with anyone in the Temple, nor did I incite a riot in any synagogue or on the streets of the city. 13These men certainly cannot prove the things they accuse me of doing.

14"But I admit that I follow the Way, which they call a sect. I worship the God of our ancestors, and I firmly believe the Jewish law and everything written in the books of prophecy. 15I have hope in God, just as these men do, that he will raise both the righteous and the ungodly. 16Because of this, I always try to maintain a clear conscience before God and everyone else.

17"After several years away, I returned to Jerusalem with money to aid my people and to offer sacrifices to God. 18My accusers saw me in the Temple as I was completing a purification ritual. There was no crowd around me and no rioting. 19But some Jews from the province of Asia were there—and they ought to be here to bring charges if they have anything against me! 20Ask these men here what wrongdoing the Jewish high council* found in me, 21except for one thing I said when I shouted out, 'I am on trial before you today because I believe in the resurrection of the dead!'"

22Felix, who was quite familiar with the Way, adjourned the hearing and said, "Wait until Lysias, the garrison commander, arrives. Then I will decide the case." 23He ordered an officer to keep Paul in custody but to give him some freedom and allow his friends to visit him and take care of his needs.

24A few days later Felix came with his wife, Drusilla, who was Jewish. Sending for Paul, they listened as he told them about faith in Christ Jesus. 25As he reasoned with them about righteousness and self-control and the judgment to come, Felix was terrified. "Go away for now," he replied. "When it is more convenient, I'll call for you again." 26He also hoped that Paul would bribe him, so he sent for him quite often and talked with him.

24:1 Greek *some elders and an orator.* 24:6 Some manuscripts add *We would have judged him by our law,* 7*but Lysias, the commander of the garrison, came and took him violently away from us,* 8*commanding his accusers to come before you.* 24:20 Greek *Sanhedrin.*

27Two years went by in this way; then Felix was succeeded by Porcius Festus. And because Felix wanted to gain favor with the Jewish leaders, he left Paul in prison.

## CHAPTER 25
### Paul Appears before Festus

Three days after Festus arrived in Caesarea to take over his new responsibilities, he left for Jerusalem, 2where the leading priests and other Jewish leaders met with him and made their accusations against Paul. 3They asked Festus as a favor to transfer Paul to Jerusalem. (Their plan was to waylay and kill him.) 4But Festus replied that Paul was at Caesarea and he himself would be returning there soon. 5So he said, "Those of you in authority can return with me. If Paul has done anything wrong, you can make your accusations."

6Eight or ten days later he returned to Caesarea, and on the following day Paul's trial began. 7On Paul's arrival in court, the Jewish leaders from Jerusalem gathered around and made many serious accusations they couldn't prove. 8Paul denied the charges. "I am not guilty," he said. "I have committed no crime against the Jewish laws or the Temple or the Roman government."

9Then Festus, wanting to please the Jews, asked him, "Are you willing to go to Jerusalem and stand trial before me there?"

10But Paul replied, "No! This is the official Roman court, so I ought to be tried right here. You know very well I am not guilty. 11If I have done something worthy of death, I don't refuse to die. But if I am innocent, neither you nor anyone else has a right to turn me over to these men to kill me. I appeal to Caesar!"

12Festus conferred with his advisers and then replied, "Very well! You have appealed to Caesar, and to Caesar you shall go!"

13A few days later King Agrippa arrived with his sister, Bernice,* to pay their respects to Festus. 14During their stay of several days, Festus discussed Paul's case with the king. "There is a prisoner here," he told him, "whose case was left for me by Felix. 15When I was in Jerusalem, the leading priests and other Jewish leaders pressed charges against him and asked me to sentence him. 16Of course, I quickly pointed out to them that Roman law does not convict people without a trial. They are given an opportunity to defend themselves face to face with their accusers.

17"When they came here for the trial, I called the case the very next day and ordered Paul brought in. 18But the accusations made against him weren't at all what I expected. 19It was something about their religion and about someone called Jesus who died, but whom Paul insists is alive. 20I was perplexed as to how to conduct an investigation of this kind, and I asked him whether he would be willing to stand trial on these charges in Jerusalem. 21But Paul appealed to the emperor. So I ordered him back to jail until I could arrange to send him to Caesar."

22"I'd like to hear the man myself," Agrippa said.

And Festus replied, "You shall—tomorrow!"

### Paul Speaks to Agrippa

23So the next day Agrippa and Bernice arrived at the auditorium with great pomp, accompanied by military officers and prominent men of the city. Festus ordered that Paul be brought in. 24Then Festus said, "King Agrippa and all present, this is the man whose death is demanded both by the local Jews and by those in Jerusalem. 25But in my opinion he has done nothing worthy of death. However, he appealed his case to the emperor, and I decided to send him. 26But what shall I write the emperor? For there is no real charge against him. So I have brought him before all of you, and especially you, King Agrippa, so that after we examine him, I might have something to write. 27For it doesn't seem reasonable to send a prisoner to the emperor without specifying the charges against him!"

## CHAPTER 26

Then Agrippa said to Paul, "You may speak in your defense."

So Paul, with a gesture of his hand, started his defense: 2"I am fortunate, King Agrippa, that you are the one hearing my defense against all these accusations made by the Jewish leaders, 3for I know you are an expert on Jewish customs and controversies. Now please listen to me patiently!

4"As the Jewish leaders are well aware, I was given a thorough Jewish training from my earliest childhood among my own people and in Jerusalem. 5If they would admit it, they know that I have been a member of the Pharisees, the strictest sect of our religion. 6Now I am on trial because I am looking forward to the fulfillment

25:13 Greek *Agrippa the king and Bernice arrived.*

of God's promise made to our ancestors. 7In fact, that is why the twelve tribes of Israel worship God night and day, and they share the same hope I have. Yet, O king, they say it is wrong for me to have this hope! 8Why does it seem incredible to any of you that God can raise the dead?

9"I used to believe that I ought to do everything I could to oppose the followers of Jesus of Nazareth.* 10Authorized by the leading priests, I caused many of the believers in Jerusalem to be sent to prison. And I cast my vote against them when they were condemned to death. 11Many times I had them whipped in the synagogues to try to get them to curse Christ. I was so violently opposed to them that I even hounded them in distant cities of foreign lands.

12"One day I was on such a mission to Damascus, armed with the authority and commission of the leading priests. 13About noon, Your Majesty, a light from heaven brighter than the sun shone down on me and my companions. 14We all fell down, and I heard a voice saying to me in Aramaic,* 'Saul, Saul, why are you persecuting me? It is hard for you to fight against my will.*'

15" 'Who are you, sir?' I asked.

"And the Lord replied, 'I am Jesus, the one you are persecuting. 16Now stand up! For I have appeared to you to appoint you as my servant and my witness. You are to tell the world about this experience and about other times I will appear to you. 17And I will protect you from both your own people and the Gentiles. Yes, I am going to send you to the Gentiles, 18to open their eyes so they may turn from darkness to light, and from the power of Satan to God. Then they will receive forgiveness for their sins and be given a place among God's people, who are set apart by faith in me.'

19"And so, O King Agrippa, I was not disobedient to that vision from heaven. 20I preached first to those in Damascus, then in Jerusalem and throughout all Judea, and also to the Gentiles, that all must turn from their sins and turn to God—and prove they have changed by the good things they do. 21Some Jews arrested me in the Temple for preaching this, and they tried to kill me. 22But God protected me so that I am still alive today to tell these facts to everyone, from the least to the greatest. I teach nothing except what the prophets and Moses said would happen—23that the Messiah would suffer and be

the first to rise from the dead as a light to Jews and Gentiles alike."

24Suddenly, Festus shouted, "Paul, you are insane. Too much study has made you crazy!"

25But Paul replied, "I am not insane, Most Excellent Festus. I am speaking the sober truth. 26And King Agrippa knows about these things. I speak frankly, for I am sure these events are all familiar to him, for they were not done in a corner! 27King Agrippa, do you believe the prophets? I know you do—"

28Agrippa interrupted him. "Do you think you can make me a Christian so quickly?"*

29Paul replied, "Whether quickly or not, I pray to God that both you and everyone here in this audience might become the same as I am, except for these chains."

30Then the king, the governor, Bernice, and all the others stood and left. 31As they talked it over they agreed, "This man hasn't done anything worthy of death or imprisonment." 32And Agrippa said to Festus, "He could be set free if he hadn't appealed to Caesar!"

## CHAPTER 27
*Paul Sails for Rome*

When the time came, we set sail for Italy. Paul and several other prisoners were placed in the custody of an army officer named Julius, a captain of the Imperial Regiment. 2And Aristarchus, a Macedonian from Thessalonica, was also with us. We left on a boat whose home port was Adramyttium; it was scheduled to make several stops at ports along the coast of the province of Asia.

3The next day when we docked at Sidon, Julius was very kind to Paul and let him go ashore to visit with friends so they could provide for his needs. 4Putting out to sea from there, we encountered headwinds that made it difficult to keep the ship on course, so we sailed north of Cyprus between the island and the mainland. 5We passed along the coast of the provinces of Cilicia and Pamphylia, landing at Myra, in the province of Lycia. 6There the officer found an Egyptian ship from Alexandria that was bound for Italy, and he put us on board.

7We had several days of rough sailing, and after great difficulty we finally neared Cnidus. But the wind was against us, so we sailed down to the leeward side of Crete, past the cape of Salmone. 8We struggled along the coast with great difficulty

26:9 Greek *oppose the name of Jesus the Nazarene.* 26:14a Or *Hebrew.* 26:14b Greek *It is hard for you to kick against the oxgoads.* 26:28 Or "A little more, and your arguments would make me a Christian."

and finally arrived at Fair Havens, near the city of Lasea. 9We had lost a lot of time. The weather was becoming dangerous for long voyages by then because it was so late in the fall,* and Paul spoke to the ship's officers about it.

10"Sirs," he said, "I believe there is trouble ahead if we go on—shipwreck, loss of cargo, injuries, and danger to our lives." 11But the officer in charge of the prisoners listened more to the ship's captain and the owner than to Paul. 12And since Fair Havens was an exposed harbor—a poor place to spend the winter—most of the crew wanted to go to Phoenix, farther up the coast of Crete, and spend the winter there. Phoenix was a good harbor with only a southwest and northwest exposure.

### The Storm at Sea

13When a light wind began blowing from the south, the sailors thought they could make it. So they pulled up anchor and sailed along close to shore. 14But the weather changed abruptly, and a wind of typhoon strength (a "northeaster," they called it) caught the ship and blew it out to sea. 15They couldn't turn the ship into the wind, so they gave up and let it run before the gale.

16We sailed behind a small island named Cauda,* where with great difficulty we hoisted aboard the lifeboat that was being towed behind us. 17Then we banded the ship with ropes to strengthen the hull. The sailors were afraid of being driven across to the sandbars of Syrtis off the African coast, so they lowered the sea anchor and were thus driven before the wind.

18The next day, as gale-force winds continued to batter the ship, the crew began throwing the cargo overboard. 19The following day they even threw out the ship's equipment and anything else they could lay their hands on. 20The terrible storm raged unabated for many days, blotting out the sun and the stars, until at last all hope was gone.

21No one had eaten for a long time. Finally, Paul called the crew together and said, "Men, you should have listened to me in the first place and not left Fair Havens. You would have avoided all this injury and loss. 22But take courage! None of you will lose your lives, even though the ship will go down. 23For last night an angel of the God to whom I belong and whom I serve stood beside me, 24and he said, 'Don't be afraid, Paul, for you

27:9 Greek because the fast was now already gone by. This fast happened on the Day of Atonement (Yom Kippur), which occurred in late September or early October. 27:16 Some manuscripts read Clauda.

will surely stand trial before Caesar! What's more, God in his goodness has granted safety to everyone sailing with you.' 25So take courage! For I believe God. It will be just as he said. 26But we will be shipwrecked on an island."

### The Shipwreck

27About midnight on the fourteenth night of the storm, as we were being driven across the Sea of Adria,* the sailors sensed land was near. 28They took soundings and found the water was only 120 feet deep. A little later they sounded again and found only 90 feet.* 29At this rate they were

27:27 The Sea of Adria is in the central Mediterranean; it is not to be confused with the Adriatic Sea. 27:28 Greek 20 fathoms . . . 15 fathoms [37 meters . . . 27 meters].

## Share Your Own Story
Read ACTS 26:1-23

Another useful tool in our "evangelistic toolbox" is the story, or testimony, of how we came to personally know Jesus Christ. Paul used this method effectively when he appeared before King Agrippa. As was often his style, he began his presentation of the gospel by explaining how he had personally come into a relationship with Christ. Then he segued into the proclamation of the gospel message (verses 19-23).

Every believer has a testimony. Some may be more dramatic than others. Such was the case with Paul, formerly the notorious Saul of Tarsus, an aggressive persecutor of the church. Regardless of how incredible your testimony may seem, your personal salvation story will help you find common ground with a nonbeliever. You can tell him or her of your former life and attitude before coming to Christ, then explain the changes that came afterward. When a nonbeliever sees that you can relate to his or her own life, he or she may be more open to what you have to say.

Why don't you take a moment to think about the changes that have taken place in your life now that you are a Christian? You may even want to write down your testimony so that you will be ready to share it at the next opportunity.

afraid we would soon be driven against the rocks along the shore, so they threw out four anchors from the stern and prayed for daylight. 30Then the sailors tried to abandon the ship; they lowered the lifeboat as though they were going to put out anchors from the prow. 31But Paul said to the commanding officer and the soldiers, "You will all die unless the sailors stay aboard." 32So the soldiers cut the ropes and let the boat fall off.

33As the darkness gave way to the early morning light, Paul begged everyone to eat. "You haven't touched food for two weeks," he said. 34"Please eat something now for your own good. For not a hair of your heads will perish." 35Then he took some bread, gave thanks to God before them all, and broke off a piece and ate it. 36Then everyone was encouraged, 37and all 276 of us began eating—for that is the number we had aboard. 38After eating, the crew lightened the ship further by throwing the cargo of wheat overboard.

39When morning dawned, they didn't recognize the coastline, but they saw a bay with a beach and wondered if they could get between the rocks and get the ship safely to shore. 40So they cut off the anchors and left them in the sea. Then they lowered the rudders, raised the foresail, and headed toward shore. 41But the ship hit a shoal and ran aground. The bow of the ship stuck fast, while the stern was repeatedly smashed by the force of the waves and began to break apart.

42The soldiers wanted to kill the prisoners to make sure they didn't swim ashore and escape. 43But the commanding officer wanted to spare Paul, so he didn't let them carry out their plan. Then he ordered all who could swim to jump overboard first and make for land, 44and he told the others to try for it on planks and debris from the broken ship. So everyone escaped safely ashore!

CHAPTER **28**
*Paul on the Island of Malta*
Once we were safe on shore, we learned that we were on the island of Malta. 2The people of the island were very kind to us. It was cold and rainy, so they built a fire on the shore to welcome us and warm us.

3As Paul gathered an armful of sticks and was laying them on the fire, a poisonous snake, driven out by the heat, fastened itself onto his hand. 4The people of the island saw it hanging there and said to each other, "A murderer, no doubt! Though he escaped the sea, justice will not permit him to live." 5But Paul shook off the snake into the fire and was unharmed. 6The people waited for him to swell up or suddenly drop dead. But when they had waited a long time and saw no harm come to him, they changed their minds and decided he was a god.

7Near the shore where we landed was an estate belonging to Publius, the chief official of the island. He welcomed us courteously and fed us for three days. 8As it happened, Publius's father was ill with fever and dysentery. Paul went in and prayed for him, and laying his hands on him, he healed him. 9Then all the other sick people on the island came and were cured. 10As a result we were showered with honors, and when the time came to sail, people put on board all sorts of things we would need for the trip.

*Paul Arrives at Rome*
11It was three months after the shipwreck that we set sail on another ship that had wintered at the island—an Alexandrian ship with the twin gods* as its figurehead. 12Our first stop was Syracuse,* where we stayed three days. 13From there we sailed across to Rhegium.* A day later a south wind began blowing, so the following day we sailed up the coast to Puteoli. 14There we found some believers,* who invited us to stay with them seven days. And so we came to Rome.

15The brothers and sisters* in Rome had heard we were coming, and they came to meet us at the Forum* on the Appian Way. Others joined us at The Three Taverns.* When Paul saw them, he thanked God and took courage.

16When we arrived in Rome, Paul was permitted to have his own private lodging, though he was guarded by a soldier.

*Paul Preaches at Rome under Guard*
17Three days after Paul's arrival, he called together the local Jewish leaders. He said to them, "Brothers, I was arrested in Jerusalem and handed over to the Roman government, even though I had done nothing against our people or the customs of our ancestors. 18The Romans tried me and wanted to release me, for they found no cause for the death sentence. 19But

28:11 The *twin gods* were the Roman gods Castor and Pollux. 28:12 *Syracuse* was on the island of Sicily. 28:13 *Rhegium* was on the southern tip of Italy. 28:14 Greek *brothers*. 28:15a Greek *brothers*. 28:15b *The Forum* was about 43 miles (70 kilometers) from Rome. 28:15c *The Three Taverns* was about 35 miles (57 kilometers) from Rome.

when the Jewish leaders protested the decision, I felt it necessary to appeal to Caesar, even though I had no desire to press charges against my own people. 20I asked you to come here today so we could get acquainted and so I could tell you that I am bound with this chain because I believe that the hope of Israel—the Messiah— has already come."

21They replied, "We have heard nothing against you. We have had no letters from Judea or reports from anyone who has arrived here. 22But we want to hear what you believe, for the only thing we know about these Christians* is that they are denounced everywhere."

23So a time was set, and on that day a large number of people came to Paul's house. He told them about the Kingdom of God and taught them about Jesus from the Scriptures—from the five books of Moses and the books of the prophets. He began lecturing in the morning and went on into the evening. 24Some believed and some didn't. 25But after they had argued back and forth among themselves, they left with this final word from Paul: "The Holy Spirit was right

when he said to our ancestors through Isaiah the prophet,

26 'Go and say to my people,
 You will hear my words,
  but you will not understand;
 you will see what I do,
  but you will not perceive its meaning.
27 For the hearts of these people are hardened,
  and their ears cannot hear,
  and they have closed their eyes—
 so their eyes cannot see,
  and their ears cannot hear,
  and their hearts cannot understand,
 and they cannot turn to me
  and let me heal them.'*

28So I want you to realize that this salvation from God is also available to the Gentiles, and they will accept it."*

30For the next two years, Paul lived in his own rented house.* He welcomed all who visited him, 31proclaiming the Kingdom of God with all boldness and teaching about the Lord Jesus Christ. And no one tried to stop him.

28:22 Greek *this sect.* 28:26-27 Isa 6:9-10. 28:28 Some manuscripts add verse 29, *And when he had said these words, the Jews departed, greatly disagreeing with each other.* 28:30 Or *at his own expense.*

# Romans

*Greetings from Paul*

This letter is from Paul, Jesus Christ's slave, chosen by God to be an apostle and sent out to preach his Good News. 2This Good News was promised long ago by God through his prophets in the holy Scriptures. 3It is the Good News about his Son, Jesus, who came as a man, born into King David's royal family line. 4And Jesus Christ our Lord was shown to be the Son of God when God powerfully raised him from the dead by means of the Holy Spirit.* 5Through Christ, God has given us the privilege and authority to tell Gentiles everywhere what God has done for them, so that they will believe and obey him, bringing glory to his name.

6You are among those who have been called to belong to Jesus Christ, 7dear friends in Rome. God loves you dearly, and he has called you to be his very own people.

May grace and peace be yours from God our Father and the Lord Jesus Christ.

## God's Good News

8Let me say first of all that your faith in God is becoming known throughout the world. How I thank God through Jesus Christ for each one of you. 9God knows how often I pray for you. Day and night I bring you and your needs in prayer to God, whom I serve with all my heart* by telling others the Good News about his Son.

10One of the things I always pray for is the opportunity, God willing, to come at last to see you. 11For I long to visit you so I can share a spiritual blessing with you that will help you grow strong in the Lord. 12I'm eager to encourage you in your faith, but I also want to be encouraged by yours. In this way, each of us will be a blessing to the other.

13I want you to know, dear brothers and sisters,* that I planned many times to visit you, but I was prevented until now. I want to work among you and see good results, just as I have done among other Gentiles. 14For I have a great sense of obligation to people in our culture and to people in other cultures,* to the educated and uneducated alike. 15So I am eager to come to you in Rome, too, to preach God's Good News.

16For I am not ashamed of this Good News about Christ. It is the power of God at work, saving everyone who believes—Jews first and also Gentiles. 17This Good News tells us how God makes us right in his sight. This is accomplished from start to finish by faith. As the Scriptures say, "It is through faith that a righteous person has life."*

## God's Anger at Sin

18But God shows his anger from heaven against all sinful, wicked people who push the truth away from themselves.* 19For the truth about God is known to them instinctively.* God has put this knowledge in their hearts. 20From the time the world was created, people have seen the earth and sky and all that God made. They can clearly see his invisible qualities—his eternal power and divine nature. So they have no excuse whatsoever for not knowing God.

21Yes, they knew God, but they wouldn't worship him as God or even give him thanks. And they began to think up foolish ideas of what God was like. The result was that their minds became dark and confused. 22Claiming to be wise, they became utter fools instead. 23And instead of worshiping the glorious, ever-living

1:4 Or *the Spirit of holiness.* 1:9 Or *in my spirit.* 1:13 Greek *brothers.* 1:14 Greek *to Greeks and to barbarians.* 1:17 Hab 2:4. 1:18 Or *who prevent the truth from being known.* 1:19 Greek *is manifest in them.*

God, they worshiped idols made to look like mere people, or birds and animals and snakes.

24So God let them go ahead and do whatever shameful things their hearts desired. As a result, they did vile and degrading things with each other's bodies. 25Instead of believing what they knew was the truth about God, they deliberately chose to believe lies. So they worshiped the things God made but not the Creator himself, who is to be praised forever. Amen.

26That is why God abandoned them to their shameful desires. Even the women turned against the natural way to have sex and instead indulged in sex with each other. 27And the men, instead of having normal sexual relationships with women, burned with lust for each other. Men did shameful things with other men and, as a result, suffered within themselves the penalty they so richly deserved.

28When they refused to acknowledge God, he abandoned them to their evil minds and let them do things that should never be done. 29Their lives became full of every kind of wickedness, sin, greed, hate, envy, murder, fighting, deception, malicious behavior, and gossip. 30They are backstabbers, haters of God, insolent, proud, and boastful. They are forever inventing new ways of sinning and are disobedient to their parents. 31They refuse to understand, break their promises, and are heartless and unforgiving. 32They are fully aware of God's death penalty for those who do these things, yet they go right ahead and do them anyway. And, worse yet, they encourage others to do them, too.

## CHAPTER 2
### God's Judgment of Sin

You may be saying, "What terrible people you have been talking about!" But you are just as bad, and you have no excuse! When you say they are wicked and should be punished, you are condemning yourself, for you do these very same things. 2And we know that God, in his justice, will punish anyone who does such things. 3Do you think that God will judge and condemn others for doing them and not judge you when you do them, too? 4Don't you realize how kind, tolerant, and patient God is with you? Or don't you care? Can't you see how kind he has been in giving you time to turn from your sin?

5But no, you won't listen. So you are storing up terrible punishment for yourself because of

2:24 Isa 52:5.

your stubbornness in refusing to turn from your sin. For there is going to come a day of judgment when God, the just judge of all the world, 6will judge all people according to what they have done. 7He will give eternal life to those who persist in doing what is good, seeking after the glory and honor and immortality that God offers. 8But he will pour out his anger and wrath on those who live for themselves, who refuse to obey the truth and practice evil deeds. 9There will be trouble and calamity for everyone who keeps on sinning—for the Jew first and also for the Gentile. 10But there will be glory and honor and peace from God for all who do good—for the Jew first and also for the Gentile. 11For God does not show favoritism.

12God will punish the Gentiles when they sin, even though they never had God's written law. And he will punish the Jews when they sin, for they do have the law. 13For it is not merely knowing the law that brings God's approval. Those who obey the law will be declared right in God's sight. 14Even when Gentiles, who do not have God's written law, instinctively follow what the law says, they show that in their hearts they know right from wrong. 15They demonstrate that God's law is written within them, for their own consciences either accuse them or tell them they are doing what is right. 16The day will surely come when God, by Jesus Christ, will judge everyone's secret life. This is my message.

### The Jews and the Law

17If you are a Jew, you are relying on God's law for your special relationship with him. You boast that all is well between yourself and God. 18Yes, you know what he wants; you know right from wrong because you have been taught his law. 19You are convinced that you are a guide for the blind and a beacon light for people who are lost in darkness without God. 20You think you can instruct the ignorant and teach children the ways of God. For you are certain that in God's law you have complete knowledge and truth.

21Well then, if you teach others, why don't you teach yourself? You tell others not to steal, but do you steal? 22You say it is wrong to commit adultery, but do you do it? You condemn idolatry, but do you steal from pagan temples? 23You are so proud of knowing the law, but you dishonor God by breaking it. 24No wonder the Scriptures say, "The world blasphemes the name of God because of you."*

# What Happens to Those Who Have Never Heard the Gospel?
Read ROMANS 1:18-20

Sometimes the person who asks this question is not so much concerned about those who have never heard the gospel. Rather, this person may be more concerned about trying to put up a "smoke screen" to keep you—the Christian—from showing his or her need for God. We might remind that person that God is loving and compassionate, and that he will deal fairly and justly with those who have never heard the gospel. But the person who asks you this question needs to recognize that knowledge brings responsibility. Those who know the truth of the gospel will be held accountable.

As we know from the Bible, God will judge us according to what we know of him (see Luke 12:48, p. 88). We will not be held accountable for what we do not know. Still, that does not excuse us from all responsibility. Otherwise we might say, "Ignorance is bliss." But this is not to say that the person who has not heard of Jesus will never know of him.

We, as humans, no matter where we live on God's earth, were born with a soul, an emptiness, a sense that life should have meaning and purpose. In spite of that spiritual longing, we have disregarded God and his Word. But if we are truly seeking God, he will reveal himself to us. We find proof of this in Acts 10:1-48 (pp. 150–151). There, a man named Cornelius—a religious man who constantly prayed to God—asked the Lord to reveal himself to him. Although Cornelius may have heard of Jesus Christ, he did not know God's plan for salvation. But that did not stop God from answering his prayer by sending the apostle Peter to preach the gospel to him. When Cornelius heard that wonderful message, he believed!

The Bible tells us that God is unchanging (see James 1:17, p. 299). He is the same yesterday, today, and tomorrow. If he heard Cornelius's prayer, he will also hear the prayers of those who do not know him but desire to.

BIG QUESTIONS

---

25The Jewish ceremony of circumcision is worth something only if you obey God's law. But if you don't obey God's law, you are no better off than an uncircumcised Gentile. 26And if the Gentiles obey God's law, won't God give them all the rights and honors of being his own people? 27In fact, uncircumcised Gentiles who keep God's law will be much better off than you Jews who are circumcised and know so much about God's law but don't obey it.

28For you are not a true Jew just because you were born of Jewish parents or because you have gone through the Jewish ceremony of circumcision. 29No, a true Jew is one whose heart is right with God. And true circumcision is not a cutting of the body but a change of heart produced by God's Spirit. Whoever has that kind of change seeks praise from God, not from people.

CHAPTER 3
*God Remains Faithful*
Then what's the advantage of being a Jew? Is

there any value in the Jewish ceremony of circumcision? 2Yes, being a Jew has many advantages. First of all, the Jews were entrusted with the whole revelation of God.*

3True, some of them were unfaithful; but just because they broke their promises, does that mean God will break his promises? 4Of course not! Though everyone else in the world is a liar, God is true. As the Scriptures say, "He will be proved right in what he says, and he will win his case in court."*

5"But," some say, "our sins serve a good purpose, for people will see God's goodness when he declares us sinners to be innocent. Isn't it unfair, then, for God to punish us?" (That is actually the way some people talk.) 6Of course not! If God is not just, how is he qualified to judge the world? 7"But," some might still argue, "how can God judge and condemn me as a sinner if my dishonesty highlights his truthfulness and brings him more glory?" 8If you follow that kind of thinking, however, you might as

3:2-Greek *the oracles of God.*   3:4 Ps 51:4.

well say that the more we sin the better it is!
Those who say such things deserve to be condemned, yet some slander me by saying this is
what I preach!

*All People Are Sinners*
⁹Well then, are we Jews better than others?* No,
not at all, for we have already shown that all
people, whether Jews or Gentiles, are under the
power of sin. ¹⁰As the Scriptures say,

"No one is good—
    not even one.
¹¹ No one has real understanding;
    no one is seeking God.
¹² All have turned away from God;
    all have gone wrong.
No one does good,
    not even one."*
¹³ "Their talk is foul, like the stench from an
        open grave.
    Their speech is filled with lies."
"The poison of a deadly snake drips from
        their lips."*
¹⁴    "Their mouths are full of cursing and
        bitterness."*
¹⁵ "They are quick to commit murder.
¹⁶    Wherever they go, destruction and
        misery follow them.
¹⁷ They do not know what true peace is."*
¹⁸    "They have no fear of God to restrain
        them."*

¹⁹Obviously, the law applies to those to
whom it was given, for its purpose is to keep
people from having excuses and to bring the
entire world into judgment before God. ²⁰For no
one can ever be made right in God's sight by
doing what his law commands. For the more we
know God's law, the clearer it becomes that we
aren't obeying it.

*Christ Took Our Punishment*
²¹But now God has shown us a different way of
being right in his sight—not by obeying the law
but by the way promised in the Scriptures long
ago. ²²We are made right in God's sight when we
trust in Jesus Christ to take away our sins. And
we all can be saved in this same way, no matter
who we are or what we have done.
²³For all have sinned; all fall short of God's
glorious standard. ²⁴Yet now God in his gracious
kindness declares us not guilty. He has done this
through Christ Jesus, who has freed us by taking

away our sins. ²⁵For God sent Jesus to take the
punishment for our sins and to satisfy God's
anger against us. We are made right with God
when we believe that Jesus shed his blood, sacrificing his life for us. God was being entirely fair
and just when he did not punish those who
sinned in former times. ²⁶And he is entirely fair
and just in this present time when he declares
sinners to be right in his sight because they
believe in Jesus.
²⁷Can we boast, then, that we have done anything to be accepted by God? No, because our
acquittal is not based on our good deeds. It is
based on our faith. ²⁸So we are made right with
God through faith and not by obeying the law.
²⁹After all, God is not the God of the Jews
only, is he? Isn't he also the God of the Gentiles?
Of course he is. ³⁰There is only one God, and
there is only one way of being accepted by him.
He makes people right with himself only by
faith, whether they are Jews or Gentiles. ³¹Well
then, if we emphasize faith, does this mean that
we can forget about the law? Of course not! In
fact, only when we have faith do we truly fulfill
the law.

CHAPTER **4**
*The Faith of Abraham*
Abraham was, humanly speaking, the founder
of our Jewish nation. What were his experiences concerning this question of being saved
by faith? ²Was it because of his good deeds
that God accepted him? If so, he would have
had something to boast about. But from God's
point of view Abraham had no basis at all for
pride. ³For the Scriptures tell us, "Abraham
believed God, so God declared him to be righteous."*
⁴When people work, their wages are not a
gift. Workers earn what they receive. ⁵But people
are declared righteous because of their faith, not
because of their work.
⁶King David spoke of this, describing the
happiness of an undeserving sinner who is declared to be righteous:

⁷ "Oh, what joy for those whose
        disobedience is forgiven,
    whose sins are put out of sight.
⁸ Yes, what joy for those
    whose sin is no longer counted against
        them by the Lord."*

3:9 Greek *Are we better?*  3:10-12 Pss 14:1-3; 53:1-3.  3:13 Pss 5:9; 140:3.  3:14 Ps 10:7.  3:15-17 Isa 59:7-8.  3:18 Ps 36:1.  4:3 Gen
15:6.  4:7-8 Ps 32:1-2.

## If God Is So Good, Why Do Bad Things Happen to His People? Read ROMANS 5:1-5

Sickness, war, accidents, natural disasters, tragedies—they come to the just and the unjust, the Christian and the non-Christian, the moral and the immoral. Yet, if God is so good and all-powerful, why doesn't he just wipe out evil things in this world? This question often arises after any tragedy, but especially when it affects people who you would think should be "immune" to such things.

In addressing this question, it is important to remember that God originally created the world perfect. But he also gave man the freedom to obey or disobey. When Adam sinned, death and suffering became an inevitable part of life (verse 12). Yet, as the Christian thinker C. S. Lewis observed, it is idle for us to speculate about the *origin* of evil. The problem we all face is the *fact* of evil. The only *solution* to the fact of evil is God's solution, Jesus Christ [Paul Little, *How to Give Away Your Faith* (Downers Grove, Ill.: InterVarsity Press, 1966), p. 72].

How is Jesus Christ the solution to the fact of evil? The moment you surrendered your life to Jesus Christ, you entered into the master plan that God has for you. Though it is true that you may not know what the future holds, you know who holds the future. And he has promised that all things work together for good to those that love God (see Romans 8:28, p. 185). Not just the good things, but all things.

That is easy to say when things are going smoothly. But when something unexpected comes into the picture, we may wonder if God is paying attention. That is when we need to realize that God is painting on a large canvas. He is looking at the big picture. We only see what is in front of us at the given moment.

God will allow many events to come into our life—good things, bad things, things that make sense, things that make no sense at all. But every one of these incidents in our lives serves as a part of his plan for us. Tragedy in itself is not good. But God can take tragedy and hardship and use them for his glory. As God's children, we know that everything that happens to us first goes through his screen of protection. And he will never give us more than we can handle (see 1 Corinthians 10:13, p. 208). For that reason we can follow the advice in verse 3 and rejoice. We have the assurance that God is working in our lives to strengthen and develop our character. More important, he will never leave our side (see Hebrews 13:5, p. 298).

**BIG QUESTIONS?**

9Now then, is this blessing only for the Jews, or is it for Gentiles, too? Well, what about Abraham? We have been saying he was declared righteous by God because of his faith. 10But how did his faith help him? Was he declared righteous only after he had been circumcised, or was it before he was circumcised? The answer is that God accepted him first, and then he was circumcised later!

11The circumcision ceremony was a sign that Abraham already had faith and that God had already accepted him and declared him to be righteous—even before he was circumcised. So Abraham is the spiritual father of those who have faith but have not been circumcised. They are made right with God by faith. 12And Abraham is also the spiritual father of those who have been circumcised, but only if they have the same kind of faith Abraham had before he was circumcised.

13It is clear, then, that God's promise to give the whole earth to Abraham and his descendants was not based on obedience to God's law, but on the new relationship with God that comes by faith. 14So if you claim that God's promise is for those who obey God's law and think they are "good enough" in God's sight, then you are saying that faith is useless. And in that case, the promise is also meaningless. 15But the law brings punishment on those who try to obey it. (The only way to avoid breaking the law is to have no law to break!)

16So that's why faith is the key! God's promise is given to us as a free gift. And we are certain to receive it, whether or not we follow Jewish customs, if we have faith like Abraham's. For Abraham is the father of all who believe. ¹⁷That is what the Scriptures mean when God told him, "I have made you the father of many nations."* This happened because Abraham believed in the God who brings the dead back to life and who brings into existence what didn't exist before.

¹⁸When God promised Abraham that he would become the father of many nations, Abraham believed him. God had also said, "Your descendants will be as numerous as the stars,"* even though such a promise seemed utterly impossible! ¹⁹And Abraham's faith did not weaken, even though he knew that he was too old to be a father at the age of one hundred and that Sarah, his wife, had never been able to have children.

²⁰Abraham never wavered in believing God's promise. In fact, his faith grew stronger, and in this he brought glory to God. ²¹He was absolutely convinced that God was able to do anything he promised. ²²And because of Abraham's faith, God declared him to be righteous.

²³Now this wonderful truth—that God declared him to be righteous—wasn't just for Abraham's benefit. ²⁴It was for us, too, assuring us that God will also declare us to be righteous if we believe in God, who brought Jesus our Lord back from the dead. ²⁵He was handed over to die because of our sins, and he was raised from the dead to make us right with God.

CHAPTER **5**
*Faith Brings Joy*
Therefore, since we have been made right in God's sight by faith, we have peace with God because of what Jesus Christ our Lord has done for us. ²Because of our faith, Christ has brought us into this place of highest privilege where we now stand, and we confidently and joyfully look forward to sharing God's glory.

³We can rejoice, too, when we run into problems and trials, for we know that they are good for us—they help us learn to endure. ⁴And endurance develops strength of character in us, and character strengthens our confident expectation of salvation. ⁵And this expectation will not disappoint us. For we know how dearly God loves us, because he has given us the Holy Spirit to fill our hearts with his love.

⁶When we were utterly helpless, Christ came at just the right time and died for us sinners. ⁷Now, no one is likely to die for a good person,

though someone might be willing to die for a person who is especially good. ⁸But God showed his great love for us by sending Christ to die for us while we were still sinners. ⁹And since we have been made right in God's sight by the blood of Christ, he will certainly save us from God's judgment. ¹⁰For since we were restored to friendship with God by the death of his Son while we were still his enemies, we will certainly be delivered from eternal punishment by his life. ¹¹So now we can rejoice in our wonderful new relationship with God—all because of what our Lord Jesus Christ has done for us in making us friends of God.

*Adam and Christ Contrasted*
¹²When Adam sinned, sin entered the entire human race. Adam's sin brought death, so death spread to everyone, for everyone sinned. ¹³Yes, people sinned even before the law was given. And though there was no law to break, since it had not yet been given, ¹⁴they all died anyway—even though they did not disobey an explicit commandment of God, as Adam did. What a contrast between Adam and Christ, who was yet to come! ¹⁵And what a difference between our sin and God's generous gift of forgiveness. For this one man, Adam, brought death to many through his sin. But this other man, Jesus Christ, brought forgiveness to many through God's bountiful gift. ¹⁶And the result of God's gracious gift is very different from the result of that one man's sin. For Adam's sin led to condemnation, but we have the free gift of being accepted by God, even though we are guilty of many sins. ¹⁷The sin of this one man, Adam, caused death to rule over us, but all who receive God's wonderful, gracious gift of righteousness will live in triumph over sin and death through this one man, Jesus Christ.

¹⁸Yes, Adam's one sin brought condemnation upon everyone, but Christ's one act of righteousness makes all people right in God's sight and gives them life. ¹⁹Because one person disobeyed God, many people became sinners. But because one other person obeyed God, many people will be made right in God's sight.

²⁰God's law was given so that all people could see how sinful they were. But as people sinned more and more, God's wonderful kindness became more abundant. ²¹So just as sin ruled over all people and brought them to death, now

4:17 Gen 17:5.    4:18 Gen 15:5.

God's wonderful kindness rules instead, giving us right standing with God and resulting in eternal life through Jesus Christ our Lord.

## CHAPTER 6
### Sin's Power Is Broken

Well then, should we keep on sinning so that God can show us more and more kindness and forgiveness? ²Of course not! Since we have died to sin, how can we continue to live in it? ³Or have you forgotten that when we became Christians and were baptized to become one with Christ Jesus, we died with him? ⁴For we died and were buried with Christ by baptism. And just as Christ was raised from the dead by the glorious power of the Father, now we also may live new lives.

⁵Since we have been united with him in his death, we will also be raised as he was. ⁶Our old sinful selves were crucified with Christ so that sin might lose its power in our lives. We are no longer slaves to sin. ⁷For when we died with Christ, we were set free from the power of sin. ⁸And since we died with Christ, we know we will also share his new life. ⁹We are sure of this because Christ rose from the dead, and he will never die again. Death no longer has any power over him. ¹⁰He died once to defeat sin, and now he lives for the glory of God. ¹¹So you should consider yourselves dead to sin and able to live for the glory of God through Christ Jesus.

¹²Do not let sin control the way you live;* do not give in to its lustful desires. ¹³Do not let any part of your body become a tool of wickedness, to be used for sinning. Instead, give yourselves completely to God since you have been given new life. And use your whole body as a tool to do what is right for the glory of God. ¹⁴Sin is no longer your master, for you are no longer subject to the law, which enslaves you to sin. Instead, you are free by God's grace.

### Freedom to Obey God

¹⁵So since God's grace has set us free from the law, does this mean we can go on sinning? Of course not! ¹⁶Don't you realize that whatever you choose to obey becomes your master? You can choose sin, which leads to death, or you can choose to obey God and receive his approval. ¹⁷Thank God! Once you were slaves of sin, but now you have obeyed with all your heart the new teaching God has given you. ¹⁸Now you are free from sin, your old master,

6:12 Or *Do not let sin reign in your body, which is subject to death.*

and you have become slaves to your new master, righteousness.

¹⁹I speak this way, using the illustration of slaves and masters, because it is easy to understand. Before, you let yourselves be slaves of impurity

## God's Spirit Will Help You Overcome Sin Read ROMANS 8:9-14

This powerful passage of Scripture contains some critical truths we need to know about letting the Holy Spirit lead our lives. Remember, once you became a Christian, God gave you his Holy Spirit to help you live out your faith, guide your steps, empower your witness, and, as this passage attests, overcome sin. Look at four key points the apostle Paul makes here:

**1. You Are Controlled by a New Nature.** Your old, sinful nature will still try to get a hand on the steering wheel. But now your new nature is in the driver's seat, and your old nature has become like an annoying backseat driver. You can either give in to your old nature's nagging and bad directions, or you can ignore it and let the Holy Spirit direct your path.

**2. Even Though You Will Face Physical Death, You Will Not Face Spiritual Death.** As a believer, physical death is simply a transition to eternal life in heaven. You have been spared from spiritual death, which leads to everlasting torment and hell (see Revelation 21:8, p. 347). This important fact should reassure you when the devil tries to throw doubts your way.

**3. The Same Spirit of God That Raised Jesus from the Dead Resides in *You*.** Did you catch that? The Holy Spirit, who had the power to raise Jesus from the dead, now lives in you! If that is indeed true—and God's Word says it is—just think of the supernatural power you now have in your life to resist sin!

**4. We Do Not Have to Give In to Our Sinful Nature and Urges.** Paul wasn't talking about New Year's resolutions here. If we try to live a morally upright, godly life in our own strength, we will fail—and fail miserably. But, if we rely on the power of the Holy Spirit to help us, we will be overcomers.

FIRST STEPS

## Our Lives Should Show That God Is at Work in Our Hearts
Read ROMANS 7:4

While we still live on this side of heaven, we will always struggle between the desire to obey God and the desire to follow our sinful instincts. Even the apostle Paul knew what it was like to struggle with sin. In the verses surrounding this text, he describes the six keys to winning this battle and living a life that not only pleases God, but shows that God is working in our heart:

**1. Admit the Power of Sin in Your Life (see Romans 7:14, p. 183).** Recognize that you have that "combustible nature" within you, a vulnerability to the enticements of sin. If we fail to see our potential weaknesses, we are even more vulnerable to fall to them. The Bible warns against such an attitude, saying, "If you think you are standing strong, be careful, for you too may fall into the same sin" (1 Corinthians 10:12).

**2. Realize That You Are Powerless to Change on Your Own (see Romans 7:18, p. 183).** Your sinful nature is the source of the problem. You will never "master" sin and live a life pleasing to God on your own. Apart from God, you can do nothing.

**3. Become "Fed Up" with Your Condition and Cry for Help (see Romans 7:24, p. 183).** You cannot control evil in your life by simply determining to do so. You have to come to the end of yourself and ask for God's help in this struggle.

**4. Accept Your Freedom (see Romans 7:25, p. 183).** Take the hand of help that is offered to you by Jesus.

**5. Accept God's Forgiveness and Lack of Condemnation (see Romans 8:1-2, pp. 183–184).** Because of your unique union with Christ, God will forgive you—not condemn you—when you acknowledge your failures, struggles, and broken commitments.

**6. Cut the Instinctive Actions of Your Sinful Nature (see Romans 8:3-8, p. 184).** The only way to stop committing instinctive sinful actions is to stop living by your sinful nature and start

living by the power of the Holy Spirit. How do you do this? As verse 6 implies, you must relinquish control of your mind to the Spirit. When you do this, you will be "controlled by the Holy Spirit [and] think about things that please the Spirit" (Romans 8:5).

You will always have the potential to sin. But God has given you the power to overcome sin through his Holy Spirit. The key to drawing on his power is to be obedient to the Holy Spirit.

CORNER STONES

and lawlessness. Now you must choose to be slaves of righteousness so that you will become holy.

20In those days, when you were slaves of sin, you weren't concerned with doing what was right. 21And what was the result? It was not good, since now you are ashamed of the things you used to do, things that end in eternal doom. 22But now you are free from the power of sin and have become slaves of God. Now you do those things that lead to holiness and result in eternal life. 23For the wages of sin is death, but the free gift of God is eternal life through Christ Jesus our Lord.

7:1 Greek *brothers.*

CHAPTER **7**
*No Longer Bound to the Law*
Now, dear brothers and sisters*—you who are familiar with the law—don't you know that the law applies only to a person who is still living? 2Let me illustrate. When a woman marries, the law binds her to her husband as long as he is alive. But if he dies, the laws of marriage no longer apply to her. 3So while her husband is alive, she would be committing adultery if she married another man. But if her husband dies, she is free from that law and does not commit adultery when she remarries.

4So this is the point: The law no longer holds

you in its power, because you died to its power when you died with Christ on the cross. And now you are united with the one who was raised from the dead. As a result, you can produce good fruit, that is, good deeds for God. 5When we were controlled by our old nature, sinful desires were at work within us, and the law aroused these evil desires that produced sinful deeds, resulting in death. 6But now we have been released from the law, for we died with Christ, and we are no longer captive to its power. Now we can really serve God, not in the old way by obeying the letter of the law, but in the new way, by the Spirit.

## God's Law Reveals Our Sin

7Well then, am I suggesting that the law of God is evil? Of course not! The law is not sinful, but it was the law that showed me my sin. I would never have known that coveting is wrong if the law had not said, "Do not covet."* 8But sin took advantage of this law and aroused all kinds of forbidden desires within me! If there were no law, sin would not have that power.

9I felt fine when I did not understand what the law demanded. But when I learned the truth, I realized I had broken the law and was a sinner, doomed to die. 10So the good law, which was supposed to show me the way of life, instead gave me the death penalty. 11Sin took advantage of the law and fooled me; it took the good law and used it to make me guilty of death. 12But still, the law itself is holy and right and good.

13But how can that be? Did the law, which is good, cause my doom? Of course not! Sin used what was good to bring about my condemnation. So we can see how terrible sin really is. It uses God's good commandment for its own evil purposes.

## Struggling with Sin

14The law is good, then. The trouble is not with the law but with me, because I am sold into slavery, with sin as my master. 15I don't understand myself at all, for I really want to do what is right, but I don't do it. Instead, I do the very thing I hate. 16I know perfectly well that what I am doing is wrong, and my bad conscience shows that I agree that the law is good. 17But I can't help myself, because it is sin inside me that makes me do these evil things.

18I know I am rotten through and through so far as my old sinful nature is concerned. No matter which way I turn, I can't make myself do

7:7 Exod 20:17; Deut 5:21.

right. I want to, but I can't. 19When I want to do good, I don't. And when I try not to do wrong, I do it anyway. 20But if I am doing what I don't want to do, I am not really the one doing it; the sin within me is doing it.

21It seems to be a fact of life that when I want to do what is right, I inevitably do what is wrong. 22I love God's law with all my heart. 23But there is another law at work within me that is at war with my mind. This law wins the fight and makes me a slave to the sin that is still within me. 24Oh, what a miserable person I am! Who will free me from this life that is dominated by sin?* 25Thank God! The answer is in Jesus Christ our Lord. So you see how it is: In my mind I really want to obey God's law, but because of my sinful nature I am a slave to sin.

## CHAPTER 8
### Life in the Spirit

So now there is no condemnation for those who belong to Christ Jesus. 2For the power* of the life-giving Spirit has freed you* through Christ Jesus

7:24 Greek *from this body of death?* 8:2a Greek *the law;* also in 8:2b.

## Prayer Is Not a Solitary Experience Read ROMANS 8:26-27

Have you ever wondered what to say to God? Perhaps you have a sick friend that you don't know how to pray for. Or maybe you are unsure of how to pray for your spiritual needs. This portion of Scripture will encourage you. From the moment you asked Jesus to be your personal Lord and Savior, you received a resident guest in your heart: the Holy Spirit.

One of the many things he does is to help you in prayer—especially at those times when you don't know what to pray. As you realize how intimately God is involved in your prayers, you will begin to feel a unique closeness to your Father in heaven. You may even discover a freshness in your prayer life that you never had before.

The next time you don't know what to pray for, ask the Holy Spirit to help you voice your concerns and needs to God.

## Live to Please God Read ROMANS 8:5-8

Living to please God may seem like a daunting task. And for some, it is. They struggle to live up to a list of do's and don'ts. They try to obtain God's favor through acts of kindness and compassion. They attempt to "appease" God for their sinful behavior by going to church or making a "confession." But this passage—in fact, this entire chapter in Romans—lets you know that it *is* possible to live a life that is pure and pleasing to God.

The beginning verses of this chapter explain that once we enter into a relationship with Jesus Christ, God frees us from the "vicious circle" of sin and death through the power of his Holy Spirit. This terminology illustrates the basis of our freedom: In essence, the Holy Spirit you received by accepting Jesus Christ into your life has made you a "slave" of Jesus Christ—not a "slave" of your sinful nature.

The apostle Paul often identified himself as a slave of Jesus Christ in his writings. He used the word *doulos,* which means "servant by choice." This word was readily understood by those in the Roman culture. A "doulos," or "bondslave," was a slave who had been granted freedom by his master, but who loved his master so deeply that he voluntarily chose to continue on as that master's servant. Likewise, Paul was not a slave to Christ because he had to be; he was a slave to Christ because he *wanted* to be. He had totally surrendered himself to his Master.

The only way to be free from sin is to be "bound" to Jesus. Unless you completely surrender your life to the Lord, all of your efforts to lead a pure life will be futile. That old sinful nature will continue to rear its ugly head and influence your thoughts and actions. But if you are a bondslave

of Jesus, following the leading of the Holy Spirit (verse 5), you will not serve God out of fear and duty but out of love and gratitude. Your service will not be motivated by a desire to earn God's approval but will be motivated by a desire to be close to Jesus, recognizing that you already have that approval because of what Jesus did for you. This "blessed" bondage gives you the will, the power, and the motivation to live a life that is pleasing to God.

CORNER STONES

from the power of sin that leads to death. ³The law of Moses could not save us, because of our sinful nature. But God put into effect a different plan to save us. He sent his own Son in a human body like ours, except that ours are sinful. God destroyed sin's control over us by giving his Son as a sacrifice for our sins. ⁴He did this so that the requirement of the law would be fully accomplished for us* who no longer follow our sinful nature but instead follow the Spirit.

⁵Those who are dominated by the sinful nature think about sinful things, but those who are controlled by the Holy Spirit think about things that please the Spirit. ⁶If your sinful nature controls your mind, there is death. But if the Holy Spirit controls your mind, there is life and peace. ⁷For the sinful nature is always hostile to God. It never did obey God's laws, and it never will. ⁸That's why those who are still

under the control of their sinful nature can never please God.

⁹But you are not controlled by your sinful nature. You are controlled by the Spirit if you have the Spirit of God living in you. (And remember that those who do not have the Spirit of Christ living in them are not Christians at all.) ¹⁰Since Christ lives within you, even though your body will die because of sin, your spirit is alive* because you have been made right with God. ¹¹The Spirit of God, who raised Jesus from the dead, lives in you. And just as he raised Christ from the dead, he will give life to your mortal body by this same Spirit living within you.

¹²So, dear brothers and sisters,* you have no obligation whatsoever to do what your sinful nature urges you to do. ¹³For if you keep on following it, you will perish. But if through the power of the Holy Spirit you turn from it* and

8:2b Some manuscripts read *me.* 8:4 Or *accomplished by us.* 8:10 Or *the Spirit will bring you eternal life.* 8:12 Greek *brothers*; also in 8:29. 8:13 Greek *put it to death.*

its evil deeds, you will live. <sup>14</sup>For all who are led by the Spirit of God are children* of God.

<sup>15</sup>So you should not be like cowering, fearful slaves. You should behave instead like God's very own children, adopted into his family*— calling him "Father, dear Father."* <sup>16</sup>For his Holy Spirit speaks to us deep in our hearts and tells us that we are God's children. <sup>17</sup>And since we are his children, we will share his treasures— for everything God gives to his Son, Christ, is ours, too. But if we are to share his glory, we must also share his suffering.

*The Future Glory*

<sup>18</sup>Yet what we suffer now is nothing compared to the glory he will give us later. <sup>19</sup>For all creation is waiting eagerly for that future day when God will reveal who his children really are. <sup>20</sup>Against its will, everything on earth was subjected to God's curse. <sup>21</sup>All creation anticipates the day when it will join God's children in glorious freedom from death and decay. <sup>22</sup>For we know that all creation has been groaning as in the pains of childbirth right up to the present time. <sup>23</sup>And even we Christians, although we have the Holy Spirit within us as a foretaste of future glory, also groan to be released from pain and suffering. We, too, wait anxiously for that day when God will give us our full rights as his children,* including the new bodies he has promised us. <sup>24</sup>Now that we are saved, we eagerly look forward to this freedom. For if you already have something, you don't need to hope for it. <sup>25</sup>But if we look forward to something we don't have yet, we must wait patiently and confidently.

<sup>26</sup>And the Holy Spirit helps us in our distress. For we don't even know what we should pray for, nor how we should pray. But the Holy Spirit prays for us with groanings that cannot be expressed in words. <sup>27</sup>And the Father who knows all hearts knows what the Spirit is saying, for the Spirit pleads for us believers in harmony with God's own will. <sup>28</sup>And we know that God causes everything to work together* for the good of those who love God and are called according to his purpose for them. <sup>29</sup>For God knew his people in advance, and he chose them to become like his Son, so that his Son would be the firstborn, with many brothers and sisters. <sup>30</sup>And having chosen them, he called them to come to

8:14 Greek *sons;* also in 8:19.  8:15a Greek *You received a spirit of sonship.*  8:15b Greek *"Abba, Father." Abba* is an Aramaic term for *"father."*  8:23 Greek *wait anxiously for sonship.*  8:28 Some manuscripts read *And we know that everything works together.*

## Unconditionally Surrender Your Life Read ROMANS 12:1-2

This passage of Scripture is what we call a conditional promise. The last part of verse 2 contains the promise. Yet if we want to discover God's perfect will for our lives, we must meet the three conditions mentioned at the beginning of these verses.

**1. We Must Present Ourselves to God as Living Sacrifices.** We need to recognize that we, as Christians, belong to God. The Bible tells us that we no longer own our bodies because Christ paid for them when he died on the cross (see 1 Corinthians 6:19b-20, p. 204). Because our bodies belong to him, we must refrain from sinning. This is what is meant by living sacrifice—putting aside our own will and replacing it with God's.

**2. We Must Not Be Conformed to This World.** The next step to prepare our hearts to know the will of God is to keep from copying "the behavior and customs of this world." When the Bible speaks of the "world," it is not referring to the earth. Rather it is speaking of the mentality and thinking of the times—the spiritually bankrupt mind-set that is hostile toward the things of God and primarily focuses on mankind's own selfish desires.

**3. We Must Be Transformed by the Renewing of Our Minds.** One of the best ways to become "a new and different person" is to literally saturate your mind and heart with those things that spiritually build you up. You can do this by studying God's Word, singing hymns and praises, spending time in prayer, and fellowshiping with other believers. As the apostle Paul tells us, "Fix your thoughts on what is true and honorable and right. Think about things that are pure and lovely and admirable. Think about things that are excellent and worthy of praise" (Philippians 4:8).

As we take these preliminary steps, we will be able to more accurately discern the will of God for our lives.

him. And he gave them right standing with himself, and he promised them his glory.

## Nothing Can Separate Us from God's Love
31What can we say about such wonderful things as these? If God is for us, who can ever be against us? 32Since God did not spare even his own Son but gave him up for us all, won't God, who gave us Christ, also give us everything else?

33Who dares accuse us whom God has chosen for his own? Will God? No! He is the one who has given us right standing with himself. 34Who then will condemn us? Will Christ Jesus? No, for he is the one who died for us and was raised to life for us and is sitting at the place of highest honor next to God, pleading for us.

35Can anything ever separate us from Christ's love? Does it mean he no longer loves us if we have trouble or calamity, or are persecuted, or are hungry or cold or in danger or threatened with death? 36(Even the Scriptures say, "For your sake we are killed every day; we are being slaughtered like sheep."*) 37No, despite all these things, overwhelming victory is ours through Christ, who loved us.

38And I am convinced that nothing can ever separate us from his love. Death can't, and life can't. The angels can't, and the demons can't. Our fears for today, our worries about tomorrow, and even the powers of hell can't keep God's love away. 39Whether we are high above the sky or in the deepest ocean, nothing in all creation will ever be able to separate us from the love of God that is revealed in Christ Jesus our Lord.

CHAPTER **9**
## God's Selection of Israel
In the presence of Christ, I speak with utter truthfulness—I do not lie—and my conscience

and the Holy Spirit confirm that what I am saying is true. 2My heart is filled with bitter sorrow and unending grief 3for my people, my Jewish brothers and sisters.* I would be willing to be forever cursed—cut off from Christ!—if that would save them. 4They are the people of Israel, chosen to be God's special children.* God revealed his glory to them. He made covenants with them and gave his law to them. They have the privilege of worshiping him and receiving his wonderful promises. 5Their ancestors were great people of God, and Christ himself was a Jew as far as his human nature is concerned. And he is God, who rules over everything and is worthy of eternal praise! Amen.*

6Well then, has God failed to fulfill his promise to the Jews? No, for not everyone born into a Jewish family is truly a Jew! 7Just the fact that they are descendants of Abraham doesn't make them truly Abraham's children. For the Scriptures say, "Isaac is the son through whom your descendants will be counted,"* though Abraham had other children, too. 8This means that Abraham's physical descendants are not necessarily children of God. It is the children of the promise who are considered to be Abraham's children. 9For God had promised, "Next year I will return, and Sarah will have a son."*

10This son was our ancestor Isaac. When he grew up, he married Rebekah, who gave birth to twins. 11But before they were born, before they had done anything good or bad, she received a message from God. (This message proves that God chooses according to his own plan, 12not according to our good or bad works.) She was told, "The descendants of your older son will serve the descendants of your younger son."* 13In the words of the Scriptures, "I loved Jacob, but I rejected Esau."*

8:36 Ps 44:22.  9:3 Greek *my brothers.*  9:4 Greek *chosen for sonship.*  9:5 Or *May God, who rules over everything, be praised forever. Amen.*  9:7 Gen 21:12.  9:9 Gen 18:10; 14.  9:12 Gen 25:23.  9:13 Mal 1:2-3.

# OFF AND RUNNING
## Keep Your Spiritual Zeal Alive Read ROMANS 12:11

This verse not only encourages us to keep our zeal for God alive, but it commands us to do so. Another meaning of the phrase "serve the Lord enthusiastically" is to have a burning heart for God. The importance of this is seen in the book of Revelation. There Jesus warned the church in Laodicea that they were in danger of being "spit . . . out of [his] mouth" because they were lukewarm (Revelation 3:15-16). In essence, they had lost the fire of their spiritual zeal and were an offense to Christ. Therefore, Jesus told them to repent or he would reject them.

So what can be done to keep our spiritual zeal alive? We can keep our spiritual fire fueled by spending time

14What can we say? Was God being unfair? Of course not! 15For God said to Moses,

"I will show mercy to anyone I choose,
and I will show compassion to anyone I
choose."*

16So receiving God's promise is not up to us. We can't get it by choosing it or working hard for it. God will show mercy to anyone he chooses.

17For the Scriptures say that God told Pharaoh, "I have appointed you for the very purpose of displaying my power in you, and so that my fame might spread throughout the earth."* 18So you see, God shows mercy to some just because he wants to, and he chooses to make some people refuse to listen.

19Well then, you might say, "Why does God blame people for not listening? Haven't they simply done what he made them do?"

20No, don't say that. Who are you, a mere human being, to criticize God? Should the thing that was created say to the one who made it, "Why have you made me like this?" 21When a potter makes jars out of clay, doesn't he have a right to use the same lump of clay to make one jar for decoration and another to throw garbage into? 22God has every right to exercise his judgment and his power, but he also has the right to be very patient with those who are the objects of his judgment and are fit only for destruction. 23He also has the right to pour out the riches of his glory upon those he prepared to be the objects of his mercy—24even upon us, whom he selected, both from the Jews and from the Gentiles.

25Concerning the Gentiles, God says in the prophecy of Hosea,

"Those who were not my people,
I will now call my people.
And I will love those
whom I did not love before."*

26And,

"Once they were told,
'You are not my people.'
But now he will say,
'You are children of the living God.'*"

27Concerning Israel, Isaiah the prophet cried out,

"Though the people of Israel are as
numerous as the sand on the
seashore,
only a small number will be saved.
28 For the Lord will carry out his sentence
upon the earth
quickly and with finality."*

29And Isaiah said in another place,

"If the Lord Almighty
had not spared a few of us,
we would have been wiped out
as completely as Sodom and
Gomorrah."*

### Israel's Unbelief

30Well then, what shall we say about these things? Just this: The Gentiles have been made right with God by faith, even though they were not seeking him. 31But the Jews, who tried so hard to get right with God by keeping the law, never succeeded. 32Why not? Because they were trying to get right with God by keeping the law and being good instead of by depending on faith. They stumbled over the great rock in their path. 33God warned them of this in the Scriptures when he said,

9:15 Exod 33:19.   9:17 Exod 9:16.   9:25 Hos 2:23.   9:26 Greek *You are sons of the living God.* Hos 1:10.   9:27-28 Isa 10:22-23.   9:29 Isa 1:9.

with God's people in fellowship and prayer. We can also feed the fire with constant input from God's Word. As two discouraged disciples realized, listening to the words of Jesus can rekindle a person's zeal for God: "They said to each other, 'Didn't our hearts feel strangely warm as he talked with us on the road and explained the Scriptures to us?'." (Luke 24:32).

What is your spiritual temperature? Are you passionate about the Lord you serve? Do you make the most of every opportunity to tell others about Jesus? The English evangelist John Wesley once said, "Give me a hundred men who love God with all of their hearts and fear nothing but sin, and I will move the world." If you are aglow with the Spirit, serving the Lord with zeal and enthusiasm, your life *will* make a difference.

## Our Peace Continues As We Follow the Holy Spirit Read ROMANS 8:5-8

Even if you are a Christian, you still must struggle with your sinful nature. However, if you allow God's Holy Spirit to control your life, that struggle will be much less intense. For, as this passage says, you will want to live to please God.

If you follow your old evil desires, you "can never please God" (verse 8). Your life—whether you realize it or not—will be empty. But if you live the Spirit-controlled life, you will experience "life and peace" (verse 6). To enter into the Spirit-controlled life, follow the advice of the apostle Paul, "Let heaven fill your thoughts. Do not think only about things down here on earth. For you died when Christ died, and your real life is hidden with Christ in God" (Colossians 3:2-3).

**CORNER STONES**

"I am placing a stone in Jerusalem* that
   causes people to stumble,
   and a rock that makes them fall.*
But anyone who believes in him
   will not be disappointed.*"

CHAPTER **10**

Dear brothers and sisters,* the longing of my heart and my prayer to God is that the Jewish people might be saved. 2I know what enthusiasm they have for God, but it is misdirected zeal. 3For they don't understand God's way of making people right with himself. Instead, they are clinging to their own way of getting right with God by trying to keep the law. They won't go along with God's way. 4For Christ has accomplished the whole purpose* of the law. All who believe in him are made right with God.

*Salvation Is for Everyone*

5For Moses wrote that the law's way of making a person right with God requires obedience to all of its commands.* 6But the way of getting right with God through faith says, "You don't need to go to heaven" (to find Christ and bring him down to help you). 7And it says, "You don't need to go to the place of the dead" (to bring Christ back to life again). 8Salvation that comes from trusting Christ—which is the message we preach—is already within easy reach. In fact, the Scriptures say, "The message is close at hand; it is on your lips and in your heart."* 9For if you confess with your mouth that Jesus is Lord and believe in your heart that God raised him from the dead, you will be saved.

10For it is by believing in your heart that you are made right with God, and it is by confessing with your mouth that you are saved. 11As the Scriptures tell us, "Anyone who believes in him will not be disappointed.*" 12Jew and Gentile are the same in this respect. They all have the same Lord, who generously gives his riches to all who ask for them. 13For "Anyone who calls on the name of the Lord will be saved."*

14But how can they call on him to save them unless they believe in him? And how can they believe in him if they have never heard about him? And how can they hear about him unless someone tells them? 15And how will anyone go and tell them without being sent? That is what the Scriptures mean when they say, "How beautiful are the feet of those who bring good news!"*

16But not everyone welcomes the Good News, for Isaiah the prophet said, "Lord, who has believed our message?"* 17Yet faith comes from listening to this message of good news— the Good News about Christ.

18But what about the Jews? Have they actually heard the message? Yes, they have:

"The message of God's creation has gone
   out to everyone,
   and its words to all the world."*

19But did the people of Israel really understand? Yes, they did, for even in the time of Moses, God had said,

"I will rouse your jealousy by blessing other
   nations.
I will make you angry by blessing the
   foolish Gentiles."*

9:33a Greek *in Zion.*   9:33b Isa 8:14.   9:33c Or *will not be put to shame.* Isa 28:16.   10:1 Greek *Brothers.*   10:4 Or *the end.*   10:5 Lev 18:5.   10:6-8 Deut 30:12-14.   10:11 Or *will not be put to shame.* Isa 28:16.   10:13 Joel 2:32.   10:15 Isa 52:7.   10:16 Isa 53:1.   10:18 Ps 19:4.   10:19 Deut 32:21.

## How Should I View Authority? Read ROMANS 13:1-2

When dealing with the subject of authority—particularly how one should act toward those in the government—the Bible gives us some important things to consider.

**God Raises Up Rulers.** It is true that not every government official has been obedient to God. In fact, far too many have directly violated his Word. Yet God has allowed certain people to rule for his purposes. In the Old Testament God often allowed certain "evil" countries to come to power in order to punish Israel for their wrongdoing and to remind them of their need to return to God. Therefore, we need to respect those in authority, since God has divinely appointed them.

**God Uses Those in Government Who Fear Him.** While God is ultimately in control of every event that takes place in the world, he still uses his people in strategic positions of power. When Queen Esther, a Jew, faced the prospect of seeing her people put to death, her Uncle Mordecai challenged her with these words: "If you keep quiet at a time like this, deliverance for the Jews will arise from some other place, but you and your relatives will die. What's more, who can say but that you have been elevated to the palace for just such a time as this" (Esther 4:14)? Certainly, God does not forbid us to be part of the political process. Sometimes he will even use Christians in government to accomplish his purposes.

**We Are to Be a Witness to Those in Authority.** Your obedience to the laws of the land serves as a witness to the God you serve. Peter, addressing the early Christians who were suffering persecution under the cruel tyranny of Nero, still challenged believers to be law-abiding citizens (see 1 Peter 2:13-15, p. 307).

**Our Allegiance to God Should Always Come First.** What about those times when a law or government does something that directly contradicts God's law? We are accountable to a higher authority. In the Old Testament we read how Daniel defied the king's decree that forbade people to pray to anyone but him (Daniel 6:1-28). Daniel knew that God had said to worship him alone, so he obeyed God's law instead of man's. As you may recall, he was sent to the lions' den, but God spared his life by shutting the lions' mouths. In the New Testament, Peter told the high priest, when he had been warned not to talk about Jesus, "We must obey God rather than human authority" (Acts 5:29). In more recent times, Christians in Communist and Muslim countries continue to share Christ and distribute Bibles, despite laws that make such actions illegal.

Perhaps the best approach to those in authority over us is to follow the advice found in 1 Peter 2:17: "Fear God. Show respect for the king." Here we see a perfect balance, for as we fear God in our daily lives, we will live above reproach and be examples to those in authority. At the same time, we will be able to discern when human laws contradict the divine laws established by God.

*BIG QUESTIONS*

---

20And later Isaiah spoke boldly for God:

"I was found by people
    who were not looking for me.
I showed myself to those
    who were not asking for me."*

21But regarding Israel, God said,

"All day long I opened my arms to them,
    but they kept disobeying me and arguing
    with me."*

10:20 Isa 65:1.   10:21 Isa 65:2.

CHAPTER **11**
*God's Mercy on Israel*

I ask, then, has God rejected his people, the Jews? Of course not! Remember that I myself am a Jew, a descendant of Abraham and a member of the tribe of Benjamin.

2No, God has not rejected his own people, whom he chose from the very beginning. Do you remember what the Scriptures say about this? Elijah the prophet complained to God about the people of Israel and said, 3 "Lord, they have killed your prophets and torn down your altars. I alone am left, and now they are trying to kill me, too."*

4And do you remember God's reply? He said, "You are not the only one left. I have seven thousand others who have never bowed down to Baal!"*

5It is the same today, for not all the Jews have turned away from God. A few* are being saved as a result of God's kindness in choosing them. 6And if they are saved by God's kindness, then it is not by their good works. For in that case, God's wonderful kindness would not be what it really is—free and undeserved.

7So this is the situation: Most of the Jews have not found the favor of God they are looking for so earnestly. A few have—the ones God has chosen—but the rest were made unresponsive. 8As the Scriptures say,

"God has put them into a deep sleep.
To this very day he has shut their eyes so
    they do not see,
    and closed their ears so they do not hear."*

9David spoke of this same thing when he said,

"Let their bountiful table become a snare,
    a trap that makes them think all is well.
Let their blessings cause them to stumble.
10 Let their eyes go blind so they cannot see,
    and let their backs grow weaker and
        weaker."*

11Did God's people stumble and fall beyond recovery? Of course not! His purpose was to make his salvation available to the Gentiles, and then the Jews would be jealous and want it for themselves. 12Now if the Gentiles were enriched because the Jews turned down God's offer of salvation, think how much greater a blessing the world will share when the Jews finally accept it.

13I am saying all of this especially for you Gentiles. God has appointed me as the apostle to the Gentiles. I lay great stress on this, 14for I want to find a way to make the Jews want what you Gentiles have, and in that way I might save some of them. 15For since the Jews' rejection meant that God offered salvation to the rest of the world, how much more wonderful their acceptance will be. It will be life for those who were dead! 16And since Abraham and the other patriarchs were holy, their children will also be holy.* For if the roots of the tree are holy, the branches will be, too.

17But some of these branches from Abraham's tree, some of the Jews, have been broken off. And you Gentiles, who were branches from a wild olive tree, were grafted in. So now you also receive the blessing God has promised Abraham and his children, sharing in God's rich nourishment of his special olive tree. 18But you must be careful not to brag about being grafted in to replace the branches that were broken off. Remember, you are just a branch, not the root.

19"Well," you may say, "those branches were broken off to make room for me." 20Yes, but remember—those branches, the Jews, were broken off because they didn't believe God, and you are there because you do believe. Don't think highly of yourself, but fear what could happen. 21For if God did not spare the branches he put there in the first place, he won't spare you either.

22Notice how God is both kind and severe. He is severe to those who disobeyed, but kind to you as you continue to trust in his kindness. But if you stop trusting, you also will be cut off. 23And if the Jews turn from their unbelief, God will graft them back into the tree again. He has the power to do it.

24For if God was willing to take you who were, by nature, branches from a wild olive tree and graft you into his own good tree—a very unusual thing to do—he will be far more eager to graft the Jews back into the tree where they belong.

## God's Mercy Is for Everyone

25I want you to understand this mystery, dear brothers and sisters,* so that you will not feel proud and start bragging. Some of the Jews have hard hearts, but this will last only until the complete number of Gentiles comes to Christ. 26And so all Israel will be saved. Do you remember what the prophets said about this?

"A Deliverer will come from Jerusalem,*
    and he will turn Israel* from all ungodliness.
27 And then I will keep my covenant with them
    and take away their sins."*

28Many of the Jews are now enemies of the Good News. But this has been to your benefit, for God has given his gifts to you Gentiles. Yet the Jews are still his chosen people because of his promises to Abraham, Isaac, and Jacob. 29For God's gifts and his call can never be withdrawn. 30Once, you Gentiles were rebels against God, but when the Jews refused his mercy, God was merciful to you instead.

11:3 1 Kgs 19:10, 14.  11:4 1 Kgs 19:18.  11:5 Greek *A remnant.*  11:8 Deut 29:4; Isa 29:10.  11:9-10 Ps 69:22-23.  11:16 Greek *If the dough offered as firstfruits is holy, so is the whole lump.*  11:25 Greek *brothers.*  11:26a Greek *from Zion.*  11:26b Greek *Jacob.*  11:26-27 Isa 59:20-21.

³¹And now, in the same way, the Jews are the rebels, and God's mercy has come to you. But someday they,* too, will share in God's mercy. ³²For God has imprisoned all people in their own disobedience so he could have mercy on everyone.

³³Oh, what a wonderful God we have! How great are his riches and wisdom and knowledge! How impossible it is for us to understand his decisions and his methods! ³⁴For who can know what the Lord is thinking? Who knows enough to be his counselor?* ³⁵And who could ever give him so much that he would have to pay it back? ³⁶For everything comes from him; everything exists by his power and is intended for his glory. To him be glory evermore. Amen.

## CHAPTER 12
### A Living Sacrifice to God

And so, dear brothers and sisters,* I plead with you to give your bodies to God. Let them be a living and holy sacrifice—the kind he will accept. When you think of what he has done for you, is this too much to ask? ²Don't copy the behavior and customs of this world, but let God transform you into a new person by changing the way you think. Then you will know what God wants you to do, and you will know how good and pleasing and perfect his will really is.

³As God's messenger, I give each of you this warning: Be honest in your estimate of yourselves, measuring your value by how much faith God has given you. ⁴Just as our bodies have many parts and each part has a special function, ⁵so it is with Christ's body. We are all parts of his one body, and each of us has different work to do. And since we are all one body in Christ, we belong to each other, and each of us needs all the others.

⁶God has given each of us the ability to do certain things well. So if God has given you the ability to prophesy, speak out when you have faith that God is speaking through you. ⁷If your gift is that of serving others, serve them well. If you are a teacher, do a good job of teaching. ⁸If your gift is to encourage others, do it! If you have money, share it generously. If God has given you leadership ability, take the responsibility seriously. And if you have a gift for showing kindness to others, do it gladly.

⁹Don't just pretend that you love others. Really love them. Hate what is wrong. Stand on the side of the good. ¹⁰Love each other with genuine affection,* and take delight in honoring each other. ¹¹Never be lazy in your work, but serve the Lord enthusiastically.

¹²Be glad for all God is planning for you. Be patient in trouble, and always be prayerful. ¹³When God's children are in need, be the one to help them out. And get into the habit of inviting guests home for dinner or, if they need lodging, for the night.

¹⁴If people persecute you because you are a Christian, don't curse them; pray that God will

---

## Put on God's Armor
Read ROMANS 13:11-14

Another way the last verse of this text has been translated is "Be Christ's men from head to foot, and give no chances to the flesh to have its fling." In other words, we need to "clothe ourselves" with Christ. To do this, you need to let him be a part of everything that you do. Let him go with you everywhere you go. Let him act through you in every decision you make. Remember these three simple truths as you strive to obey Christ:

**1. Time Is Short.** Jesus Christ will return soon, and we need to be the best possible witness for him that we can be.

**2. Live in the Light.** As Ephesians 5:8 says, "For though your hearts were once full of darkness, now you are full of light from the Lord, and your behavior should show it!" The more you live in God's light, the less you will want to be influenced by the darkness of the world around you.

**3. Rely upon Christ for Your Strength.** You will never be able to stand against the temptations of life on your own. As you follow Christ and his example, you will find it much easier to avoid spiritual pitfalls. As it has been said, "The best defense is a good offense."

Some people want to put God in a little compartment. They will worship God from nine to eleven on Sunday morning, but the rest of the week is theirs. That is not the Christian life. As true followers of Jesus Christ, we need to be identified with our Master twenty-four hours a day, seven days a week, for the rest of our lives.

---

11:31 Some manuscripts read *But now they;* other manuscripts read *But they.*   11:34 See Isa 40:13.   12:1 Greek *brothers.*
12:10 Greek *with brotherly love.*

bless them. 15When others are happy, be happy with them. If they are sad, share their sorrow. 16Live in harmony with each other. Don't try to act important, but enjoy the company of ordinary people. And don't think you know it all!

17Never pay back evil for evil to anyone. Do things in such a way that everyone can see you are honorable. 18Do your part to live in peace with everyone, as much as possible.

19Dear friends, never avenge yourselves. Leave that to God. For it is written,

"I will take vengeance;
   I will repay those who deserve it,"*
   says the Lord.

20Instead, do what the Scriptures say:

"If your enemies are hungry, feed them.
If they are thirsty, give them something to
   drink,
   and they will be ashamed of what they
      have done to you."*

21Don't let evil get the best of you, but conquer evil by doing good.

## CHAPTER 13
### Respect for Authority
Obey the government, for God is the one who put it there. All governments have been placed in power by God. 2So those who refuse to obey the laws of the land are refusing to obey God, and punishment will follow. 3For the authorities do not frighten people who are doing right, but they frighten those who do wrong. So do what they say, and you will get along well. 4The authorities are sent by God to help you. But if you are doing something wrong, of course you should be afraid, for you will be punished. The authorities are established by God for that very purpose, to punish those who do wrong. 5So you must obey the government for two reasons: to keep from being punished and to keep a clear conscience.

6Pay your taxes, too, for these same reasons. For government workers need to be paid so they can keep on doing the work God intended them to do. 7Give to everyone what you owe them: Pay your taxes and import duties, and give respect and honor to all to whom it is due.

### Love Fulfills God's Requirements
8Pay all your debts, except the debt of love for others. You can never finish paying that! If you love your neighbor, you will fulfill all the requirements of God's law. 9For the commandments against adultery and murder and stealing and coveting—and any other commandment— are all summed up in this one commandment: "Love your neighbor as yourself."* 10Love does no wrong to anyone, so love satisfies all of God's requirements.

11Another reason for right living is that you know how late it is; time is running out. Wake up, for the coming of our salvation is nearer now than when we first believed. 12The night is almost gone; the day of salvation will soon be here. So don't live in darkness. Get rid of your evil deeds. Shed them like dirty clothes. Clothe yourselves with the armor of right living, as those who live in the light. 13We should be decent and true in everything we do, so that everyone can approve of our behavior. Don't participate in wild parties and getting drunk, or in adultery and immoral living, or in fighting and jealousy. 14But let the Lord Jesus Christ take control of you, and don't think of ways to indulge your evil desires.

## CHAPTER 14
### The Danger of Criticism
Accept Christians who are weak in faith, and don't argue with them about what they think is right or wrong. 2For instance, one person believes it is all right to eat anything. But another believer who has a sensitive conscience will eat only vegetables. 3Those who think it is all right to eat anything must not look down on those who won't. And those who won't eat certain foods must not condemn those who do, for God

12:19 Deut 32:35.   12:20 Greek *and you will heap burning coals on their heads.* Prov 25:21-22.   13:9 Lev 19:18.

## OFF AND RUNNING ▰▰▰▰

### Could This Activity Cause Other Christians to Stumble in Their Faith? Read ROMANS 14:15

Don't do anything that will bring criticism against yourself, even if you know that a certain activity is all right. What we do and become has a direct effect on others—not only for our has accepted them. ⁴Who are you to condemn God's servants? They are responsible to the Lord, so let him tell them whether they are right or wrong. The Lord's power will help them do as they should.

⁵In the same way, some think one day is more holy than another day, while others think every day is alike. Each person should have a personal conviction about this matter. ⁶Those who have a special day for worshiping the Lord are trying to honor him. Those who eat all kinds of food do so to honor the Lord, since they give thanks to God before eating. And those who won't eat everything also want to please the Lord and give thanks to God. ⁷For we are not our own masters when we live or when we die. ⁸While we live, we live to please the Lord. And when we die, we go to be with the Lord. So in life and in death, we belong to the Lord. ⁹Christ died and rose again for this very purpose, so that he might be Lord of those who are alive and of those who have died.

¹⁰So why do you condemn another Christian*? Why do you look down on another Christian? Remember, each of us will stand personally before the judgment seat of God. ¹¹For the Scriptures say,

" 'As surely as I live,' says the Lord,
'every knee will bow to me
    and every tongue will confess allegiance
    to God.'"*

¹²Yes, each of us will have to give a personal account to God. ¹³So don't condemn each other anymore. Decide instead to live in such a way that you will not put an obstacle in another Christian's path.

¹⁴I know and am perfectly sure on the authority of the Lord Jesus that no food, in and of itself, is wrong to eat. But if someone believes it is wrong, then for that person it is wrong. ¹⁵And if another Christian is distressed by what you eat, you are not acting in love if you eat it. Don't let your eating ruin someone for whom Christ died.

¹⁶Then you will not be condemned for doing something you know is all right.

¹⁷For the Kingdom of God is not a matter of what we eat or drink, but of living a life of goodness and peace and joy in the Holy Spirit. ¹⁸If you serve Christ with this attitude, you will please God. And other people will approve of you, too. ¹⁹So then, let us aim for harmony in the church and try to build each other up.

²⁰Don't tear apart the work of God over what you eat. Remember, there is nothing wrong with these things in themselves. But it is wrong to eat anything if it makes another person stumble. ²¹Don't eat meat or drink wine or do anything else if it might cause another Christian to stumble. ²²You may have the faith to believe that there is nothing wrong with what you are doing, but keep it between yourself and God. Blessed are those who do not condemn themselves by doing something they know is all right. ²³But if people have doubts about whether they should eat something, they shouldn't eat it. They would be condemned for not acting in faith before God. If you do anything you believe is not right, you are sinning.

## CHAPTER 15
### Living to Please Others
We may know that these things make no difference, but we cannot just go ahead and do them to please ourselves. We must be considerate of the doubts and fears of those who think these things are wrong. ²We should please others. If we do what helps them, we will build them up in the Lord. ³For even Christ didn't please himself. As the Scriptures say, "Those who insult you are also insulting me."* ⁴Such things were written in the Scriptures long ago to teach us. They give us hope and encouragement as we wait patiently for God's promises.

⁵May God, who gives this patience and encouragement, help you live in complete harmony with each other—each with the attitude of Christ Jesus toward the other. ⁶Then all of you can join

**14:10** Greek *your brother;* also in 14:10b, 13, 15, 21.  **14:11** Isa 45:23.  **15:3** Ps 69:9.

life here on this earth, but also for eternity. We not only need to live our lives conscious of God's opinion, but we also need to live our lives with consideration for others. We do not want to do anything that has the potential of causing another Christian brother or sister to stumble or fall.

together with one voice, giving praise and glory to God, the Father of our Lord Jesus Christ.

⁷So accept each other just as Christ has accepted you; then God will be glorified. ⁸Remember that Christ came as a servant to the Jews to show that God is true to the promises he made to their ancestors. ⁹And he came so the Gentiles might also give glory to God for his mercies to them. That is what the psalmist meant when he wrote:

"I will praise you among the Gentiles;
  I will sing praises to your name."*

¹⁰And in another place it is written,

"Rejoice, O you Gentiles,
  along with his people, the Jews."*

¹¹And yet again,

"Praise the Lord, all you Gentiles;
  praise him, all you people of the earth."*

¹²And the prophet Isaiah said,

"The heir to David's throne* will come,
  and he will rule over the Gentiles.
  They will place their hopes on him."*

¹³So I pray that God, who gives you hope, will keep you happy and full of peace as you believe in him. May you overflow with hope through the power of the Holy Spirit.

*Paul's Reason for Writing*
¹⁴I am fully convinced, dear brothers and sisters,* that you are full of goodness. You know these things so well that you are able to teach others all about them. ¹⁵Even so, I have been bold enough to emphasize some of these points, knowing that all you need is this reminder from me. For I am, by God's grace, ¹⁶a special messenger from Christ Jesus to you Gentiles. I bring you the Good News and offer you up as a fragrant sacrifice to God so that you might be pure and pleasing to him by the

Holy Spirit. ¹⁷So it is right for me to be enthusiastic about all Christ Jesus has done through me in my service to God. ¹⁸I dare not boast of anything else. I have brought the Gentiles to God by my message and by the way I lived before them. ¹⁹I have won them over by the miracles done through me as signs from God—all by the power of God's Spirit. In this way, I have fully presented the Good News of Christ all the way from Jerusalem clear over into Illyricum.*

²⁰My ambition has always been to preach the Good News where the name of Christ has never been heard, rather than where a church has already been started by someone else. ²¹I have been following the plan spoken of in the Scriptures, where it says,

"Those who have never been told about
  him will see,
  and those who have never heard of him
  will understand."*

²²In fact, my visit to you has been delayed so long because I have been preaching in these places.

*Paul's Travel Plans*
²³But now I have finished my work in these regions, and after all these long years of waiting, I am eager to visit you. ²⁴I am planning to go to Spain, and when I do, I will stop off in Rome. And after I have enjoyed your fellowship for a little while, you can send me on my way again.

²⁵But before I come, I must go down to Jerusalem to take a gift to the Christians there. ²⁶For you see, the believers in Greece* have eagerly taken up an offering for the Christians in Jerusalem, who are going through such hard times. ²⁷They were very glad to do this because they feel they owe a real debt to them. Since the Gentiles received the wonderful spiritual blessings of the Good News from the Jewish Christians, they feel the least they can do in return is help them financially. ²⁸As soon as I have deliv-

15:9 Ps 18:49.  15:10 Deut 32:43.  15:11 Ps 117:1.  15:12a Greek *The root of Jesse.*  15:12b Isa 11:10.  15:14 Greek *brothers;* also in 15:30.  15:19 *Illyricum* was a region northeast of Italy.  15:21 Isa 52:15.  15:26 Greek *Macedonia and Achaia,* the northern and southern regions of Greece.

# OFF AND RUNNING

## Do I Have an Uneasy Conscience about This Activity?
Read ROMANS 14:23

When it comes to participating in questionable activities, it is easy to rationalize joining in because others are doing it. Yet this verse places the responsibility of your choice squarely on your shoulders. You may protest and say, "Well, so-and-so is doing it!" But you are not that person. You must be obedient to what God tells *you* to do.

ered this money and completed this good deed of theirs, I will come to see you on my way to Spain. [29]And I am sure that when I come, Christ will give me a great blessing for you.

[30]Dear brothers and sisters, I urge you in the name of our Lord Jesus Christ to join me in my struggle by praying to God for me. Do this because of your love for me, given to you by the Holy Spirit. [31]Pray that I will be rescued from those in Judea who refuse to obey God. Pray also that the Christians there will be willing to accept the donation I am bringing them. [32]Then, by the will of God, I will be able to come to you with a happy heart, and we will be an encouragement to each other.

[33]And now may God, who gives us his peace, be with you all. Amen.

## CHAPTER 16
### Paul Greets His Friends

Our sister Phoebe, a deacon in the church in Cenchrea, will be coming to see you soon. [2]Receive her in the Lord, as one who is worthy of high honor. Help her in every way you can, for she has helped many in their needs, including me.

[3]Greet Priscilla and Aquila. They have been co-workers in my ministry for Christ Jesus. [4]In fact, they risked their lives for me. I am not the only one who is thankful to them; so are all the Gentile churches. [5]Please give my greetings to the church that meets in their home.

Greet my dear friend Epenetus. He was the very first person to become a Christian in the province of Asia. [6]Give my greetings to Mary, who has worked so hard for your benefit. [7]Then there are Andronicus and Junia,* my relatives,* who were in prison with me. They are respected among the apostles and became Christians before I did. Please give them my greetings. [8]Say hello to Ampliatus, whom I love as one of the Lord's own children, [9]and Urbanus, our co-worker in Christ, and beloved Stachys.

[10]Give my greetings to Apelles, a good man whom Christ approves. And give my best regards to the members of the household of Aristobulus. [11]Greet Herodion, my relative.* Greet the Christians in the household of Narcissus. [12]Say hello to Tryphena and Tryphosa, the Lord's workers, and to dear Persis, who has worked so hard for the Lord. [13]Greet Rufus, whom the Lord picked out to be his very own; and also his dear mother, who has been a mother to me.

[14]And please give my greetings to Asyncritus, Phlegon, Hermes, Patrobas, Hermas, and the brothers and sisters* who are with them. [15]Give my greetings to Philologus, Julia, Nereus and his sister, and to Olympas and all the other believers who are with them. [16]Greet each other in Christian love.* All the churches of Christ send you their greetings.

### Paul's Final Instructions

[17]And now I make one more appeal, my dear brothers and sisters. Watch out for people who cause divisions and upset people's faith by teaching things that are contrary to what you have been taught. Stay away from them. [18]Such people are not serving Christ our Lord; they are serving their own personal interests. By smooth talk and glowing words they deceive innocent people. [19]But everyone knows that you are obedient to the Lord. This makes me very happy. I want you to see clearly what is right and to stay innocent of any wrong. [20]The God of peace will soon crush Satan under your feet. May the grace of our Lord Jesus Christ be with you.

[21]Timothy, my fellow worker, and Lucius, Jason, and Sosipater, my relatives, send you their good wishes.

[22]I, Tertius, the one who is writing this letter for Paul, send my greetings, too, as a Christian brother.

16:7a Or *Junias;* some manuscripts read *Julia.*   16:7b Or *compatriots;* also in 16:21.   16:11 Or *compatriot.*   16:14 Greek *brothers;* also in 16:17.   16:16 Greek *with a sacred kiss.*

How do you know when you should not participate in a certain activity? God's Holy Spirit will often give you an uneasy conscience about something you should not be doing. For example, you may have a sense that you are in the wrong place, with the wrong people, about to do the wrong thing. Or, you may have a lack of peace in your heart about an activity in which you are participating. When this happens, it is up to you to pay attention to your conscience and follow through by being obedient to God.

## Knowing Whom You Belong to and What the Future Holds Brings True Joy Read ROMANS 15:13

This verse touches upon three important facets of the Christian life that should give you great joy:

**1. You Have a New Identity.** When you accept Jesus Christ into your life, God gives you a new identity. You discover that you are not merely some product of random chance. You are not a speck in the universe. You are a child of God. And as God's child you can rest assured that you will be loved and cared for by your heavenly Father.

**2. You Have Power to Face Life.** With that new identity and hope in Christ, you also have the promise of the Holy Spirit's presence and power in your life. The Holy Spirit works constantly in your heart, helping you to understand God's Word and to transform your attitudes and behavior (see "Who Is the Holy Spirit?" p. A12). An expanded translation of this verse says that by the power of the Holy Spirit, your whole life and outlook will be "radiant with hope." God has not left you to face life on your own. He has promised to guide and strengthen you with his Spirit.

**3. You Have Hope for the Future.** As a Christian, you have the hope and knowledge that there is life beyond the grave. Your last breath on earth will be followed by your first breath in heaven. We know this is true, because God has promised it in his Word (see "What Is Heaven?" p. A5). This verse asserts that your belief in Jesus and his promises to us as his followers will fill you with joy and peace.

The world offers many roads to happiness: sex, money, power, personal success. But they are all cheap and worthless substitutes in comparison to knowing that you are God's child and that you have the hope of heaven. This is the only road to lasting—indeed, eternal—joy.

**CORNERSTONES**

---

23Gaius says hello to you. I am his guest, and the church meets here in his home. Erastus, the city treasurer, sends you his greetings, and so does Quartus, a Christian brother.*

25God is able to make you strong, just as the Good News says. It is the message about Jesus Christ and his plan for you Gentiles, a plan kept secret from the beginning of time. 26But now as the prophets* foretold and as the eternal God has commanded, this message is made known to all Gentiles everywhere, so that they might believe and obey Christ. 27To God, who alone is wise, be the glory forever through Jesus Christ. Amen.

16:23 Some manuscripts add verse 24, *May the grace of our Lord Jesus Christ be with you all. Amen.* 16:26 Greek *the prophetic writings.*

# 1 Corinthians

## CHAPTER 1

### Greetings from Paul

This letter is from Paul, chosen by the will of God to be an apostle of Christ Jesus, and from our brother Sosthenes.

2We are writing to the church of God in Corinth, you who have been called by God to be his own holy people. He made you holy by means of Christ Jesus, just as he did all Christians everywhere—whoever calls upon the name of Jesus Christ, our Lord and theirs.

3May God our Father and the Lord Jesus Christ give you his grace and peace.

### Paul Gives Thanks to God

4I can never stop thanking God for all the generous gifts he has given you, now that you belong to Christ Jesus. 5He has enriched your church with the gifts of eloquence and every kind of knowledge. 6This shows that what I told you about Christ is true. 7Now you have every spiritual gift you need as you eagerly wait for the return of our Lord Jesus Christ. 8He will keep you strong right up to the end, and he will keep you free from all blame on the great day when our Lord Jesus Christ returns. 9God will surely do this for you, for he always does just what he says, and he is the one who invited you into this wonderful friendship with his Son, Jesus Christ our Lord.

### Divisions in the Church

10Now, dear brothers and sisters,* I appeal to you by the authority of the Lord Jesus Christ to stop arguing among yourselves. Let there be real harmony so there won't be divisions in the church. I plead with you to be of one mind, united in thought and purpose. 11For some members of Chloe's household have told me about your arguments, dear brothers and sisters. 12Some of you are saying, "I am a follower of Paul." Others are saying, "I follow Apollos," or "I follow Peter,*" or "I follow only Christ." 13Can Christ be divided into pieces?

Was I, Paul, crucified for you? Were any of you baptized in the name of Paul? 14I thank God that I did not baptize any of you except Crispus and Gaius, 15for now no one can say they were baptized in my name. 16(Oh yes, I also baptized the household of Stephanas. I don't remember baptizing anyone else.) 17For Christ didn't send me to baptize, but to preach the Good News—and not with clever speeches and high-sounding ideas, for fear that the cross of Christ would lose its power.

### The Wisdom of God

18I know very well how foolish the message of the cross sounds to those who are on the road to destruction. But we who are being saved recognize this message as the very power of God. 19As the Scriptures say,

"I will destroy human wisdom
and discard their most brilliant ideas."*

20So where does this leave the philosophers, the scholars, and the world's brilliant debaters? God has made them all look foolish and has shown their wisdom to be useless nonsense. 21Since God in his wisdom saw to it that the world would never find him through human wisdom, he has used our foolish preaching to save all who believe. 22God's way seems foolish to the Jews because they want a sign from heaven to prove it is true. And it is foolish to the Greeks because they believe only what agrees with their own wisdom. 23So when we preach that Christ

1:10 Greek brothers; also in 1:11, 26.   1:12 Greek Cephas.   1:19 Isa 29:14.

## Overlooking Petty Issues Frees Us to Experience Joy
Read 1 CORINTHIANS 1:10-17

In Paul's first letter to the Corinthians, he addressed several problems the church of Corinth was experiencing. One of the church's problems was that the believers were dividing the church by aligning themselves under the teachings of one apostle or another, rather than focusing on the joy of their salvation. Paul, therefore, rebuked the Corinthians for dividing the church over such a petty issue, reminding them that it is Christ they follow and serve, not Apollos, Paul, or Peter.

Like the Corinthians, we can get bogged down in issues that not only divide the church but really don't matter. When we immerse ourselves in petty issues, we rob ourselves of experiencing the joy that Christ has given us. That is because advocating these issues can become more important to us than salvation itself. It is then that we can become obsessed with others' adherence to our point of view rather than their faith in Christ. However, ignoring petty issues is liberating. It frees us to focus on our own salvation and experience the joy of Christ's forgiveness.

How do we do this? Here are four ways to overlook petty issues and experience joy in Christ:

**1. Be Single-Minded in Purpose.** The purpose of our life is to serve Christ (see Philippians 1:21, p. 247).

**2. Adopt God's Priorities As Your Own.** Put God first, others second, and yourself third (see Philippians 2:5-6, p. 248).

**3. Keep Moving Forward Spiritually.** Acknowledge that you haven't "arrived" spiritually, and keep pressing on to know God more (see Philippians 3:13-14, p. 250).

**4. Have a Rejoicing Mind.** Don't rejoice in circumstances, but rejoice in God and his faithfulness (see Philippians 4:4-5, p. 250).

Failure to maintain the joy of the Lord in our personal lives leads to spiritual breakdown. Failure to keep the joy of the Lord in our churches cripples the cause of Christ. Let his joy overflow from your life.

**CORNER STONES**

---

was crucified, the Jews are offended, and the Gentiles say it's all nonsense. 24But to those called by God to salvation, both Jews and Gentiles,* Christ is the mighty power of God and the wonderful wisdom of God. 25This "foolish" plan of God is far wiser than the wisest of human plans, and God's weakness is far stronger than the greatest of human strength.

26Remember, dear brothers and sisters, that few of you were wise in the world's eyes, or powerful, or wealthy when God called you. 27Instead, God deliberately chose things the world considers foolish in order to shame those who think they are wise. And he chose those who are powerless to shame those who are powerful. 28God chose things despised by the world, things counted as nothing at all, and used them to bring to nothing what the world considers important, 29so that no one can ever boast in the presence of God.

30God alone made it possible for you to be in Christ Jesus. For our benefit God made Christ to be wisdom itself. He is the one who made us acceptable to God. He made us pure and holy, and he gave himself to purchase our freedom. 31As the Scriptures say,

"The person who wishes to boast
  should boast only of what the Lord has
  done."*

## CHAPTER 2
*Paul Preaches Wisdom*

Dear brothers and sisters,* when I first came to you I didn't use lofty words and brilliant ideas to tell you God's message.* 2For I decided to concentrate only on Jesus Christ and his death on the cross. 3I came to you in weakness—timid and trembling. 4And my message and my preaching were very plain. I did not use wise and

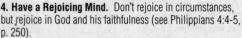

1:24 Greek *Greeks.*  1:31 Jer 9:24.  2:1a Greek *Brothers.*  2:1b Greek *mystery;* other manuscripts read *testimony.*

persuasive speeches, but the Holy Spirit was powerful among you. ⁵I did this so that you might trust the power of God rather than human wisdom.

⁶Yet when I am among mature Christians, I do speak with words of wisdom, but not the kind of wisdom that belongs to this world, and not the kind that appeals to the rulers of this world, who are being brought to nothing. ⁷No, the wisdom we speak of is the secret wisdom of God,* which was hidden in former times, though he made it for our benefit before the world began. ⁸But the rulers of this world have not understood it; if they had, they would never have crucified our glorious Lord. ⁹That is what the Scriptures mean when they say,

"No eye has seen, no ear has heard,
    and no mind has imagined
what God has prepared
    for those who love him."*

¹⁰But we know these things because God has revealed them to us by his Spirit, and his Spirit searches out everything and shows us even God's deep secrets. ¹¹No one can know what anyone else is really thinking except that person alone, and no one can know God's thoughts except God's own Spirit. ¹²And God has actually given us his Spirit (not the world's spirit) so we can know the wonderful things God has freely given us. ¹³When we tell you this, we do not use words of human wisdom. We speak words given to us by the Spirit, using the Spirit's words to explain spiritual truths.* ¹⁴But people who aren't Christians can't understand these truths from God's Spirit. It all sounds foolish to them because only those who have the Spirit can understand what the Spirit means. ¹⁵We who have the Spirit understand these things, but others can't understand us at all. ¹⁶How could they? For,

"Who can know what the Lord is thinking?
    Who can give him counsel?"*

But we can understand these things, for we have the mind of Christ.

CHAPTER 3
*Paul and Apollos, Servants of Christ*
Dear brothers and sisters,* when I was with you I couldn't talk to you as I would to mature

2:7 Greek *we speak God's wisdom in a mystery.*   2:9 Isa 64:4.   2:13 Or *explaining spiritual truths in spiritual language,* or *explaining spiritual truths to spiritual people.*   2:16 Isa 40:13.   3:1a Greek *Brothers.*

Christians. I had to talk as though you belonged to this world or as though you were infants in the Christian life.* ²I had to feed you with milk and not with solid food, because you couldn't handle anything stronger. And you still aren't ready, ³for you are still controlled by your own sinful desires. You are jealous of one another and quarrel with each other. Doesn't that prove you are controlled by your own desires? You are acting like people who don't belong to the Lord.

3:1b Greek *in Christ.*

## Understand the Simplicity of the Gospel Read 1 CORINTHIANS 2:1-5

Paul reminds us in this text that the heartbeat of the gospel message is the story of the life, death, and resurrection of Jesus Christ. The apostles emphasized this message in their preaching throughout the New Testament—especially in the book of Acts, which chronicles the start of the early church. As you share your faith with others, keep in mind these two points demonstrated in the apostles' own efforts to spread the gospel:

**1. Remember the Simplicity of the Gospel.** People need to know that they are sinners and that their sin separates them from God. But Jesus came to bring God and humankind together. When he died on the cross, the sins of humankind were placed upon him, and the penalty for those sins was paid in full. Three days after his crucifixion, he rose from the dead, proving that he was the true Son of God, the only one who could pay for our sins.

**2. Recognize the Power of the Gospel.** Although our message is simple, it is incredibly powerful. Paul wrote, "For I am not ashamed of this Good News about Christ. It is the power of God at work, saving everyone who believes" (Romans 1:16). The word Paul uses to describe the power of the gospel is the root for our English words *dynamite* and *dynamic.*

Remember there is power in the simple message of the life, death, and resurrecton of Jesus Christ. We should not be ashamed of it but boldly proclaim it.

## The Value of Our Work on Earth Will Be Tested
Read 1 CORINTHIANS 3:10-15

The British preacher Alan Redpath once said, "It is possible to have a saved soul and a lost life." In other words, it is possible to be saved and forgiven of one's sin but to waste one's life by not serving the Lord.

That is what Paul warned the Corinthians about in this passage. Here Paul describes another judgment—besides the Great White Throne Judgment—specifically for believers. You might call it the Christian's award ceremony. Yet it won't be like any awards ceremony on earth. There the quality of our work for the Lord will be tested, as well as our motives for doing it. Our reward will reflect what we have or haven't done with the talents and abilities God has given us.

One day you are going to stand before Jesus. When you do, you want to be welcomed into the arms of Jesus and hear him say, "Well done, my good and faithful servant" (Matthew 25:21).

Be an "expert builder." Take the gifts and abilities God has given you—however insignificant they may seem to you—and use them for his glory. Then you will have a saved soul *and* an abundant life.

**CORNER STONES**

4When one of you says, "I am a follower of Paul," and another says, "I prefer Apollos," aren't you acting like those who are not Christians?*

5Who is Apollos, and who is Paul, that we should be the cause of such quarrels? Why, we're only servants. Through us God caused you to believe. Each of us did the work the Lord gave us. 6My job was to plant the seed in your hearts, and Apollos watered it, but it was God, not we, who made it grow. 7The ones who do the planting or watering aren't important, but God is important because he is the one who makes the seed grow. 8The one who plants and the one who waters work as a team with the same purpose. Yet they will be rewarded individually, according to their own hard work. 9We work together as partners who belong to God. You are God's field, God's building—not ours.

10Because of God's special favor to me, I have laid the foundation like an expert builder. Now others are building on it. But whoever is building on this foundation must be very careful. 11For no one can lay any other foundation than the one we already have—Jesus Christ. 12Now anyone who builds on that foundation may use gold, silver, jewels, wood, hay, or straw. 13But there is going to come a time of testing at the judgment day to see what kind of work each builder has done. Everyone's work will be put through the fire to see whether or not it keeps its value. 14If the work survives the fire, that builder will receive a reward. 15But if the work is burned up, the builder will suffer great loss. The builders themselves will be saved, but like someone escaping through a wall of flames.

16Don't you realize that all of you together are the temple of God and that the Spirit of God lives in* you? 17God will bring ruin upon anyone who ruins this temple. For God's temple is holy, and you Christians are that temple.

18Stop fooling yourselves. If you think you are wise by this world's standards, you will have to become a fool so you can become wise by God's standards. 19For the wisdom of this world is foolishness to God. As the Scriptures say,

"God catches those who think they are wise
in their own cleverness."*

20And again,

"The Lord knows the thoughts of the wise,
that they are worthless."*

21So don't take pride in following a particular leader. Everything belongs to you: 22Paul and Apollos and Peter*; the whole world and life and death; the present and the future. Everything belongs to you, 23and you belong to Christ, and Christ belongs to God.

3:4 Greek *aren't you merely human?*  3:16 Or *among.*  3:19 Job 5:13.  3:20 Ps 94:11.  3:22 Greek *Cephas.*

# Does God Approve of Alternative Lifestyles? Read 1 CORINTHIANS 6:9-10, 15-20

In this day and age we hear a lot of talk about "alternative lifestyles." But what does God have to say about homosexuality, living together as an unmarried couple, or being promiscuous? While some say that God is accepting of any relationship, the Bible paints a very different picture. Just because these relationships exist does not make them right. In fact, God clearly labels them as sin.

**About Homosexuality.** Saying that homosexuality is wrong is not a popular thing to do in our culture today. Yet God is not concerned with what is and what is not popular. He is concerned with people's salvation and their obedience to his Word. Just because homosexuality is viewed as an acceptable lifestyle does not mean that it is not a sin. God declared it to be just that when he gave his law to the Israelites (see Leviticus 18:22). Paul reiterated God's command on abstaining from homosexual sex in his letter to the Romans (see Romans 1:26-27, p. 176), as well as in some of his other letters to the early church.

**About Living Together before Marriage and Premarital Sex.** Have you ever thought that something was OK to do because "everybody is doing it"? Today, couples living together outside of marriage has become acceptable. In addition, it seems that premarital sex is the norm, rather than the exception. But God has not given his approval of these relationships (see Hebrews 13:4, p. 297). Although God created sex, he did not intend us to have it before marriage. That is because he created sex to be a means by which a husband and wife would grow closer in their relationship. He did not create sex to be something cheaply enjoyed outside the bonds of marital commitment, which is what living together and premarital sex are.

**About Promiscuity.** *Promiscuity* is a word that we do not hear as often today as we used to. The problem with promiscuity is that it involves having many sexual partners. We know from God's Word that he intended us to have one sexual partner—our spouse. When a person has more than one partner (with the exception of remarriage after a spouse's death or a divorce on solid biblical grounds), he or she is involved in sexual immorality, if not married, or adultery, if married (see Ephesians 5:3, p. 243, and Matthew 5:27-28, p. 7).

Some have questions about whether God's Word on these subjects still applies to us today, or if it was simply meant for the people of that particular time and culture. The Word of the Lord stands forever (see 1 Peter 1:25, p. 306). Consequently, these instructions apply just as much to us today as they did to their original audience centuries ago.

God gave us our sexual desires to enjoy within the bounds of marriage (see 1 Corinthians 7:1-5, p. 204). If you go against God's divinely instituted plan and do not repent, you will reap the consequences—not only in this life, but in eternity. For you cannot be close to God if you are engaged in any immoral behavior. At the same time, you won't be engaged in this type of behavior if you are truly close to God.

BIG QUESTIONS?

CHAPTER **4**
*Paul and the Corinthians*
So look at Apollos and me as mere servants of Christ who have been put in charge of explaining God's secrets. ²Now, a person who is put in charge as a manager must be faithful. ³What about me? Have I been faithful? Well, it matters very little what you or anyone else thinks. I don't even trust my own judgment on this point. ⁴My conscience is clear, but that isn't what matters. It is the Lord himself who will examine me and decide.

⁵So be careful not to jump to conclusions before the Lord returns as to whether or not

someone is faithful. When the Lord comes, he will bring our deepest secrets to light and will reveal our private motives. And then God will give to everyone whatever praise is due.

6Dear brothers and sisters,* I have used Apollos and myself to illustrate what I've been saying. If you pay attention to the Scriptures,* you won't brag about one of your leaders at the expense of another. 7What makes you better than anyone else? What do you have that God hasn't given you? And if all you have is from God, why boast as though you have accomplished something on your own?

8You think you already have everything you need! You are already rich! Without us you have become kings! I wish you really were on your thrones already, for then we would be reigning with you! 9But sometimes I think God has put us apostles on display, like prisoners of war at the end of a victor's parade, condemned to die. We have become a spectacle to the entire world—to people and angels alike.

10Our dedication to Christ makes us look like fools, but you are so wise! We are weak, but you are so powerful! You are well thought of, but we are laughed at. 11To this very hour we go hungry and thirsty, without enough clothes to keep us warm. We have endured many beatings, and we have no homes of our own. 12We have worked wearily with our own hands to earn our living. We bless those who curse us. We are patient with those who abuse us. 13We respond gently when evil things are said about us. Yet we are treated like the world's garbage, like everybody's trash—right up to the present moment.

14I am not writing these things to shame you, but to warn you as my beloved children. 15For even if you had ten thousand others to teach you about Christ, you have only one spiritual father. For I became your father in Christ Jesus when I

preached the Good News to you. 16So I ask you to follow my example and do as I do.

17That is the very reason I am sending Timothy—to help you do this. For he is my beloved and trustworthy child in the Lord. He will remind you of what I teach about Christ Jesus in all the churches wherever I go.

18I know that some of you have become arrogant, thinking I will never visit you again. 19But I will come—and soon—if the Lord will let me, and then I'll find out whether these arrogant people are just big talkers or whether they really have God's power. 20For the Kingdom of God is not just fancy talk; it is living by God's power. 21Which do you choose? Should I come with punishment and scolding, or should I come with quiet love and gentleness?

## CHAPTER 5
*Paul Condemns Spiritual Pride*

I can hardly believe the report about the sexual immorality going on among you, something so evil that even the pagans don't do it. I am told that you have a man in your church who is living in sin with his father's wife. 2And you are so proud of yourselves! Why aren't you mourning in sorrow and shame? And why haven't you removed this man from your fellowship?

3Even though I am not there with you in person, I am with you in the Spirit.* Concerning the one who has done this, I have already passed judgment 4in the name of the Lord Jesus. You are to call a meeting of the church,* and I will be there in spirit, and the power of the Lord Jesus will be with you as you meet. 5Then you must cast this man out of the church and into Satan's hands, so that his sinful nature will be destroyed* and he himself* will be saved when the Lord returns.

6How terrible that you should boast about your spirituality, and yet you let this sort of thing

4:6a Greek *Brothers.*   4:6b Or *You must learn not to go beyond "what is written," so that.*   5:3 Or *in spirit.*   5:4 Or *In the name of the Lord Jesus, you are to call a meeting of the church.*   5:5a Or *so that he will die;* Greek reads *for the destruction of the flesh.*   5:5b Greek *and the spirit.*

# OFF AND RUNNING ▰▰▰
## Does This Activity Bring Me under Its Power?
Read 1 CORINTHIANS 6:12

Some have mistakenly assumed that following Christ means drudgingly obeying a list of "do's and don'ts." In reality, the Christian life, if lived according to Scripture, is one of joy and satisfaction. This verse serves as a case in point. To follow the principle laid out here is not overly restricting but truly liberating!
Some people are controlled by pleasure. For example, they may live for a certain sport and become so

go on. Don't you realize that if even one person is allowed to go on sinning, soon all will be affected? 7Remove this wicked person from among you so that you can stay pure.* Christ, our Passover Lamb, has been sacrificed for us. 8So let us celebrate the festival, not by eating the old bread* of wickedness and evil, but by eating the new bread* of purity and truth.

9When I wrote to you before, I told you not to associate with people who indulge in sexual sin. 10But I wasn't talking about unbelievers who indulge in sexual sin, or who are greedy or are swindlers or idol worshipers. You would have to leave this world to avoid people like that. 11What I meant was that you are not to associate with anyone who claims to be a Christian* yet indulges in sexual sin, or is greedy, or worships idols, or is abusive, or a drunkard, or a swindler. Don't even eat with such people.

12It isn't my responsibility to judge outsiders, but it certainly is your job to judge those inside the church who are sinning in these ways. 13God will judge those on the outside; but as the Scriptures say, "You must remove the evil person from among you."*

## CHAPTER 6
### Avoiding Lawsuits with Christians
When you have something against another Christian, why do you file a lawsuit and ask a secular court to decide the matter, instead of taking it to other Christians to decide who is right? 2Don't you know that someday we Christians are going to judge the world? And since you are going to judge the world, can't you decide these little things among yourselves? 3Don't you realize that we Christians will judge angels? So you should surely be able to resolve ordinary disagreements here on earth. 4If you have legal disputes about such matters, why do you go to outside judges who are not

respected by the church? 5I am saying this to shame you. Isn't there anyone in all the church who is wise enough to decide these arguments? 6But instead, one Christian* sues another—right in front of unbelievers!

7To have such lawsuits at all is a real defeat for you. Why not just accept the injustice and leave it at that? Why not let yourselves be cheated? 8But instead, you yourselves are the ones who do wrong and cheat even your own Christian brothers and sisters.*

### Avoiding Sexual Sin
9Don't you know that those who do wrong will have no share in the Kingdom of God? Don't fool yourselves. Those who indulge in sexual sin, who are idol worshipers, adulterers, male prostitutes, homosexuals, 10thieves, greedy people, drunkards, abusers, and swindlers—none of these will have a share in the Kingdom of God. 11There was a time when some of you were just like that, but now your sins have been washed away,* and you have been set apart for God. You have been made right with God because of what the Lord Jesus Christ and the Spirit of our God have done for you.

12You may say, "I am allowed to do anything." But I reply, "Not everything is good for you." And even though "I am allowed to do anything," I must not become a slave to anything. 13You say, "Food is for the stomach, and the stomach is for food." This is true, though someday God will do away with both of them. But our bodies were not made for sexual immorality. They were made for the Lord, and the Lord cares about our bodies. 14And God will raise our bodies from the dead by his marvelous power, just as he raised our Lord from the dead. 15Don't you realize that your bodies are actually parts of Christ? Should a man take his body, which belongs to Christ, and join

5:6-7 Greek Don't you realize that even a little leaven spreads quickly through the whole batch of dough? 7Purge out the old leaven so that you can be a new batch of dough, just as you are already unleavened. 5:8a Greek not with old leaven. 5:8b Greek but with unleavened [bread]. 5:11 Greek a brother. 5:13 Deut 17:7. 6:6 Greek one brother. 6:8 Greek brothers. 6:11 Or you have been cleansed.

fanatical about it that it turns into an obsession. Others may be hooked on soap operas, food, or some particular habit that has them under its power. Yet, as a Christian, you should only want to be controlled by and under the power of Jesus Christ.

We need to so treasure our relationship with God—and the ensuing freedom from sin it has brought—that we jealously guard that relationship, wanting no thing or person to get in its way. As the Psalmist prayed, we, too, should pray, "Search me, O God, and know my heart; test me and know my thoughts. Point out anything in me that offends you, and lead me along the path of everlasting life" (Psalm 139:23-24).

it to a prostitute? Never! 16And don't you know that if a man joins himself to a prostitute, he becomes one body with her? For the Scriptures say, "The two are united into one."* 17But the person who is joined to the Lord becomes one spirit with him.

18Run away from sexual sin! No other sin so clearly affects the body as this one does. For sexual immorality is a sin against your own body. 19Or don't you know that your body is the temple of the Holy Spirit, who lives in you and was given to you by God? You do not belong to yourself, 20for God bought you with a high price. So you must honor God with your body.

CHAPTER **7**
*Instruction on Marriage*

Now about the questions you asked in your letter. Yes, it is good to live a celibate life. 2But because there is so much sexual immorality, each man should have his own wife, and each woman should have her own husband.

3The husband should not deprive his wife of sexual intimacy, which is her right as a married woman, nor should the wife deprive her husband. 4The wife gives authority over her body to her husband, and the husband also gives authority over his body to his wife. 5So do not deprive each other of sexual relations. The only exception to this rule would be the agreement of both husband and wife to refrain from sexual intimacy for a limited time, so they can give themselves more completely to prayer. Afterward they should come together again so that Satan won't be able to tempt them because of their lack of self-control. 6This is only my sug-

gestion. It's not meant to be an absolute rule. 7I wish everyone could get along without marrying, just as I do. But we are not all the same. God gives some the gift of marriage, and to others he gives the gift of singleness.

8Now I say to those who aren't married and to widows—it's better to stay unmarried, just as I am. 9But if they can't control themselves, they should go ahead and marry. It's better to marry than to burn with lust.

10Now, for those who are married I have a command that comes not from me, but from the Lord.* A wife must not leave her husband. 11But if she does leave him, let her remain single or else go back to him. And the husband must not leave his wife.

12Now, I will speak to the rest of you, though I do not have a direct command from the Lord. If a Christian man* has a wife who is an unbeliever and she is willing to continue living with him, he must not leave her. 13And if a Christian woman has a husband who is an unbeliever, and he is willing to continue living with her, she must not leave him. 14For the Christian wife brings holiness to her marriage, and the Christian husband brings holiness to his marriage. Otherwise, your children would not have a godly influence, but now they are set apart for him. 15(But if the husband or wife who isn't a Christian insists on leaving, let them go. In such cases the Christian husband or wife is not required to stay with them, for God wants his children to live in peace.) 16You wives must remember that your husbands might be converted because of you. And you husbands must remember that your wives might be converted because of you.

6:16 Gen 2:24.  7:10 See Matt 5:32; 19:9; Mark 10:11-12; Luke 16:18.  7:12 Greek *a brother.*

# OFF AND RUNNING ▟▟▟

## Marriage Is Not for Everyone Read 1 CORINTHIANS 7:1-40

Contrary to what popular opinion suggests, God has given some the ability to remain "happily unmarried." Verse 35 of this passage reminds us that, when it comes to marrying, it is vitally important to make sure that your decision "will help you serve the Lord best." If you are contemplating marriage, here are four important things to consider:

**1. Take Time Getting to Know One Another.** Don't rush into marriage. If you are really in love with someone, you will want to build your friendship with that person as well. That is the foundation of your marriage. As Benjamin Franklin humorously said, "Keep your eyes wide open before marriage and half shut afterwards"—not the other way around!

**2. Test the Depth of Your Love.** Love is more than some gooey emotion. It is a commitment. In the Greek language, love was described in three different ways: *eros* (physical attraction), *philos* (love between friends), and *agape* (unconditional love). Marriages that are simply based upon *eros* or *phileo* love are destined for

17You must accept whatever situation the Lord has put you in, and continue on as you were when God first called you. This is my rule for all the churches. 18For instance, a man who was circumcised before he became a believer should not try to reverse it. And the man who was uncircumcised when he became a believer should not be circumcised now. 19For it makes no difference whether or not a man has been circumcised. The important thing is to keep God's commandments.

20You should continue on as you were when God called you. 21Are you a slave? Don't let that worry you—but if you get a chance to be free, take it. 22And remember, if you were a slave when the Lord called you, the Lord has now set you free from the awful power of sin. And if you were free when the Lord called you, you are now a slave of Christ. 23God purchased you at a high price. Don't be enslaved by the world.* 24So, dear brothers and sisters,* whatever situation you were in when you became a believer, stay there in your new relationship with God.

25Now, about the young women who are not yet married. I do not have a command from the Lord for them. But the Lord in his kindness has given me wisdom that can be trusted, and I will share it with you. 26Because of the present crisis,* I think it is best to remain just as you are. 27If you have a wife, do not end the marriage. If you do not have a wife, do not get married. 28But if you do get married, it is not a sin. And if a young woman gets married, it is not a sin. However, I am trying to spare you the extra problems that come with marriage.

29Now let me say this, dear brothers and sis-ters: The time that remains is very short, so husbands should not let marriage be their major concern. 30Happiness or sadness or wealth should not keep anyone from doing God's work. 31Those in frequent contact with the things of the world should make good use of them without becoming attached to them, for this world and all it contains will pass away. 32In everything you do, I want you to be free from the concerns of this life. An unmarried man can spend his time doing the Lord's work and thinking how to please him. 33But a married man can't do that so well. He has to think about his earthly responsibilities and how to please his wife. 34His interests are divided. In the same way, a woman who is no longer married or has never been married can be more devoted to the Lord in body and in spirit, while the married woman must be concerned about her earthly responsibilities and how to please her husband.

35I am saying this for your benefit, not to place restrictions on you. I want you to do whatever will help you serve the Lord best, with as few distractions as possible. 36But if a man thinks he ought to marry his fiancée because he has trouble controlling his passions and time is passing, it is all right; it is not a sin. Let them marry. 37But if he has decided firmly not to marry and there is no urgency and he can control his passion, he does well not to marry. 38So the person who marries does well, and the person who doesn't marry does even better.

39A wife is married to her husband as long as he lives. If her husband dies, she is free to marry whomever she wishes, but this must be a marriage acceptable to the Lord.* 40But in my opinion it

7:23 Greek *don't become slaves of people.*    7:24 Greek *brothers;* also in 7:29.    7:26 Or *pressures of life.*    7:39 Or *but only to a Christian;* Greek reads *but only in the Lord.*

---

trouble, but marriages built around the *agape* love that Christ displayed will last. Emotions will come and go, but true love is far more than that. The Bible says, "Many waters cannot quench love; neither can rivers drown it" (Song of Songs 8:7).

**3. Make Sure of Your Commitment.** Ask yourself the following questions: Are you ready to spend the rest of your life with this person? Can you see yourselves going through parenthood together? Are you willing to make sacrifices in relationships, hobbies, and even your career for the sake of your marriage?

**4. Consider Your Witness for Christ.** If this other person is not a believer, don't even consider marriage. Scripture gives stern warnings against being teamed with those who are unbelievers (2 Corinthians 6:14, p. 222). You need to also consider the spiritual implications of this relationship. Will the two of you together be a more effective and powerful witness for Christ than the two of you apart?

Whether you marry or remain single, learn to be content in whatever situation the Lord places you. Then you will possess one of the keys to true happiness.

will be better for her if she doesn't marry again, and I think I am giving you counsel from God's Spirit when I say this.

## CHAPTER 8
### Food Sacrificed to Idols

Now let's talk about food that has been sacrificed to idols. You think that everyone should agree with your perfect knowledge. While knowledge may make us feel important, it is love that really builds up the church. 2Anyone who claims to know all the answers doesn't really know very much. 3But the person who loves God is the one God knows and cares for.

4So now, what about it? Should we eat meat that has been sacrificed to idols? Well, we all know that an idol is not really a god and that there is only one God and no other. 5According to some people, there are many so-called gods and many lords, both in heaven and on earth. 6But we know that there is only one God, the Father, who created everything, and we exist for him. And there is only one Lord, Jesus Christ, through whom God made everything and through whom we have been given life.

7However, not all Christians realize this. Some are accustomed to thinking of idols as being real, so when they eat food that has been offered to idols, they think of it as the worship of real gods, and their weak consciences are violated. 8It's true that we can't win God's approval by what we eat. We don't miss out on anything if we don't eat it, and we don't gain anything if we do. 9But you must be careful with this freedom of yours. Do not cause a brother or sister with a weaker conscience to stumble.

10You see, this is what can happen: Weak Christians who think it is wrong to eat this food will see you eating in the temple of an idol. You

know there's nothing wrong with it, but they will be encouraged to violate their conscience by eating food that has been dedicated to the idol. 11So because of your superior knowledge, a weak Christian,* for whom Christ died, will be destroyed. 12And you are sinning against Christ when you sin against other Christians* by encouraging them to do something they believe is wrong. 13If what I eat is going to make another Christian sin, I will never eat meat again as long as I live—for I don't want to make another Christian stumble.

## CHAPTER 9
### Paul Gives Up His Rights

Do I not have as much freedom as anyone else?* Am I not an apostle? Haven't I seen Jesus our Lord with my own eyes? Isn't it because of my hard work that you are in the Lord? 2Even if others think I am not an apostle, I certainly am to you, for you are living proof that I am the Lord's apostle.

3This is my answer to those who question my authority as an apostle.* 4Don't we have the right to live in your homes and share your meals? 5Don't we have the right to bring a Christian wife* along with us as the other disciples and the Lord's brothers and Peter* do? 6Or is it only Barnabas and I who have to work to support ourselves? 7What soldier has to pay his own expenses? And have you ever heard of a farmer who harvests his crop and doesn't have the right to eat some of it? What shepherd takes care of a flock of sheep and isn't allowed to drink some of the milk? 8And this isn't merely human opinion. Doesn't God's law say the same thing? 9For the law of Moses says, "Do not keep an ox from eating as it treads out the grain."* Do you suppose God was thinking only about oxen when

8:11 Greek *brother;* also in 8:13.   8:12 Greek *brothers.*   9:1 Greek *Am I not free?*   9:3 Greek *those who examine me.*   9:5a Greek *a sister, a wife.*   9:5b Greek *Cephas.*   9:9 Deut 25:4.

## OFF AND RUNNING ▰▰▰▰
### A Christian Should Not Leave a Non-Christian Spouse
Read 1 CORINTHIANS 7:12-16

While it is easy to rationalize leaving an unbelieving spouse who does not support or encourage your faith, it is not biblical. As Paul reiterates here, divorce is not God's intent for married couples. In the case of a Christian and non-Christian spouse, there are two additional reasons to remain married:

**1. A Christian Spouse Serves as a Witness to an Unbelieving Spouse.** A Christian may play an important role in winning his or her spouse to the Lord. Scripture says that the Christian wife of a nonbelieving husband can have a powerful influence on her spouse through her godly actions and he said this? 10Wasn't he also speaking to us? Of course he was. Just as farm workers who plow fields and thresh the grain expect a share of the harvest, Christian workers should be paid by those they serve.

11We have planted good spiritual seed among you. Is it too much to ask, in return, for mere food and clothing? 12If you support others who preach to you, shouldn't we have an even greater right to be supported? Yet we have never used this right. We would rather put up with anything than put an obstacle in the way of the Good News about Christ.

13Don't you know that those who work in the Temple get their meals from the food brought to the Temple as offerings? And those who serve at the altar get a share of the sacrificial offerings. 14In the same way, the Lord gave orders that those who preach the Good News should be supported by those who benefit from it. 15Yet I have never used any of these rights. And I am not writing this to suggest that I would like to start now. In fact, I would rather die than lose my distinction of preaching without charge. 16For preaching the Good News is not something I can boast about. I am compelled by God to do it. How terrible for me if I didn't do it!

17If I were doing this of my own free will, then I would deserve payment. But God has chosen me and given me this sacred trust, and I have no choice. 18What then is my pay? It is the satisfaction I get from preaching the Good News without expense to anyone, never demanding my rights as a preacher.

19This means I am not bound to obey people just because they pay me, yet I have become a servant of everyone so that I can bring them to Christ. 20When I am with the Jews, I become one of them so that I can bring them to Christ. When I am with those who follow the Jewish laws, I do the same, even though I am not subject to the law, so that I can bring them to Christ. 21When I am with the Gentiles who do not have the Jewish law,* I fit in with them as much as I can. In this way, I gain their confidence and bring them to Christ. But I do not discard the law of God; I obey the law of Christ.

22When I am with those who are oppressed, I share their oppression so that I might bring them to Christ. Yes, I try to find common ground with everyone so that I might bring them to Christ. 23I do all this to spread the Good News, and in doing so I enjoy its blessings.

24Remember that in a race everyone runs, but only one person gets the prize. You also must run in such a way that you will win. 25All athletes practice strict self-control. They do it to win a prize that will fade away, but we do it for an eternal prize. 26So I run straight to the goal with purpose in every step. I am not like a boxer who misses his punches.* 27I discipline my body like an athlete, training it to do what it should. Otherwise, I fear that after preaching to others I myself might be disqualified.

## CHAPTER 10
*Warnings against Idolatry*

I don't want you to forget, dear brothers and sisters,* what happened to our ancestors in the wilderness long ago. God guided all of them by sending a cloud that moved along ahead of them, and he brought them all safely through the waters of the sea on dry ground. 2As followers of Moses, they were all baptized in the cloud and the sea. 3And all of them ate the same miraculous* food, 4and all of them drank the same miraculous water. For they all drank from the miraculous rock that traveled with them, and that rock was Christ. 5Yet after all this, God

9:21 Greek *those without the law.* 9:26 Or *I am not just shadowboxing.* 10:1 Greek *brothers.* 10:3 Greek *spiritual;* also in 10:4.

---

example, which may encourage him to come to faith in Christ (see 1 Peter 3:1-2, p. 308). The same is true for Christian husbands.

**2. A Christian Spouse Can Influence the Couple's Children for Christ.** If you separate, as Paul states, there is a good chance your children may not come to faith. It will help them to see your faith in the context of a united family.

If, however, your unbelieving spouse abandons you, and you have done everything you could to keep the marriage together, God will not hold you to that relationship. This is one of the few marriage "release clauses" found in Scripture. God will not force you to stay married to an unbelieving partner who doesn't want to stay married to you.

was not pleased with most of them, and he destroyed them in the wilderness.

6These events happened as a warning to us, so that we would not crave evil things as they did 7or worship idols as some of them did. For the Scriptures say, "The people celebrated with feasting and drinking, and they indulged themselves in pagan revelry."* 8And we must not engage in sexual immorality as some of them did, causing 23,000 of them to die in one day. 9Nor should we put Christ* to the test, as some of them did and then died from snakebites. 10And don't grumble as some of them did, for that is why God sent his angel of death to destroy them. 11All these events happened to them as examples for us. They were written down to warn us, who live at the time when this age is drawing to a close.

12If you think you are standing strong, be careful, for you, too, may fall into the same sin. 13But remember that the temptations that come into your life are no different from what others experience. And God is faithful. He will keep the temptation from becoming so strong that you can't stand up against it. When you are tempted, he will show you a way out so that you will not give in to it.

14So, my dear friends, flee from the worship of idols. 15You are reasonable people. Decide for yourselves if what I am about to say is true. 16When we bless the cup at the Lord's Table, aren't we sharing in the benefits of the blood of Christ? And when we break the loaf of bread, aren't we sharing in the benefits of the body of Christ? 17And we all eat from one loaf, showing that we are one body. 18And think about the nation of Israel; all who eat the sacrifices are united by that act.

19What am I trying to say? Am I saying that the idols to whom the pagans bring sacrifices are real gods and that these sacrifices are of some value? 20No, not at all. What I am saying is that these sacrifices are offered to demons, not to God. And I don't want any of you to be partners with demons. 21You cannot drink from the cup of the Lord and from the cup of demons, too. You cannot eat at the Lord's Table and at the table of demons, too. 22What? Do you dare to rouse the Lord's jealousy as Israel did? Do you think we are stronger than he is?

23You say, "I am allowed to do anything"— but not everything is helpful. You say, "I am allowed to do anything"—but not everything is beneficial. 24Don't think only of your own good. Think of other Christians and what is best for them.

25Here's what you should do. You may eat any meat that is sold in the marketplace. Don't ask whether or not it was offered to idols, and then your conscience won't be bothered. 26For "the earth is the Lord's, and everything in it."*

27If someone who isn't a Christian asks you home for dinner, go ahead; accept the invitation if you want to. Eat whatever is offered to you and don't ask any questions about it. Your conscience should not be bothered by this. 28But suppose someone warns you that this meat has been offered to an idol. Don't eat it, out of consideration for the conscience of the one who told you. 29It might not be a matter of conscience for you, but it is for the other person.

Now, why should my freedom be limited by what someone else thinks? 30If I can thank God for the food and enjoy it, why should I be condemned for eating it? 31Whatever you eat or drink or whatever you do, you must do all for the glory of God. 32Don't give offense to Jews or Gentiles or the church of God. 33That is the plan I follow, too. I try to please everyone in everything I do. I don't just do what I like or what is best for me, but what is best for them so they may be saved.

CHAPTER **11**

And you should follow my example, just as I follow Christ's.

*Instructions for Public Worship*

2I am so glad, dear friends, that you always keep me in your thoughts and you are following the Christian teaching I passed on to you. 3But there is one thing I want you to know: A man is responsible to Christ, a woman is responsible to her husband, and Christ is responsible to God. 4A man dishonors Christ* if he covers his head while praying or prophesying. 5But a woman dishonors her husband* if she prays or prophesies without a covering on her head, for this is the same as shaving her head. 6Yes, if she refuses to wear a head covering, she should cut off all her hair. And since it is shameful for a woman to have her hair cut or her head shaved, then she should wear a covering.* 7A man should not wear anything on his head when worshiping, for man is God's glory, made in God's own image,

10:7 Exod 32:6. 10:9 Some manuscripts read *the Lord.* 10:26 Ps 24:1. 11:4 Greek *his head.* 11:5 Greek *her head.* 11:6 Or *then she should have long hair.*

but woman is the glory of man. 8For the first man didn't come from woman, but the first woman came from man. 9And man was not made for woman's benefit, but woman was made for man. 10So a woman should wear a covering on her head as a sign of authority because the angels are watching.

11But in relationships among the Lord's people, women are not independent of men, and men are not independent of women. 12For although the first woman came from man, all men have been born from women ever since, and everything comes from God.

13What do you think about this? Is it right for a woman to pray to God in public without covering her head? 14Isn't it obvious that it's disgraceful for a man to have long hair? 15And isn't it obvious that long hair is a woman's pride and joy? For it has been given to her as a covering. 16But if anyone wants to argue about this, all I can say is that we have no other custom than this, and all the churches of God feel the same way about it.

*Order at the Lord's Supper*

17But now when I mention this next issue, I cannot praise you. For it sounds as if more harm than good is done when you meet together. 18First of all, I hear that there are divisions among you when you meet as a church, and to some extent I believe it. 19But, of course, there must be divisions among you so that those of you who are right will be recognized!

20It's not the Lord's Supper you are concerned about when you come together. 21For I am told that some of you hurry to eat your own meal without sharing with others. As a result, some go hungry while others get drunk. 22What? Is this really true? Don't you have your own homes for eating and drinking? Or do you really want to disgrace the church of God and shame the poor? What am I supposed to say about these things? Do you want me to praise you? Well, I certainly do not!

23For this is what the Lord himself said, and I pass it on to you just as I received it. On the night when he was betrayed, the Lord Jesus took a loaf of bread, 24and when he had given thanks, he broke it and said, "This is my body, which is given* for you. Do this in remembrance of me." 25In the same way, he took the cup of wine after supper, saying, "This cup is the new covenant between God and you, sealed by the shedding of

11:24 Some manuscripts read *broken.*

my blood. Do this in remembrance of me as often as you drink it." 26For every time you eat this bread and drink this cup, you are announcing the Lord's death until he comes again.

27So if anyone eats this bread or drinks this cup of the Lord unworthily, that person is guilty of sinning against the body and the blood of the Lord. 28That is why you should examine yourself before eating the bread and drinking from the cup. 29For if you eat the bread or drink the cup unworthily, not honoring the body of Christ,* you are eating and drinking God's judgment upon yourself. 30That is why many of you are weak and sick and some have even died.

11:29 Greek *the body;* some manuscripts read *the Lord's body.*

## Rejoice Because Victory Is Yours in Christ Jesus
Read 1 CORINTHIANS 10:13

God realizes that we as humans will be tempted by one thing or another in this world. Fortunately for us, God cares so deeply about us that he has taken action to help us through times of temptation. This verse provides two rays of hope for you when you are tempted:

**1. Jesus Understands Your Situation.** Any temptation you are facing or will face has been faced before. Better yet, Jesus understands what it is like to be tempted, for the Bible teaches that he can sympathize with us, for he "faced all of the same temptations we do, yet he did not sin" (Hebrews 4:15).

**2. God Will Always Give You the Strength to Get Through the Temptation.** When you face temptation, God will always give you the power to resist it or give you a way to escape it. Sometimes the way out of temptation is literal. For instance, if you are at the movie theater and an explicit sexual scene appears on the screen, the way of escape means walking out of the theater. At other times, it may mean relying on God's Holy Spirit to give you the power to resist.

The next time you are tempted or tested, remember this: God will allow hardship in the life of the Christian, but it will always be filtered through the screen of his love. He will never give you more than you can handle.

FIRST STEPS

31But if we examine ourselves, we will not be examined by God and judged in this way. 32But when we are judged and disciplined by the Lord, we will not be condemned with the world. 33So, dear brothers and sisters,* when you gather for the Lord's Supper, wait for each other. 34If you are really hungry, eat at home so you won't bring judgment upon yourselves when you meet together.

I'll give you instructions about the other matters after I arrive.

## CHAPTER 12
### Spiritual Gifts

And now, dear brothers and sisters,* I will write about the special abilities the Holy Spirit gives to each of us, for I must correct your misunderstandings about them. 2You know that when you were still pagans you were led astray and swept along in worshiping speechless idols. 3So I want you to know how to discern what is truly from God: No one speaking by the Spirit of God can curse Jesus, and no one is able to say, "Jesus is Lord," except by the Holy Spirit.

4Now there are different kinds of spiritual gifts, but it is the same Holy Spirit who is the source of them all. 5There are different kinds of service in the church, but it is the same Lord we are serving. 6There are different ways God works in our lives, but it is the same God who does the work through all of us. 7A spiritual gift is given to each of us as a means of helping the entire church.

8To one person the Spirit gives the ability to give wise advice; to another he gives the gift of special knowledge. 9The Spirit gives special faith to another, and to someone else he gives the power to heal the sick. 10He gives one person the power to perform miracles, and to another the ability to prophesy. He gives someone else the ability to know whether it is really the Spirit of God or another spirit that is speaking. Still an-

other person is given the ability to speak in unknown languages,* and another is given the ability to interpret what is being said. 11It is the one and only Holy Spirit who distributes these gifts. He alone decides which gift each person should have.

### One Body with Many Parts

12The human body has many parts, but the many parts make up only one body. So it is with the body of Christ. 13Some of us are Jews, some are Gentiles, some are slaves, and some are free. But we have all been baptized into Christ's body by one Spirit, and we have all received the same Spirit.*

14Yes, the body has many different parts, not just one part. 15If the foot says, "I am not a part of the body because I am not a hand," that does not make it any less a part of the body. 16And if the ear says, "I am not part of the body because I am only an ear and not an eye," would that make it any less a part of the body? 17Suppose the whole body were an eye—then how would you hear? Or if your whole body were just one big ear, how could you smell anything?

18But God made our bodies with many parts, and he has put each part just where he wants it. 19What a strange thing a body would be if it had only one part! 20Yes, there are many parts, but only one body. 21The eye can never say to the hand, "I don't need you." The head can't say to the feet, "I don't need you."

22In fact, some of the parts that seem weakest and least important are really the most necessary. 23And the parts we regard as less honorable are those we clothe with the greatest care. So we carefully protect from the eyes of others those parts that should not be seen, 24while other parts do not require this special care. So God has put the body together in such a way that extra honor and care are given to those parts that have less dignity. 25This makes for harmony among

11:33 Greek *brothers*. 12:1 Greek *brothers*. 12:10 Or *in tongues*; also in 12:28, 30. 12:13 Greek *we were all given one Spirit to drink.*

## OFF AND RUNNING
### Does This Activity Build Me Up Spiritually?
Read 1 CORINTHIANS 10:23

This verse tackles the issue of whether certain activities will be spiritually constructive in your life—even if it falls into a so-called "gray" area. A more literal translation of that verse is "All things are permissible, but not all things promote growth in Christian character." The next time you question whether you should be seeing a certain movie, participating in a specific activity, or engaging in a certain habit, ask yourself the following questions:

the members, so that all the members care for each other equally. 26If one part suffers, all the parts suffer with it, and if one part is honored, all the parts are glad.

27Now all of you together are Christ's body, and each one of you is a separate and necessary part of it. 28Here is a list of some of the members that God has placed in the body of Christ:

> first are apostles,
> second are prophets,
> third are teachers,
> then those who do miracles,
> those who have the gift of healing,
> those who can help others,
> those who can get others to work together,
> those who speak in unknown languages.

29Is everyone an apostle? Of course not. Is everyone a prophet? No. Are all teachers? Does everyone have the power to do miracles? 30Does everyone have the gift of healing? Of course not. Does God give all of us the ability to speak in unknown languages? Can everyone interpret unknown languages? No! 31And in any event, you should desire the most helpful gifts.

### Love Is the Greatest

First, however, let me tell you about something else that is better than any of them!

## CHAPTER 13

If I could speak in any language in heaven or on earth* but didn't love others, I would only be making meaningless noise like a loud gong or a clanging cymbal. 2If I had the gift of prophecy, and if I knew all the mysteries of the future and knew everything about everything, but didn't love others, what good would I be? And if I had the gift of faith so that I could speak to a mountain and make it move, without love I would be no good to anybody. 3If I gave everything I have

to the poor and even sacrificed my body, I could boast about it;* but if I didn't love others, I would be of no value whatsoever.

4Love is patient and kind. Love is not jealous or boastful or proud 5or rude. Love does not demand its own way. Love is not irritable, and it keeps no record of when it has been wronged. 6It is never glad about injustice but rejoices whenever the truth wins out. 7Love never gives up, never loses faith, is always hopeful, and endures through every circumstance.

8Love will last forever, but prophecy and speaking in unknown languages* and special knowledge will all disappear. 9Now we know only a little, and even the gift of prophecy reveals little! 10But when the end comes, these special gifts will all disappear.

11It's like this: When I was a child, I spoke and thought and reasoned as a child does. But when I grew up, I put away childish things. 12Now we see things imperfectly as in a poor mirror, but then we will see everything with perfect clarity.* All that I know now is partial and incomplete, but then I will know everything completely, just as God knows me now.

13There are three things that will endure—faith, hope, and love—and the greatest of these is love.

## CHAPTER 14
### The Gifts of Tongues and Prophecy

Let love be your highest goal, but also desire the special abilities the Spirit gives, especially the gift of prophecy. 2For if your gift is the ability to speak in tongues,* you will be talking to God but not to people, since they won't be able to understand you. You will be speaking by the power of the Spirit, but it will all be mysterious. 3But one who prophesies is helping others grow in the Lord, encouraging and comforting them. 4A person who speaks in tongues is strength-

13:1 Greek *in tongues of people and angels.*   13:3 Some manuscripts read *and even gave my body to be burned.*   13:8 Or *in tongues.*
13:12 Greek *see face to face.*   14:2 Or *in unknown languages;* also in 14:4, 5, 13, 14, 18, 22, 28, 39.

- Will this activity make the things of this world more appealing than the things of God?
- Will it keep me from prayer?
- Will it diminish my hunger for God's Word?
- Will it spiritually tear me down by pulling me away from other Christian believers?

You do not have time for anything that would make this world more attractive, dull your desire for prayer, take away your appetite for Bible study, or keep you from Christian fellowship. Instead, look for things that will benefit and build your Christian character.

ened personally in the Lord, but one who speaks a word of prophecy strengthens the entire church.

5I wish you all had the gift of speaking in tongues, but even more I wish you were all able to prophesy. For prophecy is a greater and more useful gift than speaking in tongues, unless someone interprets what you are saying so that the whole church can get some good out of it.

6Dear brothers and sisters,* if I should come to you talking in an unknown language,* how would that help you? But if I bring you some revelation or some special knowledge or some prophecy or some teaching—that is what will help you. 7Even musical instruments like the flute or the harp, though they are lifeless, are examples of the need for speaking in plain language. For no one will recognize the melody unless the notes are played clearly. 8And if the bugler doesn't sound a clear call, how will the soldiers know they are being called to battle? 9And it's the same for you. If you talk to people in a language they don't understand, how will they know what you mean? You might as well be talking to an empty room.

10There are so many different languages in the world, and all are excellent for those who understand them, 11but to me they mean nothing. I will not understand people who speak those languages, and they will not understand me. 12Since you are so eager to have spiritual gifts, ask God for those that will be of real help to the whole church.

13So anyone who has the gift of speaking in tongues should pray also for the gift of interpretation in order to tell people plainly what has been said. 14For if I pray in tongues, my spirit is praying, but I don't understand what I am saying.

15Well then, what shall I do? I will do both. I will pray in the spirit,* and I will pray in words I understand. I will sing in the spirit, and I will sing in words I understand. 16For if you praise God only in the spirit, how can those who don't understand you praise God along with you? How can they join you in giving thanks when they don't understand what you are saying? 17You will be giving thanks very nicely, no doubt, but it doesn't help the other people present.

18I thank God that I speak in tongues more than all of you. 19But in a church meeting I would much rather speak five understandable

words that will help others than ten thousand words in an unknown language.

20Dear brothers and sisters, don't be childish in your understanding of these things. Be innocent as babies when it comes to evil, but be mature and wise in understanding matters of this kind. 21It is written in the Scriptures,*

"I will speak to my own people
    through unknown languages
    and through the lips of foreigners.
But even then, they will not listen to me,"*
    says the Lord.

22So you see that speaking in tongues is a sign, not for believers, but for unbelievers; prophecy, however, is for the benefit of believers, not unbelievers. 23Even so, if unbelievers or people who don't understand these things come into your meeting and hear everyone talking in an unknown language, they will think you are crazy. 24But if all of you are prophesying, and unbelievers or people who don't understand these things come into your meeting, they will be convicted of sin, and they will be condemned by what you say. 25As they listen, their secret thoughts will be laid bare, and they will fall down on their knees and worship God, declaring, "God is really here among you."

### A Call to Orderly Worship

26Well, my brothers and sisters, let's summarize what I am saying. When you meet, one will sing, another will teach, another will tell some special revelation God has given, one will speak in an unknown language, while another will interpret what is said. But everything that is done must be useful to all and build them up in the Lord. 27No more than two or three should speak in an unknown language. They must speak one at a time, and someone must be ready to interpret what they are saying. 28But if no one is present who can interpret, they must be silent in your church meeting and speak in tongues to God privately.

29Let two or three prophesy, and let the others evaluate what is said. 30But if someone is prophesying and another person receives a revelation from the Lord, the one who is speaking must stop. 31In this way, all who prophesy will have a turn to speak, one after the other, so that everyone will learn and be encouraged. 32Remember that people who prophesy are in control of their spirit and can wait their turn.

14:6a Greek *brothers;* also in 14:20, 26, 39.    14:6b Or *in tongues;* also in 14:19, 23, 26, 27.    14:15 Or *in the Spirit;* also in 14:15b, 16.
14:21a Greek *in the law.*    14:21b Isa 28:11-12.

33For God is not a God of disorder but of peace, as in all the other churches.*

34Women should be silent during the church meetings. It is not proper for them to speak. They should be submissive, just as the law says. 35If they have any questions to ask, let them ask their husbands at home, for it is improper for women to speak in church meetings.*

36Do you think that the knowledge of God's word begins and ends with you Corinthians? Well, you are mistaken! 37If you claim to be a prophet or think you are very spiritual, you should recognize that what I am saying is a command from the Lord himself. 38But if you do not recognize this, you will not be recognized.*

39So, dear brothers and sisters, be eager to prophesy, and don't forbid speaking in tongues. 40But be sure that everything is done properly and in order.

## CHAPTER 15
*The Resurrection of Christ*

Now let me remind you, dear brothers and sisters,* of the Good News I preached to you before. You welcomed it then and still do now, for your faith is built on this wonderful message. 2And it is this Good News that saves you if you firmly believe it—unless, of course, you believed something that was never true in the first place.

3I passed on to you what was most important and what had also been passed on to me—that Christ died for our sins, just as the Scriptures said. 4He was buried, and he was raised from the dead on the third day, as the Scriptures said. 5He was seen by Peter* and then by the twelve apostles. 6After that, he was seen by more than five hundred of his followers* at one time, most of whom are still alive, though some have died by now. 7Then he was seen by James and later by all the apostles. 8Last of all, I saw him, too, long after the others, as though I had been born at the wrong time. 9For I am the least of all the apostles, and I am not worthy to be called an apostle after the way I persecuted the church of God.

10But whatever I am now, it is all because God poured out his special favor on me—and not without results. For I have worked harder than all the other apostles, yet it was not I but God who was working through me by his grace. 11So

14:33 The phrase *as in all the other churches* could be joined to the beginning of 14:34. 14:35 Some manuscripts place verses 34-35 after 14:40. 14:38 Some manuscripts read *If you are ignorant of this, stay in your ignorance.* 15:1 Greek *brothers;* also in 15:31, 50, 58. 15:5 Greek *Cephas.* 15:6 Greek *the brothers.*

## You Have a Place in the Church Read 1 CORINTHIANS 12:12-27

The apostle Paul used this illustration of the physical body to drive home an important point: Every single person has a vital role to play in the body of Christ. That means God has a specific purpose for *you* to carry out in your local church, and it is up to you to fill that purpose, with God's help. This passage explains why this is so important.

**The Church Consists of Different People with Different Roles.** When God designed the church, he did not intend for its members to be "Christian clones." Instead, he chose to use the various groups and spiritual gifts found throughout the church to bring attention to the person who unifies us: Jesus Christ (see Ephesians 3:10-11, p. 239). When the church operates as God intended, it serves as a powerful witness to a watching world.

**No One Person Is More Valuable than Another.** No gift of the Holy Spirit is "better" than another. Therefore, each individual has a special place of significance within the body of Christ. Even though your role may not seem as visible as others—for instance, God may be using you to visit convalescent homes while someone else leads a Bible study—your role is just as vital.

**We Need One Another to Function as God Intended.** If you fail to use the special gifts and abilities God has given you, you do a disservice to the church. God wants you to realize the importance of working together and building friendships with other committed Christians. One could liken the church to a group of coals burning brightly together. Each coal not only emanates its own heat, but also helps to keep the others hot, all the while benefiting from their warmth, as well. If you were to isolate one of those coals from the others, it would only be a matter of time until its heat dissipated. The same holds true for us as believers. We need one another to function as individuals and as the body of Christ.

FIRST STEPS

## Love Surpasses All Spiritual Gifts  Read 1 CORINTHIANS 13:1-13

This passage gives one of the most complete descriptions of love in the Bible. More importantly, it shows that love needs to be the one thing in life we seek more than anything else. For without it, whatever we do or say really has no lasting value. Compare the love described here with the superficial love found in this world:

- God says love should be directed toward others (verses 1-3).
  The world says love should be directed toward ourselves.
- God says love is patient and kind (verse 4).
  The world says love satisfies your immediate needs.
- God says love is never jealous or envious (verse 4).
  The world says love means that you deserve the "best."
- God says love is never boastful or proud (verse 4).
  The world says love isn't necessary to make people respect you.
- God says love is never rude (verse 5).
  The world says love lets you act as you please.
- God says love does not demand its own way (verse 5).
  The world says love gets in the way of what is in it for me.
- God says love is not irritable or touchy, and it holds no grudges (verse 5).
  The world says love takes a backseat when it comes to seeking revenge.
- God says love rejoices in justice and truth (verse 6).
  The world says love understands—even ignores—evil.
- God says love is loyal (verse 7).
  The world says love should be self-serving.

The kind of love God wants you to give others is impossible to "manufacture" on our own. You might say that it is a "supernatural" love. It is a natural outflow of God's presence in our lives. That is why the Bible says, "[God] has given us the Holy Spirit to fill our hearts with his love" (Romans 5:5).

If you feel your love for others is falling short of God's ideal, ask the Holy Spirit to strengthen you in this area. Your relationships with others will never be the same.

**CORNER STONES**

it makes no difference whether I preach or they preach. The important thing is that you believed what we preached to you.

### The Resurrection of the Dead

12But tell me this—since we preach that Christ rose from the dead, why are some of you saying there will be no resurrection of the dead? 13For if there is no resurrection of the dead, then Christ has not been raised either. 14And if Christ was not raised, then all our preaching is useless, and your trust in God is useless. 15And we apostles would all be lying about God, for we have said that God raised Christ from the grave, but that can't be true if there is no resurrection of the dead. 16If there is no resurrection of the dead, then Christ has not been raised. 17And if Christ has not been raised, then your faith is useless, and you are still under condemnation for your sins. 18In that case, all who have died believing in Christ have perished! 19And if we have hope in Christ only for this life, we are the most miserable people in the world.

20But the fact is that Christ has been raised from the dead. He has become the first of a great harvest of those who will be raised to life again.

21So you see, just as death came into the world through a man, Adam, now the resurrection from the dead has begun through another man, Christ. 22Everyone dies because all of us are related to Adam, the first man. But all who are related to Christ, the other man, will be given new life. 23But there is an order to this resurrection: Christ was raised first; then when Christ comes back, all his people will be raised.

24After that the end will come, when he will turn the Kingdom over to God the Father, having put down all enemies of every kind.* 25For Christ must reign until he humbles all his enemies beneath his feet. 26And the last enemy to be destroyed is death. 27For the Scriptures say, "God has given him authority over all things."* (Of course, when it says "authority over all things," it does not include God himself, who gave Christ his authority.) 28Then, when he has conquered all things, the Son will present himself to God, so that God, who gave his Son authority over all things, will be utterly supreme over everything everywhere.

29If the dead will not be raised, then what point is there in people being baptized for those who are dead? Why do it unless the dead will someday rise again?

30And why should we ourselves be continually risking our lives, facing death hour by hour? 31For I swear, dear brothers and sisters, I face death daily. This is as certain as my pride in what the Lord Jesus Christ has done in you. 32And what value was there in fighting wild beasts—those men of Ephesus*—if there will be no resurrection from the dead? If there is no resurrection,

"Let's feast and get drunk,
    for tomorrow we die!"*

33Don't be fooled by those who say such things, for "bad company corrupts good character." 34Come to your senses and stop sinning. For to your shame I say that some of you don't even know God.

## The Resurrection Body

35But someone may ask, "How will the dead be raised? What kind of bodies will they have?" 36What a foolish question! When you put a seed into the ground, it doesn't grow into a plant unless it dies first. 37And what you put in the ground is not the plant that will grow, but only a dry little seed of wheat or whatever it is you are planting. 38Then God gives it a new body—just the kind he wants it to have. A different kind of plant grows from each kind of seed. 39And just as there are different kinds of seeds and plants, so also there are different kinds of flesh— whether of humans, animals, birds, or fish.

40There are bodies in the heavens, and there are bodies on earth. The glory of the heavenly bodies is different from the beauty of the earthly bodies. 41The sun has one kind of glory, while the moon and stars each have another kind. And even the stars differ from each other in their beauty and brightness.

42It is the same way for the resurrection of the dead. Our earthly bodies, which die and decay, will be different when they are resurrected, for they will never die. 43Our bodies now disappoint us, but when they are raised, they will be full of glory. They are weak now, but when they are raised, they will be full of power. 44They are natural human bodies now, but when they are raised, they will be spiritual bodies. For just as there are natural bodies, so also there are spiritual bodies.

45The Scriptures tell us, "The first man, Adam, became a living person."* But the last Adam—that is, Christ—is a life-giving Spirit. 46What came first was the natural body, then the spiritual body comes later. 47Adam, the first man, was made from the dust of the earth, while Christ, the second man, came from heaven. 48Every human being has an earthly body just like Adam's, but our heavenly bodies will be just like Christ's. 49Just as we are now like Adam, the man of the earth, so we will someday be like Christ, the man from heaven.

50What I am saying, dear brothers and sisters, is that flesh and blood cannot inherit the Kingdom of God. These perishable bodies of ours are not able to live forever.

51But let me tell you a wonderful secret God has revealed to us. Not all of us will die, but we will all be transformed. 52It will happen in a moment, in the blinking of an eye, when the last trumpet is blown. For when the trumpet sounds, the Christians who have died* will be raised with transformed bodies. And then we who are living will be transformed so that we will never die. 53For our perishable earthly bodies must be transformed into heavenly bodies that will never die.

54When this happens—when our perishable earthly bodies have been transformed into heavenly bodies that will never die—then at last the Scriptures will come true:

"Death is swallowed up in victory.*
55 O death, where is your victory?
    O death, where is your sting?"*

56For sin is the sting that results in death, and the law gives sin its power. 57How we thank God,

15:24 Greek *every ruler and every authority and power.*   15:27 Ps 8:6.   15:32a Greek *fighting wild beasts in Ephesus.*   15:32b Isa 22:13.
15:45 Gen 2:7.   15:52 Greek *the dead.*   15:54 Isa 25:8.   15:55 Hos 13:14.

who gives us victory over sin and death through Jesus Christ our Lord!

58So, my dear brothers and sisters, be strong and steady, always enthusiastic about the Lord's work, for you know that nothing you do for the Lord is ever useless.

## CHAPTER 16
### The Collection for Jerusalem

Now about the money being collected for the Christians in Jerusalem: You should follow the same procedures I gave to the churches in Galatia. 2On every Lord's Day,* each of you should put aside some amount of money in relation to what you have earned and save it for this offering. Don't wait until I get there and then try to collect it all at once. 3When I come I will write letters of recommendation for the messengers you choose to deliver your gift to Jerusalem. 4And if it seems appropriate for me also to go along, then we can travel together.

### Paul's Final Instructions

5I am coming to visit you after I have been to Macedonia, for I am planning to travel through Macedonia. 6It could be that I will stay awhile with you, perhaps all winter, and then you can send me on my way to the next destination. 7This time I don't want to make just a short visit and then go right on. I want to come and stay awhile, if the Lord will let me. 8In the meantime, I will be staying here at Ephesus until the Festival of Pentecost, 9for there is a wide-open door for a great work here, and many people are responding. But there are many who oppose me.

10When Timothy comes, treat him with respect. He is doing the Lord's work, just as I am.

11Don't let anyone despise him. Send him on his way with your blessings when he returns to me. I am looking forward to seeing him soon, along with the other brothers.

12Now about our brother Apollos—I urged him to join the other brothers when they visit you, but he was not willing to come right now. He will be seeing you later, when the time is right.

13Be on guard. Stand true to what you believe. Be courageous. Be strong. 14And everything you do must be done with love.

15You know that Stephanas and his household were the first to become Christians in Greece,* and they are spending their lives in service to other Christians. I urge you, dear brothers and sisters,* 16to respect them fully and others like them who serve with such real devotion. 17I am so glad that Stephanas, Fortunatus, and Achaicus have come here. They have been making up for the help you weren't here to give me. 18They have been a wonderful encouragement to me, as they have been to you, too. You must give proper honor to all who serve so well.

### Paul's Final Greetings

19The churches here in the province of Asia* greet you heartily in the Lord, along with Aquila and Priscilla and all the others who gather in their home for church meetings. 20 All the brothers and sisters here have asked me to greet you for them. Greet each other in Christian love.*

21Here is my greeting, which I write with my own hand—PAUL.

22If anyone does not love the Lord, that person is cursed. Our Lord, come!*

23May the grace of the Lord Jesus be with you. 24My love to all of you in Christ Jesus.*

16:2 Greek *every first day of the week.* 16:15a Greek *were the firstfruits in Achaia,* the southern region of the Greek peninsula. 16:15b Greek *brothers;* also in 16:20. 16:19 *Asia* was a Roman province in what is now western Turkey. 16:20 Greek *with a sacred kiss.* 16:22 From Aramaic, *Marana tha.* 16:24 Some manuscripts add *Amen.*

# 2 Corinthians

## CHAPTER 1

### Greetings from Paul

This letter is from Paul, appointed by God to be an apostle of Christ Jesus, and from our dear brother Timothy.

We are writing to God's church in Corinth and to all the Christians throughout Greece.*

2May God our Father and the Lord Jesus Christ give you his grace and peace.

### God Offers Comfort to All

3All praise to the God and Father of our Lord Jesus Christ. He is the source* of every mercy and the God who comforts us. 4He comforts us in all our troubles so that we can comfort others. When others are troubled, we will be able to give them the same comfort God has given us. 5You can be sure that the more we suffer for Christ, the more God will shower us with his comfort through Christ. 6So when we are weighed down with troubles, it is for your benefit and salvation! For when God comforts us, it is so that we, in turn, can be an encouragement to you. Then you can patiently endure the same things we suffer. 7We are confident that as you share in suffering, you will also share God's comfort.

8I think you ought to know, dear brothers and sisters,* about the trouble we went through in the province of Asia. We were crushed and completely overwhelmed, and we thought we would never live through it. 9In fact, we expected to die. But as a result, we learned not to rely on ourselves, but on God who can raise the dead. 10And he did deliver us from mortal danger. And we are confident that he will continue to deliver us. 11He will rescue us because you are helping by praying for us. As a result, many will give thanks to God because so many people's prayers for our safety have been answered.

### Paul's Change of Plans

12We can say with confidence and a clear conscience that we have been honest* and sincere in all our dealings. We have depended on God's grace, not on our own earthly wisdom. That is how we have acted toward everyone, and especially toward you. 13My letters have been straightforward, and there is nothing written between the lines and nothing you can't understand. I hope someday you will fully understand us, 14even if you don't fully understand us now. Then on the day when our Lord Jesus comes back again, you will be proud of us in the same way we are proud of you.

15Since I was so sure of your understanding and trust, I wanted to give you a double blessing. 16I wanted to stop and see you on my way to Macedonia and again on my return trip. Then you could send me on my way to Judea.

17You may be asking why I changed my plan. Hadn't I made up my mind yet? Or am I like people of the world who say yes when they really mean no? 18As surely as God is true, I am not that sort of person. My yes means yes 19because Jesus Christ, the Son of God, never wavers between yes and no. He is the one whom Timothy, Silas,* and I preached to you, and he is the divine Yes—God's affirmation. 20For all of God's promises have been fulfilled in him. That is why we say "Amen" when we give glory to God through Christ. 21It is God who gives us, along with you, the ability to stand firm for Christ.* He has commissioned us, 22and he has identified us as his own by placing the Holy Spirit in our hearts as the first installment of everything he will give us.

1:1 Greek Achaia, the southern region of the Greek peninsula.   1:3 Greek the Father.   1:8 Greek brothers.   1:12 Some manuscripts read holy.   1:19 Greek Silvanus.   1:21 Or who has identified us and you as genuine Christians.

23Now I call upon God as my witness that I am telling the truth. The reason I didn't return to Corinth was to spare you from a severe rebuke. 24But that does not mean we want to tell you exactly how to put your faith into practice.* We want to work together with you so you will be full of joy as you stand firm in your faith.

## CHAPTER 2

So I said to myself, "No, I won't do it. I won't make them unhappy with another painful visit." 2For if I cause you pain and make you sad, who is going to make me glad? 3That is why I wrote as I did in my last letter, so that when I do come, I will not be made sad by the very ones who ought to give me the greatest joy. Surely you know that my happiness depends on your happiness. 4How painful it was to write that letter! Heartbroken, I cried over it. I didn't want to hurt you, but I wanted you to know how very much I love you.

### Forgiveness for the Sinner

5I am not overstating it when I say that the man who caused all the trouble hurt your entire church more than he hurt me. 6He was punished enough when most of you were united in your judgment against him. 7Now it is time to forgive him and comfort him. Otherwise he may become so discouraged that he won't be able to recover. 8Now show him that you still love him.

9I wrote to you as I did to find out how far you would go in obeying me. 10When you forgive this man, I forgive him, too. And when I forgive him (for whatever is to be forgiven), I do so with Christ's authority for your benefit, 11so that Satan will not outsmart us. For we are very familiar with his evil schemes.

### Ministers of the New Covenant

12Well, when I came to the city of Troas to preach the Good News of Christ, the Lord gave me tremendous opportunities. 13But I couldn't rest because my dear brother Titus hadn't yet arrived with a report from you. So I said goodbye and went on to Macedonia to find him.

14But thanks be to God, who made us his captives and leads us along in Christ's triumphal procession. Now wherever we go he uses us to tell others about the Lord and to spread the Good News like a sweet perfume. 15Our lives are a fragrance presented by Christ to God. But this fragrance is perceived differently by those being saved and by those perishing. 16To those who are perishing we are a fearful smell of death and doom. But to those who are being saved we are a life-giving perfume. And who is adequate for such a task as this? 17You see, we are not like those hucksters—and there are many of them— who preach just to make money. We preach God's message with sincerity and with Christ's authority. And we know that the God who sent us is watching us.

## CHAPTER 3

Are we beginning again to tell you how good we are? Some people need to bring letters of recommendation with them or ask you to write letters of recommendation for them. 2But the only letter of recommendation we need is you yourselves! Your lives are a letter written in our* hearts, and everyone can read it and recognize our good work among you. 3Clearly, you are a letter from Christ prepared by us. It is written not with pen and ink, but with the Spirit of the living God. It is carved not on stone, but on human hearts.

4We are confident of all this because of our great trust in God through Christ. 5It is not that we think we can do anything of lasting value by ourselves. Our only power and success come from God. 6He is the one who has enabled us to represent his new covenant. This is a covenant, not of written laws, but of the Spirit. The old way ends in death; in the new way, the Holy Spirit gives life.

### The Glory of the New Covenant

7That old system of law etched in stone led to death, yet it began with such glory that the people of Israel could not bear to look at Moses' face. For his face shone with the glory of God, even though the brightness was already fading away. 8Shouldn't we expect far greater glory when the Holy Spirit is giving life? 9If the old covenant, which brings condemnation, was glorious, how much more glorious is the new covenant, which makes us right with God! 10In fact, that first glory was not glorious at all compared with the overwhelming glory of the new covenant. 11So if the old covenant, which has been set aside, was full of glory, then the new covenant, which remains forever, has far greater glory.

12Since this new covenant gives us such confidence, we can be very bold. 13We are not like

1:24 Greek *want to lord it over your faith.*   3:2 Some manuscripts read *your.*

Moses, who put a veil over his face so the people of Israel would not see the glory fading away. 14But the people's minds were hardened, and even to this day whenever the old covenant is being read, a veil covers their minds so they cannot understand the truth. And this veil can be removed only by believing in Christ. 15Yes, even today when they read Moses' writings, their hearts are covered with that veil, and they do not understand.

16But whenever anyone turns to the Lord, then the veil is taken away. 17Now, the Lord is the Spirit, and wherever the Spirit of the Lord is, he gives freedom. 18And all of us have had that veil removed so that we can be mirrors that brightly reflect* the glory of the Lord. And as the Spirit of the Lord works within us, we become more and more like him and reflect his glory even more.

CHAPTER **4**

*Treasure in Perishable Containers*

And so, since God in his mercy has given us this wonderful ministry, we never give up. 2We reject all shameful and underhanded methods. We do not try to trick anyone, and we do not distort the word of God. We tell the truth before God, and all who are honest know that.

3If the Good News we preach is veiled from anyone, it is a sign that they are perishing. 4Satan, the god of this evil world, has blinded the minds of those who don't believe, so they are unable to see the glorious light of the Good News that is shining upon them. They don't understand the message we preach about the glory of Christ, who is the exact likeness of God.

5We don't go around preaching about ourselves; we preach Christ Jesus, the Lord. All we say about ourselves is that we are your servants because of what Jesus has done for us. 6For God, who said, "Let there be light in the darkness,". has made us understand that this light is the brightness of the glory of God that is seen in the face of Jesus Christ.

7But this precious treasure—this light and power that now shine within us—is held in perishable containers, that is, in our weak bodies.* So everyone can see that our glorious power is from God and is not our own.

8We are pressed on every side by troubles, but we are not crushed and broken. We are perplexed, but we don't give up and quit. 9We are

3:18 Or *so that we can see in a mirror.* 4:7 Greek *But we have this treasure in earthen vessels.*

hunted down, but God never abandons us. We get knocked down, but we get up again and keep going. 10Through suffering, these bodies of o. s constantly share in the death of Jesus so that the life of Jesus may also be seen in our bodies.

11Yes, we live under constant danger of death because we serve Jesus, so that the life of Jesus will be obvious in our dying bodies. 12So we live in the face of death, but it has resulted in eternal life for you.

13But we continue to preach because we have the same kind of faith the psalmist had when he said, "I believed in God, and so I speak."* 14We know that the same God who raised our Lord Jesus will also raise us with Jesus and present us to himself along with you. 15All of these things are for your benefit. And as God's grace brings more and more people to Christ, there will be great thanksgiving, and God will receive more and more glory.

16That is why we never give up. Though our bodies are dying, our spirits are* being renewed

4:13 Ps 116:10.   4:16 Greek *our inner being is.*

---

## Trials Help Us Comfort Others Read 2 CORINTHIANS 1:3-7

The apostle Paul penned these words from personal experience. He had seen his share of suffering over the years—particularly for the sake of the gospel of Jesus Christ. He was thrown into prison on more than one occasion, but he continued to praise God and share his faith in Christ. He was shipwrecked, abandoned by former friends, pelted by stones, and left for dead. His faith, however, remained firm. Why? Because he learned to draw his comfort from the Lord. This then enabled him to be a greater source of comfort to those around him.

The next time someone ridicules or rejects you because of your commitment to Christ, remember Paul's words. You do not need to fear trials in your life. No matter how great a hardship you face, realize that Jesus *will* comfort and strengthen you. In turn, you will be better equipped to comfort those around you who suffer the same hardships.

## What Are Satan's Abilities? Read 2 CORINTHIANS 4:3-4

Ever since Satan lost his privileges and was cast to this earth, he has been using his abilities to oppose the work that God has been seeking to accomplish. Paul's second letter to the Corinthians reveals at least three of Satan's abilities:

**1. He Is the God of This World.** This becomes more and more evident as you survey the increasing wickedness around you. While Christ conquered sin and death at the cross, this world is still flawed and evil. But Satan will lose his reign in this world when Christ returns to establish his Kingdom on earth.

**2. He Blinds the Minds of Unbelievers.** According to this text, Satan wants to keep those who do not have a relationship with God from coming to God. The unbelieving mind has a difficult time understanding the message of the gospel because Satan has darkened or blinded that person's mind. Yet Christ can break through that barrier (see 2 Timothy 2:24-26, p. 277).

**3. He Is a Master Counterfeiter.** One of Satan's greatest abilities is deception. He is good at deception because he makes lies look like truth. Paul describes Satan as someone who disguises himself as an angel of light (see 2 Corinthians 11:14, p. 226). That is, he fools people by making them think the lies he offers are truth. His lies take on various forms, such as cults and false doctrines. But we can discern the difference between truth and error when we test them against what is found in God's Word.

**CORNER STONES**

---

every day. 17For our present troubles are quite small and won't last very long. Yet they produce for us an immeasurably great glory that will last forever! 18So we don't look at the troubles we can see right now; rather, we look forward to what we have not yet seen. For the troubles we see will soon be over, but the joys to come will last forever.

CHAPTER **5**
*New Bodies*

For we know that when this earthly tent we live in is taken down—when we die and leave these bodies—we will have a home in heaven, an eternal body made for us by God himself and not by human hands. 2We grow weary in our present bodies, and we long for the day when we will put on our heavenly bodies like new clothing. 3For we will not be spirits without bodies, but we will put on new heavenly bodies. 4Our dying bodies make us groan and sigh, but it's not that we want to die and have no bodies at all. We want to slip into our new bodies so that these dying bodies will be swallowed up by everlasting life. 5God himself has prepared us for this, and as a guarantee he has given us his Holy Spirit.

**5:14a** Or *urges us on.*

6So we are always confident, even though we know that as long as we live in these bodies we are not at home with the Lord. 7That is why we live by believing and not by seeing. 8Yes, we are fully confident, and we would rather be away from these bodies, for then we will be at home with the Lord. 9So our aim is to please him always, whether we are here in this body or away from this body. 10For we must all stand before Christ to be judged. We will each receive whatever we deserve for the good or evil we have done in our bodies.

*We Are God's Ambassadors*

11It is because we know this solemn fear of the Lord that we work so hard to persuade others. God knows we are sincere, and I hope you know this, too. 12Are we trying to pat ourselves on the back again? No, we are giving you a reason to be proud of us, so you can answer those who brag about having a spectacular ministry rather than having a sincere heart before God. 13If it seems that we are crazy, it is to bring glory to God. And if we are in our right minds, it is for your benefit. 14Whatever we do, it is because Christ's love controls us.* Since we believe that Christ died for everyone, we also believe that we have all died to the old life we used to live.* ¹⁵He died for everyone so that those who receive his new life will no longer live to please themselves. Instead, they will live to please Christ, who died and was raised for them.

¹⁶So we have stopped evaluating others by what the world thinks about them. Once I mistakenly thought of Christ that way, as though he were merely a human being. How differently I think about him now! ¹⁷What this means is that those who become Christians become new persons. They are not the same anymore, for the old life is gone. A new life has begun!

¹⁸All this newness of life is from God, who brought us back to himself through what Christ did. And God has given us the task of reconciling people to him. ¹⁹For God was in Christ, reconciling the world to himself, no longer counting people's sins against them. This is the wonderful message he has given us to tell others. ²⁰We are Christ's ambassadors, and God is using us to speak to you. We urge you, as though Christ himself were here pleading with you, "Be reconciled to God!" ²¹For God made Christ, who never sinned, to be the offering for our sin, so that we could be made right with God through Christ.

## CHAPTER 6

As God's partners,* we beg you not to reject this marvelous message of God's great kindness. ²For God says,

"At just the right time, I heard you.
    On the day of salvation, I helped you."*

Indeed, God is ready to help you right now. Today is the day of salvation.

### Paul's Hardships

³We try to live in such a way that no one will be hindered from finding the Lord by the way we act, and so no one can find fault with our ministry. ⁴In everything we do we try to show that we are true ministers of God. We patiently endure troubles and hardships and calamities of every kind. ⁵We have been beaten, been put in jail, faced angry mobs, worked to exhaustion, endured sleepless nights, and gone without food. ⁶We have proved ourselves by our purity, our understanding, our patience, our kindness, our sincere love, and the power of the Holy Spirit.*

5:14b Greek *Since one died on behalf of all, then all died.*   6:1 Or *As we work together.*   6:2 Isa 49:8.   6:6 Or *the holiness of spirit.*

## Trials Are Survivable
Read 2 CORINTHIANS 4:7-18

When we face trials in our lives, we can do one of two things. We can either become self-absorbed with our problems and say, "Look at how tough things are!" Or we can keep our eyes on Jesus and say, "This is only temporary." The apostle Paul was able to focus on the temporary nature of his problems because he accepted five important facts:

**1. Our Bodies Are Weak and Mortal.** Paul wasn't the type to be caught up in his bodily aches and pains. He didn't strive for the perfect body or the perfect image because he knew his body was a "perishable container." The Bible does not teach that we should neglect our bodies, but it does say that spiritual exercise is more important and beneficial (see 1 Timothy 4:8, p. 272).

**2. God's Power Is Displayed in Our Weakness.** If we become overly obsessed with ourselves, we will never give God the chance to work through our lives. Paul recognized that God's glory shines through our weaknesses.

**3. God Does Not Abandon Us.** Even though we may be "crushed" and "perplexed," we have the hope that God will protect and strengthen us through these trials.

**4. Trials Can Be Witnessing Opportunities.** When people see the inner strength we have in Christ, they will take notice. This is well illustrated in the story of Paul and Silas, who were put in prison for preaching the gospel (see Acts 16:16-36, p. 158). Though they had been whipped and had their legs clamped in stocks in a damp, dark dungeon, they began to pray and worship the Lord in song. In an unusual string of events, these men were able to lead their jailer, as well as his entire family, to the Lord. Paul and Silas's godly attitude, which enabled them to rejoice in such a time of trouble, prepared the soil of this man's heart, opening him up to the gospel they preached.

**5. We Have the Hope of Heaven.** These trials are only a momentary blink in time compared to the eternal joys and blessings of heaven.

## When Does a Christian Enter Heaven? Read 2 CORINTHIANS 5:6-9

Some people teach that when we die we go into a state of suspended animation. Then later on we are called into the presence of God. But this passage clearly explains that when a believer dies, he or she will go directly to heaven to "be at home with the Lord." This is illustrated in at least two other instances in Scripture:

**1. The Thief on the Cross.** As Jesus was being crucified, a thief hanging on a cross next to him asked Jesus to remember him when Jesus entered his Kingdom. To this request, Jesus replied, "*Today* you will be with me in paradise" (Luke 23:40-43).

**2. The Apostle Paul.** The apostle Paul wrote, "I long to go and be with Christ" (Philippians 1:23). He didn't say, "I long to depart and be suspended in a soul sleep for a few thousand years." Paul understood better than most this truth about entering heaven, because he had already had a glimpse of heaven. It is probable that when Paul had been stoned, he died and entered the

presence of the Lord. But God still had work for Paul to do on earth. So he sent Paul back to earth to carry out God's work (see 2 Corinthians 12:2-4, p. 227).

The moment you take your last breath on earth, you will take your first breath in heaven. So don't be afraid of death. Instead, enjoy your life in Christ on earth, and spend the rest of your time here introducing others to the one with whom you will spend eternity.

CORNER STONES

---

7We have faithfully preached the truth. God's power has been working in us. We have righteousness as our weapon, both to attack and to defend ourselves. 8We serve God whether people honor us or despise us, whether they slander us or praise us. We are honest, but they call us impostors. 9We are well known, but we are treated as unknown. We live close to death, but here we are, still alive. We have been beaten within an inch of our lives. 10Our hearts ache, but we always have joy. We are poor, but we give spiritual riches to others. We own nothing, and yet we have everything.

11Oh, dear Corinthian friends! We have spoken honestly with you. Our hearts are open to you. 12If there is a problem between us, it is not because of a lack of love on our part, but because you have withheld your love from us. 13I am talking now as I would to my own children. Open your hearts to us!

### The Temple of the Living God

14Don't team up with those who are unbelievers. How can goodness be a partner with wickedness? How can light live with darkness? 15What harmony can there be between Christ and the Devil*? How can a believer be a part-

ner with an unbeliever? 16And what union can there be between God's temple and idols? For we are the temple of the living God. As God said:

> "I will live in them
> and walk among them.
> I will be their God,
> and they will be my people.*
> 17 Therefore, come out from them
> and separate yourselves from them, says the Lord.
> Don't touch their filthy things,
> and I will welcome you.*
> 18 And I will be your Father,
> and you will be my sons and daughters,
> says the Lord Almighty.*"

## CHAPTER 7

Because we have these promises, dear friends, let us cleanse ourselves from everything that can defile our body or spirit. And let us work toward complete purity because we fear God.

### Paul's Joy at the Church's Repentance

2Please open your hearts to us. We have not done wrong to anyone. We have not led anyone

6:15 Greek *and Beliar.*   6:16 Lev 26:12; Ezek 37:27.   6:17 Isa 52:11; Ezek 20:34.   6:18 2 Sam 7:14.

astray. We have not taken advantage of anyone. ³I'm not saying this to condemn you, for I said before that you are in our hearts forever. We live or die together with you. ⁴I have the highest confidence in you, and my pride in you is great. You have greatly encouraged me; you have made me happy despite all our troubles.

⁵When we arrived in Macedonia there was no rest for us. Outside there was conflict from every direction, and inside there was fear. ⁶But God, who encourages those who are discouraged, encouraged us by the arrival of Titus. ⁷His presence was a joy, but so was the news he brought of the encouragement he received from you. When he told me how much you were looking forward to my visit, and how sorry you were about what had happened, and how loyal your love is for me, I was filled with joy!

⁸I am no longer sorry that I sent that letter to you, though I was sorry for a time, for I know that it was painful to you for a little while. ⁹Now I am glad I sent it, not because it hurt you, but because the pain caused you to have remorse and change your ways. It was the kind of sorrow God wants his people to have, so you were not harmed by us in any way. ¹⁰For God can use sorrow in our lives to help us turn away from sin and seek salvation. We will never regret that kind of sorrow. But sorrow without repentance is the kind that results in death.

¹¹Just see what this godly sorrow produced in you! Such earnestness, such concern to clear yourselves, such indignation, such alarm, such longing to see me, such zeal, and such a readiness to punish the wrongdoer. You showed that you have done everything you could to make things right. ¹²My purpose was not to write about who did the wrong or who was wronged. I wrote to you so that in the sight of God you could show how much you really do care for us. ¹³We have been encouraged by this.

In addition to our own encouragement, we were especially delighted to see how happy Titus was at the way you welcomed him and set his mind at ease. ¹⁴I had told him how proud I was of you—and you didn't disappoint me. I have always told you the truth, and now my boasting to Titus has also proved true! ¹⁵Now he cares for you more than ever when he remembers the way you listened to him and welcomed him with such respect and deep concern. ¹⁶I am very happy now because I have complete confidence in you.

## CHAPTER 8
*A Call to Generous Giving*

Now I want to tell you, dear brothers and sisters,* what God in his kindness has done for the churches in Macedonia. ²Though they have been going through much trouble and hard times, their wonderful joy and deep poverty have overflowed in rich generosity. ³For I can testify that they gave not only what they could

8:1 Greek *brothers.*

---

### Recognize That You Are a New Creation Read 2 CORINTHIANS 5:14-17

Although outwardly you may appear to be the same person, when you received Christ you underwent a radical heart transplant. You literally became a "new person" (or "creation") inside. This short passage of Scripture highlights some encouraging points as you endeavor to be obedient to God.

• As "new creations," Christ's love compels us to please God rather than ourselves.
• As "new creations," we can look beyond the "packaging" of a person to what is inside.
• As "new creations," we have become altogether different people.
• As "new creations," we have been given a clean slate, a fresh start, and a new nature.

The new nature you have received is like a tender little flower. It takes time and effort to cultivate. You may find it hard at times to obey God and leave certain old habits behind at first. But as you cultivate that new nature by spending more time with God through activities like prayer and Bible study, you will notice changes as the weeks, months, and years go by.

A man from India was heard to compare our new spiritual nature and our old selfish one to two dogs constantly fighting with each other. He went on to say that he could determine which dog would win. When asked how he determined which dog won, his response was, "The one I feed the most, of course." When you take time to "feed" your new spiritual nature (as you are doing right now), you give it the edge in this ongoing conflict between good and evil.

FIRST STEPS

afford but far more. And they did it of their own free will. ⁴They begged us again and again for the gracious privilege of sharing in the gift for the Christians in Jerusalem. ⁵Best of all, they went beyond our highest hopes, for their first action was to dedicate themselves to the Lord and to us for whatever directions God might give them.

⁶So we have urged Titus, who encouraged your giving in the first place, to return to you and encourage you to complete your share in this ministry of giving. ⁷Since you excel in so many ways—you have so much faith, such gifted speakers, such knowledge, such enthusiasm, and such love for us*—now I want you to excel also in this gracious ministry of giving. ⁸I am not saying you must do it, even though the other churches are eager to do it. This is one way to prove your love is real.

⁹You know how full of love and kindness our Lord Jesus Christ was. Though he was very rich, yet for your sakes he became poor, so that by his poverty he could make you rich.

¹⁰I suggest that you finish what you started a year ago, for you were the first to propose this idea, and you were the first to begin doing something about it. ¹¹Now you should carry this project through to completion just as enthusiastically as you began it. Give whatever you can according to what you have. ¹²If you are really eager to give, it isn't important how much you are able to give. God wants you to give what you have, not what you don't have. ¹³Of course, I don't mean you should give so much that you suffer from having too little. I only mean that there should be some equality. ¹⁴Right now you have plenty and can help them. Then at some other time they can share with you when you need it. In this way, everyone's needs will be met. ¹⁵Do you remember what the Scriptures say about this? "Those who gathered a lot had nothing left over, and those who gathered only a little had enough."*

### Titus and His Companions

¹⁶I am thankful to God that he has given Titus the same enthusiasm for you that I have. ¹⁷He welcomed our request that he visit you again. In fact, he himself was eager to go and see you. ¹⁸We are also sending another brother with Titus. He is highly praised in all the churches as a preacher of the Good News. ¹⁹He was appointed by the churches to accompany us as we take the offering to Jerusalem*—a service that glorifies the Lord and shows our eagerness to help. ²⁰By traveling together we will guard against any suspicion, for we are anxious that no one should find fault with the way we are handling this generous gift. ²¹We are careful to be honorable before the Lord, but we also want everyone else to know we are honorable.

²²And we are also sending with them another brother who has been thoroughly tested and has shown how earnest he is on many occasions. He is now even more enthusiastic because of his increased confidence in you. ²³If anyone asks about Titus, say that he is my partner who works with me to help you. And these brothers are representatives* of the churches. They are splendid examples of those who bring glory to Christ. ²⁴So show them your love, and prove to all the churches that our boasting about you is justified.

CHAPTER **9**
### The Collection for Christians in Jerusalem

I really don't need to write to you about this gift for the Christians in Jerusalem.* ²For I know how eager you are to help, and I have been boasting to our friends in Macedonia that you Christians in Greece* were ready to send an offering a year ago. In fact, it was your enthusiasm that stirred up many of them to begin helping. ³But I am sending these brothers just to be sure that you really are ready, as I told them you would be, with your money all collected. I don't want it to turn out that I was wrong in my boasting about you. ⁴I would be humiliated—

8:7 Some manuscripts read *love from us to you.*   8:15 Exod 16:18.   8:19 See 1 Cor 16:3-4.   8:23 Greek *apostles.*   9:1 Greek *about the offering for the saints.*   9:2 Greek *Achaia,* the southern region of the Greek peninsula.

## OFF AND RUNNING
### Avoid Relationships That Could Cause You to Sin
Read 2 CORINTHIANS 6:14–7:1

As a Christian, you should avoid anything that would compromise your relationship with Jesus. That includes entering into a relationship, business deal, or any other association that would tempt you to lower your standards or discredit your integrity. When you team up with someone who does not love and fear the Lord, that relationship can dramatically weaken you spiritually.

and so would you—if some Macedonian Christians came with me, only to find that you still weren't ready after all I had told them! 5So I thought I should send these brothers ahead of me to make sure the gift you promised is ready. But I want it to be a willing gift, not one given under pressure.

6Remember this—a farmer who plants only a few seeds will get a small crop. But the one who plants generously will get a generous crop. 7You must each make up your own mind as to how much you should give. Don't give reluctantly or in response to pressure. For God loves the person who gives cheerfully. 8And God will generously provide all you need. Then you will always have everything you need and plenty left over to share with others. 9As the Scriptures say,

"Godly people give generously to the poor.
 Their good deeds will never be forgotten."*

10For God is the one who gives seed to the farmer and then bread to eat. In the same way, he will give you many opportunities to do good, and he will produce a great harvest of generosity* in you.

11Yes, you will be enriched so that you can give even more generously. And when we take your gifts to those who need them, they will break out in thanksgiving to God. 12So two good things will happen—the needs of the Christians in Jerusalem will be met, and they will joyfully express their thanksgiving to God. 13You will be glorifying God through your generous gifts. For your generosity to them will prove that you are obedient to the Good News of Christ. 14And they will pray for you with deep affection because of the wonderful grace of God shown through you.

15Thank God for his Son—a gift too wonderful for words!*

CHAPTER **10**
*Paul Defends His Authority*
Now I, Paul, plead with you. I plead with the gentleness and kindness that Christ himself

would use, even though some of you say I am bold in my letters but timid in person. 2I hope it won't be necessary, but when I come I may have to be very bold with those who think we act from purely human motives. 3We are human, but we don't wage war with human plans and methods. 4We use God's mighty weapons, not mere worldly weapons, to knock down the Devil's strongholds. 5With these weapons we break down every proud argument that keeps people from knowing God. With these weapons we conquer their rebellious ideas, and we teach them to obey Christ. 6And we will punish those who remained disobedient after the rest of you became loyal and obedient.

7The trouble with you is that you make your decisions on the basis of appearance.* You must recognize that we belong to Christ just as much as those who proudly declare that they belong to Christ. 8I may seem to be boasting too much about the authority given to us by the Lord. But this authority is to build you up, not to tear you down. And I will not be put to shame by having my work among you destroyed.

9Now this is not just an attempt to frighten you by my letters. 10For some say, "Don't worry about Paul. His letters are demanding and forceful, but in person he is weak, and his speeches are really bad!" 11The ones who say this must realize that we will be just as demanding and forceful in person as we are in our letters.

12Oh, don't worry; I wouldn't dare say that I am as wonderful as these other men who tell you how important they are! But they are only comparing themselves with each other, and measuring themselves by themselves. What foolishness!

13But we will not boast of authority we do not have. Our goal is to stay within the boundaries of God's plan for us, and this plan includes our working there with you. 14We are not going too far when we claim authority over you, for we were the first to travel all the way to you with the

9:9 Ps 112:9.   9:10 Greek *righteousness.*   9:15 Greek *Thank God for his indescribable gift.*   10:7 Or *Look at the obvious facts.*

God does not want us to avoid all interaction with nonbelievers. Jesus himself spent time with the "sinners" and social outcasts of his day in order to share the message of salvation. God just wants us to keep from being so closely connected to unbelievers that it ultimately affects our faith and behavior, tempting us to compromise our witness for and obedience to God.

Good News of Christ. 15Nor do we claim credit for the work someone else has done. Instead, we hope that your faith will grow and that our work among you will be greatly enlarged. 16Then we will be able to go and preach the Good News in other places that are far beyond you, where no one else is working. Then there will be no question about being in someone else's territory. 17As the Scriptures say,

"The person who wishes to boast
should boast only of what the Lord has done."*

18When people boast about themselves, it doesn't count for much. But when the Lord commends someone, that's different!

## CHAPTER 11
### Paul and the False Apostles

I hope you will be patient with me as I keep on talking like a fool. Please bear with me. 2I am jealous for you with the jealousy of God himself. For I promised you as a pure bride* to one husband, Christ. 3But I fear that somehow you will be led away from your pure and simple devotion to Christ, just as Eve was deceived by the serpent. 4You seem to believe whatever anyone tells you, even if they preach about a different Jesus than the one we preach, or a different Spirit than the one you received, or a different kind of gospel than the one you believed. 5But I don't think I am inferior to these "super apostles." 6I may not be a trained speaker, but I know what I am talking about. I think you realize this by now, for we have proved it again and again.

7Did I do wrong when I humbled myself and honored you by preaching God's Good News to you without expecting anything in return? 8I "robbed" other churches by accepting their contributions so I could serve you at no cost. 9And when I was with you and didn't have enough to live on, I did not ask you to help me. For the brothers who came from Macedonia brought me another gift. I have never yet asked you for any support, and I never will. 10As surely as the truth of Christ is in me, I will never stop boasting about this all over Greece.* 11Why? Because I don't love you? God knows I do.

12But I will continue doing this to cut the ground out from under the feet of those who boast that their work is just like ours. 13These people are false apostles. They have fooled you by disguising themselves as apostles of Christ.

14But I am not surprised! Even Satan can disguise himself as an angel of light. 15So it is no wonder his servants can also do it by pretending to be godly ministers. In the end they will get every bit of punishment their wicked deeds deserve.

### Paul's Many Trials

16Once again, don't think that I have lost my wits to talk like this. But even if you do, listen to me, as you would to a foolish person, while I also boast a little. 17Such bragging is not something the Lord wants, but I am acting like a fool. 18And since others boast about their human achievements, I will, too. 19After all, you, who think you are so wise, enjoy listening to fools! 20You put up with it when they make you their slaves, take everything you have, take advantage of you, put on airs, and slap you in the face. 21I'm ashamed to say that we were not strong enough to do that!

But whatever they dare to boast about—I'm talking like a fool again—I can boast about it, too. 22They say they are Hebrews, do they? So am I. And they say they are Israelites? So am I. And they are descendants of Abraham? So am I. 23They say they serve Christ? I know I sound like a madman, but I have served him far more! I have worked harder, been put in jail more often, been whipped times without number, and faced death again and again. 24Five different times the Jews gave me thirty-nine lashes. 25Three times I was beaten with rods. Once I was stoned. Three times I was shipwrecked. Once I spent a whole night and a day adrift at sea. 26I have traveled many weary miles. I have faced danger from flooded rivers and from robbers. I have faced danger from my own people, the Jews, as well as from the Gentiles. I have faced danger in the cities, in the deserts, and on the stormy seas. And I have faced danger from men who claim to be Christians but are not.* 27I have lived with weariness and pain and sleepless nights. Often I have been hungry and thirsty and have gone without food. Often I have shivered with cold, without enough clothing to keep me warm.

28Then, besides all this, I have the daily burden of how the churches are getting along. 29Who is weak without my feeling that weakness? Who is led astray, and I do not burn with anger?

30If I must boast, I would rather boast about the things that show how weak I am. 31God, the

10:17 Jer 9:24.   11:2 Greek *a virgin.*   11:10 Greek *Achaia.*   11:26 Greek *from false brothers.*

Father of our Lord Jesus, who is to be praised forever, knows I tell the truth. ³²When I was in Damascus, the governor under King Aretas kept guards at the city gates to catch me. ³³But I was lowered in a basket through a window in the city wall, and that's how I got away!

## CHAPTER 12
*Paul's Vision and His Thorn in the Flesh*
This boasting is all so foolish, but let me go on. Let me tell about the visions and revelations I received from the Lord. ²I* was caught up into the third heaven fourteen years ago. ³Whether my body was there or just my spirit, I don't know; only God knows. ⁴But I do know that I* was caught up into paradise and heard things so astounding that they cannot be told. ⁵That experience is something worth boasting about, but I am not going to do it. I am going to boast only about my weaknesses. ⁶I have plenty to boast about and would be no fool in doing it, because I would be telling the truth. But I won't do it. I don't want anyone to think more highly of me than what they can actually see in my life and my message, ⁷even though I have received wonderful revelations from God. But to keep me from getting puffed up, I was given a thorn in my flesh, a messenger from Satan to torment me and keep me from getting proud.

⁸Three different times I begged the Lord to take it away. ⁹Each time he said, "My gracious favor is all you need. My power works best in your weakness." So now I am glad to boast about my weaknesses, so that the power of Christ may work through me. ¹⁰Since I know it is all for Christ's good, I am quite content with my weaknesses and with insults, hardships, persecutions, and calamities. For when I am weak, then I am strong.

*Paul's Concern for the Corinthians*
¹¹You have made me act like a fool—boasting like this. You ought to be writing commendations for me, for I am not at all inferior to these "super apostles," even though I am nothing at all. ¹²When I was with you, I certainly gave you every proof that I am truly an apostle, sent to you by God himself. For I patiently did many signs and wonders and miracles among you. ¹³The only thing I didn't do, which I do in the other churches, was to become a burden to you. Please forgive me for this wrong!

¹⁴Now I am coming to you for the third time,

12:2 Greek *I know a man in Christ who.* 12:4 Greek *he.*

## What Happens When You Give? Read 2 CORINTHIANS 9:6-14

One of Paul's goals in his ministry was to mend the division that existed between Jewish and Gentile believers. To do this, he took up a gift offering from the Gentile believers to be given to the needy Jewish believers in Jerusalem. Apparently the believers in Corinth were lagging behind in their giving. So Paul, in this portion of 2 Corinthians, wrote of the benefits of giving to God and the work of his church. Here are three important truths from this passage about our giving as believers:

**1. Our Motives Are Important.** The passage says that God prizes cheerful givers (verse 7). The word *cheerfully* could also be translated as "hilariously." We should give hilariously, joyfully—not out of mere duty or guilt. As Jesus said, it is truly "more blessed to give than to receive" (Acts 20:35).

**2. As We Give, God Will Give to Us.** You can't outgive God (verses 8, 10). As Jesus said, "If you give, you will receive. Your gift will return to you in full measure, pressed down, shaken together to make room for more, and running over. Whatever measure you use in giving—large or small—it will be used to measure what is given back to you" (Luke 6:38). Coming back to our motive for giving, we should not fall into the trap of "giving to get." We should give because God has so graciously and generously given to us.

**3. Others Are Helped because of Our Financial Help.** We should always be on the lookout to help Christian brothers and sisters who are in need. Paul was not speaking of the tithe you give, but an offering above and beyond your tithe (verses 11-14). Our tithe goes to the church. Our offerings go to other situations, like helping those in need. When these people receive our gifts, they see that our faith is deeper than mere words.

When you give to the Lord's work, that money, which really had no effect in any spiritual sense before, will be used to touch the lives of others for the glory of God. God is looking for openhanded people— people upon whom he can pour out his blessings, and who, in turn, will give it to others.

and I will not be a burden to you. I don't want what you have; I want you. And anyway, little children don't pay for their parents' food. It's the other way around; parents supply food for their children. 15I will gladly spend myself and all I have for your spiritual good, even though it seems that the more I love you, the less you love me.

16Some of you admit I was not a burden to you. But they still think I was sneaky and took advantage of you by trickery. 17But how? Did any of the men I sent to you take advantage of you? 18When I urged Titus to visit you and sent our other brother with him, did Titus take advantage of you? No, of course not! For we both have the same Spirit and walk in each other's steps, doing things the same way.

19Perhaps you think we are saying all this just to defend ourselves. That isn't it at all. We tell you this as Christ's servants, and we know that God is listening. Everything we do, dear friends, is for your benefit. 20For I am afraid that when I come to visit you I won't like what I find, and then you won't like my response. I am afraid that I will find quarreling, jealousy, outbursts of anger, selfishness, backstabbing, gossip, conceit, and disorderly behavior. 21Yes, I am afraid that when I come, God will humble me again because of you. And I will have to grieve because many of you who sinned earlier have not repented of your impurity, sexual immorality, and eagerness for lustful pleasure.

CHAPTER **13**
*Paul's Final Advice*
This is the third time I am coming to visit you. As the Scriptures say, "The facts of every case must be established by the testimony of two or three witnesses."* 2I have already warned those who had been sinning when I was there on my second visit. Now I again warn them and all

others, just as I did before, that this next time I will not spare them.

3I will give you all the proof you want that Christ speaks through me. Christ is not weak in his dealings with you; he is a mighty power among you. 4Although he died on the cross in weakness, he now lives by the mighty power of God. We, too, are weak, but we live in him and have God's power—the power we use in dealing with you.

5Examine yourselves to see if your faith is really genuine. Test yourselves. If you cannot tell that Jesus Christ is among you,* it means you have failed the test. 6I hope you recognize that we have passed the test and are approved by God.

7We pray to God that you will not do anything wrong. We pray this, not to show that our ministry to you has been successful, but because we want you to do right even if we ourselves seem to have failed. 8Our responsibility is never to oppose the truth, but to stand for the truth at all times. 9We are glad to be weak, if you are really strong. What we pray for is your restoration to maturity.

10I am writing this to you before I come, hoping that I won't need to deal harshly with you when I do come. For I want to use the authority the Lord has given me to build you up, not to tear you down.

*Paul's Final Greetings*
11Dear brothers and sisters,* I close my letter with these last words: Rejoice. Change your ways. Encourage each other. Live in harmony and peace. Then the God of love and peace will be with you.

12Greet each other in Christian love.* All the Christians here send you their greetings.

13May the grace of our Lord Jesus Christ, the love of God, and the fellowship of the Holy Spirit be with you all.*

13:1 Deut 19:15.   13:5 Or *in you.*   13:11 Greek *brothers.*   13:12 Greek *with a sacred kiss.*   13:12-13 Some English versions divide verse 12 into verses 12 and 13, and then verse 13 becomes verse 14.

# Galatians

## CHAPTER 1

### Greetings from Paul

This letter is from Paul, an apostle. I was not appointed by any group or by human authority. My call is from Jesus Christ himself and from God the Father, who raised Jesus from the dead. ²All the brothers and sisters* here join me in sending greetings to the churches of Galatia.

³May grace and peace be yours from God our Father and from the Lord Jesus Christ. ⁴He died for our sins, just as God our Father planned, in order to rescue us from this evil world in which we live. ⁵That is why all glory belongs to God through all the ages of eternity. Amen.

### There Is Only One Good News

⁶I am shocked that you are turning away so soon from God, who in his love and mercy called you to share the eternal life he gives through Christ. You are already following a different way ⁷that pretends to be the Good News but is not the Good News at all. You are being fooled by those who twist and change the truth concerning Christ.

⁸Let God's curse fall on anyone, including myself, who preaches any other message than the one we told you about. Even if an angel comes from heaven and preaches any other message, let him be forever cursed. ⁹I will say it again: If anyone preaches any other gospel than the one you welcomed, let God's curse fall upon that person.

¹⁰Obviously, I'm not trying to be a people pleaser! No, I am trying to please God. If I were still trying to please people, I would not be Christ's servant.

### Paul's Message Comes from Christ

¹¹Dear brothers and sisters, I solemnly assure you that the Good News of salvation which I preach is not based on mere human reasoning or logic. ¹²For my message came by a direct revelation from Jesus Christ himself. No one else taught me.

¹³You know what I was like when I followed the Jewish religion—how I violently persecuted the Christians.* I did my best to get rid of them. ¹⁴I was one of the most religious Jews of my own age, and I tried as hard as possible to follow all the old traditions of my religion.

¹⁵But then something happened! For it pleased God in his kindness to choose me and call me, even before I was born! What undeserved mercy! ¹⁶Then he revealed his Son to me* so that I could proclaim the Good News about Jesus to the Gentiles. When all this happened to me, I did not rush out to consult with anyone else; ¹⁷nor did I go up to Jerusalem to consult with those who were apostles before I was. No, I went away into Arabia and later returned to the city of Damascus. ¹⁸It was not until three years later that I finally went to Jerusalem for a visit with Peter* and stayed there with him for fifteen days. ¹⁹And the only other apostle I met at that time was James, our Lord's brother. ²⁰You must believe what I am saying, for I declare before God that I am not lying. ²¹Then after this visit, I went north into the provinces of Syria and Cilicia. ²²And still the Christians in the churches in Judea didn't know me personally. ²³All they knew was that people were saying, "The one who used to persecute us now preaches the very faith he tried to destroy!" ²⁴And they gave glory to God because of me.

## CHAPTER 2

### The Apostles Accept Paul

Then fourteen years later I went back to Jerusalem again, this time with Barnabas; and Titus

---

1:2 Greek *brothers;* also in 1:11.   1:13 Greek *the church of God.*   1:16 Or *in me.*   1:18 Greek *Cephas.*

## Why Christians Need the Holy Spirit Read GALATIANS 5:16-26

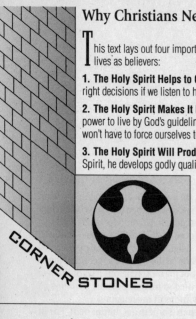

T his text lays out four important reasons we need to let the Holy Spirit have full control of our lives as believers:

**1. The Holy Spirit Helps to Conquer Our Sin Nature.** The Holy Spirit will help us make the right decisions if we listen to his advice.

**2. The Holy Spirit Makes It Easier to Follow God's Guidelines.** The Holy Spirit gives us the power to live by God's guidelines. If we listen to and follow the Holy Spirit's promptings, then we won't have to force ourselves to obey the Lord. That is because we will want to obey him.

**3. The Holy Spirit Will Produce Godly Qualities in Our Lives.** When we live by the Holy Spirit, he develops godly qualities (known as the fruit of the Spirit) in our lives.

**4. The Holy Spirit Encourages Us to Seek God's Approval above Man's.** We will seek God's glory above our own when we follow the Holy Spirit's leading.

In essence, the Holy Spirit enables Christians to live lives that are pleasing to God—something that is impossible to do on our own. He makes following Christ a joy rather than a duty.

**CORNER STONES**

---

came along, too. ²I went there because God revealed to me that I should go. While I was there I talked privately with the leaders of the church. I wanted them to understand what I had been preaching to the Gentiles. I wanted to make sure they did not disagree, or my ministry would have been useless. ³And they did agree. They did not even demand that my companion Titus be circumcised, though he was a Gentile.*

⁴Even that question wouldn't have come up except for some so-called Christians there—false ones, really*—who came to spy on us and see our freedom in Christ Jesus. They wanted to force us, like slaves, to follow their Jewish regulations. ⁵But we refused to listen to them for a single moment. We wanted to preserve the truth of the Good News for you.

⁶And the leaders of the church who were there had nothing to add to what I was preaching. (By the way, their reputation as great leaders made no difference to me, for God has no favorites.) ⁷They saw that God had given me the responsibility of preaching the Good News to the Gentiles, just as he had given Peter the responsibility of preaching to the Jews. ⁸For the same God who worked through Peter for the benefit of the Jews worked through me for the

benefit of the Gentiles. ⁹In fact, James, Peter,* and John, who were known as pillars of the church, recognized the gift God had given me, and they accepted Barnabas and me as their co-workers. They encouraged us to keep preaching to the Gentiles, while they continued their work with the Jews. ¹⁰The only thing they suggested was that we remember to help the poor, and I have certainly been eager to do that.

*Paul Confronts Peter*

¹¹But when Peter came to Antioch, I had to oppose him publicly, speaking strongly against what he was doing, for it was very wrong. ¹²When he first arrived, he ate with the Gentile Christians, who don't bother with circumcision. But afterward, when some Jewish friends of James came, Peter wouldn't eat with the Gentiles anymore because he was afraid of what these legalists would say. ¹³Then the other Jewish Christians followed Peter's hypocrisy, and even Barnabas was influenced to join them in their hypocrisy.

¹⁴When I saw that they were not following the truth of the Good News, I said to Peter in front of all the others, "Since you, a Jew by birth, have discarded the Jewish laws and are living like a Gentile, why are you trying to make these

2:3 Greek *a Greek*.　2:4 Greek *some false brothers*.　2:9 Greek *Cephas*; also in 2:11, 14.

Gentiles obey the Jewish laws you abandoned? 15You and I are Jews by birth, not 'sinners' like the Gentiles. 16And yet we Jewish Christians know that we become right with God, not by doing what the law commands, but by faith in Jesus Christ. So we have believed in Christ Jesus, that we might be accepted by God because of our faith in Christ—and not because we have obeyed the law. For no one will ever be saved by obeying the law."*

17But what if we seek to be made right with God through faith in Christ and then find out that we are still sinners? Has Christ led us into sin? Of course not! 18Rather, I make myself guilty if I rebuild the old system I already tore down. 19For when I tried to keep the law, I realized I could never earn God's approval. So I died to the law so that I might live for God. I have been crucified with Christ. 20I myself no longer live, but Christ lives in me. So I live my life in this earthly body by trusting in the Son of God, who loved me and gave himself for me. 21I am not one of those who treats the grace of God as meaningless. For if we could be saved by keeping the law, then there was no need for Christ to die.

CHAPTER **3**
*The Law and Faith in Christ*
Oh, foolish Galatians! What magician has cast an evil spell on you? For you used to see the meaning of Jesus Christ's death as clearly as though I had shown you a signboard with a picture of Christ dying on the cross. 2Let me ask you this one question: Did you receive the Holy Spirit by keeping the law? Of course not, for the Holy Spirit came upon you only after you believed the message you heard about Christ. 3Have you lost your senses? After starting your Christian lives in the Spirit, why are you now trying to become perfect by your own human effort? 4You have suffered so much for the Good News. Surely it was not in vain, was it? Are you now going to just throw it all away?

5I ask you again, does God give you the Holy Spirit and work miracles among you because you obey the law of Moses? Of course not! It is because you believe the message you heard about Christ.

6In the same way, "Abraham believed God, so God declared him righteous because of his

faith."* 7The real children of Abraham, then, are all those who put their faith in God.

8What's more, the Scriptures looked forward to this time when God would accept the Gentiles, too, on the basis of their faith. God promised this good news to Abraham long ago when he said, "All nations will be blessed through you."* 9And so it is: All who put their faith in Christ share the same blessing Abraham received because of his faith.

10But those who depend on the law to make them right with God are under his curse, for the Scriptures say, "Cursed is everyone who does not observe and obey all these commands that are written in God's Book of the Law."* 11Consequently, it is clear that no one can ever be right with God by trying to keep the law. For the Scriptures say, "It is through faith that a righteous person has life."* 12How different from this way of faith is the way of law, which says, "If you wish to find life by obeying the law, you must obey all of its commands."* 13But Christ has rescued us from the curse pronounced by the law. When he was hung on the cross, he took upon himself the curse for our wrongdoing. For it is written in the Scriptures, "Cursed is everyone who is hung on a tree."* 14Through the work of Christ Jesus, God has blessed the Gentiles with the same blessing he promised to Abraham, and we Christians receive the promised Holy Spirit through faith.

*The Law and God's Promises*
15Dear brothers and sisters,* here's an example from everyday life. Just as no one can set aside or amend an irrevocable agreement, so it is in this case. 16God gave the promise to Abraham and his child.* And notice that it doesn't say the promise was to his children,* as if it meant many descendants. But the promise was to his child—and that, of course, means Christ. 17This is what I am trying to say: The agreement God made with Abraham could not be canceled 430 years later when God gave the law to Moses. God would be breaking his promise. 18For if the inheritance could be received only by keeping the law, then it would not be the result of accepting God's promise. But God gave it to Abraham as a promise.

19Well then, why was the law given? It was given to show people how guilty they are. But this system of law was to last only until the coming of the child to whom God's promise was made. And there is this further difference. God gave his laws to angels to give to Moses, who was the mediator between God and the people. 20Now a mediator is needed if two people enter into an agreement, but God acted on his own when he made his promise to Abraham.

21Well then, is there a conflict between God's law and God's promises? Absolutely not! If the law could have given us new life, we could have been made right with God by obeying it. 22But the Scriptures have declared that we are all prisoners of sin, so the only way to receive God's promise is to believe in Jesus Christ.

23Until faith in Christ was shown to us as the way of becoming right with God, we were guarded by the law. We were kept in protective custody, so to speak, until we could put our faith in the coming Savior.

### God's Children through Faith

24Let me put it another way. The law was our guardian and teacher to lead us until Christ came. So now, through faith in Christ, we are made right with God. 25But now that faith in Christ has come, we no longer need the law as our guardian. 26So you are all children* of God through faith in Christ Jesus. 27And all who have been united with Christ in baptism have been made like him. 28There is no longer Jew or Gentile,* slave or free, male or female. For you are all Christians—you are one in Christ Jesus. 29And now that you belong to Christ, you are the true children of Abraham. You are his heirs, and now all the promises God gave to him belong to you.

### CHAPTER 4

Think of it this way. If a father dies and leaves great wealth for his young children, those children are not much better off than slaves until they grow up, even though they actually own everything their father had. 2They have to obey their guardians until they reach whatever age their father set.

3And that's the way it was with us before Christ came. We were slaves to the spiritual powers of this world. 4But when the right time came, God sent his Son, born of a woman, subject to the law. 5God sent him to buy freedom for us who were slaves to the law, so that he could adopt us as his very own children.* 6And because you Gentiles have become his children, God has sent the Spirit of his Son into your hearts, and now you can call God your dear Father.* 7Now you are no longer a slave but God's own child.* And since you are his child, everything he has belongs to you.

### Paul's Concern for the Galatians

8Before you Gentiles knew God, you were slaves to so-called gods that do not even exist. 9And now that you have found God (or should I say, now that God has found you), why do you want to go back again and become slaves once more to the weak and useless spiritual powers of this world? 10You are trying to find favor with God by what you do or don't do on certain days or months or seasons or years. 11I fear for you. I am afraid that all my hard work for you was worth nothing. 12Dear brothers and sisters,* I plead with you to live as I do in freedom from these things, for I have become like you Gentiles were—free from the law.

You did not mistreat me when I first preached to you. 13Surely you remember that I was sick when I first brought you the Good News of Christ. 14But even though my sickness was revolting to you, you did not reject me and turn me away. No, you took me in and cared for me as though I were an angel from God or even Christ Jesus himself. 15Where is that joyful spirit

3:26 Greek *sons.* 3:28 Greek *Jew or Greek.* 4:5 Greek *sons;* also in 4:6. 4:6 Greek *into your hearts, crying, "Abba, Father." Abba* is an Aramaic term for "father." 4:7 Greek *son;* also in 4:7b. 4:12 Greek *brothers;* also in 4:28, 31.

## OFF AND RUNNING

### Find a Close Christian Friend Read GALATIANS 6:1-3

God never intended us to be "solo" Christians. That is why one of the first things you should do after becoming a Christian is find some good, solid Christian friends. Although God wants us to turn to him first in times of trouble, he also knows that we need Christian brothers and sisters here on earth to help us through our difficulties—and they need us, too. Here are three things to look for in a Christian friend:

**1. A True Christian Friend Will Let You Know When You Sin.** A true friend will care enough about your spiritual condition to tell you the truth. The Bible says, "Wounds from a friend are better than many kisses from an enemy" (Proverbs 27:6).

we felt together then? In those days, I know you would gladly have taken out your own eyes and given them to me if it had been possible. 16Have I now become your enemy because I am telling you the truth?

17Those false teachers who are so anxious to win your favor are not doing it for your good. They are trying to shut you off from me so that you will pay more attention to them. 18Now it's wonderful if you are eager to do good, and especially when I am not with you. 19But oh, my dear children! I feel as if I am going through labor pains for you again, and they will continue until Christ is fully developed in your lives. 20How I wish I were there with you right now, so that I could be more gentle with you. But at this distance I frankly don't know what else to do.

### Abraham's Two Children

21Listen to me, you who want to live under the law. Do you know what the law really says? 22The Scriptures say that Abraham had two sons, one from his slave-wife and one from his freeborn wife.* 23The son of the slave-wife was born in a human attempt to bring about the fulfillment of God's promise. But the son of the freeborn wife was born as God's own fulfillment of his promise.

24Now these two women serve as an illustration of God's two covenants. Hagar, the slave-wife, represents Mount Sinai where people first became enslaved to the law. 25And now Jerusalem is just like Mount Sinai in Arabia, because she and her children live in slavery. 26But Sarah, the free woman, represents the heavenly Jerusalem. And she is our mother. 27That is what Isaiah meant when he prophesied,

"Rejoice, O childless woman!
Break forth into loud and joyful song,
    even though you never gave birth to a child.

For the woman who could bear no children
    now has more than all the other
        women!"*

28And you, dear brothers and sisters, are children of the promise, just like Isaac. 29And we who are born of the Holy Spirit are persecuted by those who want us to keep the law, just as Isaac, the child of promise, was persecuted by Ishmael, the son of the slave-wife.

30But what do the Scriptures say about that? "Get rid of the slave and her son, for the son of the slave woman will not share the family inheritance with the free woman's son."* 31So, dear brothers and sisters, we are not children of the slave woman, obligated to the law. We are children of the free woman, acceptable to God because of our faith.

### CHAPTER 5
### Freedom in Christ

So Christ has really set us free. Now make sure that you stay free, and don't get tied up again in slavery to the law.

2Listen! I, Paul, tell you this: If you are counting on circumcision to make you right with God, then Christ cannot help you. 3I'll say it again. If you are trying to find favor with God by being circumcised, you must obey all of the regulations in the whole law of Moses. 4For if you are trying to make yourselves right with God by keeping the law, you have been cut off from Christ! You have fallen away from God's grace.

5But we who live by the Spirit eagerly wait to receive everything promised to us who are right with God through faith. 6For when we place our faith in Christ Jesus, it makes no difference to God whether we are circumcised or not circumcised. What is important is faith expressing itself in love.

4:22 See Gen 16:15; 21:2-3.   4:27 Isa 54:1.   4:30 Gen 21:10.

**2. A True Christian Friend Is Humble.** If you fall spiritually, a friend who is a strong Christian can be counted upon to help restore you without spreading rumors. That is because this friend realizes that he or she is just as susceptible to sin as you are.

**3. A True Christian Friend Will Help Carry Your Burdens.** He will weep with you when you weep and rejoice with you when you rejoice (see Romans 12:15, p. 192).

Having a friend who is a strong Christian is not just a benefit—it is a necessity! And that is how Jesus wants it to be. Therefore, build your Christian friendships, and in so doing, you will help strengthen yourself and the body of Christ.

7You were getting along so well. Who has interfered with you to hold you back from following the truth? 8It certainly isn't God, for he is the one who called you to freedom. 9But it takes only one wrong person among you to infect all the others—a little yeast spreads quickly through the whole batch of dough! 10I am trusting the Lord to bring you back to believing as I do about these things. God will judge that person, whoever it is, who has been troubling and confusing you.

11Dear brothers and sisters,* if I were still preaching that you must be circumcised—as some say I do—why would the Jews persecute me? The fact that I am still being persecuted proves that I am still preaching salvation through the cross of Christ alone. 12I only wish that those troublemakers who want to mutilate you by circumcision would mutilate themselves.*

13For you have been called to live in freedom—not freedom to satisfy your sinful nature, but freedom to serve one another in love. 14For the whole law can be summed up in this one command: "Love your neighbor as yourself."* 15But if instead of showing love among yourselves you are always biting and devouring one another, watch out! Beware of destroying one another.

## Living by the Spirit's Power
16So I advise you to live according to your new life in the Holy Spirit. Then you won't be doing what your sinful nature craves. 17The old sinful nature loves to do evil, which is just opposite from what the Holy Spirit wants. And the Spirit gives us desires that are opposite from what the sinful nature desires. These two forces are constantly fighting each other, and your choices are never free from this conflict. 18But when you are directed by the Holy Spirit, you are no longer subject to the law.

19When you follow the desires of your sinful nature, your lives will produce these evil results: sexual immorality, impure thoughts, eagerness for lustful pleasure, 20idolatry, participation in demonic activities, hostility, quarreling, jealousy, outbursts of anger, selfish ambition, divisions, the feeling that everyone is wrong except those in your own little group, 21envy, drunkenness, wild parties, and other kinds of sin. Let me tell you again, as I have before, that anyone living that sort of life will not inherit the Kingdom of God.

22But when the Holy Spirit controls our lives, he will produce this kind of fruit in us: love, joy, peace, patience, kindness, goodness, faithfulness, 23gentleness, and self-control. Here there is no conflict with the law.

24Those who belong to Christ Jesus have nailed the passions and desires of their sinful nature to his cross and crucified them there. 25If we are living now by the Holy Spirit, let us follow the Holy Spirit's leading in every part of our lives. 26Let us not become conceited, or irritate one another, or be jealous of one another.

## CHAPTER 6
### We Reap What We Sow
Dear brothers and sisters, if another Christian* is overcome by some sin, you who are godly should gently and humbly help that person back onto the right path. And be careful not to fall into the same temptation yourself. 2Share each other's troubles and problems, and in this way obey the law of Christ. 3If you think you are too important to help someone in need, you are only fooling yourself. You are really a nobody.

4Be sure to do what you should, for then you will enjoy the personal satisfaction of having done your work well, and you won't need to compare yourself to anyone else. 5For we are each responsible for our own conduct.

6Those who are taught the word of God should help their teachers by paying them.

7Don't be misled. Remember that you can't ignore God and get away with it. You will always reap what you sow! 8Those who live only to satisfy their own sinful desires will harvest the consequences of decay and death. But those who live to please the Spirit will harvest everlasting life from the Spirit. 9So don't get tired of doing what is good. Don't get discouraged and give up, for we will reap a harvest of blessing at the appropriate time. 10Whenever we have the opportunity, we should do good to everyone, especially to our Christian brothers and sisters.

### Paul's Final Advice
11Notice what large letters I use as I write these closing words in my own handwriting. 12Those who are trying to force you to be circumcised are doing it for just one reason. They don't want to be persecuted for teaching that the cross of Christ alone can save. 13And even those who

5:11 Greek *Brothers.* 5:12 Or *castrate themselves;* Greek reads *cut themselves off.* 5:14 Lev 19:18. 6:1 Greek *Brothers, if a man.*

advocate circumcision don't really keep the whole law. They only want you to be circumcised so they can brag about it and claim you as their disciples.

14As for me, God forbid that I should boast about anything except the cross of our Lord Jesus Christ. Because of that cross,* my interest in this world died long ago, and the world's interest in me is also long dead. 15It doesn't make any difference now whether we have been circumcised or not. What counts is whether we really have been changed into new and different people. 16May God's mercy and peace be upon all those who live by this principle. They are the new people of God.*

17From now on, don't let anyone trouble me with these things. For I bear on my body the scars that show I belong to Jesus.

18My dear brothers and sisters,* may the grace of our Lord Jesus Christ be with you all. Amen.

6:14 Or *Because of him.*   6:16 Greek *the Israel of God.*   6:18 Greek *Brothers.*

# Ephesians

## CHAPTER 1

### Greetings from Paul

This letter is from Paul, chosen by God to be an apostle of Christ Jesus.

It is written to God's holy people in Ephesus,* who are faithful followers of Christ Jesus.

2May grace and peace be yours, sent to you from God our Father and Jesus Christ our Lord.

### Spiritual Blessings

3How we praise God, the Father of our Lord Jesus Christ, who has blessed us with every spiritual blessing in the heavenly realms because we belong to Christ. 4Long ago, even before he made the world, God loved us and chose us in Christ to be holy and without fault in his eyes. 5His unchanging plan has always been to adopt us into his own family by bringing us to himself through Jesus Christ. And this gave him great pleasure.

6So we praise God for the wonderful kindness he has poured out on us because we belong to his dearly loved Son. 7He is so rich in kindness that he purchased our freedom through the blood of his Son, and our sins are forgiven. 8He has showered his kindness on us, along with all wisdom and understanding.

9God's secret plan has now been revealed to us; it is a plan centered on Christ, designed long ago according to his good pleasure. 10And this is his plan: At the right time he will bring everything together under the authority of Christ—everything in heaven and on earth. 11Furthermore, because of Christ, we have received an inheritance from God,* for he chose us from the beginning, and all things happen just as he decided long ago. 12God's purpose was that we who were the first to trust in Christ should praise our glorious God. 13And now you also have heard the truth, the Good News that God saves you. And when you believed in Christ, he identified you as his own by giving you the Holy Spirit, whom he promised long ago. 14The Spirit is God's guarantee that he will give us everything he promised and that he has purchased us to be his own people. This is just one more reason for us to praise our glorious God.

### Paul's Prayer for Spiritual Wisdom

15Ever since I first heard of your strong faith in the Lord Jesus and your love for Christians everywhere, 16I have never stopped thanking God for you. I pray for you constantly, 17asking God, the glorious Father of our Lord Jesus Christ, to give you spiritual wisdom and understanding, so that you might grow in your knowledge of God. 18I pray that your hearts will be flooded with light so that you can understand the wonderful future he has promised to those he called. I want you to realize what a rich and glorious inheritance he has given to his people.*

19I pray that you will begin to understand the incredible greatness of his power for us who believe him. This is the same mighty power 20that raised Christ from the dead and seated him in the place of honor at God's right hand in the heavenly realms. 21Now he is far above any ruler or authority or power or leader or anything else in this world or in the world to come. 22And God has put all things under the authority of Christ, and he gave him this authority for the benefit of the church. 23And the church is his body; it is filled by Christ, who fills everything everywhere with his presence.

1:1 Some manuscripts do not include *in Ephesus.*  1:11 Or *we have become God's inheritance.*  1:18 Or *realize how much God has been honored by acquiring his people.*

## Why God Gives Us the Holy Spirit Read EPHESIANS 1:13-14

You might say that the Holy Spirit is our "identifying mark" as a Christian. In this text we see three specific reasons God gives us his Holy Spirit:

**1. The Holy Spirit Is a Promise.** Once again, Scripture reminds us that God has promised to send the Holy Spirit to all those who have heard the good news of the gospel and trusted Christ as Savior.

**2. The Holy Spirit Is a Seal.** The Holy Spirit serves as a mark of ownership, showing that we belong to God.

**3. The Holy Spirit Is a Guarantee.** The Holy Spirit also represents God's pledge to bring us to our final spiritual inheritance. This word could also be translated as a "first installment" or "deposit," signifying that his sealing in our lives is a foretaste of much more to come!

God gives us the Holy Spirit not only to enable us to live out the Christian life but to prove that we are precious in his sight.

**CORNER STONES**

---

CHAPTER **2**

*Made Alive with Christ*

Once you were dead, doomed forever because of your many sins. 2You used to live just like the rest of the world, full of sin, obeying Satan, the mighty prince of the power of the air. He is the spirit at work in the hearts of those who refuse to obey God. 3All of us used to live that way, following the passions and desires of our evil nature. We were born with an evil nature, and we were under God's anger just like everyone else.

4But God is so rich in mercy, and he loved us so very much, 5that even while we were dead because of our sins, he gave us life when he raised Christ from the dead. (It is only by God's special favor that you have been saved!) 6For he raised us from the dead along with Christ, and we are seated with him in the heavenly realms—all because we are one with Christ Jesus. 7And so God can always point to us as examples of the incredible wealth of his favor and kindness toward us, as shown in all he has done for us through Christ Jesus.

8God saved you by his special favor when you believed. And you can't take credit for this; it is a gift from God. 9Salvation is not a reward for the good things we have done, so none of us can boast about it. 10For we are God's masterpiece. He has created us anew in Christ Jesus, so that we can do the good things he planned for us long ago.

*Oneness and Peace in Christ*

11Don't forget that you Gentiles used to be outsiders by birth. You were called "the uncircumcised ones" by the Jews, who were proud of their circumcision, even though it affected only their bodies and not their hearts. 12In those days you were living apart from Christ. You were excluded from God's people, Israel, and you did not know the promises God had made to them. You lived in this world without God and without hope. 13But now you belong to Christ Jesus. Though you once were far away from God, now you have been brought near to him because of the blood of Christ.

14For Christ himself has made peace between us Jews and you Gentiles by making us all one people. He has broken down the wall of hostility that used to separate us. 15By his death he ended the whole system of Jewish law that excluded the Gentiles. His purpose was to make peace between Jews and Gentiles by creating in himself one new person from the two groups. 16Together as one body, Christ reconciled both groups to God by means of his death, and our hostility toward each other was put to death. 17He has brought this Good News of peace to you Gentiles who were far away from him, and to us Jews who were near. 18Now all of us, both Jews and Gentiles, may come to the Father through the same Holy Spirit because of what Christ has done for us.

## A Temple for the Lord

¹⁹So now you Gentiles are no longer strangers and foreigners. You are citizens along with all of God's holy people. You are members of God's family. ²⁰We are his house, built on the foundation of the apostles and the prophets. And the cornerstone is Christ Jesus himself. ²¹We who believe are carefully joined together, becoming a holy temple for the Lord. ²²Through him you Gentiles are also joined together as part of this dwelling where God lives by his Spirit.

## CHAPTER 3

### God's Secret Plan Revealed

I, Paul, am a prisoner of Christ Jesus because of my preaching to you Gentiles. ²As you already know, God has given me this special ministry of announcing his favor to you Gentiles. ³As I briefly mentioned earlier in this letter, God himself revealed his secret plan to me. ⁴As you read what I have written, you will understand what I know about this plan regarding Christ. ⁵God did not reveal it to previous generations, but now he has revealed it by the Holy Spirit to his holy apostles and prophets.

⁶And this is the secret plan: The Gentiles have an equal share with the Jews in all the riches inherited by God's children. Both groups have believed the Good News, and both are part of the same body and enjoy together the promise of blessings through Christ Jesus. ⁷By God's special favor and mighty power, I have been given the wonderful privilege of serving him by spreading this Good News.

⁸Just think! Though I did nothing to deserve it, and though I am the least deserving Christian there is, I was chosen for this special joy of telling the Gentiles about the endless treasures available to them in Christ. ⁹I was chosen to explain to everyone this plan that God, the Creator of all things, had kept secret from the beginning.

¹⁰God's purpose was to show his wisdom in all its rich variety to all the rulers and authorities in the heavenly realms. They will see this when Jews and Gentiles are joined together in his church. ¹¹This was his plan from all eternity, and it has now been carried out through Christ Jesus our Lord.

¹²Because of Christ and our faith in him, we can now come fearlessly into God's presence, assured of his glad welcome. ¹³So please don't despair because of what they are doing to me

here. It is for you that I am suffering, so you should feel honored and encouraged.

### Paul's Prayer for Spiritual Empowering

¹⁴When I think of the wisdom and scope of God's plan, I fall to my knees and pray to the Father,* ¹⁵the Creator of everything in heaven and on earth. ¹⁶I pray that from his glorious, unlimited resources he will give you mighty inner strength through his Holy Spirit. ¹⁷And I pray that Christ will be more and more at home in your hearts as you trust in him. May your roots go down deep into the soil of God's marvelous love. ¹⁸And may you have the power to under-

3:14 Some manuscripts read *the Father of our Lord Jesus Christ.*

## Why the Church Needs You
Read EPHESIANS 4:11-16

Not only do you need the church, but the church needs you! As God's child, you are blessed with unique spiritual gifts and talents that can be used to benefit the body of Christ. You can use these gifts in at least two ways to benefit fellow believers:

**1. The Gifts God Gives You Promote Spiritual Maturity.** God wants you to grow spiritually. In order for this to happen, he has placed gifted people in the church to fulfill different aspects of ministry. If the pastor, teacher, evangelist, and others properly carry out their duties, this not only helps to promote your spiritual growth, but also equips you to do better work for him. For this to take place, however, you must be "fitted together perfectly," with "each part [doing] its own special work, [helping] the other parts grow."

**2. The Gifts God Gives You Bless Others.** Although you may not hold a prominent position in your church, you may be able to encourage others, care for the sick or those in need, financially support a ministry outreach, or even clean restrooms. If you fail to regularly fellowship in a church with other believers, you are neglecting a tremendous opportunity to use what God has given you.

## God Saved Us for a Purpose Read EPHESIANS 2:10

**A**s a nonbeliever, you had nothing to motivate you to live righteously. You may have searched for purpose and meaning in life but found nothing satisfying. As a believer, however, you are "God's workmanship," which means that his Spirit is working in your life to make you more like Christ and to give you a purpose for living.

This verse describes part of the purpose God has for your life as his child—to do good works by helping others. The amazing and wonderful truth about God's purpose for your life is that he had plans for you to do good works long before you even existed. He has already scheduled the days and events of your life with opportunities to tangibly share his love with others (see Ephesians 2:10, p. 238).

The next time you see a neighbor in trouble, hear about a friend struggling with a problem, notice a coworker in distress, or see a stranger who genuinely needs a helping hand—take hold of this opportunity God has placed in your path. Let your "light shine" (see Matthew 5:16, p. 7) because you are his child.

**CORNER STONES**

stand, as all God's people should, how wide, how long, how high, and how deep his love really is. ¹⁹May you experience the love of Christ, though it is so great you will never fully understand it. Then you will be filled with the fullness of life and power that comes from God.

²⁰Now glory be to God! By his mighty power at work within us, he is able to accomplish infinitely more than we would ever dare to ask or hope. ²¹May he be given glory in the church and in Christ Jesus forever and ever through endless ages. Amen.

CHAPTER **4**
*Unity in the Body*
Therefore I, a prisoner for serving the Lord, beg you to lead a life worthy of your calling, for you have been called by God. ²Be humble and gentle. Be patient with each other, making allowance for each other's faults because of your love. ³Always keep yourselves united in the Holy Spirit, and bind yourselves together with peace.

⁴We are all one body, we have the same Spirit, and we have all been called to the same glorious future. ⁵There is only one Lord, one faith, one baptism, ⁶and there is only one God and Father, who is over us all and in us all and living through us all. ⁷However, he has given each one of us a special gift according to the generosity of Christ. ⁸That is why the Scriptures say,

"When he ascended to the heights,
he led a crowd of captives
and gave gifts to his people."*

⁹Notice that it says "he ascended." This means that Christ first came down to the lowly world in which we live.* ¹⁰The same one who came down is the one who ascended higher than all the heavens, so that his rule might fill the entire universe.

¹¹He is the one who gave these gifts to the church: the apostles, the prophets, the evangelists, and the pastors and teachers. ¹²Their responsibility is to equip God's people to do his work and build up the church, the body of Christ, ¹³until we come to such unity in our faith and knowledge of God's Son that we will be mature and full grown in the Lord, measuring up to the full stature of Christ.

¹⁴Then we will no longer be like children, forever changing our minds about what we believe because someone has told us something different or because someone has cleverly lied to us and made the lie sound like the truth. ¹⁵Instead, we will hold to the truth in love, becoming more and more in every way like Christ, who is the head of his body, the church. ¹⁶Under his direction, the whole body is fitted together perfectly. As each part does its own special work, it helps the other parts grow, so that the whole body is healthy and growing and full of love.

4:8 Ps 68:18.   4:9 Or *to the lowest parts of the earth.*

# What Are Spiritual Gifts? Read EPHESIANS 4:11-16

God has chosen people to do his work. He chose this course of action for reasons only he knows and understands. From a human perspective, we may wonder if this was the best decision. After all, "the sky was the limit" concerning what God could have done. He could have chosen to use angels to speak to lost humanity. He certainly used them on many significant occasions throughout Scripture. Or God could have created a special category of messengers that would never fail him—a "sin-proof" instrument that would faithfully proclaim his Word. For that matter, God himself could have simply poked his face through the heavens and said, "Hello, world! I'm God, and you're not!" But God has chosen men and women to do his work among humankind.

As we seek to follow and be used by Jesus Christ, we need to utilize all that he has made available to us. One of the great blessings Jesus has given to his church and to us as individuals is the gifts of the Spirit. Why has he given these gifts? The Bible has this to say about the vital role they play in the lives of believers:

**Spiritual Gifts Enable Us to Grow in the Knowledge of Christ.** Some people get sidetracked with spiritual gifts and become more obsessed with the gifts than with Jesus. Believers begin to follow signs and wonders, instead of signs and wonders following believers. This is a sign of spiritual immaturity. The Christian writer/preacher A. B. Simpson wrote these insightful words:

Once it was the blessing, now it is the Lord.
Once it was the feeling, now it is his Word.
Once his gifts I wanted, now the Giver own.
Once I sought for healing, now himself alone.

Attaining spiritual gifts is not the goal—they are the gateway. They are not a hobby to play with—they are tools to build with, weapons to fight with. We will be more effective as we put them to use for God's glory and not our own.

**Spiritual Gifts Are to Be Used.** It is possible to let a gift go unused. In doing this, however, you disobey God and cheat the church of a blessing. For this reason, we must use those unique gifts he has given us. In fact, it must be insulting to God for us to demean some gift his Holy Spirit has instilled in our life by saying that it just isn't important enough to use.

**Each Spiritual Gift Has a Special Place in the Body of Christ.** Every gift that God has placed in the body of Christ, the church, is important. Some gifts such as preaching, teaching, and prophesying may seem more important than others such as hospitality or service. But God has given all of these gifts to build up his church. None of these gifts should be looked down upon or treated lightly.

BIG QUESTIONS

*Living as Children of Light*

17With the Lord's authority let me say this: Live no longer as the ungodly* do, for they are hopelessly confused. 18Their closed minds are full of darkness; they are far away from the life of God because they have shut their minds and hardened their hearts against him. 19They don't care anymore about right and wrong, and they have given themselves over to immoral ways. Their lives are filled with all kinds of impurity and greed.

20But that isn't what you were taught when you learned about Christ. 21Since you have heard all about him and have learned the truth that is in Jesus, 22throw off your old evil nature and your former way of life, which is rotten through and through, full of lust and deception. 23Instead, there must be a spiritual renewal of your thoughts and attitudes. 24You must display a new nature because you are a new person, created in God's likeness—righteous, holy, and true.

25So put away all falsehood and "tell your neighbor the truth"* because we belong to each

4:17 Greek *Gentiles.* 4:25 Zech 8:16.

other. 26And "don't sin by letting anger gain control over you."* Don't let the sun go down while you are still angry, 27for anger gives a mighty foothold to the Devil.

28If you are a thief, stop stealing. Begin using your hands for honest work, and then give generously to others in need. 29Don't use foul or abusive language. Let everything you say be good and helpful, so that your words will be an encouragement to those who hear them.

30And do not bring sorrow to God's Holy Spirit by the way you live. Remember, he is the one who has identified you as his own, guaran-

4:26 Ps 4:4.

teeing that you will be saved on the day of redemption.

31Get rid of all bitterness, rage, anger, harsh words, and slander, as well as all types of malicious behavior. 32Instead, be kind to each other, tenderhearted, forgiving one another, just as God through Christ has forgiven you.

## CHAPTER 5
*Living in the Light*

Follow God's example in everything you do, because you are his dear children. 2Live a life

# OFF AND RUNNING

## Husbands and Wives Have Distinct Roles in Marriage Read EPHESIANS 5:21-33

The reason so many marriages fail is that husbands, wives, or both do not obey the standards God has laid out in Scripture. In this text, we find the specific roles God has given the husband and the wife.

### God's Plan for the Husband.

• He is to be the head of his wife as Christ is the head of the church

True authority in the marriage relationship has been given by God to the husband. From the beginning, God designated the man as the leader in the marriage relationship (verse 23). Like Christ, a husband should be firm and decisive but also humble and unselfish. Before a husband can expect his wife to submit to him, though, he has to submit to Christ.

• He must love his wife as Christ loved the church

Jesus said, "I . . . came here not to be served but to serve others, and to give my life as a ransom for many" (Matthew 20:28). To love as Jesus loved means that a husband focuses primarily on his wife's needs, not his own (verse 25). The wife's submission hinges upon the husband's fulfillment of this role. Just as the church loves Jesus because of his incredible display of love for it, so the wife will love and submit to her husband as she sees his demonstration of love toward her. One heart burning with love sets another on fire.

• He must encourage his wife's spiritual growth

One of the husband's first priorities is to make sure his wife has a good relationship with God (verse 26). He is to encourage his wife's spiritual growth, recognizing that it affects her personal happiness as a woman, wife, and mother.

• He must love his wife as he loves himself

A husband must recognize that he and his wife are actually "one." Therefore, he must do for his wife what he would do for himself. He should give her needs as much attention as he would his own (verses 28-29).

### God's Plan for the Wife.

• She must submit to her husband's leadership

Just as a wife submits to God, seeking his will above her own, so she must submit to her husband and his decisions (verses 21, 24).

These guidelines for the husband and the wife become much easier to follow if they respect the first code of conduct listed: "Submit to one another out of reverence for Christ" (verse 21). The word used for *submit* is a term that means "to arrange or rank under." In other words, we need to put the needs of our spouse before our own—in the fear of God. As we do that, our marriages will flourish as God intended—and you will be a living illustration of Christ's love for the church to an unbelieving world. For marriage is not so much *finding* the right person as it is *being* the right person.

filled with love for others, following the example of Christ, who loved you and gave himself as a sacrifice to take away your sins. And God was pleased, because that sacrifice was like sweet perfume to him.

³Let there be no sexual immorality, impurity, or greed among you. Such sins have no place among God's people. ⁴Obscene stories, foolish talk, and coarse jokes—these are not for you. Instead, let there be thankfulness to God. ⁵You can be sure that no immoral, impure, or greedy person will inherit the Kingdom of Christ and of God. For a greedy person is really an idolater who worships the things of this world. ⁶Don't be fooled by those who try to excuse these sins, for the terrible anger of God comes upon all those who disobey him. ⁷Don't participate in the things these people do. ⁸For though your hearts were once full of darkness, now you are full of light from the Lord, and your behavior should show it! ⁹For this light within you produces only what is good and right and true.

¹⁰Try to find out what is pleasing to the Lord. ¹¹Take no part in the worthless deeds of evil and darkness; instead, rebuke and expose them. ¹²It is shameful even to talk about the things that ungodly people do in secret. ¹³But when the light shines on them, it becomes clear how evil these things are. ¹⁴And where your light shines, it will expose their evil deeds. This is why it is said,

"Awake, O sleeper,
    rise up from the dead,
    and Christ will give you light."

*Living by the Spirit's Power*

¹⁵So be careful how you live, not as fools but as those who are wise. ¹⁶Make the most of every opportunity for doing good in these evil days. ¹⁷Don't act thoughtlessly, but try to understand what the Lord wants you to do. ¹⁸Don't be drunk with wine, because that will ruin your life. Instead, let the Holy Spirit fill and control you. ¹⁹Then you will sing psalms and hymns and spiritual songs among yourselves, making music to the Lord in your hearts. ²⁰And you will always give thanks for everything to God the Father in the name of our Lord Jesus Christ.

*Spirit-Guided Relationships: Wives and Husbands*

²¹And further, you will submit to one another out of reverence for Christ. ²²You wives will submit to your husbands as you do to the Lord. ²³For a husband is the head of his wife as Christ is the head of his body, the church; he gave his life to be her Savior. ²⁴As the church submits to Christ, so you wives must submit to your husbands in everything.

²⁵And you husbands must love your wives

## Realize Who Is Tempting You
Read EPHESIANS 6:10-12

In the Bible, the Christian life is not simply compared to a war—it is actually called a war! As in any battle, it helps to know your enemy. In this case, our enemy is the same one who faced off against Christ in the wilderness: the devil. He is incensed that you have surrendered your life to Christ, and he also sees you as a potential threat to his kingdom. But the encouraging news is that the devil is not as powerful as he would like you to think. Here are two things the devil doesn't want you to know:

**1. The Devil Was Conquered by Jesus.** When Jesus Christ died on the cross, he disarmed the devil and his demon powers. They could no longer control and condemn people for their sin. In addition, they could no longer keep the penalty of death hanging above people's heads (see Colossians 2:13-15, p. 255; Hebrews 2:14, p. 287; 1 John 3:8-9, pp. 319–320). The fact that Jesus defeated the devil does not mean that the devil has no power today. But it does mean that he does not have the upper hand.

**2. The Devil Has Definite Limitations.** Satan would love to have us think that he is God's equal, but God has given us power to defeat him (see James 4:7, p. 303). Most important, before he can bring one temptation or hardship our way, he has to go through the protective hedge of Jesus Christ.

Temptation will come your way in the Christian life. But if you are wise, you will cling to the Lord that much tighter when the devil comes with his enticements. Then, once you have stood through the temptation, you will be stronger. As Martin Luther once said, "One Christian who has been tempted is worth a thousand who haven't."

FIRST STEPS

## Christ's Love Sets the Standard Read EPHESIANS 5:2

Think back for a moment to when you were a child. What if your parents had never demonstrated how to use a fork and spoon. Then one day they placed you at a table with these utensils and said, "Eat!" You would have had no idea how to use them to get food into your mouth. Consequently, you would have made a mess.

Fortunately, when it comes to loving others, God has given us the greatest example: Jesus Christ. He knew that the best way to teach us how to love was to show us how it is done, and throughout the Gospels, we can see Jesus' love in action. Of course the greatest display of Christ's love for us was when he took the punishment we deserved by dying on the cross. Because of that tremendous sacrifice, we are obligated to love others. Scripture says, "Pay all your debts, except the debt of love for others. You can never finish paying that!" (Romans 13:8). Because we will never match the depth of love God has for us, we will never be able to fully repay the debt of love we owe him. That is why we have to keep giving out that same kind of love to others.

Perhaps you have grown up in a home where love was seldom expressed, or you have had a distorted view of love, and you feel that you are incapable of truly loving others. Take heart, for as this passage says, you can look to Jesus as your example.

When Christ becomes the standard of your love, you will understand what the apostle Paul meant when he said that Christ's love controls us (see 2 Corinthians 5:14, pp. 220–221).

**CORNER STONES**

---

with the same love Christ showed the church. He gave up his life for her ²⁶to make her holy and clean, washed by baptism and God's word.* ²⁷He did this to present her to himself as a glorious church without a spot or wrinkle or any other blemish. Instead, she will be holy and without fault. ²⁸In the same way, husbands ought to love their wives as they love their own bodies. For a man is actually loving himself when he loves his wife. ²⁹No one hates his own body but lovingly cares for it, just as Christ cares for his body, which is the church. ³⁰And we are his body.

³¹As the Scriptures say, "A man leaves his father and mother and is joined to his wife, and the two are united into one."* ³²This is a great mystery, but it is an illustration of the way Christ and the church are one. ³³So again I say, each man must love his wife as he loves himself, and the wife must respect her husband.

## CHAPTER 6

### Children and Parents

Children, obey your parents because you belong to the Lord, for this is the right thing to do. ²"Honor your father and mother." This is the

first of the Ten Commandments that ends with a promise. ³And this is the promise: If you honor your father and mother, "you will live a long life, full of blessing."*

⁴And now a word to you fathers. Don't make your children angry by the way you treat them. Rather, bring them up with the discipline and instruction approved by the Lord.

### Slaves and Masters

⁵Slaves, obey your earthly masters with deep respect and fear. Serve them sincerely as you would serve Christ. ⁶Work hard, but not just to please your masters when they are watching. As slaves of Christ, do the will of God with all your heart. ⁷Work with enthusiasm, as though you were working for the Lord rather than for people. ⁸Remember that the Lord will reward each one of us for the good we do, whether we are slaves or free.

⁹And in the same way, you masters must treat your slaves right. Don't threaten them; remember, you both have the same Master in heaven, and he has no favorites.

### The Whole Armor of God

¹⁰A final word: Be strong with the Lord's mighty

**5:26** Greek *having cleansed her by the washing of water with the word.*   **5:31** Gen 2:24.   **6:2-3** Exod 20:12; Deut 5:16.

power. [11]Put on all of God's armor so that you will be able to stand firm against all strategies and tricks of the Devil. [12]For we are not fighting against people made of flesh and blood, but against the evil rulers and authorities of the unseen world, against those mighty powers of darkness who rule this world, and against wicked spirits in the heavenly realms.

[13]Use every piece of God's armor to resist the enemy in the time of evil, so that after the battle you will still be standing firm. [14]Stand your ground, putting on the sturdy belt of truth and the body armor of God's righteousness. [15]For shoes, put on the peace that comes from the Good News, so that you will be fully prepared.* [16]In every battle you will need faith as your shield to stop the fiery arrows aimed at you by Satan.* [17]Put on salvation as your helmet, and take the sword of the Spirit, which is the word of God. [18]Pray at all times and on every occasion in the power of the Holy Spirit. Stay alert and be persistent in your prayers for all Christians everywhere.

[19]And pray for me, too. Ask God to give me the right words as I boldly explain God's secret plan that the Good News is for the Gentiles, too.* [20]I am in chains now for preaching this message as God's ambassador. But pray that I will keep on speaking boldly for him, as I should.

## Final Greetings

[21]Tychicus, a much loved brother and faithful helper in the Lord's work, will tell you all about how I am getting along. [22]I am sending him to you for just this purpose. He will let you know how we are, and he will encourage you.

[23]May God give you peace, dear brothers and sisters,* and love with faith, from God the Father and the Lord Jesus Christ. [24]May God's grace be upon all who love our Lord Jesus Christ with an undying love.

6:15 Or *For shoes, put on the readiness to preach the Good News of peace with God.*   6:16 Greek *by the evil one.*   6:19 Greek *explain the mystery of the gospel.*   6:23 Greek *brothers.*

# Philippians

## CHAPTER 1

### Greetings from Paul

This letter is from Paul and Timothy, slaves of Christ Jesus.

It is written to all of God's people in Philippi, who believe in Christ Jesus, and to the elders* and deacons.

2May God our Father and the Lord Jesus Christ give you grace and peace.

### Paul's Thanksgiving and Prayer

3Every time I think of you, I give thanks to my God. 4I always pray for you, and I make my requests with a heart full of joy 5because you have been my partners in spreading the Good News about Christ from the time you first heard it until now. 6And I am sure that God, who began the good work within you, will continue his work until it is finally finished on that day when Christ Jesus comes back again.

7It is right that I should feel as I do about all of you, for you have a very special place in my heart. We have shared together the blessings of God, both when I was in prison and when I was out, defending the truth and telling others the Good News. 8God knows how much I love you and long for you with the tender compassion of Christ Jesus. 9I pray that your love for each other will overflow more and more, and that you will keep on growing in your knowledge and understanding. 10For I want you to understand what really matters, so that you may live pure and blameless lives until Christ returns. 11May you always be filled with the fruit of your salvation*—those good things that are produced in your life by Jesus Christ—for this will bring much glory and praise to God.

### Paul's Joy That Christ Is Preached

12And I want you to know, dear brothers and sisters,* that everything that has happened to me here has helped to spread the Good News. 13For everyone here, including all the soldiers in the palace guard, knows that I am in chains because of Christ. 14And because of my imprisonment, many of the Christians* here have gained confidence and become more bold in telling others about Christ.

15Some are preaching out of jealousy and rivalry. But others preach about Christ with pure motives. 16They preach because they love me, for they know the Lord brought me here to defend the Good News. 17Those others do not have pure motives as they preach about Christ. They preach with selfish ambition, not sincerely, intending to make my chains more painful to me. 18But whether or not their motives are pure, the fact remains that the message about Christ is being preached, so I rejoice. And I will continue to rejoice. 19For I know that as you pray for me and as the Spirit of Jesus Christ helps me, this will all turn out for my deliverance.

### Paul's Life for Christ

20For I live in eager expectation and hope that I will never do anything that causes me shame, but that I will always be bold for Christ, as I have been in the past, and that my life will always honor Christ, whether I live or I die. 21For to me, living is for Christ, and dying is even better. 22Yet if I live, that means fruitful service for Christ. I really don't know which is better. 23I'm torn between two desires: Sometimes I want to live, and sometimes I long to go and be with Christ. That would be far better for me, 24but it is better for you that I live.

1:1 Greek *overseers*.   1:11 Greek *the fruit of righteousness*.   1:12 Greek *brothers*.   1:14 Greek *brothers in the Lord*.

## Jesus Is Human Read PHILIPPIANS 2:5-11

This passage of Scripture paints a touching portrait of the Savior while letting us in on some key truths concerning Christ's divinity and humanity. In essence, it shows why we should worship and emulate Jesus in our lives.

**Jesus Veiled His Deity without Voiding It.** There was never a moment in the life of Jesus when he suddenly "became" God. He was God before he entered this world as a little baby. And he remained God after he became man. When the Scripture says that "made himself nothing," it does not mean that he ceased being God. He simply veiled his deity. But he never voided it. He always was and always will be God.

**Jesus Experienced Our Experiences.** Another way of saying that Jesus took the disguise of a slave is to say that "he emptied himself." Again, this does not mean that he emptied himself of his deity, but that he emptied himself of the privileges of deity. For instance, he never performed a miracle for his own benefit. He walked this earth as a man, not a spirit. He experienced human limitations. Jesus—God in human form—experienced hunger. He endured sorrow. He grew tired. He felt the sting of loneliness. He felt the pressure of temptation. For these reasons, we can be assured that our God understands what we are going through (see Hebrews 2:17-18, p. 287).

**Jesus' Lordship Will Be Acknowledged by All.** Regardless of what anyone thinks of Jesus now, in the end every knee will bow and every tongue will confess that Jesus Christ is Lord. The authority of the Bible backs this claim. Christ's divine nature, which he veiled at times during his time on earth, will then be clearly visible for all to see.

CORNER STONES

---

25I am convinced of this, so I will continue with you so that you will grow and experience the joy of your faith. 26Then when I return to you, you will have even more reason to boast about what Christ Jesus has done for me.

### Live as Citizens of Heaven

27But whatever happens to me, you must live in a manner worthy of the Good News about Christ, as citizens of heaven. Then, whether I come and see you again or only hear about you, I will know that you are standing side by side, fighting together for the Good News. 28Don't be intimidated by your enemies. This will be a sign to them that they are going to be destroyed, but that you are going to be saved, even by God himself. 29For you have been given not only the privilege of trusting in Christ but also the privilege of suffering for him. 30We are in this fight together. You have seen me suffer for him in the past, and you know that I am still in the midst of this great struggle.

CHAPTER **2**
*Unity through Humility*

Is there any encouragement from belonging to Christ? Any comfort from his love? Any fellowship together in the Spirit? Are your hearts tender and sympathetic? 2Then make me truly happy by agreeing wholeheartedly with each other, loving one another, and working together with one heart and purpose.

3Don't be selfish; don't live to make a good impression on others. Be humble, thinking of others as better than yourself. 4Don't think only about your own affairs, but be interested in others, too, and what they are doing.

### Christ's Humility and Exaltation

5Your attitude should be the same that Christ Jesus had. 6Though he was God, he did not demand and cling to his rights as God. 7He made himself nothing;* he took the humble position of a slave and appeared in human form.* 8And in human form he obediently humbled himself even further by dying a criminal's death on a cross. 9Because of this, God

2:7a Or *He laid aside his mighty power and glory.*   2:7b Greek *and was born in the likeness of men and was found in appearance as a man.*

raised him up to the heights of heaven and gave him a name that is above every other name, ¹⁰so that at the name of Jesus every knee will bow, in heaven and on earth and under the earth, ¹¹and every tongue will confess that Jesus Christ is Lord, to the glory of God the Father.

## Shine Brightly for Christ

¹²Dearest friends, you were always so careful to follow my instructions when I was with you. And now that I am away you must be even more careful to put into action God's saving work in your lives, obeying God with deep reverence and fear. ¹³For God is working in you, giving you the desire to obey him and the power to do what pleases him.

¹⁴In everything you do, stay away from complaining and arguing, ¹⁵so that no one can speak a word of blame against you. You are to live clean, innocent lives as children of God in a dark world full of crooked and perverse people. Let your lives shine brightly before them. ¹⁶Hold tightly to the word of life, so that when Christ returns, I will be proud that I did not lose the race and that my work was not useless. ¹⁷But even if my life is to be poured out like a drink offering to complete the sacrifice of your faithful service (that is, if I am to die for you), I will rejoice, and I want to share my joy with all of you. ¹⁸And you should be happy about this and rejoice with me.

## Paul Commends Timothy

¹⁹If the Lord Jesus is willing, I hope to send Timothy to you soon. Then when he comes back, he can cheer me up by telling me how you are getting along. ²⁰I have no one else like Timothy, who genuinely cares about your welfare. ²¹All the others care only for themselves and not for what matters to Jesus Christ. ²²But you know how Timothy has proved himself. Like a son with his father, he has helped me in preaching the Good News. ²³I hope to send him to you just as soon as I find out what is going to happen to me here. ²⁴And I have confidence from the Lord that I myself will come to see you soon.

## Paul Commends Epaphroditus

²⁵Meanwhile, I thought I should send Epaphroditus back to you. He is a true brother, a faithful worker, and a courageous soldier. And he was your messenger to help me in my need. ²⁶Now I am sending him home again, for he has been longing to see you, and he was very distressed

that you heard he was ill. ²⁷And he surely was ill; in fact, he almost died. But God had mercy on him—and also on me, so that I would not have such unbearable sorrow.

²⁸So I am all the more anxious to send him back to you, for I know you will be glad to see him, and that will lighten all my cares. ²⁹Welcome him with Christian love* and with great joy, and be sure to honor people like him. ³⁰For he risked his life for the work of Christ, and he was at the point of death while trying to do for me the things you couldn't do because you were far away.

## CHAPTER 3
*The Priceless Gain of Knowing Christ*

Whatever happens, dear brothers and sisters,* may the Lord give you joy. I never get tired of telling you this. I am doing this for your own good.

²Watch out for those dogs, those wicked men and their evil deeds, those mutilators who say you must be circumcised to be saved. ³For we who worship God in the Spirit* are the only ones who are truly circumcised. We put no confidence in human effort. Instead, we boast about what Christ Jesus has done for us.

⁴Yet I could have confidence in myself if anyone could. If others have reason for confidence in their own efforts, I have even more! ⁵For I was circumcised when I was eight days old, having been born into a pure-blooded Jewish family that is a branch of the tribe of Benjamin. So I am a real Jew if there ever was one! What's more, I was a member of the Pharisees, who demand the strictest obedience to the Jewish law. ⁶And zealous? Yes, in fact, I harshly persecuted the church. And I obeyed the Jewish law so carefully that I was never accused of any fault.

⁷I once thought all these things were so very important, but now I consider them worthless because of what Christ has done. ⁸Yes, everything else is worthless when compared with the priceless gain of knowing Christ Jesus my Lord. I have discarded everything else, counting it all as garbage, so that I may have Christ ⁹and become one with him. I no longer count on my own goodness or my ability to obey God's law, but I trust Christ to save me. For God's way of making us right with himself depends on faith. ¹⁰As a result, I can really know Christ and experience the mighty power that raised him from the dead. I can learn what it means to suffer with him, sharing in his death, ¹¹so that, somehow, I can experience the resurrection from the dead!

2:29 Greek *in the Lord.*   3:1 Greek *brothers;* also in 3:13, 17.   3:3 Or *in spirit;* some manuscripts read *worship by the Spirit of God.*

*Pressing toward the Goal*

12I don't mean to say that I have already achieved these things or that I have already reached perfection! But I keep working toward that day when I will finally be all that Christ Jesus saved me for and wants me to be. 13No, dear brothers and sisters, I am still not all I should be,* but I am focusing all my energies on this one thing: Forgetting the past and looking forward to what lies ahead, 14I strain to reach the end of the race and receive the prize for which God, through Christ Jesus, is calling us up to heaven.*

15I hope all of you who are mature Christians will agree on these things. If you disagree on some point, I believe God will make it plain to you. 16But we must be sure to obey the truth we have learned already.

17Dear brothers and sisters, pattern your lives after mine, and learn from those who follow our example. 18For I have told you often before, and I say it again with tears in my eyes, that there are many whose conduct shows they are really enemies of the cross of Christ. 19Their future is eternal destruction. Their god is their appetite, they brag about shameful things, and all they think about is this life here on earth. 20But we are citizens of heaven, where the Lord Jesus Christ lives. And we are eagerly waiting for him to return as our Savior. 21He will take these weak mortal bodies of ours and change them into glorious bodies like his own, using the same mighty power that he will use to conquer everything, everywhere.

CHAPTER **4**

Dear brothers and sisters,* I love you and long to see you, for you are my joy and the reward for my work. So please stay true to the Lord, my dear friends.

*Paul's Final Thoughts*

2And now I want to plead with those two women, Euodia and Syntyche. Please, because you belong to the Lord, settle your disagreement. 3And I ask you, my true teammate,* to help these women, for they worked hard with me in telling others the Good News. And they worked with Clement and the rest of my co-workers, whose names are written in the Book of Life.

4Always be full of joy in the Lord. I say it again—rejoice! 5Let everyone see that you are considerate in all you do. Remember, the Lord is coming soon.

6Don't worry about anything; instead, pray about everything. Tell God what you need, and thank him for all he has done. 7If you do this, you will experience God's peace, which is far more wonderful than the human mind can understand. His peace will guard your hearts and minds as you live in Christ Jesus.

8And now, dear brothers and sisters, let me say one more thing as I close this letter. Fix your thoughts on what is true and honorable and right. Think about things that are pure and lovely and admirable. Think about things that are excellent and worthy of praise. 9Keep putting into practice all you learned from me and

3:13 Some manuscripts read *I am not all I should be.*   3:14 Or *from heaven.*   4:1 Greek *brothers;* also in 4:8.   4:3 Greek *true yokefellow,* or *loyal Syzygus.*

# OFF AND RUNNING ▰▰▰

## Place Christ before All Else Read PHILIPPIANS 3:4-8

As verses 4-6 attest, the apostle Paul was the epitome of a good Jew. He had been born a member of God's chosen people and had flawlessly kept God's laws. But when Paul met Jesus on the road to Damascus (see Acts 9:1-19, pp. 148–149), Paul realized that everything he was living for was taking him in the wrong direction. For that reason he counted everything else in life—his reputation, his achievements, his pursuits, his possessions—worthless, so that his sole pursuit would be in knowing and serving Jesus.

Do you, like Paul, place Christ above everything else in your life? If you are not sure, ask yourself the following questions: How do you spend your time? What dominates your thoughts? Where are your priorities? What motivates you? If the most important thing in your life is Jesus, then your life will revolve around getting to know him more and more. You will want to spend time learning about his nature, his will, and his purposes for you in his Word. And you will truly be able to say that you have discovered "the priceless gain of knowing Christ Jesus."

heard from me and saw me doing, and the God of peace will be with you.

## Paul's Thanks for Their Gifts

10How grateful I am, and how I praise the Lord that you are concerned about me again. I know you have always been concerned for me, but for a while you didn't have the chance to help me. 11Not that I was ever in need, for I have learned how to get along happily whether I have much or little. 12I know how to live on almost nothing or with everything. I have learned the secret of living in every situation, whether it is with a full stomach or empty, with plenty or little. 13For I can do everything with the help of Christ who gives me the strength I need. 14But even so, you have done well to share with me in my present difficulty.

15As you know, you Philippians were the only ones who gave me financial help when I brought you the Good News and then traveled on from Macedonia. No other church did this. 16Even when I was in Thessalonica you sent help more than once. 17I don't say this because I want a gift from you. What I want is for you to receive a well-earned reward because of your kindness.

18At the moment I have all I need—more than I need! I am generously supplied with the gifts you sent me with Epaphroditus. They are a sweet-smelling sacrifice that is acceptable to God and pleases him. 19And this same God who takes care of me will supply all your needs from his glorious riches, which have been given to us in Christ Jesus. 20Now glory be to God our Father forever and ever. Amen.

## Paul's Final Greetings

21Give my greetings to all the Christians there. The brothers who are with me here send you their greetings. 22And all the other Christians send their greetings, too, especially those who work in Caesar's palace.

23May the grace of the Lord Jesus Christ be with your spirit.

## Prayer Helps Us Overcome Worry Read PHILIPPIANS 4:6-7

Have you ever been gripped by worry or fear? Worry is a completely unproductive emotion. It is the advance interest we pay on troubles that seldom come. But these verses give us the best antidote for worry—prayer. God wants to be the first one we turn to in times of worry or crisis. When we do, he promises a special blessing if we do the following four things:

**1. Stop Worrying and Start Praying.** Don't ever think that your need is too insignificant for God's attention. He wants us to pray about *everything*.

**2. Tell God Your Needs.** Even though God is all-knowing and is well aware of your situation, he desires that you verbalize your needs to him and place them in his hands.

**3. Present Your Requests with Thanks.** Instead of praying with feelings of doubt, we can thank God for his answers in advance because of the promises he has made to us in his Word.

**4. Receive God's Peace.** Once you do these things, verse 7 says that you will experience God's peace. In the original Greek text, this verse literally means that God's peace will "mount a guard or garrison" around your heart and mind to keep and protect you during those difficult times in your life.

The next time you are tempted to worry about something, channel into prayer all of the energy you would have put into worry. Say something like, "Lord, here is my problem. It looms ever larger in my path, so I am putting it into your hands. I am not going to worry, Lord. Instead, I am going to trust you. I am even going to thank you in advance for what you will do, because you know what you are doing." This may not always be an easy thing to do, but if you want to overcome worry and experience God's peace, it is something you must consciously do.

FIRST STEPS

# Colossians

## Greetings from Paul

This letter is from Paul, chosen by God to be an apostle of Christ Jesus, and from our brother Timothy.

²It is written to God's holy people in the city of Colosse, who are faithful brothers and sisters* in Christ.

May God our Father give you grace and peace.

## Paul's Thanksgiving and Prayer

³We always pray for you, and we give thanks to God the Father of our Lord Jesus Christ, ⁴for we have heard that you trust in Christ Jesus and that you love all of God's people. ⁵You do this because you are looking forward to the joys of heaven—as you have been ever since you first heard the truth of the Good News. ⁶This same Good News that came to you is going out all over the world. It is changing lives everywhere, just as it changed yours that very first day you heard and understood the truth about God's great kindness to sinners.

⁷Epaphras, our much loved co-worker, was the one who brought you the Good News. He is Christ's faithful servant, and he is helping us in your place.* ⁸He is the one who told us about the great love for others that the Holy Spirit has given you.

⁹So we have continued praying for you ever since we first heard about you. We ask God to give you a complete understanding of what he wants to do in your lives, and we ask him to make you wise with spiritual wisdom. ¹⁰Then the way you live will always honor and please the Lord, and you will continually do good, kind things for others. All the while, you will learn to know God better and better.

¹¹We also pray that you will be strengthened with his glorious power so that you will have all the patience and endurance you need. May you be filled with joy, ¹²always thanking the Father, who has enabled you to share the inheritance that belongs to God's holy people, who live in the light. ¹³For he has rescued us from the one who rules in the kingdom of darkness, and he has brought us into the Kingdom of his dear Son. ¹⁴God has purchased our freedom with his blood* and has forgiven all our sins.

## Christ Is Supreme

¹⁵Christ is the visible image of the invisible God. He existed before God made anything at all and is supreme over all creation.* ¹⁶Christ is the one through whom God created everything in heaven and earth. He made the things we can see and the things we can't see—kings, kingdoms, rulers, and authorities. Everything has been created through him and for him. ¹⁷He existed before everything else began, and he holds all creation together.

¹⁸Christ is the head of the church, which is his body. He is the first of all who will rise from the dead,* so he is first in everything. ¹⁹For God in all his fullness was pleased to live in Christ, ²⁰and by him God reconciled everything to himself. He made peace with everything in heaven and on earth by means of his blood on the cross. ²¹This includes you who were once so far away from God. You were his enemies, separated from him by your evil thoughts and actions, ²²yet now he has brought you back as his friends. He has done this through his death on the cross in his own human body. As a result, he has brought you into the very presence of God, and you are holy and blameless as you stand before him

1:2 Greek *faithful brothers*.   1:7 Greek *he is ministering on your behalf*; other manuscripts read *he is ministering on our behalf*.   1:14 Some manuscripts do not include *with his blood*.   1:15 Greek *He is the firstborn of all creation*.   1:18 Greek *He is the beginning, the firstborn from the dead*.

## Jesus Is Divine Read COLOSSIANS 1:15-20

The most crucial truth of the Christian faith is that Jesus Christ, though he came to earth as a man, was in fact God. This passage lays out six important details about Jesus' divinity and his work in heaven and on earth:

**1. Jesus Is Eternal.** Being God, Jesus never had a beginning, nor does he have an end (verse 15). The apostle John knew this. In John 1:1, he refers to Jesus as the Word and says that "in the beginning the Word already existed."

**2. Jesus Is the Creator of All Things.** This concept makes the whole idea of Jesus' coming as a Savior to this earth so amazing. He understood the way people acted and the hardness of humans' hearts because he created them (verse 16). Yet he loved people so much he was willing to come down to earth and die in order to redeem all humankind.

**3. Jesus Holds Everything Together.** Jesus has and always will be in control (verses 16-17). Our world is not in some chaotic state but has been created with a purpose in mind—to ultimately bring glory to Christ.

**4. Jesus Is the Head of the Church.** The church was not established by a group of people but by God himself. Although some leaders in the church may let us down at times, we must remember that Christ, the true head of this body of believers (verse 18), will never fail us.

**5. Jesus Is the Leader of All Who Will Rise from the Dead.** Christ was the first to actually defeat death and return to life in a resurrected body (verse 18). For that reason, we who follow him have the hope—and the evidence—that we, too, will one day rise again after death to spend eternity with him.

**6. Jesus Is the Only Way to Peace with God.** God was never surprised that man sinned in the Garden of Eden. The Bible even records that Jesus' sacrifice on the cross was known before "the world was made" (Revelation 13:8). That means that God had already made a provision for our sins long before Adam ate the forbidden fruit (verse 20).

Jesus was much more than a mere prophet, teacher, or messenger. In reality, Jesus was nothing less than God himself come to the earth. To deny this central truth is to deny the basis of the Christian faith. Remember, it was this truth that motivated the Christians of the first century to turn their world "upside down" for the sake of the gospel (see Acts 17:6, p. 159).

CORNER STONES

without a single fault. 23But you must continue to believe this truth and stand in it firmly. Don't drift away from the assurance you received when you heard the Good News. The Good News has been preached all over the world, and I, Paul, have been appointed by God to proclaim it.

### Paul's Work for the Church

24I am glad when I suffer for you in my body, for I am completing what remains of Christ's sufferings for his body, the church. 25God has given me the responsibility of serving his church by proclaiming his message in all its fullness to you Gentiles. 26This message was kept secret for centuries and generations past, but now it has been revealed to his own holy people. 27For it has pleased God to tell his people that the riches and glory of Christ are for you Gentiles, too. For this is the secret: Christ lives in you, and this is your assurance that you will share in his glory.

28So everywhere we go, we tell everyone about Christ. We warn them and teach them with all the wisdom God has given us, for we want to present them to God, perfect* in their relationship to Christ. 29I work very hard at this, as I depend on Christ's mighty power that works within me.

## CHAPTER 2

I want you to know how much I have agonized for you and for the church at Laodicea, and for many other friends who have never known me personally. 2My goal is that they will be encouraged and knit together by strong ties of love. I want them to have full confidence because they have complete understanding of God's secret plan, which is Christ himself. 3In him lie hidden all the treasures of wisdom and knowledge.

4I am telling you this so that no one will be able to deceive you with persuasive arguments. 5For though I am far away from you, my heart is with you. And I am very happy because you are living as you should and because of your strong faith in Christ.

### Freedom from Rules and New Life in Christ

6And now, just as you accepted Christ Jesus as your Lord, you must continue to live in obedience to him. 7Let your roots grow down into him and draw up nourishment from him, so you will grow in faith, strong and vigorous in the truth you were taught. Let your lives overflow with thanksgiving for all he has done.

8Don't let anyone lead you astray with empty philosophy and high-sounding nonsense that come from human thinking and from the evil powers of this world,* and not from Christ. 9For in Christ the fullness of God lives in a human body,* 10and you are complete through your union with Christ. He is the Lord over every ruler and authority in the universe.

11When you came to Christ, you were "circumcised," but not by a physical procedure. It was a spiritual procedure—the cutting away of your sinful nature. 12For you were buried with Christ when you were baptized. And with him you were raised to a new life because you trusted the mighty power of God, who raised Christ from the dead.

13You were dead because of your sins and because your sinful nature was not yet cut away. Then God made you alive with Christ. He forgave all our sins. 14He canceled the record that contained the charges against us. He

took it and destroyed it by nailing it to Christ's cross. 15In this way, God disarmed the evil rulers and authorities. He shamed them publicly by his victory over them on the cross of Christ.

16So don't let anyone condemn you for what you eat or drink, or for not celebrating certain holy days or new-moon ceremonies or Sabbaths. 17For these rules were only shadows of the real thing, Christ himself. 18Don't let anyone condemn you by insisting on self-denial. And don't let anyone say you must worship angels, even though they say they have had visions about this. These people claim to be so humble, but their sinful minds have

---

## Let God Occupy Your Thoughts Read COLOSSIANS 3:2-4

A song in the church says, "Turn your eyes upon Jesus. Look full in his wonderful face. And the things of earth will grow strangely dim in the light of his glory and grace." These are good words to live by, for one of the strongest deterrents against returning to your old way of life is to focus upon your Savior and future. As a believer, you have been promised eternal life, the hope of heaven, and the assurance of spending eternity in the presence of God. When you think about that, the trappings of this world begin to lose their appeal.

The next time you feel inclined to dabble with your old life, or feel weighed down by the worries of this world, or fear that you won't make it as a Christian, remember to do these things:

- Keep your eyes on your final destination.
- Realize that worry should not be a part of your life.
- Picture yourself as dead to this world and alive in Christ.
- Remember that your Redeemer is returning.

If you allow these truths to occupy your thoughts, you will find it much easier to obey God and say no to the alluring, but damaging, enticements of this sinful world.

---

1:28 Or *mature.*   2:8 Or *from the basic principles of this world;* also in 2:20.   2:9 Greek *in him dwells all the fullness of the Godhead bodily.*

## God's Peace Needs to Rule in Our Hearts Read COLOSSIANS 3:15

One of the most obvious identifying marks of a Christian is peace. As Paul points out in this verse, the peace a Christian has comes from Christ and "rules" in a Christian's heart. The Greek verb Paul uses for *rule* suggests that Christ's peace is to act as an "umpire" or a judge in our lives, deciding our outlook and mood in the midst of all circumstances.

What characterizes Christ's peace? Here are a few more biblical descriptions:

- It is not anxious about anything but trusts God (see Philippians 4:6-7, p. 250).
- It doesn't doubt that God is in control (see Mark 4:35-41, pp. 47–48).
- It doesn't forget God's blessings and answers to prayer (see Philippians 4:6, p. 250).
- It should be present in our relationships (see Romans 12:18, p. 192).
- It comes from Christ alone (see John 16:33, p. 128).

- It is produced by the Holy Spirit (see Galatians 5:22, p. 234).
- It promotes peace with others (see James 3:18, p. 302).

Does the peace of Christ rule in your life? If not, you are not living as Jesus really intends you to live. Give God your worries and concerns, and ask him to replace them with his peace. This peace will not only calm your heart, but it will also help encourage harmony between you and your Christian brothers and sisters.

**CORNER STONES**

---

made them proud. ¹⁹But they are not connected to Christ, the head of the body. For we are joined together in his body by his strong sinews, and we grow only as we get our nourishment and strength from God.

²⁰You have died with Christ, and he has set you free from the evil powers of this world. So why do you keep on following rules of the world, such as, ²¹"Don't handle, don't eat, don't touch." ²²Such rules are mere human teaching about things that are gone as soon as we use them. ²³These rules may seem wise because they require strong devotion, humility, and severe bodily discipline. But they have no effect when it comes to conquering a person's evil thoughts and desires.

CHAPTER **3**
*Living the New Life*

Since you have been raised to new life with Christ, set your sights on the realities of heaven, where Christ sits at God's right hand in the place of honor and power. ²Let heaven fill your thoughts. Do not think only about things down

---

# OFF AND RUNNING

### Avoid Aggravating Your Children Read COLOSSIANS 3:20-21

While discipline is necessary in the lives of children, it is equally necessary that discipline be tempered with love. This means that parents should not scold or nag their children, especially when disciplining them. Other words that have been used for scold and nag are *exasperate* and *aggravate*. The word *aggravate* means to irritate, enrage, harass, tease, and add fuel to the flame.

When discipline is administered in an aggravating manner, the consequences can be devastating. Children may not only be angry with their parents and resent them, but children may also disrespect and dishonor their parents. Even worse, they may one day end their relationship with their parents or act out violently against them.

If you really want your children to honor you as a parent, then you must discipline them with love, praise them when they obey, and train them in the instruction of the Lord.

here on earth. ³For you died when Christ died, and your real life is hidden with Christ in God. ⁴And when Christ, who is your* real life, is revealed to the whole world, you will share in all his glory.

⁵So put to death the sinful, earthly things lurking within you. Have nothing to do with sexual sin, impurity, lust, and shameful desires. Don't be greedy for the good things of this life, for that is idolatry. ⁶God's terrible anger will come upon those who do such things. ⁷You used to do them when your life was still part of this world. ⁸But now is the time to get rid of anger, rage, malicious behavior, slander, and dirty language. ⁹Don't lie to each other, for you have stripped off your old evil nature and all its wicked deeds. ¹⁰In its place you have clothed yourselves with a brand-new nature that is continually being renewed as you learn more and more about Christ, who created this new nature within you. ¹¹In this new life, it doesn't matter if you are a Jew or a Gentile,* circumcised or uncircumcised, barbaric, uncivilized,* slave, or free. Christ is all that matters, and he lives in all of us.

¹²Since God chose you to be the holy people whom he loves, you must clothe yourselves with tenderhearted mercy, kindness, humility, gentleness, and patience. ¹³You must make allowance for each other's faults and forgive the person who offends you. Remember, the Lord forgave you, so you must forgive others. ¹⁴And the most important piece of clothing you must wear is love. Love is what binds us all together in perfect harmony. ¹⁵And let the peace that comes from Christ rule in your hearts. For as members of one body you are all called to live in peace. And always be thankful.

¹⁶Let the words of Christ, in all their richness, live in your hearts and make you wise. Use his words to teach and counsel each other. Sing psalms and hymns and spiritual songs to God with thankful hearts. ¹⁷And whatever you do or say, let it be as a representative of the Lord Jesus, all the while giving thanks through him to God the Father.

### Instructions for Christian Households

¹⁸You wives must submit to your husbands, as is fitting for those who belong to the Lord. ¹⁹And you husbands must love your wives and never treat them harshly.

²⁰You children must always obey your parents, for this is what pleases the Lord. ²¹Fathers,

don't aggravate your children. If you do, they will become discouraged and quit trying.

²²You slaves must obey your earthly masters in everything you do. Try to please them all the time, not just when they are watching you. Obey them willingly because of your reverent fear of the Lord. ²³Work hard and cheerfully at whatever you do, as though you were working for the Lord rather than for people. ²⁴Remember that the Lord will give you an inheritance as your reward, and the Master you are serving is Christ. ²⁵But if you do what is wrong, you will be paid back for the wrong you have done. For God has no favorites who can get away with evil.

## CHAPTER 4

You slave owners must be just and fair to your slaves. Remember that you also have a Master—in heaven.

### An Encouragement for Prayer

²Devote yourselves to prayer with an alert mind and a thankful heart. ³Don't forget to pray for us, too, that God will give us many opportunities to preach about his secret plan—that Christ is also for you Gentiles. That is why I am here in chains. ⁴Pray that I will proclaim this message as clearly as I should.

⁵Live wisely among those who are not Christians, and make the most of every opportunity. ⁶Let your conversation be gracious and effective so that you will have the right answer for everyone.

### Paul's Final Instructions and Greetings

⁷Tychicus, a much loved brother, will tell you how I am getting along. He is a faithful helper who serves the Lord with me. ⁸I have sent him on this special trip to let you know how we are doing and to encourage you. ⁹I am also sending Onesimus, a faithful and much loved brother, one of your own people. He and Tychicus will give you all the latest news.

¹⁰Aristarchus, who is in prison with me, sends you his greetings, and so does Mark, Barnabas's cousin. And as you were instructed before, make Mark welcome if he comes your way. ¹¹Jesus (the one we call Justus) also sends his greetings. These are the only Jewish Christians among my co-workers; they are working with me here for the Kingdom of God. And what a comfort they have been!

¹²Epaphras, from your city, a servant of Christ Jesus, sends you his greetings. He always prays

3:4 Some manuscripts read *our.*   3:11a Greek *Greek.*   3:11b Greek *Barbarian, Scythian.*

# OFF AND RUNNING

## Work As If You Are Working for the Lord
Read COLOSSIANS 3:22-24

While the world says to work for the sake of your own welfare, Jesus says to work out of your desire to please him. While the world says to work hard to get ahead, Jesus says to work hard to show the world who you are really working for. When you work as though you are working for the Lord, your whole outlook changes.

Do you want to revolutionize your attitude toward your job? Then take this verse to heart. If you are a mother at home, tackle the dishes, laundry, and cooking as if you are serving the Lord, not just your family. If you work in an office, take care of your tasks and treat your co-workers as you would the Lord himself. Your work may be unappreciated and underpaid in this life, but God promises to give you your full reward in heaven (verse 24).

---

earnestly for you, asking God to make you strong and perfect, fully confident of the whole will of God. ¹³I can assure you that he has agonized for you and also for the Christians in Laodicea and Hierapolis.

¹⁴Dear Doctor Luke sends his greetings, and so does Demas. ¹⁵Please give my greetings to our Christian brothers and sisters* at Laodicea, and to Nympha and those who meet in her house.

4:15 Greek *brothers.*

¹⁶After you have read this letter, pass it on to the church at Laodicea so they can read it, too. And you should read the letter I wrote to them. ¹⁷And say to Archippus, "Be sure to carry out the work the Lord gave you."

¹⁸Here is my greeting in my own handwriting—PAUL.

Remember my chains.

May the grace of God be with you.

# OFF AND RUNNING

## Keep Your Conversation Gracious Read COLOSSIANS 4:6

Witnessing to others about the Lord can be a bit intimidating at first. We never know what kind of response we will receive. But if you follow the three steps found in these verses, you will become much more effective at sharing your faith:

**1. Tell the Good News.** Center your conversation on the simple gospel message: (1) Man is separated from God by sin; (2) God sent his Son, Jesus Christ, to die on the cross and pay the price for our sin; and (3) if we will turn from that sin, embrace Christ as Savior and Lord, and follow him, we can be forgiven and have a relationship with God.

**2. Be Wise When Sharing Your Faith.** Use discernment. Don't push the subject of your faith if you sense the person is not interested. On the other hand, don't end the conversation if you feel the person is sincerely interested. Remember, God softens a person's heart. You simply present the message.

**3. Let Your Conversation Be Gracious and Sensible.** Don't rely upon sophisticated arguments to prove your point. Let Christ's love shine through you as you speak. Another translation adds that your conversation should also be "seasoned with salt." In other words, give the person a thirst to learn more about Christ.

Jesus communicated his message in a unique way to each individual. We must do the same. The more we share our faith, the easier that will become.

# 1 Thessalonians

## CHAPTER 1

*Greetings from Paul*

This letter is from Paul, Silas,* and Timothy.

It is written to the church in Thessalonica, you who belong to God the Father and the Lord Jesus Christ.

May his grace and peace be yours.

*The Faith of the Thessalonian Believers*

2We always thank God for all of you and pray for you constantly. 3As we talk to our God and Father about you, we think of your faithful work, your loving deeds, and your continual anticipation of the return of our Lord Jesus Christ.

4We know that God loves you, dear brothers and sisters,* and that he chose you to be his own people. 5For when we brought you the Good News, it was not only with words but also with power, for the Holy Spirit gave you full assurance that what we said was true. And you know that the way we lived among you was further proof of the truth of our message. 6So you received the message with joy from the Holy Spirit in spite of the severe suffering it brought you. In this way, you imitated both us and the Lord. 7As a result, you yourselves became an example to all the Christians in Greece.* 8And now the word of the Lord is ringing out from you to people everywhere, even beyond Greece, for wherever we go we find people telling us about your faith in God. We don't need to tell them about it, 9for they themselves keep talking about the wonderful welcome you gave us and how you turned away from idols to serve the true and living God. 10And they speak of how you are looking forward to the coming of God's Son from heaven—

Jesus, whom God raised from the dead. He is the one who has rescued us from the terrors of the coming judgment.

## CHAPTER 2

*Paul Remembers His Visit*

You yourselves know, dear brothers and sisters,* that our visit to you was not a failure. 2You know how badly we had been treated at Philippi just before we came to you and how much we suffered there. Yet our God gave us the courage to declare his Good News to you boldly, even though we were surrounded by many who opposed us. 3So you can see that we were not preaching with any deceit or impure purposes or trickery.

4For we speak as messengers who have been approved by God to be entrusted with the Good News. Our purpose is to please God, not people. He is the one who examines the motives of our hearts. 5Never once did we try to win you with flattery, as you very well know. And God is our witness that we were not just pretending to be your friends so you would give us money! 6As for praise, we have never asked for it from you or anyone else. 7As apostles of Christ we certainly had a right to make some demands of you, but we were as gentle among you as a mother* feeding and caring for her own children. 8We loved you so much that we gave you not only God's Good News but our own lives, too.

9Don't you remember, dear brothers and sisters, how hard we worked among you? Night and day we toiled to earn a living so that our expenses would not be a burden to anyone there as we preached God's Good News among

---

1:1 Greek *Silvanus.*  1:4 Greek *brothers.*  1:7 Greek *Macedonia and Achaia,* the northern and southern regions of Greece; also in 1:8.
2:1 Greek *brothers;* also in 2:9, 14, 17.  2:7 Some manuscripts read *we were as infants among you; we were as a mother.*

## Our Love Should Grow Read 1 THESSALONIANS 3:12-13

Too many of us think that love is some emotional thing that comes and goes. Yet this passage suggests that our love should not only remain steady but that it should also *grow*. This may seem like an impossible task on our own—and it is. That is why the apostle Paul says, "May the *Lord* make your love grow." You cannot manufacture sincere love. Christ's love must motivate and compel you (see 2 Corinthians 5:14, pp. 220-221). This love, in turn, will help to strengthen your heart, keep you from sin, and make you holy so that you can be guiltless when Christ returns.

If your love toward God and others seems stagnant, it is likely you have distanced yourself from the Source of that love. Return to the Lord and ask him to refill and refresh your love for him, then look for ways to share that love with others.

**CORNER STONES**

you. ¹⁰You yourselves are our witnesses—and so is God—that we were pure and honest and faultless toward all of you believers. ¹¹And you know that we treated each of you as a father treats his own children. ¹²We pleaded with you, encouraged you, and urged you to live your lives in a way that God would consider worthy. For he called you into his Kingdom to share his glory.

¹³And we will never stop thanking God that when we preached his message to you, you didn't think of the words we spoke as being just our own. You accepted what we said as the very word of God—which, of course, it was. And this word continues to work in you who believe.

¹⁴And then, dear brothers and sisters, you suffered persecution from your own countrymen. In this way, you imitated the believers in God's churches in Judea who, because of their belief in Christ Jesus, suffered from their own people, the Jews.

¹⁵For some of the Jews had killed their own prophets, and some even killed the Lord Jesus. Now they have persecuted us and driven us out. They displease God and oppose everyone ¹⁶by trying to keep us from preaching the Good News

## OFF AND RUNNING

### Encourage Your Children's Spiritual Growth
Read 1 THESSALONIANS 2:11-12

The apostle Paul compared his relationship with the Thessalonians to that of a father with his children. Although this passage doesn't necessarily deal with the father-child relationship, it does show three ways in which fathers play an important role in developing their children's faith:

**1. Fathers Encourage Children in Their Faith.** One way in which fathers can do this is to live out their faith before their children. Doing this will show children how one's faith affects the way a person lives.

**2. Fathers Comfort Children in Their Faith.** Be available for your children when they face challenges to their faith.

**3. Fathers Urge Children to Grow in Their Faith.** Set rules and boundaries that will help establish the moral foundation children need to live a life pleasing to God.

Fathers may not be able to be with their children twenty-four hours a day, but they can help build conviction in their children's lives so that their children will make the right choices. This is one of the most important investments fathers will ever make.

to the Gentiles, for fear some might be saved. By doing this, they continue to pile up their sins. But the anger of God has caught up with them at last.

*Timothy's Good Report about the Church*

17Dear brothers and sisters, after we were separated from you for a little while (though our hearts never left you), we tried very hard to come back because of our intense longing to see you again. 18We wanted very much to come, and I, Paul, tried again and again, but Satan prevented us. 19After all, what gives us hope and joy, and what is our proud reward and crown? It is you! Yes, you will bring us much joy as we stand together before our Lord Jesus when he comes back again. 20For you are our pride and joy.

CHAPTER **3**

Finally, when we could stand it no longer, we decided that I should stay alone in Athens, 2and we sent Timothy to visit you. He is our co-worker for God and our brother in proclaiming the Good News of Christ. We sent him to strengthen you; to encourage you in your faith, 3and to keep you from becoming disturbed by the troubles you were going through. But, of course, you know that such troubles are going to happen to us Christians. 4Even while we were with you, we warned you that troubles would soon come—and they did, as you well know.

5That is why, when I could bear it no longer, I sent Timothy to find out whether your faith was still strong. I was afraid that the Tempter had gotten the best of you and that all our work had been useless. 6Now Timothy has just returned, bringing the good news that your faith and love are as strong as ever. He reports that you remember our visit with joy and that you want to see us just as much as we want to see you. 7So we have been greatly comforted, dear brothers and sisters,* in all of our own crushing troubles and suffering, because you have remained strong in your faith. 8It gives us new life, knowing you remain strong in the Lord.

9How we thank God for you! Because of you we have great joy in the presence of God. 10Night and day we pray earnestly for you, asking God to let us see you again to fill up anything that may still be missing in your faith.

11May God himself, our Father, and our Lord Jesus make it possible for us to come to you very soon. 12And may the Lord make your love grow and overflow to each other and to everyone else,

3:7 Greek *brothers*.

## Act upon What God Has Already Revealed in Scripture
Read 1 THESSALONIANS 4:1-5

We often wonder what God's will may be for us concerning a particular situation. Yet Scripture reveals certain things that are clearly the will of God for every believer—without exception. Here are four things Scripture reveals as God's will:

**1. God Wants Us to Live under the Control of the Holy Spirit.** God doesn't want us to fill our life with cheap substitutes, like alcohol, possessions, or worldly pursuits. Instead, he wants us to seek to live under the control of the Holy Spirit (see Ephesians 5:18, p. 243), who produces such attributes as love, joy, peace, patience, kindness, goodness, faithfulness, gentleness, and self-control in our lives. To be controlled by anything or anyone else is outside the will of God.

**2. God Wants Us to Live a Pure and Holy Life.** It is the clear will of God that we as Christians live sexually pure lives (verses 4-5). The only sexual relationship God will bless is that of a man and woman committed to each other in marriage. Premarital and extramarital sexual relationships are never the will of God for the believer, under any circumstances.

**3. God Wants Us to Have an Attitude of Gratitude.** No matter what happens, God wants us to be thankful, recognizing that he is in control of all the circumstances that surround our life (see 1 Thessalonians 5:18, p. 264). He has promised to work all things together for good in the life of the Christian. We can rejoice that he has a purpose in mind for whatever we are going through.

**4. God Wants Everyone to Come to Repentance.** God makes it clear that he desires to see more people come into a relationship with him (see 2 Peter 3:9, p. 315). For that reason, you should take advantage of every opportunity you have to pray for or witness to someone who needs Christ.

## Avoid Adulterous Relationships Read 1 THESSALONIANS 4:1-8

This passage gives some strong reasons as to why we should avoid sexual immorality at all costs. Beyond that, there are at least six more damaging consequences the sin of adultery causes:

**1. Adultery Inflicts Incredible Pain on the Adulterer's Spouse.** A married adulterer violates the oneness with his or her mate by entering into this bond with another person. This sin is so serious that Jesus said it could be grounds for divorce (see Matthew 19:9, p. 27). While a marriage can survive the pain of adultery with God's help, the level of trust will never be the same.

**2. Adultery Does Irreparable Damage to the Adulterer.** Though God will forgive the person who commits this sin, others will not forgive this person so quickly. This person's reputation will be tarnished, and Satan will undoubtedly riddle him or her with guilt.

**3. Adultery Tremendously Hurts the Adulterer's Children.** A person who commits this sin may never fully regain his or her children's trust. Worse yet, the adulterer's children may even follow in his or her footsteps and fall to that same sin later in life.

**4. Believers Who Commit Adultery Give the Church a Bad Reputation.** Scripture teaches that when one part of the body of Christ suffers, we all suffer (see 1 Corinthians 12:26, p. 211). All Christians are representatives of the church. And when a Christian's sin is exposed, that person has hurt the reputation of the church—especially if that person is in a position of leadership.

**5. Adultery Hurts the Cause of Christ.** Such behavior hurts a Christian's witness and damages his or her credibility.

**6. Adultery Is a Sin against the Lord.** This should be the primary motive for living a pure life.

As Paul reminds us in this text, God has given us his *Holy* Spirit to live in us. The more his Spirit fills and controls our life, the less likely we will be to give in to the temptation of adultery.

CORNER STONES

---

just as our love overflows toward you. <sup>13</sup>As a result, Christ will make your hearts strong, blameless, and holy when you stand before God our Father on that day when our Lord Jesus comes with all those who belong to him.

4:1 Greek *brothers;* also in 4:10, 13.

CHAPTER **4**
*Live to Please God*
Finally, dear brothers and sisters,* we urge you in the name of the Lord Jesus to live in a way that pleases God, as we have taught you. You are

---

# OFF AND RUNNING

### Strive to Be Responsible Read 1 THESSALONIANS 4:11-12

As a Christian, you should strive to be the best worker you can be. If you don't, then you disgrace the Lord you serve by doing less than quality work. However, if you work hard and lead a responsible life, you will have many more opportunities to share your faith, because people will respect you.

Consider Joseph of the Old Testament. Although he had been sold into slavery by his own brothers, he worked diligently in every position he held. And his hard work made a difference. The Bible doing this already, and we encourage you to do so more and more. ²For you remember what we taught you in the name of the Lord Jesus. ³God wants you to be holy, so you should keep clear of all sexual sin. ⁴Then each of you will control your body* and live in holiness and honor— ⁵not in lustful passion as the pagans do, in their ignorance of God and his ways.

⁶Never cheat a Christian brother in this matter by taking his wife, for the Lord avenges all such sins, as we have solemnly warned you before. ⁷God has called us to be holy, not to live impure lives. ⁸Anyone who refuses to live by these rules is not disobeying human rules but is rejecting God, who gives his Holy Spirit to you.

⁹But I don't need to write to you about the Christian love* that should be shown among God's people. For God himself has taught you to love one another. ¹⁰Indeed, your love is already strong toward all the Christians* in all of Macedonia. Even so, dear brothers and sisters, we beg you to love them more and more. ¹¹This should be your ambition: to live a quiet life, minding your own business and working with your hands, just as we commanded you before. ¹²As a result, people who are not Christians will respect the way you live, and you will not need to depend on others to meet your financial needs.

### The Hope of the Resurrection

¹³And now, brothers and sisters, I want you to know what will happen to the Christians who have died so you will not be full of sorrow like people who have no hope. ¹⁴For since we believe that Jesus died and was raised to life again, we also believe that when Jesus comes, God will bring back with Jesus all the Christians who have died.

¹⁵I can tell you this directly from the Lord: We who are still living when the Lord returns will not rise to meet him ahead of those who are in their graves. ¹⁶For the Lord himself will come down from heaven with a commanding shout, with the call of the archangel, and with the trumpet call of God. First, all the Christians who have died will rise from their graves. ¹⁷Then, together with them, we who are still alive and remain on the earth will be caught up in the clouds to meet the Lord in the air and remain with him forever. ¹⁸So comfort and encourage each other with these words.

## CHAPTER 5

I really don't need to write to you about how and when all this will happen, dear brothers and sisters.* ²For you know quite well that the day of the Lord will come unexpectedly, like a thief in the night. ³When people are saying, "All is well; everything is peaceful and secure," then disaster will fall upon them as suddenly as a woman's birth pains begin when her child is about to be born. And there will be no escape.

⁴But you aren't in the dark about these things, dear brothers and sisters, and you won't be surprised when the day of the Lord comes like a thief. ⁵For you are all children of the light and of the day; we don't belong to darkness and night. ⁶So be on your guard, not asleep like the others. Stay alert and be sober. ⁷Night is the time for sleep and the time when people get drunk. ⁸But let us who live in the light think clearly, protected by the body armor of faith and love, and wearing as our helmet the confidence of our salvation. ⁹For God decided to save us through our Lord Jesus Christ, not to pour out his anger on us. ¹⁰He died for us so that we can live with him forever, whether we are dead or alive at the time of his return. ¹¹So encourage each other and build each other up, just as you are already doing.

### Paul's Final Advice

¹²Dear brothers and sisters, honor those who are your leaders in the Lord's work. They work hard

4:4 Or *will know how to take a wife for himself;* Greek reads *will know how to possess his own vessel.* 4:9 Greek *brotherly love.* 4:10 Greek *the brothers.* 5:1 Greek *brothers;* also in 5:4, 12, 14, 25, 26, 27.

records, "The LORD was with Joseph and blessed him greatly as he served in the home of his Egyptian master. Potiphar noticed this and realized that the LORD was with Joseph, giving him success in everything he did" (Genesis 39:2-3).

You can't expect others to take your message seriously if they don't see that you are serious in what you do. Don't draw attention to yourself by your laziness. Instead, draw attention to the Lord by your diligence. Your faithful, responsible lifestyle will be your greatest sermon.

among you and warn you against all that is wrong. 13Think highly of them and give them your wholehearted love because of their work. And remember to live peaceably with each other.

14Brothers and sisters, we urge you to warn those who are lazy. Encourage those who are timid. Take tender care of those who are weak. Be patient with everyone.

15See that no one pays back evil for evil, but always try to do good to each other and to everyone else.

16Always be joyful. 17Keep on praying. 18No matter what happens, always be thankful, for this is God's will for you who belong to Christ Jesus.

19Do not stifle the Holy Spirit. 20Do not scoff at prophecies, 21but test everything that is said. Hold on to what is good. 22Keep away from every kind of evil.

### Paul's Final Greetings

23Now may the God of peace make you holy in every way, and may your whole spirit and soul and body be kept blameless until that day when our Lord Jesus Christ comes again. 24God, who calls you, is faithful; he will do this.

25Dear brothers and sisters, pray for us.

26Greet all the brothers and sisters in Christian love.*

27I command you in the name of the Lord to read this letter to all the brothers and sisters.

28And may the grace of our Lord Jesus Christ be with all of you.

5:26 Greek *with a holy kiss.*

# OFF AND RUNNING ////

## Think of Ways to Encourage, Praise, and Build Up Others Read 1 THESSALONIANS 5:11

Do the words you use truly benefit and leave a positive impression upon those to whom you speak? In this passage Paul stresses the importance of speaking wholesomely. Below are three insights from this passage that will help you make your conversations more meaningful:

**1. Do Not Use Bad Language.** As Christians, our speech should be positive and uplifting, not vulgar and crude. Such speech draws attention away from Christ and does nothing to encourage others.

**2. Listen before You Speak.** Don't just pretend to be interested—*really* listen. You won't know what would be helpful to say to an individual unless you understand his or her needs, questions, and hurts. James instructs us to be quick to listen and slow to speak (see James 1:19, p. 299).

**3. Strive to Honor Christ in What You Say.** The greatest way we can bless or encourage others with our conversation is to point them to our Savior. This verse has also been translated to say that we should use "words suitable for the occasion, which God can use to help other people." For instance, when someone begins talking about a hurt in his or her life, take that opportunity to somehow bring the hope that Jesus Christ gives you into that discussion.

Unfortunately, with our busy, hectic lives, the quality of our conversations with others often suffers. Our discussions seem to revolve around "surface" issues like the weather, sports events, the latest headline, or our workday. Yet, as Christians, we should go the "extra mile" to make our conversations more meaningful so that those who listen to us will be encouraged and refreshed by what we say. Those who follow Paul's advice will not only develop deeper friendships, but will also be effective witnesses for the Lord.

# 2 Thessalonians

## CHAPTER 1

### Greetings from Paul

This letter is from Paul, Silas,* and Timothy.

It is written to the church in Thessalonica, you who belong to God our Father and the Lord Jesus Christ.

²May God our Father and the Lord Jesus Christ give you grace and peace.

### Encouragement during Persecution

³Dear brothers and sisters,* we always thank God for you, as is right, for we are thankful that your faith is flourishing and you are all growing in love for each other. ⁴We proudly tell God's other churches about your endurance and faithfulness in all the persecutions and hardships you are suffering. ⁵But God will use this persecution to show his justice. For he will make you worthy of his Kingdom, for which you are suffering, ⁶and in his justice he will punish those who persecute you. ⁷And God will provide rest for you who are being persecuted and also for us when the Lord Jesus appears from heaven. He will come with his mighty angels, ⁸in flaming fire, bringing judgment on those who don't know God and on those who refuse to obey the Good News of our Lord Jesus. ⁹They will be punished with everlasting destruction, forever separated from the Lord and from his glorious power ¹⁰when he comes to receive glory and praise from his holy people. And you will be among those praising him on that day, for you believed what we testified about him.

¹¹And so we keep on praying for you, that our God will make you worthy of the life to which he called you. And we pray that God, by his power, will fulfill all your good intentions and faithful deeds. ¹²Then everyone will give honor to the name of our Lord Jesus because of you, and you will be honored along with him. This is all made possible because of the undeserved favor of our God and Lord, Jesus Christ.*

## CHAPTER 2

### Events prior to the Lord's Second Coming

And now, brothers and sisters,* let us tell you about the coming again of our Lord Jesus Christ and how we will be gathered together to meet him. ²Please don't be so easily shaken and troubled by those who say that the day of the Lord has already begun. Even if they claim to have had a vision, a revelation, or a letter supposedly from us, don't believe them. ³Don't be fooled by what they say.

For that day will not come until there is a great rebellion against God and the man of lawlessness is revealed—the one who brings destruction.* ⁴He will exalt himself and defy every god there is and tear down every object of adoration and worship. He will position himself in the temple of God, claiming that he himself is God. ⁵Don't you remember that I told you this when I was with you? ⁶And you know what is holding him back, for he can be revealed only when his time comes.

⁷For this lawlessness is already at work secretly, and it will remain secret until the one who is holding it back steps out of the way. ⁸Then the man of lawlessness will be revealed, whom the Lord Jesus will consume with the breath of his mouth and destroy by the splendor of his coming. ⁹This evil man will come to do the work of Satan with counterfeit power and signs and miracles. ¹⁰He will use every kind of wicked

---

1:1 Greek *Silvanus.* 1:3 Greek *brothers.* 1:12 Or *of our God and the Lord Jesus Christ.* 2:1 Greek *brothers;* also in 2:13, 15. 2:3 Greek *the son of destruction.*

## What Is the Worst Punishment of Hell? Read 2 THESSALONIANS 1:7-10

As this passage states, the real agony of those who go to hell is that they will be eternally separated from the Lord. To understand how terrible a punishment this is, examine the consequences of being separated from God's presence:

**Judgment.** When Christ comes back, nonbelievers will face a judgment that believers will not. At this judgment nonbelievers will have their deeds revealed before everyone and then will be sentenced to spend eternity in the lake of fire (see Revelation 20:11-15, p. 347).

**Everlasting Destruction.** In hell, nonbelievers will be doomed to exist in unending torment with the Devil and his demons. The torment that they will endure is described by Jesus as an unquenchable, eternal fire (see Matthew 18:8, p. 26, and Matthew 25:41, p. 36). Nonbelievers will spend eternity in agony.

**Regret.** Jesus used many parables to describe the Kingdom of Heaven—who would get into it, and who would not. Those who don't get into the Kingdom are pictured as "weeping and gnashing [their] teeth" (Matthew 13:42). Their response—weeping and gnashing of teeth—is one of regret when they realize what they will be missing out on for eternity.

**Hopelessness.** Because their punishment is everlasting, nonbelievers have no hope of their condition ever improving. Their existence is not only one of agony, but of despair.

Those who know Christ have much to gain. Those who do not, have everything to lose.

**CORNER STONES**

---

deception to fool those who are on their way to destruction because they refuse to believe the truth that would save them. ¹¹So God will send great deception upon them, and they will believe all these lies. ¹²Then they will be condemned for not believing the truth and for enjoying the evil they do.

### Believers Should Stand Firm
¹³As for us, we always thank God for you, dear brothers and sisters loved by the Lord. We are thankful that God chose you to be among the first* to experience salvation, a salvation that came through the Spirit who makes you holy and by your belief in the truth. ¹⁴He called you to salvation when we told you the Good News; now you can share in the glory of our Lord Jesus Christ.

¹⁵With all these things in mind, dear brothers and sisters, stand firm and keep a strong grip on everything we taught you both in person and by letter.

¹⁶May our Lord Jesus Christ and God our Father, who loved us and in his special favor gave us everlasting comfort and good hope, ¹⁷comfort your hearts and give you strength in every good thing you do and say.

## CHAPTER 3
### Paul's Request for Prayer
Finally, dear brothers and sisters,* I ask you to pray for us. Pray first that the Lord's message will spread rapidly and be honored wherever it goes, just as when it came to you. ²Pray, too, that we will be saved from wicked and evil people, for not everyone believes in the Lord. ³But the Lord is faithful; he will make you strong and guard you from the evil one.* ⁴And we are confident in the Lord that you are practicing the things we commanded you, and that you always will. ⁵May the Lord bring you into an ever deeper understanding of the love of God and the endurance that comes from Christ.

### An Exhortation to Proper Living
⁶And now, dear brothers and sisters, we give you this command with the authority of our Lord Jesus Christ: Stay away from any Christian* who lives in idleness and doesn't follow

2:13 Some manuscripts read *God chose you from the very beginning.* 3:1 Greek *brothers;* also in 3:6, 13. 3:3 Or *from evil.* 3:6 Greek *brother;* also in 3:15.

the tradition of hard work we gave you. [7]For you know that you ought to follow our example. We were never lazy when we were with you. [8]We never accepted food from anyone without paying for it. We worked hard day and night so that we would not be a burden to any of you. [9]It wasn't that we didn't have the right to ask you to feed us, but we wanted to give you an example to follow. [10]Even while we were with you, we gave you this rule: "Whoever does not work should not eat."

[11]Yet we hear that some of you are living idle lives, refusing to work and wasting time meddling in other people's business. [12]In the name of the Lord Jesus Christ, we appeal to such people—no, we command them: Settle down and get to work. Earn your own living. [13]And I say to the rest of you, dear brothers and sisters, never get tired of doing good.

[14]Take note of those who refuse to obey what we say in this letter. Stay away from them so they will be ashamed. [15]Don't think of them as enemies, but speak to them as you would to a Christian who needs to be warned.

## Paul's Final Greetings

[16]May the Lord of peace himself always give you his peace no matter what happens. The Lord be with you all.

[17]Now here is my greeting, which I write with my own hand—PAUL. I do this at the end of all my letters to prove that they really are from me.

[18]May the grace of our Lord Jesus Christ be with you all.

# 1 Timothy

## CHAPTER 1

### Greetings from Paul

This letter is from Paul, an apostle of Christ Jesus, appointed by the command of God our Savior and by Christ Jesus our hope.

²It is written to Timothy, my true child in the faith.

May God our Father and Christ Jesus our Lord give you grace, mercy, and peace.

### Warnings against False Teachings

³When I left for Macedonia, I urged you to stay there in Ephesus and stop those who are teaching wrong doctrine. ⁴Don't let people waste time in endless speculation over myths and spiritual pedigrees.* For these things only cause arguments; they don't help people live a life of faith in God.* ⁵The purpose of my instruction is that all the Christians there would be filled with love that comes from a pure heart, a clear conscience, and sincere faith.

⁶But some teachers have missed this whole point. They have turned away from these things and spend their time arguing and talking foolishness. ⁷They want to be known as teachers of the law of Moses, but they don't know what they are talking about, even though they seem so confident. ⁸We know these laws are good when they are used as God intended. ⁹But they were not made for people who do what is right. They are for people who are disobedient and rebellious, who are ungodly and sinful, who consider nothing sacred and defile what is holy, who murder their father or mother or other people. ¹⁰These laws are for people who are sexually immoral, for homosexuals and slave traders, for liars and oath breakers, and for those who do anything else that contradicts the right teaching ¹¹that comes from the glorious Good News entrusted to me by our blessed God.

### Paul's Gratitude for God's Mercy

¹²How thankful I am to Christ Jesus our Lord for considering me trustworthy and appointing me to serve him, ¹³even though I used to scoff at the name of Christ. I hunted down his people, harming them in every way I could. But God had mercy on me because I did it in ignorance and unbelief. ¹⁴Oh, how kind and gracious the Lord was! He filled me completely with faith and the love of Christ Jesus.

¹⁵This is a true saying, and everyone should believe it: Christ Jesus came into the world to save sinners—and I was the worst of them all. ¹⁶But that is why God had mercy on me, so that Christ Jesus could use me as a prime example of his great patience with even the worst sinners. Then others will realize that they, too, can believe in him and receive eternal life. ¹⁷Glory and honor to God forever and ever. He is the eternal King, the unseen one who never dies; he alone is God. Amen.

### Timothy's Responsibility

¹⁸Timothy, my son, here are my instructions for you, based on the prophetic words spoken about you earlier. May they give you the confidence to fight well in the Lord's battles. ¹⁹Cling tightly to your faith in Christ, and always keep your conscience clear. For some people have deliberately violated their consciences; as a result, their faith has been shipwrecked. ²⁰Hymenaeus and Alexander are two examples of this. I turned them over to Satan so they would learn not to blaspheme God.

1:4a Greek *in myths and endless genealogies, which cause speculation.*   1:4b Greek *a stewardship of God in faith.*

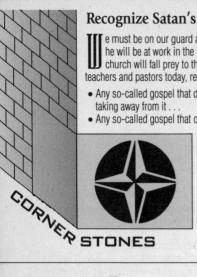

## Recognize Satan's Strategies Read 1 TIMOTHY 4:1-2

We must be on our guard against Satan's clever counterfeits, because, as this passage tells us, he will be at work in the last days (which we are in). In fact, we are warned that some in the church will fall prey to these aberrant ideas and teachings. Therefore, as you listen to various teachers and pastors today, remember this:

- Any so-called gospel that distorts the message of Jesus as found in the Bible by adding to it or taking away from it . . .
- Any so-called gospel that offers Christianity without Christ or the Cross . . .
    - Any so-called gospel that promises forgiveness without repentance . . .
    - Any so-called gospel that presents the hope of heaven without the reality of hell . . .

    . . . is not the gospel, but a "watered-down" version that will give you a false assurance. Such teachings are extremely hazardous to your spiritual health. Stay away from them at all costs.

CORNER STONES

CHAPTER **2**

*Instructions about Worship*

I urge you, first of all, to pray for all people. As you make your requests, plead for God's mercy upon them, and give thanks. ²Pray this way for kings and all others who are in authority, so that we can live in peace and quietness, in godliness and dignity. ³This is good and pleases God our Savior, ⁴for he wants everyone to be saved and to understand the truth. ⁵For there is only one God and one Mediator who can reconcile God and people. He is the man Christ Jesus. ⁶He gave his life to purchase freedom for everyone. This is the message that God gave to the world at the proper time. ⁷And I have been chosen—this is the absolute truth—as a preacher and apostle to teach the Gentiles about faith and truth.

⁸So wherever you assemble, I want men to pray with holy hands lifted up to God, free from anger and controversy. ⁹And I want women to be modest in their appearance. They should wear decent and appropriate clothing and not draw attention to themselves by the way they fix their hair or by wearing gold or pearls or expensive clothes. ¹⁰For women who claim to be devoted to God should make themselves attractive by the good things they do.

¹¹Women should listen and learn quietly and submissively. ¹²I do not let women teach men or have authority over them. Let them listen quietly. ¹³For God made Adam first, and afterward he made Eve. ¹⁴And it was the woman, not Adam, who was deceived by Satan, and sin was the result. ¹⁵But women will be saved through childbearing* and by continuing to live in faith, love, holiness, and modesty.

CHAPTER **3**

*Leaders in the Church*

It is a true saying that if someone wants to be an elder,* he desires an honorable responsibility. ²For an elder must be a man whose life cannot be spoken against. He must be faithful to his wife.* He must exhibit self-control, live wisely, and have a good reputation. He must enjoy having guests in his home and must be able to teach. ³He must not be a heavy drinker or be violent. He must be gentle, peace loving, and not one who loves money. ⁴He must manage his own family well, with children who respect and obey him. ⁵For if a man cannot manage his own household, how can he take care of God's church?

⁶An elder must not be a new Christian, because he might be proud of being chosen so soon, and the Devil will use that pride to make him fall.* ⁷Also, people outside the church must speak well of him so that he will not fall into the Devil's trap and be disgraced.

⁸In the same way, deacons must be people who are respected and have integrity. They must

2:15 Or *will be saved by accepting their role as mothers,* or *will be saved by the birth of the Child.* 3:1 Greek *overseer;* also in 3:2. 3:2 Greek *be the husband of one wife;* also in 3:12. 3:6 Or *he might fall into the same judgment as the Devil.*

not be heavy drinkers and must not be greedy for money. 9They must be committed to the revealed truths of the Christian faith and must live with a clear conscience. 10Before they are appointed as deacons, they should be given other responsibilities in the church as a test of their character and ability. If they do well, then they may serve as deacons.

11In the same way, their wives* must be respected and must not speak evil of others. They must exercise self-control and be faithful in everything they do.

12A deacon must be faithful to his wife, and he must manage his children and household well. 13Those who do well as deacons will be rewarded with respect from others and will have increased confidence in their faith in Christ Jesus.

### The Truths of Our Faith

14I am writing these things to you now, even though I hope to be with you soon, 15so that if I can't come for a while, you will know how people must conduct themselves in the household of God. This is the church of the living God, which is the pillar and support of the truth. 16Without question, this is the great mystery of our faith:

> Christ* appeared in the flesh
>     and was shown to be righteous by the
>         Spirit.*
> He was seen by angels
>     and was announced to the nations.
> He was believed on in the world
>     and was taken up into heaven.*

## CHAPTER 4
### Warnings against False Teachers

Now the Holy Spirit tells us clearly that in the last times some will turn away from what we believe; they will follow lying spirits and teachings that come from demons. 2These teachers are hypocrites and liars. They pretend to be religious, but their consciences are dead.* 3They will say it is wrong to be married and wrong to eat certain foods. But God created those foods to be eaten with thanksgiving by people who know and believe the truth. 4Since everything God created is good, we should not reject any of it. We may receive it gladly, with thankful hearts. 5For we know it is made holy by the word of God and prayer.

### A Good Servant of Christ Jesus

6If you explain this to the brothers and sisters,* you will be doing your duty as a worthy servant of Christ Jesus, one who is fed by the message of faith and the true teaching you have followed. 7Do not waste time arguing over godless ideas and old

---

## Can You Enjoy Wealth?
Read 1 TIMOTHY 6:17-19

The Lord can and may bless you with riches. They may not necessarily be the material kind. As verse 6 of this chapter says, "true religion with contentment is great wealth." Still, if God does bless you with material riches, he requires three things of you:

**1. Do Not Be Arrogant or Put Your Ultimate Hope in Your Wealth.** As verse 10 of this chapter says, "For the love of money is at the root of all kinds of evil. And some people, craving money, have wandered from the faith and pierced themselves with many sorrows." Wealth is not sinful. Wealth is not godly. It all depends on the heart of the wealthy person. There are godly people who are wealthy, and there are ungodly people who are poor—as well as vice versa. The question you must always ask yourself is, "Do I possess my possessions, or do my possessions possess me?"

**2. Enjoy What God Has Given You.** If God blesses you materially, don't feel guilty about it. Be thankful, realizing that he wants you to enjoy what you have.

**3. Be Generous, Do Good, and Share Your Wealth with Others.** With wealth comes responsibility. Recognize that you are a steward of what God has given you, and invest what you have in his work.

If you follow these three principles, they will help you be content with whatever you have. When you give God total control of this area of your life, you will never be controlled by your wealth—or by the wealth you wish you had.

---

3:11 Or *the women deacons.* The Greek word can be translated *women* or *wives.*   3:16a Greek *Who;* some manuscripts read *God.*
3:16b Or *in his spirit.*   3:16c Greek *in glory.*   4:2 Greek *are seared.*
4:6 Greek *brothers.*

wives' tales. Spend your time and energy in training yourself for spiritual fitness. 8Physical exercise has some value, but spiritual exercise is much more important, for it promises a reward in both this life and the next. 9This is true, and everyone should accept it. 10We work hard and suffer much* in order that people will believe the truth, for our hope is in the living God, who is the Savior of all people, and particularly of those who believe.

11Teach these things and insist that everyone learn them. 12Don't let anyone think less of you because you are young. Be an example to all believers in what you teach, in the way you live, in your love, your faith, and your purity. 13Until I get there, focus on reading the Scriptures to the church, encouraging the believers, and teaching them.

14Do not neglect the spiritual gift you received through the prophecies spoken to you when the elders of the church laid their hands on you. 15Give your complete attention to these matters. Throw yourself into your tasks so that everyone will see your progress. 16Keep a close watch on yourself and on your teaching. Stay true to what is right, and God will save you and those who hear you.

## CHAPTER 5

Never speak harshly to an older man,* but appeal to him respectfully as though he were your own father. Talk to the younger men as you would to your own brothers. 2Treat the older women as you would your mother, and treat the younger women with all purity as your own sisters.

### Advice about Widows, Elders, and Slaves

3The church should care for any widow who has no one else to care for her. 4But if she has children or grandchildren, their first responsibility is to show godliness at home and repay their parents by taking care of them. This is something that pleases God very much.

5But a woman who is a true widow, one who is truly alone in this world, has placed her hope in God. Night and day she asks God for help and spends much time in prayer. 6But the widow who lives only for pleasure is spiritually dead. 7Give these instructions to the church so that the widows you support* will not be criticized.

8But those who won't care for their own relatives, especially those living in the same household, have denied what we believe. Such people are worse than unbelievers.

9A widow who is put on the list for support must be a woman who is at least sixty years old and was faithful to her husband.* 10She must be well respected by everyone because of the good she has done. Has she brought up her children well? Has she been kind to strangers? Has she served other Christians humbly?* Has she helped those who are in trouble? Has she always been ready to do good?

11The younger widows should not be on the list, because their physical desires will overpower their devotion to Christ and they will want to remarry. 12Then they would be guilty of breaking their previous pledge. 13Besides, they are likely to become lazy and spend their time gossiping from house to house, getting into other people's business and saying things they shouldn't. 14So I advise these younger widows to marry again, have children, and take care of their own homes. Then the enemy will not be able to say anything against them. 15For I am afraid that some of them have already gone astray and now follow Satan.

16If a Christian woman has relatives who are widows, she must take care of them and not put the responsibility on the church. Then the church can care for widows who are truly alone.

17Elders who do their work well should be paid well,* especially those who work hard at both preaching and teaching. 18For the Scripture says, "Do not keep an ox from eating as it treads out the grain." And in another place, "Those who work deserve their pay!"*

19Do not listen to complaints against an elder unless there are two or three witnesses to accuse him. 20Anyone who sins should be rebuked in front of the whole church so that others will have a proper fear of God.

21I solemnly command you in the presence of God and Christ Jesus and the holy angels to obey these instructions without taking sides or showing special favor to anyone. 22Never be in a hurry about appointing an elder. Do not participate in the sins of others. Keep yourself pure.

23Don't drink only water. You ought to drink a little wine for the sake of your stomach because you are sick so often.

24Remember that some people lead sinful lives, and everyone knows they will be judged. But there are others whose sin will not be re-

---

4:10 Some manuscripts read *and strive.* 5:1 Or *an elder.* 5:7 Or *so the church;* Greek reads *so they.* 5:9 Greek *was the wife of one man.* 5:10 Greek *Has she washed the feet of saints?* 5:17 Greek *should be worthy of double honor.* 5:18 Deut 25:4; Luke 10:7.

vealed until later. [25]In the same way, everyone knows how much good some people do, but there are others whose good deeds won't be known until later.

## CHAPTER  6

Christians who are slaves should give their masters full respect so that the name of God and his teaching will not be shamed. [2]If your master is a Christian, that is no excuse for being disrespectful. You should work all the harder because you are helping another believer* by your efforts.

### False Teaching and True Riches

Teach these truths, Timothy, and encourage everyone to obey them. [3]Some false teachers may deny these things, but these are the sound, wholesome teachings of the Lord Jesus Christ, and they are the foundation for a godly life. [4]Anyone who teaches anything different is both conceited and ignorant. Such a person has an unhealthy desire to quibble over the meaning of words. This stirs up arguments ending in jealousy, fighting, slander, and evil suspicions. [5]These people always cause trouble. Their minds are corrupt, and they don't tell the truth. To them religion is just a way to get rich.

[6]Yet true religion with contentment is great wealth. [7]After all, we didn't bring anything with us when we came into the world, and we certainly cannot carry anything with us when we die. [8]So if we have enough food and clothing, let us be content. [9]But people who long to be rich fall into temptation and are trapped by many foolish and harmful desires that plunge them into ruin and destruction. [10]For the love of money is at the root of all kinds of evil. And some people, craving money, have wandered from the faith and pierced themselves with many sorrows.

6:2 Greek *a brother.*

### Paul's Final Instructions

[11]But you, Timothy, belong to God; so run from all these evil things, and follow what is right and good. Pursue a godly life, along with faith, love, perseverance, and gentleness. [12]Fight the good fight for what we believe. Hold tightly to the eternal life that God has given you, which you have confessed so well before many witnesses. [13]And I command you before God, who gives life to all, and before Christ Jesus, who gave a good testimony before Pontius Pilate, [14]that you obey his commands with all purity. Then no one can find fault with you from now until our Lord Jesus Christ returns. [15]For at the right time Christ will be revealed from heaven by the blessed and only almighty God, the King of kings and Lord of lords. [16]He alone can never die, and he lives in light so brilliant that no human can approach him. No one has ever seen him, nor ever will. To him be honor and power forever. Amen.

[17]Tell those who are rich in this world not to be proud and not to trust in their money, which will soon be gone. But their trust should be in the living God, who richly gives us all we need for our enjoyment. [18]Tell them to use their money to do good. They should be rich in good works and should give generously to those in need, always being ready to share with others whatever God has given them. [19]By doing this they will be storing up their treasure as a good foundation for the future so that they may take hold of real life.

[20]Timothy, guard what God has entrusted to you. Avoid godless, foolish discussions with those who oppose you with their so-called knowledge. [21]Some people have wandered from the faith by following such foolishness.

May God's grace be with you all.

# 2 Timothy

## CHAPTER 1
### Greetings from Paul

This letter is from Paul, an apostle of Christ Jesus by God's will, sent out to tell others about the life he has promised through faith in Christ Jesus.

²It is written to Timothy, my dear son.

May God our Father and Christ Jesus our Lord give you grace, mercy, and peace.

### Encouragement to Be Faithful

³Timothy, I thank God for you. He is the God I serve with a clear conscience, just as my ancestors did. Night and day I constantly remember you in my prayers. ⁴I long to see you again, for I remember your tears as we parted. And I will be filled with joy when we are together again.

⁵I know that you sincerely trust the Lord, for you have the faith of your mother, Eunice, and your grandmother, Lois. ⁶This is why I remind you to fan into flames the spiritual gift God gave you when I laid my hands on you. ⁷For God has not given us a spirit of fear and timidity, but of power, love, and self-discipline. ⁸So you must never be ashamed to tell others about our Lord. And don't be ashamed of me, either, even though I'm in prison for Christ. With the strength God gives you, be ready to suffer with me for the proclamation of the Good News.

⁹It is God who saved us and chose us to live a holy life. He did this not because we deserved it, but because that was his plan long before the world began—to show his love and kindness to us through Christ Jesus. ¹⁰And now he has made all of this plain to us by the coming of Christ Jesus, our Savior, who broke the power of death and showed us the way to everlasting life

through the Good News. ¹¹And God chose me to be a preacher, an apostle, and a teacher of this Good News.

¹²And that is why I am suffering here in prison. But I am not ashamed of it, for I know the one in whom I trust, and I am sure that he is able to guard what I have entrusted to him* until the day of his return.

¹³Hold on to the pattern of right teaching you learned from me. And remember to live in the faith and love that you have in Christ Jesus. ¹⁴With the help of the Holy Spirit who lives within us, carefully guard what has been entrusted to you.

¹⁵As you know, all the Christians who came here from the province of Asia have deserted me; even Phygelus and Hermogenes are gone. ¹⁶May the Lord show special kindness to Onesiphorus and all his family because he often visited and encouraged me. He was never ashamed of me because I was in prison. ¹⁷When he came to Rome, he searched everywhere until he found me. ¹⁸May the Lord show him special kindness on the day of Christ's return. And you know how much he helped me at Ephesus.

## CHAPTER 2
### A Good Soldier of Christ Jesus

Timothy, my dear son, be strong with the special favor God gives you in Christ Jesus. ²You have heard me teach many things that have been confirmed by many reliable witnesses. Teach these great truths to trustworthy people who are able to pass them on to others.

³Endure suffering along with me, as a good soldier of Christ Jesus. ⁴And as Christ's soldier, do not let yourself become tied up in the affairs of this life, for then you cannot satisfy the one

1:12 Or *what has been entrusted to me.*

## Guard the Content of Your Thoughts Read 2 TIMOTHY 2:22

I n Paul's second letter to Timothy, he gave Timothy helpful advice on how to live a pure life. This advice included (1) recognizing his potential to sin; (2) avoiding influences that could inspire youthful lust; (3) pursuing faith, love, and peace; and (4) spending time with other believers whose hearts are pure.

One of the more difficult challenges of living a pure life is guarding the content of our thoughts. It has been said, "You can't stop a bird from flying over your head, but you can stop it from building a nest in your hair." In the same way, we cannot stop an impure or wicked thought from "knocking" on the door of our imagination, but we certainly can keep that door closed and locked.

If we don't, and we allow tempting thoughts to infiltrate our mind, we may fall, allowing our old nature to prevail.

The good news is that even though each one of us is still capable of falling, we don't have to. If we stay close to the Lord and follow Paul's advice in this verse, we will be building a strong "fortress" around our life—including our thoughts—and it will be harder for Satan's arrows of temptation to get through.

### CORNER STONES

who has enlisted you in his army. ⁵Follow the Lord's rules for doing his work, just as an athlete either follows the rules or is disqualified and wins no prize. ⁶Hardworking farmers are the first to enjoy the fruit of their labor. ⁷Think about what I am saying. The Lord will give you understanding in all these things.

⁸Never forget that Jesus Christ was a man born into King David's family and that he was raised from the dead. This is the Good News I preach. ⁹And because I preach this Good News, I am suffering and have been chained like a criminal. But the word of God cannot be chained. ¹⁰I am willing to endure anything if it will bring salvation and eternal glory in Christ Jesus to those God has chosen.

¹¹This is a true saying:

If we die with him,
  we will also live with him.
¹² If we endure hardship,
  we will reign with him.
If we deny him,
  he will deny us.
¹³ If we are unfaithful,
  he remains faithful,
  for he cannot deny himself.

### An Approved Worker

¹⁴Remind everyone of these things, and command them in God's name to stop fighting over words. Such arguments are useless, and they can ruin those who hear them. ¹⁵Work hard so God can approve you. Be a good worker, one who does not need to be ashamed and who correctly explains the word of truth. ¹⁶Avoid godless, foolish discussions that lead to more and more ungodliness. ¹⁷This kind of talk spreads like cancer. Hymenaeus and Philetus are examples of this. ¹⁸They have left the path of truth, preaching the lie that the resurrection of the dead has already occurred; and they have undermined the faith of some.

¹⁹But God's truth stands firm like a foundation stone with this inscription: "The Lord knows those who are his,"* and "Those who claim they belong to the Lord must turn away from all wickedness."*

²⁰In a wealthy home some utensils are made of gold and silver, and some are made of wood and clay. The expensive utensils are used for special occasions, and the cheap ones are for everyday use. ²¹If you keep yourself pure, you will be a utensil God can use for his purpose. Your life will be clean, and you will be ready for the Master to use you for every good work.

²²Run from anything that stimulates youthful lust. Follow anything that makes you want to do right. Pursue faith and love and peace, and enjoy the companionship of those who call on the Lord with pure hearts.

²³Again I say, don't get involved in foolish,

2:19a Num 16:5.   2:19b See Isa 52:11.

ignorant arguments that only start fights. 24The Lord's servants must not quarrel but must be kind to everyone. They must be able to teach effectively and be patient with difficult people. 25They should gently teach those who oppose the truth. Perhaps God will change those people's hearts, and they will believe the truth. 26Then they will come to their senses and escape from the Devil's trap. For they have been held captive by him to do whatever he wants.

## CHAPTER 3
### The Dangers of the Last Days

You should also know this, Timothy, that in the last days there will be very difficult times. 2For people will love only themselves and their money. They will be boastful and proud, scoffing at God, disobedient to their parents, and ungrateful. They will consider nothing sacred. 3They will be unloving and unforgiving; they will slander others and have no self-control; they will be cruel and have no interest in what is good. 4They will betray their friends, be reckless, be puffed up with pride, and love pleasure rather than God. 5They will act as if they are religious, but they will reject the power that could make them godly. You must stay away from people like that.

6They are the kind who work their way into people's homes and win the confidence of* vulnerable women who are burdened with the guilt of sin and controlled by many desires. 7Such women are forever following new teachings, but they never understand the truth. 8And these teachers fight the truth just as Jannes and Jambres fought against Moses. Their minds are depraved, and their faith is counterfeit. 9But they won't get away with this for long. Someday everyone will recognize what fools they are, just as happened with Jannes and Jambres.

### Paul's Charge to Timothy

10But you know what I teach, Timothy, and how I live, and what my purpose in life is. You know my faith and how long I have suffered. You know my love and my patient endurance. 11You know how much persecution and suffering I have endured. You know all about how I was persecuted in Antioch, Iconium, and Lystra—but the Lord delivered me from all of it. 12Yes, and everyone who wants to live a godly life in Christ Jesus will suffer persecution. 13But evil people and impostors will flour-

3:6 Greek and take captive.

ish. They will go on deceiving others, and they themselves will be deceived.

14But you must remain faithful to the things you have been taught. You know they are true, for you know you can trust those who taught you. 15You have been taught the holy Scriptures from childhood, and they have given you the wisdom to receive the salvation that comes by trusting in Christ Jesus. 16All Scripture is inspired by God and is useful to teach us what is true and to make us realize what is wrong in our lives. It straightens us out and teaches us to do

---

## Studying the Bible Is Necessary for Our Spiritual Growth Read 2 TIMOTHY 3:16-17

The primary reason we should study the Bible is because it was inspired by the Creator of the universe to guide us through this adventure called life. This passage of Scripture gives us three more reasons why we should make the Bible part of our day-to-day life:

**1. The Bible Teaches Us What Is True.** The Bible is the only book we need to discover the foundational truths of how to know and walk with God. Some aberrant religious groups or cults insist we need another book to help us interpret what the Bible says. But the Bible needs no outside interpretation. It speaks for itself. In fact, the best commentary on the Bible is the Bible.

**2. The Bible Shows Us What Is Wrong in Our Lives.** God's Word serves to reprove us or to make us aware when we are headed in the wrong direction.

**3. The Bible Helps Us Do What Is Right.** If we read and meditate on God's Word, we will be molded into the man or woman God wants us to be.

When we allow the Bible to teach us in these three areas, we are told that we will be prepared and equipped to do good to everyone (see 2 Timothy 3:14-16). Our foundation will be solid, our motives pure, and our character more refined. What better reasons are there to make a commitment to stick with Bible study!

what is right. 17It is God's way of preparing us in every way, fully equipped for every good thing God wants us to do.

## CHAPTER 4

And so I solemnly urge you before God and before Christ Jesus—who will someday judge the living and the dead when he appears to set up his Kingdom: 2Preach the word of God. Be persistent, whether the time is favorable or not. Patiently correct, rebuke, and encourage your people with good teaching.

3For a time is coming when people will no longer listen to right teaching. They will follow their own desires and will look for teachers who will tell them whatever they want to hear. 4They will reject the truth and follow strange myths.

5But you should keep a clear mind in every situation. Don't be afraid of suffering for the Lord. Work at bringing others to Christ. Complete the ministry God has given you.

### Paul's Final Words

6As for me, my life has already been poured out as an offering to God. The time of my death is near. 7I have fought a good fight, I have finished the race, and I have remained faithful. 8And now the prize awaits me—the crown of righteousness that the Lord, the righteous Judge, will give me on that great day of his return. And the prize is not just for me but for all who eagerly look forward to his glorious return.

9Please come as soon as you can. 10Demas has deserted me because he loves the things of

this life and has gone to Thessalonica. Crescens has gone to Galatia, and Titus has gone to Dalmatia. 11Only Luke is with me. Bring Mark with you when you come, for he will be helpful to me. 12I sent Tychicus to Ephesus. 13When you come, be sure to bring the coat I left with Carpus at Troas. Also bring my books, and especially my papers.*

14Alexander the coppersmith has done me much harm, but the Lord will judge him for what he has done. 15Be careful of him, for he fought against everything we said.

16The first time I was brought before the judge, no one was with me. Everyone had abandoned me. I hope it will not be counted against them. 17But the Lord stood with me and gave me strength, that I might preach the Good News in all its fullness for all the Gentiles to hear. And he saved me from certain death.* 18Yes, and the Lord will deliver me from every evil attack and will bring me safely to his heavenly Kingdom. To God be the glory forever and ever. Amen.

### Paul's Final Greetings

19Give my greetings to Priscilla and Aquila and those living at the household of Onesiphorus. 20Erastus stayed at Corinth, and I left Trophimus sick at Miletus.

21Hurry so you can get here before winter. Eubulus sends you greetings, and so do Pudens, Linus, Claudia, and all the brothers and sisters.*

22May the Lord be with your spirit. Grace be with you all.

4:13 Greek *especially the parchments.*    4:17 Greek *from the mouth of a lion.*    4:21 Greek *brothers.*

# Titus

## CHAPTER 1
### Greetings from Paul

This letter is from Paul, a slave of God and an apostle of Jesus Christ. I have been sent to bring faith to those God has chosen and to teach them to know the truth that shows them how to live godly lives. ²This truth gives them the confidence of eternal life, which God promised them before the world began—and he cannot lie. ³And now at the right time he has revealed this Good News, and we announce it to everyone. It is by the command of God our Savior that I have been trusted to do this work for him.

⁴This letter is written to Titus, my true child in the faith that we share.

May God the Father and Christ Jesus our Savior give you grace and peace.

### Titus's Work in Crete

⁵I left you on the island of Crete so you could complete our work there and appoint elders in each town as I instructed you. ⁶An elder must be well thought of for his good life. He must be faithful to his wife,* and his children must be believers who are not wild or rebellious. ⁷An elder* must live a blameless life because he is God's minister. He must not be arrogant or quick-tempered; he must not be a heavy drinker, violent, or greedy for money. ⁸He must enjoy having guests in his home and must love all that is good. He must live wisely and be fair. He must live a devout and disciplined life. ⁹He must have a strong and steadfast belief in the trustworthy message he was taught; then he will be able to encourage others with right teaching and show those who oppose it where they are wrong.

¹⁰For there are many who rebel against right teaching; they engage in useless talk and deceive people. This is especially true of those who insist on circumcision for salvation. ¹¹They must be silenced. By their wrong teaching, they have already turned whole families away from the truth. Such teachers only want your money. ¹²One of their own men, a prophet from Crete, has said about them, "The people of Crete are all liars; they are cruel animals and lazy gluttons." ¹³This is true. So rebuke them as sternly as necessary to make them strong in the faith. ¹⁴They must stop listening to Jewish myths and the commands of people who have turned their backs on the truth.

¹⁵Everything is pure to those whose hearts are pure. But nothing is pure to those who are corrupt and unbelieving, because their minds and consciences are defiled. ¹⁶Such people claim they know God, but they deny him by the way they live. They are despicable and disobedient, worthless for doing anything good.

## CHAPTER 2
### Promote Right Teaching

But as for you, promote the kind of living that reflects right teaching. ²Teach the older men to exercise self-control, to be worthy of respect, and to live wisely. They must have strong faith and be filled with love and patience.

³Similarly, teach the older women to live in a way that is appropriate for someone serving the Lord. They must not go around speaking evil of others and must not be heavy drinkers. Instead, they should teach others what is good. ⁴These older women must train the younger women to love their husbands and their children, ⁵to live wisely and be pure, to take care of their homes, to do good, and to be submissive to their husbands. Then they will not bring shame on the word of God.

1:6 Or have only one wife, or be married only once; Greek reads be the husband of one wife.   1:7 Greek overseer.

## We Need to Set an Example for Others Read TITUS 2:6-8

This passage gives some practical reasons and ways to live out your faith. Though these words were written to Titus, a leader in the early church, they apply to anyone whose life influences the lives of others. That is, the passage speaks to all of us! Take a moment to ponder these simple, yet useful, thoughts:

### How Should We Behave?

- We need to be self-controlled and serious about life.
- We should do good deeds often as an example to others.
- We should love the truth.
- We should be earnest and serious in our pursuit of truth.
- We should think before we speak, making sure that our conversation is sound and sensible.

### Why Should We Live Godly Lives?

- We represent God, who is holy.
- We are an example to others, particularly young people and new believers.
- Our behavior will silence our critics.

**CORNER STONES**

6In the same way, encourage the young men to live wisely in all they do. 7And you yourself must be an example to them by doing good deeds of every kind. Let everything you do reflect the integrity and seriousness of your teaching. 8Let your teaching be so correct that it can't be criticized. Then those who want to argue will be ashamed because they won't have anything bad to say about us.

9Slaves must obey their masters and do their best to please them. They must not talk back 10or steal, but they must show themselves to be entirely trustworthy and good. Then they will make the teaching about God our Savior attractive in every way.

11For the grace of God has been revealed, bringing salvation to all people. 12And we are instructed to turn from godless living and sinful pleasures. We should live in this evil world with self-control, right conduct, and devotion to

## OFF AND RUNNING

### Create a Spiritual Hunger in Those around You
Read TITUS 2:9-10

While we are not slaves, this verse could easily apply to workers and employees today—or to anyone who is asked to do something for someone else. Jesus gave a unique example of how this works when he told his disciples, "If a soldier demands that you carry his gear for a mile, carry it two miles" (Matthew 5:41). At that time, Roman law gave soldiers the right to retain private citizens to carry their pack for a mile. Yet Jesus told his disciples to go above and beyond that request. In so doing, they would have a "captive audience" for presenting the gospel.

Today, when everyone seems to be demanding his or her rights, this verse is a direct contradiction to the current wave of thinking. But it all comes back to our frame of reference as Christians: Our goal on earth is not to win our own rights, but to win people to our Lord.

Your work may be difficult. You may even think it is mundane and insignificant. But it is not. God has placed you in your place of employment for a reason—to let your light shine. Your dedicated work may be just the thing that wins your employer or supervisor to Christ. So look for opportunities to "go the extra mile."

God, 13while we look forward to that wonderful event when the glory of our great God and Savior, Jesus Christ, will be revealed. 14He gave his life to free us from every kind of sin, to cleanse us, and to make us his very own people, totally committed to doing what is right. 15You must teach these things and encourage your people to do them, correcting them when necessary. You have the authority to do this, so don't let anyone ignore you or disregard what you say.

CHAPTER **3**
*Do What Is Good*
Remind your people to submit to the government and its officers. They should be obedient, always ready to do what is good. 2They must not speak evil of anyone, and they must avoid quarreling. Instead, they should be gentle and show true humility to everyone.

3Once we, too, were foolish and disobedient. We were misled by others and became slaves to many wicked desires and evil pleasures. Our lives were full of evil and envy. We hated others, and they hated us.

4But then God our Savior showed us his kindness and love. 5He saved us, not because of the good things we did, but because of his mercy. He washed away our sins and gave us a new life through the Holy Spirit.* 6He generously poured out the Spirit upon us because of what Jesus Christ our Savior did. 7He declared us not

guilty because of his great kindness. And now we know that we will inherit eternal life. 8These things I have told you are all true. I want you to insist on them so that everyone who trusts in God will be careful to do good deeds all the time. These things are good and beneficial for everyone.

*Paul's Final Remarks and Greetings*
9Do not get involved in foolish discussions about spiritual pedigrees* or in quarrels and fights about obedience to Jewish laws. These kinds of things are useless and a waste of time. 10If anyone is causing divisions among you, give a first and second warning. After that, have nothing more to do with that person. 11For people like that have turned away from the truth. They are sinning, and they condemn themselves.

12I am planning to send either Artemas or Tychicus to you. As soon as one of them arrives, do your best to meet me at Nicopolis as quickly as you can, for I have decided to stay there for the winter. 13Do everything you can to help Zenas the lawyer and Apollos with their trip. See that they are given everything they need. 14For our people should not have unproductive lives. They must learn to do good by helping others who have urgent needs.

15Everybody here sends greetings. Please give my greetings to all of the believers who love us.
May God's grace be with you all.

3:5 Greek *He saved us through the washing of regeneration and renewing of the Holy Spirit.*    3:9 Greek *discussions and genealogies.*

# Philemon

### Greetings from Paul

This letter is from Paul, in prison for preaching the Good News about Christ Jesus, and from our brother Timothy.

It is written to Philemon, our much loved co-worker, 2and to our sister Apphia and to Archippus, a fellow soldier of the cross. I am also writing to the church that meets in your house. 3May God our Father and the Lord Jesus Christ give you grace and peace.

### Paul's Thanksgiving and Prayer

4I always thank God when I pray for you, Philemon, 5because I keep hearing of your trust in the Lord Jesus and your love for all of God's people. 6You are generous because of your faith. And I am praying that you will really put your generosity to work, for in so doing you will come to an understanding of all the good things we can do for Christ. 7I myself have gained much joy and comfort from your love, my brother, because your kindness has so often refreshed the hearts of God's people.

### Paul's Appeal for Onesimus

8That is why I am boldly asking a favor of you. I could demand it in the name of Christ because it is the right thing for you to do, 9but because of our love, I prefer just to ask you. So take this as a request from your friend Paul, an old man, now in prison for the sake of Christ Jesus. 10My plea is that you show kindness to Onesimus. I think of him as my own son because he became a believer as a result of my ministry here in prison. 11Onesimus* hasn't been of much use to you in the past, but now he is very useful to

both of us. 12I am sending him back to you, and with him comes my own heart.

13I really wanted to keep him here with me while I am in these chains for preaching the Good News, and he would have helped me on your behalf. 14But I didn't want to do anything without your consent. And I didn't want you to help because you were forced to do it but because you wanted to. 15Perhaps you could think of it this way: Onesimus ran away for a little while so you could have him back forever. 16He is no longer just a slave; he is a beloved brother, especially to me. Now he will mean much more to you, both as a slave and as a brother in the Lord.

17So if you consider me your partner, give him the same welcome you would give me if I were coming. 18If he has harmed you in any way or stolen anything from you, charge me for it. 19I, Paul, write this in my own handwriting: "I will repay it." And I won't mention that you owe me your very soul!

20Yes, dear brother, please do me this favor for the Lord's sake. Give me this encouragement in Christ. 21I am confident as I write this letter that you will do what I ask and even more!

22Please keep a guest room ready for me, for I am hoping that God will answer your prayers and let me return to you soon.

### Paul's Final Greetings

23Epaphras, my fellow prisoner in Christ Jesus, sends you his greetings. 24So do Mark, Aristarchus, Demas, and Luke, my co-workers.

25The grace of the Lord Jesus Christ be with your spirit.

11 Onesimus means "useful."

# Hebrews

## CHAPTER 1

### Jesus Christ Is God's Son

Long ago God spoke many times and in many ways to our ancestors through the prophets. 2But now in these final days, he has spoken to us through his Son. God promised everything to the Son as an inheritance, and through the Son he made the universe and everything in it. 3The Son reflects God's own glory, and everything about him represents God exactly. He sustains the universe by the mighty power of his command. After he died to cleanse us from the stain of sin, he sat down in the place of honor at the right hand of the majestic God of heaven.

### Christ Is Greater Than the Angels

4This shows that God's Son is far greater than the angels, just as the name God gave him is far greater than their names. 5For God never said to any angel what he said to Jesus:

"You are my Son.
Today I have become your Father."*

And again God said,

"I will be his Father,
and he will be my Son."*

6And then, when he presented his honored* Son to the world, God said, "Let all the angels of God worship him."* 7God calls his angels

"messengers swift as the wind,
and servants made of flaming fire."*

8But to his Son he says,

"Your throne, O God, endures forever and
ever.
Your royal power is expressed in
righteousness.
9 You love what is right and hate what is
wrong.
Therefore God, your God, has anointed
you,
pouring out the oil of joy on you more
than on anyone else."*

10And,

"Lord, in the beginning you laid the
foundation of the earth,
and the heavens are the work of your
hands.
11 Even they will perish, but you remain
forever.
They will wear out like old clothing.
12 You will roll them up like an old coat.
They will fade away like old clothing.
But you are always the same;
you will never grow old."*

13And God never said to an angel, as he did to his Son,

"Sit in honor at my right hand
until I humble your enemies,
making them a footstool under your
feet."*

14But angels are only servants. They are spirits sent from God to care for those who will receive salvation.

## CHAPTER 2

### A Warning against Drifting Away

So we must listen very carefully to the truth we have heard, or we may drift away from it. 2The

---

1:5a Or *Today I reveal you as my Son.* Ps 2:7.   1:5b 2 Sam 7:14.   1:6a Greek *firstborn.*   1:6b Deut 32:43.   1:7 Ps 104:4.   1:8-9 Ps 45:6-7.
1:10-12 Ps 102:25-27.   1:13 Ps 110:1.

## Why Did God Create Angels? Read HEBREWS 1:4-14

Throughout the ages, people have been fascinated with and awed by angels. Some have even tried to worship them. But it is important to understand that angels are distinctly different from God's Son, Jesus Christ. One significant area of distinction is creation. Angels are created beings, while Jesus is not. Because angels are created, it is wrong to worship them.

If they are not to be worshiped, then what did God create angels for? God created angels for several reasons, three of which are the following:

**1. Angels Worship God.** As verse 6 attests, one of the reasons God created angels was to worship him. Some people may think this is egotistical, but consider how many people worship professional athletes and other celebrities. These people by comparison have done nothing to earn or be worthy of the worship they receive. God, on the other hand, has created angels and humans and given them life. In addition, God is majestic beyond our understanding, so worshiping him is simply the natural response of being in his presence. For it is an incredible privilege to be in the presence of God. Only God is worthy of worship, and his creation, which includes angels, should worship him.

**2. Angels Serve as God's Messengers.** God uses angels to deliver messages to his followers on earth (verse 7). The Bible records a few instances of this. In Luke 1 God sent an angel to tell Mary that she would give birth to the Messiah. An angel was also sent to Jesus' tomb to tell his followers that he had risen from the dead (Matthew 28).

**3. Angels Minister to God's Followers.** God also created angels to minister to his followers (verse 14). In Acts 12, an angel freed Peter from prison before he was to be tried in public for being a follower of Christ.

While angels play a significant role in the lives of believers, we must be careful that we do not give them the honor and praise that should be reserved for Jesus Christ alone.

CORNER STONES

---

message God delivered through angels has always proved true, and the people were punished for every violation of the law and every act of disobedience. ³What makes us think that we can escape if we are indifferent to this great salvation that was announced by the Lord Jesus himself? It was passed on* to us by those who heard him speak, ⁴and God verified the message by signs and wonders and various miracles and by giving gifts of the Holy Spirit whenever he chose to do so.

### Jesus, the Man

⁵And furthermore, the future world we are talking about will not be controlled by angels. ⁶For somewhere in the Scriptures it says,

"What is man that you should think of him,
and the son of man* that you should
care for him?

⁷ For a little while you made him lower than
the angels,
and you crowned him with glory and
honor.*

⁸ You gave him authority over all things."*

Now when it says "all things," it means nothing is left out. But we have not yet seen all of this happen. ⁹What we do see is Jesus, who "for a little while was made lower than the angels" and now is "crowned with glory and honor" because he suffered death for us. Yes, by God's grace, Jesus tasted death for everyone in all the world. ¹⁰And it was only right that God—who made everything and for whom everything was made—should bring his many children into glory. Through the suffering of Jesus, God made him a perfect leader, one fit to bring them into their salvation.

2:3 Or *and confirmed.* 2:6 Or *Son of Man.* 2:7 Some manuscripts add *You put him in charge of everything you made.* 2:6-8 Ps 8:4-6.

## Why Would a Good God Send Anyone to Hell? Read HEBREWS 2:2-3

If God loves people, why doesn't he just save everyone? Perhaps you have asked this question or know someone who has. While the question is good, it places the blame for people's damnation on the wrong person: God.

God does not want anyone to spend eternity in hell. In fact, he earnestly desires that everyone spend all eternity with him in heaven. Scripture tells us, "[God] does not want anyone to perish, so he is giving more time for everyone to repent" (2 Peter 3:9). Throughout the Bible we see God's loving and patient invitation for us to come to him:

- "Come to me, all of you who are weary and carry heavy burdens, and I will give you rest." (Matthew 11:28)
- "'Come.' Let the thirsty ones come—anyone who wants to. Let them come and drink the water of life without charge." (Revelation 22:17)

The truth is that there are some things only God can do—such as cleanse us of our sin, forgive us, and justify us. At the same time, there are some things only we can do—such as come to him, believe in him, and repent of our sins. While God does indeed love everyone (see John 3:16, p. 109; and Romans 5:8, p. 180), he has given us a wonderful but dangerous gift. That gift is called "free will." It is the ability to choose between right and wrong, good and evil, God and Satan, and heaven and hell. God will not force his salvation and forgiveness upon our lives. It is our choice to say yes or no.

Anyone who ends up in hell is there because of his or her willful and deliberate decision to reject God's offer of forgiveness. As the famous British author C. S. Lewis put it, "The gates of hell are locked from the inside."

---

[11]So now Jesus and the ones he makes holy have the same Father. That is why Jesus is not ashamed to call them his brothers and sisters.* [12]For he said to God,

"I will declare the wonder of your name to my brothers and sisters.*
I will praise you among all your people."

[13]He also said, "I will put my trust in him." And in the same context he said, "Here I am—together with the children God has given me."* [14]Because God's children are human beings—made of flesh and blood—Jesus also became flesh and blood by being born in human form. For only as a human being could he die, and only by dying could he break the power of the Devil, who had the power of death. [15]Only in this way could he deliver those who have lived all their lives as slaves to the fear of dying.

[16]We all know that Jesus came to help the descendants of Abraham, not to help the angels. [17]Therefore, it was necessary for Jesus to be in every respect like us, his brothers and sisters, so that he could be our merciful and faithful High Priest before God. He then could offer a sacrifice that would take away the sins of the people. [18]Since he himself has gone through suffering and temptation, he is able to help us when we are being tempted.

## CHAPTER 3
### Jesus Is Greater Than Moses
And so, dear brothers and sisters who belong to God* and are bound for heaven, think about this Jesus whom we declare to be God's Messenger and High Priest. [2]For he was faithful to God, who appointed him, just as Moses served faithfully and was entrusted with God's entire house. [3]But Jesus deserves far more glory than Moses, just as a person who builds a fine house deserves more praise than the house itself. [4]For every house has a builder, but God is the one who made everything.

[5]Moses was certainly faithful in God's house, but only as a servant. His work was an illustration of the truths God would reveal later. [6]But Christ, the faithful Son, was in charge of the entire household. And we are God's household, if we keep up our courage and remain confident

2:11 Greek *his brothers*; also in 2:17.   2:12 Greek *my brothers.* Ps 22:22.   2:13 Isa 8:17-18.   3:1 Greek *And so, holy brothers.*

in our hope in Christ. 7That is why the Holy Spirit says,

"Today you must listen to his voice.
8 Don't harden your hearts against him
    as Israel did when they rebelled,
    when they tested God's patience in the
        wilderness.
9 There your ancestors tried my patience,
    even though they saw my miracles for
        forty years.
10 So I was angry with them, and I said,
    'Their hearts always turn away from me.
    They refuse to do what I tell them.'
11 So in my anger I made a vow:
    'They will never enter my place of rest.'"*

12Be careful then, dear brothers and sisters.* Make sure that your own hearts are not evil and unbelieving, turning you away from the living God. 13You must warn each other every day, as long as it is called "today," so that none of you will be deceived by sin and hardened against God. 14For if we are faithful to the end, trusting God just as firmly as when we first believed, we will share in all that belongs to Christ. 15But never forget the warning:

"Today you must listen to his voice.
    Don't harden your hearts against him
    as Israel did when they rebelled."*

16And who were those people who rebelled against God, even though they heard his voice? Weren't they the ones Moses led out of Egypt? 17And who made God angry for forty years? Wasn't it the people who sinned, whose bodies fell in the wilderness? 18And to whom was God speaking when he vowed that they would never enter his place of rest? He was speaking to those who disobeyed him. 19So we see that they were not allowed to enter his rest because of their unbelief.

CHAPTER **4**
## Promised Rest for God's People
God's promise of entering his place of rest still stands, so we ought to tremble with fear that some of you might fail to get there. 2For this Good News—that God has prepared a place of rest—has been announced to us just as it was to them. But it did them no good because they didn't believe what God told them.* 3For only we who believe can enter his place of rest. As for those who didn't believe, God said,

"In my anger I made a vow:
    'They will never enter my place of rest.'"*

even though his place of rest has been ready since he made the world. 4We know it is ready because the Scriptures mention the seventh day, saying, "On the seventh day God rested from all his work."* 5But in the other passage God said, "They will never enter my place of rest."* 6So God's rest is there for people to enter. But those who formerly heard the Good News failed to enter because they disobeyed God. 7So God set another time for entering his place of rest, and that time is today. God announced this through David a long time later in the words already quoted:

"Today you must listen to his voice.
    Don't harden your hearts against him."*

8This new place of rest was not the land of Canaan, where Joshua led them. If it had been, God would not have spoken later about another day of rest. 9So there is a special rest* still waiting for the people of God. 10For all who enter into God's rest will find rest from their labors, just as God rested after creating the world. 11Let us do our best to enter that place of rest. For anyone who disobeys God, as the people of Israel did, will fall.

12For the word of God is full of living power. It is sharper than the sharpest knife, cutting deep into our innermost thoughts and desires. It exposes us for what we really are. 13Nothing in all creation can hide from him. Everything is naked and exposed before his eyes. This is the God to whom we must explain all that we have done.

## Christ Is Our High Priest
14That is why we have a great High Priest who has gone to heaven, Jesus the Son of God. Let us cling to him and never stop trusting him. 15This High Priest of ours understands our weaknesses, for he faced all of the same temptations we do, yet he did not sin. 16So let us come boldly to the throne of our gracious God. There we will receive his mercy, and we will find grace to help us when we need it.

CHAPTER **5**
Now a high priest is a man chosen to represent other human beings in their dealings with God. He presents their gifts to God and offers their sacrifices for sins. 2And because he is human, he

3:7-11 Ps 95:7-11.   3:12 Greek *brothers*.   3:15 Ps 95:7-8.   4:2 Some manuscripts read *they didn't share the faith of those who listened [to God]*.   4:3 Ps 95:11.   4:4 Gen 2:2.   4:5 Ps 95:11.   4:7 Ps 95:7-8.   4:9 Or *Sabbath rest*.

is able to deal gently with the people, though they are ignorant and wayward. For he is subject to the same weaknesses they have. ³That is why he has to offer sacrifices, both for their sins and for his own sins. ⁴And no one can become a high priest simply because he wants such an honor. He has to be called by God for this work, just as Aaron was.

⁵That is why Christ did not exalt himself to become High Priest. No, he was chosen by God, who said to him,

"You are my Son.
    Today I have become your Father.*"

⁶And in another passage God said to him,

"You are a priest forever
    in the line of Melchizedek."*

⁷While Jesus was here on earth, he offered prayers and pleadings, with a loud cry and tears, to the one who could deliver him out of death. And God heard his prayers because of his reverence for God. ⁸So even though Jesus was God's Son, he learned obedience from the things he suffered. ⁹In this way, God qualified him as a perfect High Priest, and he became the source of eternal salvation for all those who obey him. ¹⁰And God designated him to be a High Priest in the line of Melchizedek.

## A Call to Spiritual Growth

¹¹There is so much more we would like to say about this. But you don't seem to listen, so it's hard to make you understand. ¹²You have been Christians a long time now, and you ought to be teaching others. Instead, you need someone to teach you again the basic things a beginner must learn about the Scriptures.* You are like babies who drink only milk and cannot eat solid food. ¹³And a person who is living on milk isn't very far along in the Christian life and doesn't know much about doing what is right. ¹⁴Solid food is for those who are mature, who have trained themselves to recognize the difference between right and wrong and then do what is right.

## CHAPTER 6

So let us stop going over the basics of Christianity* again and again. Let us go on instead and become mature in our understanding. Surely we don't need to start all over again with the importance of turning away from evil deeds and placing our faith in God. ²You don't need further

instruction about baptisms, the laying on of hands, the resurrection of the dead, and eternal judgment. ³And so, God willing, we will move forward to further understanding.

⁴For it is impossible to restore to repentance those who were once enlightened—those who have experienced the good things of heaven and shared in the Holy Spirit, ⁵who have tasted the goodness of the word of God and the power of the age to come—⁶and who then turn away from God. It is impossible to bring such people to repentance again because they are nailing the Son of God to the cross again by rejecting him, holding him up to public shame.

⁷When the ground soaks up the rain that falls on it and bears a good crop for the farmer, it has the blessing of God. ⁸But if a field bears thistles and thorns, it is useless. The farmer will condemn that field and burn it.

⁹Dear friends, even though we are talking like this, we really don't believe that it applies to you. We are confident that you are meant for better things, things that come with salvation. ¹⁰For God is not unfair. He will not forget how hard you have worked for him and how you have shown your love to him by caring for other Christians, as you still do. ¹¹Our great desire is that you will keep right on loving others as long as life lasts, in order to make certain that what you hope for will come true. ¹²Then you will not become spiritually dull and indifferent. Instead, you will follow the example of those who are going to inherit God's promises because of their faith and patience.

## God's Promises Bring Hope

¹³For example, there was God's promise to Abraham. Since there was no one greater to swear by, God took an oath in his own name, saying:

¹⁴ "I will certainly bless you richly,
    and I will multiply your descendants into
        countless millions."*

¹⁵Then Abraham waited patiently, and he received what God had promised.

¹⁶When people take an oath, they call on someone greater than themselves to hold them to it. And without any question that oath is binding. ¹⁷God also bound himself with an oath, so that those who received the promise could be perfectly sure that he would never change his mind. ¹⁸So God has given us both his promise and his oath. These two things are un-

5:5 Or *Today I reveal you as my Son.* Ps 2:7.    5:6 Ps 110:4.    5:12 Or *about the oracles of God.*    6:1 Or *the basics about Christ.*    6:14 Gen 22:17.

changeable because it is impossible for God to lie. Therefore, we who have fled to him for refuge can take new courage, for we can hold on to his promise with confidence.

19This confidence is like a strong and trustworthy anchor for our souls. It leads us through the curtain of heaven into God's inner sanctuary. 20Jesus has already gone in there for us. He has become our eternal High Priest in the line of Melchizedek.

CHAPTER **7**
*Melchizedek Is Compared to Abraham*
This Melchizedek was king of the city of Salem and also a priest of God Most High. When Abraham was returning home after winning a great battle against many kings, Melchizedek met him and blessed him. 2Then Abraham took a tenth of all he had won in the battle and gave it to Melchizedek. His name means "king of justice." He is also "king of peace" because *Salem* means "peace." 3There is no record of his father or mother or any of his ancestors—no beginning or end to his life. He remains a priest forever, resembling the Son of God.

4Consider then how great this Melchizedek was. Even Abraham, the great patriarch of Israel, recognized how great Melchizedek was by giving him a tenth of what he had taken in battle. 5Now the priests, who are descendants of Levi, are commanded in the law of Moses to collect a tithe from all the people, even though they are their own relatives.* 6But Melchizedek, who was not even related to Levi, collected a tenth from Abraham. And Melchizedek placed a blessing upon Abraham, the one who had already received the promises of God. 7And without question, the person who has the power to bless is always greater than the person who is blessed.

8In the case of Jewish priests, tithes are paid to men who will die. But Melchizedek is greater than they are, because we are told that he lives on. 9In addition, we might even say that Levi's descendants, the ones who collect the tithe, paid a tithe to Melchizedek through their ancestor Abraham. 10For although Levi wasn't born yet, the seed from which he came was in Abraham's loins when Melchizedek collected the tithe from him.

11And finally, if the priesthood of Levi could have achieved God's purposes—and it was that priesthood on which the law was based—why did God need to send a different priest from the line of Melchizedek, instead of from the line of Levi and Aaron?*

12And when the priesthood is changed, the law must also be changed to permit it. 13For the one we are talking about belongs to a different tribe, whose members do not serve at the altar. 14What I mean is, our Lord came from the tribe of Judah, and Moses never mentioned Judah in connection with the priesthood.

*Christ Is like Melchizedek*
15The change in God's law is even more evident from the fact that a different priest, who is like Melchizedek, has now come. 16He became a priest, not by meeting the old requirement of belonging to the tribe of Levi, but by the power of a life that cannot be destroyed. 17And the psalmist pointed this out when he said of Christ,

"You are a priest forever
   in the line of Melchizedek."*

18Yes, the old requirement about the priesthood was set aside because it was weak and useless. 19For the law made nothing perfect, and now a better hope has taken its place. And that is how we draw near to God.

20God took an oath that Christ would always be a priest, but he never did this for any other priest. 21Only to Jesus did he say,

"The Lord has taken an oath
   and will not break his vow:
   'You are a priest forever.'"*

22Because of God's oath, it is Jesus who guarantees the effectiveness of this better covenant.

23Another difference is that there were many priests under the old system. When one priest died, another had to take his place. 24But Jesus remains a priest forever; his priesthood will never end. 25Therefore he is able, once and forever, to save* everyone who comes to God through him. He lives forever to plead with God on their behalf.

26He is the kind of high priest we need because he is holy and blameless, unstained by sin. He has now been set apart from sinners, and he has been given the highest place of honor in heaven. 27He does not need to offer sacrifices every day like the other high priests. They did this for their own sins first and then for the sins of the people. But Jesus did this once for all when he sacrificed himself on the cross. 28Those

7:5 Greek *their brothers, who are descendants of Abraham.* 7:11 Greek *according to the order of Aaron.* 7:17 Ps 110:4. 7:21 Ps 110:4. 7:25 Or *able to save completely.*

who were high priests under the law of Moses were limited by human weakness. But after the law was given, God appointed his Son with an oath, and his Son has been made perfect forever.

## CHAPTER 8
### Christ Is Our High Priest

Here is the main point: Our High Priest sat down in the place of highest honor in heaven, at God's right hand. ²There he ministers in the sacred tent, the true place of worship that was built by the Lord and not by human hands.

³And since every high priest is required to offer gifts and sacrifices, our High Priest must make an offering, too. ⁴If he were here on earth, he would not even be a priest, since there already are priests who offer the gifts required by the law of Moses. ⁵They serve in a place of worship that is only a copy, a shadow of the real one in heaven. For when Moses was getting ready to build the Tabernacle, God gave him this warning: "Be sure that you make everything according to the design I have shown you here on the mountain."* ⁶But our High Priest has been given a ministry that is far superior to the ministry of those who serve under the old laws, for he is the one who guarantees for us a better covenant with God, based on better promises.

⁷If the first covenant had been faultless, there would have been no need for a second covenant to replace it. ⁸But God himself found fault with the old one when he said:

"The day will come, says the Lord,
    when I will make a new covenant
    with the people of Israel and Judah.
⁹ This covenant will not be like the one
    I made with their ancestors
    when I took them by the hand
    and led them out of the land of Egypt.
They did not remain faithful to my
        covenant,
    so I turned my back on them, says the
        Lord.
¹⁰ But this is the new covenant I will make
        with the people of Israel on that day, says
        the Lord:
I will put my laws in their minds
    so they will understand them,
and I will write them on their hearts
    so they will obey them.
I will be their God,
    and they will be my people.

¹¹ And they will not need to teach their
        neighbors,
    nor will they need to teach their family,
    saying, 'You should know the Lord.'
For everyone, from the least to the greatest,
    will already know me.
¹² And I will forgive their wrongdoings,
    and I will never again remember their
        sins."*

¹³When God speaks of a new covenant, it means he has made the first one obsolete. It is now out of date and ready to be put aside.

## CHAPTER 9
### Old Rules about Worship

Now in that first covenant between God and Israel, there were regulations for worship and a sacred tent here on earth. ²There were two rooms in this tent. In the first room were a lampstand, a table, and loaves of holy bread on the table. This was called the Holy Place. ³Then there was a curtain, and behind the curtain was the second room called the Most Holy Place. ⁴In that room were a gold incense altar and a wooden chest called the Ark of the Covenant, which was covered with gold on all sides. Inside the Ark were a gold jar containing some manna, Aaron's staff that sprouted leaves, and the stone tablets of the covenant with the Ten Commandments written on them. ⁵The glorious cherubim were above the Ark. Their wings were stretched out over the Ark's cover, the place of atonement. But we cannot explain all of these things now.

⁶When these things were all in place, the priests went in and out of the first room* regularly as they performed their religious duties. ⁷But only the high priest goes into the Most Holy Place, and only once a year, and always with blood, which he offers to God to cover his own sins and the sins the people have committed in ignorance. ⁸By these regulations the Holy Spirit revealed that the Most Holy Place was not open to the people as long as the first room and the entire system it represents were still in use.

⁹This is an illustration pointing to the present time. For the gifts and sacrifices that the priests offer are not able to cleanse the consciences of the people who bring them. ¹⁰For that old system deals only with food and drink and ritual washing—external regulations that are in effect only until their limitations can be corrected.

8:5 Exod 25:40; 26:30.    8:8-12 Jer 31:31-34.    9:6 Greek *first tent*; also in 9:8.

## Christ Is the Perfect Sacrifice

11So Christ has now become the High Priest over all the good things that have come. He has entered that great, perfect sanctuary in heaven, not made by human hands and not part of this created world. 12Once for all time he took blood into that Most Holy Place, but not the blood of goats and calves. He took his own blood, and with it he secured our salvation forever.

13Under the old system, the blood of goats and bulls and the ashes of a young cow could cleanse people's bodies from ritual defilement. 14Just think how much more the blood of Christ will purify our hearts from deeds that lead to death so that we can worship the living God. For by the power of the eternal Spirit, Christ offered himself to God as a perfect sacrifice for our sins. 15That is why he is the one who mediates the new covenant between God and people, so that all who are invited can receive the eternal inheritance God has promised them. For Christ died to set them free from the penalty of the sins they had committed under that first covenant.

16Now when someone dies and leaves a will, no one gets anything until it is proved that the person who wrote the will* is dead.* 17The will goes into effect only after the death of the person who wrote it. While the person is still alive, no one can use the will to get any of the things promised to them.

18That is why blood was required under the first covenant as a proof of death. 19For after Moses had given the people all of God's laws, he took the blood of calves and goats, along with water, and sprinkled both the book of God's laws and all the people, using branches of hyssop bushes and scarlet wool. 20Then he said, "This blood confirms the covenant God has made with you."* 21And in the same way, he sprinkled blood on the sacred tent and on everything used for worship. 22In fact, we can say that according to the law of Moses, nearly everything was purified by sprinkling with blood. Without the shedding of blood, there is no forgiveness of sins.

23That is why the earthly tent and everything in it—which were copies of things in heaven—had to be purified by the blood of animals. But the real things in heaven had to be purified with far better sacrifices than the blood of animals.

24For Christ has entered into heaven itself to appear now before God as our Advocate.* He did not go into the earthly place of worship, for that was merely a copy of the real Temple in heaven. 25Nor did he enter heaven to offer himself again and again, like the earthly high priest who enters the Most Holy Place year after year to offer the blood of an animal. 26If that had been necessary, he would have had to die again and again, ever since the world began. But no! He came once for all time, at the end of the age, to remove the power of sin forever by his sacrificial death for us.

27And just as it is destined that each person dies only once and after that comes judgment, 28so also Christ died only once as a sacrifice to take away the sins of many people. He will come again but not to deal with our sins again. This time he will bring salvation to all those who are eagerly waiting for him.

## CHAPTER 10
## Christ's Sacrifice Once for All

The old system in the law of Moses was only a shadow of the things to come, not the reality of the good things Christ has done for us. The sacrifices under the old system were repeated again and again, year after year, but they were never able to provide perfect cleansing for those who came to worship. 2If they could have provided perfect cleansing, the sacrifices would have stopped, for the worshipers would have been purified once for all time, and their feelings of guilt would have disappeared.

3But just the opposite happened. Those yearly sacrifices reminded them of their sins year after year. 4For it is not possible for the blood of bulls and goats to take away sins. 5That is why Christ, when he came into the world, said,

"You did not want animal sacrifices and
grain offerings.
But you have given me a body so that I
may obey you.
6  No, you were not pleased with animals
burned on the altar
or with other offerings for sin.
7  Then I said, 'Look, I have come to do your
will, O God—
just as it is written about me in the
Scriptures.'"*

8Christ said, "You did not want animal sacrifices or grain offerings or animals burned on the altar or other offerings for sin, nor were you pleased with them" (though they are required by the law

9:16a Or *covenant*.    9:16b Or *Now when someone makes a covenant, it is necessary to ratify it with the death of a sacrifice*.    9:20 Exod 24:8.
9:24 Greek *on our behalf*.    10:5-7 Ps 40:6-8.

of Moses). 9Then he added, "Look, I have come to do your will." He cancels the first covenant in order to establish the second. 10And what God wants is for us to be made holy by the sacrifice of the body of Jesus Christ once for all time.

11Under the old covenant, the priest stands before the altar day after day, offering sacrifices that can never take away sins. 12But our High Priest offered himself to God as one sacrifice for sins, good for all time. Then he sat down at the place of highest honor at God's right hand. 13There he waits until his enemies are humbled as a footstool under his feet. 14For by that one offering he perfected forever all those whom he is making holy.

15And the Holy Spirit also testifies that this is so. First he says,

16 "This is the new covenant I will make
    with my people on that day, says the
      Lord:
I will put my laws in their hearts
    so they will understand them,
and I will write them on their minds
    so they will obey them."

17Then he adds,

"I will never again remember
    their sins and lawless deeds."*

18Now when sins have been forgiven, there is no need to offer any more sacrifices.

*A Call to Persevere*

19And so, dear brothers and sisters,* we can boldly enter heaven's Most Holy Place because of the blood of Jesus. 20This is the new, life-giving way that Christ has opened up for us through the sacred curtain, by means of his death for us.*

21And since we have a great High Priest who rules over God's people, 22let us go right into the presence of God, with true hearts fully trusting him. For our evil consciences have been sprinkled with Christ's blood to make us clean, and our bodies have been washed with pure water.

23Without wavering, let us hold tightly to the hope we say we have, for God can be trusted to keep his promise. 24Think of ways to encourage one another to outbursts of love and good deeds. 25And let us not neglect our meeting together, as some people do, but encourage and warn each other, especially now that the day of his coming back again is drawing near.

26Dear friends, if we deliberately continue

10:16-17 Jer 31:33-34.    10:19 Greek *brothers.*    10:20 Greek *his flesh.*

# Why We Need Fellowship with Other Believers
Read HEBREWS 10:25

Involvement in a local church is necessary for the spiritual growth of all Christians, and it is something we never outgrow. For the new believer, moreover, such interaction is critical for four reasons:

**1. Fellowship Provides Us with Encouragement and Love.** As Christians, we need a place where we can be encouraged in our faith and be reminded that we are a member of God's family. When we go to church, we are surrounded by others who share our love for Christ. Being in the presence of other believers can encourage us to live for Christ, as well as give us a sense of belonging and acceptance that we don't receive from the world.

**2. Fellowship Allows Us to Learn from Spiritually Mature Christians.** In the biblical account of the early church, we are told how the apostle Paul's friends, Priscilla and Aquila, took time to help another believer learn more about Jesus (see Acts 18:26, p. 161). Likewise, younger Christians in the church today will have the opportunity to gain spiritual wisdom and insight from more mature Christians.

**3. Fellowship Helps Us Discern False Teachings.** The Bible warns of false teachers and teachings, to which the young believer is especially susceptible because he or she lacks basic Bible understanding. A healthy, Bible-teaching church will encourage young believers in their growth and help them discern truth from error.

**4. Fellowship Prepares Us for Christ's Return.** As the day for Christ's return comes closer, we need to help each other through difficult times and keep our problems in perspective. We also need to encourage each other to live holy lives and to share God's Good News with others in the time that remains. God wants the body of Christ to stand out and be a light in these ever darkening days.

## Christ Endured Great Pain for Us Read HEBREWS 12:1-3

Throughout the New Testament, the Christian life is compared to a race. With that in mind, we need to realize that it is not a short sprint, but a long-distance run. Sometimes, as we are participating in this race, we can grow discouraged by circumstances or by what others say to us. But just as a successful runner must "keep his eyes on the prize," we, too, must remember what this race is all about. We must bear in mind for whom and to whom we are running: Jesus Christ. In essence, we need to "keep our eyes on Jesus."

Corrie ten Boom, a Dutch Christian who survived the horrors of Hitler's concentration camps during World War II, often said, "Look within and be depressed. Look without and be distressed. Look at Jesus and be at rest."

God will see us through to the end. He has given us his word: "And I am sure that God, who began the good work within you, will continue his work until it is finally finished on that day when Christ Jesus comes back again" (Philippians 1:6).

**CORNER STONES**

sinning after we have received a full knowledge of the truth, there is no other sacrifice that will cover these sins. 27There will be nothing to look forward to but the terrible expectation of God's judgment and the raging fire that will consume his enemies. 28Anyone who refused to obey the law of Moses was put to death without mercy on the testimony of two or three witnesses. 29Think how much more terrible the punishment will be for those who have trampled on the Son of God and have treated the blood of the covenant as if it were common and unholy. Such people have insulted and enraged the Holy Spirit who brings God's mercy to his people.

30For we know the one who said,

"I will take vengeance.
I will repay those who deserve it."

He also said,

"The Lord will judge his own people."*

31It is a terrible thing to fall into the hands of the living God.

32Don't ever forget those early days when you first learned about Christ. Remember how you remained faithful even though it meant terrible suffering. 33Sometimes you were exposed to public ridicule and were beaten, and sometimes you helped others who were suffering the same things. 34You suffered along with those who were thrown into jail. When all you owned was

taken from you, you accepted it with joy. You knew you had better things waiting for you in eternity.

35Do not throw away this confident trust in the Lord, no matter what happens. Remember the great reward it brings you! 36Patient endurance is what you need now, so you will continue to do God's will. Then you will receive all that he has promised.

37 "For in just a little while,
    the Coming One will come and not delay.
38 And a righteous person will live by faith.
    But I will have no pleasure in anyone who turns away."*

39But we are not like those who turn their backs on God and seal their fate. We have faith that assures our salvation.

CHAPTER **11**
*Great Examples of Faith*
What is faith? It is the confident assurance that what we hope for is going to happen. It is the evidence of things we cannot yet see. 2God gave his approval to people in days of old because of their faith.

3By faith we understand that the entire universe was formed at God's command, that what we now see did not come from anything that can be seen.

10:30 Deut 32:35-36.   10:37-38 Hab 2:3-4.

⁴It was by faith that Abel brought a more acceptable offering to God than Cain did. God accepted Abel's offering to show that he was a righteous man. And although Abel is long dead, he still speaks to us because of his faith.

⁵It was by faith that Enoch was taken up to heaven without dying—"suddenly he disappeared because God took him."* But before he was taken up, he was approved as pleasing to God. ⁶So, you see, it is impossible to please God without faith. Anyone who wants to come to him must believe that there is a God and that he rewards those who sincerely seek him.

⁷It was by faith that Noah built an ark to save his family from the flood. He obeyed God, who warned him about something that had never happened before. By his faith he condemned the rest of the world and was made right in God's sight.

⁸It was by faith that Abraham obeyed when God called him to leave home and go to another land that God would give him as his inheritance. He went without knowing where he was going. ⁹And even when he reached the land God promised him, he lived there by faith—for he was like a foreigner, living in a tent. And so did Isaac and Jacob, to whom God gave the same promise. ¹⁰Abraham did this because he was confidently looking forward to a city with eternal foundations, a city designed and built by God.

¹¹It was by faith that Sarah together with Abraham was able to have a child, even though they were too old and Sarah was barren. Abraham believed that God would keep his promise.* ¹²And so a whole nation came from this one man, Abraham, who was too old to have any children—a nation with so many people that, like the stars of the sky and the sand on the seashore, there is no way to count them.

¹³All these faithful ones died without receiving what God had promised them, but they saw it all from a distance and welcomed the promises of God. They agreed that they were no more than foreigners and nomads here on earth. ¹⁴And obviously people who talk like that are looking forward to a country they can call their own. ¹⁵If they had meant the country they came from, they would have found a way to go back. ¹⁶But they were looking for a better place, a heavenly homeland. That is why God is not ashamed to be called their God, for he has prepared a heavenly city for them.

¹⁷It was by faith that Abraham offered Isaac as a sacrifice when God was testing him. Abraham, who had received God's promises, was ready to sacrifice his only son, Isaac, ¹⁸though God had promised him, "Isaac is the son through whom your descendants will be counted."* ¹⁹Abraham assumed that if Isaac died, God was able to bring him back to life again. And in a sense, Abraham did receive his son back from the dead.

²⁰It was by faith that Isaac blessed his two sons, Jacob and Esau. He had confidence in what God was going to do in the future.

²¹It was by faith that Jacob, when he was old and dying, blessed each of Joseph's sons and bowed in worship as he leaned on his staff.

²²And it was by faith that Joseph, when he was about to die, confidently spoke of God's bringing the people of Israel out of Egypt. He was so sure of it that he commanded them to carry his bones with them when they left!

²³It was by faith that Moses' parents hid him for three months. They saw that God had given them an unusual child, and they were not afraid of what the king might do.

²⁴It was by faith that Moses, when he grew up, refused to be treated as the son of Pharaoh's daughter. ²⁵He chose to share the oppression of God's people instead of enjoying the fleeting pleasures of sin. ²⁶He thought it was better to suffer for the sake of the Messiah than to own the treasures of Egypt, for he was looking ahead to the great reward that God would give him. ²⁷It was by faith that Moses left the land of Egypt. He was not afraid of the king. Moses kept right on going because he kept his eyes on the one who is invisible. ²⁸It was by faith that Moses commanded the people of Israel to keep the Passover and to sprinkle blood on the doorposts so that the angel of death would not kill their firstborn sons.

²⁹It was by faith that the people of Israel went right through the Red Sea as though they were on dry ground. But when the Egyptians followed, they were all drowned.

³⁰It was by faith that the people of Israel marched around Jericho seven days, and the walls came crashing down.

³¹It was by faith that Rahab the prostitute did not die with all the others in her city who refused to obey God. For she had given a friendly welcome to the spies.

³²Well, how much more do I need to say? It would take too long to recount the stories of

the faith of Gideon, Barak, Samson, Jephthah, David, Samuel, and all the prophets. [33]By faith these people overthrew kingdoms, ruled with justice, and received what God had promised them. They shut the mouths of lions, [34]quenched the flames of fire, and escaped death by the edge of the sword. Their weakness was turned to strength. They became strong in battle and put whole armies to flight. [35]Women received their loved ones back again from death.

But others trusted God and were tortured, preferring to die rather than turn from God and be free. They placed their hope in the resurrection to a better life. [36]Some were mocked, and their backs were cut open with whips. Others were chained in dungeons. [37]Some died by stoning, and some were sawed in half; others were killed with the sword. Some went about in skins of sheep and goats, hungry and oppressed and mistreated. [38]They were too good for this world. They wandered over deserts and mountains, hiding in caves and holes in the ground.

[39]All of these people we have mentioned received God's approval because of their faith, yet none of them received all that God had promised. [40]For God had far better things in mind for us that would also benefit them, for they can't receive the prize at the end of the race until we finish the race.*

CHAPTER **12**
*God's Discipline Proves His Love*
Therefore, since we are surrounded by such a huge crowd of witnesses to the life of faith, let us strip off every weight that slows us down, especially the sin that so easily hinders our progress. And let us run with endurance the race that God has set before us. [2]We do this by keeping our eyes on Jesus, on whom our faith depends from start to finish.* He was willing to die a shameful death on the cross because of the joy he knew would be his afterward. Now he is seated in the place of highest honor beside God's throne in heaven. [3]Think about all he endured when sinful people did such terrible things to him, so that you don't become weary and give up. [4]After all, you have not yet given your lives in your struggle against sin.

11:40 Greek *for us, for they apart from us can't finish.* 12:2 Or *Jesus, the Originator and Perfecter of our faith.*

# OFF AND RUNNING

## Keeping Your Marriage Strong Read HEBREWS 13:4

Tragically, many people do not take marriage seriously today. They forget that their vows are made before God and include the words "till death do us part." So what steps can you take to keep from becoming another marriage "casualty"? Here are four principles that will help you to maintain a strong and flourishing marriage:

**1. Walk with God.** As you cultivate and deepen your fellowship with God, you will have the power, the will, and the resources to stand when temptation comes knocking.

**2. Walk with Your Spouse.** Keep the friendship and romance alive in your marriage. Remember what you did when you first started courting your spouse. Compliment one another. Spend time together. Be genuinely interested in one another's lives. Try your best to look attractive for each other. Treat your partner with respect. Take practical steps to keep that fire of love burning.

**3. Don't Walk on Thin Ice.** It is dangerous to form close relationships with those who do not love God as you do. You must avoid potentially dangerous and flirtatious relationships at all costs. Find Christian friends (of the same sex) who can be honest with you if they think you are heading into dangerous territory.

**4. Count the Cost.** Remember the price that comes with adultery and immorality. Are you ready to face the shame? Are you prepared for the disgrace and distrust you will bring upon your spouse and children—as well as the cause of Christ? A few moments of pleasure will result in a lifetime of regret.

An intense love for God and for your husband or wife will see you through the rough waters of sexual temptation. Don't be an easy target for Satan's arrows. Keep moving forward in your relationship with Christ and with your spouse.

⁵And have you entirely forgotten the encouraging words God spoke to you, his children? He said,

"My child, don't ignore it when the Lord
disciplines you,
and don't be discouraged when he
corrects you.
⁶ For the Lord disciplines those he loves,
and he punishes those he accepts as his
children."*

⁷As you endure this divine discipline, remember that God is treating you as his own children. Whoever heard of a child who was never disciplined? ⁸If God doesn't discipline you as he does all of his children, it means that you are illegitimate and are not really his children after all. ⁹Since we respect our earthly fathers who disciplined us, should we not all the more cheerfully submit to the discipline of our heavenly Father and live forever*?

¹⁰For our earthly fathers disciplined us for a few years, doing the best they knew how. But God's discipline is always right and good for us because it means we will share in his holiness. ¹¹No discipline is enjoyable while it is happening—it is painful! But afterward there will be a quiet harvest of right living for those who are trained in this way.

¹²So take a new grip with your tired hands and stand firm on your shaky legs. ¹³Mark out a straight path for your feet. Then those who follow you, though they are weak and lame, will not stumble and fall but will become strong.

## A Call to Listen to God

¹⁴Try to live in peace with everyone, and seek to live a clean and holy life, for those who are not holy will not see the Lord. ¹⁵Look after each other so that none of you will miss out on the special favor of God. Watch out that no bitter root of unbelief rises up among you, for whenever it springs up, many are corrupted by its poison. ¹⁶Make sure that no one is immoral or godless like Esau. He traded his birthright as the oldest son for a single meal. ¹⁷And afterward, when he wanted his father's blessing, he was rejected. It was too late for repentance, even though he wept bitter tears.

¹⁸You have not come to a physical mountain, to a place of flaming fire, darkness, gloom, and whirlwind, as the Israelites did at Mount Sinai when God gave them his laws. ¹⁹For they heard an awesome trumpet blast and a voice with a message so terrible that they begged God to stop speaking. ²⁰They staggered back under God's command: "If even an animal touches the mountain, it must be stoned to death."* ²¹Moses himself was so frightened at the sight that he said, "I am terrified and trembling."*

²²No, you have come to Mount Zion, to the city of the living God, the heavenly Jerusalem, and to thousands of angels in joyful assembly. ²³You have come to the assembly of God's firstborn children, whose names are written in heaven. You have come to God himself, who is the judge of all people. And you have come to the spirits of the redeemed in heaven who have now been made perfect. ²⁴You have come to Jesus, the one who mediates the new covenant between God and people, and to the sprinkled blood, which graciously forgives instead of crying out for vengeance as the blood of Abel did.

²⁵See to it that you obey God, the one who is speaking to you. For if the people of Israel did not escape when they refused to listen to Moses, the earthly messenger, how terrible our danger if we reject the One who speaks to us from heaven! ²⁶When God spoke from Mount Sinai his voice shook the earth, but now he makes another promise: "Once again I will shake not only the earth but the heavens also."* ²⁷This means that the things on earth will be shaken, so that only eternal things will be left.

²⁸Since we are receiving a kingdom that cannot be destroyed, let us be thankful and please God by worshiping him with holy fear and awe. ²⁹For our God is a consuming fire.

## CHAPTER 13
### Concluding Words

Continue to love each other with true Christian love.* ²Don't forget to show hospitality to strangers, for some who have done this have entertained angels without realizing it! ³Don't forget about those in prison. Suffer with them as though you were there yourself. Share the sorrow of those being mistreated, as though you feel their pain in your own bodies.

⁴Give honor to marriage, and remain faithful to one another in marriage. God will surely judge people who are immoral and those who commit adultery.

12:5-6 Prov 3:11-12.    12:9 Or *really live.*    12:20 Exod 19:13.    12:21 Deut 9:19.    12:26 Hag 2:6.    13:1 Greek *with brotherly love.*

5Stay away from the love of money; be satisfied with what you have. For God has said,

"I will never fail you.
I will never forsake you."*

6That is why we can say with confidence,

"The Lord is my helper,
so I will not be afraid.
What can mere mortals do to me?"*

7Remember your leaders who first taught you the word of God. Think of all the good that has come from their lives, and trust the Lord as they do.

8Jesus Christ is the same yesterday, today, and forever. 9So do not be attracted by strange, new ideas. Your spiritual strength comes from God's special favor, not from ceremonial rules about food, which don't help those who follow them.

10We have an altar from which the priests in the Temple on earth have no right to eat. 11Under the system of Jewish laws, the high priest brought the blood of animals into the Holy Place as a sacrifice for sin, but the bodies of the animals were burned outside the camp. 12So also Jesus suffered and died outside the city gates in order to make his people holy by shedding his own blood. 13So let us go out to him outside the camp and bear the disgrace he bore. 14For this world is not our home; we are looking forward to our city in heaven, which is yet to come.

15With Jesus' help, let us continually offer our

sacrifice of praise to God by proclaiming the glory of his name. 16Don't forget to do good and to share what you have with those in need, for such sacrifices are very pleasing to God.

17Obey your spiritual leaders and do what they say. Their work is to watch over your souls, and they know they are accountable to God. Give them reason to do this joyfully and not with sorrow. That would certainly not be for your benefit.

18Pray for us, for our conscience is clear and we want to live honorably in everything we do. 19I especially need your prayers right now so that I can come back to you soon.

20-21And now, may the God of peace, who brought again from the dead our Lord Jesus, equip you with all you need for doing his will. May he produce in you, through the power of Jesus Christ, all that is pleasing to him. Jesus is the great Shepherd of the sheep by an everlasting covenant, signed with his blood. To him be glory forever and ever. Amen.

22I urge you, dear brothers and sisters,* please listen carefully to what I have said in this brief letter.

23I want you to know that our brother Timothy is now out of jail. If he comes here soon, I will bring him with me to see you.

24Give my greetings to all your leaders and to the other believers there. The Christians from Italy send you their greetings.

25May God's grace be with you all.

13:5 Deut 31:6, 8.   13:6 Ps 118:6.   13:22 Greek *brothers.*

# OFF AND RUNNING

## Our Needs Must Come Last Read HEBREWS 13:11-13

Jesus gave us the ultimate example to follow in meekness. Jesus, who is God, came to this earth and humbled himself in an incredible way by becoming a man. It is important to note that he never at any time ceased being God. But he did lay aside the privileges of deity to experience genuine human conditions, such as sorrow, anger, weariness, and pain (see Philippians 2:3-11, pp. 248–249). Yet the most dramatic act of his meekness came when he went to a cross to be crucified. Although he was led away to die, no one took his life. That is because Jesus could have called down legions of angels to rescue him. But instead he "suffered and died" for us. How should Christ's attitude affect the way we treat others? In short, we must put the needs of others before our own. During Jesus' earthly ministry, he always had time for others. We should follow his example. Here is a simple acrostic that will help you keep your priorities in order:

**J** is for Jesus.
**O** is for others.
**Y** is for yourself.

If you put the will of God first and the needs of others above your own, you will find joy.

# James

## Greetings from James

This letter is from James, a slave of God and of the Lord Jesus Christ.

It is written to Jewish Christians scattered among the nations.*

Greetings!

## Faith and Endurance

2Dear brothers and sisters,* whenever trouble comes your way, let it be an opportunity for joy. 3For when your faith is tested, your endurance has a chance to grow. 4So let it grow, for when your endurance is fully developed, you will be strong in character and ready for anything.

5If you need wisdom—if you want to know what God wants you to do—ask him, and he will gladly tell you. He will not resent your asking. 6But when you ask him, be sure that you really expect him to answer, for a doubtful mind is as unsettled as a wave of the sea that is driven and tossed by the wind. 7People like that should not expect to receive anything from the Lord. 8They can't make up their minds. They waver back and forth in everything they do.

9Christians who are* poor should be glad, for God has honored them. 10And those who are rich should be glad, for God has humbled them. They will fade away like a flower in the field. 11The hot sun rises and dries up the grass; the flower withers, and its beauty fades away. So also, wealthy people will fade away with all of their achievements.

12God blesses the people who patiently endure testing. Afterward they will receive the crown of life that God has promised to those who love him. 13And remember, no one who wants to do wrong should ever say, "God is tempting me." God is never tempted to do wrong, and he never tempts anyone else either. 14Temptation comes from the lure of our own evil desires. 15These evil desires lead to evil actions, and evil actions lead to death. 16So don't be misled, my dear brothers and sisters.

17Whatever is good and perfect comes to us from God above, who created all heaven's lights.* Unlike them, he never changes or casts shifting shadows. 18In his goodness he chose to make us his own children by giving us his true word. And we, out of all creation, became his choice possession.

## Listening and Doing

19My dear brothers and sisters, be quick to listen, slow to speak, and slow to get angry. 20Your anger can never make things right in God's sight.

21So get rid of all the filth and evil in your lives, and humbly accept the message God has planted in your hearts, for it is strong enough to save your souls.

22And remember, it is a message to obey, not just to listen to. If you don't obey, you are only fooling yourself. 23For if you just listen and don't obey, it is like looking at your face in a mirror but doing nothing to improve your appearance. 24You see yourself, walk away, and forget what you look like. 25But if you keep looking steadily into God's perfect law—the law that sets you free—and if you do what it says and don't forget what you heard, then God will bless you for doing it.

26If you claim to be religious but don't control your tongue, you are just fooling yourself, and your religion is worthless. 27Pure and last-

1:1 Greek To the twelve tribes in the dispersion. 1:2 Greek brothers; also in 1:16, 19. 1:9 Greek The brother who is. 1:17 Greek from above, from the Father of lights.

## Life's Trials Will Make You Stronger Read JAMES 1:2-4

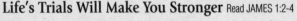

One of the keys to growing and being able to effectively continue in the Christian life is enduring. A key aspect of endurance is patience. The word used for "endurance" in verse 3 is the Greek word *hupomone,* which means "a patient enduring."

This cheerful, enduring patience, which helps us to continue in our Christian walk, actually comes—and develops—in times of testing and hardship. During these trials or "storms of life," our spiritual roots grow deeper, thus strengthening our faith. If we had our way, most of us would probably try to avoid these difficult times in our lives. Yet God promises that he will never give us more than we can handle (see 1 Corinthians 10:13, p. 208).

These times of trial and testing will make us either better or bitter. It really is up to us and the outlook we choose to take. If we can learn to walk in our relationship with God on the basis of faith as opposed to mere feeling, we will grow stronger and, as this passage says, "be strong in character and ready for anything."

**CORNER STONES**

---

ing religion in the sight of God our Father means that we must care for orphans and widows in their troubles, and refuse to let the world corrupt us.

## CHAPTER 2
*A Warning against Prejudice*

My dear brothers and sisters,* how can you claim that you have faith in our glorious Lord Jesus Christ if you favor some people more than others?

2For instance, suppose someone comes into your meeting* dressed in fancy clothes and expensive jewelry, and another comes in who is poor and dressed in shabby clothes. 3If you give special attention and a good seat to the rich person, but you say to the poor one, "You can stand over there, or else sit on the floor"—well, 4doesn't this discrimination show that you are guided by wrong motives?

5Listen to me, dear brothers and sisters. Hasn't God chosen the poor in this world to be rich in faith? Aren't they the ones who will inherit the kingdom God promised to those who love him? 6And yet, you insult the poor man! Isn't it the rich who oppress you and drag you into court? 7Aren't they the ones who slander Jesus Christ, whose noble name you bear?

8Yes indeed, it is good when you truly obey our Lord's royal command found in the Scriptures: "Love your neighbor as yourself."* 9But if you pay special attention to the rich, you are committing a sin, for you are guilty of breaking that law.

10And the person who keeps all of the laws except one is as guilty as the person who has broken all of God's laws. 11For the same God who said, "Do not commit adultery," also said, "Do not murder."* So if you murder someone, you have broken the entire law, even if you do not commit adultery.

12So whenever you speak, or whatever you do, remember that you will be judged by the law of love, the law that set you free. 13For there will be no mercy for you if you have not been merciful to others. But if you have been merciful, then God's mercy toward you will win out over his judgment against you.

*Faith without Good Deeds Is Dead*

14Dear brothers and sisters, what's the use of saying you have faith if you don't prove it by your actions? That kind of faith can't save anyone. 15Suppose you see a brother or sister who needs food or clothing, 16and you say, "Well, good-bye and God bless you; stay warm and eat well"—but then you don't give that person any food or clothing. What good does that do?

17So you see, it isn't enough just to have faith. Faith that doesn't show itself by good deeds is no faith at all—it is dead and useless.

---

2:1 Greek *brothers;* also in 2:5, 14.   2:2 Greek *synagogue.*   2:8 Lev 19:18.   2:11 Exod 20:13-14; Deut 5:17-18.

18Now someone may argue, "Some people have faith; others have good deeds." I say, "I can't see your faith if you don't have good deeds, but I will show you my faith through my good deeds."

19Do you still think it's enough just to believe that there is one God? Well, even the demons believe this, and they tremble in terror! 20Fool! When will you ever learn that faith that does not result in good deeds is useless?

21Don't you remember that our ancestor Abraham was declared right with God because of what he did when he offered his son Isaac on the altar? 22You see, he was trusting God so much that he was willing to do whatever God told him to do. His faith was made complete by what he did—by his actions. 23And so it happened just as the Scriptures say: "Abraham believed God, so God declared him to be righteous."* He was even called "the friend of God."* 24So you see, we are made right with God by what we do, not by faith alone.

25Rahab the prostitute is another example of this. She was made right with God by her actions—when she hid those messengers and sent them safely away by a different road. 26Just as the body is dead without a spirit, so also faith is dead without good deeds.

## CHAPTER 3
*Controlling the Tongue*

Dear brothers and sisters,* not many of you should become teachers in the church, for we who teach will be judged by God with greater strictness.

2We all make many mistakes, but those who control their tongues can also control themselves in every other way. 3We can make a large horse turn around and go wherever we want by means of a small bit in its mouth. 4And a tiny rudder makes a huge ship turn wherever the pilot wants it to go, even though the winds are strong. 5So also, the tongue is a small thing, but what enormous damage it can do. A tiny spark can set a great forest on fire. 6And the tongue is a flame of fire. It is full of wickedness that can ruin your whole life. It can turn the entire course of your life into a blazing flame of destruction, for it is set on fire by hell itself.

7People can tame all kinds of animals and birds and reptiles and fish, 8but no one can tame the tongue. It is an uncontrollable evil, full of deadly poison. 9Sometimes it praises our Lord and Father, and sometimes it breaks out into curses against those who have been made in the image of God. 10And so blessing and cursing come pouring out of the same mouth. Surely, my brothers and sisters, this is not right! 11Does a spring of water bubble out with both fresh water and bitter water? 12Can you pick olives from a fig tree or figs from a grapevine? No, and you can't draw fresh water from a salty pool.

*True Wisdom Comes from God*

13If you are wise and understand God's ways, live a life of steady goodness so that only good deeds will pour forth. And if you don't brag about the good you do, then you will be truly

## Prayer Allows Us to Voice Our Requests to God
Read JAMES 4:2-3

There may come a time in your life when you wonder why you are not growing in your faith. Or you might wonder why you don't ever have the opportunity to lead others to Christ. When you ask yourself these kinds of questions, you may be able to answer them with another question: "Have I asked God to help me in this area?"

Understand that this passage does not advocate that you "demand" things from God as though he were some "cosmic butler," prepared to answer your every beck and call. Yet it is equally wrong to fail to ask him to help meet your needs or to bless your life and spiritually strengthen you. God wants to bless you because you are his child. Unfortunately, many of us fail to receive what God has for us because we don't pray.

Take a moment to look at your own spiritual progress. Do you want to have a better understanding of the Bible? Are you looking for some Christian friends? Do you want the Lord to show you what your gifts and talents are? God wants to bless you, but he may be just waiting for your invitation to do so.

FIRST STEPS

2:23a Gen 15:6.   2:23b See Isa 41:8.   3:1 Greek *brothers;* also in 3:10.

## We Must Live Out Our Faith Read JAMES 2:14-17

While you do not need to change your lifestyle before you come to Christ, once you do come to Christ, your lifestyle should show tangible changes. If it does not, then one could doubt whether Christ has really come into your life. The way you live should reflect what you believe. As John the Baptist said, "Prove by the way you live that you have really turned from your sins and turned to God" (Luke 3:8).

James brings out another important reason for backing up our faith with our actions in verses 15 and 16: It makes it easier to share our faith with others. When people see that we genuinely care about them as individuals, then they will be much more open to hearing about what motivates us.

Can people see Jesus in the way you live? If not, it is time to move Jesus into the "pilot seat" of your life.

**CORNER STONES**

---

wise! 14But if you are bitterly jealous and there is selfish ambition in your hearts, don't brag about being wise. That is the worst kind of lie. 15For jealousy and selfishness are not God's kind of wisdom. Such things are earthly, unspiritual, and motivated by the Devil. 16For wherever there is jealousy and selfish ambition, there you will find disorder and every kind of evil.

17But the wisdom that comes from heaven is first of all pure. It is also peace loving, gentle at all times, and willing to yield to others. It is full of mercy and good deeds. It shows no partiality and is always sincere. 18And those who are peacemakers will plant seeds of peace and reap a harvest of goodness.

CHAPTER **4**
*Drawing Close to God*

What is causing the quarrels and fights among you? Isn't it the whole army of evil desires at war within you? 2You want what you don't have, so you scheme and kill to get it. You are jealous for what others have, and you can't possess it, so you fight and quarrel to take it away from them. And yet the reason you don't have what you want is that you don't ask God for it. 3And even when you do ask, you don't get it because your whole motive is wrong—you want only what will give you pleasure.

4You adulterers! Don't you realize that friendship with this world makes you an enemy of God? I say it again, that if your aim is to enjoy

## OFF AND RUNNING

### Control Your Tongue Read JAMES 3:1-12

It has been said that "A lie is halfway around the world while truth is still putting its shoes on." This illustrates the power of malicious speech. One unfounded rumor, one careless remark, one morsel of gossip can cause the greatest devastation. How correct James was when he wrote that the tongue is a flame of fire and full of wickedness.

Unfortunately, it is the sins of the tongue—backbiting, gossip, and tearing down another person—that we often excuse. We think that because we do not murder, commit adultery, or steal we are basically good people. But James makes it clear that certain kinds of speech are wrong. The content of a Christian's conversation should reflect what has happened in his or her heart. After all, part of the fruit, or evidence, of the Holy Spirit's presence in our lives is self-control (see Galatians 5:22-23, p. 234). The person who has no control over his or her tongue is usually "out of control" in other areas of life. But the person who has discipline over this area of life has yielded to the control of the Holy Spirit and will undoubtedly be able to keep other areas of his or her life in check as well.

this world, you can't be a friend of God. ⁵What do you think the Scriptures mean when they say that the Holy Spirit, whom God has placed within us, jealously longs for us to be faithful*? ⁶He gives us more and more strength to stand against such evil desires. As the Scriptures say,

"God sets himself against the proud,
but he shows favor to the humble."*

⁷So humble yourselves before God. Resist the Devil, and he will flee from you. ⁸Draw close to God, and God will draw close to you. Wash your hands, you sinners; purify your hearts, you hypocrites. ⁹Let there be tears for the wrong things you have done. Let there be sorrow and deep grief. Let there be sadness instead of laughter, and gloom instead of joy. ¹⁰When you bow down before the Lord and admit your dependence on him, he will lift you up and give you honor.

### Warning against Judging Others
¹¹Don't speak evil against each other, my dear brothers and sisters.* If you criticize each other and condemn each other, then you are criticizing and condemning God's law. But you are not a judge who can decide whether the law is right or wrong. Your job is to obey it. ¹²God alone, who made the law, can rightly judge among us. He alone has the power to save or to destroy. So what right do you have to condemn your neighbor?

### Warning about Self-Confidence
¹³Look here, you people who say, "Today or tomorrow we are going to a certain town and will stay there a year. We will do business there and make a profit." ¹⁴How do you know what will happen tomorrow? For your life is like the morning fog—it's here a little while, then it's gone. ¹⁵What you ought to say is, "If the Lord wants us to, we will live and do this or that." ¹⁶Otherwise you will be boasting about your own plans, and all such boasting is evil. ¹⁷Remember, it is sin to know what you ought to do and then not do it.

## CHAPTER 5
### Warning to the Rich
Look here, you rich people, weep and groan with anguish because of all the terrible troubles ahead of you. ²Your wealth is rotting away, and

your fine clothes are moth-eaten rags. ³Your gold and silver have become worthless. The very wealth you were counting on will eat away your flesh in hell.* This treasure you have accumulated will stand as evidence against you on the day of judgment. ⁴For listen! Hear the cries of the field workers whom you have cheated of

---

### Resist the Devil  Read JAMES 4:7-8

Satan recognizes the value of getting a foothold in the realm of our thoughts. He knows that sin is not merely a matter of actions and deeds, but something within the heart and the mind that eventually leads to the sinful action. Here are four practical and effective ways to "resist" the Devil and his temptations:

**1. Submit Yourself to God.** When you submit yourself to God, you are acknowledging his authority in your life. Because God is holy, which means pure and without sin, he will help you live a life that is pleasing to him. But in order to do this, you must submit to his authority.

**2. Resist the Devil.** To resist the Devil means to not give in to temptation when it presents itself. Giving in to temptation is an open invitation for the Devil and his demons to continually tempt you. But if you resist giving in to sin, the Devil will flee from you, meaning that he will give up tempting you for the time being.

**3. Draw Close to God.** The closer you get to God, the more you distance yourself from your old partner, the Devil. And the more time you spend with the Lord, through Bible study and prayer, the less likely you will be to fall. As Psalm 16:8 says, "I am always thinking of the LORD; and because he is so near, I never need to stumble or fall."

**4. Wash Your Hands and Purify Your Hearts.** This set of instructions is a call to repentance for all those who are harboring sin in their life. To harbor sin in your life is to give the Devil an opportunity to work in you and through you. But God is the one who should work in your life, not the Devil. If you are harboring sin in any area of your life, stop doing it, confess it to God, and ask him to forgive you and then work through you.

FIRST STEPS

---

4:5 Or the spirit that God placed within us tends to envy, or the Holy Spirit, whom God has placed within us, opposes our envy.   4:6 Prov 3:34.
4:11 Greek brothers.   5:3 Or will eat your flesh like fire.

## What Do Demons Believe? Read JAMES 2:19

**B**elieve it or not, in some ways demons are quite orthodox in their beliefs. They recognize that Jesus is indeed the Son of God. In Matthew's Gospel, the demons say to Jesus, "Why are you bothering us, Son of God? You have no right to torture us before God's appointed time!" (Matthew 8:29). Clearly the demons understand Jesus' awesome power—and they shudder in fear at the thought of him!

Interestingly enough, many people today do not even accept that Jesus is God's Son. Yet, even if you do believe in God, these verses show that it is not enough to keep you from going to hell. Belief without obedience is worthless. Those who settle for less than a total commitment to Christ may find themselves in the company of the demons at the time of judgment.

**CORNER STONES**

---

their pay. The wages you held back cry out against you. The cries of the reapers have reached the ears of the Lord Almighty.

⁵You have spent your years on earth in luxury, satisfying your every whim. Now your hearts are nice and fat, ready for the slaughter. ⁶You have condemned and killed good people who had no power to defend themselves against you.

### Patience in Suffering

⁷Dear brothers and sisters,* you must be patient as you wait for the Lord's return. Consider the farmers who eagerly look for the rains in the fall and in the spring. They patiently wait for the precious harvest to ripen. ⁸You, too, must be patient. And take courage, for the coming of the Lord is near.

⁹Don't grumble about each other, my brothers and sisters, or God will judge you. For look! The great Judge is coming. He is standing at the door!

¹⁰For examples of patience in suffering, dear brothers and sisters, look at the prophets who spoke in the name of the Lord. ¹¹We give great honor to those who endure under suffering. Job is an example of a man who endured patiently. From his experience we see how the Lord's plan finally ended in good, for he is full of tenderness and mercy.

¹²But most of all, my brothers and sisters, never take an oath, by heaven or earth or any-

5:7 Greek *brothers;* also in 5:9, 10, 12, 19.

thing else. Just say a simple yes or no, so that you will not sin and be condemned for it.

### The Power of Prayer

¹³Are any among you suffering? They should keep on praying about it. And those who have reason to be thankful should continually sing praises to the Lord.

¹⁴Are any among you sick? They should call for the elders of the church and have them pray over them, anointing them with oil in the name of the Lord. ¹⁵And their prayer offered in faith will heal the sick, and the Lord will make them well. And anyone who has committed sins will be forgiven.

¹⁶Confess your sins to each other and pray for each other so that you may be healed. The earnest prayer of a righteous person has great power and wonderful results. ¹⁷Elijah was as human as we are, and yet when he prayed earnestly that no rain would fall, none fell for the next three and a half years! ¹⁸Then he prayed for rain, and down it poured. The grass turned green, and the crops began to grow again.

### Restore Wandering Believers

¹⁹My dear brothers and sisters, if anyone among you wanders away from the truth and is brought back again, ²⁰you can be sure that the one who brings that person back will save that sinner from death and bring about the forgiveness of many sins.

# 1 Peter

## CHAPTER 1

### Greetings from Peter

This letter is from Peter, an apostle of Jesus Christ.

I am writing to God's chosen people who are living as foreigners in the lands of Pontus, Galatia, Cappadocia, the province of Asia, and Bithynia. 2God the Father chose you long ago, and the Spirit has made you holy. As a result, you have obeyed Jesus Christ and are cleansed by his blood.

May you have more and more of God's special favor and wonderful peace.

### The Hope of Eternal Life

3All honor to the God and Father of our Lord Jesus Christ, for it is by his boundless mercy that God has given us the privilege of being born again. Now we live with a wonderful expectation because Jesus Christ rose again from the dead. 4For God has reserved a priceless inheritance for his children. It is kept in heaven for you, pure and undefiled, beyond the reach of change and decay. 5And God, in his mighty power, will protect you until you receive this salvation, because you are trusting him. It will be revealed on the last day for all to see. 6So be truly glad!* There is wonderful joy ahead, even though it is necessary for you to endure many trials for a while.

7These trials are only to test your faith, to show that it is strong and pure. It is being tested as fire tests and purifies gold—and your faith is far more precious to God than mere gold. So if your faith remains strong after being tried by fiery trials, it will bring you much praise and glory and honor on the day when Jesus Christ is revealed to the whole world.

8You love him even though you have never seen him. Though you do not see him, you trust him; and even now you are happy with a glorious, inexpressible joy. 9Your reward for trusting him will be the salvation of your souls.

10This salvation was something the prophets wanted to know more about. They prophesied about this gracious salvation prepared for you, even though they had many questions as to what it all could mean. 11They wondered what the Spirit of Christ within them was talking about when he told them in advance about Christ's suffering and his great glory afterward. They wondered when and to whom all this would happen. 12They were told that these things would not happen during their lifetime, but many years later, during yours. And now this Good News has been announced by those who preached to you in the power of the Holy Spirit sent from heaven. It is all so wonderful that even the angels are eagerly watching these things happen.

### A Call to Holy Living

13So think clearly and exercise self-control. Look forward to the special blessings that will come to you at the return of Jesus Christ. 14Obey God because you are his children. Don't slip back into your old ways of doing evil; you didn't know any better then. 15But now you must be holy in everything you do, just as God—who chose you to be his children—is holy. 16For he himself has said, "You must be holy because I am holy."*

17And remember that the heavenly Father to whom you pray has no favorites when he judges. He will judge or reward you according to what you do. So you must live in reverent fear of him during your time as foreigners here on earth. 18For you know that God paid a ransom to save

1:6 Or *So you are truly glad.*  1:16 Lev 11:44-45; 19:2; 20:7.

## How the Holy Spirit Works with the Father and the Son
Read 1 PETER 1:2

The Holy Spirit has the distinct honor of being one of the three members of the Trinity—the other two members being God the Father and Jesus Christ, his Son. This particular verse shows how the Holy Spirit works with the Father and the Son in the life of a believer:

- The Father chooses us and makes us his children.
- Jesus redeems us, having died for us while we were still sinners.
  - The Holy Spirit draws us to the Lord and continues to work in our lives to make us pleasing to God.

As you can see, all three members of the Trinity work in concert to bring us into a relationship with God. For that reason, we see that the Holy Spirit is indeed an integral part of what has been called "the Godhead."

**CORNER STONES**

you from the empty life you inherited from your ancestors. And the ransom he paid was not mere gold or silver. ¹⁹He paid for you with the precious lifeblood of Christ, the sinless, spotless Lamb of God. ²⁰God chose him for this purpose long before the world began, but now in these final days, he was sent to the earth for all to see. And he did this for you.

²¹ Through Christ you have come to trust in God. And because God raised Christ from the dead and gave him great glory, your faith and hope can be placed confidently in God. ²²Now you can have sincere love for each other as brothers and sisters* because you were cleansed from your sins when you accepted the truth of the Good News. So see to it that you really do love each other intensely with all your hearts.*

²³For you have been born again. Your new life did not come from your earthly parents because the life they gave you will end in death. But this new life will last forever because it comes from the eternal, living word of God. ²⁴As the prophet says,

"People are like grass that dies away;
their beauty fades as quickly as the
beauty of wildflowers.
The grass withers,
and the flowers fall away.
²⁵ But the word of the Lord will last forever."*

And that word is the Good News that was preached to you.

CHAPTER **2**

So get rid of all malicious behavior and deceit. Don't just pretend to be good! Be done with hypocrisy and jealousy and backstabbing. ²You must crave pure spiritual milk so that you can grow into the fullness of your salvation. Cry out for this nourishment as a baby cries for milk, ³now that you have had a taste of the Lord's kindness.

*Living Stones for God's House*
⁴Come to Christ, who is the living cornerstone of God's temple. He was rejected by the people, but he is precious to God who chose him.

⁵And now God is building you, as living stones, into his spiritual temple. What's more, you are God's holy priests, who offer the spiritual sacrifices that please him because of Jesus Christ. ⁶As the Scriptures express it,

"I am placing a stone in Jerusalem,*
a chosen cornerstone,
and anyone who believes in him
will never be disappointed.*"

⁷Yes, he is very precious to you who believe. But for those who reject him,

"The stone that was rejected by the builders
has now become the cornerstone."*

⁸And the Scriptures also say,

"He is the stone that makes people stumble,
the rock that will make them fall."*

1:22a Greek *can have brotherly love.*   1:22b Some manuscripts read *with a pure heart.*   1:24-25 Isa 40:6-8.   2:6a Greek *in Zion.*   2:6b Or *will never be put to shame.* Isa 28:16.   2:7 Ps 118:22.   2:8 Isa 8:14.

They stumble because they do not listen to God's word or obey it, and so they meet the fate that has been planned for them.

9But you are not like that, for you are a chosen people. You are a kingdom of priests, God's holy nation, his very own possession. This is so you can show others the goodness of God, for he called you out of the darkness into his wonderful light.

10 "Once you were not a people;
    now you are the people of God.
Once you received none of God's mercy;
    now you have received his mercy."*

11Dear brothers and sisters, you are foreigners and aliens here. So I warn you to keep away from evil desires because they fight against your very souls. 12Be careful how you live among your unbelieving neighbors. Even if they accuse you of doing wrong, they will see your honorable behavior, and they will believe and give honor to God when he comes to judge the world.*

### Respecting People in Authority

13For the Lord's sake, accept all authority—the king as head of state, 14and the officials he has appointed. For the king has sent them to punish all who do wrong and to honor those who do right. 15It is God's will that your good lives should silence those who make foolish accusations against you. 16You are not slaves; you are free. But your freedom is not an excuse to do evil. You are free to live as God's slaves. 17Show respect for everyone. Love your Christian brothers and sisters.* Fear God. Show respect for the king.

### Slaves

18You who are slaves must accept the authority of your masters. Do whatever they tell you—not only if they are kind and reasonable, but even if they are harsh. 19For God is pleased with you when, for the sake of your conscience, you patiently endure unfair treatment. 20Of course, you get no credit for being patient if you are beaten for doing wrong. But if you suffer for doing right and are patient beneath the blows, God is pleased with you. 21This suffering is all part of what God has called you to. Christ, who suffered for you, is your example. Follow in his steps. 22He never sinned, and he never deceived anyone. 23He

did not retaliate when he was insulted. When he suffered, he did not threaten to get even. He left his case in the hands of God, who always judges fairly. 24He personally carried away our sins in his own body on the cross so we can be dead to sin and live for what is right. You have been healed by his wounds! 25Once you were wandering like lost sheep. But now you have turned to your Shepherd, the Guardian of your souls.

## Trials Sharpen Our Faith
### Read 1 PETER 1:3-7

God has selected you for a choice work. But before he can use you, he must toughen the grain of your life. He does this by allowing you to go through difficulties so that your faith can be tested and purified. While this process may not be enjoyable, this passage of Scripture gives us four insights into what we should remember during the testing of our faith, so that our faith will be stronger in the end:

**1. Remember *Whose* You Are.** You are God's child (verse 3).

**2. Remember *What* God Has Promised You.** God has promised you the priceless gift of eternal life (verse 4).

**3. Remember *Who* Will See You Through.** God will protect you until you reach your final destination: heaven (verses 5-6).

**4. Remember *Why* God Lets You Go through Trials.** God wants to test the genuineness of your faith so that your life will result in praise and glory when Jesus returns (verse 7).

Although it is great to spend time on a "spiritual mountaintop," so to speak, we cannot stay there forever. More often than not, at the bottom of that mountain lies cold, hard reality. Yet fruit grows best in the "valleys" (the hard times of life), not on the mountaintops (when everything is going well). Our greatest character development takes place when we take what we have learned on the mountaintop and put it into practice in the valley.

2:10 Hos 1:6, 9; 2:23.   2:12 Or *on the day of visitation.*   2:17 Greek *Love the brotherhood.*

## Knowing and Trusting God Is the Source of Inexpressible Joy
Read 1 PETER 1:8

Many people today are seeking joy and happiness but are not finding it. Perhaps they don't understand what happiness really is. At best, they will only find fleeting happiness from possessions, pleasures, or accomplishments. But the joy God gives is not merely some emotional feeling. It is not affected by our circumstances. In fact, it is an unchanging, natural by-product of our faith in Jesus Christ.

As you trust in Jesus and look forward to his return, you will be filled with an "inexpressible joy." It won't be just some sort of emotional high, but it will be a deep, supernatural experience of contentedness based upon the fact that your life is right with God. And this lasting joy and happiness will sustain you for the rest of your life.

**CORNER STONES**

CHAPTER **3**

### Wives
In the same way, you wives must accept the authority of your husbands, even those who refuse to accept the Good News. Your godly lives will speak to them better than any words. They will be won over ²by watching your pure, godly behavior.

³Don't be concerned about the outward beauty that depends on fancy hairstyles, expensive jewelry, or beautiful clothes. ⁴You should be known for the beauty that comes from within, the unfading beauty of a gentle and quiet spirit, which is so precious to God. ⁵That is the way the holy women of old made themselves beautiful. They trusted God and accepted the authority of their husbands. ⁶For instance, Sarah obeyed her husband, Abraham, when she called him her master. You are her daughters when you do what is right without fear of what your husbands might do.

### Husbands
⁷In the same way, you husbands must give honor to your wives. Treat her with understanding as you live together. She may be weaker than you are, but she is your equal partner in God's gift of new life. If you don't treat her as you should, your prayers will not be heard.

### All Christians
⁸Finally, all of you should be of one mind, full of sympathy toward each other, loving one another with tender hearts and humble minds. ⁹Don't repay evil for evil. Don't retaliate when people say unkind things about you. Instead, pay them back with a blessing. That is what God wants you to do, and he will bless you for it. ¹⁰For the Scriptures say,

"If you want a happy life and good days,
    keep your tongue from speaking evil,
    and keep your lips from telling lies.
¹¹ Turn away from evil and do good.
    Work hard at living in peace with others.
¹² The eyes of the Lord watch over those who
    do right,
    and his ears are open to their prayers.

## OFF AND RUNNING

### Never Use Vulgar Speech  Read 1 PETER 3:10

One thing that should certainly change when we come to Christ is the way we talk. If we continue using God's name in vain or keep telling dirty jokes, something is not right. Ephesians 4:29 says, "Don't use foul or abusive language." When we become indifferent to the way we speak (or the way others speak around us), we are downplaying the destructiveness of sin and doing a disservice to the Lord.

But the Lord turns his face
against those who do evil."*

### Suffering for Doing Good

13Now, who will want to harm you if you are eager to do good? 14But even if you suffer for doing what is right, God will reward you for it. So don't be afraid and don't worry. 15Instead, you must worship Christ as Lord of your life. And if you are asked about your Christian hope, always be ready to explain it. 16But you must do this in a gentle and respectful way. Keep your conscience clear. Then if people speak evil against you, they will be ashamed when they see what a good life you live because you belong to Christ. 17Remember, it is better to suffer for doing good, if that is what God wants, than to suffer for doing wrong!

18Christ also suffered when he died for our sins once for all time. He never sinned, but he died for sinners that he might bring us safely home to God. He suffered physical death, but he was raised to life in the Spirit.*

19So he went and preached to the spirits in prison—20those who disobeyed God long ago when God waited patiently while Noah was building his boat. Only eight people were saved from drowning in that terrible flood.* 21And this is a picture of baptism, which now saves you by the power of Jesus Christ's resurrection. Baptism is not a removal of dirt from your body; it is an appeal to God from* a clean conscience.

22Now Christ has gone to heaven. He is seated in the place of honor next to God, and all the angels and authorities and powers are bowing before him.

## CHAPTER 4
### Living for God

So then, since Christ suffered physical pain, you must arm yourselves with the same attitude he had, and be ready to suffer, too. For if you are willing to suffer for Christ, you have decided to stop sinning. 2And you won't spend the rest of your life chasing after evil desires, but you will be anxious to do the will of God. 3You have had enough in the past of the evil things that godless people enjoy—their immorality and lust, their feasting and drunkenness and wild parties, and their terrible worship of idols.

4Of course, your former friends are very surprised when you no longer join them in the wicked things they do, and they say evil things about you. 5But just remember that they will have to face God, who will judge everyone, both the living and the dead. 6That is why the Good News was preached even to those who have died—so that although their bodies were punished with death, they could still live in the spirit as God does.

7The end of the world is coming soon. Therefore, be earnest and disciplined in your prayers. 8Most important of all, continue to show deep love for each other, for love covers a multitude of sins. 9Cheerfully share your home with those who need a meal or a place to stay.

10God has given gifts to each of you from his great variety of spiritual gifts. Manage them well so that God's generosity can flow through you. 11Are you called to be a speaker? Then speak as though God himself were speaking through you. Are you called to help others? Do it with all the strength and energy that God supplies. Then God will be given glory in everything through Jesus Christ. All glory and power belong to him forever and ever. Amen.

### Suffering for Being a Christian

12Dear friends, don't be surprised at the fiery trials you are going through, as if something strange were happening to you. 13Instead, be very glad—because these trials will make you partners with Christ in his suffering, and afterward you will have the wonderful joy of sharing his glory when it is displayed to all the world.

3:10-12 Ps 34:12-16.   3:18 Or *spirit.*   3:20 Greek *saved through water.*   3:21 Or *for.*

If you find that this area is a trouble spot for you, commit it to God, and he will begin by cleaning up your thoughts. Then consciously replace that coarse language with praise and thankfulness to God for his goodness. As you focus upon God's goodness, your mind will be less filled with the perverse and wicked thoughts of this world.

# Our Conduct Should Cause Others to Glorify Christ
Read 1 PETER 2:9-12

Have you ever felt like your life wasn't really important in the grand scheme of things? Have you ever wondered if it was possible to make a difference in the world around you? These verses show that you can—and should—play a significant role in this world.

**Remember Who You Are.** First, think about who you are. Christians need to be different than those who do not know the Lord. Your godly lifestyle, priorities, and outlook should set you apart from nonbelievers.

**Make a Difference.** We are not to isolate ourselves from the world. God has placed us in this world so that our lives can have an impact on the people with whom we come into contact. Our Christian character and lifestyle will expose those who are living an ungodly life and confront them with the life-changing message of the gospel.

In many ways, the holiest moment of a church service is when God's people go out the doors of the church and into the world. That is when your godly living will cause people to ask, "What makes you different?"

Some people may criticize, ridicule, or persecute you for living a godly life. Others, however, may come to know Jesus as a result of your faithful obedience to God's Word. If they do, they will glorify God for your testimony and their newfound salvation.

CORNER STONES

---

¹⁴Be happy if you are insulted for being a Christian, for then the glorious Spirit of God will come upon you. ¹⁵If you suffer, however, it must not be for murder, stealing, making trouble, or prying into other people's affairs. ¹⁶But it is no shame to suffer for being a Christian. Praise God for the privilege of being called by his wonderful name! ¹⁷For the time has come for judgment, and it must begin first among God's own children. And if even we Christians must be judged, what terrible fate awaits those who have never believed God's Good News? ¹⁸And

"If the righteous are barely saved,
what chance will the godless and sinners have?"*

¹⁹So if you are suffering according to God's will, keep on doing what is right, and trust yourself to the God who made you, for he will never fail you.

## CHAPTER 5
*Advice for Elders and Young Men*
And now, a word to you who are elders in the churches. I, too, am an elder and a witness to the sufferings of Christ. And I, too, will share his glory and his honor when he returns. As a fellow elder,

4:18 Prov 11:31.  5:5 Prov 3:34.  5:9 Greek *your brothers.*

this is my appeal to you: ²Care for the flock of God entrusted to you. Watch over it willingly, not grudgingly—not for what you will get out of it, but because you are eager to serve God. ³Don't lord it over the people assigned to your care, but lead them by your good example. ⁴And when the head Shepherd comes, your reward will be a never-ending share in his glory and honor.

⁵You younger men, accept the authority of the elders. And all of you, serve each other in humility, for

"God sets himself against the proud,
but he shows favor to the humble."*

⁶So humble yourselves under the mighty power of God, and in his good time he will honor you. ⁷Give all your worries and cares to God, for he cares about what happens to you.

⁸Be careful! Watch out for attacks from the Devil, your great enemy. He prowls around like a roaring lion, looking for some victim to devour. ⁹Take a firm stand against him, and be strong in your faith. Remember that your Christian brothers and sisters* all over the world are going through the same kind of suffering you are.

¹⁰In his kindness God called you to his eter-

nal glory by means of Jesus Christ. After you have suffered a little while, he will restore, support, and strengthen you, and he will place you on a firm foundation. [11]All power is his forever and ever. Amen.

## Peter's Final Greetings

[12]I have written this short letter to you with the help of Silas,* whom I consider a faithful brother. My purpose in writing is to encourage you and assure you that the grace of God is with you no matter what happens.

[13]Your sister church here in Rome* sends you greetings, and so does my son Mark. [14]Greet each other in Christian love.*

Peace be to all of you who are in Christ.

5:12 Greek Silvanus.   5:13 Greek The elect one in Babylon. Babylon was probably a code name for Rome.   5:14 Greek with a kiss of love.

# 2 Peter

## CHAPTER 1

### Greetings from Peter

This letter is from Simon* Peter, a slave and apostle of Jesus Christ.

I am writing to all of you who share the same precious faith we have, faith given to us by Jesus Christ, our God and Savior, who makes us right with God.

2May God bless you with his special favor and wonderful peace as you come to know Jesus, our God and Lord,* better and better.

### Growing in the Knowledge of God

3As we know Jesus better, his divine power gives us everything we need for living a godly life. He has called us to receive his own glory and goodness! 4And by that same mighty power, he has given us all of his rich and wonderful promises. He has promised that you will escape the decadence all around you caused by evil desires and that you will share in his divine nature.

5So make every effort to apply the benefits of these promises to your life. Then your faith will produce a life of moral excellence. A life of moral excellence leads to knowing God better. 6Knowing God leads to self-control. Self-control leads to patient endurance, and patient endurance leads to godliness. 7Godliness leads to love for other Christians,* and finally you will grow to have genuine love for everyone. 8The more you grow like this, the more you will become productive and useful in your knowledge of our Lord Jesus Christ. 9But those who fail to develop these virtues are blind or, at least, very shortsighted. They have already forgotten that God has cleansed them from their old life of sin.

10So, dear brothers and sisters,* work hard to prove that you really are among those God has called and chosen. Doing this, you will never stumble or fall away. 11And God will open wide the gates of heaven for you to enter into the eternal Kingdom of our Lord and Savior Jesus Christ.

### Paying Attention to Scripture

12I plan to keep on reminding you of these things—even though you already know them and are standing firm in the truth. 13Yes, I believe I should keep on reminding you of these things as long as I live. 14But the Lord Jesus Christ has shown me that my days here on earth are numbered and I am soon to die.* 15So I will work hard to make these things clear to you. I want you to remember them long after I am gone.

16For we were not making up clever stories when we told you about the power of our Lord Jesus Christ and his coming again. We have seen his majestic splendor with our own eyes. 17And he received honor and glory from God the Father when God's glorious, majestic voice called down from heaven, "This is my beloved Son; I am fully pleased with him." 18We ourselves heard the voice when we were there with him on the holy mountain.

19Because of that, we have even greater confidence in the message proclaimed by the prophets. Pay close attention to what they wrote, for their words are like a light shining in a dark place—until the day Christ appears and his brilliant light shines in your hearts.* 20Above all, you must understand that no prophecy in Scripture ever came from the prophets themselves* 21or because they wanted to prophesy. It was the Holy Spirit who moved the prophets to speak from God.

1:1 Greek Simeon. 1:2 Or come to know God and Jesus our Lord. 1:7 Greek brotherly love. 1:10 Greek brothers. 1:14 Greek I must soon put off this earthly tent. 1:19 Or until the day dawns and the morning star rises in your hearts. 1:20 Or is a matter of one's own interpretation.

## God Is Loving and Just Read 2 PETER 3:3-9

The scoffers described in this passage mistook Christ's delayed return to earth to mean that there would be no final judgment at all. Because everything "remained exactly the same since the world was first created," they not only doubted Christ's return but forgot about God's judgment in the past. More importantly, these scoffers overlooked God's love and mercy. It is for their sake that God is restraining his judgment because "he does not want anyone to perish."

This passage shows two important and seemingly contradictory aspects of God's character: love and justice. The Bible tells us that God is love. In spite of his extensive knowledge of our sinfulness and unworthiness, he has declared, "I will never fail you. I will never forsake you" (Hebrews 13:5). One of the clearest demonstrations of his love is found at the cross on which Jesus died for us: "But God showed his great love for us by sending Christ to die for us while we were still sinners" (Romans 5:8).

God's love, however, is often misunderstood. Many think that because he loves us, he won't judge us. But his love for us does not negate the fact that he is also just. Scripture clearly and repeatedly makes the point that only the godly will see his face. Therefore, we can be certain that our sins must be dealt with. For those who have accepted God's gift of salvation—Jesus' death on the cross—their sins have been forgiven. For those who haven't accepted this gift, God's judgment is certain.

Every day is another opportunity for nonbelievers to come to faith in Jesus Christ. It is also evidence of the tremendous love God has for his creation. In his holiness God is unapproachable, but in his love he approaches us. The next time you are tempted to doubt God's tender love for you, just take a long, hard look at the cross, and remember that it was not the nails that held Jesus there, but his love for you and others!

**CORNER STONES**

---

## CHAPTER 2

### The Danger of False Teachers

But there were also false prophets in Israel, just as there will be false teachers among you. They will cleverly teach their destructive heresies about God and even turn against their Master who bought them. Theirs will be a swift and terrible end. [2]Many will follow their evil teaching and shameful immorality. And because of them, Christ and his true way will be slandered. [3]In their greed they will make up clever lies to get hold of your money. But God condemned them long ago, and their destruction is on the way.

[4]For God did not spare even the angels when they sinned; he threw them into hell,* in gloomy caves* and darkness until the judgment day. [5]And God did not spare the ancient world—except for Noah and his family of seven. Noah warned the world of God's righteous judgment. Then God destroyed the whole world of ungodly people with a vast flood. [6]Later, he turned the cities of Sodom and Gomorrah into heaps of ashes and swept them off the face of the earth. He made them an example of what will happen to ungodly people. [7]But at the same time, God rescued Lot out of Sodom because he was a good man who was sick of all the immorality and wickedness around him. [8]Yes, he was a righteous man who was distressed by the wickedness he saw and heard day after day.

[9]So you see, the Lord knows how to rescue godly people from their trials, even while punishing the wicked right up until the day of judgment. [10]He is especially hard on those who follow their own evil, lustful desires and who despise authority. These people are proud and arrogant, daring even to scoff at the glorious ones* without so much as trembling. [11]But the angels, even though they are far greater in power and strength than these false

2:4a Greek *Tartaros*.  2:4b Some manuscripts read *chains of gloom*.  2:10 *The glorious ones* are probably evil angels; also in 2:11.

teachers, never speak out disrespectfully against* the glorious ones.

12These false teachers are like unthinking animals, creatures of instinct, who are born to be caught and killed. They laugh at the terrifying powers they know so little about, and they will be destroyed along with them. 13Their destruction is their reward for the harm they have done. They love to indulge in evil pleasures in broad daylight. They are a disgrace and a stain among you. They revel in deceitfulness while they feast with you. 14They commit adultery with their eyes, and their lust is never satisfied. They make a game of luring unstable people into sin. They train themselves to be greedy; they are doomed and cursed. 15They have wandered off the right road and followed the way of Balaam son of Beor,* who loved to earn money by doing wrong. 16But Balaam was stopped from his mad course when his donkey rebuked him with a human voice.

17These people are as useless as dried-up springs of water or as clouds blown away by the wind—promising much and delivering nothing. They are doomed to blackest darkness. 18They brag about themselves with empty, foolish boasting. With lustful desire as their bait, they lure back into sin those who have just escaped from such wicked living. 19They promise freedom, but they themselves are slaves to sin and corruption. For you are a slave to whatever controls you. 20And when people escape from the wicked ways of the world by learning about our Lord and Savior Jesus Christ and then get tangled up with sin and become its slave again, they are worse off than before. 21It would be better if they had never known the right way to live than to know it and then reject the holy commandments that were given to them. 22They make these proverbs come true: "A dog returns to its vomit,"* and "A washed pig returns to the mud."

## CHAPTER 3
### The Day of the Lord Is Coming

This is my second letter to you, dear friends, and in both of them I have tried to stimulate your wholesome thinking and refresh your memory. 2I want you to remember and understand what the holy prophets said long ago and what our Lord and Savior commanded through your apostles.

3First, I want to remind you that in the last days there will be scoffers who will laugh at the truth and do every evil thing they desire. 4This will be their argument: "Jesus promised to come back, did he? Then where is he? Why, as far back as anyone can remember, everything has remained exactly the same since the world was first created."

5They deliberately forget that God made the heavens by the word of his command, and he brought the earth up from the water and surrounded it with water. 6Then he used the water to destroy the world with a mighty flood. 7And God has also commanded that the heavens and the earth will be consumed by fire on the day of judgment, when ungodly people will perish.

8But you must not forget, dear friends, that a day is like a thousand years to the Lord, and a thousand years is like a day. 9The Lord isn't really being slow about his promise to return, as some people think. No, he is being patient for your sake. He does not want anyone to perish, so he is giving more time for everyone to repent. 10But the day of the Lord will come as unexpectedly as a thief. Then the heavens will pass away with a terrible noise, and everything in them will disappear in fire, and the earth and everything on it will be exposed to judgment.*

11Since everything around us is going to melt away, what holy, godly lives you should be living! 12You should look forward to that day and hurry it along—the day when God will set the heavens on fire and the elements will melt away in the flames. 13But we are looking forward to the new heavens and new earth he has promised, a world where everyone is right with God.

14And so, dear friends, while you are waiting for these things to happen, make every effort to live a pure and blameless life. And be at peace with God.

15And remember, the Lord is waiting so that people have time to be saved. This is just as our beloved brother Paul wrote to you with the wisdom God gave him—16speaking of these things in all of his letters. Some of his comments are hard to understand, and those who are ignorant and unstable have twisted his letters around to mean something quite different from what he meant, just as they do the other parts of Scripture—and the result is disaster for them.

2:11 Greek *never bring blasphemous judgment from the Lord against.* 2:15 Other manuscripts read *Bosor.* 2:22 Prov 26:11. 3:10 Some manuscripts read *will be burned up.*

## Keep an Eternal Perspective Read 2 PETER 3:10-11

If Jesus were to come today, would you be embarrassed by what you are doing? That is a good question to ask yourself each morning—and especially those times when immoral thoughts pop into your head. Jesus emphasized the importance of keeping a pure heart when he said, "God blesses those whose hearts are pure, for they shall see God" (Matthew 5:8).

A literal definition of the word *pure* is "without hypocrisy," or "single." In other words, Jesus says that we must have a singular, sincere devotion to him in order to see God.

The Bible reminds us that the hope of the coming return of Jesus Christ can have a spiritually purifying effect on our lives: "And all who believe this will keep themselves pure, just as Christ is pure" (1 John 3:3). As we recognize the holiness of God and his imminent return, we should pray along with the psalmist, "Teach me your ways, O LORD, that I may live according to your truth! Grant me purity of heart, that I may honor you" (Psalm 86:11).

**CORNER STONES**

---

*Peter's Final Words*

17 I am warning you ahead of time, dear friends, so that you can watch out and not be carried away by the errors of these wicked people. I don't want you to lose your own secure footing. 18 But grow in the special favor and knowledge of our Lord and Savior Jesus Christ.

To him be all glory and honor, both now and forevermore. Amen.

# 1 John

## CHAPTER 1

### Introduction

The one who existed from the beginning* is the one we have heard and seen. We saw him with our own eyes and touched him with our own hands. He is Jesus Christ, the Word of life. 2This one who is life from God was shown to us, and we have seen him. And now we testify and announce to you that he is the one who is eternal life. He was with the Father, and then he was shown to us. 3We are telling you about what we ourselves have actually seen and heard, so that you may have fellowship with us. And our fellowship is with the Father and with his Son, Jesus Christ.

4We are writing these things so that our* joy will be complete.

### Living in the Light

5This is the message he has given us to announce to you: God is light and there is no darkness in him at all. 6So we are lying if we say we have fellowship with God but go on living in spiritual darkness. We are not living in the truth. 7But if we are living in the light of God's presence, just as Christ is, then we have fellowship with each other, and the blood of Jesus, his Son, cleanses us from every sin.

8If we say we have no sin, we are only fooling ourselves and refusing to accept the truth. 9But if we confess our sins to him, he is faithful and just to forgive us and to cleanse us from every wrong. 10If we claim we have not sinned, we are calling God a liar and showing that his word has no place in our hearts.

## CHAPTER 2

My dear children, I am writing this to you so that you will not sin. But if you do sin, there is someone to plead for you before the Father. He is Jesus Christ, the one who pleases God completely.* 2He is the sacrifice for our sins. He takes away not only our sins but the sins of all the world.

3And how can we be sure that we belong to him? By obeying his commandments. 4If someone says, "I belong to God," but doesn't obey God's commandments, that person is a liar and does not live in the truth. 5But those who obey God's word really do love him. That is the way to know whether or not we live in him. 6Those who say they live in God should live their lives as Christ did.

### A New Commandment

7Dear friends, I am not writing a new commandment, for it is an old one you have always had, right from the beginning. This commandment—to love one another—is the same message you heard before. 8Yet it is also new. This commandment is true in Christ and is true among you, because the darkness is disappearing and the true light is already shining.

9If anyone says, "I am living in the light," but hates a Christian brother or sister,* that person is still living in darkness. 10Anyone who loves other Christians* is living in the light and does not cause anyone to stumble. 11Anyone who hates a Christian brother or sister is living and walking in darkness. Such a person is lost, having been blinded by the darkness.

12I am writing to you, my dear children,
because your sins have been forgiven
because of Jesus.

13I am writing to you who are mature

1:1 Greek What was from the beginning.   1:4 Some manuscripts read your.   2:1 Greek Jesus Christ, the righteous.   2:9 Greek his brother; also in 2:11.   2:10 Greek his brother.

## Our Love for Others Mirrors the Condition of Our Heart
Read 1 JOHN 2:9-11

Being a Christian involves more than just vocalizing our love to God. It also means demonstrating God's love to others. Humanly speaking, it is much easier to dislike someone than it is to love him or her. Grudges and resentment come easily. Yet bitterness toward others is a poison. Not only does it affect our relationships with other people, but it spiritually blinds us as well. Worse yet, harboring bitterness toward other people is a sin that can lead to other sins.

If you are having trouble loving others, then you need to learn how to walk "in the light." How do you do that? Verse 6 of this chapter says, "Those who say they live in God should live their lives as Christ did." Take a look at the way you treat the people in your life; then compare your relationships with Jesus' relationships in the Gospels (Matthew, Mark, Luke, and John). Here is a sampling of what you will find:

- Jesus reached out to the unlovable (see Luke 19:1-10, pp. 96–97).
- Jesus gave a second chance to a friend who had let him down (see John 18:25-27, p. 129, and John 21:15-19, pp. 133–134).
- Jesus showed patience toward those who questioned him (see John 20:24-28, p. 133).
- Jesus cared for the sick (see Luke 5:12-16, p. 73).
- Jesus initiated conversations with those whom others despised (see John 4:4-42, pp. 110–111).
- Jesus wept with those who grieved (see John 11:1-44, pp. 119–120).

Ask God to help you love as Jesus loved, and you will see some radical changes in your heart and your life.

CORNER STONES

because you know Christ, the one who is from the beginning.

I am writing to you who are young because you have won your battle with Satan.

14I have written to you, children, because you have known the Father.

I have written to you who are mature

because you know Christ, the one who is from the beginning.

I have written to you who are young because you are strong with God's word living in your hearts, and you have won your battle with Satan.

15Stop loving this evil world and all that it offers you, for when you love the world, you show that

## OFF AND RUNNING
### Make Sure Your Friendships Honor God Read 1 JOHN 1:7

What is the key to having a friendship that honors God? First, make sure that you are walking in obedience to God, "living in the light of God's presence." If you are not committed to obeying God, then you will probably make friends with those who also lack this commitment. Any relationship that does not encourage you to live obediently to God and entices you to sin dishonors God.

On the other hand, if you are committed to obeying God, you will seek out friends who are also committed to him. As you walk with those who share the same love for the Lord as you have, you will be filled with joy and have greater impetus to keep from sinning. And your friendships will honor God.

you do not have the love of the Father in you. 16For the world offers only the lust for physical pleasure, the lust for everything we see, and pride in our possessions. These are not from the Father. They are from this evil world. 17And this world is fading away, along with everything it craves. But if you do the will of God, you will live forever.

18Dear children, the last hour is here. You have heard that the Antichrist is coming, and already many such antichrists have appeared. From this we know that the end of the world has come. 19These people left our churches because they never really belonged with us; otherwise they would have stayed with us. When they left us, it proved that they do not belong with us. 20But you are not like that, for the Holy Spirit has come upon you,* and all of you know the truth. 21So I am writing to you not because you don't know the truth but because you know the difference between truth and falsehood. 22And who is the great liar? The one who says that Jesus is not the Christ. Such people are antichrists, for they have denied the Father and the Son. 23Anyone who denies the Son doesn't have the Father either. But anyone who confesses the Son has the Father also.

24So you must remain faithful to what you have been taught from the beginning. If you do, you will continue to live in fellowship with the Son and with the Father. 25And in this fellowship we enjoy the eternal life he promised us.

26I have written these things to you because you need to be aware of those who want to lead you astray. 27But you have received the Holy Spirit,* and he lives within you, so you don't need anyone to teach you what is true. For the Spirit teaches you all things, and what he teaches is true—it is not a lie. So continue in what he has taught you, and continue to live in Christ.

28And now, dear children, continue to live in fellowship with Christ so that when he returns, you will be full of courage and not shrink back from him in shame. 29Since we know that God is always right, we also know that all who do what is right are his children.

CHAPTER **3**
*Living as Children of God*
See how very much our heavenly Father loves us, for he allows us to be called his children, and we really are! But the people who belong to this world don't know God, so they don't under-

2:20 Greek *But you have an anointing from the Holy One.*
2:27 Greek *the anointing.*

stand that we are his children. 2Yes, dear friends, we are already God's children, and we can't even imagine what we will be like when Christ returns. But we do know that when he comes we will be like him, for we will see him as he really is. 3And all who believe this will keep themselves pure, just as Christ is pure.

4Those who sin are opposed to the law of God, for all sin opposes the law of God. 5And you know that Jesus came to take away our sins, for there is no sin in him. 6So if we continue to live in him, we won't sin either. But those who keep on sinning have never known him or understood who he is.

7Dear children, don't let anyone deceive you about this: When people do what is right, it is because they are righteous, even as Christ is righteous. 8But when people keep on sinning, it shows they belong to the Devil, who has been sinning since the beginning. But the Son of God came to destroy these works of the Devil. 9Those who have

## A Disciple Walks as Jesus Walked Read 1 JOHN 2:3-6

If you call yourself a disciple, you need to follow in Jesus' footsteps. As verse 6 says, you need to "live [your life] as Christ did." Another translation says that you should "walk as he walked."

Walking implies a steady motion—you put one foot in front of the other, and you keep moving. That is the way we should follow Christ. We need to stick with it and be consistent. How do you practically live as Christ did?

- Make time for God and his Word every single day.
- Spend time in prayer with the Lord throughout the day.
- Take time to be with God's people.

There is a tremendous benefit to the disciple who stays close to Christ. By walking as he walked, the Bible tells us we will have help to keep us from sinning (see 1 John 3:6, p. 319). For that reason, one of the greatest identifying marks of a disciple is that his or her walk resembles the Master's.

## Understand the Difference between the True Gospel and a False Gospel Read 1 JOHN 4:1-3

False teachings are not unique to our times. They cropped up in the days of the early church as well. When John wrote this passage, a teaching called Gnosticism (which means "to know") had become popular. It taught that Jesus was a mere human being, born by natural procreation. It also claimed that "the Christ" came upon Jesus at his baptism and left him before his crucifixion. This, of course, was false and unscriptural. Yet it is important to note that this heresy is still taught by some today.

As this text says, we need to "test" these teachings to see if they really come from God. Since false teachers don't carry ID cards, here are three simple questions to ask of anyone you may suspect of being a false teacher:

**1. What Is Their Ultimate Hope?** Some hope to make a better world. Mormons expect to be equal with God. They also hope that each Mormon couple will be given their own planet to populate. Jehovah's Witnesses believe God will come back to earth at the end of time and establish a paradise here. They hope to live in this paradise on earth. But the hope for the Christian is to spend eternity with Jesus Christ in heaven.

**2. What Is the Basis for This Hope?** Do they teach that you can only get to heaven by living a good life? Do they say that you obtain salvation by faith in Jesus Christ and by performing certain things or rituals, like baptism, keeping the Sabbath, or other works? You must beware of the "and's." The Bible says, "God saved you by his special favor when you believed. And you can't take credit for this; it is a gift from God. Salvation is not a reward for the good things we have done, so none of us can boast about it" (Ephesians 2:8-9).

**3. How Do They View Jesus Christ?** Another earmark of a false teacher preaching a false gospel is what he or she claims about the person of Jesus Christ. This is really the central and primary issue. Many cults seek to make their teachings more "palatable" to those in the church by including Jesus Christ in their teachings. They may even use terms like "saved" and "born again," and speak of Jesus dying on the cross. Interestingly enough, some teachings may pass the first two tests but fail this ultimate test, which is believing that Jesus was resurrected from the dead.

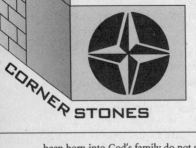

Any attempts to cast doubt upon the Bible's sufficiency should be rejected. Any "broadness" that would admit any other way to God outside of Christ is false. To say that Jesus is not the only way to God is to call Jesus a liar! Anytime Jesus, "the unique Son of God," is reduced to merely *"a* son of God" or one of many prophets from God, it is erroneous. The best way to know the false is to be familiar with the true: God's Word, the Bible.

**CORNERSTONES**

---

been born into God's family do not sin, because God's life is in them. So they can't keep on sinning, because they have been born of God. ¹⁰So now we can tell who are children of God and who are children of the Devil. Anyone who does not obey God's commands and does not love other Christians* does not belong to God.

### Love One Another

¹¹This is the message we have heard from the beginning: We should love one another. ¹²We must not be like Cain, who belonged to the evil one and killed his brother. And why did he kill him? Because Cain had been doing what was evil, and his brother had been doing what was right. ¹³So don't be surprised, dear brothers and sisters,* if the world hates you.

¹⁴If we love our Christian brothers and sisters, it proves that we have passed from death to eternal life. But a person who has no love is still dead. ¹⁵Anyone who hates another Christian* is really a murderer at heart. And you know that

3:10 Greek *his brother.*   3:13 Greek *brothers;* also in 3:14, 16.   3:15 Greek *his brother.*

# How Can I Tell the Difference between True and False Teachings about God? Read 1 JOHN 4:1-2

The Bible tells us that we must be especially careful in these "last days," for the coming Antichrist and false prophet will perform signs and miracles and deceive many (see 2 Thessalonians 2:9-10, pp. 265–266).

So how does one tell the true gospel from a counterfeit or false gospel? Here are four tests you can apply to make sure the teachings you hear really come from God:

**1. Does the Teaching Recognize Jesus Christ as the Son of God and the Only Way of Salvation?** Proper teaching must agree that Jesus Christ is God's unique Son, and that he "became a human being" (verse 2). Most cults deny Christ's deity, recognizing him only as a great teacher or, as Jehovah's Witnesses claim, simply God's first created creature. So find out what this teaching has to say about Jesus.

**2. Does the Teaching Agree with Scripture?** The apostle Paul commended the Bereans because "they searched the Scriptures day after day to check up on [their statements] to see if they were really teaching the truth" (Acts 17:11). Don't simply take some pastor or teacher's word as gospel without examining it in the light of God's Word first.

**3. If Miracles Are Involved, Do They Bring Glory to God or to Someone Else?** Remember, God is not the only one who can do miracles. As mentioned above, the Antichrist will deceive many with his miraculous wonders. Satan is a great imitator. In the last days, "false messiahs and false prophets will rise up and perform great miraculous signs and wonders so as to deceive, if possible, even God's chosen ones" (Matthew 24:24). Do not accept any miracle at face value. Make sure that the person through whom the miracle comes has a strong personal relationship with Jesus Christ (see Matthew 7:21-23, p. 12). More important, be certain the miracle glorifies Jesus Christ and does not contradict what Scripture teaches.

**4. Is the Teaching Widely Accepted by the World at Large?** Contrary to conventional wisdom, the more popular a teaching is does not make it a more "correct" teaching. For instance, relativism, or the idea that each person can live the way he or she wants to as long as he or she is true to himself or herself, is a popular belief. However, we know that God's Word teaches differently. As shown in this passage, if the message is really from God, the world won't listen to it (1 John 4:6).

The more you study the "real thing"—God's Word—the more you will be able to quickly identify the counterfeits. And remember, "the Spirit who lives in you is greater than the spirit who lives in the world" (1 John 4:4).

BIG QUESTIONS

murderers don't have eternal life within them. 16We know what real love is because Christ gave up his life for us. And so we also ought to give up our lives for our Christian brothers and sisters. 17But if anyone has enough money to live well and sees a brother or sister in need and refuses to help—how can God's love be in that person?

18Dear children, let us stop just saying we love each other; let us really show it by our actions. 19It is by our actions that we know we are living in the truth, so we will be confident when we stand before the Lord, 20even if our hearts condemn us. For God is greater than our hearts, and he knows everything.

21Dear friends, if our conscience is clear, we

can come to God with bold confidence. ²²And we will receive whatever we request because we obey him and do the things that please him. ²³And this is his commandment: We must believe in the name of his Son, Jesus Christ, and love one another, just as he commanded us. ²⁴Those who obey God's commandments live in fellowship with him, and he with them. And we know he lives in us because the Holy Spirit lives in us.

## CHAPTER 4
### Discerning False Prophets

Dear friends, do not believe everyone who claims to speak by the Spirit. You must test them to see if the spirit they have comes from God. For there are many false prophets in the world. ²This is the way to find out if they have the Spirit of God: If a prophet acknowledges that Jesus Christ became a human being, that person has the Spirit of God. ³If a prophet does not acknowledge Jesus, that person is not from God. Such a person has the spirit of the Antichrist. You have heard that he is going to come into the world, and he is already here.

⁴But you belong to God, my dear children. You have already won your fight with these false prophets, because the Spirit who lives in you is greater than the spirit who lives in the world. ⁵These people belong to this world, so they speak from the world's viewpoint, and the world listens to them. ⁶But we belong to God; that is why those who know God listen to us. If they do not belong to God, they do not listen to us. That is how we know if someone has the Spirit of truth or the spirit of deception.

### Loving One Another

⁷Dear friends, let us continue to love one another, for love comes from God. Anyone who loves is born of God and knows God. ⁸But anyone who does not love does not know God—for God is love.

⁹God showed how much he loved us by sending his only Son into the world so that we might have eternal life through him. ¹⁰This is real love. It is not that we loved God, but that he loved us and sent his Son as a sacrifice to take away our sins.

¹¹Dear friends, since God loved us that much, we surely ought to love each other. ¹²No one has ever seen God. But if we love each other, God lives in us, and his love has been brought to full expression through us.

¹³And God has given us his Spirit as proof that we live in him and he in us. ¹⁴Furthermore, we have seen with our own eyes and now testify that the Father sent his Son to be the Savior of the world. ¹⁵All who proclaim that Jesus is the Son of God have God living in them, and they live in God. ¹⁶We know how much God loves us, and we have put our trust in him.

God is love, and all who live in love live in God, and God lives in them. ¹⁷And as we live in God, our love grows more perfect. So we will not be afraid on the day of judgment, but we can face him with confidence because we are like Christ here in this world.

¹⁸Such love has no fear because perfect love expels all fear. If we are afraid, it is for fear of judgment, and this shows that his love has not been perfected in us. ¹⁹We love each other* as a result of his loving us first.

²⁰If someone says, "I love God," but hates a Christian brother or sister,* that person is a liar; for if we don't love people we can see, how can

4:19 Or *We love him;* Greek reads *We love.*   4:20 Greek *brother;* also in 4:21.

## OFF AND RUNNING ◢◢◢◢◢
### Pray Expecting to Get Answers  Read 1 JOHN 5:14-15

Prayer is not getting your will in heaven. It is getting God's will on earth. Prayer is not an argument with God in which you try to persuade him to move things your way. Prayer is an exercise in which his Spirit enables you to move yourself his way. Prayer is not overcoming God's reluctance. It is laying hold of his willingness.

We like to gravitate toward the latter part of these verses. But don't forget the first part. You have to first "stay in Christ" by maintaining a healthy, ongoing relationship with him. When that happens, you will see your will coming in line with his, and your requests will begin to mirror what Christ wants to do in your life and the lives of those around you. At that point, you can be assured that God is listening to you and will answer your prayers.

we love God, whom we have not seen? 21And God himself has commanded that we must love not only him but our Christian brothers and sisters, too.

## CHAPTER 5
### Faith in the Son of God

Everyone who believes that Jesus is the Christ is a child of God. And everyone who loves the Father loves his children, too. 2We know we love God's children if we love God and obey his commandments. 3Loving God means keeping his commandments, and really, that isn't difficult. 4For every child of God defeats this evil world by trusting Christ to give the victory. 5And the ones who win this battle against the world are the ones who believe that Jesus is the Son of God.

6And Jesus Christ was revealed as God's Son by his baptism in water and by shedding his blood on the cross*—not by water only, but by water and blood. And the Spirit also gives us the testimony that this is true. 7So we have these three witnesses*—8the Spirit, the water, and the blood—and all three agree. 9Since we believe human testimony, surely we can believe the testimony that comes from God. And God has testified about his Son. 10All who believe in the Son of God know that this is true. Those who don't believe this are actually calling God a liar because they don't believe what God has testified about his Son.

11And this is what God has testified: He has given us eternal life, and this life is in his Son. 12So whoever has God's Son has life; whoever does not have his Son does not have life.

### Conclusion

13I write this to you who believe in the Son of God, so that you may know you have eternal life. 14And we can be confident that he will listen to us whenever we ask him for anything in line with his will. 15And if we know he is listening when we make our requests, we can be sure that he will give us what we ask for.

16If you see a Christian brother or sister* sinning in a way that does not lead to death, you should pray, and God will give that person life. But there is a sin that leads to death, and I am not saying you should pray for those who commit it. 17Every wrong is sin, but not all sin leads to death.

18We know that those who have become part of God's family do not make a practice of sinning, for God's Son holds them securely, and the evil one cannot get his hands on them. 19We know that we are children of God and that the world around us is under the power and control of the evil one. 20And we know that the Son of God has come, and he has given us understanding so that we can know the true God. And now we are in God because we are in his Son, Jesus Christ. He is the only true God, and he is eternal life.

21Dear children, keep away from anything that might take God's place in your hearts.*

5:6 Greek This is he who came by water and blood. 5:7 Some very late manuscripts add in heaven—the Father, the Word, and the Holy Spirit, and these three are one. And we have three witnesses on earth. 5:16 Greek your brother. 5:21 Greek keep yourselves from idols.

# 2 John

## Greetings

This letter is from John the Elder.*

It is written to the chosen lady and to her children,* whom I love in the truth, as does everyone else who knows God's truth—²the truth that lives in us and will be in our hearts forever.

³May grace, mercy, and peace, which come from God our Father and from Jesus Christ his Son, be with us who live in truth and love.

## Live in the Truth

⁴How happy I was to meet some of your children and find them living in the truth, just as we have been commanded by the Father.

⁵And now I want to urge you, dear lady, that we should love one another. This is not a new commandment, but one we had from the beginning. ⁶Love means doing what God has commanded us, and he has commanded us to love one another, just as you heard from the beginning.

⁷Many deceivers have gone out into the world. They do not believe that Jesus Christ came to earth in a real body. Such a person is a deceiver and an antichrist. ⁸Watch out, so that you do not lose the prize for which we* have been working so hard. Be diligent so that you will receive your full reward. ⁹For if you wander beyond the teaching of Christ, you will not have fellowship with God. But if you continue in the teaching of Christ, you will have fellowship with both the Father and the Son.

¹⁰If someone comes to your meeting and does not teach the truth about Christ, don't invite him into your house or encourage him in any way. ¹¹Anyone who encourages him becomes a partner in his evil work.

## Conclusion

¹²Well, I have much more to say to you, but I don't want to say it in a letter. For I hope to visit you soon and to talk with you face to face. Then our joy will be complete.

¹³Greetings from the children of your sister,* chosen by God.

1a Greek *From the elder.*   1b Or *the church God has chosen and her members,* or *the chosen Kyria and her children.*   8 Some manuscripts read *you.*   13 Or *from the members of your sister church.*

# 3 John

## Greetings

This letter is from John the Elder.*

It is written to Gaius, my dear friend, whom I love in the truth.

²Dear friend, I am praying that all is well with you and that your body is as healthy as I know your soul is. ³Some of the brothers recently returned and made me very happy by telling me about your faithfulness and that you are living in the truth. ⁴I could have no greater joy than to hear that my children live in the truth.

## Caring for the Lord's Workers

⁵Dear friend, you are doing a good work for God when you take care of the traveling teachers* who are passing through, even though they are strangers to you. ⁶They have told the church here of your friendship and your loving deeds. You do well to send them on their way in a manner that pleases God. ⁷For they are traveling for the Lord* and accept nothing from those who are not Christians.* ⁸So we ourselves should support them so that we may become partners with them for the truth.

⁹I sent a brief letter to the church about this, but Diotrephes, who loves to be the leader, does not acknowledge our authority. ¹⁰When I come, I will report some of the things he is doing and the wicked things he is saying about us. He not only refuses to welcome the traveling teachers, he also tells others not to help them. And when they do help, he puts them out of the church.

¹¹Dear friend, don't let this bad example influence you. Follow only what is good. Remember that those who do good prove that they are God's children, and those who do evil prove that they do not know God. ¹²But everyone speaks highly of Demetrius, even truth itself. We ourselves can say the same for him, and you know we speak the truth.

## Conclusion

¹³I have much to tell you, but I don't want to do it in a letter. ¹⁴For I hope to see you soon, and then we will talk face to face.

¹⁵May God's peace be with you.

Your friends here send you their greetings. Please give my personal greetings to each of our friends there.

1 Greek *From the elder.*   5 Greek *the brothers;* also in verse 10.   7a Greek *the Name.*   7b Greek *from Gentiles.*

# Jude

## Greetings from Jude

This letter is from Jude, a slave of Jesus Christ and a brother of James.

I am writing to all who are called to live in the love of God the Father and the care of Jesus Christ.

2 May you receive more and more of God's mercy, peace, and love.

## The Danger of False Teachers

3 Dearly loved friends, I had been eagerly planning to write to you about the salvation we all share. But now I find that I must write about something else, urging you to defend the truth of the Good News.* God gave this unchanging truth once for all time to his holy people. 4 I say this because some godless people have wormed their way in among you, saying that God's forgiveness allows us to live immoral lives. The fate of such people was determined long ago, for they have turned against our only Master and Lord, Jesus Christ.

5 I must remind you—and you know it well—that even though the Lord* rescued the whole nation of Israel from Egypt, he later destroyed every one of those who did not remain faithful. 6 And I remind you of the angels who did not stay within the limits of authority God gave them but left the place where they belonged. God has kept them chained in prisons of darkness, waiting for the day of judgment. 7 And don't forget the cities of Sodom and Gomorrah and their neighboring towns, which were filled with sexual immorality and every kind of sexual perversion. Those cities were destroyed by fire and are a warning of the eternal fire that will punish all who are evil.

8 Yet these false teachers, who claim authority from their dreams, live immoral lives, defy authority, and scoff at the power of the glorious ones.* 9 But even Michael, one of the mightiest of the angels, did not dare accuse Satan of blasphemy, but simply said, "The Lord rebuke you." (This took place when Michael was arguing with Satan about Moses' body.) 10 But these people mock and curse the things they do not understand. Like animals, they do whatever their instincts tell them, and they bring about their own destruction. 11 How terrible it will be for them! For they follow the evil example of Cain, who killed his brother. Like Balaam, they will do anything for money. And like Korah, they will perish because of their rebellion.

12 When these people join you in fellowship meals celebrating the love of the Lord, they are like dangerous reefs that can shipwreck you.* They are shameless in the way they care only about themselves. They are like clouds blowing over dry land without giving rain, promising much but producing nothing. They are like trees without fruit at harvesttime. They are not only dead but doubly dead, for they have been pulled out by the roots. 13 They are like wild waves of the sea, churning up the dirty foam of their shameful deeds. They are wandering stars, heading for everlasting gloom and darkness.

14 Now Enoch, who lived seven generations after Adam, prophesied about these people. He said,

"Look, the Lord is coming
    with thousands of his holy ones.
15 He will bring the people of the world
    to judgment.

3 Greek *to contend for the faith.*   5 Some manuscripts read *Jesus.*   8 *The glorious ones* are probably evil angels.   12 Or *they are contaminants among you,* or *they are stains.*

He will convict the ungodly of all the evil
things
they have done in rebellion
and of all the insults that godless sinners
have spoken against him."*

16These people are grumblers and complainers, doing whatever evil they feel like. They are loud-mouthed braggarts, and they flatter others to get favors in return.

## A Call to Remain Faithful

17But you, my dear friends, must remember what the apostles of our Lord Jesus Christ told you, 18that in the last times there would be scoffers whose purpose in life is to enjoy themselves in every evil way imaginable. 19Now they are here, and they are the ones who are creating divisions among you. They live by natural instinct because they do not have God's Spirit living in them.

20But you, dear friends, must continue to build your lives on the foundation of your holy faith. And continue to pray as you are directed by the Holy Spirit.* 21Live in such a way that God's love can bless you as you wait for the eternal life that our Lord Jesus Christ in his mercy is going to give you. 22Show mercy to those whose faith is wavering. 23Rescue others by snatching them from the flames of judgment. There are still others to whom you need to show mercy, but be careful that you aren't contaminated by their sins.*

## A Prayer of Praise

24And now, all glory to God, who is able to keep you from stumbling, and who will bring you into his glorious presence innocent of sin and with great joy. 25All glory to him, who alone is God our Savior, through Jesus Christ our Lord. Yes, glory, majesty, power, and authority belong to him, in the beginning, now, and forevermore. Amen.

14-15 The quotation comes from the Apocrypha: Enoch 1:9.   20 Greek *Pray in the Holy Spirit.*   23 Greek *mercy, hating even the clothing stained by the flesh.*

# Revelation

## Prologue

This is a revelation from* Jesus Christ, which God gave him concerning the events that will happen soon. An angel was sent to God's servant John so that John could share the revelation with God's other servants. ²John faithfully reported the word of God and the testimony of Jesus Christ—everything he saw.

³God blesses the one who reads this prophecy to the church, and he blesses all who listen to it and obey what it says. For the time is near when these things will happen.

## John's Greeting to the Seven Churches

⁴This letter is from John to the seven churches in the province of Asia. Grace and peace from the one who is, who always was, and who is still to come; from the sevenfold Spirit* before his throne; ⁵and from Jesus Christ, who is the faithful witness to these things, the first to rise from the dead, and the commander of all the rulers of the world.

All praise to him who loves us and has freed us from our sins by shedding his blood for us. ⁶He has made us his kingdom and his priests who serve before God his Father. Give to him everlasting glory! He rules forever and ever! Amen!

⁷Look! He comes with the clouds of heaven. And everyone will see him—even those who pierced him. And all the nations of the earth will weep because of him. Yes! Amen!

⁸"I am the Alpha and the Omega—the beginning and the end," says the Lord God. "I am the one who is, who always was, and who is still to come, the Almighty One."

## Vision of the Son of Man

⁹I am John, your brother. In Jesus we are partners in suffering and in the Kingdom and in patient endurance. I was exiled to the island of Patmos for preaching the word of God and speaking about Jesus. ¹⁰It was the Lord's Day, and I was worshiping in the Spirit.* Suddenly, I heard a loud voice behind me, a voice that sounded like a trumpet blast. ¹¹It said, "Write down what you see, and send it to the seven churches: Ephesus, Smyrna, Pergamum, Thyatira, Sardis, Philadelphia, and Laodicea."

¹²When I turned to see who was speaking to me, I saw seven gold lampstands. ¹³And standing in the middle of the lampstands was the Son of Man.* He was wearing a long robe with a gold sash across his chest. ¹⁴His head and his hair were white like wool, as white as snow. And his eyes were bright like flames of fire. ¹⁵His feet were as bright as bronze refined in a furnace, and his voice thundered like mighty ocean waves. ¹⁶He held seven stars in his right hand, and a sharp two-edged sword came from his mouth. And his face was as bright as the sun in all its brilliance.

¹⁷When I saw him, I fell at his feet as dead. But he laid his right hand on me and said, "Don't be afraid! I am the First and the Last. ¹⁸I am the living one who died. Look, I am alive forever and ever! And I hold the keys of death and the grave.* ¹⁹Write down what you have seen—both the things that are now happening and the things that will happen later. ²⁰This is the meaning of the seven stars you saw in my right hand and the seven gold lampstands: The seven stars are the angels of* the seven churches, and the seven lampstands are the seven churches.

1:1 Or of.   1:4 Greek the seven spirits.   1:10 Or in spirit.   1:13 Or one who looked like a man; Greek reads one like a son of man. See Dan 7:13.   1:18 Greek and Hades.   1:20 Or the messengers for.

## Jesus Has an Eternal Dominion Read REVELATION 1:4-8

This passage of Scripture confirms two important aspects about Jesus Christ: his majesty and dominion. Yet Jesus is distinctly different than any type of royalty or government we are familiar with. The following six points show that difference:

**1. He Is the First to Rise from Death and Die No More.** Christ gives us a glimpse of what will happen after we die.

**2. He Is Greater than Any King in All the Earth.** He is Lord over all creation—no earthly leader can make that claim.

**3. He Loves Us and Demonstrated His Love by His Death.** Rarely has someone in authority over others offered to die in their place.

**4. He Has Set Us Free from Our Sins and Given Us a Place of Honor in His Kingdom.** For those of us who have received Jesus into our lives, he has given us a place of tremendous privilege and access to the throne of God.

**5. He Will Return Again in Triumph.** This king will draw the attention of the entire universe with his return.

**6. He Is Eternal.** He always has been and always will be. No one else but God could make that claim.

Some people have a rather stereotypical view of Jesus. They picture him as most artists have, with long, flowing hair—perhaps a staff in his hand and a lamb wrapped around his neck. Yet the Bible never does give us a description of Jesus' physical appearance. If it did, we would undoubtedly worship the image instead of the Lord. This description of Christ in Revelation—though it does not give us a physical picture—allows us to see the glorified Christ. And this Christ is full of power and majesty.

CORNER STONES

## CHAPTER 2

*The Message to the Church in Ephesus*

"Write this letter to the angel of* the church in Ephesus. This is the message from the one who holds the seven stars in his right hand, the one who walks among the seven gold lampstands:

2 "I know all the things you do. I have seen your hard work and your patient endurance. I know you don't tolerate evil people. You have examined the claims of those who say they are apostles but are not. You have discovered they are liars. 3 You have patiently suffered for me without quitting. 4 But I have this complaint against you. You don't love me or each other as you did at first! 5 Look how far you have fallen from your first love! Turn back to me again and work as you did at first. If you don't, I will come and remove your lampstand from its place among the churches. 6 But there is

this about you that is good: You hate the deeds of the immoral Nicolaitans, just as I do.

7 "Anyone who is willing to hear should listen to the Spirit and understand what the Spirit is saying to the churches. Everyone who is victorious will eat from the tree of life in the paradise of God.

*The Message to the Church in Smyrna*

8 "Write this letter to the angel of the church in Smyrna. This is the message from the one who is the First and the Last, who died and is alive:

9 "I know about your suffering and your poverty—but you are rich! I know the slander of those opposing you. They say they are Jews, but they really aren't because theirs is a synagogue of Satan. 10 Don't be afraid of what you are about to suffer. The Devil will throw some of you into prison

2:1 Or *the messenger for;* also in 2:8, 12, 18.

and put you to the test. You will be persecuted for 'ten days.' Remain faithful even when facing death, and I will give you the crown of life.

11 "Anyone who is willing to hear should listen to the Spirit and understand what the Spirit is saying to the churches. Whoever is victorious will not be hurt by the second death.

### The Message to the Church in Pergamum

12 "Write this letter to the angel of the church in Pergamum. This is the message from the one who has a sharp two-edged sword:

13 "I know that you live in the city where that great throne of Satan is located, and yet you have remained loyal to me. And you refused to deny me even when Antipas, my faithful witness, was martyred among you by Satan's followers. 14 And yet I have a few complaints against you. You tolerate some among you who are like Balaam, who showed Balak how to trip up the people of Israel. He taught them to worship idols by eating food offered to idols and by committing sexual sin. 15 In the same way, you have some Nicolaitans among you—people who follow the same teaching and commit the same sins. 16 Repent, or I will come to you suddenly and fight against them with the sword of my mouth.

17 "Anyone who is willing to hear should listen to the Spirit and understand what the Spirit is saying to the churches. Everyone who is victorious will eat of the manna that has been hidden away in heaven. And I will give to each one a white stone, and on the stone will be engraved a new name that no one knows except the one who receives it.

### The Message to the Church in Thyatira

18 "Write this letter to the angel of the church in Thyatira. This is the message from the Son of God, whose eyes are bright like flames of fire, whose feet are like polished bronze:

19 "I know all the things you do—your love, your faith, your service, and your patient endurance. And I can see your constant improvement in all these things. 20 But I have this complaint against you. You are permitting that woman—that Jezebel who calls herself a prophet—to lead my servants astray. She is encouraging them to worship idols, eat food offered to idols, and commit sexual sin. 21 I gave her time to repent, but she would not turn away from her immorality. 22 Therefore, I will throw her upon a sickbed, and she will suffer greatly with all who commit adultery with her, unless they turn away from all their evil deeds. 23 I will strike her children dead. And all the churches will know that I am the one who searches out the thoughts and intentions of every person. And I will give to each of you whatever you deserve. 24 But I also have a message for the rest of you in Thyatira who have not followed this false teaching ('deeper truths,' as they call them—depths of Satan, really). I will ask nothing more of you 25 except that you hold tightly to what you have until I come.

26 "To all who are victorious, who obey me to the very end, I will give authority over all the nations. 27 They will rule the nations with an iron rod and smash them like clay pots. 28 They will have the same authority I received from my Father, and I will also give them the morning star! 29 Anyone who is willing to hear should listen to the Spirit and understand what the Spirit is saying to the churches.

## CHAPTER 3

### The Message to the Church in Sardis

"Write this letter to the angel of* the church in Sardis. This is the message from the one who has the sevenfold Spirit* of God and the seven stars:

"I know all the things you do, and that you have a reputation for being alive—but you are dead. 2 Now wake up! Strengthen what little remains, for even what is left is at the point of death. Your deeds are far from right in the sight of God. 3 Go back to what you heard and believed at first; hold to it firmly and turn to me again. Unless you do, I will come upon you suddenly, as unexpected as a thief.

4 "Yet even in Sardis there are some who have not soiled their garments with evil deeds. They will walk with me in white, for they are worthy. 5 All who are victorious will be clothed in white. I will never erase their names from the Book of Life, but I will announce before my Father and his angels

3:1a Or *the messenger for;* also in 3:7, 14.   3:1b Greek *the seven spirits.*

that they are mine. 6Anyone who is willing to hear should listen to the Spirit and understand what the Spirit is saying to the churches.

### The Message to the Church in Philadelphia

7"Write this letter to the angel of the church in Philadelphia. This is the message from the one who is holy and true. He is the one who has the key of David. He opens doors, and no one can shut them; he shuts doors, and no one can open them.

8"I know all the things you do, and I have opened a door for you that no one can shut. You have little strength, yet you obeyed my word and did not deny me. 9Look! I will force those who belong to Satan—those liars who say they are Jews but are not—to come and bow down at your feet. They will acknowledge that you are the ones I love.

10"Because you have obeyed my command to persevere, I will protect you from the great time of testing that will come upon the whole world to test those who belong to this world. 11Look, I am coming quickly. Hold on to what you have, so that no one will take away your crown. 12All who are victorious will become pillars in the Temple of my God, and they will never have to leave it. And I will write my God's name on them, and they will be citizens in the city of my God—the new Jerusalem that comes down from heaven from my God. And they will have my new name inscribed upon them. 13Anyone who is willing to hear should listen to the Spirit and understand what the Spirit is saying to the churches.

### The Message to the Church in Laodicea

14"Write this letter to the angel of the church in Laodicea. This is the message from the one who is the Amen—the faithful and true witness, the ruler* of God's creation:

15"I know all the things you do, that you are neither hot nor cold. I wish you were one or the other! 16But since you are like lukewarm water, I will spit you out of my mouth! 17You say, 'I am rich. I have everything I want. I don't need a thing!' And you don't realize that you are wretched and miserable and poor and blind and naked. 18I advise you to buy gold from me—gold that has been purified by fire. Then you will be rich. And also buy white garments so you will not be shamed by your nakedness. And buy ointment for your eyes so you will be able to see. 19I am the one who corrects and disciplines everyone I love. Be diligent and turn from your indifference.

20"Look! Here I stand at the door and knock. If you hear me calling and open the door, I will come in, and we will share a meal as friends. 21I will invite everyone who is victorious to sit with me on my throne, just as I was victorious and sat with my Father on his throne. 22Anyone who is willing to hear should listen to the Spirit and understand what the Spirit is saying to the churches."

## CHAPTER 4
### Worship in Heaven

Then as I looked, I saw a door standing open in heaven, and the same voice I had heard before spoke to me with the sound of a mighty trumpet blast. The voice said, "Come up here, and I will show you what must happen after these things." 2And instantly I was in the Spirit,* and I saw a throne in heaven and someone sitting on it! 3The one sitting on the throne was as brilliant as gemstones—jasper and carnelian. And the glow of an emerald circled his throne like a rainbow. 4Twenty-four thrones surrounded him, and twenty-four elders sat on them. They were all clothed in white and had gold crowns on their heads. 5And from the throne came flashes of lightning and the rumble of thunder. And in front of the throne were seven lampstands with burning flames. They are the seven spirits* of God. 6In front of the throne was a shiny sea of glass, sparkling like crystal.

In the center and around the throne were four living beings, each covered with eyes, front and back. 7The first of these living beings had the form of a lion; the second looked like an ox; the third had a human face; and the fourth had the form of an eagle with wings spread out as though in flight. 8Each of these living beings had six wings, and their wings were covered with eyes, inside and out. Day after day and night after night they keep on saying,

3:14 Or *the source.*   4:2 Or *in spirit.*   4:5 See 1:4 and 3:1, where the same expression is translated *the sevenfold Spirit.*

"Holy, holy, holy is the Lord God
Almighty—
the one who always was, who is, and
who is still to come."

9Whenever the living beings give glory and
honor and thanks to the one sitting on the
throne, the one who lives forever and ever, 10the
twenty-four elders fall down and worship the
one who lives forever and ever. And they lay
their crowns before the throne and say,

11 "You are worthy, O Lord our God,
to receive glory and honor and power.
For you created everything,
and it is for your pleasure that they exist
and were created."

## CHAPTER 5
### The Lamb Opens the Scroll

And I saw a scroll in the right hand of the one
who was sitting on the throne. There was writing
on the inside and the outside of the scroll, and
it was sealed with seven seals. 2And I saw a
strong angel, who shouted with a loud voice:
"Who is worthy to break the seals on this scroll
and unroll it?" 3But no one in heaven or on
earth or under the earth was able to open the
scroll and read it.

4Then I wept because no one could be found
who was worthy to open the scroll and read it.
5But one of the twenty-four elders said to me,
"Stop weeping! Look, the Lion of the tribe of
Judah, the heir to David's throne,* has conquered. He is worthy to open the scroll and
break its seven seals."

6I looked and I saw a Lamb that had been
killed but was now standing between the throne
and the four living beings and among the
twenty-four elders. He had seven horns and
seven eyes, which are the seven spirits* of God
that are sent out into every part of the earth. 7He
stepped forward and took the scroll from the
right hand of the one sitting on the throne. 8And
as he took the scroll, the four living beings and
the twenty-four elders fell down before the
Lamb. Each one had a harp, and they held gold
bowls filled with incense—the prayers of God's
people!

9And they sang a new song with these words:

"You are worthy to take the scroll
and break its seals and open it.

For you were killed, and your blood has
ransomed people for God
from every tribe and language and
people and nation.
10 And you have caused them to become
God's kingdom and his priests.
And they will reign* on the earth."

11Then I looked again, and I heard the singing
of thousands and millions of angels around the
throne and the living beings and the elders.
12And they sang in a mighty chorus:

"The Lamb is worthy—the Lamb who was
killed.
He is worthy to receive power and riches
and wisdom and strength
and honor and glory and blessing."

13And then I heard every creature in heaven
and on earth and under the earth and in the sea.
They also sang:

"Blessing and honor and glory and power
belong to the one sitting on the throne
and to the Lamb forever and ever."

14And the four living beings said, "Amen!"
And the twenty-four elders fell down and worshiped God and the Lamb.

## CHAPTER 6
### The Lamb Breaks the First Six Seals

As I watched, the Lamb broke the first of the
seven seals on the scroll. Then one of the four
living beings called out with a voice that
sounded like thunder, "Come!" 2I looked up
and saw a white horse. Its rider carried a bow,
and a crown was placed on his head. He rode out
to win many battles and gain the victory.

3When the Lamb broke the second seal, I
heard the second living being say, "Come!"
4And another horse appeared, a red one. Its rider
was given a mighty sword and the authority to
remove peace from the earth. And there was war
and slaughter everywhere.

5When the Lamb broke the third seal, I heard
the third living being say, "Come!" And I looked
up and saw a black horse, and its rider was
holding a pair of scales in his hand. 6And a voice
from among the four living beings said, "A loaf
of wheat bread or three loaves of barley for a
day's pay.* And don't waste* the olive oil and
wine."

7And when the Lamb broke the fourth seal, I

5:5 Greek *the root of David.*  5:6 See note on 4:5.  5:10 Some manuscripts read *they are reigning.*  6:6a Greek *A choinix of wheat for a
denarius, and 3 choinix of barley for a denarius.*  6:6b Or *hurt.*

## What Will Life in Heaven Be Like? Read REVELATION 7:13-17

The apostle Paul had a taste of heaven, either through a vision or by actually dying. He wrote about his experience in 2 Corinthians 12:2-4. Upon entering God's presence, he said, "I was caught up into paradise." The word *paradise* literally means "the royal garden of a king with all kinds of fruit and flowers." This passage of Scripture shows us four aspects of the life we will live in the wonderful place called paradise:

**1. We Will Live a Life without Fear and Worry.** Heaven is a place of protection (verse 15). We will have no reason to fear anything there. We won't find bars on windows, crime on the streets, or any other type of violence. God will be our shelter.

**2. We Will Live a Life without Need.** Heaven is a place of complete sufficiency (verse 16). Hunger and thirst will not be a part of our vocabulary there. That is because the Lord will feed us and quench our thirst.

**3. We Will Live a Life without Pain.** Heaven is a place of comfort (verse 16). Elsewhere, the Bible says that in heaven "there will be no more death or sorrow or crying or pain" (Revelation 21:4). Our heavenly bodies will not be subjected to the illnesses, aches, and pains that we know so well here on earth.

**4. We Will Live a Life without Sorrow.** Heaven is a place of joy (verse 17). Being in God's presence is a joyful and wonderful experience. Sorrow will not be found in heaven, and God will wipe away all of our tears.

While we can look forward to the glories of heaven, one thing far outweighs them all: the fact that we will be able to spend eternity with Jesus. Dwight L. Moody once wrote, "It is not the jeweled walls and pearly gates that are going to make heaven attractive. It is being with God." May that truth inspire you as you live out your life on this earth.

CORNER STONES

heard the fourth living being say, "Come!" ⁸And I looked up and saw a horse whose color was pale green like a corpse. And Death was the name of its rider, who was followed around by the Grave.* They were given authority over one-fourth of the earth, to kill with the sword and famine and disease* and wild animals.

⁹And when the Lamb broke the fifth seal, I saw under the altar the souls of all who had been martyred for the word of God and for being faithful in their witness. ¹⁰They called loudly to the Lord and said, "O Sovereign Lord, holy and true, how long will it be before you judge the people who belong to this world for what they have done to us? When will you avenge our blood against these people?" ¹¹Then a white robe was given to each of them. And they were told to rest a little longer until the full number of their brothers and sisters*—their fellow servants of Jesus—had been martyred.

¹²I watched as the Lamb broke the sixth seal, and there was a great earthquake. The sun became as dark as black cloth, and the moon became as red as blood. ¹³Then the stars of the sky fell to the earth like green figs falling from trees shaken by mighty winds. ¹⁴And the sky was rolled up like a scroll and taken away. And all of the mountains and all of the islands disappeared. ¹⁵Then the kings of the earth, the rulers, the generals, the wealthy people, the people with great power, and every slave and every free person—all hid themselves in the caves and among the rocks of the mountains. ¹⁶And they cried to the mountains and the rocks, "Fall on us and hide us from the face of the one who sits on the throne and from the wrath of the Lamb. ¹⁷For the great day of their wrath has come, and who will be able to survive?"

6:8a Greek *by Hades.*   6:8b Greek *death.*   6:11 Greek *their brothers.*

## CHAPTER 7
*God's People Will Be Preserved*
Then I saw four angels standing at the four corners of the earth, holding back the four winds from blowing upon the earth. Not a leaf rustled in the trees, and the sea became as smooth as glass. 2And I saw another angel coming from the east, carrying the seal of the living God. And he shouted out to those four angels who had been given power to injure land and sea, 3"Wait! Don't hurt the land or the sea or the trees until we have placed the seal of God on the foreheads of his servants."

4And I heard how many were marked with the seal of God. There were 144,000 who were sealed from all the tribes of Israel:

| | | |
|---|---|---|
| 5 | from Judah | 12,000 |
| | from Reuben | 12,000 |
| | from Gad | 12,000 |
| 6 | from Asher | 12,000 |
| | from Naphtali | 12,000 |
| | from Manasseh | 12,000 |
| 7 | from Simeon | 12,000 |
| | from Levi | 12,000 |
| | from Issachar | 12,000 |
| 8 | from Zebulun | 12,000 |
| | from Joseph | 12,000 |
| | from Benjamin | 12,000 |

*Praise from the Great Multitude*
9After this I saw a vast crowd, too great to count, from every nation and tribe and people and language, standing in front of the throne and before the Lamb. They were clothed in white and held palm branches in their hands. 10And they were shouting with a mighty shout, "Salvation comes from our God on the throne and from the Lamb!"

11And all the angels were standing around the throne and around the elders and the four living beings. And they fell face down before the throne and worshiped God. 12They said,

"Amen! Blessing and glory and wisdom
  and thanksgiving and honor and power
  and strength
  belong to our God forever and forever.
  Amen!"

13Then one of the twenty-four elders asked me, "Who are these who are clothed in white? Where do they come from?"

14And I said to him, "Sir, you are the one who knows."

Then he said to me, "These are the ones coming out of the great tribulation. They washed their robes in the blood of the Lamb and made them white. 15That is why they are standing in front of the throne of God, serving him day and night in his Temple. And he who sits on the throne will live among them and shelter them. 16They will never again be hungry or thirsty, and they will be fully protected from the scorching noontime heat. 17For the Lamb who stands in front of the throne will be their Shepherd. He will lead them to the springs of life-giving water. And God will wipe away all their tears."

## CHAPTER 8
*The Lamb Breaks the Seventh Seal*
When the Lamb broke the seventh seal, there was silence throughout heaven for about half an hour. 2And I saw the seven angels who stand before God, and they were given seven trumpets.

3Then another angel with a gold incense burner came and stood at the altar. And a great quantity of incense was given to him to mix with the prayers of God's people, to be offered on the gold altar before the throne. 4The smoke of the incense, mixed with the prayers of the saints, ascended up to God from the altar where the angel had poured them out. 5Then the angel filled the incense burner with fire from the altar and threw it down upon the earth; and thunder crashed, lightning flashed, and there was a terrible earthquake.

*The First Four Trumpets*
6Then the seven angels with the seven trumpets prepared to blow their mighty blasts.

7The first angel blew his trumpet, and hail and fire mixed with blood were thrown down upon the earth, and one-third of the earth was set on fire. One-third of the trees were burned, and all the grass was burned.

8Then the second angel blew his trumpet, and a great mountain of fire was thrown into the sea. And one-third of the water in the sea became blood. 9And one-third of all things living in the sea died. And one-third of all the ships on the sea were destroyed.

10Then the third angel blew his trumpet, and a great flaming star fell out of the sky, burning like a torch. It fell upon one-third of the rivers and on the springs of water. 11The name of the star was Bitterness.* It made one-third of the

8:11 Greek *Wormwood.*

water bitter, and many people died because the water was so bitter.

12Then the fourth angel blew his trumpet, and one-third of the sun was struck, and one-third of the moon, and one-third of the stars, and they became dark. And one-third of the day was dark and one-third of the night also.

13Then I looked up. And I heard a single eagle crying loudly as it flew through the air, "Terror, terror, terror to all who belong to this world because of what will happen when the last three angels blow their trumpets."

## CHAPTER 9
### The Fifth Trumpet Brings the First Terror

Then the fifth angel blew his trumpet, and I saw a star that had fallen to earth from the sky, and he was given the key to the shaft of the bottomless pit. 2When he opened it, smoke poured out as though from a huge furnace, and the sunlight and air were darkened by the smoke.

3Then locusts came from the smoke and descended on the earth, and they were given power to sting like scorpions. 4They were told not to hurt the grass or plants or trees but to attack all the people who did not have the seal of God on their foreheads. 5They were told not to kill them but to torture them for five months with agony like the pain of scorpion stings. 6In those days people will seek death but will not find it. They will long to die, but death will flee away!

7The locusts looked like horses armed for battle. They had gold crowns on their heads, and they had human faces. 8Their hair was long like the hair of a woman, and their teeth were like the teeth of a lion. 9They wore armor made of iron, and their wings roared like an army of chariots rushing into battle. 10They had tails that stung like scorpions, with power to torture people. This power was given to them for five months. 11Their king is the angel from the bottomless pit; his name in Hebrew is *Abaddon*, and in Greek, *Apollyon*—the Destroyer.

12The first terror is past, but look, two more terrors are coming!

### The Sixth Trumpet Brings the Second Terror

13Then the sixth angel blew his trumpet, and I heard a voice speaking from the four horns of the gold altar that stands in the presence of God. 14And the voice spoke to the sixth angel who held the trumpet: "Release the four angels who are bound at the great Euphrates River." 15And the four angels who had been prepared for this

hour and day and month and year were turned loose to kill one-third of all the people on earth. 16They led an army of 200 million mounted troops—I heard an announcement of how many there were.

17And in my vision, I saw the horses and the riders sitting on them. The riders wore armor that was fiery red and sky blue and yellow. The horses' heads were like the heads of lions, and fire and smoke and burning sulfur billowed from their mouths. 18One-third of all the people on earth were killed by these three plagues—by the fire and the smoke and burning sulfur that came from the mouths of the horses. 19Their power was in their mouths, but also in their tails. For their tails had heads like snakes, with the power to injure people.

20But the people who did not die in these plagues still refused to turn from their evil deeds. They continued to worship demons and idols made of gold, silver, bronze, stone, and wood—idols that neither see nor hear nor walk! 21And they did not repent of their murders or their witchcraft or their immorality or their thefts.

## CHAPTER 10
### The Angel and the Small Scroll

Then I saw another mighty angel coming down from heaven, surrounded by a cloud, with a rainbow over his head. His face shone like the sun, and his feet were like pillars of fire. 2And in his hand was a small scroll, which he had unrolled. He stood with his right foot on the sea and his left foot on the land. 3And he gave a great shout, like the roar of a lion. And when he shouted, the seven thunders answered.

4When the seven thunders spoke, I was about to write. But a voice from heaven called to me: "Keep secret what the seven thunders said. Do not write it down."

5Then the mighty angel standing on the sea and on the land lifted his right hand to heaven. 6And he swore an oath in the name of the one who lives forever and ever, who created heaven and everything in it, the earth and everything in it, and the sea and everything in it. He said, "God will wait no longer. 7But when the seventh angel blows his trumpet, God's mysterious plan will be fulfilled. It will happen just as he announced it to his servants the prophets."

8Then the voice from heaven called to me again: "Go and take the unrolled scroll from the angel who is standing on the sea and on the land."

9So I approached him and asked him to give me the little scroll. "Yes, take it and eat it," he said. "At first it will taste like honey, but when you swallow it, it will make your stomach sour!" 10So I took the little scroll from the hands of the angel, and I ate it! It was sweet in my mouth, but it made my stomach sour. 11Then he said to me, "You must prophesy again about many peoples, nations, languages, and kings."

## CHAPTER 11
### The Two Witnesses

Then I was given a measuring stick, and I was told, "Go and measure the Temple of God and the altar, and count the number of worshipers. 2But do not measure the outer courtyard, for it has been turned over to the nations. They will trample the holy city for 42 months. 3And I will give power to my two witnesses, and they will be clothed in sackcloth and will prophesy during those 1,260 days."

4These two prophets are the two olive trees and the two lampstands that stand before the Lord of all the earth. 5If anyone tries to harm them, fire flashes from the mouths of the prophets and consumes their enemies. This is how anyone who tries to harm them must die. 6They have power to shut the skies so that no rain will fall for as long as they prophesy. And they have the power to turn the rivers and oceans into blood, and to send every kind of plague upon the earth as often as they wish.

7When they complete their testimony, the beast that comes up out of the bottomless pit will declare war against them. He will conquer them and kill them. 8And their bodies will lie in the main street of Jerusalem,* the city which is called "Sodom" and "Egypt," the city where their Lord was crucified. 9And for three and a half days, all peoples, tribes, languages, and nations will come to stare at their bodies. No one will be allowed to bury them. 10All the people who belong to this world will give presents to each other to celebrate the death of the two prophets who had tormented them.

11But after three and a half days, the spirit of life from God entered them, and they stood up! And terror struck all who were staring at them. 12Then a loud voice shouted from heaven, "Come up here!" And they rose to heaven in a cloud as their enemies watched.

11:8 Greek the great city.

13And in the same hour there was a terrible earthquake that destroyed a tenth of the city. Seven thousand people died in that earthquake. And everyone who did not die was terrified and gave glory to the God of heaven.

14The second terror is past, but look, now the third terror is coming quickly.

### The Seventh Trumpet Brings the Third Terror

15Then the seventh angel blew his trumpet, and there were loud voices shouting in heaven: "The whole world has now become the kingdom of our Lord and of his Christ, and he will reign forever and ever."

16And the twenty-four elders sitting on their thrones before God fell on their faces and worshiped him. 17And they said,

"We give thanks to you, Lord God Almighty,
    the one who is and who always was,
for now you have assumed your great power
    and have begun to reign.
18 The nations were angry with you,
    but now the time of your wrath has come.
It is time to judge the dead and reward your
        servants.
You will reward your prophets and your
        holy people,
    all who fear your name, from the least to
        the greatest.
And you will destroy all who have caused
        destruction on the earth."

19Then, in heaven, the Temple of God was opened and the Ark of his covenant could be seen inside the Temple. Lightning flashed, thunder crashed and roared; there was a great hailstorm, and the world was shaken by a mighty earthquake.

## CHAPTER 12
### The Woman and the Dragon

Then I witnessed in heaven an event of great significance. I saw a woman clothed with the sun, with the moon beneath her feet, and a crown of twelve stars on her head. 2She was pregnant, and she cried out in the pain of labor as she awaited her delivery.

3Suddenly, I witnessed in heaven another significant event. I saw a large red dragon with seven heads and ten horns, with seven crowns on his heads. 4His tail dragged down one-third of the stars, which he threw to the earth. He stood before the woman as she was about to give

## Who Can Thwart Satan's Agenda? Read REVELATION 12:10-12

God uses his faithful followers to ruin Satan's plans. Here we see three significant ways these martyrs for the gospel overcame the Devil's attacks:

**1. They Overcame Him by the Blood of the Lamb.** The Bible says, "Without the shedding of blood, there is no forgiveness of sins" (Hebrews 9:22). It is only through what Jesus did for us on the cross that we can approach God. These people knew that they could never go to heaven or overcome Satan's accusations on their own merit or ability. They realized that they had fallen short of God's ideal, but they also knew that the blood of Jesus "cleanses us from every sin" (1 John 1:7).

**2. They Overcame Him by Their Testimony.** The believers described in these verses had come to understand what God had done for them and were proclaiming it to others. They not only realized that they had unconditional access to God, but they also sought to "invade enemy territory" by reaching out to others with the message of the gospel.

**3. They Overcame Him by Their Attitude toward Life.** These believers did not love their lives more than Christ. They endured execution for their faith because they realized that a better life was awaiting them in heaven with Christ. As the apostle Paul said, "For to me, living is for Christ, and dying is even better" (Philippians 1:21).

History relates the story of a Christian who was persecuted by Rome for his faith. As he stood before the emperor, he was told, "Give up Christ. If you don't, I'll banish you."

The Christian replied, "You cannot banish me from Christ, for God says, 'I will never leave you or forsake you.'_"

The ruler said, "I'll confiscate your property."

The Christian patiently responded, "My treasures are laid up in heaven. You can't touch them."

The emperor shot back, "I'll kill you!"

The Christian answered, "I've been dead to the world in Christ for forty years. My life is hid with Christ in God. You can't touch it."

The emperor turned to some of the members of his court and said in disgust, "What can you do with such a fanatic?"

*May God give his church more men like this man.*

**CORNER STONES**

---

birth to her child, ready to devour the baby as soon as it was born.

⁵She gave birth to a boy who was to rule all nations with an iron rod. And the child was snatched away from the dragon and was caught up to God and to his throne. ⁶And the woman fled into the wilderness, where God had prepared a place to give her care for 1,260 days.

⁷Then there was war in heaven. Michael and the angels under his command fought the dragon and his angels. ⁸And the dragon lost the battle and was forced out of heaven. ⁹This great dragon—the ancient serpent called the Devil, or Satan, the one deceiving the whole world—was thrown down to the earth with all his angels.

12:10 Greek *brothers.*

¹⁰Then I heard a loud voice shouting across the heavens,

"It has happened at last—the salvation and power and kingdom of our God, and the authority of his Christ! For the Accuser has been thrown down to earth—the one who accused our brothers and sisters* before our God day and night. ¹¹And they have defeated him because of the blood of the Lamb and because of their testimony. And they were not afraid to die. ¹²Rejoice, O heavens! And you who live in the heavens, rejoice! But terror will come on the earth and the sea. For the Devil has come down to you in great anger, and he knows that he has little time."

13And when the dragon realized that he had been thrown down to the earth, he pursued the woman who had given birth to the child. 14But she was given two wings like those of a great eagle. This allowed her to fly to a place prepared for her in the wilderness, where she would be cared for and protected from the dragon* for a time, times, and half a time.

15Then the dragon tried to drown the woman with a flood of water that flowed from its mouth. 16But the earth helped her by opening its mouth and swallowing the river that gushed out from the mouth of the dragon. 17Then the dragon became angry at the woman, and he declared war against the rest of her children—all who keep God's commandments and confess that they belong to Jesus.

## The Beast out of the Sea

18Then he stood* waiting on the shore of the sea.

CHAPTER **13**

And now in my vision I saw a beast rising up out of the sea. It had seven heads and ten horns, with ten crowns on its horns. And written on each head were names that blasphemed God. 2This beast looked like a leopard, but it had bear's feet and a lion's mouth! And the dragon gave him his own power and throne and great authority.

3I saw that one of the heads of the beast seemed wounded beyond recovery—but the fatal wound was healed! All the world marveled at this miracle and followed the beast in awe. 4They worshiped the dragon for giving the beast such power, and they worshiped the beast. "Is there anyone as great as the beast?" they exclaimed. "Who is able to fight against him?"

5Then the beast was allowed to speak great blasphemies against God. And he was given authority to do what he wanted for forty-two months. 6And he spoke terrible words of blasphemy against God, slandering his name and all who live in heaven, who are his temple. 7And the beast was allowed to wage war against God's holy people and to overcome them. And he was given authority to rule over every tribe and people and language and nation. 8And all the people who belong to this world worshiped the beast. They are the ones whose names were not written in the Book of Life, which belongs to the Lamb who was killed before the world was made.

9Anyone who is willing to hear should listen and understand. 10The people who are destined for prison will be arrested and taken away. Those who are destined for death will be killed. But do not be dismayed, for here is your opportunity to have endurance and faith.

## The Beast out of the Earth

11Then I saw another beast come up out of the earth. He had two horns like those of a lamb, and he spoke with the voice of a dragon. 12He exercised all the authority of the first beast. And he required all the earth and those who belong to this world to worship the first beast, whose death-wound had been healed. 13He did astounding miracles, such as making fire flash down to earth from heaven while everyone was watching. 14And with all the miracles he was allowed to perform on behalf of the first beast, he deceived all the people who belong to this world. He ordered the people of the world to make a great statue of the first beast, who was fatally wounded and then came back to life. 15He was permitted to give life to this statue so that it could speak. Then the statue commanded that anyone refusing to worship it must die.

16He required everyone—great and small, rich and poor, slave and free—to be given a mark on the right hand or on the forehead. 17And no one could buy or sell anything without that mark, which was either the name of the beast or the number representing his name. 18Wisdom is needed to understand this. Let the one who has understanding solve the number of the beast, for it is the number of a man.* His number is 666.*

CHAPTER **14**
## The Lamb and the 144,000

Then I saw the Lamb standing on Mount Zion, and with him were 144,000 who had his name and his Father's name written on their foreheads. 2And I heard a sound from heaven like the roaring of a great waterfall or the rolling of mighty thunder. It was like the sound of many harpists playing together.

3This great choir sang a wonderful new song in front of the throne of God and before the four living beings and the twenty-four elders. And no one could learn this song except those 144,000 who had been redeemed from the earth. 4For they are spiritually undefiled, pure as virgins,*

12:14 Greek *the serpent;* also in 12:15. See 12:9.   12:18 Some manuscripts read *Then I stood,* and some translations put this entire sentence into 13:1.   13:18a Or *of humanity.*   13:18b Some manuscripts read *616.*   14:4a Greek *they are virgins who have not defiled themselves with women.*

## What Role Will Angels Play in the End Times? Read REVELATION 14:6-7

The Bible tells us that the last days are going to be spiritually dark. Many people will be deceived into believing "teachings that come from demons" (see 1 Timothy 4:1, p. 271), and people will become increasingly immoral, proud, and disobedient (see 2 Timothy 3:1-5, p. 277). We already see this beginning to happen. There is a fresh demand for psychics, an increasing amount of violent crime on the streets, and a blatant lack of values in much of entertainment today.

This text shows that during the Tribulation, which is generally recognized as the last seven years on earth before Christ's return, the demons will not be the only ones at work. The angels of God will fly through the heavens preaching the everlasting gospel to make sure that everyone throughout the world is aware of the upcoming judgment of God. In essence, it will be the final "wake-up call" for people to turn to Jesus Christ.

CORNER STONES

following the Lamb wherever he goes. They have been purchased from among the people on the earth as a special offering* to God and to the Lamb. 5No falsehood can be charged against them; they are blameless.

### The Three Angels

6And I saw another angel flying through the heavens, carrying the everlasting Good News to preach to the people who belong to this world—to every nation, tribe, language, and people. 7"Fear God," he shouted. "Give glory to him. For the time has come when he will sit as judge. Worship him who made heaven and earth, the sea, and all the springs of water."

8Then another angel followed him through the skies, shouting, "Babylon is fallen—that great city is fallen—because she seduced the nations of the world and made them drink the wine of her passionate immorality."

9Then a third angel followed them, shouting, "Anyone who worships the beast and his statue or who accepts his mark on the forehead or the hand 10must drink the wine of God's wrath. It is poured out undiluted into God's cup of wrath. And they will be tormented with fire and burning sulfur in the presence of the holy angels and the Lamb. 11The smoke of their torment rises forever and ever, and they will have no relief day or night, for they have worshiped the beast and his statue and have accepted the mark of his name. 12Let this encourage God's holy people to endure persecution patiently and remain firm to the end, obeying his commands and trusting in Jesus."

13And I heard a voice from heaven saying, "Write this down: Blessed are those who die in the Lord from now on. Yes, says the Spirit, they are blessed indeed, for they will rest from all their toils and trials; for their good deeds follow them!"

### The Harvest of the Earth

14Then I saw the Son of Man* sitting on a white cloud. He had a gold crown on his head and a sharp sickle in his hand.

15Then an angel came from the Temple and called out in a loud voice to the one sitting on the cloud, "Use the sickle, for the time has come for you to harvest; the crop is ripe on the earth." 16So the one sitting on the cloud swung his sickle over the earth, and the whole earth was harvested.

17After that, another angel came from the Temple in heaven, and he also had a sharp sickle. 18Then another angel, who has power to destroy the world with fire, shouted to the angel with the sickle, "Use your sickle now to gather the clusters of grapes from the vines of the earth, for they are fully ripe for judgment." 19So the angel swung his sickle on the earth and loaded the grapes into the great winepress of God's wrath. 20And the grapes were trodden in the winepress outside the city, and blood flowed from the winepress in a stream about 180 miles* long and as high as a horse's bridle.

14:4b Greek *as firstfruits.* 14:14 Or *one who looked like a man;* Greek reads *one like a son of man.* 14:20 Greek *1,600 stadia* [296 kilometers].

# CHAPTER **15**
*The Song of Moses and of the Lamb*
Then I saw in heaven another significant event, and it was great and marvelous. Seven angels were holding the seven last plagues, which would bring God's wrath to completion. ²I saw before me what seemed to be a crystal sea mixed with fire. And on it stood all the people who had been victorious over the beast and his statue and the number representing his name. They were all holding harps that God had given them. ³And they were singing the song of Moses, the servant of God, and the song of the Lamb:

"Great and marvelous are your actions,
  Lord God Almighty.
Just and true are your ways,
  O King of the nations.*
⁴ Who will not fear, O Lord, and glorify your
    name?
  For you alone are holy.
All nations will come and worship before
    you,
  for your righteous deeds have been
    revealed."

*The Seven Bowls of the Seven Plagues*
⁵Then I looked and saw that the Temple in heaven, God's Tabernacle, was thrown wide open! ⁶The seven angels who were holding the bowls of the seven plagues came from the Temple, clothed in spotless white linen* with gold belts across their chests. ⁷And one of the four living beings handed each of the seven angels a gold bowl filled with the terrible wrath of God, who lives forever and forever. ⁸The Temple was filled with smoke from God's glory and power. No one could enter the Temple until the seven angels had completed pouring out the seven plagues.

# CHAPTER **16**
Then I heard a mighty voice shouting from the Temple to the seven angels, "Now go your ways and empty out the seven bowls of God's wrath on the earth."

²So the first angel left the Temple and poured out his bowl over the earth, and horrible, malignant sores broke out on everyone who had the mark of the beast and who worshiped his statue.

³Then the second angel poured out his bowl on the sea, and it became like the blood of a corpse. And everything in the sea died.

⁴Then the third angel poured out his bowl on the rivers and springs, and they became blood. ⁵And I heard the angel who had authority over all water saying, "You are just in sending this judgment, O Holy One, who is and who always was. ⁶For your holy people and your prophets have been killed, and their blood was poured out on the earth. So you have given their murderers blood to drink. It is their just reward." ⁷And I heard a voice from the altar saying, "Yes, Lord God Almighty, your punishments are true and just."

⁸Then the fourth angel poured out his bowl on the sun, causing it to scorch everyone with its fire. ⁹Everyone was burned by this blast of heat, and they cursed the name of God, who sent all of these plagues. They did not repent and give him glory.

¹⁰Then the fifth angel poured out his bowl on the throne of the beast, and his kingdom was plunged into darkness. And his subjects ground their teeth in anguish, ¹¹and they cursed the God of heaven for their pains and sores. But they refused to repent of all their evil deeds.

¹²Then the sixth angel poured out his bowl on the great Euphrates River, and it dried up so that the kings from the east could march their armies westward without hindrance. ¹³And I saw three evil spirits that looked like frogs leap from the mouth of the dragon, the beast, and the false prophet. ¹⁴These miracle-working demons caused all the rulers of the world to gather for battle against the Lord on that great judgment day of God Almighty.

¹⁵"Take note: I will come as unexpectedly as a thief! Blessed are all who are watching for me, who keep their robes ready so they will not need to walk naked and ashamed."

¹⁶And they gathered all the rulers and their armies to a place called *Armageddon* in Hebrew. ¹⁷Then the seventh angel poured out his bowl into the air. And a mighty shout came from the throne of the Temple in heaven, saying, "It is finished!" ¹⁸Then the thunder crashed and rolled, and lightning flashed. And there was an earthquake greater than ever before in human history. ¹⁹The great city of Babylon split into three pieces, and cities around the world fell into heaps of rubble. And so God remembered all of Babylon's sins, and he made her drink the cup that was filled with the wine of his fierce wrath. ²⁰And every island disappeared, and all the

15:3 Some manuscripts read *King of the ages;* other manuscripts read *King of the saints.*   15:6 Some manuscripts read *in bright and sparkling stone.*

mountains were leveled. 21There was a terrible hailstorm, and hailstones weighing seventy-five pounds* fell from the sky onto the people below. They cursed God because of the hailstorm, which was a very terrible plague.

## CHAPTER 17
### The Great Prostitute

One of the seven angels who had poured out the seven bowls came over and spoke to me. "Come with me," he said, "and I will show you the judgment that is going to come on the great prostitute, who sits on many waters. 2The rulers of the world have had immoral relations with her, and the people who belong to this world have been made drunk by the wine of her immorality."

3So the angel took me in spirit* into the wilderness. There I saw a woman sitting on a scarlet beast that had seven heads and ten horns, written all over with blasphemies against God. 4The woman wore purple and scarlet clothing and beautiful jewelry made of gold and precious gems and pearls. She held in her hand a gold goblet full of obscenities and the impurities of her immorality. 5A mysterious name was written on her forehead: "Babylon the Great, Mother of All Prostitutes and Obscenities in the World." 6I could see that she was drunk—drunk with the blood of God's holy people who were witnesses for Jesus. I stared at her completely amazed.

7"Why are you so amazed?" the angel asked. "I will tell you the mystery of this woman and of the beast with seven heads and ten horns. 8The beast you saw was alive but isn't now. And yet he will soon come up out of the bottomless pit and go to eternal destruction. And the people who belong to this world, whose names were not written in the Book of Life from before the world began, will be amazed at the reappearance of this beast who had died.

9"And now understand this: The seven heads of the beast represent the seven hills of the city where this woman rules. They also represent seven kings. 10Five kings have already fallen, the sixth now reigns, and the seventh is yet to come, but his reign will be brief. 11The scarlet beast that was alive and then died is the eighth king. He is like the other seven, and he, too, will go to his doom. 12His ten horns are ten kings who have not yet risen to power; they will be appointed to their kingdoms for one brief moment to reign with the beast. 13They will all agree to give their

power and authority to him. 14Together they will wage war against the Lamb, but the Lamb will defeat them because he is Lord over all lords and King over all kings, and his people are the called and chosen and faithful ones."

15And the angel said to me, "The waters where the prostitute is sitting represent masses of people of every nation and language. 16The scarlet beast and his ten horns—which represent ten kings who will reign with him—all hate the prostitute. They will strip her naked, eat her flesh, and burn her remains with fire. 17For God has put a plan into their minds, a plan that will carry out his purposes. They will mutually agree to give their authority to the scarlet beast, and so the words of God will be fulfilled. 18And this woman you saw in your vision represents the great city that rules over the kings of the earth."

## CHAPTER 18
### The Fall of Babylon

After all this I saw another angel come down from heaven with great authority, and the earth grew bright with his splendor. 2He gave a mighty shout, "Babylon is fallen—that great city is fallen! She has become the hideout of demons and evil spirits, a nest for filthy buzzards, and a den for dreadful beasts. 3For all the nations have drunk the wine of her passionate immorality. The rulers of the world have committed adultery with her, and merchants throughout the world have grown rich as a result of her luxurious living."

4Then I heard another voice calling from heaven, "Come away from her, my people. Do not take part in her sins, or you will be punished with her. 5For her sins are piled as high as heaven, and God is ready to judge her for her evil deeds. 6Do to her as she has done to your people. Give her a double penalty for all her evil deeds. She brewed a cup of terror for others, so give her twice as much as she gave out. 7She has lived in luxury and pleasure, so match it now with torments and sorrows. She boasts, 'I am queen on my throne. I am no helpless widow. I will not experience sorrow.' 8Therefore, the sorrows of death and mourning and famine will overtake her in a single day. She will be utterly consumed by fire, for the Lord God who judges her is mighty."

9And the rulers of the world who took part in her immoral acts and enjoyed her great luxury will mourn for her as they see the smoke rising

16:21 Greek 1 *talent* [34 kilograms].   17:3 Or *in the Spirit.*

from her charred remains. 10They will stand at a distance, terrified by her great torment. They will cry out, "How terrible, how terrible for Babylon, that great city! In one single moment God's judgment came on her."

11The merchants of the world will weep and mourn for her, for there is no one left to buy their goods. 12She bought great quantities of gold, silver, jewels, pearls, fine linen, purple dye, silk, scarlet cloth, every kind of perfumed wood, ivory goods, objects made of expensive wood, bronze, iron, and marble. 13She also bought cinnamon, spice, incense, myrrh, frankincense, wine, olive oil, fine flour, wheat, cattle, sheep, horses, chariots, and slaves—yes, she even traded in human lives.

14"All the fancy things you loved so much are gone," they cry. "The luxuries and splendor that you prized so much will never be yours again. They are gone forever."

15The merchants who became wealthy by selling her these things will stand at a distance, terrified by her great torment. They will weep and cry. 16"How terrible, how terrible for that great city! She was so beautiful—like a woman clothed in finest purple and scarlet linens, decked out with gold and precious stones and pearls! 17And in one single moment all the wealth of the city is gone!"

And all the shipowners and captains of the merchant ships and their crews will stand at a distance. 18They will weep as they watch the smoke ascend, and they will say, "Where in all the world is there another city like this?" 19And they will throw dust on their heads to show their great sorrow. And they will say, "How terrible, how terrible for the great city! She made us all rich from her great wealth. And now in a single hour it is all gone."

20But you, O heaven, rejoice over her fate. And you also rejoice, O holy people of God and apostles and prophets! For at last God has judged her on your behalf.

21Then a mighty angel picked up a boulder as large as a great millstone. He threw it into the ocean and shouted, "Babylon, the great city, will be thrown down as violently as I have thrown away this stone, and she will disappear forever. 22Never again will the sound of music be heard there—no more harps, songs, flutes, or trumpets. There will be no industry of any kind, and no more milling of grain. 23Her nights will be dark, without a single lamp. There will be no

happy voices of brides and grooms. This will happen because her merchants, who were the greatest in the world, deceived the nations with her sorceries. 24In her streets the blood of the prophets was spilled. She was the one who slaughtered God's people all over the world."

CHAPTER **19**
*Songs of Victory in Heaven*
After this, I heard the sound of a vast crowd in heaven shouting, "Hallelujah! Salvation is from our God. Glory and power belong to him alone. 2His judgments are just and true. He has punished the great prostitute who corrupted the earth with her immorality, and he has avenged the murder of his servants." 3Again and again their voices rang, "Hallelujah! The smoke from that city ascends forever and forever!"

4Then the twenty-four elders and the four living beings fell down and worshiped God, who was sitting on the throne. They cried out, "Amen! Hallelujah!"

5And from the throne came a voice that said, "Praise our God, all his servants, from the least to the greatest, all who fear him."

6Then I heard again what sounded like the shout of a huge crowd, or the roar of mighty ocean waves, or the crash of loud thunder: "Hallelujah! For the Lord our God, the Almighty, reigns. 7Let us be glad and rejoice and honor him. For the time has come for the wedding feast of the Lamb, and his bride has prepared herself. 8She is permitted to wear the finest white linen." (Fine linen represents the good deeds done by the people of God.)

9And the angel said, "Write this: Blessed are those who are invited to the wedding feast of the Lamb." And he added, "These are true words that come from God."

10Then I fell down at his feet to worship him, but he said, "No, don't worship me. For I am a servant of God, just like you and other brothers and sisters* who testify of their faith in Jesus. Worship God. For the essence of prophecy is to give a clear witness for Jesus.*"

*The Rider on the White Horse*
11Then I saw heaven opened, and a white horse was standing there. And the one sitting on the horse was named Faithful and True. For he judges fairly and then goes to war. 12His eyes were bright like flames of fire, and on his head were many crowns. A name was written on him,

19:10a Greek brothers. 19:10b Or is the message confirmed by Jesus.

## Who Will Go to Hell? Read REVELATION 20:11-15

The event described in this passage is the final judgment of humankind, also known as the Great White Throne Judgment. The standard by which you will be judged is simple. If you have accepted God's wonderful gift of salvation through his Son, Jesus Christ, your name will be found in the Book of Life, and you will spend eternity in heaven with God. If you have chosen to reject Christ, then your final destination will be the lake of fire. No arguments. Case closed.

Sadly, many people will unwittingly choose the latter option. They do so, not because they want to spend their eternity in agony, but because they just "go with the flow." They do what everybody else does and don't think for themselves. Jesus called this choice the "easy way." In describing the way to heaven and the way to hell, Jesus said, "You can enter God's Kingdom

only through the narrow gate. The highway to hell is broad, and its gate is wide for the many who choose the easy way. But the gateway to life is small, and the road is narrow, and only a few ever find it" (Matthew 7:13-14). The only way to get off this broad road and "cancel" your reservation for hell is to make sure your name is entered into God's reservation book for heaven—the Book of Life.

## CORNER STONES

and only he knew what it meant. ¹³He was clothed with a robe dipped in blood, and his title was the Word of God. ¹⁴The armies of heaven, dressed in pure white linen, followed him on white horses. ¹⁵From his mouth came a sharp sword, and with it he struck down the nations. He ruled them with an iron rod, and he trod the winepress of the fierce wrath of almighty God. ¹⁶On his robe and thigh was written this title: King of kings and Lord of lords.

¹⁷Then I saw an angel standing in the sun, shouting to the vultures flying high in the sky: "Come! Gather together for the great banquet God has prepared. ¹⁸Come and eat the flesh of kings, captains, and strong warriors; of horses and their riders; and of all humanity, both free and slave, small and great."

¹⁹Then I saw the beast gathering the kings of the earth and their armies in order to fight against the one sitting on the horse and his army. ²⁰And the beast was captured, and with him the false prophet who did mighty miracles on behalf of the beast—miracles that deceived all who had accepted the mark of the beast and who worshiped his statue. Both the beast and his false prophet were thrown alive into the lake of fire that burns with sulfur. ²¹Their entire army was killed by the sharp sword that came out of the mouth of the one riding the white horse. And all the vultures of the sky gorged themselves on the dead bodies.

## CHAPTER 20
### The Thousand Years

Then I saw an angel come down from heaven with the key to the bottomless pit and a heavy chain in his hand. ²He seized the dragon—that old serpent, the Devil, Satan—and bound him in chains for a thousand years. ³The angel threw him into the bottomless pit, which he then shut and locked so Satan could not deceive the nations anymore until the thousand years were finished. Afterward he would be released again for a little while.

⁴Then I saw thrones, and the people sitting on them had been given the authority to judge. And I saw the souls of those who had been beheaded for their testimony about Jesus, for proclaiming the word of God. And I saw the souls of those who had not worshiped the beast or his statue, nor accepted his mark on their forehead or their hands. They came to life again, and they reigned with Christ for a thousand years. ⁵This is the first resurrection. (The rest of the dead did not come back to life until the thousand years had ended.) ⁶Blessed and holy are those who share in the first resurrection. For them the second death holds no power, but they will be priests of God and of Christ and will reign with him a thousand years.

### The Defeat of Satan

⁷When the thousand years end, Satan will be let out of his prison. ⁸He will go out to deceive the

nations from every corner of the earth, which are called Gog and Magog. He will gather them together for battle—a mighty host, as numberless as sand along the shore. 9And I saw them as they went up on the broad plain of the earth and surrounded God's people and the beloved city. But fire from heaven came down on the attacking armies and consumed them.

10Then the Devil, who betrayed them, was thrown into the lake of fire that burns with sulfur, joining the beast and the false prophet. There they will be tormented day and night forever and ever.

### The Final Judgment

11And I saw a great white throne, and I saw the one who was sitting on it. The earth and sky fled from his presence, but they found no place to hide. 12I saw the dead, both great and small, standing before God's throne. And the books were opened, including the Book of Life. And the dead were judged according to the things written in the books, according to what they had done. 13The sea gave up the dead in it, and death and the grave* gave up the dead in them. They were all judged according to their deeds. 14And death and the grave were thrown into the lake of fire. This is the second death—the lake of fire. 15And anyone whose name was not found recorded in the Book of Life was thrown into the lake of fire.

## CHAPTER 21
### The New Jerusalem

Then I saw a new heaven and a new earth, for the old heaven and the old earth had disappeared. And the sea was also gone. 2And I saw the holy city, the new Jerusalem, coming down from God out of heaven like a beautiful bride prepared for her husband.

3I heard a loud shout from the throne, saying, "Look, the home of God is now among his people! He will live with them, and they will be his people. God himself will be with them.* 4He will remove all of their sorrows, and there will be no more death or sorrow or crying or pain. For the old world and its evils are gone forever."

5And the one sitting on the throne said, "Look, I am making all things new!" And then he said to me, "Write this down, for what I tell you is trustworthy and true." 6And he also said, "It is finished! I am the Alpha and the Omega—the Beginning and the End. To all who are thirsty I will give the springs of the water of life without charge! 7All who are victorious will inherit all these blessings, and I will be their God, and they will be my children. 8But cowards who turn away from me, and unbelievers, and the corrupt, and murderers, and the immoral, and those who practice witchcraft, and idol worshipers, and all liars—their doom is in the lake that burns with fire and sulfur. This is the second death."

9Then one of the seven angels who held the seven bowls containing the seven last plagues came and said to me, "Come with me! I will show you the bride, the wife of the Lamb."

10So he took me in spirit* to a great, high mountain, and he showed me the holy city, Jerusalem, descending out of heaven from God. 11It was filled with the glory of God and sparkled like a precious gem, crystal clear like jasper. 12Its walls were broad and high, with twelve gates guarded by twelve angels. And the names of the twelve tribes of Israel were written on the gates. 13There were three gates on each side—east, north, south, and west. 14The wall of the city had twelve foundation stones, and on them were written the names of the twelve apostles of the Lamb.

15The angel who talked to me held in his hand a gold measuring stick to measure the city, its gates, and its wall. 16When he measured it, he found it was a square, as wide as it was long. In fact, it was in the form of a cube, for its length and width and height were each 1,400 miles.* 17Then he measured the walls and found them to be 216 feet thick* (the angel used a standard human measure).

18The wall was made of jasper, and the city was pure gold, as clear as glass. 19The wall of the city was built on foundation stones inlaid with twelve gems: the first was jasper, the second sapphire, the third agate, the fourth emerald, 20the fifth onyx, the sixth carnelian, the seventh chrysolite, the eighth beryl, the ninth topaz, the tenth chrysoprase, the eleventh jacinth, the twelfth amethyst.

21The twelve gates were made of pearls—each gate from a single pearl! And the main street was pure gold, as clear as glass.

22No temple could be seen in the city, for the Lord God Almighty and the Lamb are its temple. 23And the city has no need of sun or moon, for the glory of God illuminates the city, and the Lamb is its light. 24The nations of the earth will

20:13 Greek and Hades; also in 20:14.   21:3 Some manuscripts read God himself will be with them, their God.   21:10 Or in the Spirit.
21:16 Greek 12,000 stadia [2,220 kilometers].   21:17 Greek 144 cubits [65 meters].

walk in its light, and the rulers of the world will come and bring their glory to it. 25Its gates never close at the end of day because there is no night. 26And all the nations will bring their glory and honor into the city. 27Nothing evil will be allowed to enter—no one who practices shameful idolatry and dishonesty—but only those whose names are written in the Lamb's Book of Life.

CHAPTER **22**

And the angel showed me a pure river with the water of life, clear as crystal, flowing from the throne of God and of the Lamb, 2coursing down the center of the main street. On each side of the river grew a tree of life, bearing twelve crops of fruit,* with a fresh crop each month. The leaves were used for medicine to heal the nations.

3No longer will anything be cursed. For the throne of God and of the Lamb will be there, and his servants will worship him. 4And they will see his face, and his name will be written on their foreheads. 5And there will be no night there—no need for lamps or sun—for the Lord God will shine on them. And they will reign forever and ever.

6Then the angel said to me, "These words are trustworthy and true: 'The Lord God, who tells his prophets what the future holds, has sent his angel to tell you what will happen soon.'"

*Jesus Is Coming*

7"Look, I am coming soon! Blessed are those who obey the prophecy written in this scroll."

8I, John, am the one who saw and heard all these things. And when I saw and heard these things, I fell down to worship the angel who showed them to me. 9But again he said, "No, don't worship me. I am a servant of God, just like you and your brothers the prophets, as well as all who obey what is written in this scroll. Worship God!"

10Then he instructed me, "Do not seal up the prophetic words you have written, for the time is near. 11Let the one who is doing wrong continue to do wrong; the one who is vile, continue to be vile; the one who is good, continue to do good; and the one who is holy, continue in holiness."

12"See, I am coming soon, and my reward is with me, to repay all according to their deeds. 13I am the Alpha and the Omega, the First and the Last, the Beginning and the End."

14Blessed are those who wash their robes so they can enter through the gates of the city and eat the fruit from the tree of life. 15Outside the city are the dogs—the sorcerers, the sexually immoral, the murderers, the idol worshipers, and all who love to live a lie.

16"I, Jesus, have sent my angel to give you this message for the churches. I am both the source of David and the heir to his throne.* I am the bright morning star."

17The Spirit and the bride say, "Come." Let each one who hears them say, "Come." Let the thirsty ones come—anyone who wants to. Let them come and drink the water of life without charge. 18And I solemnly declare to everyone who hears the prophetic words of this book: If anyone adds anything to what is written here, God will add to that person the plagues described in this book. 19And if anyone removes any of the words of this prophetic book, God will remove that person's share in the tree of life and in the holy city that are described in this book.

20He who is the faithful witness to all these things says, "Yes, I am coming soon!"

Amen! Come, Lord Jesus!

21The grace of the Lord Jesus be with you all.

22:2 Or *12 kinds of fruit.* 22:16 Greek *I am the root and offspring of David.*

# TOPICAL
# INDEX

## COMFORT

Matthew 5:4. *God promises to comfort those who mourn.* 6
John 14:16. *God's Holy Spirit is our Comforter.* 124
John 16:33. *Jesus has overcome the world and its troubles.* 128
2 Corinthians 1:3-11. *God comforts those who are hurting.* 217
1 Thessalonians 4:18. *Christians should comfort each other.* 263
Revelation 21:3-4. *One day all pain will end.* 347

## COMMITMENT

Matthew 10:32-33. *We must be committed to Christ.* 15
Matthew 13:21. *We must remain committed to Christ in tough times.* 20
John 1:49. *Nathanael showed decisive commitment to Jesus.* 108
Acts 24:16. *Paul was committed to maintaining a clear conscience before God.* 168

## COMMUNICATION

James 1:19. *Listen more than you talk.* 299
See also: CRITICISM, GOSSIP, WITNESSING

## COMPASSION

Matthew 14:14. *Jesus is our example of compassion.* 22
Mark 3:3-5. *Compassion means helping others less fortunate.* 45
Luke 6:36. *We are to be compassionate just as God is.* 75
Luke 10:30-37. *We should have compassion even on those we do not like.* 83
Luke 15:11-32 *God has great compassion for those who have wandered from him.* 91
See also: CARING, SERVING OTHERS

## COMPLAINING

Matthew 20:1-16. *Envy can cause complaining.* 28
Philippians 2:14-16. *Do everything without complaining.* 249
Jude 1:16. *False teachers will be grumblers and complainers.* 330
See also: CONTENTMENT

## COMPROMISE

Matthew 5:25. *Sometimes we should compromise with others to be reconciled to them.* 7
Mark 15:15. *Compromise can keep us from doing what is right.* 63
2 Corinthians 6:14-18. *Some compromise can weaken our faith.* 222

## CONFESSION

Luke 3:4-18. *John called people to repent and turn from sin.* 69
James 5:16. *We should confess our sins to other believers.* 304
1 John 1:8-10. *God forgives our sins when we confess them.* 107
See also: FORGIVENESS, REPENTANCE

## CONSCIENCE

Romans 9:1. *The Holy Spirit works together with our conscience to speak to us.* 186
Romans 14:23. *Listen to your conscience.* 193
1 Timothy 1:18-19. *Keep your conscience clear.* 269
1 Timothy 3:9. *A church leader must have a clear conscience.* 271
1 Timothy 4:2. *Many false teachers have deadened their conscience.* 271
Hebrews 9:14. *Jesus' forgiveness clears our conscience.* 292
1 Peter 3:16. *Our best witness comes from a godly life and a clear conscience.* 309

## CONSEQUENCES

Matthew 7:13-14.  *The path we choose in life will have definite consequences.*  11

2 Corinthians 5:10.  *Each of us will stand before God.*  220

## CONTENTMENT

Matthew 6:25-35.  *Be content with what you have.*  10

John 3:30.  *Contentment comes when you put Jesus first.*  110

Philippians 4:10-14.  *Be content in every situation.*  251

*See also:* HAPPINESS

## COURAGE

John 16:33.  *Jesus' victory over the world gives us courage.*  128

Acts 4:31.  *God's Holy Spirit fills us with courage to proclaim Christ.*  141

1 Corinthians 16:13.  *Christians should be courageous.*  216

Ephesians 6:19-20.  *Pray for courage.*  245

Hebrews 4:16.  *Christians can pray to God with confidence.*  288

## COVENANT

Luke 22:20.  *Jesus established a new covenant in his blood.*  101

2 Corinthians 3:6.  *God's covenant brings life.*  218

Hebrews 8:6.  *The new covenant is superior to the old covenant.*  291

Hebrews 10:1.  *The old covenant foreshadowed the new covenant.*  292

## CREATION

Colossians 1:16.  *Christ was involved in Creation.*  253

Revelation 4:11.  *God the Creator is worthy of worship.*  335

Revelation 21:1-4.  *God will make a new heaven and a new earth.*  347

## CRITICISM

Matthew 7:1-6.  *Take care of your own problems before criticizing others.*  11

Luke 17:3-4.  *We should rebuke those who need correction.*  93

Galatians 5:15.  *Harsh criticism can destroy rather than help.*  234

1 Peter 3:16.  *Live above criticism.*  309

*See also:* COMMUNICATION

## CROSS

Matthew 27:31-35.  *Jesus was nailed to a cross.*  39

Mark 8:34-38.  *Following Christ requires that we shoulder our crosses.*  52

1 Corinthians 1:17-18.  *The power of the Good News comes from the power of the Cross.*  197

Ephesians 2:16.  *Jesus' death unified all Christians.*  238

Colossians 1:20-22.  *Jesus' death was a sacrifice.*  253

Colossians 2:14-15.  *Jesus' death defeated Satan.*  255

Hebrews 12:1-4.  *Jesus' cross is an example for us.*  296

## CULTS

Matthew 7:15.  *False teachers will come.*  11

John 14:6.  *Jesus is the only way to truly know God.*  123

Ephesians 4:13-14; 5:12.  *Beware of those who teach clever lies.*  240, 243

1 Thessalonians 5:21.  *We should always weigh carefully what we are being taught.*  264

2 Timothy 3:2-8.  *Beware those who teach things that do not follow God's Word.*  277

*See also:* OCCULT

Hebrews 5:14. *Mature Christians should be able to discern right and wrong.* 289
James 1:5. *Ask God for help in discerning his will.* 299

## DISCIPLESHIP
Matthew 28:19-20. *Jesus instructed his followers to make disciples.* 41
John 13:35. *Jesus' followers are known by their love.* 123
Acts 14:21-22. *Christians should help other Christians grow.* 156

## DISCIPLINE
Matthew 18:15-17. *There are definite steps to follow in dealing with those who are sinning.* 26
Acts 5:1-11. *Punishment for sin may be swift and severe.* 142
1 Corinthians 5:1-5. *Paul commanded punishment for blatant sin in the church.* 202
2 Corinthians 7:8-9. *Punishment should lead to repentance.* 223
Ephesians 6:4. *Do not discipline in anger.* 244
Hebrews 12:5-11. *Sometimes God punishes us to bring us back to himself.* 297
Revelation 3:19. *God disciplines those he loves.* 334

## DISCOURAGEMENT
Matthew 10:16-28. *Don't be discouraged by persecution.* 15
John 15:18-19. *Christ's example helps us avoid discouragement from rejection.* 125
Romans 8:35. *Christ's unending love for us can help fight discouragement.* 186
*See also:* DEPRESSION, GIVING UP, PROBLEMS

## DISCRIMINATION
Acts 10:34. *God does not discriminate among his people.* 151
Galatians 3:28. *All Christians are equally accepted by God.* 232
Colossians 3:25. *God has no favorites.* 257
James 2:1-9. *Do not discriminate against the poor.* 300

## DISHONESTY
James 5:1-4. *God will judge those who cheat others.* 303

## DOCTRINE
2 Timothy 1:13-14. *Protect sound doctrine.* 275
2 Timothy 3:16. *All sound doctrine comes from Scripture.* 277
Titus 1:6-9. *Leaders in the church must have sound doctrine.* 279
Titus 2:1. *Christians should teach correct beliefs.* 279

## DOUBT
Matthew 11:1-6. *Jesus helped remove John's doubts.* 16
John 20:24-29. *Jesus helped remove Thomas's doubts.* 133
Hebrews 3:12. *We must guard against unbelief in ourselves and others.* 288
James 1:5-8. *Don't let doubt ruin your faith.* 299
*See also:* FAITH, TRUST

## DRINKING
Luke 21:34. *Living in drunkenness and irresponsibility is dangerous.* 100
Romans 13:11-14. *Drunkenness is not fitting for a Christian.* 192
Ephesians 5:18. *Drunkenness can cause immoral behavior.* 243

## DRUGS
1 Corinthians 6:19-20. *Your body is the temple of the Holy Spirit.* 204

## EMBARRASSMENT

Romans 1:16.   *We should not be embarrassed about the gospel.*   175
Galatians 1:10.   *We should not be embarrassed about serving Christ.*   229

## EMOTIONS

John 11:35.   *At times Jesus experienced strong emotion.*   120
Ephesians 4:31.   *We must make sure that our emotions do not lead us to sin.*   242

## EMPLOYMENT

Ephesians 6:6-7.   *Work as though Jesus were your boss.*   244
Titus 2:9-10.   *Christians should do their best at their job.*   280

## ENCOURAGEMENT

Acts 9:31.   *The Holy Spirit comforts us.*   149
Romans 15:4.   *The Bible encourages us.*   193
Philippians 2:1.   *Our position in Christ encourages us.*   248
1 Thessalonians 4:18.   *We should encourage each other with thoughts of our hopeful future.*   263
1 Thessalonians 5:14.   *Encourage those who are weak and afraid.*   264
Hebrews 3:13.   *We should encourage each other not to sin.*   288
Hebrews 10:24.   *Encourage others to show love and good deeds.*   293

## ENVY

Acts 7:9.   *Envy can cause you to act rashly.*   145
Romans 1:29.   *Envy characterizes sinful people.*   176
Galatians 5:26.   *We should not envy other Christians.*   234
Titus 3:3.   *Envy has no place in a Christian's life.*   281
James 3:14-15.   *Do not harbor envy.*   302
1 Peter 2:1.   *Get rid of envy.*   306

## ETERNAL LIFE

Matthew 7:13-14.   *Jesus is the only way to eternal life.*   11
Matthew 25:46.   *The righteous will receive eternal life.*   36
John 3:15-16.   *Everyone who believes in Jesus will receive eternal life.*   109
John 5:28-29.   *Evil people will receive eternal punishment.*   112
John 10:10.   *Jesus came to give life.*   118
John 11:25.   *Jesus gives eternal life.*   120
John 14:6.   *Jesus is eternal life.*   123
Ephesians 2:8-9.   *Eternal life cannot be earned; it is received by grace.*   238
Titus 1:2.   *Eternal life comes from God.*   279
Titus 3:7.   *Eternal life gives us hope.*   281

*See also:* **FUTURE, HEAVEN**

## EVANGELISM

Matthew 5:14-16.   *Christians bring light to a spiritually dark world.*   6
Matthew 9:9-13.   *Jesus made salvation available to sinners.*   14
Matthew 28:18-20.   *Jesus sent his followers to make disciples.*   41
Acts 1:8.   *The Holy Spirit gives us power to evangelize.*   135

*See also:* **WITNESSING**

## EVIL

Romans 1:24-28.   *Sometimes God allows evil to run its course.*   176

Hebrews 9:22.  *Jesus died so we could be forgiven.*  292
1 John 1:8-9.  *God will forgive our sins as we confess them.*  107

See also: CONFESSION

## FOUL LANGUAGE
Ephesians 5:4.  *Foul language is not fitting for a Christian.*  243
Colossians 4:6.  *Our speech should reflect our relationship with God.*  257
1 Timothy 4:12.  *Our speech should be an example to others.*  272

## FREEDOM
John 8:30-36.  *Jesus can set us free from sin.*  116
Romans 5:21.  *Christians are free from sin's power.*  180
Romans 14:10-16.  *Don't use your freedom to lead others to sin.*  193
Galatians 5:1.  *Christians are free in order to serve others.*  233

See also: CHOICES, DECISIONS

## FRIENDSHIP
John 15:13-15.  *Friendship is marked by sacrifice.*  125
Acts 9:23-29.  *Barnabas was a true friend to Paul.*  149

See also: PEER PRESSURE, POPULARITY, RELATIONSHIPS

## FUTURE
John 3:16.  *Jesus came so that we could have a future of eternal life.*  109
John 14:1-4.  *Jesus said he was going to prepare a place for his followers.*  123
1 Corinthians 2:9.  *God prepares a wonderful future for his people.*  199

See also: ETERNAL LIFE, GUIDANCE

## GIFTS
Luke 12:48.  *God expects more from those who have been given more.*  88
1 Corinthians 12:1-11.  *The Holy Spirit equips believers with spiritual gifts.*  210
1 Timothy 4:14-16.  *We should use the gifts and abilities God has given us.*  272

See also: USING YOUR ABILITIES WISELY

## GIVING
Mark 9:41.  *God will reward us for giving to others.*  54
Acts 2:44-45.  *Giving should naturally flow out of our faith in Christ.*  138
1 Timothy 6:17-19.  *Wealthy people should give generously.*  273
Hebrews 13:16.  *God is pleased with our gifts.*  298
1 John 3:17.  *Giving reflects God's love.*  321

## GIVING UP
1 Corinthians 9:24-27.  *Discipline yourself for endurance.*  207
Galatians 6:9-10.  *Never get tired of doing right.*  234
Philippians 3:12-14.  *Never give up the race of obedience to Christ.*  250
2 Timothy 2:3-13.  *Don't give up even when you are suffering.*  275

See also: DEPRESSION, DISCOURAGEMENT

## GOALS
Philippians 3:12-20.  *Following Christ should be our ultimate goal.*  250
James 4:13-16.  *Make sure your goals please God.*  303

## GOD
Matthew 6:9.  *God is our father.*  9
Luke 1:37.  *God is all-powerful.*  66

John 4:24.   *God is spirit.*   110
Romans 11:33.   *God is all-knowing.*   191
Ephesians 1:17.   *God is knowable.*   237
1 Timothy 4:10.   *God is living.*   272
1 Timothy 6:15.   *God is King of kings.*   273
James 4:8.   *God will draw close to us.*   303
James 4:12.   *God is judge.*   303
1 John 4:16.   *God is love.*   322
Revelation 1:8.   *God is almighty.*   331

## GOD'S WILL
Matthew 1:18-25.   *Follow God's will even if you don't understand it.*   3
Acts 16:6-7.   *God directs events in our life.*   157
Philippians 2:13-16.   *God wants to help you do his will.*   249
James 1:2-5.   *God gives wisdom for making decisions.*   299

*See also:* BIBLE

## GOSPEL/GOOD NEWS
Matthew 28:18-19.   *Christians should tell others about the gospel.*   41
Luke 24:46-47.   *The gospel is for everyone.*   106
John 1:12.   *People should respond to the gospel with faith.*   107
Romans 1:16.   *The gospel is powerful.*   175
1 Corinthians 15:1-5.   *The gospel is that Jesus died for our sins and rose again.*   213
1 Thessalonians 1:4-5.   *Believing the gospel brings a change to life.*   259

## GOSSIP
Romans 1:29.   *Gossiping is wicked.*   176
2 Thessalonians 3:11-12.   *God hates gossiping.*   267
1 Timothy 5:13.   *Gossip should have no place among Christians.*   272
Titus 3:2.   *Don't speak evil of anyone.*   281

*See also:* COMMUNICATION, LYING

## GOVERNMENT
Romans 13:1.   *God gives authority to those in government.*   192
Titus 3:1.   *Christians should obey the government.*   281

## GRACE
Ephesians 1:7-8.   *God's grace makes salvation possible.*   237
Ephesians 2:8-9.   *God accepts us by his grace.*   238
1 Peter 1:13.   *God's grace gives us hope.*   305

## GREED
Matthew 26:14-15.   *Greed caused Judas to betray Jesus.*   36
Ephesians 5:3.   *Christians should not be greedy.*   243
Ephesians 5:5.   *People who are full of greed will not enter heaven.*   243
Titus 1:7.   *Leaders of the church must not be greedy.*   279
2 Peter 2:15.   *Greed causes some to use religion to get rich.*   315

*See also:* MATERIALISM, MONEY, POSSESSIONS

## GRIEF
Matthew 5:4.   *God promises to comfort those who grieve.*   6
John 14:16.   *God's Holy Spirit is our Comforter.*   124

John 16:33. *Jesus has overcome the world's troubles.* 128
Acts 9:31. *The Holy Spirit comforts us.* 149
Romans 15:4. *The Scriptures encourage us.* 193
2 Corinthians 1:3-11. *God comforts those who grieve.* 217
Revelation 21:3-4. *One day all grief will end.* 347

*See also:* SORROW

## GUIDANCE
Matthew 2:13-15. *Sometimes God uses unusual ways to guide us.* 4
Acts 8:26-37. *Sometimes God guides us to help others.* 148

*See also:* FUTURE, GOD'S WILL, PRAYER

## GUILT
Romans 3:9-12. *Everyone is guilty of sin.* 178
Romans 3:23-24. *Jesus Christ takes away all guilt.* 178
1 Timothy 1:12-17. *God can forgive even the most wicked of sinners.* 269

*See also:* CONFESSION, FORGIVENESS

## HAPPINESS
Matthew 5:3-12. *Jesus told his followers how to be truly happy.* 6
1 Timothy 6:6-10. *Contentedness and sincerity in our faith bring much happiness.* 273

*See also:* CONTENTMENT

## HATRED
Matthew 10:22. *Followers of Jesus will be hated.* 15
John 15:18. *Many in the world hate Jesus.* 125
Romans 12:9. *Christians should hate evil.* 191
Colossians 3:8. *Christians need to get rid of their own hatred.* 257
1 John 3:15. *Those who hate fellow Christians are murderers at heart.* 320

*See also:* ANGER, REVENGE

## HEART
Matthew 5:8. *Those who have a pure heart will see God.* 6
Luke 6:45. *Words and actions reflect what is in the heart.* 76

## HEAVEN
Matthew 5:17-20. *Actions on earth affect position in heaven.* 7
Matthew 7:13-14. *The road and gateway to heaven are very narrow.* 11
Luke 13:29. *People from all over the world will be together in heaven.* 89
John 14:2-3. *Jesus said he was preparing a place in heaven for his followers.* 123
2 Corinthians 5:2. *Our earthly bodies will be made complete in heaven.* 220
Philippians 1:23. *We can look forward to heaven.* 247
Colossians 3:1-5. *Christians should look forward to heaven.* 256
Revelation 7:17. *God is the focus of attention in heaven.* 337
Revelation 22:3-4. *There will not be any evil or sadness in heaven.* 348
Revelation 22:5. *God will be heaven's light.* 348

*See also:* ETERNAL LIFE

## HELL
Matthew 7:22-23. *Even some who do good deeds will end up in hell.* 12
Matthew 8:12. *Hell is a place of weeping.* 13
Matthew 25:41. *Hell was prepared for Satan and demons.* 36

## POPULARITY

Matthew 10:32-33.  *Don't let your concern for popularity make you ashamed of Christ.*  15

John 15:18-19.  *Following Christ will guarantee that some people will hate you.*  125

2 Corinthians 4:4.  *Satan makes his followers hate Christians.*  219

James 4:4.  *God doesn't want us to be popular with everyone.*  302

1 John 2:15-17.  *Believers must stay away from some popular activities.*  318

*See also:* PEER PRESSURE

## POSSESSIONS

Matthew 19:16-22.  *Don't let possessions keep you from following Christ.*  27

Acts 2:42-45.  *Christians should be generous in sharing their possessions.*  138

James 2:1-9.  *Don't show favoritism toward wealthy people.*  300

*See also:* GREED, MATERIALISM, MONEY

## POWER

Acts 1:8.  *Christians receive power from the Holy Spirit.*  135

Ephesians 6:17.  *God's Word is a powerful weapon.*  245

Hebrews 1:1-4.  *Jesus sustains the universe by his powerful command.*  285

James 5:16.  *Earnest prayer from a righteous person has powerful results.*  304

1 John 5:4-5.  *God gives Christians power to overcome the world.*  323

## PRAISE

*See:* WORSHIP

## PRAYER

Matthew 6:6.  *Prayer should not be done for show.*  9

Matthew 6:9-13.  *Jesus taught his disciples how to pray.*  9

Matthew 7:7-12.  *We must be persistent in prayer.*  11

Matthew 21:21-22.  *We can pray with confidence that God is able to answer our requests.*  29

Luke 18:9-14.  *Pray with an attitude of humility.*  95

John 16:23-24.  *Pray with confidence in Jesus' name.*  127

Ephesians 6:18.  *Pray all the time.*  245

2 Thessalonians 1:11.  *Pray for others.*  265

James 1:6.  *Pray without doubting.*  299

James 4:3.  *Pray with right motives.*  302

1 John 5:14-15.  *Pray according to God's will.*  323

*See also:* CHOICES, DECISIONS, GUIDANCE

## PREJUDICE

Luke 10:25-37.  *Prejudice keeps us from helping others.*  83

Acts 10:34-43.  *Jesus died for people of all nations.*  151

Galatians 3:28-29.  *All Christians are equally accepted by God.*  232

Ephesians 2:11-16.  *Christ has made it possible to remove prejudice.*  238

## PRIDE

Matthew 11:20-26.  *Pride keeps people from finding Christ.*  17

Luke 18:9-14.  *Pride cuts us off from God and others.*  95

Romans 3:27.  *There is no place for proud boasting in the Christian life.*  178

1 Corinthians 1:26-31.  *God chose to reveal himself to the humble, not to the proud.*  198

Galatians 5:22-26.  *Pride is not compatible with the fruit of the Spirit.*  234

James 4:6.  *God opposes the proud.*  303

*See also:* SELF-ESTEEM

## PROBLEMS

Matthew 11:27-30. *Jesus offers rest for the weary.* 17
Romans 8:28. *God can bring good from any problem.* 185
Philippians 1:29-30. *We should view suffering for Christ as a privilege.* 248
Philippians 3:7-11. *Our struggles allow us to share in Christ's suffering.* 249

*See also:* DEPRESSION, DISCOURAGEMENT,
FAILURE, STRESS, SUFFERING, TRIALS

## PROCRASTINATION

Matthew 25:1-13. *Do not procrastinate in securing your relationship with God.* 35
2 Corinthians 6:2. *Today is the day to be saved.* 221
Revelation 10:6. *No one can procrastinate forever.* 338

## PROPHECY

Matthew 7:21-23. *Claiming to prophesy in Jesus' name does not make you godly.* 12
Acts 2:17-18. *The Holy Spirit allows believers to prophesy.* 137
1 Corinthians 14:1-5. *Prophecy is a spiritual gift.* 211
1 Thessalonians 5:20. *We should listen to God's messages.* 264
2 Peter 1:20-21. *True prophets speak God's words.* 313

*See also:* TEACHING

## PURITY

Matthew 5:8. *The pure in heart will see God.* 6
Matthew 5:27-30. *Purity begins in the heart.* 7
Matthew 23:25-28. *Outward purity cannot substitute for inner purity.* 33
John 17:17. *Purity comes from God.* 128
Ephesians 5:1-4. *Purity ought to mark believers' lives.* 242
Philippians 3:7-11. *Give up what hinders purity.* 249
Philippians 4:8. *Our mind should think about things that are pure.* 250
1 John 3:1-3. *One day our purity will be like Christ's.* 319

*See also:* MARRIAGE, SEX/SEXUAL SIN

## QUESTIONS

Luke 7:18-23. *Christ does not rebuke us for asking sincere questions.* 76
Luke 21:12-15. *We need not be afraid when questioned about our faith.* 99
1 Peter 3:15. *We should be ready with answers when questioned about our faith.* 309

## RAPTURE

*See:* SECOND COMING OF CHRIST

## REJECTION

Matthew 13:53-58. *Jesus was rejected in his hometown.* 21
Luke 15:11-24. *God does not reject repentant sinners.* 91
John 6:58-66. *Jesus was rejected by many of his followers.* 113
Romans 1:18-32. *Rejecting God allows sin to run wild.* 175

## RELATIONSHIPS

John 14:19-21. *Our relationship with God is made possible through Jesus Christ.* 124
1 Corinthians 11:2-12. *Humility strengthens family relationships.* 208
2 Corinthians 6:14-18. *Our relationships should not compromise our faith.* 222
Ephesians 2:21-22. *We are united with all believers in God's family.* 239
2 Timothy 2:11-13. *Christians have a deep relationship with Christ.* 276

1 Peter 2:21-23. *Jesus is our example of how to handle insults and suffering.* 307
1 Peter 3:8-9. *Be tender and humble.* 308

*See also:* ANGER, HATRED

## RIGHTEOUS/RIGHTEOUSNESS
Romans 3:10-18. *We are not righteous by ourselves.* 178
Romans 4:18-25. *Righteousness is not attained by works.* 180
Galatians 3:11-21. *Trying to keep the law cannot make us righteous.* 231
Ephesians 6:14. *Our God-given righteousness is armor against Satan's attacks.* 245
Philippians 3:9. *We become righteous through faith in Christ.* 249
2 Timothy 3:16. *Studying God's Word helps us grow in righteousness.* 277
1 Peter 2:24. *Righteousness ought to characterize each believer's life.* 307

## SADNESS
*See:* GRIEF, SORROW

## SALVATION
Matthew 19:25-26. *Salvation is by God's grace alone.* 28
John 1:12-13. *Those who receive salvation become God's children.* 107
John 3:1-16. *Salvation is a work of the Holy Spirit in a person's life.* 109
John 14:6. *Jesus is the way to salvation.* 123
John 17:1-5. *Salvation involves knowing the Father through his Son, Jesus Christ.* 128
Acts 2:37-38. *Receiving salvation means we must turn from our sins.* 138
Romans 3:8. *Jesus died for our sins.* 177
Romans 3:23. *No one deserves salvation.* 178
Romans 6:23. *Salvation cannot be earned; it is a gift of God.* 182
Romans 10:8-10. *Receiving salvation is simple and personal.* 188
Ephesians 2:1-9. *Salvation is by God's grace alone.* 238
Philippians 3:4-11. *No one is good enough to be saved.* 249
Colossians 1:13-14. *Salvation means being rescued from Satan's dominion!* 253
1 Peter 1:18-19. *Our salvation was obtained by Jesus' blood.* 305

## SATAN
Matthew 4:1-11. *Satan even tempted Jesus.* 5
John 8:44. *Satan is completely evil.* 116
Ephesians 2:1-2. *Satan is the temporary ruler over this world.* 238
Ephesians 6:12. *Satan and his demons are spiritual.* 245
James 4:1-10. *Believers have the authority to resist Satan.* 302
1 Peter 5:8. *Satan is an enemy to Christians.* 310
1 John 3:7-8. *Jesus destroyed Satan's work with his death on the cross.* 319
Revelation 20:10. *Satan is a defeated enemy.* 347

## SECOND COMING OF CHRIST
Matthew 24:36. *We do not know when Jesus will return.* 35
Mark 13:26-27. *Christ's return will be unmistakable.* 60
Luke 12:35-40. *Christ's return will be joyous for those who are ready.* 87
John 12:37-50. *Christ's second coming will be a time of judgment on unbelievers.* 121
John 14:1-3. *At Christ's second coming we will be with him forever.* 123
Acts 1:10-11. *We have the promise that Christ will one day return.* 135
1 Corinthians 15:51-57. *When Christ returns, believers will be resurrected in new bodies.* 215

*See also:* CONSCIENCE, CONSEQUENCES, TEMPTATION

## SINGLENESS

Matthew 19:12.   *Some people remain single to work for God's Kingdom.*   27

1 Corinthians 7:7-8.   *God gives some people the gift of singleness.*   204

1 Corinthians 7:25-31.   *Sometimes singleness is best in certain situations.*   205

1 Corinthians 7:32-35.   *Single people have more time to focus on service for God.*   205

## SORROW

Matthew 5:4.   *God promises comfort to those who experience sorrow.*   6

2 Corinthians 7:10-11.   *God may use sorrow to point out sin and draw us back to him.*   223

1 Thessalonians 4:13-18.   *Christians can look to their hopeful future to help alleviate sorrow.*   263

Revelation 21:3-4.   *Sorrow will not exist in God's Kingdom.*   347

*See also:* GRIEF

## SOUL

Matthew 10:28.   *People cannot destroy your soul.*   15

Matthew 22:36-40.   *We are to love God with our whole being—heart, soul, and mind.*   32

Mark 8:34-38.   *It is of no value to gain the world but lose your soul.*   52

## SPIRITUAL GIFTS

Romans 12:3-8.   *God expects us to use our gifts.*   191

1 Corinthians 12:4-11.   *God gives us our spiritual gifts.*   210

Ephesians 4:11-13.   *Spiritual gifts build up the body of Christ.*   240

Hebrews 2:4.   *God distributes spiritual gifts according to his will.*   286

## STRESS

Romans 8:31-39.   *God is always with us.*   186

2 Corinthians 4:8-12.   *God is with us during stressful times.*   219

Philippians 4:4-9.   *Praying about everything helps us not to worry.*   250

## SUBMISSION

Matthew 26:36-44.   *Christ is the perfect example of submission to the Father's will.*   37

Luke 14:27.   *Following Christ requires submission to him.*   90

1 Corinthians 11:2-16.   *Harmonious relationships require submission to authority.*   208

Ephesians 5:21-33.   *Marriage calls for mutual submission.*   243

James 4:7-10.   *Submit to God.*   303

*See also:* OBEDIENCE

## SUFFERING

Matthew 16:21-26.   *Christ's followers will face suffering.*   24

Romans 8:18-21.   *The curse of sin has brought suffering.*   185

2 Corinthians 1:3-7.   *Our suffering helps us comfort others who are suffering.*   217

2 Corinthians 4:17-18.   *Our suffering will end in glory.*   220

Hebrews 2:11-18.   *Jesus can help us in our suffering.*   287

1 Peter 2:21-24.   *We should imitate Christ's response to suffering.*   307

Revelation 21:4.   *There will be no suffering in Christ's Kingdom.*   347

*See also:* PROBLEMS, TRIALS, TRUST

## TEACHING

2 Timothy 2:2.   *Christians are to teach each other God's truth.*   275

2 Timothy 2:24-26.   *We should be patient as we teach God's truth to others.*   277

Titus 2:1-15.   *Christians should teach each other how to live for God.*   279

*See also:* WITNESSING

## TEMPTATION

Matthew 4:1-11.   *Jesus experienced temptation and overcame it.*   5

1 Corinthians 10:13.   *God will provide a way of escape from every temptation.*   208

1 Timothy 6:11-12.   *Paul encouraged Timothy to run from temptation and pursue godliness.*   273

2 Timothy 2:22.   *We are to run from temptation and pursue good things.*   276

Hebrews 2:16-18.   *Jesus can help us when we are tempted.*   287

Hebrews 4:15-16.   *Christ can help us, for he, too, has faced temptation.*   288

James 1:13-15.   *God never tempts people to sin.*   299

*See also:* SIN

## THANKFULNESS

Luke 17:11-18.   *Always thank God for his blessings.*   93

Acts 3:7-11.   *Thankfulness brings praise to God.*   138

Ephesians 2:4-10.   *Be thankful for salvation and God's grace.*   238

Philippians 4:6.   *We should thank God for all he has done.*   250

Colossians 3:15-17.   *Our life should be characterized by thankfulness to God.*   257

1 Thessalonians 5:16-18.   *We are called to give thanks in all circumstances!*   264

*See also:* BLESSING

## TRIALS

Matthew 11:28-30.   *Christ promises us rest for our souls.*   17

John 15:18.   *Jesus understands our struggles.*   125

John 16:33.   *We can have peace in trials.*   128

Romans 5:1-5.   *Trials help us learn to endure.*   180

Romans 8:28.   *God causes everything to work together for the good of his people.*   185

2 Corinthians 6:3-13.   *Believers can expect to suffer for their faith.*   221

James 1:2-4.   *God can use trials to help us grow.*   299

*See also:* SUFFERING

## TRUST

Philippians 1:6.   *We can trust God to complete the good work he has begun in us.*   247

*See also:* DOUBT, FAITH

## TRUTH

John 8:31-32.   *The truth will set us free.*   116

John 14:6.   *Jesus Christ is the truth.*   123

John 17:17.   *God's Word is truth.*   128

1 John 1:5-7.   *We must not only believe the truth but also live by it.*   317

## UNBELIEVERS

John 17:14-19.   *Christians are called to live holy lives among unbelievers.*   128

Romans 8:9.   *Unbelievers do not have the Holy Spirit.*   184

2 Corinthians 6:14-18.   *We should avoid situations that force us to compromise our beliefs.*   222

1 John 5:10-12.   *Believing in Jesus Christ is essential for eternal life.*   323

# Bibles At Cost

To Order Additional Copies 1-800-778-8865
(or refer to last page)

## New Believer's Full Study
## New Testament

## Find a Bible Teaching Church!

| To Find a Church | National Phone Number |
|---|---|
| Assembly of God | (417) 862-2781 |
| Calvary Chapel | (714) 979-4422 |
| Church of God | (800) 741-7721 |
| Conservative Baptist | (630) 653-5350 |
| Evangelical Free | (800) 745-2202 |
| Lutheran Church | (773) 380-2700 |
| Church of the Nazarene | (816) 333-7000 |
| Presbyterian Church | (502) 569-5000 |
| Southern Baptist | (615) 244-2355 |
| United Methodist Church | (800) 251-8140 |

## Become Involved in an Outreach Ministry

| To help or join a ministry | Contact |
|---|---|
| Able Ministries - Bibles for Africa | (877) 432-4332 |
| Christian Businessmen's Committee | (800) 566-2262 |
| Crisis Pregnancy Care Net | (800) 359-HELP |
| Fellowship of Christian Athletes | (800) 289-0909 |
| Harvest Crusade - Greg Laurie | (800) CRUSADE |
| Luis Palau Evangelistic Assoc. | (503) 614-1500 |
| Jesus Video Project | (888) JESUS36 |
| Youth for Christ | (800) 843-9000 |
| Youth With A Mission | (619) 420-1900 |

www.biblesatcost.com          A Bible Distribution Ministry

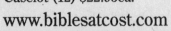